W9-COB-587

THE PAINTINGS OF
NICOLAS POUSSIN

A CRITICAL CATALOGUE
BY ANTHONY BLUNT

THE PAINTINGS OF
NICOLAS POUSSIN

A CRITICAL CATALOGUE
BY ANTHONY BLUNT

PHAIDON

MADE IN GREAT BRITAIN

PRINTED AT THE ABERDEEN UNIVERSITY PRESS

BOUND BY A. W. BAIN AND CO. LTD · LONDON

CONTENTS

THE PAINTINGS OF
NICOLAS POUSSIN

INTRODUCTION

THE FOLLOWING CATALOGUE contains entries for all the paintings which I believe to be by Nicolas Poussin and which survive either in the original or in copies or engravings. Paintings which are attributed to him in early documents but of which no visual record survives are listed in a separate section, and those which I believe to be wrongly attributed to Poussin are dealt with in a further list of rejected works. Small reproductions of all paintings in the first category have been included for ready reference. They are also reproduced on a larger scale in the plate volume of the monograph.

Almost all the paintings listed in the catalogue are discussed in the text volume; the references to them can be traced through its index, and cross references have only been given in the catalogue entries in cases where the discussion in the text substantially affects either the history or the iconography of the paintings in question.

I have attempted to trace the pedigrees of the pictures catalogued below, but in many cases it is impossible to be certain whether a particular entry in, say, a guide book or a sale catalogue refers to the picture under discussion or another similar composition, perhaps now lost.

Generally speaking I have avoided making comments on the condition of pictures, unless there is some very obvious need to do so, since I believe that, unless one has the opportunity of making, or studying the results of, a full technical examination, it is very easy to be misled by examination of the surface of a picture with the unaided eye.

Under the heading 'Bibliography' I have of necessity been selective, since to give every reference in every book and article to every picture would have made the catalogue unprintable and would have led to the important items being swamped by those of minor significance. I have aimed at giving all references before 1800, but I have been ruthless in leaving out those in later works which add nothing of importance to our knowledge of a particular picture.

In the case of guide books I have generally quoted the earliest edition in which the picture in question is mentioned, and have only included references to later editions when they add something specific to its history. In a few cases, e.g. the *St. Erasmus*, I have omitted all reference to guide books, since the picture is mentioned in every edition of every guide book to Rome.

After some hesitation it was decided in general not to include in the catalogue entries references to exhibitions where the paintings had been shown, on the grounds that these rarely added new information. A few exceptions were made, e.g. for the Poussin exhibitions at the Louvre in 1960 and at Rouen in 1961, and references were also included to any 19th century exhibitions where the fact that a picture was lent provided a clue to the owner at a particular time.

I have listed such copies of originals as are known to me and are relevant. Copies on snuffboxes, fans, etc., have not been included, but the few instances in which Poussin's compositions have been translated into sculpture have been noted. It must also be made clear that the copies listed may not all be distinct, since there is often no means of saying whether versions recorded in different sales or collections are identical or different. It may be thought tendentious to class as 'copies' paintings which are no longer traceable, but this is based on the belief that Poussin never repeated himself exactly. It is hardly necessary to say that the list of copies cannot be complete; there must be, for instance, many, perhaps hundreds of copies of Poussin's religious compositions in French churches, and those that I have listed are simply those known to me through printed sources or personal observation.

It is also no doubt the case that many French painters of the nineteenth century made copies of Poussin which have escaped me. For instance, it was pointed out to me by Dr. Phoebe Pool, unfortunately too late for the references to be included in the catalogue, that Fantin-Latour copied several of Poussin's pictures in the Louvre.

Engravings after Poussin's compositions are listed with references to A. Andresen's *Nicolas Poussin. Verzeichniss der nach seinen Gemälden gefertigten Kupferstiche*, of 1863, and Georges Wildenstein's two articles in the *Gazette des Beaux-Arts* of 1955 and 1958. In general engravings made after the publication of Andresen's list have not been included, unless they have some particular importance.

Preparatory drawings and drawings after paintings are listed with reference, where possible, to W. Friedlaender and A. Blunt, *The Drawings of Nicolas Poussin. A catalogue raisonné*.

Unless otherwise stated, paintings are in oil on canvas; dimensions are given in centimetres, height preceding width.

The catalogue entries are arranged by subject roughly on the pattern of Smith's *Catalogue raisonné*. The arrangement has, however, been slightly simplified, so that the pictures are grouped in the following categories:

1. Portraits (Nos. 1–2)
2. Old Testament and Jewish history (Nos. 3–37)
3. New Testament, including the life of the Virgin (Nos. 38–94)
4. Post-New Testament Saints (Nos. 95–104)
5. The Sacraments (Nos. 105–18)
6. Allegory (Nos. 119–25)
7. Classical subjects, including both mythology and history (Nos. 126–201)
8. Subjects from Tasso (Nos. 202–7)
9. Landscapes (Nos. 208–17)
10. Sculpture (Nos. 218–31).

All the classical subjects have been put into one section, owing to the difficulty of drawing a precise line of demarcation between mythology and history.

As regards the dating of pictures, I have in general quoted the opinions of those who have studied this problem carefully, but, since I believe that in many cases it is impossible to arrive at a precise dating owing to the lack of evidence, the views which I have myself expressed are often vague, suggesting a dating to a period of years rather than to a single year.

The preparation of this catalogue was continued for several years after the manuscript of the text volume was handed to the publishers. There may, therefore, be certain details in the one which disagree with those given in the other. In any such case it may be assumed that the opinion expressed in the catalogue supersedes that in the text volume.

Some readers may think that I have been too severe in this catalogue and that I have rejected paintings for which a case can be made as genuine works of Poussin. If this is so I am sure that other critics will soon adjust the balance, but I believe that at the present stage of Poussin studies the first aim should be to establish a canon of works which can be ascribed to the artist with a high degree of probability. In the eighteenth and nineteenth centuries, when paintings by Poussin were in great demand and in short supply, dealers and collectors had no scruples about putting his name to works which were certainly by imitators, sometimes even by imitators of a later generation. I have dealt with some aspects of this problem in a series of articles in the *Burlington Magazine* in which I have attempted to put together certain groups of pictures, which can, I believe, be attributed to specific painters. Of these some, like Jean Lemaire or Karel Philips Spierincks, are namable; others I dubbed with fancy names such as 'The Hovingham

Master' or 'The Master of the Clumsy Children'. One of these, 'The Silver Birch Master', has since been identified as the young Gaspar Dughet and in the present catalogue I am proposing a new figure, 'The Heytesbury Master' (see R112), who in my opinion is responsible for a group of erotic mythological paintings which have been ascribed to Poussin. In this way I have attempted to sift the Poussin Apocrypha and so to define his real work more clearly; but there are other paintings ascribed to Poussin which, though very close to him in style, are in my view not from his own hand and yet cannot be connected with any of the known or supposed followers. These I have listed in the catalogue of Rejected Works below, giving as far as possible my reason for not accepting them. I am aware, however, that in some cases my opinion may not be shared by others, particularly when I challenge the authenticity of paintings such as the Munich *Midas before Bacchus* which has, as far as I know, never been doubted. I should like to emphasize, however, that I have only come to reject these works after careful study and after much thought. I have omitted in this catalogue all reference to the *Rebecca* recently published by Mr. Denis Mahon (Bibl. 1434), as I have been unable to examine the original in its cleaned state.

There are still many parts of the 'penumbra' around Poussin which are not clear. In particular his relations with Pier Francesco Mola, Testa and Castiglione need further investigation. In the case of Mola Mr. Richard Cocke in the dissertation which he is just completing has, in my opinion, established a clear canon of his works and has produced much information which will help to clarify the artist's relation to Poussin. On the whole his paintings only seem to show the direct influence of Poussin for a single relatively short period in the 1650's, but Mr. Cocke has convincingly shown that he is the author of a celebrated group of drawings, most of which were in the Crozat sale under the name of Poussin, but which have been rejected by modern critics. Testa is being studied by various scholars and it is to be hoped that a similar clarification will take place. The problem of Castiglione is much more complex since we know almost nothing of his paintings—as opposed to his drawings and etchings—during his early years in Rome, where, it is now known from unpublished documents discovered by Miss Ann Percy, he was already established by 1632 and where he was still working in 1651. There is, however, every reason to suppose that he was in fairly close touch with Poussin at any rate for part of that time, and there are works, such as the little *Satyr* in the Galleria Nazionale, Rome, and the *Bacchus and Ariadne* in the Prado, which show a puzzling blend of features characteristic of Castiglione with others typical of the early Poussin.

In the compilation of this catalogue I have received help from a great number of friends. First and foremost I must thank Professor Ellis Waterhouse, who has brought to my attention a large number of paintings by or connected with Poussin and has generously allowed me to draw on his unrivalled knowledge in tracing the pedigrees of Poussin's paintings. I am also indebted to Mrs. Peter Coope, Dr. Anita Brookner, Mrs. Frances Vivian and Mrs. Allan Braham for help in checking bibliographical references and entries in sale catalogues. The whole catalogue has been typed, checked and indexed by Miss Elsa Scheerer, with the result that many wrong references and errors of detail have been removed. In spite of all this help, however, I have no doubt that errors will have remained in some at least of the many thousands of references which the catalogue contains and I shall be very grateful to readers who spot them and are kind enough to let me have their corrections.

ABBREVIATIONS USED IN THE CATALOGUE

Actes   *Actes du Colloque International Nicolas Poussin*, Paris, 1960

Andresen   A. Andresen, *Nicolas Poussin, Verzeichniss der nach seinen Gemälden gefertigten Kupferstiche*, Leipzig, 1863. Bibl. 500

Andresen-Wildenstein   French translation by G. Wildenstein. Bibl. 500a

Bailly   N. Bailly, *Inventaire des tableaux du Roy rédigé en 1709 et 1710*, ed. Engerand, Paris, 1899. Bibl. 131

Baldinucci   F. Baldinucci, *Notizie de' professori del disegno da Cimabue in quà*, Florence, 1767–73. Bibl. 85a

Bardon   F. M. Dandré Bardon, *Traité de peinture*, Paris, 1765. Bibl. 220

Bartsch   A. Bartsch, *Le peintre-graveur*, Leipzig, 1854-70. Bibl. 463

Bellori   Giovanni Pietro Bellori, *Le Vite de' pittori, scultori et architetti moderni*, Rome, 1672. Bibl. 56

Buchanan   W. Buchanan, *Memoirs of paintings . . .* , London, 1824. Bibl. 376

Cartari   Vincenzo Cartari, *Le Imagini de i dei degli antichi*, Venice, 1587.

Chantelou, 1885   P. Fréart de Chantelou, *Journal du voyage du Cavalier Bernin en France*, Paris, 1885. Bibl. 41

Chantelou, 1960   Parts reprinted in J. Thuillier, 'Pour un "Corpus Pussinianum" ', *Actes*, II 1960. Bibl. 41e

Comptes des bâtiments   J. Guiffrey, *Comptes des bâtiments du roi sous le règne de Louis XIV*, Paris, 1881–1901. Bibl. 39

Correspondance   N. Poussin, *Correspondance de Nicolas Poussin*, ed. Ch. Jouanny, Paris, 1911. Bibl. 3a

CR   W. Friedlaender and A. Blunt, *The Drawings of Nicolas Poussin. A catalogue raisonné*, London, 1939– (In progress). Bibl. 944

Davies and Blunt   M. Davies and A. Blunt, 'Some corrections and additions to M. Wildenstein's "Graveurs de Poussin au XVIIᵉ siècle" ', *Gazette des Beaux-Arts*, 1962, II, pp. 205 ff. Bibl. 1363

Dézallier, 1745   A. J. Dézallier d'Argenville, *Abrégé de la vie des plus fameux peintres . . .* , Paris, 1745. Bibl. 178

Dézallier, 1762   2nd ed., Paris, 1762. Bibl. 178a

Exposition Poussin (Louvre)   Louvre, Paris: *Exposition Poussin*, 1960. Second edition. Bibl. 1266

Exposition Poussin (Rouen)   Musée des Beaux-Arts, Rouen: *Exposition Nicolas Poussin et son temps*, 1961. Bibl. 1341

Félibien   A. Félibien, *Entretiens sur les vies . . . des plus excellens peintres . . .* , Trévoux, 1725. Bibl. 44c

Florent Le Comte   Florent Le Comte, *Cabinet des singularitez d'architecture, peinture, sculpture et graveure*, Brussels, 1702. Bibl. 119a

Friedlaender, 1914   W. Friedlaender, *Nicolas Poussin*, Munich 1914. Bibl. 722

Friedlaender, 1933   W. Friedlaender, "Nicolas Poussin", Thieme-Becker, XXVII, 1933, pp. 321 ff. Bibl. 875

Gault de Saint-Germain   P. M. Gault de Saint-Germain, *Vie de Nicolas Poussin . . .* , Paris, 1806. Bibl. 330

Grautoff   O. Grautoff, *Nicolas Poussin: sein Werk und sein Leben*, Munich, 1914. Bibl. 723

Inventaire général, Ecole française   *Inventaire général des dessins du Musée du Louvre et du Musée de Versailles. Ecole française*, Paris, 1907–38.

Jamot   P. Jamot, *Connaissance de Poussin*, Paris, 1948. Bibl. 1031

Landon   C. P. Landon, *Vies et œuvres des peintres les plus célèbres de toutes les écoles*, Paris, 1803–17. Bibl. 326

Licht   F. S. Licht, *Die Entwicklung der Landschaft in den Werken von Nicolas Poussin*, Basle and Stuttgart, 1954. Bibl. 1102

L'ideale classico (Bologna)   Palazzo dell' Archiginnasio, Bologna: *L'ideale classico del seicento in Italia e la pittura di Paesaggio*, 1962. Bibl. 1369

Loménie de Brienne   L. H. Loménie, Comte de Brienne, *Discours sur les ouvrages des plus excellens peintres anciens et nouveaux avec un traité de la peinture composé et imaginé par Mʳᵉ L. H. de L. C. de B. Reclus*, printed in J. Thuillier, 'Pour un "Corpus Pussinianum" ', *Actes*, II, 1960, pp. 210 ff. Bibl. 108

Magne, 1914   E. Magne, *Nicolas Poussin, Premier Peintre du Roi, 1594-1665*, Brussels and Paris, 1914. Bibl. 724

Magne, 1928   New ed., Paris, 1928. Bibl. 724a

Mémoires inédits. *Mémoires inédits sur la vie et les ouvrages des membres de l'Académie Royale de Peinture et de Sculpture*, ed. L. Dussieux and others, Paris, 1887. Bibl. 102

Passeri   G. Passeri, *Vite de' pittori, scultori ed architetti che anno lavorato in Roma, morti del 1641 fino al 1673*, ed. J. Hess, Leipzig and Vienna, 1934. Bibl. 75b

Procès-verbaux   *Académie Royale de Peinture et de Sculpture, Procès-verbaux*, ed. Anatole de Montaiglon, Paris, 1875–1909. Bibl. 13

Richardson, *Account*   J. Richardson, *An account of the statues . . . and pictures in Italy, France, etc.*, London, 1722. Bibl. 149

Richardson, *Traité*   J. Richardson, *Traité de la peinture*, Amsterdam, 1728. Bibl. 154

Sandrart   J. von Sandrart, *Teutsche Academie . . .* , ed. A. R. Peltzer, Munich, 1925. Bibl. 67b.

Smith   J. Smith, *A catalogue raisonné of the works of the most eminent Dutch, Flemish and French painters*, London, 1829-42. Bibl. 390

Testament   'Testament et inventaires des biens, . . . de Claudine Bouzonnet Stella (1693-1697)', ed. J. Guiffrey, Nouvelles Archives de l'Art Français, 1877, pp. 1 ff. Bibl. 107

Wildenstein   G. Wildenstein, 'Les graveurs de Poussin au XVIIe siècle, *Gazette des Beaux-Arts*, 1958. Bibl. 1186

CATALOGUE

SELF-PORTRAITS

1. SELF-PORTRAIT. 78×65 cm. Inscribed: NICOLAVS POVSSINVS ANDELYENSIS ACADEMICVS ROMANVS PRIMVS PICTOR ORDINARIVS LVDOVICI IVSTI REGIS GALLIÆ. ANNO Domini 1649. Romæ. ÆTATIS SVÆ. 55, and on the book: DE LVMINE ET COLORE. Staatliche Museen, Gemälde-galerie, East Berlin.

HISTORY: Painted for Pointel, finished before 20.vi.1649 (*Correspondance*, p. 402) and dispatched to Paris 19.vi.1650. Seen by Bernini in Cérisier's collection in 1665 (Chantelou, 1885, p. 90, and 1960, p. 126). The Berlin picture comes from the Solly collection; bought by the museum in 1821; on deposit at Königsberg for many years as a copy of the Louvre portrait.

DRAWINGS: A red chalk drawing in the collection of René Varin at Versailles is a copy of one of the reversed engravings after the Berlin composition with a different background, consisting of a curtain on the right and, on the left, a view showing trees, an obelisk and a sphinx. The drawing appears to be by a Roman artist of the circle of Maratta.

ENGRAVINGS: 1. By Jean Pesne (Andresen, No. I; Wildenstein, No. 1).
2. Attributed to Jean Pesne (Andresen, No. X; Davies and Blunt, p. 207, No. 1).

COPIES: 1. With Gimpel fils, London (Matthew Anderson sale, Christie, London, 8.vi.1861, lot 141; Sir Richard Leighton sale, Christie, London, 1.iv.1934, lot 44; bt. Max Rothschild; Gimpel, Paris). Regarded as the original before the discovery of the Berlin painting (cf. Blunt, Bibl. 1002, p. 219; Dorival, Bibl. 1009, p. 39; Bertin-Mourot, Bibl. 1023, p. 45; Tolnay, Bibl. 1083, p. 110).

2. Musée de l'Ain, Bourg-en-Bresse.
3. National Museum, Warsaw. By Daniel Seghers. In a wreath of flowers, painted as a pair to a portrait of Rubens by the same artist (cf. Bialostocki, Bibl. 1193, Pl. 71 and Martin, Bibl. 1338.1, pp. 67 ff.).
4. Anon. (= Vigné) sale, Remy, Paris, 1.iv.1773, lot 80. Said to have been painted for Pointel, but the size (19×14 inches) does not agree with the Berlin picture.
5. Le Brun sale, Christie, London, 18.iii.1774, lot 8 (18×12 inches).
6. C. Jennens sale, Langford, London, 27.iv.1774, lot 53.
7. Lord Montfort sale, Christie, London, 16.ii.1776, lot 8; bt. G. Vandergucht; Vandergucht sale, Christie, London, 6.iii.1777, lot 33.
8. A self-portrait in the J. B. de Troy sale, Remy, Paris, 9.iv.1764, lot 84 (19×14½ inches) may be after either the Berlin or the Louvre painting, but its size indicates that it may be identical with No. 4 above.

NOTES: The artist has painted himself against a background formed by two putti—one apparently asleep and one awake—supporting a wreath and flanking a tablet which bears the inscription quoted above. The whole forms a sort of funerary monument, like the tombs carved by Poussin's friend François Duquesnoy for Adriaan Vrijburch and Ferdinand van den Eynde in S. Maria dell'Anima (rep. Mahon, Bibl. 1367, pp. 80 f.).

BIBLIOGRAPHY: *Correspondance*, pp. 355, 376, 380, 386, 390, 392, 394, 399, 402, 405, 409 f., 412, 414 ff., 457; Chantelou, 1885, p. 90, and 1960, p. 126; Félibien, IV, p. 62; Florent Le Comte, III, p. 31; Smith, No. 1; Friedlaender, 1914, p. 120; Grautoff, I, pp. 263 f.; Magne, 1914, pp. 155, 218, No. 325; Sterling, Bibl. 881, p. 134; Dorival, Bibl. 1009, pp. 39 ff.; Simon Bibl. 1078; Sterling, Bibl. 1080a, p. 135; Grohn, Bibl 1116, p. 34; *Kunsthaus, Zurich*, Bibl. 1134, No. 202; Wild, Bibl. 1184, p. 166; *Exposition Poussin (Louvre)*, No. 89 bis; Wild, Bibl. 1310; Ettlinger, Bibl. 1327, p. 198; Mahon, Bibl. 1367, p. 115.

2. SELF-PORTRAIT. 98 × 74 cm. Inscribed: EFFIGIES NICOLAI POVSSINI ANDELYENSIS PIC-
TORIS. ANNO ÆTATIS. 56. ROMÆ ANNO IVBILEI 1650. Musée du Louvre, Paris (743).

HISTORY: Painted for Paul Fréart de Chantelou; begun in September 1649 (*Correspondance*, p. 405), finished
in May 1650 (*ibid.*, p. 414). The despatch of the picture was delayed because the artist's Roman friends
wanted a copy made, but it was finally sent off, on 19.vi.1650 (*ibid.*, p. 416). In 1778 a member of the Fréart
de Chantelou family offered the *Self-Portrait* by Poussin to Louis XVI, but the king did not buy it (Magne,
1914, p. 164). The Louvre painting was acquired in 1797 from a dealer named Lerouge by means of an
exchange. Everything points to its being the original painted for Chantelou and offered to the king in
1778.

DRAWINGS: A drawing in red chalk, now at Windsor,
which formed the frontispiece to the Massimi volume
of drawings by Poussin, is a copy of the Louvre painting.

ENGRAVINGS: 1. By Jean Pesne (Andresen, No. II;
   Wildenstein No. 2; Davies and Blunt, p. 207, No. 2.
2. By C. G. Lewis (Andresen, No. III).
3. By L. J. Cathelin (Andresen, No. IV).
4. By Baltard and Voyez (Andresen, No. V).
5. By F. Lignon, 1824 (Andresen, No. VI).
6. By E. Perrot (Andresen, No. VII).
7. By A. Clouvet (Andresen, No. VIII).
8. By J. L. Potrelle (Andresen, No. IX).

COPIES: 1. Galleria degli Uffizi, Florence.
2. Musée des Beaux-Arts, Nantes. Presented by
   Philippe Caffiéri to the Académie Royale de Peinture
   et de Sculpture in 1782; sent to Nantes from the
   Louvre (cf. *Procès-verbaux*, IX, p. 130; Fontaine,
   Bibl. 692, p. 192; Thuillier, Bibl. 1297, p. 40).
3. Ecole des Beaux-Arts, Paris.

4. Galleria Pallavicini, Rome. In the collection by 1708
   (cf. Zeri, Bibl. 1216, p. 197, No. 342). Also mentioned in the eighteenth and nineteenth centuries
   (cf. Orbessan, Bibl. 232, I, p. 555; Hazlitt, Bibl.
   381a, p. 237; Thuillier, Bibl. 1298, p. 273).
5. Musée des Beaux-Arts, Rouen.
6. Formerly Alte Pinakothek, Munich.
7. On the Dublin art market, 1912 (cf. Grautoff, I, p.
   264).
8. Possibly in Cassiano dal Pozzo's collection. The
   Robert de Cotte papers (Bibl. 98a, p. 203) mention
   Son portrait peint par luy, and the Ghezzi inventory
   (Bibl. 1254, p. 325) has an entry (Nos. 73, 74): *Li due
   ritratti da 4 p. mi uno di Pietro da Cortona, e l'altro di
   Nicolò Pussino.* At one time I suggested that this
   might refer to the portrait of Poussin at Hovingham
   Hall, but now I believe this to be by Bernini (cf.
   text volume, p. 97, and Blunt, Bibl. 1426 Fr., p.
   61). It is extremely probable that Pozzo was one
   of the friends for whom copies were made before
   the original left Rome.

NOTES: In this portrait the artist has depicted himself in his studio against a background of frames and
canvases. On the left can be seen a part of a painting, on which are visible the head and shoulders of a
woman wearing a diadem ornamented with an eye in the middle. Two hands, belonging to a figure not
visible in the composition, grasp her by the shoulders. Bellori (p. 440) tells us that the woman symbolizes
painting and the two hands friendship. Tolnay (Bibl. 1083, pp. 109 ff.) has proposed a different interpretation, but there does not seem to be any reason to doubt that Bellori's is correct.

BIBLIOGRAPHY: *Correspondance*, pp. 355, 376, 380, 386,
390, 392, 394, 399, 402, 405, 409, 410, 412, 414 f., 416,
417, 418, 457; Chantelou, 1885, p. 64, and 1960, p. 124;
Félibien, IV, p. 62; Bellori, p. 440; Baldinucci, XVI,
p. 106; Florent Le Comte, III, p. 31; Landon, No. 1;
Gault de Saint-Germain, Pt. II, p. 3; Smith, No. 2;
Estrée, Bibl. 634.1, p. 501; Denio, Bibl. 640a, p. 116;
Advielle, Bibl. 652, p. 103; Desjardins, Bibl. 656, p. 99;
Waetzoldt, Bibl. 679, pp. 353 ff.; Friedlaender, 1914,
pp. 92, 120; Grautoff, I, p. 265, II, No. 141; Magne,
1914, pp. 163, 218, No. 326, and 1928, pp. 237 ff.;
Jamot, Bibl. 737, pp. 345 ff., and Bibl. 749, pp. 81 ff.;
Alpatov, Bibl. 871, pp. 113 ff.; Sterling, Bibl. 881, No.
93; Alpatov, Bibl. 882, pp. 5 ff.; Gillet, Bibl. 884, pp.
41 f.; Schapiro, Bibl. 895, pp. 264 f.; Blunt, Bibl. 1002,
pp. 219 ff.; Dorival, Bibl. 1009, pp. 39 ff.; Jamot,
p. 27; Tolnay, Bibl. 1083, pp. 109 ff.; Licht, p. 159;
Chastel, Bibl. 1197, p. 18, and Bibl. 1238, p. 300;
Hours, Bibl. 1256, p. 34; Kauffmann, Bibl. 1262, pp.
82 ff.; *Exposition Poussin (Louvre)*, No. 90; Wild, Bibl.
1311; Ettlinger, Bibl. 1327, pp. 196 ff.; Mahon, Bibl.
1367, p. 118.

THE OLD TESTAMENT

3–6. THE FOUR SEASONS. Each 118 × 160 cm. Musée du Louvre, Paris (736–739).

HISTORY: Painted, according to Félibien (IV, p. 66), for the Duc de Richelieu between 1660 and 1664. Bought with the whole of the duke's collection by Louis XIV in 1665 (Ferraton, Bibl. 1043, p. 439).

COPIES: Paintings of these subjects attributed to Poussin were in the sale of paintings from the collection of Cardinal Antonio Barberini, Sir James Palmer, and others, Davis and Millingham, London, 23.xi.1691, lot 84.

NOTES: The last works to be completed by Poussin, the *Apollo and Daphne* being left unfinished at his death. They show signs of the shakiness of his hand in old age, but in spite of this they are among the noblest examples of his late landscape style. *Winter* in particular has always aroused the interest of artists and critics, and was enthusiastically praised by men of such different tastes as Diderot, Delacroix, and Turner.

For the iconography of the Seasons, see text volume, pp. 332 ff.

BIBLIOGRAPHY: Félibien, IV, p. 66; *Mémoires inédits*, I, p. 343; Loménie de Brienne, p. 222; Florent Le Comte, III, p. 32; Piganiol de La Force, Bibl. 124, I, p. 359; Bailly, p. 313; Richardson, *Account*, p. 8, wrongly referred to as by Albani; Walpole, Bibl. 162, IX, p. 78; Dézallier, 1745, II, p. 255, and 1762, IV, p. 40; Dézallier d'Argenville, Bibl. 183d, pp. 344 ff.; Gougenot, Bibl. 184, p. 179; La Roque, Bibl. 248, I, pp. 142 f.; Landon, Nos. 206–9; Barry, Bibl. 338, I, p. 32; Smith, Nos. 296–9; Duranty, Bibl. 554, p. 281; Bonnaffé, Bibl. 572, pp. 207, 214; Gautier, Bibl. 575, p. 174; Friedlaender, 1914, pp. 100, 124, 262 ff.; Grautoff, I, pp. 283 ff., II, Nos. 156–9; Magne, 1914, pp. 156, 169, 219, No. 335; Blunt, Bibl. 972, pp. 165 f.; Jamot, p. 81; Clark, Bibl. 1040, pp. 69 f.; Ferraton, Bibl. 1043, pp. 439, 445, 446; Licht, pp. 182 ff.; Sauerländer, Bibl. 1140, pp. 169 ff.; Du Colombier, Bibl. 1246, p. 55; *Exposition Poussin (Louvre)*, Nos. 115–18; Kitson, Bibl. 1335, p. 158; Mahon, Bibl. 1338, pp. 125 f.; Friedlaender, Bibl. 1365, pp. 257 ff.; Mahon, Bibl. 1367, pp. XIV, 120 f., 129; Alpatov, Bibl. 1425, pp. 12 f.

3. SPRING or THE EARTHLY PARADISE.

ENGRAVINGS: 1. Probably by Jean Audran (Andresen, No. 436; Wildenstein, No. 174; Davies and Blunt, p. 215, No. 174).
2. By Franz Geisler, 1811 (see Andresen, Nos. 436–39).

COPIES: 1. Musée, Langres (cf. Magne, 1914, p. 219, No. 335d).
2. A painting of Creation appeared in the sale of Thomas Pelleteir at his house in Henrietta Street, Covent Garden, London, 19.iii.1712/13, lot 27. It was a pair to one of the *Deluge*, and both may therefore have been copies after the Seasons.

BIBLIOGRAPHY: See above, and Cambry, Bibl. 272a, p. 40; Gault de Saint-Germain, Pt. II, p. 59; Hazlitt, Bibl. 417, p. 167; Magne, 1914, p. 192; Courthion, Bibl. 781, p. 61; Sayce, Bibl. 1020, p. 246; Tolnay, Bibl. 1379, p. 262.

4. SUMMER or RUTH AND BOAZ.

ENGRAVING: By Jean Pesne (Andresen, No. 437; Wildenstein, No. 175).

COPY: Akademie der bildenden Künste, Vienna (936). From the Lamberg collection.

BIBLIOGRAPHY: See above, and J. B. de Champaigne (1671) in Fontaine, Bibl. 55, p. 119; *Mémoires inédits*, I, p. 349; *Exposition Poussin (Rouen)*, No. 91; *L'ideale classico (Bologna)*, No. 86.

5. AUTUMN or THE SPIES WITH THE GRAPES FROM THE PROMISED LAND.

DRAWING: Pierpont Morgan Library, New York. A copy of a lost original for the whole composition (*CR*, IV, p. 53, No. A143).

ENGRAVINGS: 1. By Jean Pesne (Andresen, No. 438; Wildenstein, No. 175).

2. Anonymous, in the *Protestant Bible*, London, 1780 (as after Salvator Rosa).

COPY: Louis Patural collection, St. Etienne (in 1956).

BIBLIOGRAPHY: See above, and *L'ideale classico* (*Bologna*), No. 87.

6. WINTER or THE FLOOD.

ENGRAVINGS By Jean Audran (Andresen, No. 439; Wildenstein, No. 176).

COPIES: 1. Musée des Beaux-Arts, Rheims (696).
2. Robert Strange, London (1769).
3. By Perron in the Angiviller collection, Paris, confiscated in 1793 (cf. Tuétey, Bibl. 295, I, p. 335).

4. Thomas Pelleteir sale, at his house, Henrietta Street, Covent Garden, London, 19.iii.1712/13, lot 37. See above, No. 3.
5. A version on slate (42 × 53 cm.) was in the Cardinal Fesch sale, George, Rome, 17ff.iii.1845, Pt. II, lot 401; appeared again in the Forcade sale, Pillet, Paris, 2.iv.1873, lot 4. Probably the painting mentioned by Smith (No. 4) as in a private collection, Rome.

NOTES: The painting was restored in 1792–93 (cf. Tuétey, Bibl. 304, p. 314).

BIBLIOGRAPHY: See above, and C. A. Coypel (1750) in *Procès-verbaux*, VI, p. 241; N. Loir (1668) in *Conférences de l'Académie . . .*, Bibl. 47a, p. 100; *Mémoires inédits*, I, p. 341; Perrault, Bibl. 113, I, p. 90; Diderot, Bibl. 211, X, p. 388; Bardon, I, pp. 144, 176, 226, II, pp. 124 f.; Boyer d'Argens, Bibl. 231, p. 301; Le Mierre, Bibl. 234, p. 56; Cambry, Bibl. 272a, p. 44; Guibal, Bibl. 273, p. 54; Gault de Saint-Germain, Pt. II, pp. 10 ff.; Opie, Bibl. 335, pp. 120 f.; Barry, Bibl. 338, I, p. 457; Ruault, Bibl. 340, p. 41; Leslie, Bibl. 413a, pp. 297, 314; Hazlitt, Bibl. 417, p. 196; Delacroix, Bibl. 453a, p. 102; Fry, Bibl. 761, p. 53; Finberg, Bibl. 934, p. 89; Jamot, p. 84; Dorival, Bibl. 1088, p. 46; Messerer, Bibl. 1175, p. 248; Bardon, Bibl. 1218, p. 129.

7. LANDSCAPE WITH HAGAR AND THE ANGEL. 98 × 73 cm. Contessa Pasolini (nata Altieri), Palazzo Altieri, Rome.

HISTORY: Nothing is known of the history of this picture, which is not mentioned in any of the Roman guides which describe the palace and its contents in some detail. On the back of the canvas is a seal, which does not look Italian and which bears an undecipherable monogram.

NOTES: The attribution to Poussin was first suggested by Professor Rudolf Wittkower. The picture is presumably a fragment, since the tents of Abraham, to which the angel is pointing (cf. Genesis, XVI, 7 ff.) must have been visible on the left. The painting is on the scale and in exactly the style of the Four Seasons and should be dated to the same years, 1660–64.

BIBLIOGRAPHY: Chastel, Bibl. 1236, p. 239.

8. ELIEZER AND REBECCA. 118 × 197 cm. Musée du Louvre, Paris (704).

HISTORY: Painted for Pointel in 1648 (Félibien, IV, p. 59). Sold by the Duc de Richelieu to Louis XIV in 1665 (Ferraton, Bibl. 1043, p. 439).

DRAWINGS: 1. Randall Davies sale, Sotheby, London, 10.ii.1947, lot 149. From the collections of the elder Richardson and the Earl of Aylesford. A copy after the painting.
2. Musée de Peinture, Alençon. Copy of one figure from the painting, with colour notes written in French.
3. Nationalmuseum, Stockholm. Drawing by Sébastien Bourdon after the painting.

ENGRAVINGS: 1. By Aegidius Rousselet, 1677 (Andresen, No. 12; Wildenstein, No. 7; but see Davies and Blunt, p. 207, No. 7).

2. Anonymous, published by Audran (Andresen, No. 13).
3. Anonymous, published by François Chéreau (Andresen, No. 14).
4. Anonymous, published by Jean Mariette (Andresen, No. 15).
5. By Aug. Boucher Desnoyers (Andresen, No. 16).
6. In the manner of Bernard Picart (Andresen, No. 17).
7. Anonymous (Andresen, No. 18).

COPIES: 1. Fitzwilliam Museum, Cambridge. Bequeathed by the founder, Richard, 7th Viscount Fitzwilliam of Merrion, in 1816.

2. Musée des Beaux-Arts, Marseilles. Partial copy by Ingres (cf. Thuillier, Bibl. 1299, p. 293).

3. Musée Ingres, Montauban. Partial copy by Ingres.

4. Mrs. Parshall, 11 Palace Gardens Terrace, London. Inherited from Wilton Castle, Co. Wexford, Ireland.

5. Private collection, Italy. From the Koscek collection, Nice.

6. With Leggatt, London (1952).

7. With Casa d'Arte, 24 Monte Napoleone, Milan (1961).

8. A 'limning' after the painting was sold in the Edward Miles and others sale, Cock and Langford, London, 3.i.1747/8, second day, lot 41.

9. Hon. Mrs. Emmott sale, Christie, London, 2.iv.1948, lot 145. From the collection of Baroness Donington.

10. Anonymous sale, Christie, London, 30.vi.1961, lot 102.

Paintings of this subject attributed to Poussin were in the following sales:

1. Empress Joséphine sale, George, Paris, 22.iv.1839, lot 7.

2. Rospigliosi sale, Guido Tavazzi, Rome, 12–24.xii.1932, lot 166, 118 × 160 cm.

BIBLIOGRAPHY: *Procès-verbaux*, III, pp. 127 f.; Chantelou, 1885, p. 159, and 1960, p. 128; Félibien, IV, pp. 59, 90, 99 ff.; P. de Champaigne (1668) in *Conférences de l'Académie . . .*, Bibl. 47a, p. 87; Bellori, p. 451; Testelin, Bibl. 80, p. 20; *Mercure Galant*, Bibl. 87, p. 13; *Mémoires inédits*, I, pp. 244 ff.; Loménie de Brienne, pp. 215, 218, 220, 224; Perrault, Bibl. 113, I, p. 90; Piganiol de La Force, Bibl. 124, I, p. 124; Florent Le Comte, I, p. 201, III, p. 30; Bailly, p. 303; (C. Saugrain), Bibl. 138a, I, p. 93; Dézallier, 1745, II, p. 254; 1762, IV, p. 39; Landon, No. 4; Gault de Saint-Germain, Pt. II, pp. 40 ff.; Paillot de Montabert, Bibl. 387, IV, p. 491; Smith, No. 6; Friedlaender, 1914, pp. 85 f., 119; Grautoff, I, p. 260, II, No. 130; Magne, 1914, pp. 155, 191, 204, No. 131; Francastel, Bibl. 883, pp. 151, 153; Finberg, Bibl. 934, p. 89; Blunt, Bibl. 972, p. 161, n. 3; Sayce, Bibl. 1020, p. 247; Jamot, p. 81; Ferraton, Bibl. 1043, pp. 439, 443, 446; Blunt, Bibl. 1086, pp. 189, 220 n. 213, and Bibl. 1086a, pp. 165, 273 n. 215; Licht, p. 144; Chastel, Bibl. 1238, p. 308; *Exposition Poussin* (*Louvre*), No. 79; Sterling, Bibl. 1290, p. 268; *L'ideale classico* (*Bologna*), No. 77; Mahon, Bibl. 1367, pp. 120, 124, 128 f.

9. ELIEZER AND REBECCA. 96·5 × 138 cm. Sir Anthony Blunt, London.

HISTORY: Bought from Duits, London, in 1933; then said to come from the Galton collection, Hadzor Hall, Cheshire, but probably the painting sold at an anon. (=E. Perfect) sale, Christie, London, 8.vii.1929, lot 73; bt. Duits. Probably the painting owned by Calonne and sold by Skinner and Dyke, London, 28.iii.1795, lot 15. According to the papers of Robert de Cotte (Bibl. 98, III, p. 152, and Bibl. 98a, p. 203) and the letters of de Brosses (Bibl. 170a, II, p. 456), Cassiano dal Pozzo owned a picture of this subject. Richardson (*Account*, p. 186) mentions a *Rachel Giving the Messengers Water*, which is evidently the same picture. It is probable that the present painting is that owned by dal Pozzo (but see Mahon, Bibl. 1434).

DRAWINGS: 1. Musée des Beaux-Arts, Lyons (*CR*, I, p. 4, No. 2).

2. Musée du Louvre, Paris. Copy of a lost original (*CR*, I, p. 4, No. A1).

ENGRAVING: The engraving by Louis Cossin, described by Andresen (No. 19), appears to agree with the painted composition, but no proof of it is at present traceable.

NOTES: The central group is reminiscent of an anonymous French engraving after Primaticcio (cf. W. M. Ivins, 'French XVI century prints', *The Metropolitan Museum of Art Bulletin*, N.S. III, 1944, p. 128). M. Sterling and Mr. Mahon (Bibl. 1367, pp. 120 f.) have proposed a very late date, c. 1660–61, for this painting, but its unusual colouring, with light blues, soft pinks, and pale greens, corresponds so exactly to the *St. Peter and St. John Healing* in the Metropolitan Museum, painted according to Félibien (IV, p. 54) in 1655, that it cannot be far removed from this painting in date.

BIBLIOGRAPHY: de Cotte, Bibl. 98, III, p. 152, and Bibl. 98a, p. 203; Richardson, *Account*, p. 186 (as *Rachel*); de Brosses, Bibl. 170a, II, p. 456; Keyssler, Bibl. 172a, II, p. 401; Magne, 1914, p. 204, No. 132; Blunt, Bibl. 910, p. 1; Lord, Bibl. 918, p. 394; *CR*, I, p. 4; Bertin-Mourot, Bibl. 999, p. 73; Blunt, Bibl. 1002, p. 219; Bertin-Mourot, Bibl. 1023, p. 45, No. IV; Haskell and Rinehart, Bibl. 1254, pp. 322, 325; *Exposition Poussin* (*Louvre*), No. 100; Rinehart, Bibl. 1281, p. 28; Mahon, Bibl. 1367, pp. 120 f., and Bibl. 1434.

10. THE EXPOSITION OF MOSES. 144 × 196 cm. Staatliche Gemäldegalerie, Dresden (720).

HISTORY: Bought by Augustus III of Saxony in 1742 from the Parisian collector Poincinet through the de Brais (Gallery catalogue). Presumably the painting seen by James Thornhill in Paris in 1717 (cf. Waterhouse, Bibl. 1308, p. 289), and perhaps that mentioned by Loménie de Brienne as belonging to Mme d'Aligre, 'fort grand par la toile et où il y a encore un grand fleuve qui ne me plaist guère' (p. 215). Brienne describes it as 'Moyse sauvé des eaux', but this may well be due to a confusion. The painting that belonged to Mme d'Aligre cannot be the Oxford picture, nor any of the surviving paintings of the Finding of Moses, all of which were in other collections when Brienne wrote. Mme d'Aligre's paintings had previously belonged to the painter Nicolas Quesnel (cf. Grouchy, Bibl. 618, p. 92).

ENGRAVING: By F. Michelis (Andresen, No. 26).   COPY: National Museum, Budapest (696). From the Esterhazy collection.

NOTES: Dated by Grautoff (II, No. 18) 1628–29; by Mahon (Bibl. 1367, p. 29, n. 84) to the earlier part of the period beginning at the end of 1627 and ending around the late summer of 1629. I agree to this in general and should propose *c.* 1627–29.

BIBLIOGRAPHY: Loménie de Brienne, p. 215; Thornhill, Bibl. 140, p. 88; Smith, No. 14; Grouchy, Bibl. 618, p. 92; Friedlaender, 1914, p. 188; Grautoff, I, pp. 15, 85, II, No. 18; Magne, 1914, p. 205, No. 147; Sayce, Bibl. 1020, p. 244; Licht, p. 90; Blunt, Bibl. 1227, p. 165; Mahon, Bibl. 1271, p. 297; Waterhouse, Bibl. 1308, p. 289; Mahon, Bibl. 1367, pp. XI, 29, 57, 62, 78.

11. THE EXPOSITION OF MOSES. 150 × 204 cm. Ashmolean Museum, Oxford.

HISTORY: Painted for Jacques Stella in 1654 (Félibien, IV, p. 64); passed by inheritance to his niece, Claudine Bouzonnet Stella, and on her death in 1697 to her niece, Marie-Anne Molandier (*Testament . . .*, Bibl. 107, pp. 18, 37, 42); bt. by the Duke of Orleans before 1727 (Dubois de Saint-Gelais, Bibl. 153, p. 350); sold in 1792 with the Italian and French pictures of the Orleans collection to Walkuers, who sold them in the same year to Laborde de Méréville; bt. in 1798 by Bryan for a group of English collectors; exhibited the same year for sale in London and acquired by Richard, Earl Temple, later 1st duke of Buckingham and Chandos (Buchanan, I, p. 152); sold by his son, the 2nd duke, Christie, at Stowe Park, 15.viii–7.x.1848, lot 420; bt. A. Robertson; Francis Gibson, Saffron Walden (d. 1859); bequeathed to his son-in-law, Lewis Fry; by descent to Miss Margery Fry; bt. from her by the museum in 1950.

ENGRAVINGS: 1. By Claudine Bouzonnet Stella, 1672 (Andresen, No. 22; Wildenstein, No. 9; Davies and Blunt, p. 209, No. 9).
2. Probably by Jean Audran (Andresen, No. 23).
3. By G. Chasteau (Andresen, No. 24).
4. Anonymous, published by Hecquet (Andresen, No. 25).

COPIES: 1. Formerly Calais Museum. Presented by Boursot; destroyed in 1940 (cf. Grautoff, II, No. 151).
2. With Ruck, London (1927); probably the same as the picture with Le Portique Gallery, Paris, 1937.

3. In tapestry (cf. Niclausse, Bibl. 920, Pl. XVI).
4. Nicolas Fouquet had a copy of an *Exposition of Moses* sent from Rome in 1656 (cf. Bonnaffé, Bibl. 572, p. 38), which was probably a copy of the Oxford rather than the Dresden picture. This may possibly be the picture recorded in the possession of the Duc de Créqui at his death in 1687 (cf. Magne, Bibl. 936, p. 180).
5. By Antoine Bouzonnet Stella, in the possession of Claudine Bouzonnet Stella (1697, *Testament . . .*, Bibl. 107, pp. 18, 37, 42).

NOTES: The City of the Pharaohs in the background is composed of a mixture of buildings, Roman and oriental, ancient and modern. On the left is the Mausoleum of Hadrian in its modernized form as the Castel S. Angelo. Further to the right is a tomb topped by a pyramid, reminiscent of the so-called Tomb of Absalom outside Jerusalem (cf. text volume, p. 204). Beside this stands a circular temple, which recalls sixteenth-century reconstructions of the so-called Temples of Vesta in Rome and at Tivoli, but is also like Bramante's Tempietto in S. Pietro in Montorio, Rome.

BIBLIOGRAPHY: Chantelou, 1885, p. 159, and 1960, p. 128; Félibien, IV, p. 64; Bellori, p. 450; *Testament . . .*, Bibl. 107, pp. 18, 37, 42; Loménie de Brienne, pp. 214, 218; Florent Le Comte, III, p. 32; (C. Saugrain), Bibl. 138a, I, pp. 159, 175; Thornhill, Bibl. 140, p. 3; Dubois de Saint-Gelais, Bibl. 153, p. 350; Dézallier, 1745, II, p. 255, and 1762, IV, p. 40; Dézallier d'Argenville, Bibl. 183, p. 72; Bardon, II, p. 125; La Roque, Bibl. 248, I, p. 111; Couché, Fontenai and Croze-Magnan, Bibl. 285, III, No. 11; Fuseli, Bibl. 322, pp. 182f; Landon, No. 7; Gault de Saint-Germain, Pt. II, p. 18; Barry, Bibl. 338, I, p. 106; Buchanan, I, p. 152; Waagen, Bibl. 384b, II, p. 493; Smith, No. 11; Friedlaender, 1914, pp. 91, 123; Grautoff, I, p. 278, II, No. 151; Magne, 1914, pp. 155, 205, No. 146; Jamot, p. 53; Blunt, Bibl. 1050, pp. 38 f.; Weigert, Bibl. 1062, p. 84; *Exposition Poussin (Louvre)*, No. 105; Waterhouse, Bibl. 1308, p. 288; Mahon, Bibl. 1338, p. 122; *L'ideale classico (Bologna)*, No. 83; Mahon, Bibl. 1367, pp. XIV, 114, 120; Dempsey, Bibl. 1391, pp. 117 f.

12. THE FINDING OF MOSES. 93 × 120 cm. A strip of 5·5 cm. added at the top and one of 3 cm. on the left. Musée du Louvre, Paris (705).

HISTORY: Painted in 1638; later belonged to André Le Nôtre (Félibien, IV, pp. 151 f.); given by him to Louis XIV in September 1693 (Guiffrey, Bibl. 697, p. 223).

DRAWING: Albertina, Vienna. Reversed copy of painting.

ENGRAVINGS: 1. By Jean Mariette, 1692 (Andresen, No. 33; Wildenstein, No. 12; Davies and Blunt, p. 208, No. 12).
2. By Van Somer (Andresen, No. 34).

COPIES: 1. Museum, Vilna.
2. In the A. L. Girodet-Trioson sale, Pérignon, Paris, 11.iv.1825, lot 437.
3. In the Cardinal Fesch sale, George, Rome, 17 ff.iii. 1845, lot 406.

NOTES: The authenticity of the picture has been doubted by Kauffmann (Bibl. 1332, p. 97).

BIBLIOGRAPHY: Chantelou, 1885, p. 222, and 1960, p. 130; Félibien, IV, pp. 151 f.; Florent Le Comte, III, p. 32; Bailly, p. 313; Dézallier, 1745, II, p. 254, and 1762, IV, p. 39; Landon, No. 8; Gault de Saint-Germain, Pt. II, pp. 31 ff.; Smith, No. 12; Friedlaender, 1914, pp. 58, 115, 191; Grautoff, I, p. 148, II, No. 77; Magne, 1914, pp. 155, 206, No. 154; Sayce, Bibl. 1020, p. 245; Jamot, pp. 25, 52, 63; Blunt, Bibl. 1050, p. 39; Licht, pp. 125 f.; Delbourgo and Petit, Bibl. 1243, p. 49; *Exposition Poussin* (*Louvre*), No. 57; Mahon, Bibl. 1269, p. 262, and Bibl. 1271, p. 304; Thuillier, Bibl. 1296, p. 85; Kauffmann, Bibl. 1332, p. 97; Kitson, Bibl. 1335, p. 154; Mahon, Bibl. 1338, pp. 119 f.; *L'ideale classico* (Bologna), No. 66; Mahon, Bibl. 1367, pp. XIII, 104, 107, 111, 113, 128, and Bibl. 1434, pp. 135 f.

13. THE FINDING OF MOSES. 121 × 195 cm. Musée du Louvre, Paris (706).

HISTORY: Painted for Pointel in 1647 (*Correspondance*, p. 372, and Félibien, IV, p. 55); acquired by the Duc de Richelieu; bt. from him by Louis XIV in 1665 (Ferraton, Bibl. 1043, pp. 439, 446).

DRAWINGS: 1. Musée du Louvre, Paris (*CR*, I, p. 5, No. 3).
2. Musée du Louvre, Paris (*CR*, I, p. 5, No. 5).
3. Museum of Fine Arts, Budapest (*CR*, I, p. 5, No. 4).
4. A further drawing in the Louvre (RF 746) is a very good copy of *CR*, No. 4.

ENGRAVINGS: 1. By Aegidius Rousselet (Andresen, No. 31; Wildenstein, No. 11; Davies and Blunt, p. 208, No. 11).

2. By Simonneau (Andresen, No. 32).

COPIES: 1. Musée des Beaux-Arts, Lille (cf. Gonse, Bibl. 538, pp. 142 f.).
2. Formerly (1897) Löwenfeld collection, Munich.
3. A variant formerly (1937) in a private collection, Brussels.
4. Schwarz sale, Lempertz, Cologne, 10.vi.1931, lot 132 (as by J. F. Millet).
5. A copy in Gobelins tapestry, Musée du Louvre, Paris (cf. Weigert, Bibl. 1062, pp. 83 f.).

NOTES: The group showing a hippopotamus hunt is taken from the Palestrina mosaic.

BIBLIOGRAPHY: *Correspondance*, pp. 327, 375; Félibien, Bibl. 73a, p. 176; *Comptes des bâtiments*, I, p. 927; Chantelou, 1885, p. 159, and 1960, p. 128; Félibien, IV, pp. 55, 149; Loménie de Brienne, pp. 211, 213, 216; Florent Le Comte, I, p. 201, III, p. 29; Piganiol de La Force, Bibl. 124, I, p. 125; Bailly, p. 304; Richardson, *Account*, p. 8 (probably refers to this picture rather than Louvre 705); Dézallier, 1745, II, p. 254, and 1762, IV, p. 39; Landon, No. 11; Smith, No. 15 (wrongly identifies his No. 13 as the Louvre painting); Bonnaffé, Bibl. 573, pp. 207, 214; Friedlaender, 1914, pp. 85, 119, 228; Grautoff, I, p. 230, II, No. 115; Magne, 1914, p. 206, No. 155; Blunt, Bibl. 972, p. 161 n. 3; Sayce, Bibl. 1020, p. 245; Ferraton, Bibl. 1043, pp. 439, 446; Blunt, Bibl. 1050, pp. 39 f.; Licht, p. 138; *Exposition Poussin* (*Louvre*), No. 78; *Exposition* (*Rouen*), No. 84; Mahon, Bibl. 1367, pp. 122 ff., 128; Dempsey, Bibl. 1391, p. 114.

14. THE FINDING OF MOSES. 116 × 177·5 cm. Mrs. Derek Schreiber, Bellasis House, Dorking, Surrey.

HISTORY: Painted for Reynon of Lyons in 1651 (Félibien, IV, p. 63); acquired by the Duc de Richelieu; exchanged with Loménie de Brienne for a landscape by Annibale Carracci (Loménie de Brienne, p. 187) before 1662 (*ibid.*, p. 115); sold by Brienne to du Housset, and by him to the Marquis de Seignelay (*ibid.*, p. 221) before 1685 (Lemaire, Bibl. 91, III, p. 264); in 1702 in the collection of Moreau (Charlotte, Duchesse d'Orléans, Bibl. 125, I, pp. 261 f.), who bought it from 'Païot' or Paillot (Davies, Bibl. 988a,

p. 182 n. 26); passed by inheritance to the Nyert family; Nyert sale, Musier, Paris, 30 ff.iii.1772, lot 19. The Schreiber painting was acquired by the first Lord Clive (cf. inventory of 1774); passed by inheritance to the Earls of Powis and so to the Styche Trust, in favour of Mrs. Schreiber, mother of the present Earl of Powis.

DRAWING: Musée du Louvre, Paris (*CR*, I, p. 6, No. 6). This drawing differs in many details from the Reynon painting, but it must be a study for it.

ENGRAVING: By A. Loir, 1677 (Andresen, No. 27; Wildenstein, No. 10; Davies and Blunt, p. 208, No. 10).

COPY: A version containing only five figures is in the Museum at Lisieux.

BIBLIOGRAPHY: Félibien, IV, p. 63; Le Maire, Bibl. 91, III, p. 264, and Bibl. 91a, p. 191; Loménie de Brienne, pp. 115, 187, 213, 221; Charlotte, Duchesse d'Orléans, Bibl. 125, I, pp. 261 f.; Landon, No. 9; Smith, No. 13; Friedlaender, 1914, p. 121; Grautoff, II, p. 254; Magne, 1914, pp. 155, 206, No. 157; Davies, Bibl. 988a, p. 181; Blunt, Bibl. 1050, pp. 39, 40; Bibl. 1086, p. 192, and Bibl. 1086a, p. 168; *Exposition Poussin* (*Louvre*), No. 102; Mahon, Bibl. 1367, pp. 120, 128; Dempsey, Bibl. 1391, p. 114.

15. MOSES TRAMPLING ON PHARAOH'S CROWN. 92 × 128 cm. Musée du Louvre, Paris (707).

HISTORY: Painted for Cardinal Camillo Massimi (Bellori, p. 450) with *Moses changing Aaron's rod into a serpent* (cf. No. 19) as a pendant; bequeathed to his brother Fabio Camillo (Orbaan, Bibl. 746, p. 517); bt. by Alvarez in Rome and sold by him to Louis XIV in 1683 (Bailly, p. 310).

DRAWINGS: 1. Royal Library, Windsor Castle (*CR*, I, p. 7, No. 9).
2. Formerly Vivant Denon collection, Paris. Rep. in a lithograph in Denon, Bibl. 385, IV, Pl. 283. Also known from a copy in the possession of the author.
3. Gabinetto Nazionale, Rome (129744). Study for the figure on the extreme left of the painting.

ENGRAVINGS: 1. By I. Bouilliard (Andresen, No. 39; Andresen-Wildenstein, No. 39).

2. By Van Somer (Andresen, No. 40; Davies and Blunt, p. 208, No. 13).

COPIES: Paintings of this subject, which may have been copies of the Louvre or the Bedford version (No. 16) appeared in the following sales:
1. Count Reventlow sale, Christie, London, 8 ff.xii. 1788, 4th day, lot 90; bt. Ogle.
2. Girodet-Trioson sale, Pérignon, Paris, 11.iv.1825, lot 437 (attributed to Stella).

NOTES: The subject, rarely treated in art, is taken from Josephus, *Antiquitates*, II, 9, 7.

This picture presents a difficult problem of dating, particularly in relation to the version at Woburn Abbey (No. 16). Grautoff dated the Louvre painting 1643–45, rather earlier than the Woburn version. In 1914 Friedlaender placed the two versions at about the same date, whereas in 1933 he suggested that the Louvre version was the later. In *CR* (I, p. 7) the date *c.* 1643 was proposed for the Woburn Abbey painting, and the Louvre picture was placed in the early fifties. In the catalogue of the Bologna exhibition (No. 73) Mr. Mahon put forward stylistic arguments in favour of the view that the Louvre version is the later of the two and dates the pictures 1643 and 1644–45 respectively.

The Woburn Abbey picture, painted for Pointel, must have been executed between 1642 and 1647, since Lebrun told Bernini in 1665 that he had seen the artist at work on it in Rome, where he spent those five years. (If his statement that it was painted 'il y a vingt ans' is to be taken literally, this would lead to the year 1645, but it must be supposed that Lebrun was talking in general terms.) Poussin had presumably been in contact with Pointel during his visit to Paris in 1640–42, since he speaks of him as a friend in a letter of 17.iii.1644 (*Correspondance*, p. 258), but it is not without significance that his patron was in Rome from the end of May 1645 to the end of July 1646 (*Correspondance*, pp. 302, 341).

On the whole the stylistic evidence points to the Louvre picture being the later of the two, and this view is confirmed by the X-ray of the *Landscape with a Roman Road* (No. 210), which shows under the picture at present visible a version of the Louvre *Moses trampling on Pharaoh's Crown*—a juxtaposition which suggests that the execution of the *Moses* and the Landscape cannot have been separated by too long an interval of time.

BIBLIOGRAPHY: (G. P. Bellori), Bibl. 36, p. 33; *Comptes des bâtiments*, II, p. 272; Félibien, IV, pp. 82, 116, 146; Bellori, p. 450; Loménie de Brienne, p. 222; Florent Le Comte, III, p. 32; Piganiol de La Force, Bibl. 124, I, p. 127; Bailly, p. 310; Dézallier, 1745, II, pp. 254, 255,

and 1762, IV, p. 39; Tuétey and Guiffrey, Bibl. 304, p. 369; Landon, No. 13; Guiffrey, Bibl. 581, I, p. 85; Friedlaender, 1914, pp. 84, 118, 225; Grautoff, I, p. 225, II, No. 110; Magne, 1914, p. 206, No. 152; Orbaan, Bibl. 746, p. 517; Blunt, Bibl. 972, p. 163, and

Bibl. 975, p. 51, No. 262; Sayce, Bibl. 1020, p. 246; Weigert, Bibl. 1062, p. 83; *Exposition Poussin (Louvre)*, No. 76; *L'ideale classico (Bologna)*, No. 73; Mahon, Bibl. 1367, p. 119.

16. MOSES TRAMPLING ON PHARAOH'S CROWN. 101×141 cm. The Duke of Bedford, Woburn Abbey.

HISTORY: Painted between 1642 and 1647 (Chantelou, 1960, p. 131) probably for Pointel, in whose possession it is first recorded; bt. at his death by Loménie de Brienne (Loménie de Brienne, pp. 213, 224); belonged to Cotteblanche in 1665 (Chantelou, 1960, pp. 128, 131); bt. by Jean Baptiste Colbert, Marquis de Seignelay, son of the minister (d. 1690; Loménie de Brienne, p. 213); presumably passed with his collection to his younger brother, Jacques Nicolas Colbert, Archbishop of Rouen (d. 1707), and then to his nephew, the Abbé de Colbert. Bt. by Philippe, Duc d'Orléans, the Regent, before 1727 (Dubois de Saint-Gelais, Bibl. 153, p. 326); sold with the French and Italian pictures in the Orleans collection to Walkuers in 1792; sold by him the same year to Laborde de Méréville; bt. in 1798 by Bryan for a group of English collectors; in Bryan's list of pictures for sale in 1798 (No. 46); bt. by the Duke of Bedford (Buchanan, I, p. 151); anon. (= Duke of Bedford) sale, Christie, London, 6.vi.1829, lot 35; bt. in.

DRAWING: Kauffmann (Bibl. 1118, p. 231,) reproduces a drawing at Düsseldorf which may be a copy of an original by Poussin now lost.

ENGRAVINGS: 1. By Etienne Baudet (Andresen, No. 35; Wildenstein, No. 13; Davies and Blunt, p. 208, No. 13).
2. Anonymous, published by H. Bonnart (Andresen, No. 36).
3. By I. Bouilliard (Andresen, No. 37).
4. Anonymous, published by Hecquet (Andresen, No. 38).

NOTES: For a discussion of the dating, see No. 15.

BIBLIOGRAPHY: Chantelou, 1885, pp. 159, 227, and 1960, pp. 128, 131; Loménie de Brienne, pp. 213, 215 f., 218, 220, 224; (C. Saugrain), Bibl. 138a, I, pp. 166, 175; Dubois de Saint-Gelais, Bibl. 153, p. 326; Dézallier, 1745, II, p. 255, and 1762, IV, p. 40; Dézallier d'Argenville, Bibl. 183, p. 60; Bardon, II, p. 125; La Roque, Bibl. 248, I, p. 107; Couché, Fontenai and Croze-Magnan, Bibl. 285, III, No. 10; Volkmann, Bibl. 290,

COPIES: 1. Musée Ingres, Montauban (cf. Thuillier, Bibl. 1299, p. 293).
2. Ritter collection, Basle (101×141 cm.).
3. Grautoff (II, No. 111) records that a copy appeared in an unspecified sale at the Hôtel Drouot, Paris, in April 1914.
4. A copy of this or the Louvre composition (No. 15) in gouache, signed *Henri Toutin,* was in an anonymous sale, Christie, London, 6.v.1949, lot 75.
5. A painting of this subject was formerly in the Palazzo Ruspoli, Rome (Rossini, Bibl. 106b, p. 85).

I, p. 284; Landon, No. 12; Barry, Bibl. 338, II, p. 75; Buchanan, I, p. 151; Waagen, Bibl. 384b, II, pp. 284, 493; Smith, No. 19; Friedlaender, 1914, p. 118; Grautoff, I, p. 225, II, No. 111; Magne, 1914, p. 206, No. 153; Blunt, Bibl. 972, p. 163; Sayce, Bibl. 1020, p. 246; Waterhouse, Bibl. 1061, p. 53; Kauffmann, Bibl. 1118, p. 232; Mahon, Bibl. 1338, p. 129.

17. MOSES AND THE DAUGHTERS OF JETHRO. Original lost. Composition known from engravings and drawings.

DRAWINGS: 1. Royal Library, Windsor Castle (*CR*, I, p. 9, Nos. 11, 12). Studies for the group of women on the *recto* and *verso* of a single sheet.
2. Royal Library, Windsor Castle (*CR*, I, p. 8, No. A3). Study for the whole composition. Classified in *CR* as a copy, but probably an original.
3. Private collection, London (*CR*, I, p. 8, No. 10). Classified in *CR* as an original, but probably a copy.
4. Mrs. Murray Danforth, Providence, Rhode Island. Study for the group of Moses and the Shepherds. Almost identical with the corresponding group in *CR*, I, p. 8, No. A3.

5. Musée du Louvre, Paris (*CR*, I, p. 9, No. 13).
6. Musée du Louvre, Paris (*CR*, I, p. 9, No. 15). Engraved by J. F. P. Peyron (Andresen, No. 45).

ENGRAVINGS: 1. By Trouvain (Andresen, No. 41; Davies and Blunt, p. 208, No. 14). The engraving has the words: *N. Poussin pinxit,* which prove that it was made from a painting, not a drawing.
2. Anonymous, published by Vallet (Andresen, No. 42; Wildenstein, No. 14).
3. By Jean Langlois (Andresen, No. 43).

NOTES: The drawings prove that Trouvain's and Vallet's engravings are both reversed. In the absence of the original it is difficult to suggest an exact date for the composition, the more so as the evidence of the drawings is conflicting. The big and finished drawing in the Louvre (*CR*, No. 15) must date from the late forties, a dating confirmed by the close connection with *CR*, No. 13, which has on the other side of the sheet sketches for the *Finding of Moses* of 1647. On the other hand the much livelier composition shown in *CR*, Nos. 10, 11, 12 and A3 suggests an earlier dating, perhaps in the late thirties. It is possible, therefore, that Poussin may have planned the composition before the journey to Paris, set it aside, and taken it up again in the late forties. There is no reference to the subject of this composition in the early sources.

BIBLIOGRAPHY: Landon, No. 15; Smith, No. 22; Grautoff, II, p. 255.

18. MOSES AND THE BURNING BUSH. 193 × 158 cm. Originally oval. The canvas was at some date made rectangular, but the additions were removed in 1960. Nationalmuseum, Copenhagen (558).

HISTORY: Commissioned by Cardinal Richelieu for the Grand Cabinet in the Palais Cardinal (later Palais Royal) in Paris (Bellori, p. 428); finished before November 1641 (see below); bequeathed with the palace and its contents to Louis XIII; mentioned by Félibien (IV, p. 151) as belonging to Louis XIV, but not listed in any of the inventories of the royal collection; perhaps, therefore, left in the Palais Royal, which had been lent to the king's brother, Philippe, Duc d'Orléans, and was given in 1692 to the latter's son Philippe, Duc de Chartres, later Duc d'Orléans and Regent during the minority of Louis XV; probably removed during the alterations made to the palace by the younger Philippe d'Orléans, and perhaps given to the king of Denmark, in whose collection it is recorded in 1761 (cf. catalogue of the Copenhagen museum).

DRAWINGS: 1. Musée du Louvre, Paris (*CR*, I, p. 10, No. A 4).
2. Royal Library, Windsor Castle (*CR*, I, p. 10, No. A 5).
Both drawings are finished versions made by studio assistants, perhaps for submission to the cardinal. In the painting the figure of God the Father in *CR*, No. A 4, is combined with that of Moses from *CR*, No. A 5.

ENGRAVING: The engraving by B. Vernesson (Andresen, No. 46; Wildenstein, No. 15) is apparently based on the Windsor drawing (*CR*, No. A 5) and not on the painting.

COPY: In the chapel of the château of Bussy-Rabutin (cf. Dumolin, Bibl. 873, p. 90). Its history is not known, but it may well have been commissioned by Roger de Bussy, Comte de Rabutin, author of the *Histoire amoureuse des Gaules*, and a contemporary of Poussin.

NOTES: The evidence about the precise date at which the *Burning Bush* was painted is as follows. On his arrival in Paris in December 1640, Poussin, according to Bellori (p. 428), embarked on painting the *Institution of the Eucharist* (No. 78), commissioned by the king for the chapel of St. Germain-en-Laye, and the *St. Francis Xavier* (No. 101), ordered by Sublet de Noyers for the Noviciate of the Jesuits, Paris. According to Bellori (*ibid.*), however, work on both the pictures was shelved, so that the artist could paint the *Burning Bush* for Richelieu. Soon afterwards he executed for the cardinal a second painting, *Time saving Truth from the attacks of Envy and Discord* (No. 122), which was to decorate the ceiling of the same room in the Palais Cardinal. Both canvases were finished by November 1641, because on the 21st of the month Poussin wrote to Pozzo that the cardinal was satisfied 'de' suoi [quadri]' (unfortunately Jouanny, *Correspondance*, p. 106, prints *del* for *de*' and translates *du sien* instead of *des siens*).

There can be little doubt that Richelieu chose the themes for both the paintings in the Grand Cabinet, and that he saw in Moses a forerunner of himself as leader of a great people through a crisis in their history. Sterling (*Exposition Poussin (Louvre)*, pp. 240 f.) has pointed out that almost the same subjects were represented in the decoration of the château de Richelieu, the only difference being that *Moses receiving the tables of the law* replaced the *Burning Bush*. The painting contains many borrowings from Raphael: the figure of Moses is based on one in the Ananias tapestry, and God the Father is taken from an engraving by Marcantonio after Raphael (cf. Stein, Bibl. 1079, p. 9).

BIBLIOGRAPHY: *Correspondance*, p. 106; Félibien, IV, p. 151; Bellori, p. 428; Passeri, p. 329; Baldinucci, XVI, p. 104; Florent Le Comte, III, p. 31; Ramdohr, Bibl. 302, pp. 113 f.; Smith, No. 24; Nielsen, Bibl. 644, p. 37; Friedlaender, 1914, pp. 117, 213; Grautoff, I, p. 213, II, No. 104; Magne, 1914, pp. 122, 126, 204, No. 129; Hourticq, Bibl. 748, pp. 23 ff.; Elling, Bibl. 889, p. 10; Blunt, Bibl. 975, p. 50, No. 246, and Bibl. 1065, p. 370 n. 2; Stein, Bibl. 1079, p. 9; Licht, p. 133; *Exposition Poussin (Louvre)*, No. 64, and pp. 240 f.

19. MOSES CHANGING AARON'S ROD INTO A SERPENT. 92×128 cm. Musée du Louvre, Paris (708).

HISTORY: See the pendant, No. 15.

DRAWINGS: 1. Musée du Louvre, Paris (*CR*, I, p. 10, No. 16).
2. Gabinetto Nazionale, Rome (129744). Study for the priest in the centre of the composition.

ENGRAVINGS: 1. By F. de Poilly (Andresen, No. 47; Wildenstein, No. 16; Davies and Blunt, p. 208, No. 16).
2. Anonymous, published by Gantrel (Andresen, No. 48).

NOTES: For the question of dating, see No. 15.

BIBLIOGRAPHY: See No. 15, and Bellori, p. 451; Loménie de Brienne, p. 222; Landon, No. 17; Smith, No. 25; Grautoff, I, p. 225, II, No. 109;

COPIES: 1. A cartoon was made by Bonemer as a preparation for the Gobelins tapestry (cf. Guiffrey, Bibl. 581, I, p. 129, and Weigert, Bibl. 1062, p. 83).
2. A painting of this subject was offered for sale by S. Pawson, London, in 1795 or 1796 (No. 16) as coming from the collection of 'Mons. July de la Live'. No such painting is, however, traceable in the La Live de Jully sale, Remy, Paris, 2 ff.v.1770.

Magne, 1914, p. 205, No. 142; Orbaan, Bibl. 746, p. 519; Delbourgo and Petit, Bibl. 1243, p. 46; *Exposition Poussin* (*Louvre*), No. 77.

20. THE CROSSING OF THE RED SEA. 154×210 cm. National Gallery of Victoria, Melbourne, Australia.

HISTORY: Painted for Amadeo dal Pozzo, marchese di Voghera, cousin of Cassiano dal Pozzo, with its pendant, the *Adoration of the Golden Calf* (No. 26); still in his palace in Turin in the 1670's (Bellori, p. 419, and Scaramuccia, Bibl. 64, p. 157); both pictures were in the collection of the Chevalier de Lorraine (d. 1702) by 1684, when the *Golden Calf* was engraved by E. Baudet (cf. No. 26); apparently in the Hôtel de Bretonvilliers in 1713 (Brice, Bibl. 89d, II, pp. 162 f.); bought through Samuel Paris in 1741 by Sir Jacob Bouverie; by descent to the Earls of Radnor; sold 1945 to Agnew's; bt. from them by the National Gallery in 1948.

DRAWINGS: 1. Hermitage Museum, Leningrad (*CR* I, p. 11, No. 17).
2. Hermitage Museum, Leningrad (*CR*, I, p. 11, No. 18).
3. Hermitage Museum, Leningrad (*CR*, I, p. 11, No. 19).
4. Musée du Louvre, Paris (*CR*, I, p. 11, No. 20).
5. Musée du Louvre, Paris (*CR*, I, p. 11, No. 21).
6. Musée des Beaux-Arts, Besançon. A copy after the painting.

7. Marquess of Northampton sale, Christie, London, 1.v.1959, lot 8. An engraver's drawing after the painting.
8. Sir Anthony Blunt collection, London. Red chalk (Isaacs sale, Sotheby, London, 27.ii.1964, lot 69, as Italian School).

ENGRAVING: Anonymous, published by E. Gantrel (Andresen, No. 49; Wildenstein, No. 17).

COPY: By Charles Lebrun. Robert Strange sale, Christie, London, 5.iii.1773, lot 107; bt. West (presumably Benjamin West).

NOTES: The catalogue of the Strange sale contains the following note on the copy by Lebrun: 'It is to be remarked that the engravings which have been published of this picture and its companion, have, in all probability, been done from these admirable copies of Le Brun, because in the print of this subject we do not find the pillar of fire behind the Moses, which is certainly in the picture painted by Poussin, in the collection of the Earl of Radnor. For what reason Le Brun had omitted this, is best known to himself.' The pillar—in fact of cloud not fire—which had been painted out in the original, reappeared when the painting was cleaned in 1960, but was in fact so much damaged that it had to be covered again.

Poussin has followed Josephus (*Antiquitates*, II, 16, 6) in showing the children of Israel taking the armour from the bodies of the dead Egyptians being washed up on the shore of the Red Sea.

The dating of this picture and its pendant presents considerable difficulties. Bellori mentions them just before discussing those which he allots to the year 1637. Grautoff dates them 1637–39; Friedlaender (1914, p. 114) 1633–37; in the Catalogue Raisonné of the drawings (*CR*, I, pp. 10 f.) *c.* 1636 is proposed. In the catalogue of the Paris exhibition (No. 37) I suggested *c.* 1634–35. Mr. Mahon (Bibl. 1367, pp. 92 ff.) proposes *c.* 1637.

It is clear that they must have been painted after the *Adoration of the Magi* of 1633 (No. 44) and well before the journey to Paris. Their Venetian character leads at first sight to the view that they would come early in this period, but Mr. Mahon points out certain features of colour which relate them to the paintings of about 1637. A dating of *c.* 1635–37 seems reasonably safe.

BIBLIOGRAPHY: *Procès-verbaux*, II, p. 278; Monconys, Bibl. 35, II, p. 496, and Bibl. 35a, p. 119; Félibien, IV, p. 24; Bellori, p. 419; Scaramuccia, Bibl. 64, p. 157, and Bibl. 64a, p. 159; Sandrart, p. 258; Baldinucci, XVI, p. 102; Brice, Bibl. 89a, I, p. 60, and Bibl. 89d, II, pp. 162 f.; Loménie de Brienne, pp. 214, 218; Vertue, Bibl. 132, XXII, pp. 105, 117; Piganiol de La Force, Bibl. 173, I, p. 347; Dézallier, 1745, II, p. 254, and 1762, IV, p. 38; Guibal, Bibl. 273, p. 30; Dulaure, Bibl. 278a, II, p. 75; Landon, No. 18; Gault de Saint-Germain, Pt. II, pp. 60 f.; Waagen, Bibl. 384b, III, p. 141, IV, p. 359; Smith, No. 26; Friedlaender, 1914, pp. 63, 114, 201; Grautoff, I, p. 164, II, No. 89; Magne, 1914, pp. 93, 206, No. 160; Davies, Bibl. 988a, p. 177; Blunt, Bibl. 1003, p. 269; Sayce, Bibl. 1020, p. 246; Blunt, Bibl. 1064, *passim*, Bibl. 1086, p. 186, and Bibl. 1086a, p. 162; Licht, p. 129; *Exposition Poussin (Louvre)*, No. 37; Mahon, Bibl. 1271, pp. 303 f.; Waterhouse, Bibl. 1308, p. 292; Mahon, Bibl. 1367, pp. XII, 79 ff., 92, 94 f., 101 f., 107.

21. THE ISRAELITES GATHERING THE MANNA. 149×200 cm. Musée du Louvre, Paris (709).

HISTORY: Painted for Paul Fréart de Chantelou; in a letter of 19.iii.1639 (*Correspondance*, pp. 19 f.) Poussin announced that it was finished, but it must have been begun the year before, and perhaps even in 1637, since Félibien (IV, p. 26) wrote of the *Manna* with the pictures which he dates to that year. Chantelou presumably sold the picture to Nicolas Fouquet, who is mentioned by Chantelou in 1665 as having owned it (1885, p. 159); probably seized when Fouquet was disgraced in 1661; certainly in the royal collection by 1667, when it was the subject of a lecture delivered to the Academy by Charles Lebrun (*Conférences*, Bibl. 47a, pp. 48 ff.).

ENGRAVINGS: 1. By G. Chasteau, 1680 (Andresen, No. 50; Wildenstein, No. 18; Davies and Blunt, p. 208, No. 18).
2. By E. Gantrel (Andresen, No. 51).
3. By H. Testelin (Andresen, No. 52) for his *Les sentiments des plus habiles peintres . . .*, 1680 (Bibl. 80).
4. Anonymous, published by B. Audran (Andresen, No. 53).
5. Anonymous, published by Poilly (Andresen, No. 54).
6. Anonymous, published by Jean Mariette (Andresen, No. 55).
7. Johannes Hainzelmann (Andresen, No. 56).
8. An engraving by Jean Pesne (Andresen, No. 309; Wildenstein, No. 108; Davies and Blunt, p. 213, No. 108) reproduces two figures from the painting adapted to represent the story of Cimon and Pero.

COPIES: 1. By Delacroix. Jacques Dupont collection, Paris (cf. Chastel, Bibl. 1238, p. 303).
2. By Degas, anon. sale, Hôtel Drouot, Paris, 9.v.1949, lot 61.
3. Comte de Bagneux collection, Château de Limezy, Normandy (in 1914; cf. Grautoff, I, p. 165).
4. By Eustache Restout. Abbey de Mondaye, near Bayeux (cf. Chennevières-Pointel, Bibl. 603, p. 99).

NOTES: For a discussion of this picture, see text volume, p. 223.

Brice states in his edition of 1687 (Bibl. 89a, I, p. 213) that the *Manna* still belonged to Chantelou, but either he was mistaken or Chantelou, having parted with the original, had replaced it by a copy.

BIBLIOGRAPHY: *Correspondance*, pp. 8 f., 12, 13, 14, 19, 20 f., 23, 267, 288; *Comptes des bâtiments*, I, p. 1347; Chantelou, 1885, p. 159, and 1960, p. 128; Félibien, IV, pp. 26 f., 120 ff.; Lebrun (1667) in *Conférences . . .*, Bibl. 47a, pp. 48 ff.; Bellori, p. 427; Testelin, Bibl. 80, pp. 28 f.; Brice, Bibl. 89a, I, p. 213; Loménie de Brienne, pp. 213, 218, 224; Perrault, Bibl. 113, I, p. 89; Florent Le Comte, I, p. 201, III, p. 26; Piganiol de La Force, Bibl. 124, I, p. 126; Bailly, p. 302; Dézallier, 1745, II, p. 254, and 1762, IV, p. 39; Gougenot, Bibl. 184, p. 179; Diderot, Bibl. 211, XI, p. 41; Hagedorn, Bibl. 215, p. 92; Bardon, I, pp. 93, 110, II, p. 125; Boyer d'Argens, Bibl. 231, p. 297; Le Mierre, Bibl. 234, p. 17; Cambry, Bibl. 272a, pp. 49, 55; Guibal, Bibl. 273, p. 30; Landon, No. 19; Gault de Saint-Germain, Pt. II, pp. 25 ff.; Barry, Bibl. 338, I, p. 458; Smith, No. 27, Rou, Bibl. 475.1, p. 22; Bonnaffé, Bibl. 572, pp. 40, 51; Friedlaender, 1914, pp. 64 ff., 116, 203; Grautoff, I, p. 165, II, No. 90; Magne, 1914, pp. 101, 103, 204, No. 133; Francastel, Bibl. 883, p. 146; Finberg, Bibl. 934, p. 89; Blunt, Bibl. 972, p. 154, Bibl. 1086, pp. 187, 189, and Bibl. 1086a, pp. 163, 165; Licht, p. 130; Thuillier, Bibl. 1161, p. 388; Wild, Bibl. 1184, p. 170; Delbourgo and Petit, Bibl. 1243, pp. 44 ff.; *Exposition Poussin (Louvre)*, No. 56; Mahon, Bibl. 1268.1, p. 354, Bibl. 1269, p. 263, and Bibl. 1271, p. 304; Seznec, Bibl. 1284, p. 345; Vanuxem, Bibl. 1302, p. 158; Mahon, Bibl. 1338, p. 120; *Exposition Poussin (Rouen)*, No. 81; *L'ideale classico (Bologna)*, No. 67; Mahon, Bibl. 1367, pp. XII f., 95, 101, 104 f., 107, 113, 115.

22. MOSES STRIKING THE ROCK. 97×133 cm. The Duke of Sutherland (on loan to the National Gallery of Scotland, Edinburgh).

HISTORY: For the details of the complicated early history of the picture, see below. Almost certainly painted for Melchior Gillier, not later than 1637; then belonged to de l'Isle Sourdière (perhaps d. 1650); later to the Président de Bellièvre and Dreux, and in 1685 to Jean Baptiste Colbert, Marquis de Seignelay (d. 1690; cf. Félibien, IV, p. 24); presumably passed with his collection to his younger brother, Jacques Nicolas Colbert, Archbishop of Rouen (d. 1707) and then to his nephew, the Abbé de Colbert (cf. Bonnaffé, Bibl. 583, p. 289); in the possession of the Duc d'Orléans by 1727 (Dubois de Saint-Gelais, Bibl. 153, p. 329, as from the Dreux collection); sold with the Italian and French pictures of the Orleans collection to Walkuers in 1792; sold by him the same year to Laborde de Méréville; bt. 1798 by Bryan for a group of English collectors; exhibited by Bryan, 1798, No. 54; bt. by the Duke of Bridgewater (Buchanan, I, p. 151); by descent to the Earls of Ellesmere and so to the Duke of Sutherland; on loan to the National Gallery of Scotland since 1946.

DRAWINGS: 1. Musée du Louvre, Paris (CR, I, p. 13, No. 23).

2. A drawing in the Museum Boymans-van Beuningen, Rotterdam, is a copy after the group in the left foreground of the painting. It appeared in the A. Kann sale, New York, 7.i.1927, lot 16.

ENGRAVINGS: 1. By E. Baudet (Andresen, No. 63; Wildenstein, No. 20; Davies and Blunt, p. 208, No. 20). A proof of the engraving was presented to the Academy by Baudet in 1684 (Procès-verbaux, II, p. 278).

2. Anonymous, published by E. Gantrel (Andresen, No. 64).

3. Anonymous, published by Cars (Andresen, No. 65).

COPIES: 1. Musée des Beaux-Arts, Angers. From the convent of the Dames de Saint-Magloire, rue St. Denis, Paris (Thuillier, Bibl. 1297, p. 38).

2. Shipley Art Gallery, Gateshead, Durham.

3. Musée des Beaux-Arts, Rouen. Copy of right-hand part of the composition only.

4. Church of St. Bernard de la Bénisson-Dieu, near Rouen (cf. Magne, 1914, p. 205, No. 148).

5. Mme Groene, Montrouge, Paris.

6. Baroness Esther Rosenkrantz, Copenhagen.

7. A copy of the group in the right foreground, present whereabouts unknown. Formerly Agar Ellis collection; Earl Grosvenor; by descent to the Dukes of Westminster; Westminster sale, Christie, London, 10.xii.1948, lot 115 (Smith, No. 293; Grautoff, I, p. 266); Swinfen-Brown sale, Christie, London, 10.xii.1948, lot 114.

NOTES: Félibien (IV, p. 24) states that the painting commissioned by Melchior Gillier later belonged to de l'Isle Sourdière, the Président de Bellièvre and Dreux, and that at the time he was writing it belonged to the marquis de Seignelay. If this is correct, this is the painting which was later in the Orleans collection, since Dubois de Saint-Gelais says that the latter had belonged to Dreux.

The identification of the early owners is not easy. Gillier belonged to the household of the Maréchal de Créqui. He lived in a house on the Île St. Louis, built for him in the late 1630's by Louis Le Vau (C. Tooth, 'The Paris houses of Louis Le Vau', unpublished dissertation, London, 1961) and died in 1669 at the age of eighty (cf. C. Petitjean and C. Wickert, Catalogue de l'oeuvre gravé de Robert Nanteuil, Paris, 1925, I, p. 199). De l'Isle Sourdière is not otherwise mentioned in the early sources. M. Wildenstein (No. 20) says that Félibien gives the owner as 'de Lisle Jourdain' and states further that he has found the inventory made at the death of François Gujet, Sieur de Lisle Jourdain, at his death in 1650, which contained a painting of the Striking of the Rock by Poussin, the size of which is given as 4×3 feet (approximately 130 × 100 cm.), which would correspond with the dimensions of the Sutherland canvas. If in fact the inventory which M. Wildenstein found is that of de l'Isle Sourdière and not of de Lisle Jourdain, the pedigree of the painting as given by Félibien would be confirmed, though it would be necessary to assume that Gillier sold the picture during his life-time. Pomponne de Bellièvre died in 1657 and so could have acquired the painting after the death of de l'Isle Sourdière. Dreux cannot be exactly identified, but there was a family of that name who produced several distinguished lawyers in the seventeenth century, though little is known of them. One, whose Christian name is not known, was a son of Pierre de Dreux and was conseiller au Parlement and later became a canon of Notre-Dame; another, also without known Christian name, became conseiller au Grand Conseil in 1637 and died in 1680 (de la Chenaye-Desbois and Badier, Dictionnaire de la Noblesse, 1863–76, VII, pp. 26 ff.). Jean Baptiste Colbert, Marquis de Seignelay, son of Louis XIV's famous minister, some of whose pictures were bought by the Regent from Seignelay's nephew, who died in 1690.

The only difficulty about identifying the Sutherland picture with that commissioned by Gillier is that Bellori (p. 421) states that Gillier's painting was executed after that for Stella (No. 23), and his description of the composition agrees not with the Sutherland painting but with the engraving attributed to Jean Lepautre after a lost version (see No. 24). Félibien, however, who would have been better informed than Bellori about Gillier's painting, which was in Paris, states that it was earlier than Stella's, but does not describe it. Bellori very likely wrote his description from the engraving, supposing it to be after Gillier's picture.

Grautoff (II, No. 91) further confuses the matter by stating, without giving any evidence, that the Sutherland picture was painted for Paul Fréart de Chantelou.

The precise dating of the picture presents some difficulties. Félibien speaks of it just before mentioning the *Camillus* executed for Le Vrillière in 1637, but it is fairly clear that the arrangement of pictures in this section of the *Entretiens* on Poussin is not intended to be strictly chronological. Mme Wild (Bibl. 1312, p. 157) wants to date it 1633–34, because Gillier left Rome with the duc de Créqui in the latter year, but there is nothing to show that the painting was executed while Gillier was in Italy. Grautoff dates it 1639–40, which is probably too late. Mahon (Bibl. 1271, p. 304) supports the dating *c.* 1637 proposed in the catalogue of the Paris exhibition (pp. 117, 155).

BIBLIOGRAPHY: Félibien, IV, pp. 24, 60, 91; Bellori, pp. 421, 427; Baldinucci, XVI, p. 102; Le Maire, Bibl. 91, III, p. 264, and Bibl. 91a, p. 191; Loménie de Brienne, p. 221; Florent Le Comte, III, p. 26; (C. Saugrain), Bibl. 138a, I, p. 175; Thornhill, Bibl. 140, p. 88; Dubois de Saint-Gelais, Bibl. 153, p. 329; Dézallier, 1745, II, p. 255, and 1762, IV, p. 40; Dézallier d'Argenville, Bibl. 183, p. 61; Bardon, II, p. 125; La Roque, Bibl. 248, I, p. 102; Cambry, Bibl. 272a, p. 40; Couché, Fontenai and Croze-Magnan, Bibl. 285, III, No. 9; Landon, No. 22; Gault de Saint-Germain, Pt. II, pp. 61 f.; Barry, Bibl. 338, I, pp. 31, 458, II, p. 80; Buchanan, I, p. 151; Waagen, Bibl. 384b, II, pp. 39, 493; Smith, No. 31; Cousin, Bibl. 456, p. 13; Friedlaender, 1914, pp. 61 f., 115, 200; Grautoff, I, p. 167, II, No. 91; Magne, 1914, pp. 93, 205, No. 148; Hourticq, Bibl. 899, p. 62; Blunt, Bibl. 975, p. 46, and Bibl. 976, p. 189; Sayce, Bibl. 1020, p. 246; Licht, p. 129; Mahon, Bibl. 1271, p. 304; Waterhouse, Bibl. 1308, p. 289; Wild, Bibl. 1312, p. 157; Mahon, Bibl. 1367, pp. XII, 102.

23. MOSES STRIKING THE ROCK. 122.5 × 193 cm. Hermitage Museum, Leningrad (1117).

HISTORY: Painted for Jacques Stella in 1649 (Félibien, IV, p. 60); bequeathed to his niece, Claudine Bouzonnet Stella, and by her to her niece, Marie Anne Molandier (*Testament . . .*, Bibl. 107, pp. 18, 37, 42); acquired by Sir Robert Walpole *c.* 1733 (Waterhouse, Bibl. 1308, p. 290); bt. with the Walpole collection by Catherine II of Russia in 1779.

DRAWINGS: 1. Hermitage Museum, Leningrad (*CR*, I, p. 13, No. 24).
2. Nationalmuseum, Stockholm (*CR*, I, p. 13, No. 25).
3. Musée du Louvre, Paris (*CR*, I, p. 13, No. 26).
4. Hermitage Museum, Leningrad (*CR*, I, p. 14, No. 27).
5. Nationalmuseum, Stockholm. By Bourdon after the painting.

ENGRAVINGS: 1. By Claudine Bouzonnet Stella (Andresen, No. 57; Wildenstein, No. 19; Davies and Blunt, p. 208, No. 19).
2. Anonymous, published by Etienne Gantrel (Andresen, No. 58).
3. By J. B. Michel (Andresen, No. 59).
4. Anonymous, published by Poilly (Andresen, No. 60).
6. Anonymous, published by Audran (Andresen, No. 61).
7. By G. C. Kilian (Andresen, No. 62).

COPIES: 1. H. Walker collection, Brookman Park, Hertfordshire. An exact copy, but extended on the right by the addition of the right-hand groups from the Sutherland painting (No. 22).
2. Justice Murnaghan, Dublin.
3. Private collection, Edinburgh.
4. With Tozzi, New York (1956).
5. Ann Murrell collection, Washington, D.C. 69.5 × 84.5 cm. Brought to the United States in 1835.
6. By Antoine Stella, in the possession of Claudine Bouzonnet Stella (*Testament . . .*, Bibl. 107, p. 57).
7. By Ranelagh Barrett, made in 1742 (Vertue, Bibl. 132, XXII, p. 112).
8. In the Convent of the Blancs-Manteaux, Paris, confiscated in 1790 (Stein, Bibl. 610, p. 42). The author states that the picture was a copy of the Hermitage version, but without giving any evidence.
9. In the P. Norton collection, lent to the Manchester exhibition in 1857. Triqueti (*Catalogue*, Bibl. 440) states explicitly that it was a copy of the version engraved by Stella.

A painting of this subject was in the Chaillon de Joinville collection, confiscated in 1793 (*Les tableaux saisis*, Bibl. 305, p. 295), but there is no means of knowing which composition it represented.

A copy of one version, unspecified, belonged to André Le Nôtre (Guiffrey, Bibl. 697, p. 243, No. 198). Its dimensions were *c.* 3×4 feet. Valued at 80 livres.

BIBLIOGRAPHY: Chantelou, 1885, p. 159, and 1960, p. 128; Félibien, IV, pp. 60, 91; Bellori, p. 419; Baldinucci, XVI, p. 102; *Testament*, Bibl. 107, pp. 18, 37, 42; Loménie de Brienne, pp. 214, 218, 221; Florent Le Comte, III, p. 31; Vertue, Bibl. 132, XXX, p. 175; Walpole, Bibl. 319, II, p. 276; Landon, No. 20; Le Breton, Bibl. 339, p. 394; Smith, No. 28; Friedlaender, 1914, p. 120; Grautoff, I, p. 263, II, No. 139; Magne, 1914, pp. 155, 206, No. 149; Goertz, Bibl. 952, II, p. 149; Sayce, Bibl. 1020, p. 246; Sterling, Bibl. 1159, p. 32; *Exposition Poussin (Louvre)*, No. 88; Panofsky, Bibl. 1273, p. 31; Waterhouse, Bibl. 1308, p. 290; Mahon, Bibl. 1367, p. 115.

24. MOSES STRIKING THE ROCK. Original lost. Composition known from an engraving.

ENGRAVING: Attributed by Andresen (No. 66) and Wildenstein (No. 21) to Jean Lepautre (cf. also Davies and Blunt, p. 208, No. 21). The engraving probably dates from before 1680, because it is dedicated to Nicolas Coquelin, who is not given the title of chancellor of the University of Paris, which he received in that year (cf. Wildenstein, *loc. cit.*).

NOTES: Bellori (p. 421) describes this composition in detail and says that it was executed for Gillier, which appears not to be the case (cf. No. 22).

Mr. Mahon (Bibl. 1271, p. 304) points out that the engraving is almost certainly in reverse, since Moses holds his rod in his left hand, and suggests that it may be after a drawing connected with the Sutherland picture, but the inscription on the engraving reads: *Nicolaus Poussin Invent. et Pinxit*, and Bellori in his description refers always to a *quadro*. Nevertheless the somewhat confused composition, based on the repetition of a single gesture—the arm raised in astonishment—may lead to a certain degree of doubt whether the engraving in fact records a fully elaborated design by Poussin.

BIBLIOGRAPHY: Bellori, p. 421; Landon, No. 21; Smith, No. 29; Friedlaender, 1914, p. 115; Magne, 1914, p. 206, No. 150; *CR*, I, p. 12; Mahon, Bibl. 1271, p. 304.

25. THE ADORATION OF THE GOLDEN CALF. 99.4×128.6 cm. Signed: *N.P. 1626*, the last figure being doubtful (see below). The M. H. de Young Memorial Museum, San Francisco.

HISTORY: This, rather than the National Gallery version (No. 26), may be the picture referred to by Sandrart (p. 258), partly because it was painted before he reached Rome, and partly because he does not mention any pendant, as he would probably have done if he was referring to the National Gallery painting. It is also probably the painting recorded in Holland in the eighteenth century. This appeared in the Quirijn van Biesum sale, Rotterdam, 18.x.1719, lot 11 (Hoet, Bibl. 195, I, p. 227), of which the size is given as 39×50 inches (=99×127 cm.), and is no doubt the picture seen by Richardson in the Flinck collection, Amsterdam, before 1722 (Richardson, *Account*, p. 1); a painting of the same subject was in the Dufresne sale, Amsterdam, 22.viii.1770, lot 101 (41×68 inches). In 1919 the San Francisco picture was with the Sackville Gallery, London, and was said to have belonged previously to the Earl of Harewood, and then to have been in the Estate of Rudolph Bottenwieser. After being sold by the Sackville Gallery it was in the E. May collection, Paris. Later it was with Heinemann, New York, from whom it was bought by the Kress Foundation and presented to the museum in 1952.

DRAWING: Royal Library, Windsor Castle (*CR*, I, p. 12, No. 22). In *CR* the drawing on the other side of the sheet is wrongly said to represent the *Rape of the Sabines*. In fact it shows the *Victory of the Israelites over the Midianites*.

ENGRAVING: By J. B. de Poilly (Andresen, No. 74; Andresen-Wildenstein, No. 74).
COPY: Staatliche Gemäldegalerie, Dresden (724). The composition is cut at the top. In the 1765 catalogue as an original by Poussin.

NOTES: The date on the painting was originally read as 1629 (Johnstone, Bibl. 738, p. 91), but Mr. Martin Davies later suggested (Bibl. 988a, p. 178) that it was in fact 1626. This view is generally accepted—though the last figure has now totally disappeared—as it fits much better with the chronology of Poussin's early period.

BIBLIOGRAPHY: Sandrart, p. 258; Richardson, *Account*, p. 1; Landon, No. 25; Gault de Saint-Germain, Pt. II, p. 61; Johnstone, Bibl. 738, p. 91; Friedlaender, Bibl. 947, pp. 1 ff.; Davies, Bibl. 988a, p. 178; Blunt, Bibl. 1003, p. 269; Bertin-Mourot, Bibl. 1023, p. 45, No. V; Blunt, Bibl. 1064, and Bibl. 1227, pp. 163, 173; Mahon, Bibl. 1271, pp. 290, 296, and Bibl. 1367, pp. IX, 3, 6, 38, 49 f., 132.

26. THE ADORATION OF THE GOLDEN CALF. 154×214 cm. National Gallery, London (5597).

HISTORY: See its pendant (No. 20). Bought by the Gallery from the Earl of Radnor in 1945.

DRAWINGS: 1. Wildenstein collection, New York (cf. Blunt, Bibl. 1064, p. 5). A copy of a lost original.
2. Museum Boymans-van Beuningen, Rotterdam. Partial copy of a lost original.
3. Hermitage Museum, Leningrad (5073). The group of dancers only. A copy after the same lost original.
4. Ecole des Beaux-Arts, Paris, From the Masson collection. A copy of the same lost original.
5. Musée des Beaux-Arts, Besançon (1164). Probably a copy after a lost original, near in composition to the painting.

ENGRAVINGS: 1. By E. Baudet (Andresen, No. 68; Wildenstein, No. 22; Davies and Blunt, p. 208, No. 22). A print was presented to the Academy in 1684 (cf. *Procès-verbaux*, II, p. 274).
2. Anonymous, published by J. F. Cars (Andresen, No. 69).
3. Anonymous, published by J. Audran (Andresen, No. 70).
4. Anonymous, published by E. Gantrel (Andresen, No. 71).
5. By L. Surugue (Andresen, No. 72).
6. Anonymous Dutch engraving (Andresen, No. 73).

COPIES: 1. Städtische Kunsthalle, Mannheim.
2. Pushkin Museum, Moscow (cf. Réau, Bibl. 826, p. 248).
3. Private collection, Northampton, England (1948).
4. A copy by Charles Lebrun was in the Robert Strange sale, Christie, London, 5.iii.1773, lot 109.
5. In Gobelins tapestry (cf. Weigert, Bibl. 1062, pp. 79 ff.).

NOTES: For the dating see the pendant, No. 20. Kauffmann (Bibl. 1395, pp. 55 ff.) shows that the *Apollo and the Muses* in the Pitti, traditionally ascribed to Giulio Romano but which he convincingly attributes to Peruzzi, and which Poussin certainly used in preparing this composition, was still in the Palazzo Rospigliosi, Rome, in the late eighteenth century, and was presumably already there in the seventeenth century and so certainly known to Poussin.

BIBLIOGRAPHY: See above, No. 20, and *Procès-verbaux*, II, p. 278; Landon, No. 24; Smith, No. 33; Friedlaender, 1914, p. 202; Grautoff, I, p. 162, II, No. 88; Magne, 1914, p. 204, Nos. 124, 125; *Exposition Poussin* (*Louvre*), No. 38; Dempsey, Bibl. 1391, p. 117; Kauffmann, Bibl. 1395, p. 57; Mahon, Bibl. 1434, p. 135.

27. THE ADORATION OF THE GOLDEN CALF; fragment. 32×45.5 cm. Mrs. John Booth, Manor Park, Southwell, Nottinghamshire.

HISTORY: Almost certainly a fragment of a picture representing the *Adoration of the Golden Calf* painted for an unnamed Neapolitan patron. Félibien, who records its existence (IV, p. 24), says that it was damaged in the Masaniello revolt of 1647, but that a fragment was saved and brought to Rome, when he saw it between 1647 and 1649. The Booth painting belonged to the Earls of Carlisle and passed by inheritance to George Howard; his sale, Christie, London, 18.ii.1944, lot 39 (as Reni); bt. Wengraf; bt. from him by Cecil Liddell and passed by inheritance in turn to his two brothers, Guy and David Liddell, and to his niece, the present owner.

NOTES: Mr. Mahon (Bibl. 1271, p. 297, and Bibl. 1367, p. 29) dates this painting to the earlier part of the period running from the end of 1627 to the middle of 1629. I should regard it as one of the more mature of the large-scale compositions leading up to the *St. Erasmus* of 1628–29.

Examination of the picture under X-rays shows that it was painted over another composition of which the axis is at right angles to the visible work (cf. text volume, fig. 72). The X-ray reveals what must be part of the background to a large composition with a view of the Colosseum and other ruins.

BIBLIOGRAPHY: Félibien, IV, p. 24; Grautoff, II, p. 255; Blunt, Bibl. 1003, p. 266; Bertin-Mourot, Bibl. 1023, p. 46, No. VI; Blunt, Bibl. 1167, p. 76, and Bibl. 1227, p. 166; *Exposition Poussin* (*Louvre*), No. 13; Mahon, Bibl. 1271, p. 297, and Bibl. 1367, pp. 24, 29, 57, 59.

28. MOSES SWEETENING THE BITTER WATERS OF MARAH. 152×210 cm. Baltimore Museum of Art, Baltimore, Maryland.

HISTORY: Perhaps belonged to André Le Nôtre (d. 1700; see below); in the first half of the eighteenth century it belonged to an unidentified Dr. Hickman, who sold it through Knapton, presumably the painter George Knapton, to Blackwood; bt. from him by Sir John Rawdon; Rawdon and others sale, Cock, London, 1744, lot 56; bt. Bragge; after passing through 'several hands' it was bought by Simon, first Earl Harcourt in 1755 (*Harcourt Papers*, Bibl. 201, III, p. 233); Harcourt sale, Christie, London, 11.vi.1948, lot 158; bt. Knoedler; bt. by the museum from Knoedler, 1958.

NOTES: In the catalogue of the Poussin exhibition (No. 11) it was suggested very tentatively that the Baltimore painting might be identified with a *Moïse* mentioned by Loménie de Brienne (pp. 212 f.) as having belonged to Richaumont and then to François Blondel, but the evidence about this picture is too vague for any identification to be possible. (It is even conceivable that Brienne has confused the subject of the picture altogether, for later (p. 224), when he speaks of the pictures inherited by Blondel from Richaumont, he mentions a *Noah* and a *Hercules*, but no *Moses*.)

There are far stronger reasons for thinking that the Baltimore picture may be one mentioned in the inventory of André Le Nôtre, made after his death in 1700. No. 205 (cf. Guiffrey, Bibl. 697, p. 244) reads: 'Item, un tableau, *Frappement de Rocher*, du Poussin, figure naturelle, de 6 pieds de long sur 4 pieds ½ de hault, prisé avec sa bordure 800 l.' The fact that Le Nôtre's picture is described as a *Striking of the Rock* is no argument against the identification, since the Baltimore picture has frequently been so described (e.g. by Grautoff, II, No. 12). The sizes of the picture in the inventory are only approximate, and the correspondence in this case is in fact quite close. More important are the words 'figure naturelle', which, though oddly phrased, can only mean 'life-size figures'. This would fit perfectly with the Baltimore picture, but there is no *Striking of the Rock*, surviving or recorded, to which it could apply. The value of 800 livres set on the picture shows it to have been a work of importance. The same value was put on a *Nativity*, which may conceivably be that now in the National Gallery, London, but the *Echo and Narcissus* (perhaps the picture at Dresden) was only valued at 300 livres, and various copies after Poussin were put down at values running from 80 to 250 livres.

The later history of the picture can largely be reconstructed from a letter written by Rebecca, Countess Harcourt, to her son in September 1755, and printed in *The Harcourt Papers, loc. cit.*:

> 'I must tell you we lately bought one of N. Poussin's pictures (Moses sweetening the waters of Maribah). 'Tis painted after the manner of Raphael; and, though a little dark, is esteemed by the best judges to be a capital picture. Knapton sold it some years ago for Dr. Hickman to Blackwood; he sold it to Lord Royden and, after passing through several hands, my Lord was so fortunate as to get it.'

'Royden' is presumably a slip for Rawdon, as the picture appears in 1744 in the sale of Sir John (later Lord) Rawdon.

The subject, very rarely depicted in the art of the Middle Ages or later, is taken from Exodus, XV, 23–26 (cf. text volume, pp. 179 ff.).

Dated by Grautoff (II, No. 12) 1627–28; by Mahon first (Bibl. 1271, p. 296) 1627 and later (Bibl. 1367, p. 29) conceivably 1628 rather than 1627. Probably an early example of the big figure compositions which culminated in the *St. Erasmus* of 1628–29.

BIBLIOGRAPHY: *Harcourt Papers*, Bibl. 201, III, p. 233; *Description of Nuneham-Courtnay*, Bibl. 315, p. 32; Waagen, Bibl. 384b, IV, p. 349; Guiffrey, Bibl. 697, p. 244; Grautoff, I, p. 79, II, No. 12; Greig, Bibl. 1030, p. 63; Milliken, Bibl. 1176, pp. 3 ff.; Blunt, Bibl. 1227, p. 168; *Exposition Poussin (Louvre)*, No. 11; Mahon, Bibl. 1271, pp. 295 f.; Waterhouse, Bibl. 1308, p. 291; Mahon, Bibl. 1367, p. 29.

29. THE VICTORY OF JOSHUA OVER THE AMALEKITES. 97.5 × 134 cm. Hermitage Museum, Leningrad (1195).

HISTORY: Presumably this painting and its pair (No. 30) are the two battle-pieces executed, according to Bellori (p. 411), during the absence from Rome of Cardinal Francesco Barberini, i.e. between March 1625 and October 1626 (cf. Mahon, Bibl. 1271, p. 290 n. 11). Mentioned in 1685 by Félibien (IV, p. 11) and in 1700 by Florent Le Comte (III, p. 24) as belonging to the Duc de Noailles, that is to say Anne Jules de Noailles, Marshal of France, who died in 1708. Presumably inherited by his eldest son, Adrien Maurice, also a Marshal of France (d. 1766), who may have sold it, since it does not appear in the sale of his collection in 1767 after his death. Almost certainly François de Dufresne sale, Winter, Amsterdam, 22.viii. 1770, lots 102, 103 (38 × 52 inches). Bought by the Empress Catherine of Russia before 1774 (Mus. Cat.).

DRAWING: A drawing in the Albertina, Vienna (rep. Grautoff, I, Pl. 3; cf. also *CR*, I, p. 17) has certain features in common with the Hermitage painting. It may possibly be a copy after a lost drawing by Poussin, but is more likely to be by an imitator.

NOTES: A pair to No. 30. According to Bellori, Poussin could only get 6 *scudi* each for this painting and its pendant. The subject is taken from Exodus, XVII, 8. The group on the right is a variant on Polidoro da Caravaggio's *Perseus and Phineus* (see text volume, Fig. 62), and the one hurling a stone from Giulio Romano's *Martyrdom of St. Stephen* in the church of S. Stefano, Genoa (cf. A. Venturi, *Storia dell' Arte Italiana*, Milan, 1901–40, IX, 2, Fig. 300).

BIBLIOGRAPHY: Félibien, IV, p. 11; Bellori, p. 411; Baldinucci, XVI, p. 99; Florent Le Comte, III, p. 24; Bottari, Bibl. 197, p. 170; Smith, No. 35; Grautoff, I, p. 65, II, No. 4; Magne, 1914, p. 204, No. 134; Blunt, Bibl. 1086, p. 183, and Bibl. 1086a, p. 159; Licht, p. 79; Sterling, Bibl. 1159, pp. 29 f.; Blunt, Bibl. 1227, p. 166; Jullian, Bibl. 1261, p. 227; *Exposition Poussin (Louvre)*, Nos. 2 and 3; Mahon, Bibl. 1271, pp. 290, 296, and Bibl. 1367, pp. IX, 5 ff., 26, 38, 132.

30. THE VICTORY OF JOSHUA OVER THE AMORITES. 97.5 × 134 cm. Pushkin Museum, Moscow (1046).

HISTORY: See the pendant, No. 29. Transferred from the Hermitage in Leningrad to the Pushkin Museum in 1927.

DRAWING: A drawing in the Fitzwilliam Museum, Cambridge, though rather weak in quality, appears to be a study for the composition.

NOTES: The subject is taken from Joshua X. The figure with the sword, on the left, is based on a celebrated composition by Polidoro da Caravaggio (see text vol., Fig. 62).

BIBLIOGRAPHY: See No. 29, and Smith, No. 36; Grautoff, I, p. 65, II, No. 5; Magne, 1914, p. 205, No. 139.

31. THE VICTORY OF GIDEON OVER THE MIDIANITES. 98 × 137 cm. Vatican Museum, Rome.

HISTORY: Nothing is known of the history of this painting, except that it came from the papal palace at Castel Gandolfo. It is possible, however, that it belonged in the eighteenth century to the Farnese family, for a painting, described as a battle and attributed to Poussin, was sold to them in 1710 by C. A. Canopi (cf. Filangieri, Bibl. 652.1, p. 287) and is mentioned by Dézallier d'Argenville (1745, II, p. 254; 1762, IV, p. 38) as 'petit morceau précieux'. It is not now traceable in the records of the Farnese collection either in Naples or at Parma. It may have remained in Rome and have been disposed of when the main collections were moved from the Palazzo Farnese to Naples.

NOTES: The subject is taken from Judges, VII.

The painting was discovered and identified as a Poussin by M. Thuillier. My own first reaction was to doubt the attribution (cf. Sterling, in *Exposition Poussin (Louvre)*, p. 216), but after seeing once more the two Russian battle-pieces (Nos. 29 and 30 above), I came round to M. Thuillier's view. The attribution and a dating of 1625–26 are now generally accepted, though M. Thuillier would date the Vatican picture slightly later than the two Russian canvases.

Poussin seems to have planned a fourth composition of this type, recorded in a drawing at Windsor Castle (cf. Blunt, Bibl. 975, p. 38, No. 180), which has on its *verso* a study for the *Golden Calf* of 1626.

BIBLIOGRAPHY: Filangieri, Bibl. 652.1, p. 287; Blunt, Bibl. 1222, p. 330; *Exposition Poussin (Louvre)*, p. 216; Thuillier, Bibl. 1298, p. 264, No. 2; *Exposition Poussin (Rouen)*, No. 73; Mahon, Bibl. 1367, pp. IX, 5 ff., 38, 132, 136.

32. THE PLAGUE AT ASHDOD. 148 × 198 cm. Musée du Louvre, Paris (710).

HISTORY: Sandrart (p. 29) lists this picture among those ordered in Rome for the King of Spain, but Miss Costello (Bibl. 1052, pp. 237 ff.) has shown that this assertion is false and that the painting was begun at the end of 1630 and bought from Poussin's studio early in 1631 by Valguarnera for 110 scudi. Between

1647 and 1649 the picture belonged to a Roman sculptor referred to as 'Matteo' (Félibien, IV, p. 20), probably Carlo Matteo, who worked under Bernini in Rome (cf. R. Battaglia, *La Cattedra Berniniana di San Pietro*, Rome, 1943, *passim*, and Wittkower, Bibl. 1125, pp. 221, 238, 246). Acquired by the Duc de Richelieu and sold by him to Louis XIV in 1665 (Ferraton, Bibl. 1043, pp. 439, 446).

DRAWINGS: No original drawings by Poussin are known for this composition. For those wrongly attributed to him, see *CR*, I, p. 17. Drawings at Holkham Hall, Norfolk, and in the City Art Gallery, Glasgow, are copies after the painting.

ENGRAVINGS: 1. By Jean Baron, after a drawing by Guillaume Courtois (Andresen, No. 78; Wildenstein, No. 23; Davies and Blunt, p. 209, No. 23).
2. By Etienne Picart, dated 1677 (Andresen, No. 77; Wildenstein, No. 24).
3. Anonymous, published by Hecquet in Paris (Andresen, No. 79).

COPIES: 1. National Gallery, London (165). In the Palazzo Colonna by 1715; probably still there in 1797; acquired in Rome by Sir Simon Clarke, from whom bought by Irvine for W. Buchanan; anon. (= Buchanan) sale, Christie, London, 12.v.1804, lot 10; sold by Buchanan to Harris; Gentleman of Fortune (? = Harris) sale, Coxe, London, 12.vi.1812, lot 14; presented to the National Gallery by the Duke of Northumberland, 1838 (cf. Davies, Bibl. 988a, p. 185).
2. Museu Nacional de Arte Antiga, Lisbon. From the collection of Jorge Husson da Câmara; presented to the museum by King Fernando of Portugal, 1866.
3. Musée Ingres, Montauban (29·5 × 40 cm). Bequeathed by Ingres in 1867.
4. Private collection, Jugoslavia (cf. Lossky, Bibl. 919, p. 177).
5. Private collection, Alost, Belgium.
6. Ordered by Valguarnera from Caroselli as soon as he had bought the original (cf. Costello, Bibl. 1052, pp. 237 ff.).
7. By Antoine Bouzonnet Stella, in the possession of his niece, Claudine Bouzonnet Stella (cf. *Testament* . . . Bibl. 107, p. 35).
8. Flavio Chigi collection, Rome, in 1693 (cf. Incisa della Rocchetta, Bibl. 1070, p. 39).
9. John Davenport sale, Christie, London, 20.ii.1801, lot 63. Described as a 'Fine Study' for the painting, but more likely to be a small copy.
10. Anonymous sale, Desmarets, Paris, 8.ii.1803, lot 53 (16 × 19 inches).

Paintings of this subject attributed to Poussin also appeared in the following sales: Robert Knight, Cock, London, 7.ii.1745, lot 50; Bragge, Prestage, London, 15 ff. ii. 1750, second day, lot 15.

NOTES: The subject is taken from Samuel V, 1–6. It may have been suggested by the great plague which struck Milan in 1630. Similar themes were treated in the seventeenth century by Pierre Mignard in his *Plague at Aegina* (engraved by Audran) and by Michiel Sweerts in a *Plague at Athens*, formerly in the Cook collection as by Poussin (cf. Longhi, Bibl. 880, pp. 271 ff.).

The background of the picture is taken almost exactly from Serlio's engraving of the *Tragic Stage* at the end of book II of his *Architettura*, which was also used by other sixteenth-century artists, notably by Paris Bordone in his *Bathsheba* at Cologne and his *Gladiatorial Combat* in Vienna.

The man holding his nose is derived from Marc'Antonio's engraving of the *Phrygian Plague* after Raphael (cf. Bellori, p. 417), which also includes fluted drums of columns like the one which occurs in the front of Poussin's composition.

BIBLIOGRAPHY: Félibien, Bibl. 11, p. 202, and Bibl. 11a, p. 80; Fouquet, Bibl. 24a, p. 103; *Comptes des bâtiments*, I, p. 993; Chantelou, 1885, p. 233, and 1960, p. 132; Félibien, IV, p. 20; P. de Champaigne in *Conférences inédites*, Bibl. 55, p. 112; Bellori, p. 414; Sandrart, pp. 29, 258, 411; Passeri, p. 326; Baldinucci, XVI, pp. 101 f.; *Mémoires inédits*, I, pp. 95, 349; *Testament* . . ., Bibl. 107, p. 35; Loménie de Brienne, pp. 213, 216, 218; Perrault, Bibl. 113, I, p. 89; Florent Le Comte, I, p. 201, III, p. 25; Piganiol de La Force, Bibl. 124, I, p. 126; Bailly, pp. 28, 38, 39; p. 303; Dézallier, 1745, II, pp. 250, 254, and 1762, IV, Dézallier d'Argenville, Bibl. 183d, p. 343; Gougenot, Bibl. 184, p. 179; Bardon, II, p. 125; Boyer d'Argens, Bibl. 231, p. 297; Le Mierre, Bibl. 234, p. 17; Nougaret, Bibl. 251, II, p. 125; Cambry, Bibl. 272a, pp. 20, 53; Fuseli, Bibl. 322, pp. 43 f., 220; Landon, No. 27; Gault de Saint-Germain, Pt. II, p. 15; Barry, Bibl. 338, I, p. 457; Smith, No. 39; Knowles, Bibl. 392, II, pp. 270 f.; Bonnaffé, Bibl. 573, pp. 207, 214; Friedlaender, 1914, pp. 36, 114, 144; Grautoff, I, p. 89, II, No. 19; Magne, 1914, pp. 84, 206, No. 162; Francastel, Bibl. 883, p. 146; Finberg, Bibl. 934, p. 89; Davies, Bibl. 988a, p. 185, No. 165; Jamot, pp. 20, 21 ff., 83, 84; Ferraton, Bibl. 1043, pp. 439, 446; Costello, Bibl. 1052, pp. 237 ff.; Licht, pp. 92, 114; Berger, Bibl. 1113, p. 168; Blunt, Bibl. 1167, p. 76, and Bibl. 1226, p. 396; Jullian, Bibl. 1261, p. 227; *Exposition Poussin (Louvre)*, No. 23; Mahon, Bibl. 1271, pp. 290, 292 f., 298; Weigert, Bibl. 1309, p. 278; Kauffmann, Bibl. 1332, p. 95; *Exposition Poussin (Rouen)*, No. 76; *L'ideale classico (Bologna)*, No. 57; Mahon, Bibl. 1367, pp. XI, 27, 29, 58, 124, 132, 134 f., 138; Reff, Bibl. 1371, p. 186.

33. THE TRIUMPH OF DAVID. 117×146 cm. Alleyn's College of God's Gift, Dulwich, London.

HISTORY: Reproduced in an engraving by S. F. Ravenet in 1776 (Andresen, No. 81), which bears the arms of John Joshua Proby, second Lord Carysfort. At an unspecified date soon after 1787 Lord Carysfort sold the painting to Charles Alexandre de Calonne (Whitley, Bibl. 828, II, p. 189), at whose sale (Skinner and Dyke, London, 23 ff.iii.1795, third day, lot 92) it was bought by Noël Desenfans. At his death in 1807 it passed with the whole collection to his friend, Sir Francis Bourgeois, who bequeathed it, together with his other pictures, to Dulwich College in 1811.

DRAWINGS: 1. Musée Condé, Chantilly (CR, I, p. 14, No. 29). This drawing has been tentatively attributed by Thuillier (Bibl. 1296, p. 82) to Charles Mellin, but the attribution can hardly be maintained.

2. Royal Library, Windsor Castle (CR, I, p. 14, No. 30).

ENGRAVING: By S. F. Ravenet, 1776 (Andresen, No. 81).

NOTES: In the catalogue of the Poussin exhibition in the Louvre (No. 9) I suggested that the Dulwich picture might be the one mentioned in various eighteenth-century guide books to Rome as being in the Palazzo Spada. In fact, however, the size and description of the Spada picture given in the inventory of the palace, drawn up in 1759, make it clear that this is not the case. The Spada painting seems in fact to be the canvas now attributed to Orazio Gentileschi (cf. Zeri, Bibl. 1109.1, p. 86, No. 175, and Thuillier, Bibl. 1298, p. 270).

Dated by Grautoff between 1623 and 1626, and by Mahon (Bibl. 1367, pp. 30 ff.) 1632–33. The latter maintains that the painting was executed within a very short period of time, whereas there is much evidence to suggest that it was worked on over a long period.

The X-rays reveal an unusually large number of pentimenti, particularly in the architectural background and in the group of figures in the left foreground. As regards the former, the arch on the extreme left is painted over a colonnade with a flat entablature, and round-headed features appear in the X-ray between the columns of the temple itself. The interpretation of this part of the X-rays is not easy, but the most probable solution seems to be as follows. In the first version of the temple Poussin followed the engraving after Giulio Romano's *Triumph of Scipio* (cf. text volume, Fig. 25)—which certainly influenced the composition as a whole—and showed a single row of columns in front of a wall articulated with niches (or perhaps blind arches). He then inserted a second row of columns, which, unlike the front row, are clearly painted over the arches, and replaced the latter with three flat-headed pedimented doors, flanked by apparently unfluted pilasters. These alterations would mean that Poussin had replaced Giulio Romano's rather curious and unclassical portico by the peristyle of an orthodox Roman temple. The closest model would be Palladio's reconstruction of the Temple of Neptune (Bk. IV, ch. 31), the only difference being that Poussin shows three doors instead of one, an unusual feature, which he may have taken from the same architect's reconstruction of the Temple of Peace (*ibid.*, ch. 6).

As Mr. Rees Jones has pointed out (Bibl. 1280, p. 308), there have also been alterations in the figures which stand in the portico, some of which were painted at the same time as the doors, whereas others are clearly superimposed on them.

The changes in the figure group in the left foreground are the most difficult to interpret. In the X-ray there are clear traces of at least two figures to the left of the man blowing the straight trumpet, but their precise form is difficult to decipher. Mr. Rees Jones has suggested that these traces in the X-rays correspond exactly to the group of three women who close the composition on the picture as we see it today, and that Poussin simply transferred the group from one position to another, without alteration, by means of a pricked cartoon, parts of which survive on the *verso* of a drawing at Chantilly. This somewhat mechanical process is unexpected in Poussin and there does not seem to be any other instance of his using it. On the other hand the evidence supplied by the X-rays seems almost conclusive. The head and shoulders of the woman in *profil perdu*, that is to say the right-hand member of the group in the painting, can be clearly seen, even in a reproduction text volume (Fig. 67), just below the trumpeter's hand. In the original full-scale X-rays several other figures are traceable in two positions, each separated from their counterpart by the same distance. It seems, however, that, as one would expect, in transferring the group, Poussin introduced certain alterations to make it suit its new context. For instance, the X-ray does not show in the right-hand group any trace of the raised hand of the middle girl, which one would expect to be clearly visible, since, in its final form, it contains a great deal of white, and it is reasonable to conclude that it was only added in the second stage.

The many changes that took place during the execution of the painting give strong grounds for thinking that the gestation of the painting was spread over a considerable period of time. This hypothesis is confirmed by the differences in execution between various parts visible in the painting itself. In particular there is a marked contrast between the group of women on the left already discussed and the kneeling woman with two babies in the middle of the foreground. The draperies of the women on the left are thinly painted, with loosely defined folds and little feeling of weight or bulk; those of the kneeling woman are clear-cut and sculptural. In the former the colours are pale and broken, whereas in the latter they are clear, strong and sharp. It is significant that the figure of the kneeling woman also differs markedly from her neighbours in the X-ray. In the first place the figure is much more heavily modelled in white, a fact which can be explained either on the grounds that it was painted over an earlier partly scraped-out version, or that it was executed in a different technique. It is difficult to decide which of these two explanations is the more likely. The second is supported by the fact that the X-ray shows not only more white lead but a completely different handling. Whereas the build-up of the other figures is in a loose technique, which only registers faintly in the X-ray, the group in the foreground is constructed of crisp, nervous strokes which follow the contours and model the forms with far greater precision than is the case in most areas of the canvas. This marked difference in technique suggests that the figure was mainly executed at a later date than the rest of the picture. On the other hand, the Windsor drawing shows that Poussin planned a group of this type, roughly in this position, from a fairly early stage—an argument in favour of the first hypothesis.

There seem, therefore, to be reasons for thinking that the execution of the composition lasted over a considerable period of time, but it is not easy to determine in what years that period falls. For evidence about the date at which the picture was planned we should naturally turn to the drawings. Unfortunately the earlier of these—the Chantilly study—is so completely different from any other surviving drawing by Poussin that it offers no help towards the solution of the problem. The Windsor drawing, on the other hand, has such strong affinities with Poussin's earliest drawings—the series made in Paris for Marino—that it cannot date from very much later. Further, it has no likeness to the Uffizi drawing for the *St. Erasmus*, which can certainly be dated to 1628. It seems therefore safe to date the inception of the composition to a period before 1628, and, since the Windsor drawing represents a relatively advanced stage of the composition, it is likely that the painting itself was begun by this date. This would fit with the similarities pointed out in text vol., p. 70, between the *David* and certain other paintings probably produced well before 1630, notably the Petit Palais *Massacre* (No. 66), the *Entry into Jerusalem* (No. 77), and the *Woman taken in Adultery* (No. 75), of which the two last, incidentally, show many pentimenti of the kind that appear in the Dulwich picture and which seem to be unknown in Poussin's paintings after about 1630. On the other hand, the *David* is far more accomplished than any of the pictures just mentioned, partly because it may have been begun slightly later, and partly because—if my hypothesis is correct—it was reworked at a considerably later date, certainly after 1631 and possibly a little later, just before the Dresden *Adoration of the Magi*.

BIBLIOGRAPHY: (R. Smirke), Bibl. 358, p. 20; Buchanan, I, p. 252, No. 92; Waagen, Bibl. 384b, II, p. 347; Smith, No. 38; Cousin, Bibl. 456, p. 16; Friedlaender, 1914, pp. 112, 149; Grautoff, I, p. 69, II, No. 6; Magne, 1914, p. 207, No. 166; Whitley, Bibl. 828, II, p. 189; Brieger, Bibl. 915, p. 346; Blunt, Bibl. 1003, p. 269 n. 5, Bibl. 1026, pp. 4 f., Bibl. 1086, p. 183, and Bibl. 1086a, p. 159; Licht, pp. 79 f.; Blunt, Bibl. 1166, p. 8, and Bibl. 1227, p. 169; *Exposition Poussin (Louvre)*, No. 9; Mahon, Bibl. 1271, pp. 292, 294 f., 300; Rees Jones, Bibl. 1280, pp. 304 ff.; Thuillier, Bibl. 1296, p. 82; Kauffmann, Bibl. 1332, p. 96; Mahon, Bibl. 1367, pp. XI, 30–36, 38–40, 47, 50, 55, 75, 82 f., 86 ff., 93, 136.

34. THE TRIUMPH OF DAVID. 100 × 130 cm. Museo del Prado, Madrid (2311).

HISTORY: Mentioned by Bellori in the *Nota delli Musei*, published anonymously in 1664 (Bibl. 36, p. 16) as belonging to Monsignor Girolamo Casanate; described in detail in the *Vite* of 1672 (p. 451), where it is stated to be still in the possession of the same prelate. Acquired by the painter Carlo Maratta (d. 1713), and bought from his heirs by Philip V of Spain, in whose collection at La Granja it is recorded in 1746 (museum catalogue).

COPIES: 1. In the collection of Jean Baptiste Boyer d'Aguilles (1645–1709; cf. Bonnaffé, Bibl. 533, p. 40). Inherited by Pierre Boyer, son of Jean Baptiste, and recorded in the second edition of the *Recueil*, edited by P. J. Mariette and published in 1744 (Bibl. 177.2, p. 14). The Boyer painting is presumably the one mentioned by Dézallier d'Argen-ville (1745, II, p. 254; 1762, IV, p. 39). It appeared in the following sales: Robert de Saint-Victor, Roux, Paris, 26 ff.xi.1822; anon. sale, Christie, London, 13.vi.1913, lot 121, bt. Wyatt (38×50 inches); anon. sale, Christie, London, 20.iv.1928, lot 40, bt. Sampson; with a Paris dealer in 1928 (presumably the painting mentioned by Grautoff (Bibl. 774, p. 105). The Boyer painting may possibly be the same as one which appeared in the Dufresne sale (Winter, Amsterdam, 22.viii.1770, lot 104) described as follows: 'Une Ordonnance Allégorique . . ., Au

milieu du Tableau on voit un Général d'Armée qu'une femme couronne de Lauriers; de plus quelque Instrumens de Guerre et des Enfans'. The size is given as 38 × 50 inches.
2. Gräfin Fürstenberg-Herdringen (cf. Grautoff, Bibl. 864, pp. 325 ff.). Said to have been commissioned from Ferdinand Voet by Franz von Fürstenberg in Rome in 1666.
3. Private collection, Sweden.
4. Henry Howard collection, Corby Castle, Cumberland (bt. in 1810); passed by descent to H. Lawson of Corby Castle.

NOTES: Described by Bellori as 'della prima maniera'. Dated by Grautoff before 1627. Friedlaender (1914) is not explicit, but says it should not be dated 'too early'. Mahon (Bibl. 1271, p. 299, and Bibl. 1367, pp. 25 ff.) proposed 1630–31. I should see it as earlier than 1630–31 and not far removed from the *Germanicus* in date.

Even inspection with the naked eye makes it clear that the picture was painted over an earlier work, traces of which show through the top layer of pigment, particularly in the form of repeated arcs of circles which suggest an architectural setting.

BIBLIOGRAPHY: (G. P. Bellori), Bibl. 36, p. 16; Bellori, p. 451; Ponz, Bibl. 238a, p. 893, par. 49; Mengs, Bibl. 264a, p. 118; Cambry, Bibl. 272a, p. 40; Landon, No. 26; Chennevières-Pointel, Bibl. 433, I, p. 143; Friedlaender, 1914, pp. 112, 178; Grautoff, I, p. 73, II, No. 9, wrongly identified with Smith, No. 37; Magne, 1914, pp. 191, 207, No. 167; Alpatov, Bibl. 882, p. 17; Emmerling, Bibl. 933, Pl. VIII; Jamot, pp. 40, 85; Licht, p. 88; Blunt, Bibl. 1227, p. 167; Mahon, Bibl. 1271, p. 299; Thuillier, Bibl. 1296, p. 78; *Exposition Poussin (Rouen)*, No. 74; Mahon, Bibl. 1367, pp. XI, 19, 25 ff., 29, 39, 40, 132; Blunt, Bibl. 1426, p. 68.

35. THE JUDGMENT OF SOLOMON. 101×150 cm. Musée du Louvre, Paris (711).

HISTORY: Bellori (p. 452) describes a composition which corresponds exactly with the Louvre painting and says that it was painted for Pointel. Félibien (IV, pp. 59 f.) adds that it was painted in 1649 and that at the time he was writing (1685) it belonged to 'Monsieur de Harlay Procureur Général', that is to say, Achille de Harlay (1629–1712), later first president of the Parlement of Paris. This pedigree is confirmed by Florent Le Comte (III, p. 31), who, writing in 1700, says that Pointel's painting had been in the collection of Harlay. The fact that he uses the past tense implies that Harlay had sold it, and confirms the view that it was actually the Pointel-Harlay picture that was bought by Louis XIV from the painter Charles Antoine Hérault in 1685 (*Comptes des bâtiments*, II, pp. 587, 664), although it is curious that Le Comte should not mention the fact that it was at the time he wrote in the royal collection. It must also be noticed that Loménie de Brienne, writing *c.* 1693–95, refers to the picture as if it still belonged to Harlay (pp. 215, 220), but he was writing from memory and was not always up-to-date in his facts. The picture does not seem to have passed directly from Pointel's heirs to Harlay, since in 1665 Chantelou (1885, p. 159) refers to a *Judgment of Solomon*—almost certainly the same picture—as belonging to 'Rambouillet', probably Nicolas du Plessis-Rambouillet, father-in-law of Tallemant des Réaux.

DRAWINGS: 1. Hermitage Museum, Leningrad (*CR*, I, p. 15, No. 31).
2. Ecole des Beaux-Arts, Paris (*CR*, I, p. 15, No. 32).
3. Musée du Louvre, Paris (*CR*, I, p. 16, No. 33).
4. Musée du Louvre, Paris (*CR*, I, p. 16; rep. by Magne, 1914, p. 146). A copy after the painting.

ENGRAVINGS: 1. By Jean Dughet (Andresen, No. 83; Wildenstein, No. 25; Davies and Blunt, p. 209, No. 25). Before 1677, since the print is dedicated to Cardinal Camillo Massimi, who died in that year.
2. By Guillaume Chasteau (Andresen, No. 82).
3. By Martial Desbois in Patin (Bibl. 103, Pl. after p. 14). The engraving, which is not recorded by

Andresen or Wildenstein, was made in Venice, since it is signed: *M Desbois Gal. sculp. Venet.*
4. Published by Etienne Gantrel (Andresen, No. 85).
5. By Antoine André Morel, dated 1825 (Andresen, No. 84).

COPIES: 1. Slingsby sale, Christie, London, 9.v.1947, lot 93.
2. Private collection, Bologna, in the eighteenth century (cf. Algarotti, Bibl. 299, XI, p. 227).
The following paintings recorded in sales may be copies of the Louvre composition: Coggs, Christie, London, 18.vii.1770, lot 27; anon., Christie, London, 14.xii.1781, lot 21; anon., Christie, London, 7.xi.1783, lot 65; Pelletan, Regnault, Paris, 14.iv.1803, lot 93.

NOTES: Many guide books and visitors to Rome mention a painting of this subject attributed to Poussin in the Palazzo Giustiniani (for which see below, p. 158 L. 7).

Winckelmann (Bibl. 203, p. 147) remarks that the head of Solomon in the Louvre painting is based on a head of Jupiter which appears on Macedonian coins.

BIBLIOGRAPHY: *Comptes des bâtiments*, II, pp. 587, 664; Chantelou, 1885, p. 159, and 1960, p. 128; Félibien, III, p. 220, IV, pp. 59 f., 341; Bellori, p. 452; Patin, Bibl. 103, p. 15; Loménie de Brienne, pp. 215, 220; Florent Le Comte, III, p. 31; Piganiol de La Force, Bibl. 124, I, pp. 128 f.; Bailly, p. 306; Dézallier, 1745, II, p. 254, and 1762, IV, p. 39; Winckelmann, Bibl. 203, I, p. 147; Cambry, Bibl. 272a, p. 25; Landon, No. 28; Gault de Saint-Germain, Pt. II, p. 51; Smith, No. 40; Haydon, Bibl. 337.1, III, p. 114; Friedlaender, 1914, pp. 89 f., 120, 237; Grautoff, I, p. 273, II, No. 133; Magne, 1914, pp. 155, 205, No. 104; Romney-Towndrow, Bibl. 866, pp. 314 f.; Blunt, Bibl. 972, p. 161 n. 3, Bibl. 1086, p. 189, and Bibl. 1086a, p. 165; *Exposition Poussin (Louvre)*, No. 87; Cummings, Bibl. 1362, pp. 146 ff.; Mahon, Bibl. 1367, pp. 115 f., 134.

36. ESTHER BEFORE AHASUERUS. 119×155 cm. Hermitage Museum, Leningrad (1755).

HISTORY: The picture is first traceable in Cérisier's collection, where it was seen by Bernini in 1665 (Chantelou, 1960, p. 126). Le Maire (Bibl. 91, III, p. 264) describes it when it belonged to Jean Baptiste Colbert, Marquis de Seignelay (1651–90). Seignelay's collection was inherited by his brother, Jacques Nicolas, Archbishop of Rouen, who died in 1707 and bequeathed it to his nephew, the Abbé de Colbert, later Comte de Seignelay (Bonnaffé, Bibl. 533, pp. 289 f.). The picture was in the collection of Philippe, Duc d'Orléans, the Regent, by 1717, when it was seen by Thornhill (cf. Bibl. 140, p. 88) in the same room as the *Sacraments*. The duke owned several paintings which had belonged to Seignelay. Some of these he acquired in 1719, when he bought the Hôtel Colbert in the rue des Petits Champs, from the Marquise de la Carte, who had owned the house since 1713 (cf. Champier and Sandoz, Bibl. 648.1, I, p. 323), but the *Esther* must have been bought separately, since it was already in his collection by 1717. It must have been sold or given away before 1727, since it is not mentioned by Dubois de Saint-Gelais in his detailed catalogue of the Orleans collection (Bibl. 153). It is probably the picture in the François de Dufresne sale, Winter, Amsterdam, 22 ff.viii.1770, lot 100, which is said to be engraved by Pesne (size 45×60 inches). It was acquired by the Empress Catherine II of Russia between 1763 and 1774 (Hermitage Museum catalogue). There does not seem to be any evidence for Grautoff's statement that the picture belonged to Lord Carysfort and Calonne.

ENGRAVINGS: 1. By Jean Pesne (Andresen, No. 88; Wildenstein, No. 26).
2. By François de Poilly (Andresen, No. 87).
3. Published at Lyons by 'Cars le fils', probably François Cars the Younger (Andresen, No. 89).
4. Signed: *I. G.* (Andresen, No. 90).

COPY: John MacArthur sale, Christie, London, 8.v. 1841, lot 54.

NOTES: The picture was greatly admired by Bernini when he saw it in Cérisier's collection. He commented that it was painted in the manner of Raphael.

Grautoff dates it 1643–45, but the massiveness of the forms, the big heads and hands, and the composition with a gap in the middle, in which appears a small distant figure apparently irrelevant to the main theme, all recall paintings of the mid-fifties, such as *St. Peter and St. John healing* (1655, No. 84) and the *Death of Sapphira* (No. 85) and justify a dating to this period.

BIBLIOGRAPHY: Chantelou, 1885, pp. 90, 159, and 1960, pp. 126, 128; Félibien, IV, p. 146; Le Maire, Bibl. 91, III, p. 264, and Bibl. 91a, p. 191; Loménie de Brienne, pp. 215, 224; Lairesse, Bibl. 129a, I, p. 244; Thornhill, Bibl. 140, p. 88; Mengs, Bibl. 264a, pp. 118, 236; Landon, No. 29; Smith, No. 42; Friedlaender, 1914, pp. 85, 126; Grautoff, I, p. 223, II, No. 108; Magne, 1914, pp. 155, 200, No. 56; Blunt, Bibl. 972, p. 161; Seznec, Bibl. 1284, p. 345.

37. THE CAPTURE OF JERUSALEM BY TITUS. 147×198·5 cm. Signed: NI POUSSIN. FEC. Kunsthistorisches Museum, Vienna (1556).

HISTORY: Commissioned by Cardinal Francesco Barberini and given by him to Prince Eggenberg, Imperial Ambassador to Urban VIII in 1638–39 (Bellori, p. 413), probably as a gift to the Emperor; recorded in the Imperial collection in 1718; later in the possession of Fürst Kaunitz; bought back from him in 1820 (Museum catalogue).

NOTES: In his first years in Rome Poussin executed a painting of this subject for Cardinal Francesco Barberini, for which a payment is recorded in February 1626 (cf. Bousquet, Bibl. 1231, p. 3 and see below, L9). According to Bellori the Cardinal commissioned a second version, which he gave to Prince Eggenberg. Bellori gives no indication of the date at which this version was executed, but the style of the painting would fit with the hypothesis that it was executed either during Eggenberg's embassy in Rome (1638–39), or shortly before it. Friedlaender (1914, p. 112) and Grautoff (II, No. 11) assume that it was painted soon after the first version, but the style of the picture makes this highly improbable.

A picture of this subject, attributed to Poussin, appeared in the undated (but eighteenth-century) sale of Sir Peter Gleane, but it is impossible to say whether it is connected with the Vienna painting or the lost composition. It is probably the same picture as one in the Ralph Palmer sale, London, 11.iv.1755, lot 35, bt. Lord Verney.

BIBLIOGRAPHY: Félibien, IV, p. 18; Bellori, p. 413; Passeri, p. 326; Baldinucci, XVI, p. 100; Florent Le Comte, III, p. 25; Smith, No. 179; Friedlaender, 1914, pp. 32, 112, 141; Grautoff, I, p. 75, II, No. 11; Magne, 1914, pp. 82, 202, No. 97; Friedlaender, 1933, p. 323; Blunt, Bibl. 972, p. 162, and Bibl. 1026, p. 4; Jamot, p. 37; Blunt, Bibl. 1227, p. 164; *Exposition Poussin* (*Louvre*), No. 39; Mahon, Bibl. 1271, pp. 303 f., and Bibl. 1367, pp. XII, 95.

38. THE ANNUNCIATION. 75 × 95 cm. Musée Condé, Chantilly (303).

HISTORY: Probably owned, and perhaps commissioned, by Cardinal Ascanio Filomarino, Archbishop of Naples, (a friend of Cardinal Francesco Barberini), who died in 1666. Passed by inheritance to the della Torre family and mentioned as being in their palace till the end of the eighteenth century (see below). The Chantilly picture was bought by the Duc d'Aumale at the Frédéric Reiset sale, Pillet, Paris, 28.iv.1879, lot 30.

DRAWING: A drawing in the Albertina, Vienna, is related in general terms to the Chantilly painting, and was published—with some reservations—as an original by Poussin in CR (I, p. 18, No. 34), but Thuillier (Bibl. 1296, p. 81) has pointed out that it is even more closely related to the fresco by Charles Mellin in S. Luigi dei Francesi, Rome, and has proposed an attribution of the drawing to Mellin, which is confirmed by its similarity in style to others reproduced by Thuillier, and to one in a private collection in New York which is a precise preparatory study for the S. Luigi fresco. Yet another similar drawing belongs to the Rhode Island School of Design, where it is ascribed to Poussin.

ENGRAVINGS: 1. By Cornelis van Caukercken (Rudrauf, Bibl. 1035, p. 9).
2. By Jean Couvay (Andresen, No. 93; Wildenstein, No. 29; Davies and Blunt, p. 209, No. 29).
3. With considerable variants, published by Etienne Jeaurat (Andresen, No. 94).

4. The group of God the Father supported by Putti was engraved by Saint-Non in *Fragments* . . . (Bibl. 240, and cf. Cayeux, Bibl. 1390.2, p. 357, No. 224) and in the *Voyage pittoresque* . . . (Bibl. 267, I, Pl. oppos. p. 114) in the latter case after a drawing by Fragonard, which was sold in the Chanler sale, Sotheby, London, 10.vi.1959, lot 17. The engraving in the *Voyage* is Smith, No. 154.

COPIES: Hermitage Museum, Leningrad (1771). Acquired by the Empress Catherine II with the Crozat collection in 1772. Engraved by Gérard Edelinck (Andresen, No. 92; Wildenstein, No. 28; Davies and Blunt, p. 209, No. 28).
Paintings of this subject attributed to Poussin are recorded as follows:
1. In the collection of Jean de La Fourcade, Lyons, c. 1672 (cf. Bonnaffé, Bibl. 583, p. 151).
2. In the collection of Paul Poisson de Bourvalais in 1706 (cf. Brice, Bibl. 89c, I, p. 225).
3. Anon. sale, Copreaux, Paris, 25 ff.vi.1779, lot 89.

NOTES: Travellers and writers of guide books from Cochin to Martyn (see bibliography below) describe the picture in the Palazzo della Torre in sufficient detail to make it clear that it corresponded in composition with the Chantilly painting. Saint-Non's engravings of the group of God the Father with putti confirm the identity. The earlier history of the della Torre picture is not precisely known, but the whole collection seems to have been formed by Cardinal Filomarino, who is known to have owned 'tre pezzi famosi' by Poussin. For a fuller account of his collection see Blunt, Bibl. 1167, pp. 79 ff.

Cochin (Bibl. 207, I, pp. 187 f.) describes it as unfinished and says that the heads are only sketched in and 'fort grises'. The Chantilly picture appears very thin in parts, and this may be due to the condition which Cochin describes rather than to rubbing during restoration.

The Chantilly picture was dated by Grautoff (II, No. 102) 1641-43, rejected as a copy by Wild (Bibl. 1185, pp. 21 f.), and dated 1627 by Mahon (Bibl. 1271, p. 297). I should in general terms agree with the last opinion, but should see the *Annunciation* as slightly before the *Germanicus*.

BIBLIOGRAPHY: Cochin, Bibl. 207, I, pp. 187 f.; La Lande, Bibl. 224a, VII, p. 57; Northall, Bibl. 227, p. 236; Richard, Bibl. 229, IV, p. 194; La Roque, Bibl. 248, III, p. 15; Canova, Bibl. 261, p. 85; Saint-Non, Bibl. 267, I, p. 114; Martyn, Bibl. 296, p. 281; Smith, Nos. 46, 154; Grautoff, I, p. 212, II, No. 102; Magne, 1914, p. 208, No. 182, p. 216, No. 285; Hourticq, Bibl. 899, p. 186; Rudrauf, Bibl. 968, p. 131; Régamey, Bibl. 1019, pp. 27 f.; Bertin-Mourot, Bibl. 1024, p. 88; Rudrauf, Bibl. 1035, p. 8; Licht, p. 133; Blunt, Bibl. 1167, pp. 80, 86; Wild, Bibl. 1185, pp. 21 f.; Blunt, Bibl. 1227, p. 167; Mahon, Bibl. 1271, p. 297.

39. THE ANNUNCIATION. 105×103 cm. Signed: POUSSIN.FACIEBAT.ANNO SALVTIS. MDCLVII.ALEX.SEPT.PONT.MAX REGNANTE.ROMA. National Gallery, London (5472).

HISTORY: This may be either the picture in the Thomas Bladen sale, Christie, London, 10.iii.1775, lot 84, or that in the Robert Udny sale, Christie, London, 19.v.1804, lot 96, which was said to have been 'continually in the Pope's chapel till very lately, when it was brought to England'. The Udny picture was in the Robert Heathcote sale, Phillips, London, 5.iv.1805, lot 45, bt. De Blyny. Possibly J. M. Raikes sale, Christie, London, 6.vi.1829, lot 37 (as from the Orleans collection). Possibly Thomas Emmerson sale, Phillips, London, 16.vi.1832, lot 119. (According to Smith (No. 45) the Raikes picture was in an anonymous sale, presumably in London, in 1836.) Thomas Wright sale, Christie, London, 7.vi.1845, lot 41, bt. Buchanan. William Buchanan sale, Christie, London, 4.vii.1846, lot 30, bt. by Evans for Scarisbrick. Charles Scarisbrick sale, Christie, London, 18.v.1861, lot 476, bt. Part. Thomas Part collection, c. 1877; sold c. 1935 by his grandson, A. E. Part, to Christopher Norris, who presented it to the National Gallery in 1944.

COPY: Alte Pinakothek, Munich (3757). On wood, with some variations. The Munich picture seems to be the original of the engravings by Pietro del Po (Andresen, No. 95) and P. van Somer (Andresen, No. 96; Wildenstein, No. 30). Accepted as an original by Wild (Bibl. 1383, p. 234), but see Blunt (Bibl. 1226, pp. 400 f.). This is presumably the painting mentioned by L. Vleughels in 1735 in his preface (Bibl. 166) as having belonged to 'Monsieur Benoit peintre de l'Académie', probably Antoine Benoit (c. 1630–1717). It is also mentioned by Magne, 1914, p. 208, No. 181.

NOTES: The inscription and the tradition that the picture came from 'the Pope's chapel' have led to the suggestion that it was painted for Alexander VII. Miss Costello, however, has recently suggested (Bibl. 1429) that the painting was designed to hang over the tomb of Cassiano dal Pozzo in S. Maria sopra Minerva.

BIBLIOGRAPHY: Smith, No. 45; Davies, Bibl. 988a, p. 176, No. 5472; Blunt, Bibl. 1000, pp. 18 ff.; Régamey, Bibl. 1019, pp. 27 f.; Bertin-Mourot, Bibl. 1023, p. 46, No. VII; Rudrauf, Bibl. 1035, pp. 8 ff.; Ladoué, Bibl. 1076, p. 364; Mahon, Bibl. 1367, pp. 119, 121; Wild, Bibl. 1383, p. 236; Costello, Bibl. 1429.

40. THE ADORATION OF THE SHEPHERDS. 98×74 cm. Signed: N. Pousin. fe. on the stone in the foreground. National Gallery, London (6277).

HISTORY: Possibly belonged to Le Nôtre and listed in the inventory taken at his death as *un grand tableau du Poussin, peint sur toile, à bordure de bois doré, représentant une* nativité, *ayant 3 pieds et demij de haut sur deux pieds de largeur* (Guiffrey, Bibl. 697, p. 248, No. 253). De Selle sale, Remy, Paris, 19 ff.ii.1761, lot 35 (stated to be engraved by Picart with dedication to Colbert; size given as 37×27½ pouces), bt. Thibauts. Sir Joshua Reynolds sale, Christie, London, 11 ff.iii.1795, fourth day, lot 97, bt. Henry Walton, presumably for Sir Thomas Beauchamp-Proctor; by descent to Jocelyn Beauchamp; sold Sotheby, London, 11.vii.1956, lot 119, bt. D. Koetser; bt. from him by the National Gallery in 1957.

DRAWINGS: 1. Christ Church, Oxford (CR, I, p. 19, No. 35). Rather weak and possibly a copy of a lost original. Another copy by Michel Corneille is in the Musée du Louvre, Paris (No. 2585).
2. British Museum, London (CR, I, p. 19, No. A 6).

ENGRAVINGS: 1. By Etienne Picart (Andresen, No. 104; Wildenstein, No. 37; Davies and Blunt, p. 210, No. 37); with dedication to Colbert (d. 1683).
2. By Pierre Drevet (Andresen, No. 105).

COPIES: 1. Church of St. Pierre, Avignon. Very much larger than the original.
2. Château de Torigny-sur-Vire (rep. H. Soulange-Bodin, *Châteaux de Normandie*, Paris 1928, I, Pl. 78).
3. Private collection, Barcelona (cf. Sterling, Bibl. 1290, p. 276).
4. Robert Draper collection, Miami, Florida. 39×30 inches. Inscribed: *Nicolo Pousin*.
5. With Wildenstein, London, in 1936. From the Dollfus and Eugène Favier collections (Grautoff, II, No. 103). This is probably the painting which appeared in the Auguiot sale, Pillet, Paris, 1 f.iii.1875, lot 55.
6. Sir W. Hillary sale, Squibb, London, 24 f.vi.1808, second day, lot 53.
7. Grosskopf sale, Frankfurt a.M., 5.v.1925, lot 53.
8. Lempertz sale, Cologne, 23.iii.1927, lot 6 (as Bassano).
9. Copy of lower half only, National Gallery, London (1862). Lord Radstock; sold Christie, London, 13.v.1826, lot 22; Samuel Rogers; sold Christie, London, 2.v.1856, lot 622, bt. Beauclerk; bequeathed to the Victoria and Albert Museum, London in 1878 by G. Mitchell; transferred to the National Gallery (Smith, No. 55; wrongly identified by him with the Reynolds version).
10. Duchess of Northumberland, Albury Park, Surrey (Smith, No. 54, wrongly identified as the Radstock-Rogers version).

NOTES: The tradition in the Beauchamp family that this is the painting which belonged to Reynolds is supported by the following passage from Dawson Turner's *Outlines in Lithography from a small collection of pictures* (Yarmouth, 1840, p. 21), where, referring to the painter Henry Walton, who is known to have bought the *Adoration* at the Reynolds sale, he writes: 'the choice collection formed by the late Sir Thomas Beauchamp-Proctor at Langley Hall, Norfolk, was mainly, if not altogether, formed by him.'

The Favier version (see No. 5 among the copies) was dated by Grautoff, who did not know the original, to 1639–42, but this is evidently too late. A dating to 1637 seems to be generally accepted (*Exposition Poussin (Louvre)*, p. 84, and Mahon, Bibl. 1367, p. 103).

BIBLIOGRAPHY: Smith, No. 53; Graves and Cronin, Bibl. 647, IV, p. 1632; Grautoff, I, p. 213, II, No. 103; Magne, 1914, p. 207, Nos. 172, 174; (Borenius), Bibl. 977, p. 270, No. 97; *The National Gallery*, Bibl. 1178, pp. 49 f.; Wild, Bibl. 1184, p. 166; *Exposition Poussin (Louvre)*, p. 84; Mahon, Bibl. 1271, pp. 303 f., and Bibl. 1367, pp. XIII, 103.

41. THE ADORATION OF THE SHEPHERDS. 98 × 134 cm. Alte Pinakothek, Munich (617).

HISTORY: Inherited in 1777 by Carl Theodor, Elector of Bavaria, from the last Wittelsbach Elector Palatine, Max Joseph III, and brought from Mannheim to Munich.

ENGRAVINGS: 1. By Jean Baptiste Nolin (Andresen, No. 102; Wildenstein, No. 35).

2. Lithograph by Ferdinand Piloty (Andresen, No. 103).

NOTES: For the question whether this or No. 42 is the painting executed for Mauroy in 1650–53, see No. 42. The style of the Munich picture suggests a slightly later period, in the mid-fifties. The head of the grey-haired shepherd is like one in *St. Peter and St. John healing* of 1655 (No. 84), and the stiff, almost grotesque pointing gesture of Joseph is reminiscent of the Richmond *Achilles among the daughters of Lycomedes* of 1656 (No. 127). The closed, sculptural design is close to that of the Johnson *Baptism* (No. 72), undocumented but probably painted *c.* 1655–57.

BIBLIOGRAPHY: Smith, No. 52; Friedlaender, 1914, pp. 122, 241; Grautoff, I, p. 278, II, No. 150; Magne, 1914, p. 207, No. 169; Blunt, Bibl. 1226, p. 400; Wild, Bibl. 1383, pp. 223 ff.

42. THE ADORATION OF THE SHEPHERDS. Private collection, Texas.

HISTORY: Acquired by the late Count Ivan Podgoursky at some time before 1939. Probably the painting commissioned from Poussin by Séraphin de Mauroy, Intendant des Finances and later French ambassador in Rome, in 1650 (*Correspondance*, p. 412), but apparently only executed in 1653 (Félibien, IV, p. 63). This picture later belonged to Joachim de Seiglière de Boisfranc (Félibien, *ibid.*).

DRAWING: A drawing on the *verso* of the study for the *Man killed by a Snake* in the Musée des Beaux-Arts at Dijon (*CR*, IV, p. 47, No. 282) shows an *Adoration of the Shepherds* which comes closer to this composition than to any other known version, though it is in reverse. It shows the Virgin, St. Joseph and the Child almost as in the painting. The ox and the ass are present but are slightly further to the left. The group of the two shepherds in the left foreground—for which Poussin made a separate study lower down on the same sheet—is close to the corresponding group in the painting, except that in the latter the shepherd lying at full length in adoration has been moved behind the one kneeling. On the extreme left of the drawing is an indication of the door of the stable, and in the right background a line indicates the join of the two walls as in the engravings. A copy of this drawing is in the Boymans-van Beuningen Museum, Rotterdam.

ENGRAVINGS: 1. By Jean Pesne (Andresen, No. 99; Wildenstein, No. 33).
2. By Pierre Lombard (*d.* 1682; Andresen, No. 100). This engraving bears the arms of the Colbert family, with a coronet, mitre and crozier. These probably refer to Jacques Nicolas Colbert, archbishop of Rouen (1655–1707), son of the minister, who inherited the collection of his elder brother Colbert de Seignelay. The presence of the arms may indicate that he owned the original.
3. By Etienne Gantrel; in the reverse sense (cf. Wildenstein, No. 33).
4. Anonymous engraving, showing the foreground group of the Lombard and Pesne prints in reverse, with a background taken from the National Gallery picture (No. 39; cf. Blunt, Bibl. 1357, p. 489).

COPY: A copy, with the composition slightly enlarged on all sides, was in 1936 in the collection of Louis Mutuelle, Auxerre.

NOTES: Various theories have been proposed to identify the *Adoration of the Shepherds* commissioned by Mauroy in 1650 (for Mauroy, who died in 1668, see A. de Boislisle, 'La Place des Victoires et la Place de Vendôme', *Mémoires de la Société de l'histoire de Paris*, XV, 1888, p. 100). The Abbé Topin believed that his picture (now belonging to the Galerie Heim, Paris; see No. 43) was Mauroy's, but the pedigree is hypothetical (cf. *Mémorial d'Aix*, Bibl. 409), and the picture itself has given rise to doubts (cf. Badt, Bibl. 1190, p. 122, and Wild, Bibl. 1383, pp. 226 ff.). Grautoff proposed the Munich picture (No. 41), but this appears to be somewhat later. Recently Doris Wild (Bibl. 1383, pp. 228 ff.) has convincingly suggested the present composition as the most probable candidate (though she did not know the painted version). Her proposal is supported by the evidence of the drawing, which is made on the back of one for a painting executed in 1648 and is, therefore, not likely to be many years later. The style of the composition would confirm a dating to the early years of the fifties.

The painting in the Texan private collection was believed by Professor Walter Friedlaender in 1941 to be the original. The picture is now covered with a thick, partly discoloured varnish and shows signs of repaint in many parts, so that it is impossible to arrive at a definite conclusion about its status, but certain parts, notably in the drapery of the shepherds, have a quality very close to that of Poussin himself.

BIBLIOGRAPHY: *Correspondance*, p. 412; Félibien, IV, p. 63; Florent Le Comte, III, p. 31; Smith, No. 51; Friedlaender, 1914, p. 122; Grautoff, II, p. 255; Magne, 1914, p. 208, No. 175; *CR*, I, p. 19; Wild, Bibl. 1383, pp. 227 f.

43. THE ADORATION OF THE SHEPHERDS. 92 × 124 cm. Galerie Heim, Paris.

HISTORY: From the collection of C. M. A. d'Arcussia (eighteenth century); bequeathed to his relatives, the Lubières family; sold with their collection at Aix-en-Provence in the early nineteenth century; bt. by the Chanoine Topin before 1818 (*Mémorial d'Aix*, Bibl. 409); bt. from his heirs by Heim in 1958. According to Topin this was the picture commissioned by Mauroy, but see No. 42.

ENGRAVINGS: By Roger (Andresen, No. 98; Wildenstein, No. 32; Davies and Blunt, p. 209, No. 32). Wildenstein notes that the print in the Bibliothèque Nationale has an inscription (in manuscript) *Mariette 1662* and concludes that a copy belonged to Mariette by that year, but there is reason to think that inscriptions of this kind are not reliable (cf. Blunt, Bibl. 1357, p. 489 note 10). He also states that the engraver is Théodore Roger, who, according to Thieme-Becker (*sub voce* F. Roger), is traceable in Bourges in 1601. The only other engraver of this name known in the seventeenth century is François Roger, who was born about 1654 and died in 1694 (cf. Thieme-Becker, *loc. cit.*).

NOTES: When it was first exhibited at Berne in 1959 (Bibl. 1205, No. 75) this picture aroused doubts. In reviewing this exhibition, Badt (Bibl. 1190, p. 122) rejected it as an original, but did not make it clear whether he regarded it as a copy after a lost original or a composition by another painter. More recently Dr. Wild also rejected it, quoting K. E. Simon as proposing an attribution to Nicolas Loir (Bibl. 1383, pp. 226 ff.).

Certain features in the painting, such as the drily and naturalistically painted details of the brick-work and straw, are uncharacteristic of Poussin, but the general conception of the picture and the painting of certain figures, notably that of the Virgin, make it impossible to doubt that it is an original by Poussin of the early 1650's. The painting has nothing to do with the coarse and clumsy style of Loir.

BIBLIOGRAPHY: Smith, No. 51; *Mémorial d'Aix*, Bibl. 409; Magne, 1914, p. 207, No. 168; Jamot, Pl. 142; Badt, Bibl. 1190, p. 122; *Kunstmuseum, Berne*, Bibl. 1205, No. 75; Wild, Bibl. 1383, pp. 226 ff.

44. THE ADORATION OF THE MAGI. 161 × 182 cm. Signed: *Accad: rom.* NICOLAVS . PVSIN *faciebat Romae. 1633*. Staatliche Gemäldegalerie, Dresden (717).

HISTORY: Probably the painting seen by Bernini in the house of Cotteblanche in 1665 (cf. Chantelou, 1885, p. 227; 1960, p. 131), which had previously belonged to Martin de Charmois, the founder of the Academy (d. 1661; cf. Bonnaffé, Bibl. 583, p. 57). According to a tradition, recorded in the Dresden catalogue, it later belonged to 'Lord Walgrave', presumably Earl Waldegrave, who was ambassador in Paris till 1740; it was perhaps left there when he quitted the post. Bought by Augustus III of Saxony in Paris through de Brais in 1742 (museum catalogue).

DRAWINGS: 1. Musée Condé, Chantilly (*CR*, I, p. 20, No. 37).

2. Musée Condé, Chantilly (*CR*, I, p. 20, No. 38).

ENGRAVINGS: 1. By Henri d'Avice (Andresen, No. 109; Wildenstein, No. 39; Davies and Blunt, p. 210, No. 39).

2. Published by Malbouré (Andresen, No. 110).

3. By G. Vallet (Andresen, No. 111).

4. By Anton and Raphael Morghen (Andresen, No. 112).

COPIES: 1. Alleyn's College of God's Gift, Dulwich (227). This is probably the painting from the collection of Sir Edward Walpole, which later belonged to Reynolds; his sale, Christie, London, 11 ff.iii.1795, fourth day, lot 98, bt. Lawrence (? = bt. in); Reynolds sale, Phillips, London, 9.v.1798, lot 47 (Smith, No. 56; Magne, 1914, p. 208, No. 177; [Borenius], Bibl. 977, p. 273, No. 98).

2. Musée de Peinture et de Sculpture, Grenoble. Said to come from the Abbey of St. Antoine-en-Viennois; confiscated in 1799 and given to the museum by the department of the Isère (cf. Thuillier, Bibl. 1299, p. 291).

3. Musée du Louvre, Paris (712). From the monastery of the Chartreux, Paris (cf. Tuétey, Bibl. 295, I, pp. 186, 294; Tuétey and Guiffrey, Bibl. 304, p. 39; Thuillier, Bibl. 1297, pp. 41 ff.).

4. Private collection, Pas de Calais (cf. *The Times*, 29.vi.1932).

5. In the collection of Jean de La Fourcade, Lyons, *c.* 1672 (cf. Bonnaffé, Bibl. 583, p. 151).

6. Des Amory sale, Amsterdam, 23.vi.1722, lot 7, with dimensions 54×60 inches, said to be engraved by Avice (cf. Hoet, Bibl. 195, I, p. 260, and *Mercure de France*, Bibl. 148, p. 128).

7. Anonymous sale, Christie, London, 25.ii.1773, lot 65 (38×53 inches).

NOTES: Bernini complained that the Magi in the Cotteblanche picture did not look like kings, a comment which confirms the view that this was actually the Dresden painting, in which their appearance is not particularly royal.

A variant of the composition, recorded in an engraving by Benoît Thiboust, inscribed: *Nicolaus Poussinus Inve* (Andresen, No. 114; Wildenstein, No. 40), is probably based on a lost drawing rather than on a painting.

It has been suggested that the very elaborate signature, unique in Poussin's work, might be due to the fact that the picture was the artist's diploma piece on his reception as a member of the Academy of St. Luke, but it has been pointed out that the dates do not fit (Poussin was a full member of the Academy by 1632) and that there is no evidence that a diploma piece was demanded (cf. Bousquet, Bibl. 1231, p. 7 n. 28, and *L'ideale classico* (*Bologna*), No. 59 bis).

BIBLIOGRAPHY: Chantelou, 1885, p. 227, and 1960, p. 131; *Mercure de France*, Bibl. 148, p. 128; *Observations historiques*, Bibl. 236, II, pp. 202 ff.; Gault de Saint-Germain, Pt. II, p. 49; Smith, No. 59; Friedlaender, 1914, pp. 39 f., 114, 150; Grautoff, I, p. 127, II, No. 58; Magne, 1914, p. 208, No. 178; Blunt, Bibl. 906, p. 134; Jamot, p. 47; Taylor, Bibl. 1036, p. 453; Blunt, Bibl. 1086, p. 186, and Bibl. 1086a, p. 162; Licht, p. 115; Bousquet, Bibl. 1231, p. 7 n. 28; Mahon, Bibl. 1269, pp. 254, 258, and Bibl. 1271, pp. 290, 293, 295, 300; Weigert, Bibl. 1309, p. 278; *L'ideale classico* (*Bologna*), No. 59 bis; Mahon, Bibl. 1367, pp. XI f., 33 ff., 39 ff., 47, 53, 55 f., 75, 80, 82 ff., 87, 93, 135, 137.

45. THE VIRGIN AND CHILD. Original lost.

HISTORY: Probably belonged to Cérisier (see below).

ENGRAVING: By Jean Pesne (Andresen, No. 116; Wildenstein, No. 41; Davies and Blunt, p. 210, No. 41).

COPY: According to Bonnaffé (Bibl. 572, p. 38) Fouquet owned a 'Vierge avec Jésus' after Poussin. If this is taken literally to mean a composition with only the Virgin and the Christ Child, then his picture was probably Cérisier's painting or a copy after it.

NOTES: In 1665 Bernini saw in the house of Cérisier a 'vierge à demi-corps' (Chantelou, 1885, p. 90, and 1960, p. 126). Of all the compositions known in the original or through engravings that engraved by Pesne is the only one to fit this description.

As far as one can judge from the engraving, the composition must have dated from the late forties or early fifties.

BIBLIOGRAPHY: Chantelou, 1885, p. 90, and 1960, p. 126; Smith, No. 61; Grautoff, II, p. 255; Magne, 1914, p. 214, No. 259.

46. THE HOLY FAMILY. 68·5 × 44·5 cm. The Detroit Institute of Arts, Detroit (54.2).

HISTORY: Painted for Stefano Roccatagliata in 1641–42 (*Correspondance*, pp. 57 ff., see below). Belonged to Le Bailli de Breteuil, Ambassador to Rome of the Order of Malta between 1759 and 1761 (drawn there by Fragonard on his first Italian visit; the drawing sold in the Chanler sale, Sotheby, London, 10.vi.1959, lot 17, inscribed: *Palais de Malte*). There was a Breteuil sale held by Lebrun in Paris in December 1760 (Lugt, 1128), but, as no copy of the catalogue survives, it is impossible to say whether the *Holy Family* was included in it; it did not appear in the sale of pictures from the same collection, Lebrun, Paris, 16 ff.i.1786. Robert Ansell sale, Christie, London, 16.ii.1771, lot 72 (as from the Breteuil collection, with dimensions 28 × 22 inches), bt. for Lord Melbourne. The Detroit picture was acquired before 1925 by Mr. and Mrs. Edgar Whitcomb of Detroit; passed by descent to Mr. and Mrs. A. D. Wilkinson; presented by them to the Institute of Arts in 1954.

DRAWINGS: 1. Royal Library, Windsor Castle (*CR*, I, p. 24, No. 40).
2. Royal Library, Windsor Castle (*CR*, I, p. 24, No. 41).

ENGRAVINGS: By Carlo Faucci, with dedication to the Bailli de Breteuil, who then owned the picture (Andresen, No. 119; Andresen-Wildenstein, No. 119).

COPY: Anon. sale, Christie, London, 1.vi.1962, lot 140 (27 × 22½ inches).

NOTES: Poussin's letters show that the painting, no doubt commissioned before the artist left Rome, was begun by April 1641 and despatched on 22.v.1642. Apart from the completion of the *Baptism* of the first series of Sacraments for Pozzo, this seems to have been the only work undertaken in Paris by Poussin, except for his official commissions.

BIBLIOGRAPHY: *Correspondance*, pp. 57, 112, 124, 137, 153, 159, 163, 165, 169; Smith, No. 68; Friedlaender, 1914, pp. 117, 214; Grautoff, II, pp. 255, 256; Magne, 1914, pp. 122, 134; Borenius, Bibl. 779, p. 92; Heil, Bibl. 823, p. 55; Friedlaender, Bibl. 947, p. 11; Blunt, Bibl. 975, p. 42; Bertin-Mourot, Bibl. 1023, p. 47, No. IX; Licht, p. 157; *Bulletin of the Detroit Institute of Arts*, Bibl. 1111, p. 13; Thuillier, Bibl. 1296, p. 85; *Exposition Poussin* (*Louvre*), No. 65; *L'ideale classico* (*Bologna*), No. 71; Mahon, Bibl. 1367, pp. XIII, 110, 121.

47. THE VIRGIN AND CHILD WITH ST. JOHN. Original lost.

HISTORY: Possibly the painting which belonged to Claudine Bouzonnet Stella (see below); Vassal de Saint-Hubert sale, Remy, Paris, 17 ff.i.1774, lot 64 (16½ × 13¾ inches, on panel); Comte de D. (= Dubarry) sale, Remy, Paris, 21 ff.xi.1774, lot 76, as from the Vassal de Saint-Hubert sale, dimensions given as 16½ × 13½ inches. The Dubarry picture is identifiable as that engraved by Pesne by the drawing made by Gabriel de Saint-Aubin in the Dubarry sale catalogue (Bibl. 204, III, No. 76).

ENGRAVING: By Jean Pesne (Andresen, No. 117; Wildenstein, No. 42; Davies and Blunt, p. 210, No. 42).

COPIES: 1. By Claudine Bouzonnet Stella (cf. *Testament . . .*, Bibl. 107, p. 34, No. 83).
2. What may have been a version of this composition appeared in the Nyert sale, Musier, Paris, 30.iii.1772, lot 6, on wood, with dimensions of 16½ × 13 inches.

NOTES: The identification of this design with one in Claudine Bouzonnet Stella's collection is based on the reference in her inventory (*Testament . . .*, Bibl. 107, p. 34, No. 83) to a painting which she describes as 'une Vierge, Jésus qui donne la benédiction à St. Jean', which fits only this composition. It is true that this picture is described as a copy by herself, but the Stella family were in the habit of making copies of paintings which belonged to them, and it is quite likely, therefore, that she owned the original. Loménie de Brienne (p. 216) refers to 'la petite vierge qui est encore chez Melle Stella aux Galleries du Louvre', but the effect of this evidence is weakened by a second reference (*ibid.*, p. 222) to the fact that Poussin had painted for Jacques Stella, uncle of Claudine Bouzonnet Stella who inherited his collection, 'une petite vierge sous un toit trois figures', which does not seem to be the same painting. It is possible, however, that the engraving does not represent the whole composition and that in the painting there was a pent-roof over the figures.

BIBLIOGRAPHY: *Testament . . .*, Bibl. 107, p. 34, No. 83; Loménie de Brienne, pp. 216, 222; Saint-Aubin, Bibl. 204, III, No. 76; Smith, No. 62; Magne, 1914, p. 214, No. 260; Hourticq, Bibl. 899, p. 69.

48. THE HOLY FAMILY WITH ST. JOHN HOLDING A CROSS. 101 × 75.5 cm. Staatliche Kunsthalle, Karlsruhe.

HISTORY: Walsh Porter sale, Christie, London, 14.iv.1810, lot 32; W. Scrope by 1832 (exhibited at the British Institution in 1832 (No. 26) as lent by Scrope; cf. Smith, No. 71); Scrope sale, Christie, London, 30.vi.1853, lot 107; Matthew Anderson sale, Christie, London, 7.vi.1861, lot 51, as from the Walsh Porter collection; Pearson sale, Paris, 18.x.1927, lot 55, with label on back indicating a provenance from the Walsh Porter and Scrope sales; with Cassirer, Berlin; Baron Thyssen, Schloss Rohoncz; sold by his heirs, and bt. by the Gallery in 1962.

ENGRAVINGS: 1. By Guillaume Chasteau (Andresen, No. 123; Wildenstein, No. 44).

2. Published by Montbard (Davies and Blunt, p. 210, No. 44).

NOTES: Dated by Grautoff (Bibl. 864, pp. 335 f.) to 1655 and identified with the *Holy Family* ordered by Chantelou for Mme de Montmort, but evidently of a far earlier period. Mahon (Bibl. 1367, pp. 19 f.) proposes 1628–29. I should tend myself to date it a little earlier, perhaps just before rather than just after the *Germanicus*, i.e. *c.* 1627.

BIBLIOGRAPHY: Smith, No. 71; Friedlaender, 1914, pp. 92, 120; Grautoff, II, pp. 255, 256; Magne, 1914, p. 214, No. 256; *Sammlung Schloss Rohoncz*, Bibl. 844, No. 262; Grautoff, Bibl. 864, pp. 335 f.; *CR*, I, pp. 21, 23 f.; Bertin-Mourot, Bibl. 1023, p. 47, No. XI; Blunt, Bibl. 1227, p. 165; *Exposition Poussin (Louvre)*, No. 17; Mahon, Bibl. 1271, p. 297, and Bibl. 1367, pp. XI, 19 f., 23, 26, 29.

49. THE HOLY FAMILY WITH ST. JOHN. 167.5 × 122 cm. Inscribed on the scroll: ECCE AGNUS DEI. Private collection, London.

HISTORY: Apparently the picture which came to England in 1822 and which belonged (by 1835) to Vittore Zanetti, an art dealer in Manchester. It was still in the possession of his family in 1909 (cf. Giolli, Bibl. 682, p. 25, with a fanciful pedigree). Marquis of Crewe sale, Christie, London, 9.xii.1955, lot 70 (as Carracci).

ENGRAVINGS: By Faustino Anderloni (*d.* 1847) after a drawing by Giovita Garavaglia (*d.* 1835; Andresen, No. 126; Andresen-Wildenstein, No. 126), with an inscription stating that the original belonged to Zanetti.

COPY: A copy of the Virgin and Child alone was in an anonymous sale, Anderson Galleries, New York, 15.iv.1926, lot 56 (as Puligo).

NOTES: This picture is related in its general scheme to No. 48. Probably painted just before 1630.

BIBLIOGRAPHY: Triqueti, Bibl. 440, p. 48; Giolli, Bibl. 682, p. 25; Blunt, Bibl. 1227, p. 165.

50. THE HOLY FAMILY WITH ST. JOHN HOLDING A CROSS. Original lost.

HISTORY: Nothing is known of the history of this picture, which is only recorded in two copies and an engraving.

ENGRAVING: By Sébastien Vouillemont (Andresen, No. 124; Wildenstein, No. 45).

COPIES: 1. Galleria Nazionale, Rome.
2. Anon. sale, Sotheby, London, 24.ii.1965, lot 87 (as Solimena).

NOTES: Judging from the engraving and the copies, the original must have been painted some time before the journey to Paris in 1640. A variant of this composition, oblong in shape, is described by Smith (No. 73) and reproduced in Landon (No. 53). Landon says his plate is after an engraving by Pesne, which is not known to Andresen or otherwise traceable.

BIBLIOGRAPHY: Smith, No. 72; Grautoff, II, p. 256; Magne, 1914, p. 214, No. 257; *CR*, I, p. 21.

51. THE HOLY FAMILY WITH ST. JOHN. 193 × 128 cm. John and Mable Ringling Museum, Sarasota, Florida.

HISTORY: Begun for 'une personne grande' (probably the Duc de Créqui), who decided not to take it; offered in August 1655, when still unfinished, to Mme de Montmort, later Mme de Chantelou, who had asked for a Madonna. The offer was withdrawn in November 1655, when the artist discovered that the painting was not after all available (*Correspondance*, pp. 436 ff., 441), and it is to be presumed that it went to the person who had originally commissioned it. The Sarasota picture is first traceable in the collection of Sir Richard Worsley (1751–1808), and passed by inheritance to the Earls of Yarborough; sold Christie, London, 12.vii.1929, lot 70, bt. Newton; with Böhler; sold by him to the Ringling Museum.

ENGRAVINGS: 1. By Alexander Voet (Andresen, No. 121; Wildenstein, No. 43; Davies and Blunt, p. 210, No. 43).
2. Published by Malbouré (Andresen, No. 122).

COPIES: 1. Meyer-Glitza collection, Hamburg. 108 × 80 cm. Inherited from Dr. Adolf Glitza (1820–94). Sold Hauswedell, Hamburg, 27.xi.1965, lot 28.
2. Church of Montmorency (Oise).

NOTES: The Sarasota picture can be certainly identified with the composition mentioned by Poussin in his letter to Chantelou, because he describes it (*Correspondance*, pp. 437 f.) as being big, as consisting of four figures, and as showing St. John in the act of begging Christ to give His blessing.

From the fact that Voet's engraving has a dedication by Jean Dughet to Jean Pointel, Andresen wrongly concluded that the picture was painted for him. Since Pointel was active in buying pictures for the Duc de Créqui (cf. Fouquet, Bibl. 24a, p. 102), it has also been suggested that the latter was the 'personne grande' who had commissioned the painting, but although the inventory of his collection, made at his death, contains two *Holy Families* by Poussin (cf. Magne, Bibl. 936, p. 186), neither of them corresponds exactly to the Sarasota painting. One is almost certainly the Fogg picture (No. 54) and the other is described as 'Une grande Vierge avec plusieurs enfants, manière dudit', which also suggests a Holy Family with adoring putti. The words 'manière dudit' are somewhat obscure. They could mean either 'in the manner of the *Achilles*', a painting mentioned two items earlier (for the complete passage, see No. 54), or 'in the manner of the aforesaid artist', i.e. Poussin. The second reading is to some extent confirmed by the fact that in spite of its size the picture was only valued at 1500 livres as opposed to 4000 for the other *Holy Family* and 4500 for the *Achilles* (No. 127).

BIBLIOGRAPHY: *Correspondance*, pp. 436, 437 f., 439, 441; Waagen, Bibl. 384b, III, p. 69; Smith, No. 70; Friedlaender, 1914, pp. 122, 242; Magne, 1914, p. 214, No. 255; Friedlaender, Bibl. 875, p. 325; Alpatov, Bibl. 882, p. 12; *CR*, I, pp. 23 f.; Magne, Bibl. 936, p. 186; Bertin-Mourot, Bibl. 1023, p. 48, No. XII; Blunt, Bibl. 1050, p. 40; *Exposition Poussin* (*Louvre*), No. 107; Mahon, Bibl. 1367, p. 120; Wild, Bibl. 1383, p. 245.

52. THE HOLY FAMILY IN THE TEMPLE. 67 × 49 cm. Musée Condé, Chantilly (304).

HISTORY: Probably painted for Cardinal Giulio Rospigliosi, later Pope Clement IX; recorded in the Palazzo Rospigliosi in the eighteenth century (see below); Frédéric Reiset collection; bt. from him by the duc d'Aumale (Lafenestre, Bibl. 567, p. 326).

DRAWING: Royal Library, Windsor Castle (*CR*, I, p. 24, No. 43).

ENGRAVINGS: 1. By Domenico Cunego (1726–1803; Andresen, No. 134).
2. Anonymous, without inscription (Andresen, No. 133).

COPIES: 1. National Gallery, London. W. B. Tiffin sale, London, 28.v.1877, lot 32, as Le Sueur; bt. by Francis Turner Palgrave and given by him to the Gallery in 1894 (Davies, Bibl. 988a, p. 186, No. 1422).
2. Palace of Pavlovsk, Russia. In the Imperial Collection since 1768 (Grautoff, II, pp. 262 f.).
3. By Jacques Stella (cf. *Testament . . .*, Bibl. 107, p. 30).

NOTES: The copy of this composition at Pavlovsk has always been attributed to Le Sueur, and that in the National Gallery long bore his name. The existence of a drawing for the composition at Windsor, manifestly by Poussin, led to the theory, the origin of which is difficult to trace, that during the visit to Paris Poussin gave Le Sueur the drawing, from which the young painter made a painted version.

Recently, however, opinion has swung away from this complicated hypothesis (cf. Wild, Bibl. 1185, pp. 17 ff.), and a careful examination of the Chantilly painting in good daylight made it clear that, though dirty, it was an original by Poussin (cf. *Exposition Poussin* (*Louvre*), No. 190). This view is strongly confirmed by the fact that a picture of this composition—almost certainly the Chantilly version—can be identified in the Palazzo Rospigliosi in the late eighteenth century. La Lande (Bibl. 224a, IV, p. 275), who saw it in 1765–66, describes it as follows: 'Sainte Anne qui conduit le petit S. Jean devant l'enfant Jésus pour l'adorer; la Vierge porte J.C., et S. Joseph est appuyé sur sa regle; tableau de Poussin, bien pensé et bien dessiné, mais dont la couleur est tout-à-fait d'un ton de pierre'. This picture is presumably the *Holy*

Family mentioned in the Rospigliosi inventory of 1713 (Zeri, Bibl. 1216, p. 308), by Manazzale in 1802 (Bibl. 308a, I, p. 127), by Laouriens in 1816 (Bibl. 356, p. 398), by Vasi in 1819 (Bibl. 298e, I, p. 251) and by Nibby in 1827 (Bibl. 383, I, p. 336). It is significant that it is omitted by Nibby in the 1838 edition. This contains (Bibl. 383a, I, p. 282) a detailed account of the pictures on the first floor, but the similar account of the second floor rooms which contained the painting by Poussin is omitted, except for the introductory phrase: 'L'appartamento del secondo piano . . . appartiene al principe Rospigliosi. Fralle molte stanze, di cui è composto, ve ne sono quattro, che contengono una raccolta di scelti quadri'. It is true that the *Madonna* is still mentioned by Melchiorri in 1840 (Bibl. 408, p. 560), but he was much less well informed and less conscientious than Nibby and seems simply to have used the latter's edition of 1827, or rather misused it, because he confuses the accounts of the first and second floors. The *Holy Family* had presumably been sold between 1827 and 1838.

If the picture was in the Palazzo Rospigliosi in the eighteenth century, it is fairly certain that it was painted for Cardinal Giulio Rospigliosi, later Pope Clement IX, an important patron of Poussin (see text volume pp. 153 ff.). This fact is of some relevance in connection with the dating of the picture.

When the connection with Le Sueur was thought to exist, there was strong evidence for dating the Windsor drawing to the Paris journey of 1640–42, but once that theory was abandoned, the argument about dating based on it broke down. In 1958 Dr. Wild (*loc. cit.*) argued that the drawing must be dated to 1647, because Poussin shows the figures undraped and because he does the same in two drawings for the *Sacraments*, executed in that year (*CR*, I, pp. 47 f., Nos. 99, 100), a conclusion which seems a little rash. Mahon (Bibl. 1367, pp. 110 ff.) dates the drawing and the painting to 1638–42 and suggests that the latter may be identical with a picture mentioned by Poussin in a letter of 28.iv.1639 (*Correspondance*, p. 20) as having been sent to Monsieur Debonaire, i.e. Louis de Bonnaire, Portemanteau du Roi. The subject of the picture is not mentioned, and since the *Holy Family* seems to have remained in Rome it is unlikely to be Bonnaire's. As regards the dating of the picture, Poussin seems to have been working for Rospigliosi in the years just before the journey to Paris (see Nos. 61, 121) and may have continued to do so immediately after his return at the end of 1642, though not for long, because the cardinal was absent from Rome from 1644 to 1653 (Mahon, Bibl. 1367, p. 115). In the present state of our knowledge it is difficult to say definitely whether the picture was painted just before or just after the Paris journey—if it had been painted during the journey, it would probably have been mentioned in the letters—but the later period, *c.* 1643, seems the more probable.

Posner (Bibl. 1436.1) points out the similarity of the composition to Caravaggio's *Madonna of Loreto* and favours a date just before the Paris journey.

BIBLIOGRAPHY: La Lande, Bibl. 224a, IV, p. 275; Magnan, Bibl. 260, I, col. 24; Hoare, Bibl. 280, I, p. 47; Ramdohr, Bibl. 287, II, p. 65; Vasi, Bibl. 298a, I, p. 251; Starke, Bibl. 306, II, p. 37; Manazzale, Bibl. 308a, I, p. 127; Laouriens, Bibl. 356, p. 398; Nibby, Bibl. 383, I, p. 336; Smith, No. 77; Melchiorri, Bibl. 408, p. 560; Lafenestre, Bibl. 567, p. 324; Grautoff, II, p. 262; Magne, 1914, p. 213, No. 237; Friedlaender, Bibl. 834, p. 257; Hourticq, Bibl. 899, p. 183; *CR*, I, p. 21; Wild, Bibl. 1185, pp. 17 ff.; *Exposition Poussin (Louvre)*, No. 190; Zeri, Bibl. 1216, p. 308; Mahon, Bibl. 1367, pp. XIII, 110 f.; Posner, Bibl. 1436.1.

53. THE HOLY FAMILY ON THE STEPS. 68·9 × 97·5 cm. National Gallery of Art, Washington (Samuel H. Kress Collection).

HISTORY: Painted for Hennequin de Fresne in 1648 (cf. Félibien, IV, p. 59) and later in the Hôtel de Guise (Florent Le Comte, III, p. 29. There does not seem to be any foundation for the suggestion which has been made that the picture belonged to François Roger de Gaignières, Equerry to the Duc de Guise, whose collection, mainly of prints and drawings, was installed in the hôtel). What is presumably the same picture reappears in the Marquis de Lassay sale, Joullain fils, Paris, 22 ff.v.1775, lot 43, with dimensions 25 × 36 inches. (It is not mentioned by Dézallier d'Argenville in the account which he gives in the 1757 edition of his *Voyage* of the Hôtel de Lassay and the pictures in it, which were acquired by the Marquis de Lassay, who died in 1738). Presumably in the Abbé Le Blanc sale, Lebrun, Paris, 14.ii.1781, lot 39; in the Comte de Vaudreuil sale, Lebrun, Paris, 26.xi.1787, lot 29 (as from the Le Blanc sale, with dimensions 27 × 38 inches); in the La Reynière sale, Lebrun, Paris, 3.iv.1793, lot 2 (as from the Vaudreuil sale, with dimensions 27 × 38 inches); Trumbull sale, Christie, London, 17 f.ii.1797, lot 81 (as from the La Reynière sale); bt. Smith; anon. sale, Christie, London, 7.iii.1801, lot 85 (as engraved by Poilly). The Washington picture was in the possession of the Duke of Sutherland by 1844 (Jameson, Bibl. 417.1, p. 197, No.

74); Duke of Sutherland sale, Christie, London, 11.vii.1913, lot 34, bt. in; bt. from the Duke by Agnew in 1947; sold to the Kress Foundation, 1949, and presented to the National Gallery.

DRAWINGS: 1. Musée des Beaux-Arts, Dijon (*CR*, I, p. 25, No. 45).
2. Pierpont Morgan Library, New York, (*CR*, I, p. 25, No. 46). Possibly a very skilful copy.
3. Musée du Louvre, Paris (*CR*, I, p. 25, No. 47).
4. Musée du Louvre, Paris (No. 758 *verso*; see Kauffmann, Bibl. 1263, p. 147).

ENGRAVINGS: 1. By Claudine Bouzonnet Stella (Andresen, No. 135; Wildenstein, No. 52; Davies and Blunt, p. 210, No. 52).
2. By Jean Baptiste de Poilly (Andresen, No. 136).

COPIES: 1. Musée, Chaumont, Haute-Marne (cf. Bertin-Mourot, Bibl. 1150, p. 6).
2. John Bryson, Oxford.
3. Earl of Caledon sale, Christie, London, 9.vi.1939, lot 62, bt. Meatyard.
4. Anon. sale, Christie, London, 21.xii.1950, lot 78 (by N. Verendal, with the figures surrounded by a wreath of flowers).

A version belonging to Mlle Thérèse Bertin-Mourot, Paris, is believed by Friedlaender to be a variant by Poussin himself. Lord Ashburton; anon. sale, Christie, London, 17.vii.1908, lot 150, bt. Whitworth; with Quinto, Paris; Lerolle, Paris, by 1914 (cf. Rouart, Bibl. 687, p. 92; Friedlaender, 1914, p. 119; Grautoff, II, reference under No. 131; Bertin-Mourot, Bibl. 1023, p.47, No. X, Bibl. 1165.1, p. 366, and Bibl. 1192, pp. 1 ff.

BIBLIOGRAPHY: Félibien, IV, p. 59; Florent Le Comte, III, p. 29; Waagen, Bibl. 384b, II, p. 66; Smith, No. 78; Jameson, Bibl. 417.1, p. 197, No. 74; Mantz, Bibl. 493, p. 367; Friedlaender, 1914, pp. 92, 119, 239; Grautoff, I, p. 269, II, No. 131; Magne, 1914, p. 213, No. 241; Blunt, Bibl. 913, p. 9; Borenius, Bibl. 914, p. 63; Bertin-Mourot, Bibl. 1023, p. 47, No. X; Blunt, Bibl. 1086, pp. 191 f., and Bibl. 1086a, pp. 167 f.; Licht, p. 157; Bertin-Mourot, Bibl. 1150, pp. 3 ff., Bibl. 1165.1, p. 366, and Bibl. 1192, pp. 1 ff.; Kauffmann, Bibl. 1262, pp. 36 ff., and Bibl. 1263, pp. 147 ff.; Ettlinger, Bibl. 1327, pp. 196 f.; Friedlaender, Bibl. 1444, p. 160.

54. THE HOLY FAMILY WITH A BATH-TUB. 98 × 129.5 cm. Fogg Art Museum, Harvard University, Cambridge, Mass.

HISTORY: If Loménie de Brienne (p. 216) is correct in his description of the *Holy Family* belonging to the Duc de Créqui ('Ce sont un grouppe d'enfans qui servent le petit Jésus au sortir du bain et dont un de ces enfans l'adore'), then it must be the Fogg painting. Moreover, the inventory of the duke's collection, made at his death in 1687 (cf. Magne, Bibl. 936, p. 186), contains the following entries under Poussin:

La Découverte d'Achille ... 4500 livres.

Vierge avec plusieurs enfants, compagne de l'Achille ... 4000 livres.

Une grande Vierge avec plusieurs enfants, manière dudit ... 1500 livres.

The second picture mentioned is probably the Fogg *Holy Family*, which is almost exactly the same size as the Richmond Achilles (No. 127), which certainly belonged to Créqui.

According to Félibien (IV, p. 62), the duke's painting was executed in 1651. The identification of the picture is made difficult, however, because the engraving after it by Jean Pesne (see below) states that the original was then in the collection of Jean Fromont de Veine. Félibien (IV, p. 152) mentions the fact that de Veine owned such a picture, but he does not say that it was the same as Créqui's, which he had referred to earlier (IV, p. 62) and, further, he describes de Veine's as 'une Vierge dans un païsage accompagnée de cinq figures', which does not agree with the Fogg picture or with any other recorded version. Florent Le Comte repeats this description exactly (III, p. 32), having referred on the previous page to the fact that Créqui 'avoit ... une Vierge dans un païsage, accompagnée de plusieurs figures', and, like Félibien, does not suggest that the two are identical. Moreover, Créqui does not seem to have sold his *Holy Family*, since two such pictures were in his possession at his death.

The most probable solution to this problem is that Créqui and de Veine each owned two *Holy Families*, one of which—the Fogg painting—passed from the former to the latter. Objections may be raised to this hypothesis on the grounds that, according to Wildenstein (No. 53), the engraving by Pesne bearing the name of de Veine must date from before 1678, i.e. nine years before Créqui's death. This statement, however, is based on the date written on Mariette's copy of the print in the Bibliothèque Nationale, and it can be shown that these dates are often unreliable (cf. Blunt, Bibl. 1357, p. 489).

The picture later appeared as follows: Mme d'Hariague sale, Mariette, Paris, 14.iv.1750, lot 10 (as painted for Froment de Veine); Peilhon sale, Remy, Paris, 16.v.1763, lot 56 (36 × 40 inches; as engraved by Pesne); Duc de Deux-Ponts (Christian IV von Zweibrücken) sale, Remy, Paris, 6.iv.1778, lot 59 (as engraved by Pesne); Robit sale, Paillet, Paris, 11 ff.v.1801, lot 88, bt. by Bryan for George Hibbert

(Buchanan, II, p. 57); Lord Radstock sale, Christie, London, 12 f.v.1826, second day, lot 33; Sir Simon Clarke sale, Christie, London, 8.v.1840, lot 49, bt. T. Hope (Smith, No. 79 and Supplement, No. 5); Hope heirlooms sale, Christie, London, 20.vi.1917, lot 68, bt. Tooth; with Trotti, Paris; bt. from him by Samuel Sachs; presented by Mrs. Sachs to the Fogg Museum.

DRAWINGS: 1. British Museum, London (CR, I, p. 28, No. 55).

2. Hermitage Museum, Leningrad (CR, I, p. 29, No. A 9). Fragment of a copy of a drawing very close to CR, No. 55.

ENGRAVING: By Jean Pesne (Andresen, No. 137; Wildenstein, No. 53).

COPIES: 1. A small version was in the Lord Radstock sale, Christie, London, 12 f.v.1826, first day, lot 44.
2. Anon. sale, Christie, London, 22.viii.1945, lot 101.
3. Anon. sale, Sotheby, London, 18.xii.1963, lot 72.

BIBLIOGRAPHY: Félibien, IV, pp. 62, 152; Loménie de Brienne, p. 216; Florent Le Comte, III, pp. 31, 32; Cambry, Bibl. 272a, p. 40; Buchanan, II, p. 57; Waagen, Bibl. 384b, II, p. 125; Smith, No. 79, and Supplement, No. 5; Friedlaender, 1914, pp. 92, 120; Grautoff, II, p. 256; Magne, 1914, p. 214, No. 251, and Bibl. 936, p. 186; CR, I, p. 22; Friedlaender, Bibl. 947, p. 14; McLanathan, Bibl. 1015, p. 2; Bertin-Mourot, Bibl. 1023, p. 48, No. XIII; Licht, p. 158; *Exposition Poussin (Louvre)*, No. 101; Mahon, Bibl. 1367, p. 118; Wild, Bibl. 1383, p. 245.

55. THE HOLY FAMILY UNDER A GROUP OF TREES. 94×122 cm. Musée du Louvre, Paris (714).

HISTORY: Loménie de Brienne states (pp. 216, 218, 222) that a *Holy Family*, engraved by Michael Natalis for the doctoral thesis of the Cardinal de Bouillon, was originally painted for 'Mme la Surintendante Fouquet', i.e. Marie de Castille, second wife of Nicolas Fouquet, whom she married in 1651. The only engraving of a *Holy Family* by Natalis corresponds to the Louvre painting here catalogued.

Friedlaender is probably wrong in identifying it with the painting executed 'pour un particulier' in 1656, which is more likely to be No. 57. The present painting was bought by Louis XIV from the painter Charles Antoine Hérault in 1685 (*Comptes des bâtiments*, II, pp. 584, 663).

DRAWINGS Hermitage Museum, Leningrad (CR, I, p. 28, No. 54). This drawing is nearer to the present composition than to any other recorded *Holy Family*, but differs from it in many details.

ENGRAVINGS: 1. By Michel Natalis (Andresen, No. 132; Wildenstein, No. 51; Davies and Blunt, p. 210, No. 51). If we may accept Brienne's statement that Natalis's engraving was made for Cardinal de

Bouillon's thesis, it must be dated to 1667, the year in which he was awarded his doctorate.
2. Published by François de Poilly (cf. Bertin-Mourot, Bibl. 1192, p. IV).

COPIES: 1. By an unidentified artist named Girard. Private collection, Rome (cf. Sterling, Bibl. 1290, pp. 273 ff.).
2. Musée des Augustins, Toulouse (cf. Grautoff, II, p. 281, and Thuillier, Bibl. 1297, p. 38).

NOTES: Friedlaender (1914, p. 123) identifies this painting with the *Holy Family* of 1656, mentioned by Félibien, but, as has been said above, this is more likely to be No. 57. Grautoff (II, No. 138) suggests the date 1648–51, and Mahon (Bibl. 1367, p. 120) 1652. I should propose the first years of the 1650's.

BIBLIOGRAPHY: *Comptes des bâtiments*, II, pp. 584, 663; Loménie de Brienne, pp. 216, 218, 222; Piganiol de La Force, Bibl. 124, I, p. 132; Bailly, p. 309; Smith, No. 80; Friedlaender, 1914, pp. 91, 123; Grautoff, I, p. 273, II, No. 138; Magne, 1914, p. 213, No. 236; Licht, p. 158; Bertin-Mourot, Bibl. 1192, p. IV; *Exposition Poussin (Louvre)*, No. 104; Sterling, Bibl. 1290, pp. 273 f.; Mahon, Bibl. 1367, p. 120.

56. THE HOLY FAMILY WITH ST. JOHN AND ST. ELIZABETH. 172×133·5 cm. Hermitage Museum, Leningrad (1213).

HISTORY: Painted for Chantelou (finished in 1655; cf. *Correspondance*, pp. 433 f.). Possibly Comte de Fraula collection, Brussels, by 1720 (Richardson, *Account*, p. 6); sold de Vos, Brussels, 21 ff.vii.1738, lot 20 (size given as 85½×60 inches, which might correspond if the frame were included; cf. Hoet, Bibl. 195, I, p. 520). Bought in Paris through Lord Waldegrave by Sir Robert Walpole (cf. Plumb, Bibl. 1278.1, p. 86); seen in his collection by Vertue in 1739 (Vertue, Bibl. 132, XXX, p. 180); bt. with the whole Walpole collection in 1779 by the Empress Catherine II of Russia.

ENGRAVINGS: 1. By Alexander Voet (Andresen, No. 130; Wildenstein, No. 49; Davies and Blunt, p. 210, No. 49).

2. François de Poilly (Andresen, No. 129; Wildenstein, No. 50; Davies and Blunt, p. 210, No. 50). In a letter of 26.vii.1655 (*Correspondance*, p. 443) Poussin speaks discouragingly about Chantelou's project for having his painting engraved by Poilly.

COPIES: No exact copies of the Hermitage painting are at present known, but several exist of an oblong composition showing the same figure group set in a landscape:

1. Formerly in the Liechtenstein collection, Vienna (101 × 141 cm.; cf. Grautoff, I, p. 271, II, p. 282); sold in 1922 to Glückselig, Vienna. Perhaps the picture which appeared in an anon. sale, Christie, London, 2.ii.1945, lot 82, and again in an anon. sale, Sotheby, London, 17.xii.1947, lot 90.

2. Grindlay sale, Christie, London, 18.i.1887, lot 866, and again in an anon. sale, Christie, London, 29.i.1960, lot 56.

3. A small version belongs to Sir Osbert Sitwell, London.

NOTES: The idea of painting a *Madonna* for Chantelou is first mentioned by Poussin in a letter of 22.xii. 1647 (*Correspondance*, p. 376). He does not appear to have worked on the project till 1653, when the *pensée* is said to have been found (*ibid.*, p. 428). The finished picture was sent off in June 1655 (*ibid.*, p. 433).

The identification of the Chantelou picture with that appearing in the Fraula sale is purely hypothetical, but according to Richardson the figures in it were life-size, and certain of Chantelou's Poussins, notably the Sacraments, were on sale in the Low Countries (in this case actually in Holland) in the early eighteenth century.

BIBLIOGRAPHY: *Correspondance*, pp. 376, 380, 387, 390, 391, 392, 394, 395, 397, 399, 401, 409, 423, 426, 428, 429, 430, 433 f., 443; Chantelou, 1885, p. 64, and 1960, p. 124; Florent Le Comte, III, p. 32; Vertue, Bibl. 132, XXX, p. 180; Richardson, *Account*, p. 6; Walpole, Bibl. 175a, II, p. 257; Smith, No. 75; Friedlaender, 1914, p. 122; Grautoff, I, p. 270, II, No. 132 and p. 256; Magne, 1914, pp. 152, 213, Nos. 242, 249; *CR*, I, pp. 23, 29 f.; Blunt, Bibl. 1050, p. 40, Bibl. 1086, p. 194, and Bibl. 1086a, p. 170; Waterhouse, Bibl. 1308, p. 290; Mahon, Bibl. 1367, p. 120.

57. THE HOLY FAMILY IN A LANDSCAPE, WITH ST. JOHN AND ST. ELIZABETH, AND ST. JOSEPH PRAYING. 68 × 51 cm. Musée du Louvre, Paris (713).

HISTORY: Probably the painting executed 'pour un particulier' in 1656 (Félibien, IV, p. 65). Bought by Louis XIV from the dealer Moule in 1685 (*Comptes des bâtiments*, II, p. 587).

DRAWING: Musée du Louvre, Paris (*CR*, I, p. 30, No. A 10). Probably a studio copy after a lost original drawing, showing several variations from the painting.

ENGRAVINGS: 1. By Jean Pesne (Andresen, No. 127; Wildenstein, No. 48).

2. Published by Etienne Gantrel (Davies and Blunt, p. 210, No. 48).

COPIES: 1. Alleyn's College of God's Gift, Dulwich, London (225).

2. Staatsgalerie, Stuttgart (355), 54 × 41 cm. In reverse, with different background.

3. Formerly Fesch collection (No. 1963 in the 1841 catalogue); sold George Rome, 22 ff.iii.1844, lot 815 (24 × 18 inches).

4. Lady Lawrance sale, Christie, London, 10.vi.1948, lot 46.

NOTES: Félibien, who is usually quite explicit about the patron for whom a work was executed, is in this case evasive and says simply, 'pour un particulier'. It is just possible that the individual concerned may have been himself and that he was concealing the fact because he had recently sold the picture. This is a pure hypothesis, but in any case the date 1656, which he gives, would fit exactly with the style of the picture.

A curious feature of the painting is that the town in the background has houses with high-pitched roofs which are quite northern in appearance.

BIBLIOGRAPHY: *Comptes des bâtiments*, II, p. 587; Félibien, IV, p. 65; Piganiol de La Force, Bibl. 124, I, p. 128; Bailly, p. 311; Gault de Saint-Germain, Pt. II, pp. 12 f.; Smith, No. 74; Friedlaender, 1914, pp. 91, 121, 240; Grautoff, I, p. 273, II, No. 137; Magne, 1914, p. 213, No. 235; Alpatov, Bibl. 882, p. 12; Licht, p. 157; *Exposition Poussin (Louvre)*, No. 112; *Exposition Poussin (Rouen)*, No. 90; Mahon, Bibl. 1367, p. 121.

58. THE HOLY FAMILY WITH SIX PUTTI. 96·5 × 133 cm. The Chatsworth Settlement, Chatsworth, Derbyshire.

HISTORY: Perhaps Raoul de la Porte, rue de Seine, Paris, in 1713 (cf. Brice, Bibl. 89d, II, p. 191); Duke of Devonshire by 1766 (cf. Martyn, Bibl. 226, I, p. 42). In the catalogue of the Leeds exhibition (Bibl. 1110, No. 26) it was suggested that this was the picture bought by Lord James Cavendish from the Andrew Hay sale, Cock, London, 20.iv.1737/8, lot 74, but it now seems that the picture from this sale passed by inheritance to Lord Chesham and was sold at Christie, London, 31.i.1930, lot 69.

DRAWING: Musée Condé, Chantilly (CR, I, p. 27, No. 53).

ENGRAVING: By Etienne Baudet (Andresen, No. 138; Wildenstein, No. 54; Davies and Blunt, p. 210, No. 54).

COPIES: 1. Formerly A. Kann collection, Paris (cf. Friedlaender, 1914, p. 120); sold 1914; Eugen Platky collection, Leipzig; on the London art market in 1938 (71 × 95 cm.); sold Stuttgart, 29.xi.1955, lot 405; probably the picture sold anon. sale, Sotheby, London, 7.xii.1960, lot 129 (27¾ × 37 inches).

2. J. Proctor sale, Christie, London, 15.v.1847, lot 27; Miss Rowse, Elgin Road, Bournemouth; sold Bournemouth, 17.vi.1953, lot 41.

3. Formerly Cardinal Fesch collection (No. 1058 in the 1841 catalogue); sold George, Rome, 22 ff.iii.1844, lot 814 (31 × 40 inches).

NOTES: The picture belonging to Raoul de la Porte is described by Brice as follows: 'la sainte famille où plusieurs enfants sont en action d'adoration, sur un fond d'architecture et de paisage.' This seems to fit the Chatsworth picture better than any other known version, though it could be taken to apply to the Fogg painting.

According to Mahon (Bibl. 1367, p. 118), Mrs. Wild has reasons, so far unpublished, for identifying the Chatsworth painting with the *Holy Family* painted for the Duc de Créqui in 1651, which is usually considered to be the picture in the Fogg Museum (No. 54). In any case the Chatsworth painting must date from *c.* 1650.

BIBLIOGRAPHY: Brice, Bibl. 89d, II, p. 191; Martyn, Bibl. 226, I, p. 42; *Morning Chronicle*, Bibl. 288, 29.iv.1788; Waagen, Bibl. 384b, II, p. 93, III, p. 347; Smith, No. 82; Grautoff, II, p. 256; Magne, 1914, p. 213, No. 243; CR, I, p. 22; Blunt, Bibl. 1001, p. 160; Bertin-Mourot, Bibl. 1023, p. 48, No. XIV; *City Art Gallery*, Leeds, Bibl. 1110, No. 26; Mahon, Bibl. 1367, pp. XIV, 118, 120.

59. THE HOLY FAMILY WITH TEN FIGURES. 79 × 106 cm. National Gallery of Ireland, Dublin (925).

HISTORY: Painted for Pointel in 1649 (Félibien, IV, p. 59); in Cérisier's collection by 1665 (Chantelou, 1885, p. 90; 1960, p. 127). The Dublin painting belonged to the Earls of Milltown by 1847 (when it was lent to the Royal Irish Art Union) and was given to the National Gallery in 1902 by Geraldine, Countess of Milltown, widow of the sixth earl.

DRAWING: Musée Condé, Chantilly (CR, I, p. 27, No. A 8). A copy, probably after a lost drawing.

ENGRAVINGS: 1. By Claudine Bouzonnet Stella, dated 1668 (Andresen, No. 139; Wildenstein, No. 55; Davies and Blunt, p. 210, No. 55).
2. By Louis Moreau, published by Etienne Gantrel (cf. Bertin-Mourot, Bibl. 1192, p. III).

COPIES: 1. M. H. de Young Museum, San Francisco (84 × 108 cm.). Said to have been in the possession of the Routier family in France till 1935; bt. by a private collector in San Francisco. Later belonged to Roscoe and Margaret Oakes, who presented it to the Museum (cf. *Exposition Poussin (Louvre)*, No. 86).

2. Formerly in the abbey of La-Ferté-sur-Crosne (Seine-et-Loire); acquired by the mayor of Le Creusot in 1793; sold by his descendants before 1914, when it was in an unidentified private collection in Paris (cf. Grautoff, II, No. 134, who gives the size as 78 × 100 cm.).

NOTES: Certain parts of the Dublin painting, particularly the wrinkled face of St. Elizabeth and parts of the column and the water to her left, are of a hardness quite unlike Poussin's usual handling and are probably due to later repainting. The other figures and the remainder of the landscape are, however, of very fine quality.

BIBLIOGRAPHY: Chantelou, 1885, p. 90, and 1960, p. 127; Félibien, IV, p. 59; Florent Le Comte, III, p. 30; Smith, No. 81, wrongly said to be in the Liechtenstein Gallery; Friedlaender, 1914, p. 120; Grautoff, I, p. 272, II, No. 134; Magne, 1914, p. 213, No. 250; Bodkin, Bibl. 858, pp. 174, 179, and Bibl. 932, p. 253; Blunt, Bibl. 972, p. 161 n. 3, and Bibl. 1050, p. 40; Licht, p. 157; Bertin-Mourot, Bibl. 1192, p. III; Blunt, Bibl. 1226, p. 400; Mahon, Bibl. 1338, p. 129; Thuillier, Bibl. 1350, p. 339; L'ideale classico (Bologna), No. 78; Mahon, Bibl. 1367, pp. XIV, 116 f.

60. THE FLIGHT INTO EGYPT. 95 × 127.5 cm. Lawrence Gowing, Lambourn, Berkshire.

HISTORY: Bought by the Rev. Heneage Finch in 1825, probably in England (communication from Colonel J. C. Wynne-Finch); passed by descent to Col. J. C. Wynne-Finch; sold Sotheby, London, 4.vii.1956, lot 142, bt. Armitage; anon. sale, Sotheby, London, 20.xi.1957, lot 111, bt. by the present owner.

DRAWING: A drawing in the M. P. Reulos collection, Paris (*Exposition Poussin* (*Louvre*), No. 128) is closely related to the painting and may be a copy after a lost original drawing.

NOTES: Dated 1627 by Mahon (Bibl. 1271), a date with which I should agree. The Virgin recalls the Chantilly *Annunciation* (No. 38), the dark wall on the left appears in the *Entry into Jerusalem* (No. 77), the *Woman taken in Adultery* (No. 75), and even the Dulwich *Triumph of David* (No. 33). The *Flight* appears to be one of the earliest of the large-figure compositions which culminated in the *St. Erasmus* (No. 97) and the *Inspiration of the Epic Poet* (No. 124), but in the classicism of its design it is much closer to the latter than the former.

BIBLIOGRAPHY: Blunt, Bibl. 1227, p. 168; *Exposition Poussin* (*Louvre*), No. 10; Mahon, Bibl. 1271, p. 296; Rees Jones, Bibl. 1280, pp. 304 ff.; Mahon, Bibl. 1367, p. 86.

61. THE FLIGHT INTO EGYPT. Original lost.

HISTORY: Painted for Cérisier in 1658 (Félibien, IV, p. 66); seen in his house by Bernini in 1665 (Chantelou, 1885, pp. 90, 222, and 1960, pp. 127, 131). Possibly the painting mentioned by Brice in 1713 (Bibl. 89d, II, p. 191) as in the collection of Raoul de la Porte. Possibly Lethières sale, Paillet, Paris, 24 ff.xi.1829, lot 133.

ENGRAVINGS: 1. Attributed to Pietro del Po (Andresen, No. 143; Wildenstein, No. 57; Davies and Blunt, p. 210, No. 57).
2. Published by J. Mariette (Andresen, No. 144).
3. Published by Audran (Andresen, No. 145).
4. By P. van Somer (Andresen, No. 146).
5. Published by Hecquet (Andresen, No. 147).
6. Published by Etienne Gantrel (Andresen, No. 148).
7. Published by Pierre Landry (cf. Wildenstein, No. 57).
8. Smith, No. 87, records a print published by Poilly.

NOTES: Thuillier (see Chantelou, 1885, pp. 127, n. 18, and 1960, p. 131 n. 38) identifies the picture which Bernini saw at Cérisier's house with the *Holy Family in Egypt* in the Hermitage (No. 65), but this is known from Poussin's letters to have been painted for Mme de Montmort. Félibien (IV, p. 66), Chantelou (1960, pp. 127, 131) and Loménie de Brienne (p. 222) all describe Cérisier's picture as the Virgin going or fleeing into Egypt, which would fit this composition and no other among the late works.

BIBLIOGRAPHY: Chantelou, 1885, pp. 90, 222, and 1960, pp. 127, 131; Félibien, IV, p. 66; Brice, Bibl. 89d, II, p. 191; Loménie de Brienne, p. 222; Florent Le Comte, III, p. 32; *Observations historiques*, Bibl. 236, II, p. 348; Smith, No. 87; Friedlaender, 1914, p. 123; Grautoff, II, p. 256; Magne, 1914, p. 155.

62. THE REST ON THE FLIGHT INTO EGYPT. Present whereabouts unknown.

HISTORY: Probably painted for Cardinal Giulio Rospigliosi, later Pope Clement IX; recorded in the Palazzo Rospigliosi (Bellori, Bibl. 36, p. 48), and at various periods till 1803 (Buchanan, II, p. 145); bought by Cardinal Fesch (No. 1053 in the 1841 catalogue, as from the Palazzo Rospigliosi); Fesch sale, George, Rome, 17 ff.iii.1845, part III, lot 398, bt. George; Forcade sale, Pillet, Paris, 2.iv.1873, lot 2 (82 × 107 cm., as from the Fesch sale); Chennevières-Pointel collection (Grautoff, II, No. 65, as a copy, and Friedlaender, 1914, p. 123, both as from the Fesch sale).

ENGRAVINGS: 1. Anonymous (Andresen, No. 152; Wildenstein, No. 58; Davies and Blunt, p. 210, No. 58).

2. By Raphael Morghen (Andresen, No. 153; Andresen-Wildenstein, No. 153).

3. By Antonio Perfetti (1818; Andresen, No. 154).

4. Anonymous, without the elephant in the background (Andresen, No. 155).

NOTES: Grautoff does not commit himself on the date of this composition, but from the place which he gives it in his catalogue one may conclude that he believed it to have been painted c. 1636. As far as can be judged from the engravings and from the poor reproduction which Grautoff gives, this is a little too early. The design has something of the classical grandeur of the Berlin *Nurture of Jupiter* (No. 162) of c. 1638–39, and the picture should be dated to these years, during which Poussin seems to have been particularly active for Cardinal Giulio Rospigliosi.

BIBLIOGRAPHY: (Bellori), Bibl. 36, p. 48; Spon and Wheler, Bibl. 66, I, p. 305; Huguetan, Bibl. 82, p. 294; Starke, Bibl. 306, II, p. 36; Buchanan, II, p. 145; Smith, No. 91; Michel, Bibl. 660, p. 234; Friedlaender, 1914, p. 123; Grautoff, I, p. 133, II, No. 65; Magne, 1914, p. 211, No. 227; Friedlaender, 1933, pp. 324 f.; Zeri, Bibl. 1216, p. 310, No. 302; Mahon, Bibl. 1367, p. 106; Blunt, Bibl. 1426, p. 62.

63. THE REST ON THE FLIGHT INTO EGYPT. 76×63 cm. Inscribed on the back of the canvas: *No. 18 Sacra famiglia Niccolo Poussin.* Dr. and Mrs. Rudolf Heineman, New York.

HISTORY: Possibly from the Palazzo della Torre, Naples (see below).

ENGRAVING: By Saint-Non, after a drawing by Fragonard (cf. Saint-Non, Bibl. 267, I, p. 114; Andresen, No. 150, and Cayeux, Bibl. 1390.2, p. 357, No. 223).

COPY: Museo di Capodimonte, Naples.

NOTES: The evidence for identifying this picture with that in the collection of the duca della Torre, which would probably have come from that of Cardinal Ascanio Filomarino (cf. Blunt, Bibl. 1167, pp. 80 ff.), is circumstantial but not negligible. The engraving of the della Torre composition by Saint-Non differs in many respects from the painting. In fact all they have in common is the group of the Virgin and Child with St. John (in a different pose) surrounded by a number of putti, presenting to Christ baskets of fruit which they have gathered from the tree under which the whole group sits. It is, however, plain from the written descriptions of the painting that, as in the case of the *Annunciation* (No. 38), the draughtsman and engraver have made a quite arbitrary selection from the composition. In his text, for instance, Saint-Non says that the Holy Family is resting beneath a tree which on their arrival 's'est couvert de fleurs et de fruits', and Cochin (Bibl. 207, I, p. 88) adds that the composition shows 'Saint Joseph dans le fond, qui lit dans un livre'. It may still be objected that the format of the Saint-Non engraving is entirely different from that of the painting, one being oblong and the other upright, but even this discrepancy would not be unusual in the plates of the *Voyage*. Giordano's *Christ driving the Traders out of the Temple* in the church of Gerolomini, for instance, is treated in an equally cavalier way, though in this case the oblong original is turned into an upright engraving; and there are other similar examples.

The hypothesis that the Heineman painting comes from a Neapolitan collection is supported by the fact that a copy of it exists in the Naples Museum. This did not form part of the original Farnese collection and therefore probably comes from a Neapolitan source; its technique would suggest that it was a copy by a local 17th century painter.

The picture is dated by Mahon early in 1627 (Bibl. 1367, p. X). I should agree that it should be placed near and probably before the *Germanicus.*

BIBLIOGRAPHY: Cochin, Bibl. 207, I, p. 188; La Lande, Bibl. 224a, VII, p. 57; Northall, Bibl. 227, p. 226; Richard, Bibl. 229, IV, p. 194; Saint-Non, Bibl. 267, I, p. 114; Martyn, Bibl. 296, p. 281; Smith, Nos. 67, 88; Dussieux, Bibl. 470, p. 301; Magne, 1914, p. 214, No. 253; Comstock, Bibl. 956, p. 143; Blunt, Bibl. 1167, pp. 80 f., 86; *Exposition Poussin (Louvre)*, No. 27; Mahon, Bibl. 1271, p. 297, and Bibl. 1367, pp. X, 52.

64. THE REST ON THE FLIGHT INTO EGYPT. 87×66 cm. Oskar Reinhart Institute, Winterthur, Switzerland.

HISTORY: Perhaps Crozat sale, Delatour, Paris, June 1751, lot 220 (34×24 inches); Thélusson sale, Folliot, Paris, 1.xii.1777, lot 31 (32×30 pouces); Marquis de Véri sale, Paillet, Paris, 12.xii.1785, lot 1, bt.

Lebrun; belonged to William Lock; sold by him to van Heythusen and by him to Desenfans (Buchanan, I, pp. 321 ff.); passed to the Marquis of Lansdowne; in Lansdowne collection when engraved by Bartolozzi in 1796; Lansdowne sale, Coxe, London, 20.iii.1806, lot 56, bt. Earl Grosvenor; by descent to the Dukes of Westminster; Westminster sale, Christie, 4.vii.1924, lot 28, bt. Wildenstein; bt. by the present owner in 1926.

ENGRAVINGS: 1. Attributed to François Roger and published by Guillaume Chasteau (Andresen, No. 140; Wildenstein, No. 56). This print only shows the lower part of the composition.
2. By Bartolozzi (Andresen, No. 141). Dated 1796.
3. Luigi Rados. Dedicated to the Marquis of Lansdowne and dated 1813.

COPIES: 1. Eric Küsel collection, Huskvarna, Sweden. From the collections of General Miolis, Wappers-Melis, and J. B. van Rooy, from whom it passed by descent to its present owner.
2. Anon. sale, Christie, London, 20.vi.1807, lot 77.
3. Anon. sale, Christie, London, 24.iv.1959, lot 41.

NOTES: Dated by Grautoff (II, No. 62) c. 1635; by Mahon (Bibl. 1367, p. 82) 1633–34. Perhaps c. 1636–37.

BIBLIOGRAPHY: Young, Bibl. 368, No. 70; Buchanan, I, pp. 321 f.; Waagen, Bibl. 384b, II, p. 172; Hazlitt, Bibl. 411, p. 92; Smith, No. 83; Grautoff, I, p. 131, II, No. 62; Magne, 1914, p. 213, No. 240; Fray, Bibl. 733, pp. 201 f.; Courthion, Bibl. 800, p. 26; Grautoff, Bibl. 864, p. 338; Licht, p. 89; Voss, Bibl. 1162, pp. 47 f.; Blunt, Bibl. 1167, p. 80 n. 31; Mahon, Bibl. 1367, pp. XII, 82 f.

65. THE HOLY FAMILY IN EGYPT. 105 × 145 cm. Hermitage Museum, Leningrad (6741).

HISTORY: Painted for Mme de Montmort, later wife of Paul Fréart de Chantelou, between November 1655 and December 1657 (*Correspondance*, pp. 439, 443, 445, 447, 448 f.); Stroganoff collection, St. Petersburg, probably bought by Count Alexander Stroganoff (1733–1811) in Paris in the 1770's; put up for sale with the Stroganoff collection by the Russian Government, Lepke, Berlin, 12.v.1931, lot 67; bt. in, and placed in the Hermitage Museum.

DRAWING: Musée Condé, Chantilly (*CR*, I, p. 30, No. 60).

ENGRAVINGS: 1. By Jean Dughet (Andresen, No. 157; Wildenstein, No. 59).

2. By François Chauveau, 1667 (Andresen, No. 158).
3. Published by Etienne Gantrel (Andresen, No. 159).
4. Published by Quenault (Andresen, No. 160).

COPY: Viscount Cobham, Hagley Hall, Worcestershire.

NOTES: For a discussion of this work, see text volume, p. 310 f.

In a recent article (Bibl. 1391) Dempsey has analysed with great penetration the use which Poussin made in this painting of the Palestrina mosaic, and has made the point that, far from being a mere follower of earlier archaeologists, Poussin was in several respects original in his interpretation of this celebrated work of Antiquity, as well as in his treatment of the story as a whole.

BIBLIOGRAPHY: *Correspondance,* pp. 439, 443, 445, 447, 448 f.; Félibien, IV, pp. 66, 148; Bellori, p. 454; Loménie de Brienne, pp. 222, 224; Florent Le Comte, III, p. 32; Du Bos, Bibl. 142, I, pp. 339 f.; Lazzarini, Bibl. 332, I, p. 26; Smith, No. 90; Waagen, Bibl. 511, p. 402; Friedlaender, 1914, pp. 98, 123; Grautoff, I, p. 280, II, No. 153; Magne, 1914, pp. 152, 161, 211, No. 228; Blunt, Bibl. 906, pp. 134 f., and Bibl. 972, pp. 162 f.; McLanathan, Bibl. 1015, p. 4; Blunt, Bibl. 1050, p. 40, Bibl. 1086, p. 194, and Bibl. 1086a, p. 170; Sterling, Bibl. 1159, p. 35; Voss, Bibl. 1162, p. 47; Alpatov, Bibl. 1217, p. 195; *Exposition Poussin (Louvre)*, No. 109; Mahon, Bibl. 1338, p. 128, and Bibl. 1367, p. 121; Dempsey, Bibl. 1391, pp. 109 ff.

66. THE MASSACRE OF THE INNOCENTS. 98 × 133 cm. Musée des Beaux-Arts de la ville de Paris (Petit-Palais), Paris.

HISTORY: Altieri collection, Rome, by 1686–87 (Sirén, Bibl. 63, p. 178); still mentioned as in the Palazzo Altieri by Vasi in 1794 (Bibl. 298a, I, p. 96), but not listed in later editions. Possibly Lethières sale, Paillet, Paris, 24 November 1829, lot 62; Collot sale, Laneuville, Paris, 29 March 1855, lot 33; stated to have been sold from the Palazzo Altieri (1.viii.1798); bt. by the Dutuit brothers and bequeathed to the city of Paris.

ENGRAVING: By Giovanni Volpato and Pietro Bettelini (Andresen, No. 164).

NOTES: Grautoff (II, p. 277) argues that the painting was begun by Poussin and finished by another hand. He was, however, probably misled by the state of the picture, which has suffered severely (Ramdohr, writing in 1787, says of it: 'hat sehr gelitten'). A considerable part of the executioner who occupies the middle of the composition is painted on a piece of later canvas inserted in the original, and the rest of this figure, together with much of the left-hand executioner, is largely restored, as is also the baby lying at the feet of the middle soldier.

The provenance of the painting can be established from the catalogue of the Collot sale, and the Altieri picture was evidently famous, since it is mentioned by visitors and the authors of guide books to Rome from 1686 to 1794.

There is in general agreement about the dating. In the catalogue of the Louvre exhibition (No. 4) I proposed 1625–26. Mr. Mahon (Bibl. 1367, p. IX) would be more precise and gives 1626. I should prefer the wider range, because, although the *Massacre* has close affinities with paintings such as the Russian battle-pieces (Nos. 29, 30) and the ex-Böhler *Woman taken in Adultery* (No. 75), the head of the mother in the left-hand foreground group is very close to those of Cleopatra's attendants in the *Augustus and Cleopatra* (No. 146), which is probably one of the first works executed by Poussin in Rome.

BIBLIOGRAPHY: Sirén, Bibl. 63, p. 178; Deseine, Bibl. 101a, I, p. 258; Rossini, Bibl. 106, p. 38, and Bibl. 106e, p. 209; Rossi, Bibl. 114, p. 537; Pinaroli, Bibl. 123, I, p. 142; Roisecco, Bibl. 150, p. 88; Keyssler, Bibl. 172, II, p. 45; Blainville, Bibl. 176, III, pp. 76 f.; La Lande, Bibl. 224a, V, p. 174; Northall, Bibl. 227, p. 316; Venuti, Bibl. 230a, II, Pt. 1, p. 678; Vasi, Bibl. 256.1, p. 53; Volkmann, Bibl. 257, II, p. 468; Magnan, Bibl. 260, III, col. 60; Chiusole, Bibl. 269, p. 52; Pimarta, Bibl. 271, p. 267; Ramdohr, Bibl. 287, III, p. 103; Vasi, Bibl. 298, I, p. 93, and Bibl. 298a, I, p. 96; Manazzale, Bibl. 308a, II, p. 234; Salmon, Bibl. 321, I, p. 51; Laouriens, Bibl. 356, p. 398; Melchiorri, Bibl. 408, p. 586; Grautoff, II, p. 277; Kauffmann, Bibl. 1203, p. 5; Blunt, Bibl. 1227, p. 170 n. 45; Ecalle, Bibl. 1249, pp. 247 ff.; *Exposition Poussin (Louvre)*, No. 4; Mahon, Bibl. 1271, p. 296; *L'ideale classico (Bologna)*, No. 54; Mahon, Bibl. 1367, p. IX.

67. THE MASSACRE OF THE INNOCENTS. 147 × 171 cm. Musée Condé, Chantilly.

HISTORY: Owned by and probably painted for the Marchese Vincenzo Giustiniani, Rome (Salerno, Bibl. 1282, p. 101, No. 153); bt. from his descendants by Lucien Bonaparte; sold by him to the Queen of Etruria; inherited by her son, the Duke of Lucca; exhibited for sale with his collection, London, 1840, No. 10; sold Phillips, London, 5.vi.1841, lot 51 (as from the Lucien Bonaparte collection); W. Buchanan sale, Christie, London, 4.vii.1846, lot 64 (as from the Borghese and Lucien Bonaparte collections); probably D. Gardner sale, Christie, London, 25.iii.1854, lot 75, bt. in; bt. in 1854 from Colnaghi's, London, by the Duc d'Aumale.

DRAWINGS: 1. Musée des Beaux-Arts, Lille (*CR*, I, p. 31, No. 61). The *verso* has red chalk sketches for the same composition.
2. Fogg Art Museum, Cambridge, Mass. A drawing by Fragonard after the painting.

ENGRAVINGS: 1. By Saint-Non (1771; Andresen, No. 163, and Cayeux, Bibl. 1390.2, p. 345, No. 141).
2. By Giovanni Folo (Andresen, No. 161).
3. By P. Bettelini (Andresen, No. 162).

COPIES: 1. Musée de Peinture et de Sculpture, Grenoble. Deposited by the State in 1799 (cf. Thuillier, Bibl. 1297, p. 38, and Bibl. 1299, p. 291).

Paintings of this subject attributed to Poussin are recorded as follows:
1. Sir John Meres sale, Cock, London, 18 ff.v.1736, 4th day, lot 103 ('after Poussin').
2. Adam sale, Christie, London, 25 ff.ii.1773, 1st day, lot 6 (38 × 53 inches), probably bt. in; Adam sale, Christie, London, 13.vi.1785, lot 58.
3. Poniatowski sale (from Florence), Christie, London, 8 f.ii.1839, 1st day, lot 138.
4. A variant by Spierre was in the Boyer d'Aguilles collection and was engraved by Coelemans.
A copy of either this picture or No. 68 was made by Potain in Rome in 1788 (cf. Montaiglon and Guiffrey, Bibl. 45, XV, pp. 242, 248, 252).

NOTES: In spite of the fact that Sandrart (p. 257) says that this painting was executed just after Poussin's return to Rome in 1642, there is general agreement in favour of dating it to the period of the *St. Erasmus*, that is to say 1628–29. The style of the picture itself suggests this phase, and the drawing at Lille is in exactly the same manner as that for the altarpiece. Another study for the main group in the *Massacre* is to be found on the *verso* of a drawing for *Bacchus-Apollo* (No. 135) in the Fitzwilliam Museum, Cambridge (repr. Blunt, Bibl. 1322, p. 436), which also contains a study for the figure of Ajax in the Windsor drawing for the *Kingdom of Flora*. When I published this drawing I pointed out that there was a certain similarity to the Chantilly *Massacre*, but at the time I thought it was not close enough to propose an actual connection. I had, however, overlooked the fact that the *verso* of the Lille drawing includes a study for the mother in the *Massacre*, which is evidently related to the lower sketch on the *verso* of the Fitzwilliam sheet. The links between the *Massacre* and other early paintings, such as the fragment of the *Golden Calf* (No. 27), the Dulwich *David* (No. 33), and the *Inspiration of the Epic Poet* (No. 124), have been pointed out in the text volume (p. 80), as well as the connection with Domenichino and the borrowings from Palladio in the architectural setting.

Skippon (Bibl. 34.1, p. 668) refers to a *Massacre of the Innocents* in the Palazzo Giustiniani, 'said to be by an Englishman', but may in fact be referring to Poussin's painting.

BIBLIOGRAPHY: Symonds, Bibl. 25; Skippon, Bibl. 34.1, p. 668; Sirén, Bibl. 63, p. 175; Sandrart, p. 257; de Cotte, Bibl. 98, III, p. 154, and Bibl. 98a, p. 203; Deseine, Bibl. 101a, II, p. 321; Bromley, Bibl. 104, p. 247; Rossini, Bibl. 106, p. 34, and Bibl. 106e, p. 209; Pinaroli, Bibl. 123, I, p. 140; de Brosses, Bibl. 170a, II, p. 428; Keyssler, Bibl. 172, II, p. 341; Blainville, Bibl. 176, III, p. 55; Dézallier, 1745, II, p. 253, and 1762, IV, p. 38; La Lande, Bibl. 224a, V, p. 119; Volkmann, Bibl. 257, II, p. 434; Magnan, Bibl. 260, III, col. 46; Chiusole, Bibl. 269, p. 51; Cambry, Bibl. 272a, p. 58; Ramdohr, Bibl. 287, III, p. 41; Vasi, Bibl. 298, II, p. 428, Bibl. 298b, II, p. 347, Bibl. 298d, I, p. 195, and Bibl. 298 f., I, p. 236; Salmon, Bibl. 321, II, p. 6; Forsyth, Bibl. 324, p. 195; Dalmazzoni, Bibl. 325a and b, p. 274; Lazzarini, Bibl. 332, I, pp. 37 f.; Laouriens, Bibl. 356, p. 318; *Rome in the nineteenth century*, Bibl. 371, III, p. 47; Gence, Bibl. 373, p. 582; Buchanan, II, p. 154; Waagen, Bibl. 384b, IV, p. 263; Smith, No. 93; Friedlaender, 1914, pp. 54 ff., 126, 189; Grautoff, I, p. 84, II, No. 17; Magne, 1914, pp. 191, 211, Nos. 216, 217; Alpatov, Bibl. 882, pp. 16, 17, 19, 25; Blunt, Bibl. 1003, p. 266; Jamot, p. 38; Blunt, Bibl. 1086, pp. 184, 185, and Bibl. 1086a, pp. 160, 161; Licht, p. 90; Blunt, Bibl. 1167, p. 79; Wild, Bibl. 1185, p. 23; Blunt, Bibl. 1226, p. 396, and Bibl. 1227, pp. 165, 175; Jullian, Bibl. 1261, p. 228; Mahon, Bibl. 1271, pp. 291, 297; Panofsky, Bibl. 1273, p. 31; Salerno, Bibl. 1282, p. 101, No. 153; Mahon, Bibl. 1367, pp. XI, 3, 24, 29, 57, 78, 86.

68. THE RETURN OF THE HOLY FAMILY FROM EGYPT. 112 × 94 cm. Alleyn's College of God's Gift, Dulwich, London (240).

HISTORY: Probably John Purling sale, White, London, 16 f.ii.1801, lot 47 ('The Flight into Egypt with the angels supporting the Cross'; dimensions 57 × 50 inches including the frame). Sale of pictures purchased by Desenfans for the King of Poland, Skinner and Dyke, London, 16 ff. iii.1802 (presumably unsold; Desenfans, Bibl. 323, I, p. 117); bequeathed by Desenfans to Sir Francis Bourgeois (1807) and by him to Dulwich College in 1811.

DRAWING: A drawing, in reverse, in the Musée des Beaux-Arts, Orléans (No. 1142c, wrongly attributed to Vouet), is after the painting, perhaps for an engraving.

COPIES: In 1816 the picture was chosen as a model for students of the Royal Academy to copy (Whitley, Bibl. 829, p. 253). No such copies are now traceable.

ENGRAVING: According to the Dulwich catalogue the picture was engraved by Bartolozzi, but I have been unable to confirm this statement.

NOTES: Generally called *The Flight into Egypt*, but the age of the Child indicates rather the return from Egypt.

Dated by Mahon (Bibl. 1367, pp. XI, 23 ff.) between the beginning of 1628 and the middle of 1629, a view with which I should agree.

A variant in the Cleveland Museum of Art, Cleveland, Ohio, presents a peculiarly difficult problem. It was bought in 1952 from Newhouse, New York, who had acquired it from the collection of the Princes of Liechtenstein, to whom it had belonged since 1733; it may have been acquired from Poincinet in Paris in 1725 (Magne, 1914, p. 210 n. 2, quotes a document which shows that a *Flight into Egypt* attributed to Poussin was in the possession of Poincinet, a member of the Duke of Orleans' household and a dealer who sold to Central European collectors; cf. No. 10). The Cleveland picture is mentioned by the following writers in the nineteenth and twentieth centuries: Waagen, Bibl. 514, I, p. 264; Denio, Bibl. 640a, p. 225; Grautoff, I, p. 149, II, No. 78; Magne, 1914, p. 210 n. 2; Mitchell, Bibl. 908, pp. 340 ff.; Francis, Bibl. 1089, pp. 211 ff.; Blunt, Bibl. 1226, p. 400; *Exposition Poussin (Louvre)*, No. 52, and Wild, Bibl. 1310. It was engraved by F. Vicira Portoensis, London, 1799.

The history of this picture is obscure, but Hilaire Pader, in *La peinture parlante* (Bibl. 21b, p. 101), published in Toulouse in 1653, gives the following very detailed description of the picture:

I'ay veu chez un Prèlat qui chérit son Pinceau
Une Vierge & son Fils sur le bord d'un ruisseau
Qui paroit à nos yeux arrouser son ouvrage:

Un batelier conduit sa nacelle au rivage,
Où la Mère pucelle, avec son chaste Espoux,
Contemplent de Iesus ce qu'il a de plus doux;

Car bien que tout le soit, la douceur de sa face
Des traicts plus adoucis toute douceur esface :
Sa belle bouche semble estre preste à parler
Pour chérir une Croix qu'il apperçoit par l'air,
Que des enfants aislés de l'empirée apportent,
Et de leurs tendres bras en coltigeant suportent,
Nos yeux verroient ses yeux tourner de toutes parts
Si ce mystique obiet n'arrestoit ses regards.
Il élève les mains & monstre par son geste
Que son coeur reconnoist la machine céleste.
La face de la Vierge invite le Chrestien
D.admirer de son Corps le pudique maintien ;

Puisque ce rare ouvrier l'a mise avec aisance,
Sans que rien soit forcé, dedans la bien-séance ;
Le manteau qu'elle porte a droit de nous charmer ;
Non parce qu'il paroist coloré d'Outremer,
Mais d'autant que les plis sont faits avec addresse,
Et font voit tout à coup la force & la tendresse.
Certes, c'est un chef-d'oeuvre, & ce chef-d'oeuvre
    est tel
Qu'il mérite à bon droit qu'on l'ait mis sur l'Autel ;
Il n'est point de Tableau, qui d'abord ne luy cède,
Et les beautés de cent luy tout seul les possède.

Pader may have seen the picture in Rome, where he spent some years, *c.* 1638–40, in which case the prelate in question might be any bishop connected with the court of Rome, but it is significant that this is the only picture of which he gives a detailed description, as if it had some special significance for him and was a picture that he had seen recently and knew well. If this is the case, the prelate must have been either the archbishop of Toulouse or the bishop of a neighbouring diocese. An obvious candidate is Gaspard de Daillon, bishop of Albi, who was in touch with Poussin while he was in Rome and acted as carrier for the two *Bacchanals* for Richelieu from Rome to Paris and then to the château of Richelieu early in 1636. He was bishop of Albi from 1635 to 1676 and is mentioned by Pierre Borel in 1649 as having 'beaucoup de tableaux' (Bonnaffé, Bibl. 583, pp. 198 f.).

Certain details in Pader's description, particularly the facts that the Child is described as holding up his hands towards the Cross and that the angels supporting it are winged, make it plain that Pader is referring to the Liechtenstein-Cleveland composition and not to the Dulwich version.

The Liechtenstein-Cleveland picture is not mentioned by Friedlaender either in his monograph of 1914 or in his article for Thieme-Becker of 1933, but it was published by Grautoff (II, No. 78) as an original. In 1937–38 Mitchell (Bibl. 908, pp. 340 ff.) described it as a school piece, on the grounds that the symbolism was less clearly expressed than in the Dulwich painting. When the painting was shown in the Poussin exhibition in Paris (No. 52) it aroused serious doubts in the minds of many students, and in the Burlington Magazine (Bibl. 1226, p. 400) I suggested that it was a copy by an Italian, possibly a Neapolitan hand.

The very coarse-grained Neapolitan canvas is otherwise unknown in Poussin's work. (It has a particularly disturbing effect on the picture owing to the fact that the paint has been heavily pressed into it in the process of relining.) The handling of the picture is surprisingly harsh and coarse for Poussin, and the contrast between the shaded and light parts of the Virgin's blue robe, unbroken by half-tones, has, as far as I know, no parallel in his work. His manner of treating such transitions in the 1630's, the period to which by its general style the picture seems to belong, is shown in the Hermitage *Tancred and Erminia* (No. 206) which was hung not far from it in Paris. The angels in the group supporting the Cross are of a type which does not seem to recur in works by Poussin dating from the thirties, though they have affinities with later works, such as the *St. Francis Xavier* (No. 101) or even the Louvre *Ecstasy of St. Paul* (No. 89) and the *Assumption* (No. 92).

This mixture of elements dating from different periods, taken in conjunction with the character of the handling and the unusual technical details, is a strong argument against the view that the picture is an original. From the present version it is difficult to say whether it is a copy of a lost original or a very adroit imitation. The fact that the composition is recorded in 1653 suggests that there must have been a painting like this from Poussin's own hand, but it is not impossible that the copyist should have altered certain details, and that the angels, for instance, represent his own variation. On the other hand by 1653 Poussin's reputation and influence were great and his style was widely imitated. It is not inconceivable that a good imitation should have been put on the market as an original in a remote province of France.

There has recently appeared a painting of the *Agony in the Garden* (cf. Blunt, Bibl. 1426, Fig. 8), which has some analogy with the Cleveland composition. In the disposition of the apostles in the foreground it seems to imply a knowledge of Poussin's drawing of the subject at Windsor, with which it has also in common the very unusual feature of a figure, without wings and apparently human, accompanying the angel who appears to Christ. It differs fundamentally, however, from the drawing in that it has a cluster of putti carrying the symbols of the Passion. These putti and the angels are very similar to those which appear

4

in the upper part of the Cleveland composition, and the existence of the *Agony* suggests that there may have been an artist who made variations and elaborations of this particular kind of composition by Poussin, since the relation of the painting of the *Agony* to Poussin's drawing is not unlike that of the Cleveland composition to the Dulwich version, and the analogy might be even closer if a drawing of the design survived.

BIBLIOGRAPHY: Desenfans, Bibl. 323, I, p. 117; Smith, No. 86; Hazlitt, Bibl. 411, p. 33; Grautoff, I, p. 149, II, p. 264; Magne, 1914, p. 210, No. 200; Posse, Bibl. 796, p. 19; Whitley, Bibl. 829, pp. 31, 253; Mitchell, Bibl. 908, pp. 340 ff.; Blunt, Bibl. 1026, p. 7; Francis, Bibl. 1089, pp. 211 f.; Mahon, Bibl. 1367, pp. X f., 23 ff., 29; Blunt, Bibl. 1426, p. 73.

69. ST. JOHN BAPTISING THE PEOPLE. 94×120 cm. Musée du Louvre, Paris (721).

HISTORY: Belonged in 1685 to André Le Nôtre (Félibien, IV, p. 152) and given by him to Louis XIV in 1693 (Bailly, p. 313).

ENGRAVINGS: 1. By Gérard Audran (Andresen, No. 165; Wildenstein, No. 61).
2. Published by G. Audran (Andresen, No. 166).
3. By Etienne Jeaurat, 1709 (Andresen, No. 167).
4. Published by J. F. Cars (Andresen, No. 168).
5. By P. Devoux (? Devaux) (Andresen, No. 169, Wildenstein, p. 350, No. IV).
6. Published by Etienne Gantrel (Andresen, No. 170).
7. By A. Verico, 1818 (Andresen, No. 170a).

COPIES: 1. Musée d'Art et d'Histoire, Narbonne (148). From the collection of Cardinal Fesch (cf. Thuillier, Bibl. 1299, p. 296).
2. Sir Edward Every sale, Christie, London, 9.ii. 1951, lot 17.
3. Anon. sale, Christie, London, 18.xii.1964, lot 83 (24½ × 33½ inches).

NOTES: Grautoff (II, No. 98) dates this picture 'before 1640' and states wrongly that it was actually painted for Le Nôtre, who would have been less than twenty-seven at the time and certainly in no position to buy pictures by Poussin. Friedlaender (1914, p. 114) dates it before 1633; Mahon (*L'ideale classico* (*Bologna*), No. 61) 1636–37. I have on previous occasions (e.g. *Exposition Poussin* (*Louvre*), No. 55) suggested 1637–38 and placed the picture later than that of the same subject in the Bührle collection. I would now, however, tend to agree with Mahon that the Louvre painting is slightly the earlier and to accept a dating of *c.* 1636–37.

BIBLIOGRAPHY: Chantelou, 1885, p. 222, and 1960, p. 130; Félibien, IV, p. 152; Sandrart, p. 258; Loménie de Brienne, p. 218; Florent Le Comte, III, p. 32; Bailly, p. 313; Thornhill, Bibl. 140, p. 3; Richardson, *Account*, p. 8; Dézallier, 1745, II, p. 255, and 1762, IV, p. 40; Smith, No. 96; Guiffrey, Bibl. 697, p. 223; Friedlaender, 1914, pp. 40, 114, 151; Grautoff, I, p. 172, II, No. 98; Magne, 1914, pp. 155, 214, No. 265; Licht, p. 131; *Exposition Poussin* (*Louvre*), No. 55; Mahon, Bibl. 1271, p. 303; Waterhouse, Bibl. 1308, p. 288; *Exposition Poussin* (*Rouen*), No. 80; *L'ideale classico* (*Bologna*), No. 61; Mahon, Bibl. 1367, pp. XIII, 104, 105.

70. ST. JOHN BAPTISING THE PEOPLE. 95.5 × 121 cm. Bührle collection, Zürich.

HISTORY: Cassiano dal Pozzo (Bellori, p. 419); by descent to his nephew; *c.* 1725 given by him to the Marchese del Buffalo with the *Seven Sacraments* as a pledge for a debt of 6000 crowns and offered for sale by Buffalo in 1729 to Louis XV (Montaiglon and Guiffrey, Bibl. 45, VIII, pp. 47, 51); recovered by Pozzo in 1730 (*ibid.*); passed through his daughter to the Boccapaduli family, probably in 1739 (cf. Nos. 105–111 below); bought by Byres for the Duke of Rutland in 1785 (Reynolds, Bibl. 281, p. 161); sold by his descendant in 1958.

ENGRAVINGS: 1. The principal group only; anonymous engraving (Andresen, No. 171; Davies and Blunt, p. 211, No. 61).
2. The same group, according to Andresen (No. 172) in the manner of Pietro del Po.

NOTES: When cleaned a few years ago, the greater part of the tree on the extreme right, now only a stump, and most of the foliage of the tree on the left were found to be additions, perhaps made when the picture came to England, and they were removed. The hills beyond the river were also found to be very much damaged.

This picture was dated by Grautoff 1638–40; by Mahon (*L'ideale classico* (*Bologna*), No. 62) *c.* 1637, but slightly later than the Louvre version (No. 69). It should be noticed that the picture is mentioned by both

Bellori (p. 419) and Félibien (IV, pp. 23 ff.) after the *Sacraments* and before the paintings dated to 1637, but it is not clear that this placing implies a dating. The picture must, at any rate, have been painted before the journey to Paris, and probably after the Richelieu *Bacchanals* of 1635–36.

BIBLIOGRAPHY: Félibien, IV, pp. 23 ff.; Montaiglon and Guiffrey, Bibl. 45, VIII, pp. 47, 51; Bellori, p. 419; Sirén, Bibl. 63, p. 187; Baldinucci, XVI, p. 102; de Cotte, Bibl. 98, III, p. 153, and Bibl. 98a, p. 203; Florent Le Comte, III, p. 25; La Lande, Bibl. 224a, V, p. 291; La Roque, Bibl. 248, II, p. 320; Canova, Bibl. 261, p. 126; Ramdohr, Bibl. 287, II, pp. 246 f.; Eller, Bibl. 410, p. 291; Friedlaender, 1914, pp. 40, 114, 152; Grautoff, I, p. 172, II, No. 97; Waterhouse, Bibl. 1096, p. 306; Licht, p. 131; Rinehart, Bibl. 1281, p. 28; *L'ideale classico (Bologna)*, No. 62; Mahon, Bibl. 1367, pp. XIII, 104, 107 ff.

71. THE BAPTISM OF CHRIST. 30×23 cm. On a cypress panel. Messrs. Wildenstein, New York.

HISTORY: Painted in 1648 for Jean, elder brother of Paul Fréart de Chantelou; Czernin collection, Vienna (277).

ENGRAVING: By J. Pesne (Andresen, No. 175; Wildenstein, No. 63).

NOTES: The identification of the painting as that executed for Jean Fréart de Chantelou, originally proposed by Friedlaender (1914, p. 119), is made certain by the fact that in one of his letters Poussin refers to it as being painted on a small panel of cypress (*Correspondance*, p. 385). In May 1645 (*ibid.*, p. 303) Poussin refers to Chantelou's request that he should paint for Jean Fréart a picture of about the same size as the *Ecstasy of St. Paul*, which he had executed for Paul Fréart (below, No. 88); by August it was decided that it should be a *Baptism* (*ibid.*, p. 317); in February 1646 Poussin writes that the design is fixed (*ibid.*, p. 330) and we may suppose that a drawing was made; in March 1648 Poussin was about to start work on it (*ibid.*, p. 381), in June it was sketched in (*ibid.*, p. 385), and it was despatched before September 13th of the same year (*ibid.*, p. 388).

BIBLIOGRAPHY: *Correspondance*, pp. 303, 317, 320, 321, 326, 330, 337, 339, 342, 362, 381, 385, 387, 388, 390, 393; Félibien, IV, p. 59; Florent Le Comte, III, p. 30; Smith, No. 95; Friedlaender, 1914, p. 119; Magne, 1914, pp. 152, 209, No. 188; *Exposition Poussin (Louvre)*, No. 85.

72. THE BAPTISM OF CHRIST. 92×129 cm. John G. Johnson Collection, Philadelphia Museum of Art, Philadelphia, Pa.

HISTORY: The stretcher has an erased stamp, which appears to be that of a sale at Christie's.

DRAWING: Albertina, Vienna (rep. Magne, 1914, Pl. opp. p. 100). Possibly a copy after a lost original drawing, since it shows an additional figure on the right.

ENGRAVINGS: 1. By Pietro del Po (Andresen, No. 173; Wildenstein, No. 62; Davies and Blunt, p. 211, No. 62).
2. By P. van Somer (Andresen, No. 174).

COPIES: 1. Earl of Wemyss, Gosford House, Midlothian; without the dove (cf. *Catalogue of the pictures at Amisfield*, Bibl. 300, pp. 77 ff., and Waagen, Bibl. 384b, IV, p. 438).

Paintings which may be either the original or the Gosford copy are recorded in the following sales:
1. Dr. Mead, Langford, London, 20 ff.iii.1754, third day, lot 51, bt. Gore.
2. Anon. sale, Langford, London, 26 ff.iii.1778, first day, lot 30; Samuel Pawson sale, London, 1795 or 1796, lot 17.

NOTES: Grautoff (II, No. 116) wrongly identifies the picture with that painted for Jean Fréart de Chantelou in 1648. In fact it was probably painted about 1655–58. The heavy figures with their big heads recall paintings such as the *St. Peter and St. John healing* of 1655 (No. 84) or the *Death of Sapphira* (No. 85). The dove in its circular radiance is very close to the National Gallery *Annunciation* of 1657 (No. 38), and the landscape has the heaviness and the grey-greens of late works such as the *Orion* (No. 169). In its general tones it is near to the *Eudamidas* (No. 152).

According to a note of Spon, dating from after 1673, a painting of this subject belonged to Jean de La Fourcade, alderman of Lyons (cf. Bonnaffé, Bibl. 583, p. 151).

BIBLIOGRAPHY: Smith, No. 94; Friedlaender, 1914, pp. 119, 227; Grautoff, I, p. 232, II, No. 116; *Exposition Poussin (Louvre)*, No. 110; Mahon, Bibl. 1367, p. 121; Wild, Bibl. 1383, pp. 241 f.

73. CHRIST AND THE WOMAN OF SAMARIA. Original lost.

HISTORY: Painted for Mme de Chantelou, wife of Paul Fréart de Chantelou, in 1662. Mentioned in April 1662 as finished, except for the head of Christ (*Correspondance*, p. 451). In November Poussin writes that he assumes that Chantelou has received it (*ibid.*, p. 452). According to an early nineteenth-century manuscript note, probably by the collector Dufourny, in the copy of the correspondence belonging to the Institut de France, the picture was at that time in the possession of 'Legrand' (cf. *Correspondance*, p. 452 n. 1).

ENGRAVINGS: 1. By J. Pesne (Andresen, No. 176; Wildenstein, No. 64).
2. By J. Hainzelmann (Andresen, No. 177).
3. Published by Drevet (Andresen, No. 178).

COPY: Private collection, New York.

Paintings of this subject ascribed to Poussin are recorded as follows:

1. Maria de Nisas Spinola collection, Genoa (cf. Ratti, Bibl. 228a, I, p. 276).

2. Anon. sale, Lebrun, Paris, 3.v.1790, lot 68 (34×43 inches).
3. J. Cocquereau sale, Arents, Brussels, 25.viii.1806, lot 79 (20×30 cm.).
4. Bugge sale, Copenhagen, 21.viii.1837, lot 478 (30× 20 inches). Perhaps the picture mentioned by Grautoff (II, p. 265) as in the Villa Konow, Copenhagen.
5. Poniatowski sale, Christie, London, 8 f.ii.1839, lot 192.

NOTES: In his letter of November 1662 (*Correspondance*, p. 452) Poussin says that this will be the last painting that he will ever execute. Félibien points out that he did not complete the *Seasons* for the Duc de Richelieu till 1664, but it is true that he did not execute any more figure paintings.

BIBLIOGRAPHY: *Correspondance*, pp. 451, 452; Chantelou, 1885, p. 222, and 1960, p. 131; Félibien, IV, p. 66; Loménie de Brienne, p. 222; Florent Le Comte, III, p. 32; Smith, No. 98; Friedlaender, 1914, p. 124; Grautoff, II, p. 255; Hourticq, Bibl. 899, p. 270.

74. CHRIST HEALING THE BLIND MEN. 119×176 cm. Musée du Louvre, Paris (715).

HISTORY: Painted for Reynon in 1650 (Félibien, IV, p. 61); in the collection of the Duc de Richelieu and sold with it to Louis XIV in 1665 (Ferraton, Bibl. 1043, pp. 439, 443, 446).

DRAWINGS: 1. Royal Library, Windsor Castle (*CR*, I, p. 31, No. 62).
2. Musée Bonnat, Bayonne (*CR*, I, p. 32, No. 63).
3. Royal Library, Windsor Castle (*CR*, I, p. 31, No. A 11). Studio drawing or copy.
4. Royal Library, Windsor Castle (*CR*, I, p. 31, No. A 12). Studio drawing or copy.

ENGRAVINGS: 1. By G. Chasteau (Andresen, No. 181; Wildenstein, No. 65; Davies and Blunt, p. 211, No. 65).
2. By L. Audran (Andresen, No. 182).
3. Published by Picart le Romain (Andresen, No. 183).
4. Published by Coypel (Andresen, No. 184).
5. Perhaps by Jean Dughet or Pietro del Po (Andresen, No. 185). The figure group, less three disciples, without the background. A print of this engraving is to be found in the Rijksmuseum, Amsterdam.

COPIES: 1. Musée des Beaux-Arts, Rheims. Bequeathed to the city by Antoine Ferrand de Monthelon in 1752.

2. City Museum and Art Gallery, Birmingham. Given in 1933 by Mrs. C. W. Lowndes.
3. National Museum, Copenhagen (560). In the inventory of the Royal Collection by 1732; then ascribed to Bourdon, but actually a free variant of Poussin's composition by an unidentified follower.
4. André Le Nôtre collection. 42×60 inches. Valued at 100 Livres (Guiffrey, Bibl. 697, p. 243).
5. Among the pictures from the Robit and other collections exhibited for sale by Bryan in 1801–02 (cf. Buchanan, II, p. 67, No. 34).
6. Lord Berwick sale, Phillips, London, 15.iv.1826, lot 186, bt. Lord Gower; by descent to the Dukes of Sutherland; Sutherland sale, Christie, London, 11.vii.1913, lot 33.
7. Isaac Pittar sale, Phillips, London, 19.iv.1842, lot 64.
8. Anon. sale, Christie, London, 6.v.1949, lot 75. In gouache, signed by Henry Toutin.

NOTES: The painting was the subject of a lecture to the Academy delivered by Bourdon on 3.xii.1667. After the lecture, which contained a detailed and highly laudatory analysis of the picture, some members of the Academy expressed their doubts whether Poussin had represented the subject with the dignity and the precision that it deserved. One person, however, suggested that the scene represented was not the healing of the blind men of Jericho (Matthew 20. 30–34), as was generally assumed, but the similar episode at Capernaum (Matthew 9. 27–31). The question was debated with much erudition in a manner highly characteristic of the Academy. No formal decision was reached, but it is clear that Félibien, who, as secretary, wrote the account of the meeting, supported the Capernaum hypothesis proposed by the unnamed person, who may indeed be Félibien himself. His arguments are cogent, but it must be noted that, although in the list of pictures sold by Richelieu to Louis XIV in 1665 the painting is simply referred to as 'les aveugles', both Bellori (p. 452) and Félibien (Bibl. 73, pp. 11 f.) specifically state that the scene is taking place at Jericho, and this view is confirmed by the inscription on the engraving by Chasteau (d. 1683).

When the picture was cleaned for the Louvre exhibition of 1960, the colours were found to be unusually light for Poussin and in some places almost strident. This led some critics to the view that it was a copy (cf. Kauffman, Bibl. 1332, p. 97). The provenance of the picture is a strong argument in its favour but is not conclusive, since at least one painting which Louis XIV owned as a Poussin, the *Mars and Venus* (reproduced by Magne, 1914, plate opposite p. 200), has been universally rejected in recent scholarship, and another, the *Nurture of Bacchus* (see catalogue No. 133), is in my opinion also not by him. Nevertheless I believe that the *Blind Men* is in fact an original. Bourdon (Bibl. 47a, p. 73) in his lecture already commented on the unusual brightness of the colour, but justifies it as appropriate to the theme, and this is no doubt the correct explanation.

BIBLIOGRAPHY: Félibien, IV, p. 61; Bourdon, in Bibl. 47a, pp. 66 ff., 129; Bellori, p. 452; Félibien, Bibl. 73, pp. 11 ff., and Bibl. 73a, p. 176; Testelin, Bibl. 80, pp. 20 f.; *Mémoires inédits*, I, pp. 101, 405; Loménie de Brienne, pp. 215, 218; Perrault, Bibl. 113, I, p. 90; Florent Le Comte, I, p. 202, III, p. 31; Piganiol de La Force, Bibl. 124, I, p. 123; Bailly, p. 301; Dézallier, 1745, II, p. 254, and 1762, IV, p. 39; Cambry, Bibl. 272a, pp. 25, 38, 56; Smith, No. 99; Duranty, Bibl. 554, p. 282; Bonnaffé, Bibl. 573, pp. 207, 214; Friedlaender, 1914, pp. 87, 121, 231; Grautoff, I, p. 262, II, No. 140; Magne, 1914, pp. 155, 209, No. 186; Jamot, p. 38; Ferraton, Bibl. 1043, pp. 439, 443, 446; Blunt, Bibl. 1050, pp. 39 f.; Licht, p. 144; *Exposition Poussin* (*Louvre*), No. 94; Kauffmann, Bibl. 1332, p. 97; Mahon, Bibl. 1367, pp. 107, 115, 118.

75. CHRIST AND THE WOMAN TAKEN IN ADULTERY. 98×135 cm. Present whereabouts unknown.

HISTORY: Perhaps Fraula sale, de Vos, Brussels, 21.vii.1738, lot 278 (41½×56 inches; cf. Hoet, Bibl. 195, I, p. 542); perhaps anon. (= Rubempré) sale, Brussels, 11.iv.1765, lot 103 (*ibid.*, III, p. 402); W. R. Cartwright (lent by him to the British Institution in 1819 (No. 47) and 1839 (No. 82); cf. Smith, Supplement, No. 1); perhaps anon. sale, Christie, London, 7.vi.1884, lot 119; probably anon. sale, Christie, London, 25.iii.1927, lot 46 (96·5×132 cm.), bt. Buck; bt. in England by Böhler, Munich, in or before 1930.

NOTES: The picture was first published by Grautoff (Bibl. 864, p. 329), but was at that time almost wholly repainted. In 1960, however, the repaint was removed and the picture was found to be an original, though very much damaged.

Grautoff dated the picture *c.* 1645, but in style it is very close indeed to *Christ's entry into Jerusalem* (No. 77) and, like it, must be dated *c.* 1626. Examination by X-rays shows that Poussin made many alterations in the picture in the course of execution.

BIBLIOGRAPHY: Hoet, Bibl. 195, I, p. 542, III, p. 402; Smith, Supplement, No. 1; Grautoff, Bibl. 864, pp. 329, 336; Blunt, Bibl. 1227, I, p. 169.

76. CHRIST AND THE WOMAN TAKEN IN ADULTERY. 122×195 cm. Musée du Louvre, Paris (716).

HISTORY: Painted for André Le Nôtre in 1653 (Félibien, IV, p. 63) and given by him to Louis XIV in 1693 (Bailly, p. 305).

DRAWING: Musée Condé, Chantilly (*CR*, I, p. 33, No. B 17). In *CR* it was suggested that the drawing was by an imitator of Poussin and the name of La Fage was tentatively proposed. This can hardly be correct, but the drawing has fairly close affinities with a painting of the subject which belonged in 1928 to the Eberhardt Gallery, Berlin, and was published by Grautoff (Bibl. 830, p. 105) as an original by Poussin, but which was actually engraved by C. Duclos in 1711 as after N. Colombel. According to the inscription on Duclos' engraving the picture was painted in Rome in 1682, and it is mentioned by Dézallier d'Argenville (1762, IV, p. 227). No drawings certainly attributed to Colombel are known, and the ascription of the Chantilly drawing to him cannot therefore be checked on stylistic grounds.

ENGRAVINGS: 1. By G. Audran (Andresen, No. 186; Wildenstein, No. 66; Davies and Blunt, p. 211, No. 66).

2. By Van Somer (Andresen, No. 187).

3. By C. M. Vermeulen (Andresen, No. 188). Dated 1679.

4. By G. Audran (Andresen, No. 189).

5. By Q. Fonbonne (Andresen, No. 190). Dated 1709.

6. Published by F. Chereau (Andresen, No. 191).

7. Anonymous (Andresen, No. 192).

8. By A. Verico (Andresen, No. 193).

COPIES: Musée des Beaux-Arts, Quimper (Magne, 1914, p. 210, No. 199).

2. Château de Dampierre (Seine-et-Marne).

NOTES: Though generally much admired, the picture was criticized by Bernini, who saw it on his visit to Paris in 1665 and quoted it as an example of Poussin's declining ability in his old age (Chantelou, Bibl. 41e, pp. 130 f.). Later Mengs speaks of it with a certain hostility and compares it unfavourably with the simplicity of Raphael (Bibl. 264a, p. 118).

BIBLIOGRAPHY: Chantelou, 1885, p. 222, and 1960, pp. 130 f.; Félibien, IV, p. 63; Bellori, p. 452; Bailly, p. 305; Richardson, *Account*, p. 8; (C. Saugrain), Bibl. 138a, I, p. 93; Dézallier, 1745, II, p. 254, and 1762, IV, p. 39; Mengs, Bibl. 264a, p. 118; Tuétey, Bibl. 304, pp. 74, 315; Gault de Saint-Germain, Pt. II, pp. 36 f.; Smith, No. 100; Delacroix, Bibl. 453a, p. 103; Guiffrey, Bibl. 697, p. 223; Friedlaender, 1914, pp. 88, 122, 232; Grautoff, I, p. 276, II, No. 148; Magne, 1914, pp. 155, 210, No. 199; Grautoff, Bibl. 864, p. 336; Finberg, Bibl. 934, p. 89; Blunt, Bibl. 975, p. 54, No. 283, and Bibl. 1050, p. 40; Licht, p. 145; Delbourgo and Petit, Bibl. 1243, pp. 50 f.; *Exposition Poussin* (*Louvre*), No. 103; Mahon, Bibl. 1338, p. 122; *Exposition Poussin* (*Rouen*), No. 88; *L'ideale classico* (*Bologna*), No. 82; Mahon, Bibl. 1367, pp. XV, 120, 129.

77. THE ENTRY OF CHRIST INTO JERUSALEM. 98×134 cm. Musée des Beaux-Arts, Nancy.

HISTORY: Mentioned by Falconet in a letter to Catherine II of Russia (25.x.1783) as having been brought from Paris by a dealer for sale in St. Petersburg and recommended by him to the Empress (Réau, Bibl. 230.1, p. 226); presumably rejected by the Empress but bought by Falconet; passed to his granddaughter, Baronne de Jankowitz, and bequeathed by her on her death in 1866 to the city of Nancy (*ibid.*, pp. VIII, X).

NOTES: The picture was rejected by Grautoff (II, pp. 275 f.), but examination after cleaning showed that it was undoubtedly an original, and it was included as such in the exhibition of *The Age of Louis XIV* in the Royal Academy, London, 1958, No. 117 (Bibl. 1165). It is in date near to the Dulwich *Triumph of David* (No. 33), the San Francisco *Golden Calf* (No. 25) and the ex-Böhler *Woman taken in Adultery* (No. 75).

The painting is unusual iconographically in that Poussin has included a group of three putti carrying a Cross, a prefiguration of the Passion which recalls the Dulwich *Return from Egypt* (No. 68).

In his letter to the Empress Catherine recommending this picture and the others brought from Paris Falconet writes: 'Je crois qu'ils peuvent tenir une bonne place avec les autres', that is to say among the pictures in the Imperial collection.

As in the case of the Böhler *Woman taken in Adultery*, X-rays revealed a large number of alterations made by Poussin while executing the painting.

BIBLIOGRAPHY: Réau, Bibl. 230.1, p. 226; Grautoff, II, pp. 275 f.; Magne, 1914, p. 210, No. 198; *Royal Academy, London*, Bibl. 1165, No. 117; Blunt, Bibl. 1166, p. 8; Badt, Bibl. 1190, p. 122; Blunt, Bibl. 1227, p. 169; Mahon, Bibl. 1271, p. 296; Rees Jones, Bibl. 1280, pp. 304 ff.; Thuillier, Bibl. 1296, p. 82, and Bibl. 1299, p. 295; Mahon, Bibl. 1367, pp. IX, 38, 132.

78. THE INSTITUTION OF THE EUCHARIST. 325×250 cm. Musée du Louvre, Paris (717).

HISTORY: Commissioned by Louis XIII in December 1640 for the chapel at Saint Germain (*Correspondance*, p. 41); in May 1641 Poussin was working on it actively (*ibid.*, p. 64); on 19 August he reports that it is still unfinished (*ibid.*, p. 91), but by 20 September it has already been set up in the chapel (*ibid.*, p. 97). The payment for the picture was made on 16 September (Robert and Montaiglon, Bibl. 550, p. 32). The picture was taken to the Louvre in 1792 (Tuétey, Bibl. 295, II, p. 164).

DRAWING: Royal Library, Windsor Castle (*CR*, I, p. 49, No. 191). Studio drawing, perhaps after the painting.

ENGRAVING: By P. Lombard (Andresen, No. 198; Wildenstein, No. 66bis).

COPIES: 1. Musée National des Beaux-Arts, Algiers (deposited by the Louvre).

2. Musée des Beaux-Arts, Caen (cf. Magne, 1914, p. 210, No. 208).

3. Formerly in the museum at Les Andelys (cf. Magne, 1914, p. 210, No. 208). Destroyed in 1940.

NOTES: The iconography of this painting has been discussed in detail by Dr. J. Montagu (Bibl. 1339, p. 311).

BIBLIOGRAPHY: *Correspondance*, pp. 41, 44, 64, 78, 80, 87, 90, 92, 97, 106; Fréart de Chambray, Bibl. 16, Preface; Chantelou, 1885, p. 83, and 1960, p. 126; Félibien, IV, p. 33; Bellori, pp. 424, 429; Passeri, pp. 328, 329; Baldinucci, XVI, pp. 103 f.; Loménie de Brienne, p. 219; Perrault, Bibl. 113, I, p. 90, and Bibl. 113a, p. 227; Florent Le Comte, III, p. 27; Bailly, p. 316; Dézallier, 1745, II, pp. 250, 254, 255, and 1762, IV, pp. 29, 39, 40; Lépicié, Bibl. 194, I, p. LXX; Dézallier d'Argenville, Bibl. 200.1, p. 158; [Maihows], Bibl. 217, pp. 233 f.; Mery, Bibl. 221, p. 222; Cambry, Bibl. 272a, pp. 22, 39; Guibal, Bibl. 273, p. 32; Dulaure, Bibl. 282, p. 231; Tuétey, Bibl. 295, II, p. 164; Smith, No. 102; Chéravay, Bibl. 544, p. 91; Robert and Montaiglon, Bibl. 550, p. 32; Friedlaender, 1914, pp. 74, 116, 210; Grautoff, I, p. 211, II, No. 100; Magne, 1914, pp. 123 ff., 210, No. 208; Blunt, Bibl. 975, p. 50, No. 247; Jamot, p. 83; Licht, p. 131; Vanuxem, Bibl. 1302, p. 160; Montagu, Bibl. 1339, p. 311.

79. THE CRUCIFIXION. 148·5 × 218·5 cm. Wadsworth Atheneum, Hartford, Conn.

HISTORY: Commissioned by the Président Jacques de Thou before May 1644 (*Correspondance*, p. 268); begun by 12.xi. 1645 (*ibid.*, p. 322) and finished by 3.vi.1646 (*ibid.*, 339); Jacques Stella, bequeathed by him to his niece, Claudine Bouzonnet Stella, and by her to her niece, Anne Molandier, in 1697 (*Testament*, Bibl. 107, pp. 18, 36, 42). Blackwood sale, Cock, London, 1744, 2nd day, lot 54, bt. Scott; Blackwood sale, London, 1751, 3rd day, lot 69; Sir Lawrence Dundas sale, Greenwood, London, 31.v.1794, lot 39, bt. Lord Ashburnham. Not in the Ashburnham sale (Christie, London, 20.vii.1850) and presumably bought back by the Dundas family, since it passed by inheritance to the Marquises of Zetland; Zetland sale, Christie, London, 27.iv.1934, lot 121, bt. Durlacher. Bt. by the Wadsworth Atheneum in 1935.

DRAWINGS: 1. Musée du Louvre, Paris (*CR*, I, p. 34, No. 66).

2. Musée du Louvre, Paris (*CR*, I, p. 34, No. 67).

3. Musée du Louvre, Paris (*CR*, I, p. 34, No. 68).

4. Museum der bildenden Künste, Leipzig (758).

ENGRAVINGS: 1. By Claudine Bouzonnet Stella (Andresen, No. 200; Wildenstein, No. 67; Davies and Blunt, p. 211, No. 67).

2. Published by E. Gantrel (Andresen, No. 201).

3. Published by Audran (Andresen, No. 202).

COPIES: 1. By Antoine Bouzonnet Stella; in the possession of his niece, Claudine Bouzonnet Stella, at her death in 1697, and bequeathed by her to her niece, Anne Molandier (*Testament*, Bibl. 107, p. 36); later in the Léon Dufourny sale, Delaroche, Paris, 22.xi.1819, lot 122.

2. Friedlaender (1914, pp. 118, 239) and Grautoff (II, No. 114) refer to a copy formerly in the Stubenrauch collection, Lankow, near Stettin (Friedlaender incorrectly states Schwerin), which, according to Grautoff, was brought from France by the Salingré family, ancestors of the Stubenrauchs. This is apparently the picture which appeared in the following sales; Montoya sale, Lepke, Berlin, 16.iv.1912, lot 153; Lorenz sale, Michaelsen, Lübeck, 28 f.x. 1913, lot 4; Jakoby sale, Michaelsen, Lübeck, 21.iv.1914, lot 529. There remains an element of doubt, however, since Grautoff and the Jakoby sale catalogue give the dimensions as 90 × 108 cm., whereas Friedlaender, no doubt following the Montoya sale catalogue, says 115 × 145 cm., but these dimensions may include the frame.

3. The Léon Dufourny sale, Delaroche, Paris, 22.xi. 1819, lot 83, included a small upright painting on paper laid down on panel, 12 × 10 inches, which is a variant of the group round the central Cross in the Hartford picture. As far as one can judge from the line-engraving in the sale catalogue, it might be of the same type as the *Annunciation* and the *Nativity* in the Alte Pinakothek, Munich, the *Noli me tangere* in the Prado, Madrid, and the *Lamentation* in the writer's possession (cf. Blunt, Bibl. 1226, pp. 400 f.).

BIBLIOGRAPHY: *Correspondance*, pp. 268, 322, 339; Félibien, IV, p. 54; Bellori, p. 453; *Testament*, Bibl. 107, pp. 18, 36, 42; Loménie de Brienne, pp. 214, 218 f.; Florent Le Comte, III, p. 29; Dézallier, 1745, II, p. 254, and 1762, IV, p. 39; Cambry, Bibl. 272a, p. 25; Barry, Bibl. 338, II, p. 314; Smith, No. 118; Friedlaender, 1914, pp. 85, 118, 229; Grautoff, I, p. 229, II, No. 114; Magne, 1914, pp. 155, 209, No. 191; Friedlaender, Bibl. 947, pp. 11 ff.; Bertin-Mourot, Bibl. 1023, p. 46, No. VIII; Hoffmann, Bibl. 1173, p. 105; Waterhouse, Bibl. 1308, p. 293; Blunt, Bibl. 1410.

80. THE DEPOSITION. 120.5 × 99 cm. Hermitage Museum, Leningrad (1200).

HISTORY: Probably J. B. Grimbergs sale, Brussels, 4.v.1716 (unnumbered). Perhaps the painting which in 1687 belonged to Pierre de Beauchamp, Maître des Ballets du Roi (cf. Brice, Bibl. 89a, I, p. 51). Bought with the collection of Count Brühl, Minister of Augustus of Saxony, in 1769.

DRAWING: V. W. Newman sale, American Art Association, 8.v.1923, lot 82. Probably by F. Chauveau for his engraving (see below).

ENGRAVINGS: 1. By F. Chauveau (Andresen, No. 204; Wildenstein, No. 68; Davies and Blunt, p. 211, No. 68). Apparently dated 1677.
2. By B. Audran (Andresen, No. 203).

COPIES: 1. Chigi collection, Castelfusano.
2. St. Rémy, Dieppe.

NOTES: Dated by Grautoff 1630–31 (II, No. 21), by Sterling (Bibl. 1159, p. 32) before 1630, by Mahon (Bibl. 1367, pp. XI, 29) between the middle of 1629 and the middle of 1630, a dating with which I should in general agree, since the painting seems to me certainly earlier than the *Plague* (No. 32).

A painting of this subject belonged to Jean de La Fourcade at a date after 1673 (Bonnaffé, Bibl. 583, p. 151).

BIBLIOGRAPHY: Brice, Bibl. 89a, I, p. 51; Smith, No. 120; Grautoff, I, p. 93, II, No. 21; Magne, 1914, p. 209, No. 193; Sterling, Bibl. 1159, p. 32; Alpatov, Bibl. 1217, p. 193; *Exposition Poussin (Louvre)*, No. 24; Mahon, Bibl. 1271, p. 297; Thuillier, Bibl. 1297, p. 43 n. 1; Mahon, Bibl. 1367, pp. XI, 29.

81. THE PIETÀ. 49 × 40 cm. Musée Thomas Henry, Cherbourg.

HISTORY: Probably painted for Cassiano dal Pozzo in collaboration with Daniel Seghers, who executed the wreath of flowers (see below); Léon Dufourny sale, 22.xi.1819, lot 82; given to the museum by the founder Thomas Henry in 1835.

NOTES: The attribution of this painting to Poussin has been much disputed. Grautoff (II, p. 263) describes it as *undiskutierbar*, and I myself rejected it when I had the opportunity of examining it in 1958 (Bibl. 1166, pp. 12 f.). Thuillier, in an unsigned note in the *Actes* of the Colloque Poussin (Bibl. 1299, p. 289), put in a plea for it, and Haskell and Rinehart (Bibl. 1254, pp. 322, 325) called attention to the possible connection with the painting in the 1715 Ghezzi inventory of the Pozzo collection. P. Rosenberg in his catalogue (*Exposition Poussin (Rouen)*, No. 100) presses the case in favour of the painting.

His plea seems to be confirmed beyond doubt by an entry in the catalogue for the sale of the Dufourny collection in 1819, which reads as follows:

81. La Vierge assise et l'enfant Jésus, demi-figures dans un ovale entouré d'une couronne de fleurs. Derrière la toile originaire, on lisait ces mots écrits de la main du Commandeur *del Pozzo*, qui avait commandé ce tableau ainsi que le pendant ci-après décrit, au Poussin et à Seghers.
'Florea corona sine spinis à P. Soc. Jesu Daniele Seghers
Belga virgo Mar. cum puero a Nicolao Poussino.'

82. Jésus-Christ, mort entre les bras de la Vierge, demi-figures dans un ovale entouré d'une couronne d'épines; derrière la première toile, était écrit de la même main:
'Sertum floreum a P. Soc. Jesu Daniele Seghers Belga
Christi pict. a Nic. Poussino.'

There can be little doubt that the pictures referred to here are those listed by Ghezzi in the Pozzo collection under Nos. 64, 65: 'le due Ghirlande de fiori del Gesuita e figure di Pussino in tela da Imp . re.' The dimensions of the Dufourny pictures are given as 54 × 42 pouces (137 × 107 cm.), which would agree with Ghezzi's *tela da Imperatore*, and a comparison of the Cherbourg picture with others by Seghers shows that the garland may well have been so big that the whole canvas was nearly three times its present height. It should be noted that the garland in the Cherbourg picture is exclusively composed of thorny plants and so corresponds to the description given in Pozzo's note.

The painting can be dated precisely to the years 1625–27, the only period when Seghers was in Rome. Its rough handling might lead one to date it later, near the Hermitage *Deposition* (No. 80), but the picture has many features in common with the San Francisco *Golden Calf* of 1626 (No. 25) and the ex-Thyssen

Holy Family (No. 48). The strong touches of red along the edges of the Virgin's fingers relate it to the Chigi *Children's Bacchanals* (Nos. 192, 193) and the Washington *Assumption* (No. 93).

BIBLIOGRAPHY: Grautoff, II, p. 263; Blunt, Bibl. 1166, pp. 12f.; Haskell and Rinehart, Bibl. 1254, pp. 322, 325; Thuillier, Bibl. 1299, p. 289; *Exposition Poussin (Rouen)*, No. 100; Blunt, Bibl. 1426, p. 64.

82. THE LAMENTATION OVER THE DEAD CHRIST. 101 × 145 cm. Alte Pinakothek, Munich (625).

HISTORY: In the collection of the Electors of Bavaria since the eighteenth century.

DRAWINGS: 1. Graphische Sammlung, Munich (*CR*, I, p. 35, No. A 13). Probably a copy after a lost original.
2. Kupferstichkabinett, Dresden. Reversed copy after the painting.

ENGRAVINGS: 1. By Remy Vuibert (Andresen, No. 207; Wildenstein, No. 70). Dated 1643.
2. By E. Gantrel (Andresen, No. 208).
3. Lithograph by F. Piloty.

COPIES: 1. National Museum, Budapest (705). Recorded in the Esterhazy collection in 1812 and bought with it by the Hungarian State in 1872.
2. Private collection, Paris.
3. Robert Strange collection, London (p. 78 of the 1769 catalogue); Strange sale, Christie, London, 7 ff.ii.1771, lot 125.
4. Forcade sale, Pillet, Paris, 2.iv.1873, lot 3, bt. Malial.
5. M. C. B. sale, Fiévez, Brussels, 10.xii.1928, lot 55.
6. Anon. sale, Christie, London, 27.xi.1959, lot 120.

NOTES: Dated by Grautoff 1628–31 (II, No. 20), by Mahon not long after the middle of 1629 (Bibl. 1367, p. 24). Perhaps slightly earlier, *c.* 1628–29.

BIBLIOGRAPHY: Smith, No. 123; Friedlaender, 1914, pp. 47, 129, 162; Grautoff, I, pp. 15, 92, 412, II, No. 20; Magne, 1914, p. 209, No. 196, p. 210, No. 209; Alpatov, Bibl. 882, p. 17; Hourticq, Bibl. 899, p. 184; Brieger, Bibl. 915, pp. 356 f.; Blunt, Bibl. 1086, p. 186, and Bibl. 1086a, p. 162; Licht, p. 94; Blunt, Bibl. 1166, p. 5; Wild, Bibl. 1184, p. 166; Blunt, Bibl. 1226, p. 402; Mahon, Bibl. 1271, p. 297; Weigert, Bibl. 1309, p. 278; Mahon, Bibl. 1367, p. 29.

83. THE LAMENTATION OVER THE DEAD CHRIST. 98 × 132 cm. National Gallery of Ireland, Dublin (214).

HISTORY: The Adriaan Bout sale, The Hague, 11.viii.1733, contains as lot 6 an *Entombment*, of which the size is given as 38 × 54 inches (Hoet, Bibl. 195, I, p. 385). These dimensions correspond more closely to the Dublin than to the Munich painting. The Dublin picture is said by Grautoff (II, No. 113) to have been bought in Rome about 1780 by Sir William Hamilton, but there does not seem to be any evidence for this statement. In the collection of the Duke of Hamilton; Hamilton Palace sale, Christie, London, 17 ff.vii. 1882, lot 1120, bt. by the Gallery.

ENGRAVING: By J. Pesne (Andresen, No. 205; Wildenstein, No. 69; Davies and Blunt, p. 211, No. 69).

COPIES: 1. In the Skä Kyrka, Färentuna Härad, Sweden.
2. Abbé Dussel, St. Saturnin, Lozère.
3. Formerly Stroganoff collection, St. Petersburg (Grautoff, II, p. 279). In grisaille, 37 × 51 cm.

NOTES: Dated by Grautoff 1643–48 (II, No. 113), by Friedlaender (1914, p. 98) 'aus der Spätzeit', by Mahon first to 1655 (Bibl. 1271, p. 304 n. 107) and later 1654–56 (Bibl. 1367, pp. 118 f.). In the second edition of the Louvre exhibition catalogue I proposed 1655–57, a dating which, though perhaps dangerously precise, still seems to me reasonable.

The figure of the Virgin is based on an engraving by Marcantonio (Bartsch, XIV, p. 40, No. 34).

BIBLIOGRAPHY: Waagen, Bibl. 384b, III, p. 300; Smith, No. 121; Friedlaender, 1914, pp. 98, 256; Grautoff, I, p. 228, II, No. 113; Magne, 1914, p. 209, No. 195; Bodkin, Bibl. 858, p. 180; Blunt, Bibl. 1050, p. 40; Licht, p. 91; *Exposition Poussin (Louvre)*, No. 96; Mahon, Bibl. 1271, p. 304 n. 107; *L'ideale classico (Bologna)*, No. 84; Mahon, Bibl. 1367, pp. 118 f., 121.

84. ST. PETER AND ST. JOHN HEALING THE LAME MAN. 126×165 cm. Metropolitan Museum, New York (24.45.2).

HISTORY: Painted in 1655 for Mercier, Treasurer of the city of Lyons (Félibien, IV, p. 64); passed from him to M. de Bordeaux, Intendant des Finances, whose secretary obtained it from him; Loménie de Brienne tried to buy it from the secretary, but his offer was refused (Loménie de Brienne, pp. 214, 222). In 1679 it belonged to Antoine Bouzonnet Stella (inscription on engraving by Claudine Bouzonnet Stella, Andresen, No. 213); bequeathed to his niece, Claudine Bouzonnet Stella, and on her death in 1697 to her niece, Anne Molandier (*Testament*, Bibl. 107, pp. 18, 43). Later in the collection of Prince Eugene of Savoy; at his death in 1736 bt. by Prince Liechtenstein; offered by him to Augustus of Saxony in 1743 through Algarotti and Brühl, but not in fact purchased (Posse, Bibl. 177, p. 39); bt. by the museum from Prince Liechtenstein in 1924.

ENGRAVINGS: 1. By Claudine Bouzonnet Stella (Andresen, No. 213; Wildenstein, No. 74; Davies and Blunt, p. 211, No. 74).
2. By Poquet (Andresen, No. 214).
3. By B. Picart (Andresen, No. 215).
4. Published by Wolff in Augsburg (Andresen, No. 216).
5. By Audran (in the Albertina; not listed by Andresen).

COPIES: 1. St. Patrice, Rouen.
2. By A. B. Stella in the inventory of his niece (who also owned the original) in 1697 (*Testament*, Bibl. 107, p. 37).
3. Lord Radstock; sold Christie, London, 12.v.1826, lot 41 (said to come from the collection of François Michel le Tellier, Marquis de Louvois; *d.* 1691); in the collection of W. Wilkins in 1837 (Smith, No. 148); E. Higginson of Saltmarshe sale, Christie, London, 6.vi.1846, lot 182 (as from Radstock collection), bt. in; E. Higginson of Saltmarshe sale, Christie, London, 16.vi.1860, lot 28, bt. Barnet.
4. Trueman Mills sale, Christie, London, 21.xi.1924, lot 125, bt. Wyatt; anon. sale, Christie, London, 22.ii.1925, lot 33; anon. sale, Christie, London, 28.vi.1935, lot 102; anon. sale, Christie, London, 26.vi.1936, lot 111 (120·5 × 178 cm.).
5. Anon. sale, Sotheby, London, 25.vi.1947, lot 163.

Pictures of this subject which may have been copies of the Metropolitan painting appeared in the following sales:
1. A Nobleman's sale, Christie, London, 14.ii.1777, lot 47.
2. C. Jennings sale, Christie, London, 25 ff.ii.1779, 2nd day, lot 43.

NOTES: A painting of this subject in the Kunsthistorisches Museum, Vienna, frequently confused with the Liechtenstein picture (e.g. Magne, *loc. cit.*), has no connection with it and is not by Poussin. It is engraved in S. von Perger's publication of the Vienna Gallery (1825).

BIBLIOGRAPHY: Félibien, IV, p. 64; *Testament*, Bibl. 107, pp. 18, 43; Loménie de Brienne, pp. 214, 222; Florent Le Comte, III, p. 32; Posse, Bibl. 177, p. 39; Smith, No. 148; Friedlaender, 1914, pp. 123, 234; Grautoff, I, p. 279, II, No. 152; Magne, 1914, pp. 155, 215, Nos. 271, 272; Burroughs, Bibl. 769, pp. 100 f.; Licht, p. 159; Sterling, Bibl. 1122, pp. 72 ff.; Mahon, Bibl. 1367, p. 120.

85. THE DEATH OF SAPPHIRA. 122×199 cm. Musée du Louvre, Paris (720).

HISTORY: Belonged to Jean Fromont de Veine in 1685 (Félibien, IV, p. 152); bt. by Louis XIV from C. A. Hérault in 1685 (*Comptes des bâtiments*, II, pp. 587, 664).

DRAWINGS: 1. Private collection, U.S.A. Formerly Richardson collection; belonged in 1960 to Professor Jacob Isaacs, London (*Exposition Poussin* (*Louvre*), No. 230).
2. Musée Fabre, Montpellier.

ENGRAVINGS: 1. By J. Pesne (Andresen, No. 217; Wildenstein, No. 75).
2. Published by Vallet (Andresen, No. 218).
3. By F. Andriot (Andresen, No. 219).
4. By L. Audran (Andresen, No. 220).
5. By R. U. Massard (Andresen, No. 221).

COPIES: 1. Château de Dampierre (Seine-et-Marne).
2. Charles Galli sale, Wright, Edinburgh, 17.i.1829, lot 120.

NOTES: The picture was restored in 1792 (Tuétey, Bibl. 304, pp. 74, 315). Dated by Grautoff 1646–53 (II, No. 149), by Mahon *c.* 1652 (Bibl. 1367, p. 120). I should prefer the slightly later date of 1654–56 which I proposed in the Louvre exhibition catalogue.

BIBLIOGRAPHY: *Comptes des bâtiments*, II, pp. 587, 664; Félibien. IV, p. 152; Bellori, p. 454; Loménie de Brienne, pp. 218, 224; Florent Le Comte, III, p. 32; Piganiol de La Force, Bibl. 124, I, p. 131; Bailly, p. 304; (C. Saugrain), Bibl. 138a, I, p. 93; Dézallier, 1745, II, p. 254, and 1762, IV, p. 39; Tuétey, Bibl. 304, pp. 74,

315; Smith, No. 149; Friedlaender, 1914, pp. 88, 126; Grautoff, I, p. 277, II, No. 149; Magne, 1914, p. 211, No. 220; Finberg, Bibl. 934, p. 89; Jamot, p. 48; Blunt, Bibl. 1050, p. 40; Licht, p. 145; Hours, Bibl. 1256, pp. 27 f.; *Exposition Poussin (Louvre)*, No. 106; *Exposition Poussin (Rouen)*, No. 89; Mahon, Bibl. 1367, p. 120.

86. LANDSCAPE WITH ST. JOHN ON PATMOS. 102×136 cm. Art Institute, Chicago.

HISTORY: Probably Robit sale, Paris, 1801, lot 91, bt. Bryan for Sir Simon Clarke (No. 29 in Bryan's catalogue of pictures exhibited in 1801–02; cf. Buchanan, II, p. 59); Clarke sale, Christie, London, 8.v. 1840, lot 39, bt. Andrew Geddes; Geddes sale, Christie, London, 12.iv.1845, lot 651, presumably bt. in; belonged to Mrs. Geddes in 1861, when it was lent to the winter exhibition at the Royal Academy, London (No. 22); said to have been sold in London in 1918 and bt. by Max Rothschild; with Fleischmann, Munich, in 1930; A. A. Munger, Chicago, 1930; presented by him to the Art Institute in the same year.

ENGRAVING: By L. de Châtillon (Andresen, No. 454; Wildenstein, No. 186.

COPIES: 1. Sir Thomas Baring in 1837 (cf. Smith, No. 316, where he wrongly identifies the Baring with the Robit painting). This may possibly be the painting sold by Lord Berwick (Phillips, London, 6 f.vi.1825, lot 163), described as 'A grand landscape with architectural buildings and Saint Luke writing the Gospel'.
2. T. C. Hinde sale, Christie, London, 8.i.1876; anon. (= Smith) sale, Christie, London, 29.x.1948, lot 146, bt. Agnew.

NOTES: For dating, see the *Landscape with St. Matthew* (No. 87).

BIBLIOGRAPHY: Buchanan, II, p. 59; Smith, No. 316; Grautoff, II, p. 259; Magne, 1914, p. 214, No. 267; Posse, Bibl. 842, p. 62; Rich, Bibl. 843, p. 113; Valentiner, Bibl. 845, No. 74; Blunt, Bibl. 972, p. 156, and Bibl. 976, pp. 186, 189; Bertin-Mourot, Bibl. 1023, p. 52, No. XXXIII; Clark, Bibl. 1040, p. 66; Licht, p. 140; *Exposition Poussin (Louvre)*, No. 68; Shearman, Bibl. 1285, p. 181.

87. LANDSCAPE WITH ST. MATTHEW. 99×135 cm. Staatliche Museen, Museum Dahlem, Berlin.

HISTORY: Presumably painted for Cardinal Francesco Barberini, since it is recorded in the Palazzo Barberini in a manuscript inventory (among the Barberini papers in the Vatican), which lists the possessions of Carlo Barberini in 1692 (*Un fiume con paesino, e campagna. e un santo che sta scrivendo e sede sopra una pietra con l'angelo al: p.mi L (?) cornice dorata del Pusino*). It is also mentioned by La Roque, who was in Rome between 1775 and 1778 (Bibl. 248, II, p. 245); passed by inheritance to the Colonna di Sciarra, no doubt through Cornelia Costanza Barberini (1716–97), who married Giulio Cesare Colonna di Sciarra in 1728 (cf. P. Picchiai, *I Barberini*, Rome, 1959, p. 260). Noted as in the Palazzo Sciarra by M. Graham in 1820 (Bibl. 365, p. 202) and bought from there by the Kaiser-Friedrich-Museum in 1873.

DRAWING: A drawing of the landscape without the figures is in the Staatliche Kunstakademie, Düsseldorf (cf. *CR*, IV, p. 52).

COPIES: 1. Earl of Strafford, Wrotham Park, Hertfordshire. Described by Waagen (Bibl. 384b, IV, pp. 321 f.). Wrongly described as a *St. John* when exhibited at the Royal Academy winter exhibition of 1881 (No. 167).
2. Romsey Church, Hampshire (hung in the Vicarage).
3. A copy was made by Félix Hyppolite Lanoue in 1858 (letter of 22.vii.1858 in the archives of the Académie de France, Rome).
4. Anon. sale, Cock, London, 1731, lot 1: 'St. John writing the Revelations with an angel.' The reference to the angel suggests that the picture probably represented St. Matthew rather than St. John.
5. R. Ansell sale, Christie, London, 15.ii.1771, lot 23 (36×48 inches).
6. L. Dufourny sale, Delaroche, Paris, 22.xi.1819, lot 91 (16×14 inches). The figures of St. Matthew and the angel only. Said to have been brought from Rome by 'feu M. Blanchard, peintre', no doubt Laurent Blanchard (c. 1762–1819).

NOTES: The identification of the picture with one in the Palazzo Barberini is based partly on the assumption that most of the Sciarra pictures came from the Barberini, and partly on the following reference in La Roque: 'Un beau paysage; par Nicolas Poussin. Placé près de la fenêtre à gauche, où l'on voit un beau St. Jérome, près duquel est un ange qui semble lui dicter.' In other cases La Roque is careless about details of subjects, calling Germanicus Brittanicus and confusing St. Erasmus with St. Andrew, so there can be no doubt that he is actually referring to the Berlin painting.

Dated by Grautoff 1646–53 (II, No. 125), by Shearman 1640–45, together with the *St. John* (Bibl. 1285,

p. 181). Mahon, in his catalogue of the 1962 Bologna exhibition (*L'ideale classico* (Bologna), No. 72), accepts the dates *c.* 1643 for the *St. Matthew* and *c.* 1644–45 for the *St. John*, which I had proposed in the catalogue of the Louvre exhibition (*Exposition Poussin* (*Louvre*), Nos. 66, 68). The grounds for this dating are as follows: the two paintings must have been planned as part of a series of the four Evangelists, and we must assume that for some reason the series was interrupted. Whereas the *St. Matthew* was delivered to the Barberini, the *St. John* apparently was not, the hypothesis that the two pictures were separated very early being supported by the fact that, whereas the *St. John* was engraved by Châtillon, the *St. Matthew* was not.

Urban VIII died in 1644, and Cardinal Francesco Barberini fell immediately into disgrace and had to flee from Rome in the following year. These events would explain the interruption of the series, since after the death of Urban Cardinal Francesco would have been in no position to order further works of art or pay for those already commissioned.

Stylistically this dating would be satisfactory. The figures, particularly those in the *St. Matthew*, are strikingly similar to the *Baptism*, now in Washington, completed in Paris in 1642, and the landscapes correspond precisely to the stage which Poussin had reached in the years immediately after his return to Rome at the end of 1642, the *St. John* being slightly the more advanced.

BIBLIOGRAPHY: La Roque, Bibl. 248, II, p. 245; Graham, Bibl. 365, p. 202; Gence, Bibl. 373, p. 582; Burckhardt, Bibl. 465b, p. 997; Friedlaender, 1914, pp. 96, 251; Grautoff, I, p. 252, II, No. 125; Magne, 1914, pp. 192, 214, No. 268, p. 217, No. 304; Royal Academy, London, Bibl. 879, No. 130; Francastel, Bibl. 883, p. 154; Blunt, Bibl. 972, p. 156, and Bibl. 976, pp. 186, 189; Dorival, Bibl. 1088, p. 47; Licht, p. 140; Wild, Bibl. 1185, p. 25; *Exposition Poussin* (*Louvre*), No. 66; Shearman, Bibl. 1285, p. 181; Wild, Bibl. 1310, 31.v.1960; *L'ideale classico* (Bologna), No. 72.

88. THE ECSTASY OF ST. PAUL. Panel 41.5 × 30 cm. John and Mable Ringling Museum, Sarasota, Florida.

HISTORY: Painted for Paul Fréart de Chantelou in 1643 (for details see below); by 1713 in the collection of Nicolas de Launay, father-in-law of Robert de Cotte, in his apartment under the Long Gallery of the Louvre (Brice, Bibl. 89d, I, p. 124); still recorded there in 1725 (Brice, Bibl. 89 f., I, p. 164); bt. by the Duc d'Orléans, presumably at Launay's death in 1727 and listed by Dubois de Saint Gelais in the Orleans collection in that year, as coming from Launay (Bibl. 153, p. 331). Sold with the Italian and French pictures of the Orleans collection in 1792 to Walkuers; sold by him the same year to Laborde de Méréville; bt. 1798 with the collection by Bryan for a group of English collectors; exhibited by Bryan for sale in 1798 (No. 28); bt. by G. W. Taylor (Buchanan, I, p. 152); Taylor sale, Christie, London, 14.vi.1823, lot 53, bt. Col. Thwaites (presumably = bt. in); Taylor sale, Erlestoke Park, 25.vii.1832, No. 159. Later belonged to Prince Woronzov; Woronzov sale, Florence, 23.iv.1900, lot 388. Probably the painting which appeared in the following sales: Dr. Adolph Hammel, Zurich, 1909, No. 108; Carl Lanz, Mannheim, 1917, No. 57 (41 × 30 cm.). Bt. in Germany by Frederick Mont; sold by him to Rosenberg and Stiebel, New York; bt. by the Museum in 1956. The fact that this is the Orleans picture is confirmed by an old label on the back, in an English early nineteenth-century hand (perhaps Taylor's), giving the provenance. There is also attached to the panel an undecipherable seal, which may be that of Prince Woronzov.

DRAWING: Hermitage Museum, Leningrad (8017; not traceable when *CR* I was published). The drawing shows the figures undraped, in poses exactly corresponding to the painting. Certainly not an original, but probably a copy after a lost drawing by Poussin.

ENGRAVINGS: 1. By J. Pesne (Andresen, No. 228; Wildenstein, No. 80; Davies and Blunt, p. 212, No. 80).
2. By J. Dughet (Andresen, No. 229).
3. By F. Natalis (Andresen, No. 230).
4. By S. Thomassin (Andresen, No. 231; Wildenstein, No. 81). Dated 1684.
5. Anonymous (Wildenstein, No. 82). The figure group of the Sarasota picture placed in the setting of the Louvre version (No. 89).

COPIES: 1. Musée des Beaux-Arts, Rennes (306). From the church of the Feuillants, Paris (Thuillier, Bibl. 1297, p. 39); deposited by the State in 1810; 42×31 cm. Mentioned by Magne (1914, p. 211, No. 226) and Thuillier (*loc. cit.*) as a copy of the Louvre picture (Thuillier, however, states that he has not been able to check its existence).
2. D. L. Green collection, England. In reverse.
3. Formerly Ehrich Gallery, New York.
4. Anon. sale, Dorotheum, Vienna, 18 f.v.1914, lot 62. On canvas, 43 × 32 cm.

Another painting of this subject, said to have come from the Orleans collection, but having quite different dimensions (22 × 28 cm.), was in the Huard sale, Defer, Paris, 6.iv.1836, lot 262.

A painting claiming to be the Chantelou version but with a manifestly false pedigree was in the D. sale, Martin, Paris, 10.xi.1820, lot 5 (canvas, 15 × 11 inches).

A carved group by B. Precht in Uppsala Cathedral is based on Poussin's composition (cf. J. Montagu, Bibl. 1368, p. 3).

NOTES: Some time before the middle of 1643 Chantelou asked Poussin to paint for him a picture which was to hang as a pair to the *Vision of Ezekiel*, which Chantelou had acquired in Italy and which he believed to be an original by Raphael. The *Ezekiel* passed with the *St. Paul* to Launay and later to the dukes of Orleans; on their arrival in England the two pictures were separated, and the *Ezekiel* passed to Lord Berwick, Sir Thomas Baring and Lord Ashburnham, and was sold as lot 26 in the Ashburnham sale at Sotheby, London, 24.vi.1953. It is generally regarded as a very good and early copy.

On 2.vii.1643 Poussin expresses his apprehension at having to execute a work in rivalry to Raphael (Félibien, IV, pp. 50 f.). By 25.viii.1643 he has found the *pensée*, which presumably means that he had made drawings, and he promises to begin the painting in the following week (*Correspondance*, p. 211). On 27.x.1643 the picture is *mis ensemble* and Poussin is leaving it to dry before retouching it (*ibid.*, p. 213). On 5.xi.1643 he writes: "Le petit St. Paul veut enquore deux jours de caresses" (*ibid.*, p. 228), and the picture was finally despatched on 4.xii.1643 (*ibid.*, p. 234).

No doubt Chantelou selected the subject as being one which would balance the *Ezekiel* and have a reference to the Saint after whom he was named.

There is no means of telling whether Sandrart (p. 258) is referring to this picture or to No. 89.

BIBLIOGRAPHY: *Correspondance*, pp. 202, 208, 211, 214, 219, 223, 225, 228, 229, 230, 234, 238, 251, 252, 261, 280, 293; Félibien, IV, pp. 50 ff.; Sandrart, p. 258; Brice, Bibl. 89d, I, p. 124, and Bibl. 89 f., I, p. 164; Florent Le Comte, III, p. 29; (C. Saugrain), Bibl. 138a, I, p. 175; Dubois de Saint-Gelais, Bibl. 139, p. 153, and Bibl. 153, p. 331; Dézallier, 1745, II, p. 255, and 1762, IV, p. 40; Dézallier d'Argenville, Bibl. 183, p. 67; Bardon, II, p. 125; La Roque, Bibl. 248, I, p. 107; Cambry, Bibl. 272a, p. 25; Couché, Fontenai and Croze-Magnan, Bibl. 285, III, Poussin, No. 12; Gault de Saint-Germain, Pt. II, pp. 6 f.; Barry, Bibl. 338, II, p. 71; Buchanan, I, p. 152; Waagen, Bibl. 384b, II, p. 493; Smith, No. 152; Friedlaender, 1914, pp. 79, 118; Grautoff, II, p. 256; Magne, 1914, pp. 147 f., 211, No. 225; Wild, Bibl. 1184, p. 166; *Exposition Poussin* (*Louvre*), No. 67.

89. THE ECSTASY OF ST. PAUL. Whole canvas 148 × 120 cm. Original size 128 × 96 cm. Musée du Louvre, Paris (722).

HISTORY: Painted for Paul Scarron in 1649–50 (for details see below); sold by him to Jabach and by him to the Duc de Richelieu (Florent Le Comte, III, p. 30); bt. with the collection of the Duc de Richelieu by Louis XIV in 1665 (Ferraton, Bibl. 1043, pp. 439, 446).

DRAWINGS: 1. Ecole des Beaux-Arts, Paris (*CR*, I, p. 37, No. 72).
2. Musée du Louvre, Paris (*CR*, I, p. 38, No. A 17). Studio drawing.
3. Musée du Louvre, Paris (32500; cf. *CR*, I, p. 38). A copy after the painting.
4. British Museum, London. Variant, probably by R. La Fage.

ENGRAVINGS: 1. By P. del Po (Andresen, No. 224; Wildenstein, No. 78).
2. By G. Chasteau (Andresen, No. 225; Wildenstein, No. 79).
3. By Laugier (Andresen, No. 226).

4. By Cossin (in the Albertina; not listed by Andresen).
5. Anonymous (Wildenstein, No. 82). Shows the figure group of the Sarasota picture in the setting of the Louvre version.

COPIES: 1. St. Louis, Versailles.
2. Anon. sale, Christie, London, 6.x.1961, lot 70 (127 × 95 cm.).
Magne mentions a painting of this subject in the church of St. Serge at Angers (1914, p. 211, No. 226), but I have not been able to check whether this is a copy of the Louvre picture or like the painting at Rennes (see No. 88) after the Sarasota version.

NOTES: Poussin first mentions Scarron's desire to own a painting by him on 2.ii.1646, but no subject is given (*Correspondance*, p. 332). On 17.i.1649 Scarron is still reminding Poussin of his promise, but nothing has been done (*ibid.*, p. 394). On 7.ii.1649 Poussin says that he had found "la disposition d'un sujet bachique" for Scarron and hopes to paint it, if the situation in Paris (the beginning of the Fronde) does not make Scarron change his mind (*ibid.*, p. 396). On 29.v.1650 he announces to Chantelou that the *St. Paul* is finished (*ibid.*, p. 415), so one must suppose that the new subject was chosen and the painting executed between the early months of 1649 and May 1650.

BIBLIOGRAPHY: *Correspondance*, pp. 332, 339, 341, 378, 386, 394, 396, 415; *Comptes des bâtiments*, I, pp. 542, 927; Félibien, IV, p. 60; Nocret, Bibl. 47a, p. 104; Le Brun, Bibl. 55, p. 77; Sandrart, p. 258; Félibien, Bibl. 73, pp. 10 f., and Bibl. 73a, p. 176; *Mémoires inédits*, I, pp. 314 ff., 404 f.; Florent Le Comte, I, p. 202, III, p. 30; Piganiol de La Force, Bibl. 124, I, p. 126; Bailly, p. 309; Dézallier, 1745, II, p. 254, and 1762, IV, p. 39; Dézallier d'Argenville, Bibl. 183d, p. 347; La Roque, Bibl. 248, I, p. 144; Smith, No. 153; Bonnaffé, Bibl. 573, pp. 207, 214; Fontaine, Bibl. 692, p. 113; Friedlaender, 1914, pp. 19, 79, 121, 238; Grautoff, I, p. 275, II, No. 146; Magne, 1914, pp. 152 ff., 211, No. 226, and Bibl. 670a, pp. 212, 247; Courthion, Bibl. 781, p. 62; Jamot, p. 39; Ferraton, Bibl. 1043, pp. 439, 446; *Exposition Poussin (Louvre)*, No. 92; Pariset, Bibl. 1274, pp. 222 f.; *Exposition Poussin (Rouen)*, No. 86; *L'ideale classico (Bologna)*, No. 80; Mahon, Bibl. 1367, p. 118.

90. THE DEATH OF THE VIRGIN. Original lost.

HISTORY: Painted for the cathedral of Notre-Dame, Paris (Bellori, p. 411; Félibien, IV, p. 10) in 1623, probably on a commission from François de Gondi, Archbishop of Paris (M. C. P. G., Bibl. 218, p. 159). It may originally have been in the chapel of St. Nicaise, at the east end of the choir, which belonged to the Gondi family, but it is first recorded in one of the chapels of the nave in 1684 (Brice, Bibl. 89a, II, p. 260). This was probably the chapel of St. Peter Martyr, since it is recorded there, over the altar, in 1749 (Dézallier d'Argenville, Bibl. 183, p. 19). In 1763 (M. C. P. G., Bibl. 218, p. 159) it was in the chapel of St. Gérald or St. Géraud. Taken to the Grands-Augustins in 1793 and to the Louvre in 1797, and sent to Brussels in 1803. The attempts of the French Government to recover the picture in 1815 failed and it remained in Belgium. It may have been destroyed in a fire in 1827, or sold in 1823 or 1827, or it may be in a church in or near Brussels (Thuillier, Bibl. 1297, p. 30).

NOTES: The appearance of the picture can be to some extent reconstructed from the surviving descriptions. As regards its dimensions, it was described in the list of pictures sent to Brussels in 1803 as measuring 6 ft. 3 inches × 4 ft. 3 inches, and in a Brussels inventory of 1809 as measuring 2 × 1.4 metres.

The most certain visual evidence is the minute sketch made by Gabriel de Saint-Aubin in the margin of his copy of the 1763 description of Notre-Dame, preserved in the library of the City of Paris (Aubert, Bibl. 216, p. 8), and reproduced in this volume. This supports the statement made in the 1763 description that the picture included the figure of François de Gondi, who appears on the right wearing a mitre.

To this evidence must be added the description in the 1809 inventory already referred to: 'Les Disciples entourent le lit sur lequel la Vierge, mourante, est exposée. Les différences d'attitude et d'expression de ces saints personnages se réunissent toutes pour exprimer un même sentiment de douleur et de regret. Deux anges paraissent dans le haut. Le fond représente un vaste espace qui, s'élevant en voûte, reçoit son jour par une arcade à l'entrée' (Thuillier, *loc. cit.*).

Various attempts have been made to identify the Notre-Dame altarpiece with surviving paintings, but none have met with approval. E. Denio (Bibl. 640a, pp. 26 ff.) proposed a painting then in the Wesendonck collection, Berlin, now in Bonn, but this is in fact a copy of a painting by Maratta in the Villa Albani. Hourticq proposed a painting in St. Etienne-du-Mont (Bibl. 813·1, pp. 162 ff.) and, when faced by Dacier (Bibl. 812, pp. 165 ff.) with Saint-Aubin's drawing, showed some ingenuity in defending his thesis, but to no avail. For a more recent hypothesis, see the next entry (No. 91).

It is possible, but not certain, that the picture was originally on panel and later transferred to canvas. According to documents published by Montaiglon (Bibl. 502), a picture of this subject by Poussin was so treated by Hacquin in about 1790, but the problem is complicated by the fact that a rival restorer, Picault, in attacking Hacquin, refers to the Poussin as 'aux Jésuites'. However, this is likely to be a mistake, since the only works painted by Poussin for the Jesuits were the scenes from the Lives of St. Ignatius and St. Francis Xavier, executed for the celebrations of 1622, definitely stated to have been on canvas, and the *Miracle of St. Francis Xavier* for the Noviciate (No. 101), which is far too big ever to have been on panel.

BIBLIOGRAPHY: Félibien, IV, p. 10; Bellori, p. 411; Brice, Bibl. 89a, II, p. 260, and Bibl. 89g, IV, p. 223; Florent Le Comte, III, p. 23; Dézallier, 1745, II, p. 254, and 1762, IV, pp. 26, 39; Dézallier d'Argenville, Bibl. 183, p. 19, and Bibl. 183c, p. 13; Aubert, Bibl. 216, p. 8; M.C.P.G., Bibl. 218, p. 159; Bardon, II, p. 124; Ponz, Bibl. 238a, p. 1702 par. 12; Papillon de La Ferté, Bibl. 252, II, p. 451; Tuétey, Bibl. 295, II, p. 221; Gault de Saint-Germain, Pt. I, p. 9; Lenoir, Bibl. 419, p. 290; Montaiglon, Bibl. 502, p. 156; Stein, Bibl. 610, p. 27; Friedlaender, 1914, pp. 10, 111; Grautoff, I, p. 41; Magne, 1914, p. 211, No. 218; Hourticq, Bibl. 813.1, pp. 162, 167, and Bibl. 899, pp. 75, 194; Mahon, Bibl. 992, pp. 41 ff.; Jamot, pp. 8, 36; Sterling, *Exposition Poussin (Louvre)*, pp. 209 ff.; Thuillier, Bibl. 1297, pp. 29 ff.; Blunt, Bibl. 1411.

91. THE DEATH OF THE VIRGIN. Water-colour on paper. 39·5 × 31 cm. Sir William Worsley, Bart., Hovingham Hall, Yorkshire.

HISTORY: Probably acquired by Thomas Worsley (1710–78), Surveyor-General of the Board of Works to George III; passed by inheritance to the present owner.

NOTES: Probably a *modello* or finished sketch for the lost painting in Notre-Dame (see No. 90).

The Hovingham water-colour agrees with descriptions of the lost painting from Notre-Dame in showing the figure of a bishop standing on the right, a detail which has no justification in legend or traditional iconography and does not seem to occur in any other version of the subject. The argument against the identification is that in Gabriel de Saint-Aubin's sketch after the painting this figure stands in the foreground, whereas in the water-colour it is partly concealed by two kneeling apostles. Two alternative explanations of this fact may be offered. First, Saint-Aubin's sketches are not always accurate, and he may have had difficulty in seeing the painting in a dark chapel. Alternatively, if the water-colour was a *modello* to be submitted to the patron, the latter may have objected that he was not given a sufficiently prominent position, and may have ordered the artist to place him in the foreground in the picture. Some support for the first hypothesis is provided by the fact that the detailed description of the painting written when it was in Brussels in 1809 makes no mention at all of the figure of the archbishop, which may therefore not have been as prominent as it appears in Saint-Aubin's drawing. Moreover, the description fits the Hovingham water-colour with remarkable accuracy in several respects: the emphasis on the expressive power of the figures, the reference to the vault in the background, broken by an arch through which the light comes, and the mention of 'deux anges', which are presumably the winged putti hovering in the top left-hand corner.

The fact that the water-colour is very Flemish in character is no argument against Poussin's authorship, since, as has been pointed out in Chapter I of the text volume, he admired and studied the works of Pourbus and other Flemish artists in Paris.

Technically the water-colour is close to the Marino drawings in many details (see text vol., Figs. 32–46). The use of wash in the background with the white paper left for the lights, and the little pointed tongues of wash to strengthen the draperies, can be paralleled in many of them. The types of women's heads are not to be found in the oblong Marino drawings, but similar heads occur in the *Minerva and the Muses* (*CR*, III, Pl. 135, No. 163), which also comes close to the *Death of the Virgin* in its general treatment of the forms.

BIBLIOGRAPHY: Sterling, *Exposition Poussin (Louvre)*, pp. 209 ff.; Thuillier, Bibl. 1297, pp. 29 ff.; Blunt, Bibl. 1411.

92. THE ASSUMPTION OF THE VIRGIN. 132 × 96·5 cm. The National Gallery of Art, Washington, D.C.

HISTORY: Belonged to the 9th Earl of Exeter in 1794; said to have come from the Palazzo Soderini, Rome (see below). Passed by descent to the 6th Marquis of Exeter, who sold it in 1962 to Messrs. Wildenstein. Bought from them by the Gallery in 1963.

DRAWING: A drawing in the Uffizi (886E), described in *CR* (I, p. 35) as 'only related to Poussin', is probably a copy of a lost original of the same period as the Washington picture, although probably not directly connected with it.

COPY: Palazzo Ruspoli, Rome. Mentioned by Rossini in 1750 (Bibl. 106b, I, p. 85) and by Roisecco in 1762 (Bibl. 150a, p. 167) as an original. At present it hangs as a pair to a painting of a *Hermit*, attributed to G. B. Castiglione, but nearer to the early Baciccio.

NOTES: The provenance from the Soderini collection has been challenged (e.g. by Salerno, Bibl. 1282, p. 97) on the grounds that no collection of this name was traceable. In fact, however, from the mid-sixteenth century the Soderini family lived in a palace near the Ripetta, which included the Mausoleum of Augustus, and owned an important collection of ancient statues (cf. Ulisse Aldroandus, *Delle statue antiche . . .*, Venice, 1556, p. 201). The palace still belonged to the family in 1678, when it is mentioned in F. Francini's *Roma antica e moderna*, Rome, 1678, p. 468), but by the beginning of the eighteenth century it had apparently been sold and belonged to a Portuguese, the Marchese Correa. After changing hands again in the nineteenth century, it was pulled down when the area round the Mausoleum of Augustus was cleared in the 1930's.

In the seventeenth century the Soderini owned paintings attributed to Salvator Rosa and Honthorst (cf. Blunt, Bibl. 1426, pp. 60 f.). Moreover, when Chantelou was in Rome on his mission to fetch Poussin, the latter showed him the Soderini chapel in S. Maria del Popolo, and Chantelou was so much interested in the frescoes which adorned it that during Poussin's visit to Paris the artist thought it worth while reporting to his patron that the author of these frescoes was passing through Paris (cf. Blunt, *ibid.*). There is, therefore, no inherent improbability in the traditional provenance.

Salerno identified the Washington picture with one mentioned in the 1638 inventory of the Giustiniani collection and in early accounts of the collection (cf. Silos, Bibl. 61, p. 120, and Sirén, Bibl. 63, p. 174). The dimensions given in the inventory (6×4 palmi, i.e. 132×88 cm.) agree very closely with those of the Washington picture. It is, of course, possible that the Giustiniani may have sold or given away their picture at an early date, a hypothesis which would be supported by the fact that it is not mentioned in any of the later accounts of the collection.

The picture is dated by Mahon (Bibl. 1367, p. XI) to the years 1631–33. In my opinion it should be dated much earlier, *c.* 1626–27, near the *Parnassus* (No. 129), the Chigi *Children's Bacchanals* (Nos. 192, 193), and the first stage of the Dulwich *David* (No. 33).

BIBLIOGRAPHY: Sandrart, p. 258; Waagen, Bibl. 384b, III, p. 406; Magne, 1914, p. 209 n. 1; Blunt, Bibl. 1227, p. 170; *Exposition Poussin (Louvre)*, No. 7; Mahon, Bibl. 1271, pp. 292, 297; Salerno, Bibl. 1282, p. 97; Mahon, Bibl. 1367, pp. XI, 32, 49, 50, 55; Blunt, Bibl. 1426, pp. 60 f.

93. THE ASSUMPTION OF THE VIRGIN. Oil on canvas partly composed of silk threads (cf. Hours, Bibl. 1256, p. 34). 57×40 cm. Musée du Louvre, Paris (718).

HISTORY: Painted for Henri d'Etampes-Valençay, French Ambassador in Rome, and finished on 21.i.1650 (*Correspondance*, p. 411); probably belonged to Louis Cauchon Hesselin, Sieur de Condé, who died in 1664 (Wildenstein, Bibl. 1164, p. 62); certainly to Séraphin de Mauroy, who died in 1668 and whose name appears on the engraving by Pesne; and to Jean Néret de la Ravoye, from whom it was bought by Louis XIV in 1685 (*Comptes des bâtiments*, II, pp. 581, 661).

DRAWING: Musée du Louvre, Paris (*CR*, I, p. 35, No. A 14). Studio drawing.

ENGRAVINGS: 1. By J. Pesne (Andresen, No. 233; Wildenstein, No. 84; Davies and Blunt, p. 212, No. 84).
2. Attributed to A. Voet (Wildenstein, No. 83; Davies and Blunt, p. 212, No. 83).
3. By J. N. Laugier (Andresen, No. 234).
4. By P. Bettelini (Andresen, No. 235).
5. By J. Dughet; dedicated to Teodora dal Pozzo (in the Albertina; not listed by Andresen).

COPIES: 1. Mrs. C. H. Hamilton, Christchurch, New Zealand.
2. Musée Fabre, Montpellier (714).
3. St. Denis-du-Saint-Sacrement, Paris (*Inventaire général des Richesses d'Art, Paris, Monuments religieux*, (Bibl. 563, III, p. 282).
4. Saintes Cathedral.
According to Magne (1914, p. 208, No. 184) there are also copies in the museum of Quimper, and in the churches of Varennes, Girolles and La Bussière, all in the Loiret.

NOTES: The painting was presumably commissioned after the arrival of Etampes-Valençay as ambassador in July 1649 (cf. C. Bittner and L. Gross, *Repertorium der diplomatischen Vertreter*, Berlin 1936, I, p. 227).

As has been pointed out by Stein (Bibl. 1079, p. 11), the group is based on Raphael's composition of *Psyche carried to Heaven*, engraved by Marcantonio (Bartsch, XV, p. 36, No. 5).

Sandrart mentions a painting of the *Assumption*, but it is not clear to which version he is referring.

BIBLIOGRAPHY: *Correspondance*, p. 411; *Comptes des bâtiments*, II, pp. 581, 661; Sandrart, p. 258; Piganiol de La Force, Bibl. 124, I, p. 146; Bailly, p. 312; Dézallier, 1745, II, pp. 254, 255, and 1762, IV, pp. 39, 40; Gault de Saint-Germain, Pt. II, pp. 39 f.; Smith, No. 142; Friedlaender, 1914, pp. 91, 121; Grautoff, I, p. 275, II, No. 147; Magne, 1914, pp. 84 n. 2, 208, No. 184; Stein, Bibl. 1079, p. 11; Wildenstein, Bibl. 1164, pp. 62, 111; Delbourgo and Petit, Bibl. 1243, pp. 49 f.; Hours, Bibl. 1256, p. 34; *Exposition Poussin (Louvre)*, No. 95; *Exposition Poussin (Rouen)*, No. 87; *L'ideale classico (Bologna)*, No. 79; Mahon, Bibl. 1367, p. 115; Wild, Bibl. 1383, p. 225.

94. THE VIRGIN PROTECTING THE CITY OF SPOLETO. Panel. 48×37 cm. Alleyn's College of God's Gift, Dulwich, London (263).

HISTORY: Perhaps painted for Cassiano dal Pozzo (see below). About 1800 belonged to Noël Desenfans; bequeathed by him to Sir Francis Bourgeois in 1807, and by him to Dulwich College in 1811.

ENGRAVING: By R. Cockburn (Andresen, No. 450).

NOTES: The painting was described in the nineteenth century as an *Assumption*, but this identification does not seem to be correct, since neither tomb nor Apostles are depicted. Moreover, the town in the middle-distance seems fairly certainly to represent Spoleto, of which Urban VIII and, after his election as pope in 1623, his nephew, Cardinal Francesco Barberini, were archbishops (Blunt, Bibl. 1026, p. 8). In the catalogue of the Louvre exhibition (*Exposition Poussin* (*Louvre*), No. 43) I suggested that the picture might have been painted for Cardinal Francesco, but it is not mentioned in any of the available accounts of the Barberini collection, and it seems more likely that it was commissioned by Pozzo, who owned a landscape of Grottaferrata, of which Cardinal Francesco was abbott, a subject which would provide an analogy to the depiction of Spoleto in the Dulwich painting (cf. Blunt, Bibl. 1426, p. 62).

X-ray examination reveals the fact that the picture is painted over a composition showing a nymph asleep in a landscape. Poussin turned the panel upside down and probably cut it down before painting the picture that we now see (cf. X-ray reproduction preceding p. 181 below).

Dated by Mahon 1636–38 (Bibl. 1367, p. XIII). I should myself still maintain my previous suggestion of *c.* 1635 (*Exposition Poussin* (*Louvre*), No. 43).

BIBLIOGRAPHY: Waagen, Bibl. 384b, II, p. 347; Magne, 1914, p. 209, No. 185; Blunt, Bibl. 1026, p. 8, and Bibl. 1167, pp. 77, 79; *Exposition Poussin* (*Louvre*), No. 43; Mahon, Bibl. 1271, p. 303; Kitson, Bibl. 1335, p. 145; Mahon, Bibl. 1367, pp. XIII, 103; Blunt, Bibl. 1462, p. 62.

5

SAINTS

95. THE MYSTIC MARRIAGE OF ST. CATHERINE. Panel. 127×167·5 cm. Sir John Heathcoat Amory, Tiverton, Devon.

HISTORY: Cassiano dal Pozzo (Haskell and Rinehart, Bibl. 1254, pp. 321, 325). In 1781 belonged to Humphrey Morice at Chiswick (Walpole, Bibl. 192, p. 78); bt. from him with his whole collection by Lord Ashburnham in 1786 (Reynolds, Bibl. 281, p. 150); Ashburnham sale, Christie, London, 20.vii.1850, lot 9; S. Woodburn sale, Christie, London, 24.vi.1853, lot 72, bt. Pearce (no size given, but the description fits the Heathcoat Amory painting. The Woodburn picture is said in the catalogue to come from the Montcalm Gallery, but no such picture appears in the Montcalm sale, Christie, London, 4 f.v.1849); perhaps anon. sale, Phillips, London, 3.vi.1856, lot 61; T. Kibble sale, Christie, London, 5.vi.1886, lot 93, (as from the Ashburnham collection), bt. Lesser. Sir Herbert Cook; by descent to Sir Francis Cook; bt. from him by Agnew's in 1946, and from them by the present owner in the same year.

NOTES: Rejected by Grautoff (II, p. 280). Dated by Mahon 1631–33 (Bibl. 1367, p. XI). In my view to be dated near the *St. Erasmus* and the large figure compositions, *c.* 1627–29. For a discussion of the dating see the *Inspiration of the Epic Poet* (No. 124).

BIBLIOGRAPHY: De Cotte, Bibl. 98, III, p. 153, and Bibl. 98a, p. 203; Walpole, Bibl. 192, p. 78; Smith, No. 146; Brockwell, Bibl. 720, III, No. 429; Grautoff, II, p. 280; Magne, 1914, p. 210, No. 213; Royal Academy, London, Bibl. 879, p. 32, No. 115; Blunt, Bibl. 1002, p. 220, and Bibl. 1003, p. 266; Bertin-Mourot, Bibl. 1023, p. 48, No. XV; Blunt, Bibl. 1086, pp. 184, 185, and Bibl. 1086a, pp. 160, 161; Licht, p. 89; Blunt, Bibl. 1167, p. 79, and Bibl. 1227, pp. 166, 176; Haskell and Rinehart, Bibl. 1254, pp. 321, 325; Mahon, Bibl. 1269, p. 250; Rinehart, Bibl. 1281, pp. 25, 29; Mahon, Bibl. 1367, pp. XI, 4, 51 f., 55, 57, 59 f., 75 f., 78.

96. ST. CECILIA. 118×88 cm. Museo del Prado, Madrid (2317).

HISTORY: Recorded as being saved from the fire in the Alcazar in Madrid in 1734.

NOTES: Dated by Grautoff 1627–28 (II, No. 13), by Mahon 1628–29 (Bibl. 1367, p. 4), and rejected by Wild (Bibl. 1312, p. 158). The picture is certainly an original, in my opinion probably painted just before rather than just after the *St. Erasmus*, that is to say 1627–28 rather than 1628–29.

BIBLIOGRAPHY: Ponz, Bibl. 238a, p. 529, par. 49; Cumberland, Bibl. 285.1, p. 85; Smith, No. 157; Grautoff, I, p. 81, II, No. 13; Magne, 1914, p. 213, No. 234; Blunt, Bibl. 1003, p. 266, and Bibl. 1227, p. 167; Mahon, Bibl. 1271, p. 296; Wild, Bibl. 1312, p. 158; Mahon, Bibl. 1367, pp. 4, 29.

97. THE MARTYRDOM OF ST. ERASMUS. 320×186 cm., with insertion of new canvas, *c.* 45×12 cm., in the two lower corners. Signed: *Nicolaus Pusin fecit*. Pinacoteca del Vaticano, Rome.

HISTORY: Commissioned for St. Peter's in February 1628; payments from June to September 1629, with a special additional payment in October 1629 (cf. Pollak, Bibl. 832, II, pp. 74 ff., 87, 272, 540 f.). For the negotiations preceding the commission, see text volume, pp. 85 ff. Replaced by a mosaic and removed to the Quirinal before 1763 (Titi, Bibl. 65d, p. 306). Taken to Paris in 1797 (Blumer, Bibl. 314, p. 333) and returned to Rome after 1815.

DRAWINGS: 1. Uffizi, Florence (*CR*, I, p. 39, No. 73).

2. Musée Bonnat, Bayonne. Copy after the painting, perhaps by Jan Bisschop.

3. Musée du Louvre, Paris (32542). Copies of individual figures from the painting. Eighteenth century, probably French.

4. Gabinetto Nazionale, Rome (FN9920). A reversed copy of the painting.

ENGRAVING: By G. M. Mitelli (Andresen, No. 237; Wildenstein, No. 86; Davies and Blunt, p. 212, No. 86).

COPIES: 1. In the seventeenth century a version described as 'une esquisse fort finie', belonged to Passart (Loménie de Brienne, p. 218). As what appears to be the original sketch remained in Italy (see No. 98), this was probably one of the small copies listed below.

2. Cathedral, La Rochelle. In reverse.

3. Principe di Palestrina, Palazzo Barberini, Rome. Grautoff (II, p. 30 under No. 15) mentions it as a copy. Thuillier (Bibl. 1298, p. 275) reports the view of the Marchese Giovanni Incisa della Rocchetta that it may well be the original sketch. Exhibited in *I Francesi a Roma*, Palazzo Braschi, Rome, 1961, No. 257.

4. Sir John Clerk, Penicuik House, Midlothian.

5. Ritter collection, Basle. Inherited from the family of Migneron-Ritter (47 × 31 cm.).

6. Private collection, Fribourg, Switzerland (cf. Reiners, Bibl. 857, pp. 43 ff.).

7. A. Dumont collection, Cambrai (cf. Mantz, Bibl. 493, p. 312).

8. 'Mr. de Bary's sale', London, undated (but eighteenth century), lot 52.

9. Martin sale, Paillet, Paris, 5.iv.1802, lot 143 (24 × 15 inches).

10. Anon. sale, Christie, London, 1.vi.1810, lot 145.

11. L. Robicquet sale, Delaroche, Paris, 23 ff.iii.1813, lot 131.

12. Girodet-Trioson sale, Pérignon, Paris, 11.iv.1825, lot 434 (22 × 11 inches).

13. Bugge sale, Haagen, Copenhagen, 21.viii.1837, lot 477 (39 × 28½ inches).

14. Mme Gentil-Chavagnac sale, George, Paris, 20.vi.1854, lot 44 (67 × 53 cm.).

A painting of this subject in the church of Garlenda, near Albenga (Liguria), attributed to Poussin and given to the church by Pier Francesco Costa, bishop of Albenga, is a free variant of the Vatican picture, apparently by a French painter of the generation of Lebrun working in Rome (cf. Ratti, Bibl. 228a, II, p. 16).

NOTES: Grautoff (II, No. 15) says that the signature is false, but both Bellori (p. 414) and Félibien (IV, p. 19) specifically state that Poussin signed the picture himself.

For the history of the commission and the relation of Poussin's composition to drawings made by Pietro da Cortona, see text volume, pp. 85 ff. Félibien (*loc. cit.*) says that Poussin obtained the commission through Pozzo, but Bernini (Chantelou, 1885, p. 146, and 1960, p. 128) told Chantelou that he was responsible for its being given to the artist. It is, of course, quite possible that both men recommended him.

M. Stein (Bibl. 1079, p. 5) has pointed out that the general composition of the *St. Erasmus* belongs to the same type as Veronese's *Martyrdom of SS. Primus and Felicianus*, now in the Museo Civico at Padua (cf. R. Pallucchini, *Veronese*, Bergamo, 1943, Pl. 62). Though the similarity exists, it is unlikely that there is any direct connection, since in Poussin's time Veronese's altarpiece was at Praglia, where Poussin is unlikely to have seen it. Both Veronese's and Poussin's compositions are more likely to derive from Titian's Pesaro altarpiece in the Frari (cf. H. Tietze, *Titian*, Vienna and London, 1937, Pl. 81), which Poussin would certainly have seen on his short visit to Venice. As Stein (*loc. cit.*) suggests, the two flying putti come from Titian's *Peter Martyr*, then in SS. Giovanni e Paolo, Venice (cf. Tietze, *op. cit.*, Pl. 300), but the similarity which he sees between the horseman in the *St. Erasmus* and one in Veronese's *Martyrdom of St. Sebastian* in S. Sebastiano, Venice (cf. G. Fiocco, *Paolo Veronese*, Bologna, 1928, Pl. XX) is perhaps not so evident. These Venetian elements were definitely due to Poussin, since they do not occur in the drawings made by Pietro da Cortona for the altarpiece, which in other respects influenced Poussin's composition.

BIBLIOGRAPHY: Mancini, Bibl. 1, II, p. 171 n. 1255; Baglione, Bibl. 4, p. 337, and Bibl. 4b, p. 69; Ferrari, Bibl. 9, p. 49; Malvasia, Bibl. 30, p. 48; Skippon, Bibl. 34.1, p. 650; Chantelou, 1885, pp. 67, 72, 146, and 1960, pp. 125 f., 128; Félibien, III, p. 227, IV, p. 19; Montaiglon and Guiffrey, Bibl. 45, XVI, pp. 449, 466; Bellori, pp. 413 f.; Sirén, Bibl. 63, pp. 157, 167; Titi, Bibl. 65d, p. 306; Sandrart, p. 257; Passeri, p. 325; Baldinucci, XVI, p. 101; Loménie de Brienne, p. 214; Bonanni, Bibl. 111, p. 111; Florent Le Comte, III, p. 25; Rogissart, Bibl. 128a, II, p. 133; De Brosses, Bibl. 170a, II, p. 463; Dézallier, 1745, II, pp. 249, 253, and 1762, IV, pp. 28, 38; Bardon, II, p. 126; La Lande, Bibl. 224a, IV, p. 404; (Weston), Bibl. 254, p. 173; Canova, Bibl. 261, p. 116, wrongly called *S. Quirino*; Cambry, Bibl. 272a, p. 20; Prunetti, Bibl. 284, p. 105; Ramdohr, Bibl. 287, II, p. 195; Martyn, Bibl. 296, p. 213; Blumer, Bibl. 314, p. 333; Smith, No. 155; Knowles, Bibl. 392, II, pp. 270 f.; Burckhardt, Bibl. 465b, p. 977; Friedlaender, 1914, pp. 35 f., 112, 143;

Grautoff, I, p. 81, II, No. 15; Magne, 1914, pp. 82, 210, No. 215; Pollak, Bibl. 832, II, pp. 87, 272, 540; Alpatov, Bibl. 882, pp. 16 f.; Brieger, Bibl. 915, p. 356; Mahon, Bibl. 992, pp. 18, 19 f.; Blunt, Bibl. 1003, p. 266; Jamot, pp. 11, 38, 83; Costello, Bibl. 1052, pp. 250 and n. 3, 264; Stein, Bibl. 1079, p. 5; Blunt, Bibl. 1086, pp. 183 f., and Bibl. 1086a, pp. 159 f.; Licht, p. 87; Hess, Bibl. 1157, pp. 262 ff.; Blunt, Bibl. 1226, p. 399, and Bibl. 1227, p. 165; Bousquet, Bibl. 1231, p. 4; Briganti, Bibl. 1232, pp. 16 ff.; Mahon, Bibl. 1269, pp. 245 ff., and Bibl. 1271, pp. 291, 295, 297; Thuillier, Bibl. 1295, pp. 52 f., Bibl. 1296, pp. 76 ff., and Bibl. 1298, p. 264; Crelly, Bibl. 1361, p. 36; Mahon, Bibl. 1367, pp. X f., 4, 19, 24, 29, 57, 75 ff., 84, 86, 133, 137. The *St. Erasmus* is also mentioned in all the guide books to Rome.

98. THE MARTYRDOM OF ST. ERASMUS. 100×74 cm. Signora Ojetti, Il Salviatino, Florence.

HISTORY: Recorded as in the Palazzo Barberini by Tessin in 1687–88 (Bibl. 63, p. 167) and almost certainly acquired by Cardinal Francesco Barberini. Passed by inheritance to the Colonna di Sciarra through the marriage of Cornelia Costanza Barberini (1716–97) to Giulio Cesare Colonna di Sciarra in 1728 (cf. P. Picchiai, *I Barberini*, Rome, 1959, p. 260). Recorded as in their palace by Manazzale in 1816 (Bibl. 308b, I, p. 207) and by Burckhardt in 1855 (Bibl. 465b, pp. 977 f.). Bt. from the Colonna di Sciarra by Fairfax Murray before 1914 (Grautoff, II, No. 14) and sold by him to Ugo Ojetti, Florence (cf. Royal Academy, London, Bibl. 879, No. 116).

COPY: Musée du Louvre, Paris. Presented by Ernest May in 1923 (99×74 cm.). This version follows the Ojetti painting in all the details in which the latter differs from the altarpiece itself.

NOTES: This painting, which is certainly from the hand of Poussin himself, is probably the *modello* made for submission to the authorities ordering the altarpiece. It is rather bigger than the normal *modello* and it is tempting at first sight to think that it might be a reduced version made by the artist for a small oratory. On the other hand, when Tessin saw it in 1687–88 (Bibl. 63, p. 167), it was hung in the state rooms of the Palazzo Barberini, together with a number of paintings and statues, and there is no reason to think that it had ever actually been in an oratory of the palace. The small version only differs from the altarpiece in minor details: the man whose head appears just below the arm of the priest and the man turning the windlass are both bare-headed, whereas in the finished picture the former wears a turban and the latter a white *bandeau*; and the vestments of the saint lying in the foreground are plain in the small picture but of rich brocade in the altarpiece itself.

BIBLIOGRAPHY: Sirén, Bibl. 63, p. 167; de Cotte, Bibl. 98, III, p. 154, and Bibl. 98a, p. 204; La Roque, Bibl. 248, II, p. 244, as *St. Andrew*; Martyn, Bibl. 296, p. 220; Vasi, Bibl. 298e, I, p. 21; Manazzale, Bibl. 308b, I, p. 207; Dalmazzone, Bibl. 325a and b, p. 200; Nibby, Bibl. 383, I, p. 78, and Bibl. 383a, I, p. 75; Melchiorri, Bibl. 408, p. 566; Burckhardt, Bibl. 465b, pp. 977 f.; Chennevières-Pointel, Bibl. 629, p. 103; Grautoff, II, No. 14; Palais Pitti, Florence, Bibl. 981, No. 17; Licht, p. 87; Thuillier, Bibl. 1298, p. 276.

99. THE VISION OF STA. FRANCESCA ROMANA. Original lost.

HISTORY: Almost certainly commissioned by Cardinal Giulio Rospigliosi, later Clement IX (see below).

ENGRAVINGS: 1. By Pietro del Po (Andresen, No. 245; Wildenstein, No. 89; Davies and Blunt, p. 212, No. 89).   2. By G. Audran (Andresen, No. 244).

NOTES: The engraving by Pietro del Po is dedicated to Cardinal Giulio Rospigliosi, and the picture is recorded in the Rospigliosi inventory made in 1713 as follows:
'No. 289. Un quadro in tela di p. 4 e 5 . . . rappresenta una *Verità* (?) con alcune Frezze in mano, una Donna che prega, una morta, un Angelo, opera di Nicolò Pusino' (Zeri, Bibl. 1216, p. 309).
It is not clear what the word read by Zeri as *Verità* really is, but the description fits the composition in all essentials.

The subject, rarely depicted, is the appearance of the Virgin to Sta. Francesca Romana, who had prayed to her to implore her to stop a plague which had struck the city of Rome (cf. Jameson, Bibl. 613, p. 152).

Since the original of the painting is lost, the problem of the date must remain unsettled, but since it appears to have been commissioned by Cardinal Rospigliosi, it must be placed either before 1644 or after 1653, because the Cardinal was absent from Rome as Nuncio in Spain during the period 1644–53 (cf.

Mahon, Bibl. 1367, p. 115). Poussin was undoubtedly working for him before the journey to Paris in 1640, but the composition as known from the engraving suggests a later date. The almost expressionless faces and the heavy drapery indicate the mid-fifties, and there is a close similarity between the pose of the saint and that of the Virgin in the National Gallery *Annunciation* of 1657.

BIBLIOGRAPHY: Gault de Saint-Germain, Pt. II, p. 31; Smith, No. 143; Jameson, Bibl. 613, p. 152; Grautoff, II, p. 256; Magne, 1914, p. 215, No. 273; Zeri, Bibl. 1216, p. 309; Blunt, Bibl. 1426, p. 66.

100. LANDSCAPE WITH ST. FRANCIS. 117×193 cm. Palace of the President of Jugoslavia, Belgrade.

HISTORY: Belonged in the seventeenth century to the Marquis de Hauterive (see below). Probably Crozat sale, Delatour, Paris, June 1751, lot 223 (43 × 72 inches, as engraved by Châtillon), and anon. (= Martin and Donjeu) sale, Basan, Paris, 7 ff.v.1778, lot 71 (5 × 7½ feet; withdrawn). Bt. by J. Böhler, Munich, in 1931, from Anthony Reyre, London; sold to Prince Paul of Jugoslavia; passed to the Jugoslav State.

ENGRAVING: Published by Châtillon (Andresen, No. 458; Wildenstein, No. 190).

COPY: Musée Ingres, Montauban (Grautoff, II, No. 124; Magne, 1914, p. 216, No. 298; 63×85 cm.). This is probably the picture recorded in the Le Doux sale, Joullain, Paris, 24.iv.1775, lot 41, in the Didot de St. Marc sale, Detouches, Paris, 26 ff.iii.1810, lot 171 (65×97 cm., the dimensions perhaps including the frame), and the Cardinal Fesch sale, George, Rome, 17 ff.iii.1845, Part II, lot 1778.

NOTES: Both Félibien (IV, p. 150) and Loménie de Brienne (p. 215) refer to the picture as belonging to the Marquis de Hauterive, but at the times they wrote (1685 and 1693–95) there does not seem to have been anyone who officially held that title. It belonged to the family of l'Aubespine, who were Seigneurs de Hauterive, but the actual title Marquis de Hauterive seems only to have been used by François de l'Aubespine, brother of the chancellor, Châteauneuf, who died in 1670. His two sons, Charles and Philippe, who were both alive when Félibien wrote, used the titles of Marquis de Châteauneuf (d. 1716) and Comte de Sagonne (d.1686; cf. Père Anselme de Ste. Marie, *Histoire généalogique et chronologique de la maison royale de France*, Paris, 1726–33, VI, pp. 558 ff.).

Although Félibien (*loc. cit.*) is quite explicit about the fact that the picture actually belonged to the Marquis de Hauterive at the time he wrote ('qui est chez Monsieur le Marquis de Hauterive'), he may have been using out-of-date information and have been referring to François de l'Aubespine, who died in 1670. Alternatively François's son, Charles, may unofficially have used the title Marquis de Hauterive, which he would have inherited from his father. This hypothesis is confirmed by the fact that in 1685 Louis XIV bought two paintings, by Bassano and Rubens, from the 'Sᵣ Marquis d'Hauterive' (*Comptes des bâtiments*, II, pp. 585, 663). It is quite possible that Charles de l'Aubespine inherited the pictures from his father, but there is no reason to believe the statement made by Grautoff (II, No. 124) that it was actually painted for a member of the Hauterive family.

The painting has usually been called either *Landscape with three Monks*, or *Les Solitaires*, or *Une solitude*, but in the catalogue of the Crozat sale it is pointed out that the monks are Franciscans, and there can be little doubt that the subject is actually St. Francis in retreat at La Verna during the days before he received the Stigmata (see text volume, pp. 293 f.). Very similar scenes are shown in a drawing by Polidoro da Caravaggio from the Fenwick collection, now in the British Museum (see text volume, Fig. 230), and in a fresco of *St. Francis receiving the Stigmata* by Girolamo Muziano, formerly in the church of SS. Apostoli, Rome, destroyed in 1730, but recorded in an engraving by Cornelis Cort (rep. J. C. J. Bierens de Haan, *L'Oeuvre gravé de Cornelis Cort*, The Hague, 1948, Pl. opp. p. 136).

The picture was dated 1645–48 by Grautoff (*loc. cit.*), who only knew the copy at Montauban. In the catalogue of the Louvre exhibition (*Exposition Poussin (Louvre)*, p. 265) Sterling suggested that it might be the *Calme* painted for Pointel as a pair to the *Orage* (cf. Félibien, IV, p. 63), which would give a date of 1651–52. Mahon (Bibl. 1338, pp. 125, 127) accepts this dating, but proposes that the picture may have been painted for Pointel as a pendant to the National Gallery *Landscape with a Man killed by a Snake* (No. 209). Although there is no direct evidence that the *St. Francis* ever belonged to Pointel, the fact that both it and the National Gallery picture appear to represent precise sites rather supports this hypothesis. As regards dating, it seems to me difficult to be precise, but I should tend to place the picture in the years 1648–50 rather than in 1651–52.

If the Belgrade and National Gallery pictures are in fact a pair, then the identity of the *Calme* remains an open question. The possibility would occur that it might be the Landscape in the Prado (No. 216; *q.v.*).

BIBLIOGRAPHY: Félibien, IV, p. 150; Loménie de Brienne, p. 215; Le Blanc, Bibl. 180, p. 156; Smith, No. 313; Friedlaender, 1914, p. 126; Blunt, Bibl. 972, p. 157; Dorival, Bibl. 1088, p. 51; Licht, p. 155; *Exposition Poussin (Louvre)*, p. 265; Mahon, Bibl. 1338, pp. 125, 127, and Bibl. 1367, p. 120.

101. THE MIRACLE OF ST. FRANCIS XAVIER. 444×234 cm. Musée du Louvre, Paris (723).

HISTORY: Commissioned by Sublet de Noyers in 1641. The commission is first mentioned in a letter of 16.vi.1641 (*Correspondance*, p. 77); on 2.vii.1641 Poussin was reading the lives of St. Ignatius and St. Francis Xavier to find a suitable subject (*ibid.*, p. 83); in August he is about to begin the picture (*ibid.*, p. 87) and was still working on it in November of the same year (*ibid.*, p. 106). Acquired by Louis XV in 1763 on the suppression of the Jesuit Order in France.

DRAWING: Hermitage Museum, Leningrad (*CR*, I, p. 39, No. A 19). Probably a copy of a lost drawing.

ENGRAVINGS: 1. Published by E. Gantrel (Andresen, No. 238; Wildenstein, No. 87; Davies and Blunt, p. 212, No. 87).
2. By P. Drevet (Andresen, No. 239; see also Davies and Blunt, p. 212 under No. 87, where the existence of this plate is doubted. It is, however, mentioned by Landon under plate CXXVI, as well as by Andresen).

COPIES: 1. Formerly in the collection of Count Fries; passed *c.* 1820 to Baron Speck von Sternburg (cf. Frimmel, Bibl. 719, I, p. 430, and Dussieux, Bibl. 470, p. 96). 23½×13 inches.
2. Dufourny sale, Delaroche, Paris, 22 ff.xi.1819, lot 87.

NOTES: Wildenstein (under No. 87) points out that the engraving by Gantrel shows the composition with considerable additions at both sides and suggests that the original may have been cut down. He quotes the correspondence between d'Angiviller and Pierre in 1788 (Bibl. 244, pp. 194 f., 198) as supporting this hypothesis, but in fact the correspondence shows fairly certainly that, although the possibility of cutting the picture was discussed, nothing was actually done. The additions are not at all consistent with Poussin's style in this painting and in fact disturb the harmony of the composition, distracting the eye from the central group, and leaving two awkward gaps in the upper corners. Further evidence is supplied by the drawing in the Hermitage, which, though not by Poussin himself, no doubt preserves the composition of an original drawing and is similar in format to the picture as it now exists. The evidence supplied by the engraving in the 'Petit Marot' (i.e. Jean Marot, *Recueil des plans profils et elevations de plusieurs palais chasteaux eglises sepultures grotes et hostels*, n.p., *c.* 1660–70) is ambiguous, because it shows the space for the altar-piece in a form slightly broader than the picture in its present state, but not nearly so broad as it appears in Gantrel's engraving.

The eighteenth-century guides (e.g. Piganiol de La Force, Bibl. 173, VI, p. 355, and Dézallier d'Argenville, Bibl. 183, p. 241) state that the altar was rebuilt in 1709, and it is conceivable that the painting may have been slightly narrowed at that stage. It was relined by Hacquin and Godefroy in 1786 (d'Angiviller, Bibl. 276, p. 161).

BIBLIOGRAPHY: *Correspondance*, pp. 77, 80, 83, 87, 92, 94, 97, 100, 106; *Basilica in honorem . . .*, Bibl. 5, and Bibl. 5a, pp. 69 f.; Fréart de Chambray, Bibl. 16, Preface; Sauval, Bibl. 23, I, p. 462, and Bibl. 23a, p. 147; *Les choses . . . remarquables de Paris*, Bibl. 29b, p. 110; Chantelou, 1885, pp. 32, 83, and 1960, pp. 124, 126; Félibien, III, pp. 205 f., IV, pp. 38 f., 48 f., 91, 118 f.; Bellori, p. 429; Passeri, p. 330; Baldinucci, XVI, p. 104; Brice, Bibl. 89a, II, p. 205, Bibl. 89 f., III, p. 377, and Bibl. 89g, III, pp. 437 ff.; Catherinot, Bibl. 94, p. 15, and Bibl. 94b, p. 196; *Mémoires inédits*, I, p. 356; Loménie de Brienne, p. 214; Perrault, Bibl. 113, I, p. 90; Florent Le Comte, III, p. 29; [C. Saugrain], Bibl. 138a, II, p. 81; Antonini, Bibl. 160b, p. 64; Piganiol de La Force, Bibl. 173, VI, p. 355; Dézallier, 1745, II, pp. 250, 254, and 1762, IV, pp. 29, 39; Dézallier d'Argenville, Bibl. 183, p. 241; Marigny, Bibl. 191, pp. 253 f., 257, 259; Lépicié, Bibl. 194, I, p. LXIX; Ponz, Bibl. 238a, p. 1733, par. 81; d'Angiviller, Bibl. 244, pp. 194 f., 198, and Bibl. 276, p. 161; Cambry, Bibl. 272a, p. 22; Guibal, Bibl. 273, p. 32; Tuétey, Bibl. 295, I, p. 292; Gault de Saint-Germain, Pt. II, p. 29; Smith, No. 158; Bürger, Bibl. 490, p. 272; Friedlaender, 1914, pp. 75 f., 116, 211; Grautoff, I, p. 212, II, No. 101; Magne, 1914, pp. 124, 126 ff., 132, 214, No. 263; Jamot, p. 83; Blunt, Bibl. 1065, p. 370; Licht, p. 131; Hess, Bibl. 1157, p. 275; Vanuxem, Bibl. 1182, pp. 88 f.; *Exposition Poussin (Louvre)*, No. 62; Mahon, Bibl. 1269, p. 260.

102. THE VIRGIN APPEARING TO ST. JAMES. 301×242 cm. Musée du Louvre, Paris (719).

HISTORY: Painted for a church in Valenciennes (Bellori, p. 414; Félibien, IV, p. 20). Duc de Richelieu; bt. with his collection by Louis XIV in 1665 (Ferraton, Bibl. 1043, pp. 439, 446).

NOTES: According to the Spanish version of the legend of St. James the Great, the Virgin appeared to him and his companions at Saragossa, seated on a column. Hence the title of *Virgén del Pilar* usually given to pictures of this subject.

According to Bellori the picture was painted for 'Valentien in Fiandra', that is to say for Valenciennes, which till its capture by Louis XIV was part of the Spanish Netherlands. Félibien is less precise, but says that it was sent 'en Flandres'.

Some confusion has been caused by the statement made by Dézallier d'Argenville in the first edition of his *Vies* (1745, II, p. 254) that the painting was in the church of Nuestra Señora del Pilar at Saragossa. This statement was copied by Palomino in the French translation of his *Museo Pictorico*, published in 1749 (Bibl. 136a, p. 180), but was corrected by Dézallier d'Argenville in the 1762 edition of his *Vies* (IV, p. 39), where he states, correctly, that the picture was in the French Royal Collection. The confusion may have been due to thinking that the painting must have been executed for the church built to commemorate the miracle which it represents, or to a confusion between Valenciennes and Valencia, where St. James is supposed to have landed.

The date of the picture can be fixed to 1629–30, since Bellori says that it was painted 'circa gl'istessi tempi' as the *St. Erasmus* of 1628–29, and Félibien says 'vers 1630'.

Sterling (*Exposition Poussin (Louvre)*, p. 223) has pointed out that there was a church of St. Jacques in Valenciennes, which contained a painting of St. James attributed to Van Dyck, now in the museum at Valenciennes. It is quite possible that Poussin's work may have been commissioned for it, perhaps through a Spaniard living in Rome, and looted during the campaigns before the Peace of the Pyrenees in 1659.

For a discussion of this painting, see text volume, p. 92.

BIBLIOGRAPHY: Chantelou, 1885, p. 234, and 1960, p. 132; Félibien, IV, p. 20; Bellori, p. 414; Baldinucci, XVI, p. 101; Loménie de Brienne, p. 214; Florent Le Comte, III, p. 25; Piganiol de La Force, Bibl. 124a, I, p. 84; Bailly, p. 307; Palomino, Bibl. 136a, p. 180; Monicart, Bibl. 144, I, p. 119; Dézallier, 1745, II, p. 254, and 1762, IV, p. 39, Dézallier d'Argenville, Bibl. 183, p. 344; Bardon, II, p. 125; La Roque, Bibl. 248, I, p. 142; Cambry, Bibl. 272a, p. 20; Smith, No. 144; Guiffrey, Bibl. 581, p. 104; Friedlaender, 1914, pp. 11, 113; Grautoff, I, p. 82, II, No. 16; Magne, 1914, pp. 84, 155, 208, No. 183; Friedlaender, 1933, p. 324; Jamot, pp. 10 f., 21 f.; Ferraton, Bibl. 1043, pp. 439, 446; Blunt, Bibl. 1086, p. 184, and Bibl. 1086a, p. 160; Licht, p. 90; Blunt, Bibl. 1167, p. 79; Hours, Bibl. 1256, p. 14; Jullian, Bibl. 1261, p. 227; *Exposition Poussin (Louvre)*, No. 15; Mahon, Bibl. 1269, pp. 247 ff., Bibl. 1271, pp. 290 f., 295, 297, and Bibl. 1367, pp. XI, 19, 22 ff., 26, 29, 57, 60, 75.

103. LANDSCAPE WITH ST. JEROME. 155×234 cm. Museo del Prado, Madrid (2304).

HISTORY: Probably commissioned by Philip IV for the palace of Buen Retiro, near Madrid, as part of a series of paintings representing anchorites, and recorded in the inventory of the pictures there made in 1700 (cf. Blunt, Bibl. 1195, pp. 389 ff.).

NOTES: Rejected by Grautoff (II, p. 268, who ascribes it to a follower of Salvator Rosa), and by myself (Bibl. 1051, p. 70) with an attribution to the 'Silver Birch Master'. On a later occasion, however, I was able to see the picture in a good light and came to the conclusion that it was certainly an original by Poussin, of about 1637–38 (cf. Bibl. 1195, pp. 389 f.), a view that has been generally accepted. I should now incline to place the picture in 1636–37, since it must perceptibly precede the 1638 *Finding of Moses* (No. 12).

BIBLIOGRAPHY: Mabilleau, Bibl. 635, p. 307; Grautoff, II, p. 268; Magne, 1914, p. 217, No. 312; Blunt, Bibl. 1051, p. 70, and Bibl. 1195, pp. 389 f.; Kitson, Bibl. 1335, pp. 145 f.; Mahon, Bibl. 1338, p. 119, and Bibl. 1367, pp. XIII, 103, 106.

104. ST. MARGARET. 220×145 cm. About 10 cm. added at the top. Galleria Sabauda, Turin (330).

HISTORY: Prince Eugene of Savoy (d. 1736); passed at his death to his niece, Princess Victoria of Savoy, who married the Duke of Sachsen-Hildburghausen; sold by her to Charles Emmanuel III, King of Sardinia, in 1741; thence by descent in the house of Savoy (Vesme, Bibl. 596, p. 251); taken to Paris in 1799 and returned to Turin after 1815 (Blumer, Bibl. 314, p. 333).

ENGRAVINGS: 1. Published by F. Bignon (Andresen,   2. Published by Mariette (Andresen, No. 242).
No. 241; Wildenstein, No. 88; Davies and Blunt,
p. 212, No. 88).

NOTES: Rejected by Grautoff (II, p. 281) as *undiskutierbar*. The authenticity of this painting was affirmed by R. Longhi in an essay written for the Festschrift for W. Friedlaender's sixtieth birthday in 1933, but never published (cf. Friedlaender, 1933, p. 323). Longhi reaffirmed his view in 1948 (Bibl. 1048, p. 5), dating the picture to the last years of the 1630's, a view which has been generally accepted.

It is not known by whom or in what circumstances the picture was commissioned, but it may well have been through the instrumentality of Cassiano dal Pozzo's cousin, Amadeo, Marchese di Voghera, who lived in Turin and had previously commissioned the *Crossing of the Red Sea* and the *Golden Calf* (Nos. 20 and 26). The *St. Margaret* is, however, not mentioned by travellers who saw Amadeo dal Pozzo's collection, and it is likely that, if he was responsible for the commission, it was on behalf of a church rather than for himself. The scale of the painting would confirm this hypothesis, but no composition of the kind seems to be recorded by travellers in Piedmont or the authors of old guide books. Alternatively Prince Eugene may have acquired the picture as loot on one of his campaigns.

In the J. F. P. Peyron sale, Regnault, Paris, 10.vi.1816, lot 70, there appeared a 'Ste. Marguerite recevant la palme du martyre', a canvas described as 'Première manière'. This may be a sketch for the Turin painting, but there is reason to think that Poussin painted another composition of the same subject, horizontal in form, which is recorded in an engraving published by one of the Bonnart family and described by Andresen (No. 243) as follows: 'Vor Gemäuer in der Mitte des Blatts auf dem Drachen kniend, sie hält in der Rechten ein kleines Kreuz; ein Engel reicht ihr einen Kranz und eine Palme. In der Mitte unten Poussin's Name, dann: s^ta MARGARETHA und gegen rechts Bonnart's Adresse', with dimensions $12\frac{2}{3} \times 18$ inches. Wildenstein (under No. 88) mentions a *Feste de Ste. Marguerite* engraved by Nicolas Bonnart, listed by R. A. Weigert (Bibl. 945, I, p. 427), but there is no indication that it is after Poussin, and it is upright in format and so cannot correspond to Andresen No. 243, of which I have been unable to trace a copy (cf. Davies and Blunt, p. 212, No. 88, and p. 218).

BIBLIOGRAPHY: Martyn, Bibl. 296, p. 26; Blumer, Bibl. 314, p. 333; Smith, No. 156; Vesme, Bibl. 596, p. 251, No. 159; Ruskin, Bibl. 662, VII, p. 324; Grautoff, II, p. 281; Magne, 1914, p. 214, No. 262; Friedlaender, 1933, p. 323; Longhi, Bibl. 1034, p. 5; *Exposition Poussin (Louvre)*, No. 58; Mahon, Bibl. 1271, p. 304; Thuillier, Bibl. 1297, p. 43, and Bibl. 1298, p. 277; *L'ideale classico (Bologna)*, No. 70; Mahon, Bibl. 1367, pp. 114, 121.

THE SACRAMENTS

105–111. THE SEVEN SACRAMENTS (First Series).

HISTORY OF THE WHOLE SERIES: Commissioned by Cassiano dal Pozzo in the second half of the 1630's (see below); the last painting of the series was despatched from Paris on 22 May 1642 (*Correspondance*, p. 153). Passed by inheritance to Cosimo Antonio dal Pozzo, grandson of Cassiano's younger brother, Carlo Antonio (Haskell and Rinehart, Bibl. 1254, p. 319). In about 1725 Cosimo Antonio gave the series of Sacraments to the Marchese del Buffalo as a pledge for a debt of six thousand crowns; in 1729 Buffalo offered them for sale to Louis XV (Montaiglon and Guiffrey, Bibl. 45, VIII, p. 40), who, however, did not buy them (*ibid.*, p. 70). By February 1730 Pozzo had redeemed his debt and recovered the pictures (*ibid.*, p. 87). Sempill (Bibl. 163), who was in Rome in 1733, and de Brosses, who was there in 1739 (Bibl. 170a, II, p. 456), both saw the pictures in the Palazzo Pamphili, perhaps owing to a transaction similar to that between Pozzo and Buffalo. They were presumably again recovered by Pozzo, since they passed by inheritance to his daughter, Maria Laura, who married a member of the Boccapaduli family in 1727. It is not known when Pozzo died, but the date 1739 on the labels attached to the stretchers of Nos. 213 and 214, recording the transference of the pictures to Maria Laura, may be connected with the execution of Pozzo's will. At an unknown date they were actually sold to Sir Robert Walpole (d. 1745), but the export was forbidden (Whitley, Bibl. 828, II, p. 75). Late in the 1770's or early in the 1780's the Sacraments were offered to Wellbore Ellis Agar for £1,500, but he refused to buy them (Reynolds, Bibl. 281, p. 164). In 1784 or 1785 they were offered to the Duke of Rutland, through Byres, who arranged for copies to be made and substituted one by one for the originals (Whitley, *loc. cit.*). The originals arrived in London in September 1786 (Reynolds, *op. cit.* p. 160), together with the *St. John baptising* (No. 70), the duke having paid £2,000 for the eight pictures (Whitley, *loc. cit.*). They were then lined and restored by Biondi (Reynolds, *op. cit.*, pp. 163, 175) and exhibited at the Royal Academy in 1787 (Whitley, *loc. cit.*). One painting, *Penance*, was destroyed in a fire at Belvoir Castle in 1816 (Eller, Bibl. 410, pp. 290 ff.; through a confusion the painting is wrongly described as a *Last Supper*), and a second, *Baptism*, was sold in about 1939 and is now in the National Gallery, Washington. The remaining five canvases are at Belvoir Castle, near Grantham.

DRAWINGS: See entries for individual pictures.

ENGRAVINGS: By Jean Dughet (Andresen, Nos. 246–252; Wildenstein, Nos. 90–96; Davies and Blunt, p. 212, Nos. 90–96).

COPIES: 1. Copies of the whole series were made by Byres to replace the originals at the time of the sale in 1785, but they are not now traceable.
2. A set of copies after the Sacraments in the Prince de Conti sale, Remy, Paris, 8 ff.iv.1777, lot 539, may have been after the Pozzo set or after those made for Chantelou (see Nos. 112–118).

NOTES: As will be seen from the history of the series recorded above, the question of its sale by the Boccapaduli was long and complicated, but certain further points may be worth recording. In a letter to the Duke of Rutland, written in October 1786, shortly after the arrival of the pictures in London, Reynolds writes that Ellis Agar was 'very much what the vulgar call *down in the mouth*' at having missed the opportunity of buying them, and that Lord Spencer 'stood next and was to have had them if your Grace had declined the purchase' (*op. cit.* pp. 164 f.).

Byres had apparently begun to replace the originals with copies even before he approached the Duke of Rutland in 1785, for La Lande, who had admired the Sacraments in 1765–66, records in the second edition of his *Voyage* (Bibl. 224a, V, p. 291, note) that 'un amateur' who had visited the palace in 1784 told him that of the seven pictures shown only two were originals, and this is confirmed by the undated letter of Byres to the Duke of Rutland, in which he first offers them to the duke for sale, where he says: 'I am in possession of four of them and the fifth is now copying' (Whitley, *loc. cit.*).

The date at which the Sacraments were begun and the order in which they were painted are not easy to determine. We only know for certain that the *Baptism* was begun just before Poussin left Rome for Paris in 1640 and was only finished in Paris in 1642 (see above).

Friedlaender (1914, p. 116) proposes 1634–40 as the date for the whole series (except *Baptism*), but makes no suggestion about the order in which they were painted. Grautoff (II, Nos. 92 ff.) is vague about the actual dating, but proposes the following order of execution: *Confirmation, Extreme Unction, Ordination, Marriage, Eucharist, Baptism* (leaving out the lost *Penance*). Mahon (Bibl. 1367, p. 106 note 315, and *L'ideale classico* (Bologna), Nos. 68, 69) places the series, excluding *Baptism*, in the years 1638–40, but does not propose any schema for the order of painting.

One piece of evidence suggests that the series may have been begun before 1638. A drawing at Windsor (*CR*, III, pp. 24 f., No. 188) has on its *verso* two studies connected with the Morrison *Triumph of Pan* (No. 136) of 1635–36, and on the left a study for the mourning woman at the left of *Extreme Unction*. As Mahon (*loc. cit.*) has pointed out, this evidence is not conclusive, because the *recto* of the sheet has sketches for the *Blind Men* of 1650 (No. 74). This argument in its turn is not final, because, whereas the style of the *recto* is, naturally, quite different from that of the *verso*, the study of the mourning woman is in the same ink and in the same style as the sketches for the *Triumph of Pan*, and seems to belong to precisely the same date. It is, therefore, possible that the series was planned about 1636, though the style of the paintings themselves suggests that they were mainly painted from 1638 onwards. They were no doubt Poussin's principal occupation during 1639, and particularly 1640, a year during which he was living, one may imagine, from day to day, under the threat of being called to Paris, and for which there are no recorded commissions. The hypothesis that the execution of the paintings may have been spread over a longer period than three years is supported by a phrase of Bellori (p. 418), copied by Félibien (IV, p. 23), who says that they were painted 'in diversi tempi'.

BIBLIOGRAPHY: *Correspondance*, pp. 125, 208, 214, 218, 225, 239, 244 f., 254, 256, 267, 440, 443; [Bellori], Bibl. 36, p. 46; Félibien, IV, pp. 23, 164; Montaiglon and Guiffrey, Bibl. 45, VIII, pp. 40, 45, 47 f., 51, 54, 58, 62, 66 f., 70, 87, 110, IX, pp. 47, 52; Bellori, p. 416; Sirén, Bibl. 63, p. 187; Titi, Bibl. 65d, p. 91; Spon and Wheler, Bibl. 66, I, p. 304; Sandrart, p. 257; Passeri, p. 327; Baldinucci, XVI, p. 102; Mabillon and Germain, Bibl. 95, I, pt. 1, p. 142; Rossini, Bibl. 106c, II, p. 230; Loménie de Brienne, p. 218; Perrault, Bibl. 113, I, p. 89; Florent Le Comte, III, p. 5; [Rogissart], Bibl. 128a, II, p. 346; Caylus, Bibl. 133, p. 297; Wright, Bibl. 146, I, p. 6; Richardson, *Account*, pp. 22, 188 f.; Antonini, Bibl. 160b, p. 154; Sempill, Bibl. 163; De Brosses, Bibl. 170, II, p. 387; Dézallier, 1745, II, p. 250, and 1762, IV, p. 28; Bardon, II, p. 126; La Lande, Bibl. 224a, V, p. 290, VI, pp. 247 f.; Richard, Bibl. 229, IV, p. 98; La Roque, Bibl. 248, II, pp. 318 ff.; Magnan, Bibl. 260, IV, col. 24; Chiusole, Bibl. 269, p. 54; Cambry, Bibl. 272a, p. 47; Guibal, Bibl. 273, p. 28; Reynolds, Bibl. 281, pp. 125 f., 139, 145, 160 ff., 163 ff., 169, 175; *Newspaper reports*, Bibl. 286; Ramdohr, Bibl. 287, II, pp. 220 ff., Vasi, Bibl. 298, I, p. 473; Manazzale, Bibl. 308a, II, p. 95; Lazzarini, Bibl. 332, I, p. 30; Gence, Bibl. 373, p. 583; Waagen, Bibl. 384b, III, p. 401; Smith, Nos. 135–141; Eller, Bibl. 410, pp. 132, 290 ff.; De Cotte, in Bibl. 433, III, p. 153, and Bibl. 1295, p. 203; Cousin, Bibl. 456, p. 11; Tonnellé, Bibl. 489, pp. 158 ff.; Friedlaender, 1914, pp. 59 ff., 116, 194 ff.; Grautoff, I, pp. 169 ff., II, Nos. 92–96, 99; Magne, 1914, pp. 87, 92 n. 3, 212, No. 229; Whitley, Bibl. 828, II, pp. 75 ff.; Borenius, Bibl. 914, p. 63; Brieger, Bibl. 915, pp. 346 f., 356, 358; Blunt, Bibl. 972, p. 162, and Bibl. 1002, p. 219; Löhneysen, Bibl. 1077, pp. 133 ff.; Blunt, Bibl. 1086, p. 187, and Bibl. 1086a, p. 163; Licht, p. 130; Haskell and Rinehart, Bibl. 1254, pp. 321, 324; Mahon, Bibl. 1269, p. 263; Rinehart, Bibl. 1281, pp. 24, 28; Mahon, Bibl. 1367, pp. XIII, 107 ff., 128, 138; du Colombier, Bibl. 1413, pp. 89 ff.

For references to individual members of the series, see the following entries.

105. BAPTISM. 95·5 × 121 cm. National Gallery of Art, Washington (Samuel H. Kress Collection).

HISTORY: See above.

DRAWINGS: 1. Musée Condé, Chantilly (*CR*, I, p. 40, No. 75).
2. Ecole des Beaux-Arts, Paris, (*CR*, I, p. 40, No. 76).

3. Musée Condé, Chantilly, (Malo, Bibl. 878, Pl. 20). A copy after the painting.

COPY: Ritter van Klarwill sale, Berlin, 17.iv.1928, lot 50 (from the Lassus collection, Paris).

NOTES: The painting was begun in Rome but brought to Paris unfinished (*Correspondance*, p. 47). Poussin was for a long time prevented from working on it by his other commissions (*ibid.*, p. 56) and it was not despatched till May 1642 (*ibid.*, p. 153). It is interesting to notice that the figures of Christ and the two angels were the last things to be painted (*ibid.* p. 124). In style the *Baptism* differs quite markedly from the other paintings in the series and is closer to the Roccatagliata *Holy Family* (No. 46).

The figure of Christ recalls Jacopino del Conte's *Baptism* in the Oratory of S. Giovanni Decollato, Rome (rep. in Voss, *Die Malerei der Spätrenaissance in Rom und Florenz,* Berlin, 1920, I, p. 141). The man putting on or pulling off his shirt is a figure which can be traced back in Italian art through Michelangelo's Cascina cartoon to Piero della Francesca's *Baptism,* and the man pulling on his stocking also comes from the Cascina cartoon.

BIBLIOGRAPHY: See above, p. 74, and *Correspondance,* pp. 47, 56, 94, 97, 112, 118, 124, 126 f., 137, 153, 159, 163, 165, 169, 175, 177; Smith, No. 135; Friedlaender, 1914, p. 76; Grautoff, II, No. 99; Magne, 1914, pp. 122, 134; Borenius, Bibl. 914, p. 63; Blunt, Bibl. 972, p. 154.

106. CONFIRMATION. 95·5 × 121 cm. Duke of Rutland, Belvoir Castle, Grantham.

HISTORY: See above.

DRAWING: Royal Library, Windsor Castle (*CR,* I, p. 43, No. 85).

ENGRAVING: By P. Van Somer (Davies and Blunt, p. 212, No. 91).

NOTES: The architecture of the church in which the scene takes place is very close to that of S. Atanasio dei Greci (see text volume, Fig. 153).

BIBLIOGRAPHY: See above, p. 74, and Smith, No. 136; Grautoff, II, No. 92; Blunt, Bibl. 1003, p. 269 n. 5; *Exposition Poussin* (*Louvre*), No. 61; Mahon, Bibl. 1271, p. 304; Rees Jones, Bibl. 1280, pp. 304 ff.; *L'ideale classico* (*Bologna*), No. 69.

107. EUCHARIST. 95·5 × 121 cm. Duke of Rutland, Belvoir Castle, Grantham.

HISTORY: See above.

BIBLIOGRAPHY: See above, p. 74 and Smith, No. 138; Grautoff, II, No. 96; Borenius, Bibl. 914, p. 63; Dorival, Bibl. 1244, p. 65; Vanuxem, Bibl. 1302, pp. 155 ff.

108. PENANCE. Original destroyed.

HISTORY: See above. The painting was destroyed in a fire at Belvoir Castle in 1816 (cf. Eller, Bibl. 410, p. 132).

ENGRAVINGS: 1. By Barrière (Davies and Blunt, p. 213, No. 93).
2. Anonymous engraving in Wilhelm Goeree, *Voorhereidselen, tot de Bybelsche Wysheid,* Amsterdam, 1690, I, p. 544.

COPIES: 1. Private collection, New York.
2. A copy was acquired by Boizot in 1793 (cf. Thuillier, Bibl. 1297, p. 39).

NOTES: Rising, who prepared the list of paintings burnt in 1816 (printed by Eller, *loc. cit.*), describes the destroyed Poussin as 'The preparation for the Passion', i.e. presumably the Last Supper, but this is evidently a confusion between the two scenes of the Sacrament series which show the Apostles lying at a meal on couches.

BIBLIOGRAPHY: See above, p. 74, and Eller, Bibl. 410, pp. 132, 290; Dorival, Bibl. 1244, I, p. 65; Vanuxem, Bibl. 1302, pp. 155 ff.

109. EXTREME UNCTION. 95·5 × 121 cm. Duke of Rutland, Belvoir Castle, Grantham.

HISTORY: See above.

DRAWING: Royal Library, Windsor Castle (*CR,* III, p. 25; Blunt, Bibl. 975, p. 46, No. 219 *v.*).

ENGRAVING: The engraving published by J. Dughet and reproduced by Wildenstein (No. 94) does not belong to Dughet's series of the Sacraments, but shows the principal figures of the Rutland version with much of the background omitted.

COPIES: 1. Formerly with A. Galanti.
2. Briand de Varras, Seigneur de la Duchère, at Lyons in the eighteenth century; brought to Paris in 1793; D. . . sale, Paillet, Paris, 20.ii.1832, lot 11 (44×66 inches); G. . . sale, Hue, Paris, 24.xii.1832, lot 43.

A painting from the Rumiantzov collection, now in the Pushkin Museum, Moscow, may be a copy of either this picture or the Sutherland version (cf. Réau, Bibl. 826, p. 248, No. 616).

BIBLIOGRAPHY: See above, and Smith, No. 141; Grautoff, II, No. 93; Blunt, Bibl. 975, p. 46, No. 219 *v.*; *L'ideale classico (Bologna)*, No. 68.

110. ORDINATION. 95·5 × 121 cm. Duke of Rutland, Belvoir Castle, Grantham.

HISTORY: See above.

DRAWING: Private collection, England. Inscribed: *Giulio Campi da Cremona*, but probably a copy of a lost original by Poussin.

ENGRAVINGS: 1. By P. Van Somer (Davies and Blunt, p. 213, No. 95).
2. The engraving published by J. Dughet, reproduced by Wildenstein (No. 95), represents the figure group of the Rutland painting (in reverse) against the landscape of the corresponding Sutherland picture (cf. Davies and Blunt, p. 213, No. 95).

COPY: Nossa Senhora dos Chagas, Lisbon.

BIBLIOGRAPHY: See above, p. 74, and Richardson, *Account*, p. 185; Smith, No. 140; Grautoff, II, No. 94; Blunt, Bibl. 972, p. 154, Bibl. 1086, pp. 187, 191, and Bibl. 1086a, pp. 163, 167; Rinehart, Bibl. 1281, p. 24.

111. MARRIAGE. 95·5 × 121 cm. Duke of Rutland, Belvoir Castle, Grantham.

HISTORY: See above.

DRAWING: Royal Library, Windsor Castle (*CR*, I, p. 44, No. 90).

COPY: Seized at Niort at the Revolution (cf. Thuillier, Bibl. 1297, p. 40).

BIBLIOGRAPHY: See above, p. 74, and Smith, No. 139; Grautoff, II, No. 95; Blunt, Bibl. 975, p. 32, No. 204; Waterhouse, Bibl. 1096, p. 306; Dorival, Bibl. 1244, p. 61.

112–118. THE SEVEN SACRAMENTS (Second Series). The Duke of Sutherland; on loan to the National Gallery of Scotland, Edinburgh.

HISTORY: Painted for Paul Fréart de Chantelou between 1644 and 1648 (see below). It is not known to whom Chantelou bequeathed them at his death, which probably took place in 1694 (Chardon, Bibl. 515, p. 163), but according to Nougaret (Bibl. 251, II, p. 128) they were bought secretly in 1714 by a merchant of Rotterdam, who took them to Holland. The name of the merchant is given by Vertue (Bibl. 132, XVIII, p. 36) as 'Mijnheer van Meyer', perhaps the J. Van Meijer of Rotterdam who owned a version of the *Camillus and the Schoolmaster of Falerii* (cf. No. 143). The Duke of Marlborough is said to have offered 50,000 Crowns for them, but the offer was refused (Nougaret, *loc. cit.*), and they were bought by Philippe, Duke of Orleans, the Regent of France, in 1716 through the agency of the Abbé (later Cardinal) Dubois (cf. Stryenski, Bibl. 718, p. 15). In 1717 Thornhill saw them in the Palais Royal (Thornhill, Bibl. 140, p. 88). They are listed by Dubois de Saint-Gelais in his catalogue of the Orleans collection, made in 1727 (Bibl. 153, pp. 333 ff.). Sold in 1792 with the Italian and French pictures of the Orleans collection to Walkuers; sold by him the same year to Laborde de Méréville; bt. in 1798 by Bryan for the Duke of Bridgewater (Buchanan, I, pp. 16 ff., 150 ff.); passed by descent to the Earls of Ellesmere, the last of whom became Duke of Sutherland in 1964.

DRAWINGS: See entries for individual pictures.

ENGRAVINGS: 1. By J. Pesne (Andresen, Nos. 274–280; Wildenstein, Nos. 97–103; Davies and Blunt, p. 213, Nos. 97–103).
2. By B. Audran (Andresen, Nos. 281–287).
3. Published by Gantrel (Andresen, Nos. 288–294).

COPIES: 1. Musée de Tessé, Le Mans. By Boinard (cf. Chardon, Bibl. 515, p. 192). Appeared in the Véron sale, Joullain, Paris, 12 ff.xii.1780.
2. Musée de Tessé, Le Mans (Nos. 175–181). Bequeathed to the museum in 1842 by J. R. Giraud (cf. *ibid.*, p. 194).
3. Academy of S. Fernando, Madrid.
4. Church of Baugency (cf. Thuillier, Bibl. 1294, p. 303).
5. St. Julien, Le Mans (Chardon, *op. cit.* p. 194).
6. Chartreuse de Villeneuve de Rouergue.
7. Formerly Abbey of Marmoutiers (cf. Thuillier, Bibl. 1297, p. 40).

8. Formerly collection of Gluc, director of the tapestry manufacture at the Gobelins, in his house at the quai Malaquais (Brice, Bibl. 89 f., IV, p. 139).

9. Prince de Conti sale, Remy, Paris, 8 ff.iv.1777, lot 539 (cf. Chennevières-Pointel, Bibl. 433, III, pp. 152, 302).

NOTES: The second series of Sacraments has its origin in a project put forward by Chantelou to have copies made of the first set belonging to Cassiano dal Pozzo. This is probably the scheme to which Poussin refers in a letter to Pozzo sent from Paris on 27.iii.1642 (*Correspondance*, p. 125), though he only speaks of copies being made of pictures belonging to Pozzo and does not specify that he is referring to the Sacraments. At this time Pozzo refused to let Chantelou have the copies made and fobbed him off with an offer of coloured drawings instead. Chantelou was, however, clearly not satisfied with this proposal and asked Poussin to approach Pozzo again. In a letter of 4.viii.1643 (*ibid.*, p. 208) Poussin says that Errard will probably copy some and that he is looking for another painter to do the rest, though again the Sacraments are not actually specified. Soon afterwards, however, in a letter of 23.ix.1643 (*ibid.*, p. 214), Poussin says that a painter called Francesco or Ciccio Napoletano, no doubt Ciccio Graziani, had agreed to copy *Confirmation* and *Extreme Unction* (*ibid.*, p. 214). The matter dragged on, accompanied by repeated lamentations from Poussin about the badness of copyists and their exorbitant prices. On 7.i.1644 he writes that Francesco Napolitano and Claude Le Rieux have promised to copy the whole series between them (*ibid.*, p. 239; Jouanny prints 'Le vieux', but as the Christian name of this artist was Reynaud, this is fairly clearly a mistake for *Le Rieux*). Shortly afterwards, on 12.i.1644 (*ibid.*, pp. 244 f.) Poussin, in despair, offers either to do the copies himself or to make a new series of different compositions. On 17.iii.1644 (*ibid.*, p. 256) he writes with renewed courage, since Chantelou has accepted enthusiastically his proposal to paint a new series. On 15.iv.1644 (*ibid.*, p. 264) he reports that the day before he had begun to work on the first canvas, which was to represent *Extreme Unction*. This was finished by 30.x. of the same year (*ibid.*, p. 288). After an interval of some months Poussin announced, on 30.iv.1645 (*ibid.*, p. 302), that he had begun *Confirmation*, which was finished by 10.xii.1645 (*ibid.*, p. 324). In 1646 he produced one picture only, *Baptism*, which was probably begun in February (*ibid.*, p. 331) and was finished by 18.xi.1646 (*ibid.*, p. 347). In 1647 the tempo increases sharply. *Penance*, which had been mentioned as a project much earlier, on 30.v.1644 (*ibid.*, p. 272) is referred to again on 4.ii.1646 (*ibid.*, p. 331), but seems to have been put aside in favour of *Baptism*, although a drawing had already been made by 25.ii.1646 (*ibid.*, p. 334). The picture had actually been started by 4.ii.1647 (*ibid.*, p. 350) and was finished by 3.vi.1647 (*ibid.*, p. 356). On the same day he announces (*ibid.*, p. 357) that he has begun *Ordination*, which was despatched by 19.viii.1647 (*ibid.*, p. 363). *Eucharist* was begun before 1.ix.1647 (*ibid.*, p. 365) and finished by 3.xi.1647 (*ibid.*, p. 367), and *Marriage* was on the easel by 24.xi.1647 (*ibid.*, p. 370) and was finished by 23.iii.1648 (*ibid.*, p. 380).

The increase in speed in 1647 was due to Chantelou's complaints, which provoked Poussin first to a series of excuses and promises and finally to real concentration on the Sacraments, to the exclusion of almost all other work. In addition to complaints about delays, we can deduce from Poussin's letters that Chantelou sometimes expressed dissatisfaction on other grounds. He was evidently disappointed by *Ordination*, and his lack of enthusiasm for it, coupled with his jealousy over the *Finding of Moses* painted for Pointel (No. 13), provoked the artist to write his celebrated letter on the Modes (see text volume, pp. 225 ff.), in which he gives his most systematic expression of his ideas about the art of painting.

BIBLIOGRAPHY: *Correspondance*, pp. 125, 208, 214, 218, 225, 237, 239, 242, 244 f., 248, 254, 256, 259 f., 261, 262, 264, 339, 343, 344, 370; *Les choses les plus remarquables de Paris*, Bibl. 29b, p. 110; Fréart de Chambray, Bibl. 32, p. 126, and Bibl. 32b, p. 111; Chantelou, 1885, pp. 62, 65 ff., 72, 146, 163, 222, and 1960, pp. 124 f., 128 f., 131; Félibien, III, p. 146, IV, pp. 23, 53, 163; Bellori, pp. 432 ff.; Sandrart, p. 257; Baldinucci, XVI, p. 105; Brice, Bibl. 89a, I, pp. 213 f., and Bibl. 89c, I, p. 440; Loménie de Brienne, pp. 214 f., 218; Perrault, Bibl. 113, I, p. 89; Florent Le Comte, III, p. 29; Vertue, Bibl. 132, XVIII, p. 36; [C. Saugrain], Bibl. 138a, I, pp. 166, 175; Thornhill, Bibl. 140, p. 88; Du Bos, Bibl. 142, I, p. 63; Wright, Bibl. 146, I, p. 6; Richardson, *Account*, pp. 8, 22; Dubois de Saint-Gelais, Bibl. 153, pp. 333 ff.; Antonini, Bibl. 160b, p. 154; Piganiol de La Force, Bibl. 173, II, p. 237; Dézallier, 1745, II, pp. 253, 255, and 1762, IV, pp. 38, 40; Le Blanc, Bibl. 180, p. 149; Dézallier d'Argenville, Bibl. 183, p. 70; Bardon, II, p. 125; Reynolds, Bibl. 235, p. 65; Ponz, Bibl. 238a, pp. 1713 f., par. 108; *Bergeret et Fragonard*, Bibl. 243, p. 264; La Roque, Bibl. 248, I, p. 110; Nougaret, Bibl. 251, II, p. 128; Pimarta, Bibl. 271, p. 269; Cambry, Bibl. 272a, pp. 25, 47; Hoare, Bibl. 280, I, p. 81; Couché, Fontenai and Croze-Magnan, Bibl. 285, III, p. 3 and Poussin Nos. 1–7; Salmon, Bibl. 321, II, p. 39; Gault de Saint-Germain, Pt. 1, p. 47; Pt. 2, pp. 52 ff.; Barry, Bibl. 338, II, pp. 64, 66, 74, 83, 88, 89; Buchanan, I, pp. 16 f., 150 f.; Westmacott, Bibl. 378.1, pp. 190 f.; Waagen, Bibl. 384b, II, pp. 39, 493; Smith, Nos. 128–134; Eller, Bibl. 410, p. 291; Hazlitt, Bibl. 411, p. 58; Cousin,

Bibl. 456, pp. 10 ff.; Tonnellé, Bibl. 489, pp. 164 ff.; Chardon, Bibl. 515, p. 163; Montaiglon, Bibl. 600, p. 118; Stryenski, Bibl. 718, pp. 15, 93 ff.; Friedlaender, 1914, pp. 80 ff., 118, 216, 218 ff.; Grautoff, I, pp. 232 ff., II, Nos. 117–123; Magne, 1914, pp. 148, 212, No. 230; Alpatov, Bibl. 882, pp. 20 f.; Marignon, Bibl. 885, pp. 73 ff.; Blunt, Bibl. 972, p. 162; Löhneysen, Bibl. 1077, pp. 133 ff.; Blunt, Bibl. 1086, pp. 190 ff., and Bibl. 1086a, pp. 166 ff.; Licht, p. 141; Mahon, Bibl. 1124, pp. 70 ff.; *Exposition Poussin* (*Louvre*), Nos. 69–75. Vanuxem, Bibl. 1302, p. 159; Mahon, Bibl. 1367, pp. XIII f., 110 f., 119, 122 ff., 127 ff., 134.

112. BAPTISM. 117×178 cm.

HISTORY: First mentioned in a letter of 4.ii.1646 (*Correspondance*, p. 331); finished by 18.xi.1646 (*ibid.*, p. 347).

DRAWINGS: 1. Musée des Beaux-Arts, Dijon (*CR*, I, p. 41, No. 77).
2. Hermitage Museum, Leningrad (*CR*, I, p. 41, No. 78.)
3. Gabinetto dei Disegni, Florence (*CR*, I, p. 41, No. 79).
4–7. Musée du Louvre, Paris (*CR*, I, p. 41, Nos. 80–83).
8. Musée Condé, Chantilly (*CR*, I, p. 41, No. 84).

COPIES: 1. Anon. sale, Christie, London, 1.viii.1957, lot 27.
2. A copy of the landscape without figures but with a boat is in the University Art Museum, Princeton.

BIBLIOGRAPHY: See above, p. 77, and *Correspondance*, pp. 331, 345, 346, 347, 348 f., 351, 352, 353, 356, 360; Félibien, IV, pp. 54 f.; Loménie de Brienne, p. 220; Smith, No. 128; Grautoff, II, No. 120; Blunt, Bibl. 972, pp. 154 f.; Royal Academy, London, Bibl. 1048, No. 65; Mahon, Bibl. 1124, pp. 74 ff.; Shearman, Bibl. 1285, p. 182.

113. CONFIRMATION. 117×178 cm.

HISTORY: Begun before 30.iv.1645 (*Correspondance*, p. 302), the reference to *Confirmation* in the letter of 11.ix.1644 (*ibid.*, pp. 282 f.) being a mistake for *Extreme Unction*; finished by 10.xii.1645 (*ibid.*, p. 324).

DRAWINGS: 1. Royal Library, Windsor Castle (*CR*, I, p. 43, No. 86).
2–4. Musée du Louvre, Paris (*CR*, I, p. 43, Nos. 87–89).
5. Royal Library, Windsor Castle (*CR*, I, p. 43, No. A 20). Described in *CR* as 'probably executed with the help of studio hands', but certainly original.

6. British Museum, London (*CR*, I, p. 43). A reversed copy of the painting; perhaps a counter-proof.

BIBLIOGRAPHY: See above, p. 77, and *Correspondance*, pp. 283, 284, 300, 302, 309, 314 f., 317 f., 320, 322, 323, 324, 326, 328, 330, 331, 332, 333, 334, 335, 337 f.; Félibien, III, p. 235, IV, p. 54; Smith, No. 129; Grautoff, II, No. 118; Blunt, Bibl. 975, pp. 45, 51.

114. EUCHARIST. 117×178 cm.

HISTORY: Begun by 1.ix.1647 (*Correspondance*, p. 365); finished by 3.xi.1647 (*ibid.*, p. 367).

DRAWINGS: 1. Musée du Louvre, Paris (*CR*, I, p. 48, No. 100).
2. Musée du Louvre, Paris (*CR*, I, p. 48, No. 101). Sheet of studies for both *Eucharist* and *Penance*.

COPIES: 1. St. Rémy, Dieppe.
2. Le Grand Andely, church.
3. St. Bertrand de Comminge, cathedral.

BIBLIOGRAPHY: See above, p. 77, and *Correspondance*, pp. 365, 367, 370, 377, 378, 381; Chambray, Bibl. 32, p. 130; Félibien, IV, pp. 55, 356 f.; Buchanan, I, p. 18; Waagen, Bibl. 384b, II, p. 39; Smith, No. 133; Grautoff, II, No. 122; Blunt, Bibl. 929, pp. 274 f., and Bibl. 972, p. 162; Dorival, Bibl. 1244, p. 65; Vanuxem, Bibl. 1302, pp. 155 ff.; Montagu, Bibl. 1339, p. 310.

115. PENANCE. 117×178 cm.

HISTORY: In a letter of 30.v.1644 (*Correspondance*, p. 272) Poussin says he is about to begin *Penance*, but he seems to have changed his plan and in fact painted the *Baptism* (q.v.) instead. *Penance* was taken up again early in 1646; a sketch, no doubt a drawing, was ready by 25.ii.1646 (*ibid.*, p. 334) and the picture itself was begun by 4.ii.1647 (*ibid.*, p. 348) and finished by 3.vi.1647 (*ibid.*, p. 356).

DRAWINGS: 1. Musée Fabre, Montpellier, (*CR*, I, p. 47, No. 99).
2. Musée du Louvre, Paris (*CR*, I, p. 47, No. 101). A sheet of studies for both *Penance* and *Eucharist*.

COPIES: 1. Private collection, Paris.
2. Anon. sale, Sotheby, London, 2.xi.1960, lot 154.

BIBLIOGRAPHY: See above, p. 77, and *Correspondance*, pp. 268, 270, 272, 331, 334, 348, 350, 351, 352, 354, 355,

356 f., 358, 360 f., 363, 364, 381; Félibien, III, p. 146, IV, p. 55; Buchanan, I, p. 18; Waagen, Bibl. 384b, II, p. 39; Smith, No. 131; Grautoff, II, No. 119; Blunt, Bibl. 929, p. 374, and Bibl. 972, p. 162; Dorival, Bibl. 1244, pp. 65 ff., Vanuxem, Bibl. 1302, pp. 155 ff.

116. EXTREME UNCTION. 117×178 cm.

HISTORY: Begun by 14.iv.1644 (*Correspondance*, p. 264); finished by 30.x.1644 (*ibid.*, p. 288).

DRAWINGS: 1. Musée du Louvre, Paris (*CR*, I, p. 49, No. 103).
2. J. Giraudoux collection, Paris (*CR*, I, p. 49, No. 102).

COPIES: 1. St. Rémy, Dieppe.
2. G. de Penguern, Nice.
3. A copy was in 1933 in the apartment of the Brazilian ambassador in the Palazzo Pamphili, Rome.

BIBLIOGRAPHY: See above, p. 77, and *Correspondance*, pp. 262, 264, 265, 266, 267, 272, 274, 281, 282, 283, 284, 285, 286, 287, 288 ff., 294, 295, 297, 314, 324, 335; Fréart de Chambray, Bibl. 32, p. 125; Félibien, IV, pp. 53, 116, 146; Bellori, pp. 432 ff.; Loménie de Brienne, p. 224; Smith, No. 134; Grautoff, II, No. 117; Magne, 1914, p. 191; Emmerling, Bibl. 933, pp. 5, 35, 68; Mahon, Bibl. 1124, pp. 70 ff.

117. ORDINATION. 117×178 cm.

HISTORY: Begun by 3.vi.1647 (*Correspondance*, p. 357); despatched by 19.viii.1647 (*ibid.*, p. 363).

DRAWINGS: 1–2. Musée du Louvre, Paris (*CR*, I, p. 46, Nos. 95, 96).
3. Formerly Blumenreich collection, Berlin (*CR*, I, p. 46, No. 97).
4. Pierpont Morgan Library, New York (*CR*, I, p. 46, No. 98). In *CR* some doubts were expressed about the authenticity of this drawing, but they were certainly not justified.

ENGRAVING: The engraving by J. Dughet (Wildenstein, No. 95) shows the landscape of the *Ordination* from the second series with the figure group from the first.

COPIES: 1. Musée des Beaux-Arts, Nîmes.

2. Musée des Beaux-Arts, Tours. From the Seminary of Tours.
3. Private collection, San Francisco. Bought in London in 1963 (62·5×89·5 cm.).
4. Anon. sale, Sotheby, London, 2.xi.1960, lot 154.
5. T. Cottrell-Dormer, Rousham Park, Oxfordshire. A copy of the landscape and architecture, with the figures of Christ and St. Peter only.

BIBLIOGRAPHY: See above, p. 77, and *Correspondance*, pp. 357, 358, 359, 361, 362, 363, 365; Félibien, IV, p. 55; Smith, No. 132; Grautoff, II, No. 121; Blunt, Bibl. 972, pp. 154 f.; Royal Academy, London, Bibl. 1048, No. 67; Blunt, Bibl. 1050, p. 40; Kauffmann, Bibl. 1332, p. 98.

118. MARRIAGE. 117×178 cm.

HISTORY: Begun by 24.xi.1647 (*Correspondance*, p. 370); finished by 23.iii.1648 (*ibid.*, p. 380).

DRAWING: Musée du Louvre, Paris (*CR*, I, p. 45, No. 91).

COPIES: 1. A copy was in 1933 in the apartment of the Brazilian ambassador in the Palazzo Pamphili, Rome.
2. A copy with the figures set against the background of Raphael's *Heliodorus* was in the collection of Mlle de Foncières, Paris, in 1963.

BIBLIOGRAPHY: See above, p. 77, and *Correspondance*, pp. 365, 366, 370, 376, 378, 379 f., 382, 383; Félibien, IV, p. 59; Loménie de Brienne, p. 220; Smith, No. 130; Grautoff, II, No. 123; Magne, 1914, p. 150; Dorival, Bibl. 1244, p. 65.

119. THE ARCADIAN SHEPHERDS. 101 × 82 cm. About 8 cm. added on the left. The Chatsworth Settlement, Chatsworth, Derbyshire.

HISTORY: Cardinal Camillo Massimi; on his death in 1677 bequeathed to his brother, Fabio Camillo Massimi (Orbaan, Bibl. 746, p. 521). Sterling (Bibl. 1122, p. 69) implies that this painting, together with its companion, the Metropolitan Museum *Midas* (No. 165), remained in the possession of the Massimi family till the second half of the eighteenth century, but neither painting is mentioned by travellers or writers of guide books to Rome in the eighteenth century, and what appears to be the Chatsworth picture is recorded in France before the end of the seventeenth century in the collection of Mme du Housset, a relation of Loménie de Brienne, who obtained it from her (pp. 215, 223). The Chatsworth picture is first mentioned in England and as in the possession of the Duke of Devonshire in 1761 by Dodsley (Bibl. 214, II, p. 227). It passed by descent through the Dukes of Devonshire till the Chatsworth Settlement was created.

ENGRAVING: By Ravenet (Andresen, No. 418; Andresen-Wildenstein, No. 418). Dated 1763.

COPY: A copy, with variants and greatly enlarged in height, belongs to Prince Massimi. It is accompanied by a copy, also enlarged, of the Metropolitan Museum *Midas* (No. 165).

NOTES: Loménie de Brienne (p. 223) refers to two versions of this composition painted by Poussin, one which had belonged to Avice—presumably No. 120—and the other 'plus petit et en hauteur que j'avois et que je tiray des mains de l'avare Made du Housset, ma parente, qui croioit que ce fust un tableau de dévotion et l'avoit pour cette raison placé dans son Oratoire'. This is almost certainly the Massimi picture, because the cardinal left heavy debts and his heirs sold many of his possessions—for instance the two paintings of the life of Moses (Nos. 15 and 19) were bought by Louis XIV in 1683.

The picture was dated by Grautoff (II, No. 43) c. 1632–35, and by Mahon to a period between, roughly, the middle of 1629 and the later part of 1630 (Bibl. 1271, pp. 298, 300, and Bibl. 1367, p. XI). I should myself agree in general with the earlier dating, certainly to one before 1631.

BIBLIOGRAPHY: Bellori, p. 448; Loménie de Brienne, pp. 215, 223; Dodsley, Bibl. 214, II, p. 227; Martyn, Bibl. 226, I, p. 43; Keate, Bibl. 242, pp. vii ff.; Waagen, Bibl. 384b, II, p. 93; Smith, No. 278; Hazlitt, Bibl. 417, p. 199; Friedlaender, 1914, pp. 47, 125, 160; Grautoff, I, p. 111, II, No. 43; Magne, 1914, p. 215, No. 280; Orbaan, Bibl. 746, p. 521; Jamot, Bibl. 788, p. 84; Royal Academy, London, Bibl. 879, No. 117; Francastel, Bibl. 883, p. 146; Panofsky, Bibl. 893, pp. 236 ff.; Hourticq, Bibl. 899, pp. 137 f.; Klein, Bibl. 901, p. 314; Weisbach, Bibl. 905, pp. 287 ff.; Blunt, Bibl. 912, pp. 96 ff.; Panofsky, Bibl. 921, pp. 305 f.; Friedlaender, Bibl. 964, pp. 23, 26; Blunt, Bibl. 1003, p. 270; Jamot, pp. 26, 40, 45, 49, 64; Bishop, Bibl. 1084, pp. 86 f.; Blunt, Bibl. 1086, pp. 185, 190, and Bibl. 1086a, pp. 161, 166; Licht, pp. 123, 164; Sterling, Bibl. 1122, pp. 68, 69; *Exposition Poussin* (Louvre), No. 19; Mahon, Bibl. 1271, pp. 298, 300; Panofsky, Bibl. 1273, pp. 45 ff.; Mahon, Bibl. 1337, p. 281, and Bibl. 1367, pp. XI, 29, 32, 53, 78, 112, 128.

120. THE ARCADIAN SHEPHERDS. 85 × 121 cm. Musée du Louvre, Paris (734).

HISTORY: Probably belonged to the Chevalier d'Avice (Loménie de Brienne, p. 223); bt. by Louis XIV from C. A. Hérault in 1685 (*Comptes des bâtiments*, II, pp. 584, 663).

DRAWING: Öffentliche Kunstsammlung, Basle. A copy by Cézanne after the head of the shepherdess (cf. Andersen, Bibl. 1388, p. 44).

ENGRAVINGS: 1. By B. Picart (Andresen, No. 417; Wildenstein, No. 167; Davies and Blunt, p. 215, No. 167).
2. By J. Mathieu (Andresen, No. 416).
3. By M. Blot (Andresen, No. 415).

COPIES: 1. Musée des Beaux-Arts, Bordeaux. Made by Alcide Girault in 1865 (87×124 cm.; cf. Magne, 1914, p. 215, No. 279).

2. Musée National de Céramique, Sèvres.

3. Kunstakademie, Vienna (940). Given by Count Lamberg.

4. Mrs. Rita Krumpholz, Muri, Berne.

5. Arthur Luttrell, Raith Hall, Yorkshire.

6. Nyert sale, Musier, Paris, 30.iii.1772, lot 5.

7. Greenwood sale, Christie, London, 22 f.ii.1773, 2nd day, lot 22.

8. Cardinal Fesch sale, George, Paris, 17 f.ii.1840, lot 49.

9. Anon. sale, Christie, London, 29.vii.1948, lot 275.

NOTES: Grautoff (II, No. 74) dated this picture 1638–39; Friedlaender (1914, p. 58) suggested that it may have been painted just before the journey to Paris, but was on the whole inclined to place it just after Poussin's return to Rome at the end of 1642. In the catalogue of the Louvre exhibition (*Exposition Poussin* (*Louvre*), No. 99) I proposed a much later dating, to the years 1650–55. This view was attacked by Mahon (Bibl. 1367, pp. XIII, 111 ff.), who maintained Grautoff's opinion. He regards the *Shepherds* as typical of the classical phase of the years just before the journey to Paris and adduces its similarity to paintings such as the 1638 *Finding of Moses*, the 1639 *Venus and Aeneas*, and the second series of Sacraments. While agreeing that there are similarities between the *Shepherds* and these paintings, I find the mood of the *Shepherds* very different and much closer to the solemnity of paintings of a much later period, such as the *Holy Family in Egypt* (No. 65), the Johnson *Baptism* (No. 72), or the late *Rebecca* (No. 9). It has in common with them the deliberate elimination of movement, so different from the frozen movement of the *Venus and Aeneas* (No. 191), and a weighty treatment of the figures and drapery, which contrasts with the elegance of Venus or even of Pharaoh's daughter. The barren landscape with its stunted trees is, as Mahon points out, unlike the rich vegetation of certain late landscapes, but it has precise parallels in the Johnson *Baptism*, the *Landscape with two Nymphs* at Chantilly (No. 208), which Mahon convincingly dates to 1659, and even with the *Autumn* of 1661–64 (No. 5). Finally I had the opportunity of seeing the *Shepherds* side by side with the Munich *Adoration of the Shepherds* (No. 41) when it was brought to Paris for a short time during the Poussin Exhibition, and there seemed to me no doubt that the two paintings dated from the same period, that is to say after 1655.

As further evidence for dating the *Shepherds* to about 1640 Mahon mentions the fact that, according to Bellori, the theme was suggested by Cardinal Giulio Rospigliosi (he even suggests, though very tentatively, that the picture may have belonged to the cardinal, but the fact that it does not appear in the 1713 inventory of paintings in the Palazzo Rospigliosi makes this unlikely), and points out that the cardinal was absent from Rome from 1644 to 1653, but this evidence could equally be used to support the view that the *Shepherds* was painted after the latter date.

The composition enjoyed great popularity in the late eighteenth century. A poem based on it, and entitled *The Monument in Arcadia*, was published by George Keate in 1775 (cf. Manwaring, Bibl. 794, p. 22), and a monument decorated with a copy of the composition in bas-relief by Scheemakers was erected in the grounds at Shugborough by James Stuart in the mid-eighteenth century (cf. Hussey, Bibl. 1100.1, pp. 1128 f.).

BIBLIOGRAPHY: *Comptes des bâtiments*, II, pp. 584, 663; Félibien, IV, p. 86; Bellori, p. 448; Florent Le Comte, III, p. 33; Loménie de Brienne, pp. 215, 223; Piganiol de La Force, Bibl. 124, I, p. 128; Bailly, p. 310; Dézallier, 1745, II, p. 255, and 1762, IV, p. 39; Diderot, Bibl. 211, XI, p. 161; Bardon, I, pp. 158 f.; Delille, Bibl. 270, Bk. IV; Cambry, Bibl. 272a, p. 46; Gault de Saint-Germain, Pt. I, p. 63 n. 11, Pt. II, pp. 4 ff.; Smith, No. 277; Burckhardt, Bibl. 465b, p. 990; Gautier, Bibl. 575, p. 174; Friedlaender, 1914, pp. 58, 125, 193; Grautoff, I, p. 147, II, No. 74; Magne, 1914, pp. 192, 215, No. 279; Lemonnier, Bibl. 791, pp. 273 ff.; Weisbach, Bibl. 846, pp. 127 ff.; Francastel, Bibl. 883, p. 146; Panofsky, Bibl. 893, pp. 223 ff.; Hourticq, Bibl. 899, pp. 138 f.; Klein, Bibl. 901, pp. 314 ff.; Weisbach, Bibl. 905, pp. 287 ff.; Panofsky, Bibl. 921, pp. 305 ff.; Bodkin, Bibl. 932, p. 254; Jamot, pp. 24 ff., 62 f., 81, 84; Bishop, Bibl. 1084, p. 87; Blunt, Bibl. 1086, p. 190, and Bibl. 1086a, p. 166; Licht, pp. 122, 164; Hours, Bibl. 1256, pp. 34 f.; *Exposition Poussin* (*Louvre*), No. 99; Mahon, Bibl. 1271, p. 304; Panofsky, Bibl. 1273, pp. 45 ff.; Sterling, Bibl. 1290, p. 268; Mahon, Bibl. 1367, pp. XIII, 111 ff., 120 f., 128.

121. A DANCE TO THE MUSIC OF TIME. 83×105 cm. On the back of the canvas: *No. 116 du C . . .* Wallace Collection, London.

HISTORY: Painted for Cardinal Giulio Rospigliosi, later Pope Clement IX (Bellori, p. 447); remained in the Palazzo Rospigliosi till after 1800 (Manazzale, Bibl. 308a, I, p. 127). Bt. from the palace by Cardinal Fesch (Gence, Bibl. 373, p. 582); No. 1056 in the 1841 catalogue of the Fesch collection; Fesch sale, George,

Rome, 17 ff.iii.1845, part II, lot 397, bt. Laneuville for the Marquis of Hertford; by bequest to Sir Richard Wallace; bequeathed to the Nation by his widow in 1897.

DRAWINGS: 1. C. L. Loyd, Lockinge House, Berkshire (*CR*, II, p. 24, No. 149).

2. A drawing in the Bibliothèque Nationale, Paris, is a copy by Francesco Arcangeli after the painting. Dated Rome, 1665.

ENGRAVINGS: 1. By J. Dughet (Andresen, No. 401; Wildenstein, No. 161; Davies and Blunt, p. 214, No. 161).

2. By B. Picart (Andresen, No. 402a).

3. By R. Morghen (Andresen, No. 400).

COPIES: 1. Musée Réattu, Arles.

2. Accademia, Venice (cf. Burckhardt, Bibl. 465b, p. 990). Perhaps the same as No. 11 below.

3. Captain C. B. Bond, Warsash, Hampshire. Bought from Sir C. Frederick, 1906.

4. The Earl of Darnley, Cobham Hall, Kent.

5. Mrs. Hamilton, 85, Abingdon Villas, London (1958). From the collection of her great-great-uncle, James Grant Fraser.

6. K. Preedy, London (rep. *Apollo*, LV, 1952, p. 31, when with Fischmann, London).

7. R. H. Ward, Paris (1938). The figure of Time only.

8. With Cassirer, Amsterdam (1948).

9. With Gallimard, Paris (cf. Vauxelles, Bibl. 678, p. 5).

10. In the Palazzo Rospigliosi in 1713 (cf. Zeri, Bibl. 1216, p. 320, No. 522).

11. Manfrin collection, Venice (cf. Giuseppe Nicoletti, *Catalogo dei Quadri esistenti nella Galleria Manfrin in Venezia*, Venice, 1856, No. 31 (82 × 108 cm.), and Graham, Bibl. 365, p. 224). Perhaps the same as No. 2 above.

12. M. . . . T. . . (= Montullé) sale, Le Brun, Paris, 22 ff.xii.1783, lot 38; Godefroy sale, Le Brun, Paris, 25.iv.1785, lot 40; anon. (= Coclers) sale, Le Brun, Paris, 9.2.1789, lot 169 (16 × 20 inches) as from the Montullé and Godefroy sales; described in detail.

13. Anon. sale, Christie, London, 26 f.v.1780, second day, lot 101.

14. R. Cosway sale, Christie, London, 3.iii.1792, lot 71.

15. Otway sale, Christie, London, 3.v.1800, lot 39.

16. Anon. sale, Christie, London, 16.i.1800, lot 69.

17. Anon. sale, Christie, London, 2.iv.1801, lot 36. The seller of the particular lot was Van Dyck; it was bought in.

18. T. G. Taylor sale, Christie, London, 5.vii.1935, lot 44. From the Carr collection, Cocken, Durham.

19. Viscount Hampden sale, Christie, London, 25.xi.1938, lot 50 (39 × 49 inches), bt. Duits.

20. Anon. sale, Sotheby, London, 29.vii.1964, lot 152 (38 × 52¼ inches).

21. Anon. sale, Sotheby, London, 24.ii.1965, lot 42 (31½ × 41¼ inches).

NOTES: According to Bellori (p. 447) the *concetto* of the picture was proposed by Cardinal Giulio Rospigliosi, for whom it was painted. The 1713 Rospigliosi inventory (Zeri, Bibl. 1216, p. 319, No. 512) describes the picture as 'Le 4 stagioni che ballano al suono del Tempo', but the allegory, which has been worked out in detail by Panofsky (Bibl. 893, pp. 241 ff.), in fact shows the four states—Poverty, Labour, Riches and Luxury—through which humanity passes in a continually repeated cycle. The putti, one holding an hour-glass and the other blowing bubbles, are well-known symbols of Vanitas, while the whole scene takes place under the eye of Apollo, who drives his chariot across the sky surrounded by the circle of the Zodiac.

Grautoff (II, No. 73) dates the picture 1638–40, whereas Friedlaender (1914, p. 80) places it in 1643–44, just after Poussin's return from Paris. Mahon (Bibl. 1367, pp. 105 f.) suggests 1637–38, and sees the *Dance* as typical of what he calls Poussin's 'pseudo-baroque' period. I should myself prefer the dating 1639–40 proposed in the Poussin exhibition catalogue (*Exhibition Poussin (Louvre)*, pp. 157, 236).

BIBLIOGRAPHY: Félibien, IV, p. 84; Bellori, p. 447; Rossini, Bibl. 106c, II, p. 125, and Bibl. 106d, p. 125; Florent Le Comte, III, p. 33; Wright, Bibl. 146, I, p. 310; Ficoroni, Bibl. 177.1, II, p. 58; Dézallier, 1762, IV, pp. 31, 39; La Lande, Bibl. 224a, IV, p. 277; Volkmann, Bibl. 257, II, p. 237; Cambry, Bibl. 272a, p. 42; Hoare, Bibl. 280, I, p. 74; Ramdohr, Bibl. 287, III, p. 62; Vasi, Bibl. 298, II, p. 319; Starke, Bibl. 306, II, p. 30; Manazzale, Bibl. 308a, I, p. 127; Gault de Saint-Germain, Pt. II, pp. 20 ff.; Laouriens, Bibl. 356, p. 398; Gence, Bibl. 373, p. 582; Buchanan, II, p. 145; Waagen, Bibl. 384b, II, p. 156; Smith, No. 279; Melchiorri, Bibl. 408, p. 560; Cousin, Bibl. 456, p. 17; Friedlaender, 1914, pp. 80, 126, 215; Grautoff, I, p. 147, II, No. 73; Magne, 1914, pp. 192, 215, No. 278; Panofsky, Bibl. 893, pp. 241 ff., 252 ff.; Jamot, pp. 24 f., 41, 81; Gombrich, Bibl. 1058, p. 190; Blunt, Bibl. 1064, p. 9, Bibl. 1086, p. 187, and Bibl. 1086a, p. 163; Licht, pp. 117, 121; Zeri, Bibl. 1216, p. 319, No. 512; Panofsky, Bibl. 1273, p. 30; Mahon, Bibl. 1367, pp. XIII, 105 f., 115.

122. TIME SAVING TRUTH FROM ENVY AND DISCORD. Circular. Diameter 297 cm. Musée du Louvre, Paris (735).

HISTORY: Commissioned by Cardinal Richelieu in 1641 for the ceiling of the Grand Cabinet in the Palais Cardinal, together with the *Moses and the Burning Bush* (No. 18) which was placed over the fireplace (Bellori, p. 429; Félibien, IV, p. 151). Bequeathed with the Palais Cardinal to Louis XIII. According to Sauval (Bibl. 23, II, p. 169) taken to Fontainebleau by Anne of Austria; inserted in the ceiling of the Cabinet du Roi in the Louvre in 1658 (Aulanier, Bibl. 1189, pp. 80 ff.); replaced by a copy made by Challe in 1752 (Guiffrey, Bibl. 598, p. 188) when the original was removed.

ENGRAVINGS: 1. By G. Audran (Andresen, No. 403; Wildenstein, No. 162; Davies and Blunt, p. 215, No. 162).
2. By B. Picart (Andresen, No. 404).
3. By P. Schenk (Andresen, No. 405).

COPIES: 1. A copy including only the two principal figures was in an anon. sale, Robinson and Fischer, London, 18.xii.1952, lot 121 (as Italian School). It may have been connected with the engraving by Denon recorded by Andresen (No. 406), which only included these figures.
2. A copy was made by Challe in 1752 to replace the original when it was moved from the ceiling of the Cabinet du Roi in the Louvre (Guiffrey, Bibl. 598, p. 188).

NOTES: According to Bellori (p. 429) this composition was painted after the *Moses and the Burning Bush*, also commissioned by Richelieu. In a letter of 21.xi.1641 (*Correspondance*, p. 106) Poussin indicates that both the paintings for the cardinal were completed by that date.

The picture was restored by Godefroy in 1777. For a detailed discussion of the allegory see Saxl (Bibl. 894).

The painting in the Musée des Beaux-Arts, Lille, listed by Grautoff (II, No. 105) as a sketch, only corresponds in the most general way with the Louvre composition and is probably a variant by a French artist of the early nineteenth century, in spite of the view put forward by Thuillier (Bibl. 1299, pp. 291 f.; see also *Exposition Poussin (Rouen)*, No. 103).

BIBLIOGRAPHY: *Correspondance*, p. 106; Sauval, Bibl. 23, II, p. 169, and Bibl. 23a, p. 149; Félibien, IV, p. 151; Bellori, p. 429; Sirén, Bibl. 63, p. 95; Passeri, p. 330; Baldinucci, XVI, p. 104; Florent Le Comte, III, p. 31; Bailly, p. 316; Richardson, *Account*, p. 8; Dézallier 1745, II, p. 255, and 1762, IV, p. 40; Dézallier d'Argenville, Bibl. 183, p. 36; Marigny, Bibl. 191, p. 357; Angiviller, Bibl. 244, p. 147; Cambry, Bibl. 272a, p. 39; Gault de Saint-Germain, Pt. II, p. 4; Smith, No. 280; Cousin, Bibl. 456, p. 17; Guiffrey, Bibl. 581, p. 101, and Bibl. 598, p. 188; Friedlaender, 1914, pp. 76, 116, 212; Grautoff, I, p. 213, II, No. 106; Magne, 1914, pp. 122, 219, No. 340; Hourticq, Bibl. 748, pp. 26 ff.; Saxl, Bibl. 894, pp. 212 ff.; Wittkower, Bibl. 909, p. 316; Jamot, pp. 24, 83; Blunt, Bibl. 1065, p. 370; Licht, p. 134; Hess, Bibl. 1157, p. 275; Aulanier, Bibl. 1189, pp. 80 ff.; *Exposition Poussin (Louvre)*, No. 63; Sterling, Bibl. 1290, p. 275; *Exposition Poussin (Rouen)*, No. 83; Mahon, Bibl. 1367, p. 121.

123. TIME SAVING TRUTH FROM ENVY AND DISCORD. Original lost.

HISTORY: Painted for Cardinal Giulio Rospigliosi, later Pope Clement IX (Bellori, p. 448). In the Palazzo Rospigliosi till about 1800 (cf. Zeri, Bibl. 1216, p. 310, No. 297, and Manazzale, Bibl. 308a, I, p. 127).

DRAWING: Royal Library, Windsor (*CR*, II, p. 25, No. 150).

ENGRAVINGS: 1. Published by J. Dughet (Andresen, No. 408; Wildenstein, No. 163). Perhaps engraved by E. Baudet (cf. Weigert, Bibl. 945, I, p. 293, No. 30).
2. By G. Folo (Andresen, No. 407).

COPIES: 1. Private collection, Switzerland (rep. *CR*, II, Fig. 17).
2. Manfrin collection, Venice (cf. G. Nicoletti, *Catalogo dei Quadri esistenti nella Galleria Manfrin in Venezia*, Venice, 1856, No. 322 (97 × 140 cm.), and Graham, Bibl. 365, p. 224).
3. Anon. (= Comte Français) sale, Constantin, Paris, 16 ff.i.1815, lot 89 (28 × 36 inches).
4. Anon. sale, Sotheby, London, 23.iii.1949, lot 114 (as Albano).
5. F. L. Kenett.

NOTES: According to Bellori (p. 448) the theme of the painting was suggested by Cardinal Giulio Rospigliosi, for whom it was executed. In *CR* (II, p. 25) a dating of 1635–40 was proposed for the drawing and by implication for the painting. These limits can, however, probably be slightly reduced, and, as far as one can judge from the engravings and the surviving copy of the painting, the original is likely to date from the last years before the journey to Paris, 1638–40.

BIBLIOGRAPHY: Félibien, IV, p. 85; Bellori, p. 448; Florent Le Comte, III, p. 33; La Lande, Bibl. 224a, IV, p. 275; Ramdohr, Bibl. 287, III, p. 63; Manazzale, Bibl. 308a, I, p. 127; Graham, Bibl. 365, p. 224; Gence, Bibl. 373, p. 583; Smith, No. 281; Grautoff, II, p. 258; Magne, 1914, p. 219, No. 341; Panofsky, Bibl. 893, p. 252; CR, II, p. 25; Blunt, Bibl. 975, p. 42; Jamot, p. 24; Zeri, Bibl. 1216, p. 310, No. 297; Mahon, Bibl. 1367, p. 115.

124. THE INSPIRATION OF THE EPIC POET. 184×214 cm. Musée du Louvre, Paris (3128).

HISTORY: Cardinal Mazarin by 1653 (see below); passed at his death either to Hortense Mancini, wife of the Duc de La Meilleraye, who became Duc de Mazarin, or to Filippo Mancini (Cosnac, Bibl. 584, pp. 271 f.). Seen by Bernini in the Palais Mazarin in 1665 (see below). Presumably the painting recorded in the Hôtel de Lassay in 1757 by Dézallier d'Argenville (Bibl. 183b, p. 415), who says that the pictures were acquired by the Marquis de Lassay, who died in 1738. The picture does not appear in the sale of his collection in 1775 and is presumably that offered to Frederick the Great by Mettra in a letter written from Paris in 1768 (Seidel, Bibl. 631, p. 91). Probably anon. sale of pictures 'consigned from abroad', Christie, London, 27 f.ii.1772, third day, lot 70 ('Apollo crowning a poet, attended by a muse, etc., very capital'). The copy of the catalogue in the Courtauld Institute has the figure 200 written against it, which may be the price fetched, and Redford (Bibl. 601.1, II, p. 280), who wrongly gives the date of the sale as 1771, states that the picture was bought by Lord Carlisle. Probably Bryan sale, Cox, Burrell and Foster, London, 19.v.1798, lot 36; according to the copy of the catalogue in the National Gallery, London, the buyer was Lord Suffolk.

Recorded in the account given by Westmacott of the collection of Thomas Hope in 1824 (Bibl. 378.1, p. 228). It is there described as 'Petrarch composing his Odes', and is visible in the engraving of the gallery given opposite p. 223. Passed by descent with the Hope collection to Henrietta Adela Hope, who married the 6th Duke of Newcastle, and bequeathed the collection to her grandson, Lord Francis Pelham Clinton-Hope. In 1884, on an order of the Court, the greater part of the collection in the London house was sold, but the Poussin seems to have remained in the possession of Lord Francis Clinton-Hope till it was bought by Fairfax Murray in 1910 after a further Court Order. It passed to Trotti and was bought by the Louvre in 1911.

COPIES: 1. Private collection, Paris (Grautoff, II, No. 80; Magne, 1914, p. 216, No. 289; Sterling, Bibl. 1290, pp. 274 f.). Belonged in the early nineteenth century to a painter named Erard; Erard sale, Henry, Paris, 23.iv.1832, lot 190; presumably bought in, since, according to Grautoff, it passed by inheritance from the Erard to the Blondel family, who owned it when he wrote.

2. Hon. Mrs. Emmott sale, Christie, London, 2.iv. 1948, lot 63 (43×58 inches). Inherited from her mother, Baroness Donington.

NOTES: The picture can be certainly identified as that in Mazarin's collection by the entries in the inventories of 1653 and 1661. In the former (Bibl. 20, p. 324, No. 266) Mazarin's painting is described as 'Apollon avec une muse et un poete couronné de lauriers, long de travers', and in that of 1661 (Cosnac, Bibl. 584, p. 318, No. 1096) the size is given as 5 ft. 4 inches by 6 ft. 4 inches. Bernini is recorded by Chantelou as particularly admiring a painting by Poussin in the Palais Mazarin, 'dont les figures sont grandes' (1885, p. 120, and 1960, p. 127), which must be the present painting, since none of the other Poussins in the collection had big figures. Mettra, in recommending the picture to Frederick the Great in 1768 (loc. cit.), says of it: 'Ce tableau est le plus capital de ce maître qui soit en France; il est pareillement dans toute sa pureté et fraicheur.'

The subject of the picture has given rise to discussion. The title which it had in the Hope collection— 'Petrarch composing his Odes' (Westmacott, loc.cit.)—cannot be correct, since the muse is certainly Calliope and the poet therefore a writer of epics not odes. In 1757 Dézallier d'Argenville (loc. cit.) calls it 'Virgile inspiré par Apollo', and in 1768 Mettra (Seidel, loc. cit.) called it 'Appollon qui couronne Virgile'. This may well be correct, since the poet is not unlike the Virgil of the 1641 title-page (cf. Wildenstein, No. 171), and the books represented, which are inscribed odissea, ilias, and eneide, would represent the major work of the Latin poet and his two Greek models. Panofsky (Bibl. 1273, pp. 45 f.), however, believes that the poet is simply the epic poet in general rather than any particular poet of that category.

The dating of the picture has given rise to even more discussion than its subject. Grautoff (II, No. 79) proposed 1636–39; Friedlaender (1914, p. 53) suggested c. 1635; Jamot (pp. 85 f.) supported a general dating to the later 1630's; and Moussali (Bibl. 1045) placed the picture just before the journey to Paris, emphasizing its similarity to Poussin's designs for title-pages made in Paris. In 1928, however, Grautoff

(Bibl. 822, p. 263) proposed a date before 1630. Friedlaender (1933, p. 325) notes Grautoff's new dating and says that Jamot proposed a similar view, but this does not appear to be the case. In my paper to the Colloque Poussin (Bibl. 1227, pp. 171 f.) I put forward a view similar to Grautoff's, and I developed this argument in the catalogue entry for the Louvre exhibition (*Exposition Poussin (Louvre)*, No. 8). This view was challenged by Mahon in the *Actes* (Bibl. 1269, p. 250) and he tentatively proposed dating the picture 1631–32, a view which he maintained more positively in later publications (Bibl. 1271, pp. 292, 295, 300, and Bibl. 1367, *passim*), with the slight modification of 1631–33 instead of 1631–32.

The external evidence about the date at which the painting was executed is slender and ambiguous. When Bernini admired it in 1665, Chantelou (*loc. cit.*) told him that 'il y avait plus de quarante ans qu'il avait été fait'. If taken literally, this statement would date the picture to 1625 at the latest, a hypothesis which only Mrs. Wild is willing to accept (Bibl. 1215, pp. 450 f.), but it is certainly a valid argument against the view that the *Inspiration* dates from just before the Paris journey. Mahon's suggestion (Bibl. 1271, p. 295 n. 58) that when Chantelou said 'forty' it was a slip for 'thirty' is ingenious but was perhaps not intended to be taken too literally. On the other hand his theory that Mazarin may have bought both the *Inspiration* and the *Diana and Endymion* (No. 149) in 1631–33 is clearly put forward as a serious suggestion (Bibl. 1268·1, p. 352), but the author does not produce any evidence to show that at that date Mazarin was either interested in buying pictures or financially in a position to do so.

Mahon's proposal to date the *Inspiration* to the years 1631–33 is, however, in great part based on the view that it shows the direct influence of Sacchi's *Divina Sapienza* and Duquesnoy's *Sta. Susanna*, and that this automatically excludes a dating before 1630.

This argument is developed at length in his *Poussiniana* (Bibl. 1367, pp. 63 ff.), in which the author brings together in the most useful manner the detailed evidence about the exact moment at which the fresco and the statue were conceived and executed—evidence which seems to me to confirm my statement, to which Mr. Mahon takes such strong exception (*ibid.*, pp. 64, 66), that the two works 'were planned at the latest in 1629'. In view of the material presented by Mr. Mahon it might at most be necessary to substitute the words 'by the end of 1629' for 'in 1629'.

In the case of the *Divina Sapienza* Mahon records the fact that on 22.xii.1629 Sacchi received a payment of 50 scudi 'a conto de suoi lavori' in the palace, and he lists the other payments to the artist, amounting to 250 scudi, made in 1630. He then asserts that the payment in December 1629 was made at the moment when the commission was given, and before any sketch or *modello* had been made. He makes this assertion as if the truth of it was self-evident, and he does not provide any arguments in favour of it. The contrary hypothesis—that the payment was made on the basis of a *modello*—is at least worthy of consideration. We know, for instance, that on 6.ix.1631 Sacchi received a payment 'a bon conto de' Cartoni che fa' for the mosaic cartoons, for which he had received the commission on 11 August (Pollak, Bibl. 832, II, p. 575). It may be the case that 'a conto' payments were made at an early stage in the production of a work, but it does not seem *prima face* obvious that a first payment of this kind must necessarily precede some sketch or model.

As far as the *Sta. Susanna* is concerned, Mahon records the fact that in December 1629 a payment was made for a block of marble for the statue (as he points out, the words *Sta. Cecilia* must be a mistake for *Sta. Susanna*). He rejects utterly the suggestion made by Mlle Fransolet that the model for the *Sta. Susanna* may actually have been made at a date considerably earlier than this; but even if Mlle Fransolet is wrong, the fact remains that the *Sta. Susanna* was commissioned at the latest in 1629 and that a block of marble was ordered for it in that year. Recently, in an important article on the chronology of Duquesnoy's early work, Noehles has strongly reaffirmed the earlier dating of the *Sta. Susanna*. He believes that it must have been conceived early in 1628 and that a model of it must have been finished at the very latest by May 1629 and probably before the end of 1628 (Bibl. 1419, pp. 91 ff.).

On Mahon's own showing, therefore, the works which he believes to have exercised so vital an influence on Poussin's *Inspiration* were at any rate conceived in 1629.

But further doubts may suggest themselves in connection with Mahon's thesis. First, why must Poussin necessarily have been the one who tagged along behind in this case? Duquesnoy was his exact contemporary, and Sacchi was five years younger; and it can hardly be denied that Poussin, though a late starter and late arrival in Rome, was fundamentally an artist of greater invention than either of the others. Finally, though it is undoubtedly the case that Poussin stood for the classical doctrines which Sacchi maintained in the disputes in the Academy of St. Luke in the 1630's, there is, in my view, so little similarity between the actual paintings of the two artists that it is difficult to talk of the influence of one on the other.

It is true that, after Domenichino left Rome in 1631, Poussin went to draw in the studio of Sacchi, but it is worth noticing that Bellori does not mention this fact at all and that Passeri, who is the only early biographer to do so (p. 326), implies that Poussin's main reason for joining the studio was that Sacchi had as a model the celebrated Caporale Leone.

As far as Duquesnoy is concerned, there is certainly a general resemblance between the *Sta. Susanna* and the muse in Poussin's *Inspiration*, but it could well be accounted for by a study of common ancient models, which is in any case likely, since the two men were close friends, had the same artistic tastes, and had for some years lived in the same house. As with Sacchi, however, it is not *a priori* obvious that Poussin must have been the learner.

Mahon rightly calls attention to the fact that the *Divina Sapienza* and the *Sta. Susanna* caused a sensation in Rome as manifestations of the new classical tendency, and there is no reason for thinking that any work of Poussin's had quite such an impact, but, as far as we know, the *Inspiration* was not, like the *Sapienza* and the *Sta. Susanna*, executed for a public place and so could not have produced so violent an impression. It could even be argued that Poussin's one public commission of the 1620's, the *St. Erasmus* of 1628–29, had in a sense prepared the way for the classical demonstration of 1629–30; for, though it is one of the most baroque works in Poussin's *oeuvre*, seen in the context of contemporary Roman painting it seems almost classical; and Sandrart, in his account of the comparison made at the time between Poussin's *St. Erasmus* and Valentin's *Sts. Processus and Martinianus*, which balanced it in St. Peter's, says that Poussin was generally allowed to have triumphed 'in denen Passionen, Affecten, und der Invention', whereas Valentin had the advantage 'in der Wahren Natürlichkeit, Stärke, Erhebung des Colorits, Harmonia der Farben' (p. 257). It is interesting to notice that, in this analysis, Poussin is credited with qualities which are generally regarded as classical, and that he is not allowed success in colour, the principal interest of the party to which, in Mahon's reading of the artist, he was attached at the time he painted the *St. Erasmus* (Bibl. 1367, pp. IX f.).

The connection with Sacchi and Duquesnoy does not, therefore, in my opinion, provide any conclusive evidence for dating the *Inspiration* to a period after 1630. I have elsewhere (Bibl. 1227, pp. 171 f., and text volume, pp. 83 ff.) set out my reasons for believing that the *Inspiration* and several other paintings with large-scale figures (the *Marriage of St. Catherine* (No. 95), and the fragment of the *Golden Calf* (No. 27)) should, like the Chantilly *Massacre* (No. 67) and the Dresden *Exposition of Moses* (No. 10), about which there is general agreement, also be dated roughly to the years 1628–29, that is to say to the period of the *St. Erasmus*.

BIBLIOGRAPHY: *Inventaire . . . Mazarin*, Bibl. 20, p. 324; Chantelou, 1885, p. 120, and 1960, p. 127; Buchanan, I, p. 290; Smith, No. 284; Cosnac, Bibl. 584, p. 318, No. 1096; Redford, Bibl. 601.1, II, p. 280; Seidel, Bibl. 631, p. 91; Jamot, Bibl. 698, pp. 177 ff.; Leprieur, Bibl. 700, pp. 161 ff.; Thiébault-Sisson, Bibl. 709, p. 20; Friedlaender, 1914, pp. 53, 128; Grautoff, I, p. 150, II, No. 79; Magne, 1914, p. 216, No. 288; Grautoff and Pevsner, Bibl. 822, p. 263; Valentiner, Bibl. 845, p. 96; Friedlaender, 1933, p. 325; Blunt, Bibl. 1003, p. 266; Jamot, pp. 22, 24, 40, 51, 64, 80 f., 85; Kleiner, Bibl. 1044, pp. 13 ff.; Moussali, Bibl. 1045, p. 1; Stein, Bibl. 1079, p. 8; Blunt, Bibl. 1086, p. 184, and Bibl. 1086a, p. 160; Licht, p. 89; Van Gelder, Bibl. 1170, p. 11; Blunt, Bibl. 1222, p. 332, Bibl. 1226, p. 399, and Bibl. 1227, pp. 171 f.; Hours, Bibl. 1256, pp. 17 ff.; *Exposition Poussin (Louvre)*, No. 8; Mahon, Bibl. 1268.1, pp. 352 ff., Bibl. 1269, pp. 250 f., Bibl. 1270, p. 457, and Bibl. 1271, pp. 292, 295, 300; Panofsky, Bibl. 1273, pp. 45 ff., 59; Wild, Bibl. 1312, pp. 157 ff.; Bibliothèque Nationale, Paris, Bibl. 1320, p. 166; Costello, Bibl. 1360, p. 137; Mahon, Bibl. 1367, pp. XI, 16 f., 39, 47, 51 ff., 57, 59 f., 75 ff., 133, 136, 137.

125. THE INSPIRATION OF THE LYRIC POET. 94 × 69·5 cm. Niedersächsische Landesgalerie, Hanover (280).

HISTORY: The Electors of Hanover, probably by 1679; sent to England in 1803 and recorded at Great Cumberland Lodge, Windsor, in 1812; presumably sent back to Hanover before 1837 (Catalogue of the Landesgalerie).

DRAWING: In the Paris sale, Munich, 29.iv.1927, lot 308. A copy after the painting.

ENGRAVING: By Ignatius van Roy (In the Albertina; not listed by Andresen).

COPY: Alleyn's College of God's Gift, Dulwich (229).

Probably the version from the Robit collection (Buchanan, II, p. 69). Noël Desenfans; bequeathed to Sir Francis Bourgeois and by him to the gallery (Hazlitt, Bibl. 411, p. 33, and Bibl. 417, p. 198; Cousin, Bibl. 456, p. 17; Jamot, p. 86).

NOTES: The theme of the painting has been exhaustively studied by Panofsky, who identifies the Muse as Euterpe and rejects previous attempts to identify the poet as Anacreon, Ovid or Propertius, seeing him simply as the type of lyric poet, just as the hero of the Louvre picture (No. 124) is the type of the epic poet. The god is a mixed deity, a Bacchus-Apollo, as in the Stockholm painting (No. 135).

The picture was dated by Grautoff (II, No. 42) 1630–35. Friedlaender (1914, p. 53) is not quite explicit but implies a date before 1635. Mahon (Bibl. 1367, p. 26) places it 'towards the end of 1630'. I believe myself that the painting must be earlier than the *Kingdom of Flora* (No. 154) and the *Plague* of 1630 (No. 32), both of which have a much firmer construction of the figures and draperies. It may even be as early as the *Holy Family with St. John* (No. 48), which I should tend to place about 1627.

BIBLIOGRAPHY: Triqueti, Bibl. 440, p. 48; Parthey, Bibl. 504, II, p. 294, No. 47; Friedlaender, 1914, pp. 53, 128, 187; Grautoff, I, p. 110, II, No. 42; Stein, Bibl. 735, p. 104 n. 3; Waldmann, Bibl. 736, p. 595; Dorner, Bibl. 782, p. 233, and Bibl. 813, pp. 26 f.; Grautoff and Pevsner, Bibl. 822, p. 263; Friedlaender, 1933, p. 324; Hourticq, Bibl. 899, pp. 180 f.; Blunt, Bibl. 912, p. 100; Emmerling, Bibl. 933, p. 40; Christoffel, Bibl. 955, p. 64, and Bibl. 1006, p. 353; Kleiner, Bibl. 1044, pp. 13 ff.; Stuttmann, Bibl. 1095, pp. 56 f.; Licht, p. 90; *Exposition Poussin (Louvre)*, No. 18; Mahon, Bibl. 1271, pp. 298 f.; Panofsky, Bibl. 1273, pp. 45 ff., 59; Costello, Bibl. 1360, pp. 137 ff.; Mahon, Bibl. 1367, pp. XI, 17, 19 f., 26, 29, 49.

126. ACHILLES AMONG THE DAUGHTERS OF LYCOMEDES. 97 × 129·5 cm. Museum of Fine Arts, Boston (463).

HISTORY: Two pictures called *La Reconnaissance d'Achille* are recorded by Dézallier d'Argenville in 1757 (Bibl. 183b, pp. 186, 415) as being in the collection of the Fermier-Général Etienne-Michel Bouret and in the Hôtel de Lassay. Nothing seems to be known of Bouret, but the Marquis de Lassay (d. 1738) made an important collection of pictures, some of which seem to have been disposed of privately by his heirs (cf. Cat. No. 124). The remainder were offered for sale on 22 ff.v.1775, but the *Achilles* does not appear in the catalogue of that sale. Since Nos. 126 and 127 are both only traceable to sales in 1777, there is no means of linking either of them with either of the two pictures recorded in 1757, but it is fairly certain that they are the two pictures which belonged to Bouret and Lassay. Probably the painting in a sale of pictures 'consigned from abroad', Christie, London, 18 f.iv.1777, lot 34. Stephen Jarrett in 1837 (Smith, No. 162); James Fenton sale, Christie, London, 26.ii.1880, lot 121 (stated to be Smith, No. 162), bt. Hudson. The Boston picture was with Reyre, London, Atri, Paris (1924), and Wildenstein (1925). Belonged to Juliana Cheyne Edwards; acquired by the museum in 1946.

DRAWINGS: 1. Hermitage Museum, Leningrad (*CR*, II, p. 3, No. 104).

2–3. Hermitage Museum, Leningrad (*CR*, II, p. 3, Nos. A 23, A 24). Both copies of a lost original. *CR* No. 105, stated to be for the Boston painting, is in fact connected with *CR*, III, p. 19, Nos. 175, 176, and is therefore related to an early stage of the *Apollo and Daphne*.

ENGRAVING: By Pietro del Po (Andresen, No. 303; Wildenstein, No. 105; Davies and Blunt, p. 213, Nos. 104–105).

COPIES: 1. Musée, Coutances (Thuillier, Bibl. 1299, p. 290).

The following pictures are recorded in collections or sales with no details, so that it is impossible to know whether they are connected with the Boston or Richmond originals (see No. 127), or with the painting of the same subject in the Louvre, wrongly ascribed to Poussin (cf. Jamot, Bibl. 744):

1. In the possession of Claudine Bouzonnet-Stella (*Testament*, Bibl. 107, p. 37).
2. Thornhill records a copy in his diary of his visit to Paris in 1717 (Bibl. 140, p. 86) in the collection of 'Mons.' Groin y.ᵉ Treasurer'. This collector is not identifiable, but if Groin is a misspelling of Gruyn, he may be a relation of the Gruyn des Bordes who built the Hôtel de Lauzun in the 1650's.
3. Sir Gregory Page Turner sale, Phillips, London, 19 f.iv.1815, second day, lot 200, bt. Baring.
4. John Knight sale, Phillips, London, 17.iii.1821, lot 37.
5. T. B. Brown sale, Phillips, London, 20.v.1856, lot 42 (described as 'The engraved version').

NOTES: The subject is taken from Hyginus (*Fab.* xcvi), but Poussin was probably stimulated to treat it by the knowledge that it was painted in antiquity by Polygnotus (Pausanias, Bk. I, *Attica*, xxii, 6) and Athenias of Maroneia (Pliny, *Hist. Nat.*, xxxv, 134).

The picture has been generally dated to 1648–50, partly on the basis of a letter on the *verso* of one original drawing in the Hermitage. In *CR* (I, p. 3) it is stated that this letter is a first draft of one sent to Chantelou on 29.viii.1650 (*Correspondance*, p. 418), and this view is repeated by Mme Kamenskaya, who later published the text of the letter and reproduced the manuscript itself (Bibl. 1394, pp. 345 ff.). Now that the full text is available it becomes clear that the draft is not actually for the letter to Chantelou, but rather for a lost letter to Chambray. This does not affect the dating, because the letter clearly refers, like the one to Chantelou, to the dedicatory letter which Chambray prefixed to his publication of the treatise of Leonardo da Vinci. This only appeared in 1651, but from the letter to Chantelou it is clear that the author must have sent Poussin a draft for his approval.

BIBLIOGRAPHY: Bellori, p. 446; *Testament*, Bibl. 107, p. 37; Smith, No. 162; Moschetti, Bibl. 706, pp. 356 f.; Friedlaender, 1914, p. 123, Bibl. 726, p. 230, and Bibl. 809, p. 141; *CR*, II, p. 3; Friedlaender, Bibl. 947, pp. 11, 13; McLanathan, Bibl. 1015, p. 2; Bertin-Mourot, Bibl. 1023, p. 51, No. XXIX; Bardon, Bibl. 1218, p. 127; Sterling, Bibl. 1290, p. 271 n. 4; Friedlaender, Bibl. 1365, pp. 252 f.

127. ACHILLES AMONG THE DAUGHTERS OF LYCOMEDES. 98×131 cm. Virginia Museum of Fine Arts, Richmond, Virginia.

HISTORY: Painted for Charles III, Duc de Créqui, in 1656 (cf. *CR*, I, p. 31); in the inventory made at his death in 1687 (Magne, Bibl. 936, p. 186). La Curne de Sainte-Palaye; Prince de Conti sale, Remy, Paris, 8 ff.iv.1777, lot 531 (as from the La Curne de Sainte-Palaye collection); Beaujon sale, Remy, Paris, 25.iv.1787, lot 83 (as from the Conti sale); W. Ellis Agar (Christie, London, sale catalogue dated 2.v.1806, lot 52, with description; 36×52 inches); bt. with the entire Agar collection before the sale by Lord Grosvenor; Grosvenor sale, Coxe, London, 27.vi.1807, lot 94; sale of pictures coming from the Agar collection, Christie, London, 21.vi.1811, lot 47 (with description). The Richmond picture was bought from Wildenstein in 1957.

DRAWING: Hermitage Museum, Leningrad (*CR*, II, p. 4, No. 106).

ENGRAVING: Attributed to Pietro del Po (Andresen,

No. 302; Wildenstein, No. 104; Davies and Blunt, p. 213, Nos. 104–105).

COPY: Musée d'Art et d'Histoire, Geneva.

NOTES: For the subject, see No. 126.

BIBLIOGRAPHY: Félibien, IV, p. 65; Bellori, p. 445; *Testament*, Bibl. 107, p. 37; Loménie de Brienne, p. 222; Florent Le Comte, III, p. 32; Smith, No. 163; Friedlaender, 1914, pp. 99, 123, 260; Magne, 1914, pp. 156, 197, No. 2; Friedlaender, Bibl. 809, pp. 141 ff.; Magne, Bibl. 936, p. 186; *CR*, II, p. 3; McLanathan, Bibl. 1015, pp. 2 ff.; Glasser, Bibl. 1171; Bardon, Bibl. 1218, p. 127; *Exposition Poussin (Louvre)*, No. 111; Mahon, Bibl. 1338, p. 127; Friedlaender, Bibl. 1365, p. 252; Mahon, Bibl. 1367, p. 143.

128. ACIS AND GALATEA. 97×135 cm. National Gallery of Ireland, Dublin (814).

HISTORY: The picture is not clearly identifiable with any mentioned in the early sources, but it was engraved in the seventeenth century by Antoine Garnier and may be the *Galatée* mentioned by Loménie de Brienne (p. 214), though unfortunately the name of the owner is illegible in Brienne's manuscript. Perhaps Bragge sale, Prestage, London, 16.ii.1750, lot 31, and John Knight sale, Phillips, London, 17.iii.1821, lot 24 (Smith, No. 240). In 1831 the Dublin picture belonged to Earl Spencer (Passavant, Bibl. 399, II, p. 37), who sold it to Sir John Leslie in 1856. It was bought from his descendants by Sir Hugh Lane, who bequeathed it to the National Gallery of Ireland in 1916.

DRAWING: A drawing, washed with water-colour, in the National Gallery of Ireland (*CR*, III, p. 36, No. A 62) shows considerable variations from the painting and is certainly not by Poussin. It may be a copy of a lost drawing, but is more likely to be the work of an imitator.

ENGRAVING: By Antoine Garnier (1611–94; Andresen, No. 386; Wildenstein, No. 135).

COPIES: 1. J. Ehrmann collection, Paris. The left half of the composition only.
2. By Antoine Bouzonnet Stella; in the possession of his niece Claudine in 1697 (*Testament*, Bibl. 107, p. 36). Size given as "2 pieds environ".
3. In the collection of A. D. J. de Pujol, Valenciennes, in 1801 (Palais des Beaux-Arts, Valenciennes, Bibl. 855.1, I, p. 9). Size given as 36×48 inches.

NOTES: The picture has on various occasions been called *Peleus and Thetis* (Bodkin, Bibl. 858, p. 180; Royal Academy London, Bibl. 879, p. 33, No. 116; Bardon, Bibl. 1218, p. 127), but it does not correspond in any way to this story. On the other hand it follows closely Ovid's account of the story of Acis and Galatea (*Metamorphoses*, XIII, 738 ff.), with the two lovers in the foreground and Polyphemus piping in the background. It is true that Poussin mentions a project for painting the Marriage of Peleus for Pozzo, but this is in a letter of 1642 (*Correspondance*, p. 130), a date which would not fit with the style of the Dublin painting.

Mahon dates the picture 'centrally in the period between mid-1629 and the beginning of 1631', i.e. presumably to the first half of 1630. I should myself see it as earlier, and quite near the *Triumph of Flora* (No. 154).

BIBLIOGRAPHY: Loménie de Brienne, p. 214; Smith, Nos. 239, 240; Passavant, Bibl. 399, II, p. 37; Grautoff, II, p. 258; Magne, 1914, p. 197, No. 3; Bodkin, Bibl. 858, p. 180; Royal Academy, London, Bibl. 879, p. 33, No. 118; Hourticq, Bibl. 899, pp. 142, 146; *CR*, III, p. 36; Bertin-Mourot, Bibl. 1023, p. 49; Bardon, Bibl. 1218, p. 127; *Connoisseur*, Bibl. 1257, p. 43; Kauffmann, Bibl. 1334, p. 116; Mahon, Bibl. 1367, pp. 29, 53.

129. APOLLO AND THE MUSES ON PARNASSUS. 145 × 197 cm. Museo del Prado, Madrid (2313).

HISTORY: Presumably the painting seen by Félibien in Rome in 1647 (Bibl. 11a, p. 80). Possibly anon. sale, Banqueting House, Whitehall, London, 2.vi.1684, lot 31 (cf. Waterhouse, Bibl. 1308, p. 285). Spanish Royal collection by 1746.

DRAWING: Wildenstein collection (CR, III, p. 20, No. 180).

ENGRAVING: By J. Dughet (Andresen, No. 392; Wildenstein, No. 138).

NOTES: For the iconography, see Panofsky (Bibl. 1273, pp. 52 ff.), who identifies the poet being received into Parnassus as Poussin's first patron, Marino.

The picture was dated 1625–29 by Grautoff (II, No. 8); Friedlaender (1914, p. 53) proposed c. 1635, and Mahon (Bibl. 1367, p. XI and *passim*) suggests 1631–33. I find it hard to believe that a work so clumsy in drawing and composition can be so late as 1630, and see confirmation of my doubts in similarities which link the picture with works of Poussin's early years. The Wildenstein drawing is not far from the Marino series in manner, and the trees—in both drawing and painting—are like the same series in their tufty foliage, attached in a curious and unnaturalistic manner to the trunks. They have nothing of the Titianesque richness of Poussin's foliage of the years after 1630. Apollo is of the same Antinous type as the corresponding figure in the Louvre *Poet* (No. 124) and the Crocus of the Dresden *Flora* (No. 155). The curious technical trick of edging the fingers with bands of crude red is also to be found in works such as the Incisa *Children's Bacchanals* (Nos. 192, 193), which are generally accepted as very early, and others, such as the Washington *Assumption* (No. 93), which I myself believe to be before 1630. Panofsky's identification of the poet with Marino and his suggestion that the picture may have been painted in his honour soon after his death would also tend to confirm the earlier dating.

BIBLIOGRAPHY: Félibien, Bibl. 11a, p. 80; Vertue, Bibl. 132, XXVI, p. 56; Smith, No. 273; Mabilleau, Bibl. 635, p. 308; Friedlaender, 1914, pp. 53, 186; Grautoff, I, p. 71, II, No. 8; Magne, 1914, p. 216, No. 291; Friedlaender, 1933, p. 323; Francastel, Bibl. 883, p. 150; Hourticq, Bibl. 899, pp. 133, 175 ff.; Blunt, Bibl. 1026, pp. 4, 7; Jamot, pp. 11, 45, 51, 86; Blunt, Bibl. 1086, p. 183, and Bibl. 1086a, p. 159; Licht, pp. 79, 82; Blunt, Bibl. 1227, p. 170; *Exposition Poussin (Louvre)*, No. 6 bis; Mahon, Bibl. 1271, pp. 292 f.; Panofsky, Bibl. 1273, pp. 45, 50 ff., 59; Waterhouse, Bibl. 1308, p. 285; Kauffmann, Bibl. 1332, p. 96; Costello, Bibl. 1360, p. 137; Mahon, Bibl. 1367, pp. XI, 31 f., 39 f., 47 ff., 54 f., 61, 75, 86, 88, 90, 136.

130. APOLLO AND DAPHNE. 97 × 131 cm. Alte Pinakothek, Munich (2334).

HISTORY: In the collection of the Electors of Bavaria by 1781.

ENGRAVINGS: By F. Chauveau, dated 1667 (Andresen, No. 339; Wildenstein, No. 118).

COPY: A copy with some variations in the Musée d'Evreux.

NOTES: Several versions of this subject are mentioned in the early sources, but it is not possible to identify any of them with certainty as the Munich painting.

The Munich picture represents the last stage of the myth. The pursuit is over; Apollo, seated with his lyre and quiver on the ground beside him, has one arm round the waist of Daphne, who is half transformed into a laurel, while with the other hand he plucks a branch which grows from her body. Peneus sits with his hand over his eyes in an attitude of mourning. On the left are four putti; one leans on an urn; another on a cornucopia, from which emerge flowers; the third carries a sheaf of wheat, and the fourth lies on his back, apparently blowing water through two straws.

This does not agree with the composition described by Bellori (p. 444), which records an earlier moment, that of the actual pursuit:

Dafne Fuggitiva

Le braccia aperte, e le mani, che si sciolgono in frondi, il volto concitato dal dolore, e li capelli sparsi al vento sono contrasegni della fuggitiva Dafne. Sdegna ella divino amante, essendo consacrata alla Dea più casta. Ma la pittura la rappresenta in quel punto, che Apolline la raggiunge, e la ritiene pigliandole un braccio. Volgesi ella indietro dolente, e spaventata, e ricorre all'aiuto del fiume Peneo suo padre che commosso al suo duolo, sedendo l'abbraccia per salvarla. Ma già ella resta immota nel senso del dolore, e della fuga, & Apolline dimostra la sua passione di rapirla, non si accorgendo ancora del suo trasmutamento. Ecco una delle Naiadi smarrita pare che voglia fuggire, e con timore si volge verso Dafne, tenendo in mano l'urna.

Bellori's description is, apart from minor details, close to the composition preserved in a drawing at Chatsworth (*CR*, III, p. 17, No. 172), which is probably a study for the lost painting. The painting itself may be the one mentioned by Sandrart (p. 258) as 'die flüchtige Daphne durch Apollo verfolgt', and by Félibien (IV, p. 151) as 'Apollon qui poursuit Daphné'. Félibien states that the picture belonged in his time to 'le Sieur Stella aux Galeries du Louvre', but this is probably a slip, for Antoine Bouzonnet Stella, nephew of Poussin's friend Jacques Stella, had died in 1682, and there does not seem to have been a male painter of the name alive in 1685. Antoine Bouzonnet Stella bequeathed all his paintings to his niece Claudine Bouzonnet Stella, who was no doubt the actual owner when Félibien wrote. She presumably sold the picture, since it does not appear in the inventories of her possessions made in 1693–97 (*Testament*, Bibl. 107). The Stella picture is also mentioned by Florent Le Comte (III, p. 31). Its later history is unknown. Another painting of the subject was in the Radstock sale, Christie, London, 12 f.v.1826, lot 41, where it was described as follows:

Apollo and Daphne; the latter, undergoing her metamorphosis, is bending back from the embrace of Apollo; a Cupid on the wing has just discharged an arrow from his bow. The river god, Peneus, and two infants in front, complete this classic group, which is painted with a strong effect of chiaroscuro—It is 26½ inches by 22.

Smith (No. 188) gives a slightly fuller description:

The disappointed lover is bending by the side of the half-transformed nymph, extending his arms to embrace the still panting unligneous part. A river deity is seated at the foot of the forming tree, bending his hoary head drowsily over his chest; a cupid stands by him; and a second is flying above, towards the metamorphosed Daphne. This excellent work of art is distinguished by high classical feeling and masterly execution.

This picture later belonged to Lord Northwick. It was in his sale (Christie, London, 25.v.1838, lot 88, as from the Radstock collection); presumably bt. in, since it reappeared in the Northwick sale, Phillips, Cheltenham, 26 ff.vii.1859, lot 1521, bt. Farrer. It was probably the picture which had belonged to Sir Gregory Page in 1761 (Dodsley, Bibl. 214, I, p. 316, with dimensions 26½×22 inches) and which later appeared in an anon. sale, Christie, London, 7.iii.1801, lot 80 (as from the Page collection).

An unidentifiable newspaper report of the sale of 1859 adds the small detail that in the Northwick collection picture Apollo is shown seated on a bank. From the description quoted above the picture seems to have been a variant of the Munich composition. Either the Radstock or the Munich picture is probably that recorded in 1641 in the collection of Philip Baldescot in Rome, with the following description: 'Un quadro con figure, d'una figura che dorme et il ratto di Dafne, con cornice indorata, di Monsù Puccino come disse' (Orbaan and Hoogewerff, Bibl. 703.2, II, p. 215).

Félibien (IV, p. 152) also mentions an 'Apollon et Daphné de la premiere maniere' belonging to 'M. Gamarre des Chasses'. This is no doubt Hubert Gamar, Gamart or Gamarre, Lieutenant des Chasses du Louvre, who is mentioned several times in Chantelou's journal of Bernini's visit to Paris (1885, pp. 166, 227, 230), and also in the *Banquet des Curieux* (Bibl. 70b, p. 170). Florent Le Comte (III, p. 32) mentions this picture, probably simply copying Félibien. There is no reason why this painting should not be the Munich picture, but no proof that it is. It is possible, moreover, that there may have been yet another composition, now lost, like the Stella picture, because a drawing exists at Chantilly which cannot be a study for the Munich painting, since it represents the actual pursuit, and yet is quite different in style and composition from the Chatsworth drawing.

The Munich picture has suffered badly. In the shaded parts of the putti on the left the pigment seems to have discoloured completely and the forms have almost disappeared. The body of Apollo appears to have been repainted and has a smooth, sticky quality of pigment quite unlike Poussin's handling. (The only analogy is with the kneeling youth in the *Sacrifice of Noah* at Tatton Hall, Cheshire, belonging to the National Trust; rep. Blunt, Bibl. 1227, Fig 133; see also below, R7).

The condition of the picture makes it difficult to date it precisely. Grautoff (II, No. 48) proposed 1630–35, and Stechow (Bibl. 868, p. 34) the early thirties, but the looseness of the forms and the cadaverous colour of Daphne and the Cupids suggest an earlier period, near to the *Echo and Narcissus* (No. 151). The type of Daphne's face, particularly in the forms of the eyes, comes close to the head of the mother in the left-hand group of the Petit Palais *Massacre* (No. 66).

BIBLIOGRAPHY: Félibien, IV, p. 152; Florent Le Comte, III, p. 32; Smith, No. 187; Friedlaender, 1914, p. 113; Grautoff, I, pp. 115 f., II, No. 48; Magne, 1914, p. 197, No. 8; Stechow, Bibl. 868, pp. 34 ff.; Blunt, Bibl. 912, pp. 96 f.; Friedlaender, Bibl. 964, p. 26; Licht, p. 111.

131. APOLLO AND DAPHNE. 155 × 200 cm. Musée du Louvre, Paris (742).

HISTORY: Given to Cardinal Camillo Massimi by Poussin in 1664, because the artist realized that he could no longer work and would therefore not be able to finish it (Bellori, p. 444, and *Nota delli musei*, Bibl. 36, p. 33); apparently sold with his palace to Cardinal Nerli, since a picture by Poussin described as 'un Apollo, che perseguita Dafne' appears in Rossi's *Descrizione di Roma moderna* of 1697 (Bibl. 114, p. 686), written when the palace belonged to the Cardinal. The picture is not mentioned in the edition of 1727, by which time the palace had been bought by Cardinal Alessandro Albani, but it reappears in Martinelli's *Roma ricercata* of 1750 (Bibl. 186, p. 168) and in Roisecco's *Roma ampliata e rinnovata* of 1762 (Bibl. 150a, p. 150); it is still mentioned in Melchiorri's *Guida metodica di Roma* of 1840 (Bibl. 408, p. 558), but the author was probably copying earlier guides without checking, since the picture was apparently by that time in France. Erard sale, Henry, Paris, 7 ff.viii.1832, lot 191; Marquis de Gouvello; bt. by the Louvre in 1869.

DRAWINGS: 1. Musée du Louvre, Paris (*CR*, III, p. 18, No. 174). Kauffmann (Bibl. 1333, p. 124) wrongly quotes me as saying that this superb drawing is a copy. I was in fact referring to *CR*, III, p. 19, No. 177.
2–3. Hermitage Museum, Leningrad (*CR*, III, p. 19, Nos. 175, 176).
4. Musée Condé, Chantilly (*CR*, II, p. 4, No. 105; there wrongly connected with the *Achilles among the Daughters of Lycomedes*, No. 126).
5. Gabinetto dei Disegni, Florence (*CR*, III, p. 18, No. A 46). Probably an original.
6. Musée du Louvre, Paris (No. 1163 *v*). A sheet of copies, of which the lower part contains figures and animals which correspond with those appearing in other drawings for the *Apollo and Daphne*.
Drawings *CR*, III, pp. 19 f., Nos. 177–179, and possibly p. 29, No. 201, are indirectly connected with the composition (see text volume, pp. 336 ff.).

NOTES: For a discussion of the iconography, see text volume, pp. 336 ff. For Poussin's use of sixteenth-century sources in this picture, see Kauffmann (Bibl. 1334, *passim*). Bellori states that the *Apollo and Daphne* was left unfinished, a fact which is obvious from an examination of the picture itself. There is no evidence about the moment at which it was begun, but since the Seasons were, according to Bellori, not finished till 1664, and the *Apollo and Daphne* is recorded as being in Massimi's collection in the same year, it must be supposed that Poussin was working on the latter at the same time that he was painting the Seasons.

BIBLIOGRAPHY: [Bellori], Bibl. 36, p. 33; Bellori, p. 444; Rossi, Bibl. 114, p. 686; Roisecco, Bibl. 150a, p. 150; Martinelli, Bibl. 186, p. 168; Melchiorri, Bibl. 408, p. 558; Friedlaender, 1914, pp. 100, 124, 267; Grautoff, I, p. 287, II, No. 160; Magne, 1914, p. 197, No. 7; Orbaan, Bibl. 746, p. 521; Hourticq, Bibl. 899, pp. 108 f.; *CR*, III, pp. 17 ff.; Blunt, Bibl. 972, pp. 165, 168; Adhémar, Bibl. 996, p. 50; Jamot, pp. 43, 84; Panofsky, Bibl. 1060, p. 27; Blunt, Bibl. 1086, pp. 194 f., and Bibl. 1086a, pp. 170 f.; Berger, Bibl. 1113, p. 167; Thuillier, Bibl. 1161, p. 389; Blunt, Bibl. 1223, p. xxvii; Hours, Bibl. 1256, p. 38; *Exposition Poussin (Louvre)*, No. 119; Wallace, Bibl. 1307, p. 15; Kauffmann, Bibl. 1332, p. 100, and Bibl. 1334, pp. 101 ff.; Mahon, Bibl. 1338, pp. 125 f.; Friedlaender, Bibl. 1365, p. 255; Mahon, Bibl. 1367, pp. XIV, 120, 121.

132. THE BIRTH OF BACCHUS. 114·5 × 167·5 cm. Fogg Art Museum, Cambridge, Mass.

HISTORY: Painted for Jacques Stella in 1657 (Félibien, IV, p. 65); mentioned in the inventory of his niece, Claudine Bouzonnet Stella (*Testament*, Bibl. 107, p. 37) as having been sold out of the family. Philippe, Duke of Orleans, by 1727 (Dubois de Saint-Gelais, Bibl. 153, p. 352). Sold in 1790 with the Italian and French pictures of the Orleans collection to Walkuers; sold by him the same year to Laborde de Méréville; bt. 1798 by Bryan; list of pictures exhibited for sale by Bryan in London, 1798, No. 250 (Buchanan, I, p. 151). John Willett Willett; sold Coxe, London, 31.v.1813 and following days, third day, lot 124, presumably bt. in; Willett sale, Christie, London, 8.iv.1819, lot 121, bt. Pinney. Chevalier Sebastian Erard collection, Paris, in 1824 (Buchanan, *loc. cit.*); sold Henry, Paris, 7 ff.viii.1832, lot 192, bt. in; sold Christie, London, 22.vi.1833, lot 35 (with dimensions 45 × 66 inches); Montcalm sale, Christie, London, 5.v.1849, lot 137 (as from the Orleans and Erard collections); Adrian Hope sale, Christie, London, 30.vi.1894, lot 55 (as from the Orleans, Willett and Erard collections), bt. Sir A. Hayter. Anon. sale, Christie, London, 20.iv.1923 (as from the Orleans, Willett, Erard and Hope collections), bt. Durlacher; bt. from Durlacher by Samuel Sachs and presented to the Fogg Art Museum by Mrs. Sachs in 1942.

DRAWING: Fogg Art Museum, Cambridge, Mass. (cf. Mongan, Bibl. 1188).

ENGRAVING : By J. Dughet (Andresen, No. 362; Wildenstein, No. 128).

COPIES: 1. Musée Fabre, Montpellier (cf. Joubin, Bibl. 750, p. 341, and Thuillier, Bibl. 1299, p. 295).
2. Haydock collection, The Mount, York. From Aston Hall, Birmingham; sold 1862; Halton Grange, Runcorn, Cheshire; sold there May 1903.
3. Rawson collection, Yorkshire.
4. By Claudine Bouzonnet Stella (*Testament*, Bibl. 107, p. 37).
5. Roussel sale, Brussels, 22 f.v.1893, lot 19.

6. Anon. sale, Sotheby, London, 30.vi.1948, lot 77, bt. Buttery (48 × 72 inches).
7. Sir M. Grove-White sale, Sotheby, London, 16.xii.1953, lot 48, bt. Dynander.
8. Anon. sale, Christie, London, 3.xi.1961, lot 39.

Pictures of this subject also appeared in the following sales:
1. Poismenu, Nagus, Paris, 8 f.iv.1779, lot 2.
2. W. G. Podd, Richards, London, 16 f.ii.1798, lot 60.
3. Bryan sale, Coxe, London, 10.v.1804, lot 34.
4. Sir H. J. Gott, Christie, London, 24.ii.1810, lot 56, bt. Hooper.
5. Raymond, Lebrun, Paris, 4.x.1811, lot 21.
6. J. Bartie, Foster, London, 20.vi.1838, lot 192.

NOTES: For a discussion of the iconography of the painting, see text volume, pp. 316 ff.

BIBLIOGRAPHY: Félibien, IV, p. 65; Bellori, p. 445; *Testament*, Bibl. 107, p. 37; Loménie de Brienne, p. 222; Florent Le Comte, III, p. 32; [C. Saugrain], Bibl. 138a, I, p. 175; Dubois de Saint-Gelais, Bibl. 153, p. 352; Dézallier, 1745, II, p. 255, and 1762, IV, p. 40; Dézallier d'Argenville, Bibl. 183, p. 62; La Roque, Bibl. 248, I, p. 103; Couché, Fontenai and Croze-Magnan, Bibl. 285, III, Poussin, No. 8; Volkmann, Bibl. 290, I, p. 282; Barry, Bibl. 338, II, p. 133; Buchanan, I, p. 151; Waagen, Bibl. 384b, II, p. 493; Smith, No. 205; Friedlaender, 1914, pp. 99, 123, 259; Grautoff, II, p. 257; Magne, 1914, pp. 155, 198, No. 12; Friedlaender, Bibl. 947, p. 14, and Bibl. 964, p. 23; Blunt, Bibl. 972, pp. 165, 166 f.; Bertin-Mourot, Bibl. 1023, p. 50, No. XXVI; Panofsky, Bibl. 1046, pp. 112 ff.; Blunt, Bibl. 1086, p. 194, and Bibl. 1086a, p. 170; Licht, p. 166; Mongan, Bibl. 1188, pp. 29 ff.; Bardon, Bibl. 1218, p. 126; Blunt, Bibl. 1223, pp. xxvii f.; Mahon, Bibl. 1338, pp. 125 f.; Friedlaender, Bibl. 1365, p. 255; Mahon, Bibl. 1367, pp. XIV, 119, 121.

133. THE NURTURE OF BACCHUS. 75 × 97 cm. National Gallery, London (39).

HISTORY: Duc de Tallard sale, Remy, Paris, 22 ff.iii.1756, lot 161; Mariette sale, Basan, Paris, 15.xi.1775 and following days, lot 18 (see below). Possibly Thomas Bowes sale, Coxe, London, 27.vi.1812, lot 88. John Knight by 1813 (*The Picture of London*, 1813, p. 324); lent by him to the British Institution in 1816 (No. 49); Knight sale, Phillips, London, 23 f.iii.1819, second day, lot 110, bt. in; Knight sale, Phillips, London, 17.iii.1821, lot 42, bt. Cholmondeley. Bequeathed to the Gallery by G. J. Cholmondeley in 1831, with a life interest to the Hon. Mrs. Phipps; entered the Gallery in 1836.

COPIES: 1. Alleyn's College of God's Gift, Dulwich (477; cf. Hazlitt, Bibl. 411, p. 33).
2. R. Hoe sale, New York, 15 ff.ii.1911, lot 54.
3. A variant is in the Musée du Louvre, Paris (729; 97 × 136 cm); see below, and cf. Piganiol de La Force, Bibl. 124, I, p. 152; Bailly, p. 315; Monicart, Bibl. 144, II, p. 376; Dézallier, 1745, II, p. 255, and 1762, IV, p. 39; Boyer d'Argens, Bibl. 231, p. 297; Smith, No. 206; Friedlaender, 1914, pp. 50, 127; Grautoff, I, p. 101, II, No. 25; Magne, 1914, p. 198, No. 15; Jamot, pp. 21 f., 49; Licht, p. 103; *Exposition Poussin (Louvre)*, No. 29; *Exposition Poussin (Rouen)*, No. 77; Blunt, Bibl. 1357, pp. 494 ff.; Mahon, Bibl. 1367, pp. 29, 53, 132.

NOTES: The identification of the National Gallery picture with that in the Mariette sale is rendered fairly certain by the small sketch made by Gabriel de Saint-Aubin in the margin of his copy of the catalogue, now in the Public Library at Boston. Davies (Bibl. 988a, p. 62) believes that the sketch is too small for any certain conclusions to be drawn from it, but in fact it seems to show the composition of the National Gallery picture; and Mariette (Bibl. 157, IV, p. 205) tells us that his picture came from the Tallard sale. In the Mariette sale the subject of the picture is given as the Nursing of Jupiter, which is certainly incorrect (see text volume, p. 123).

The National Gallery picture is apparently unfinished in certain parts of the landscape on the left, but it is unquestionably from the hand of Poussin.

The version in the Louvre, however, although it belonged to Louis XIV, has been the subject of increasing scepticism. In the second edition of the catalogue of the Louvre exhibition (No. 29) I expressed a doubt whether the whole painting could be by Poussin; Mahon had meanwhile begun to have similar doubts (Bibl. 1271, pp. 297 f.). Finally I came to the conclusion that the picture was not by Poussin at all, but by an imitator whom I dubbed 'The Master of the clumsy Children' (Bibl. 1357, pp. 494 ff.).

Grautoff, who curiously enough omits the National Gallery picture altogether, dates the Louvre version 1630–35. Mahon (Bibl. 1367, p. 21) dates the National Gallery painting to 1630. I should still hold to my earlier view and place the picture about 1629.

BIBLIOGRAPHY: Mariette, Bibl. 157, IV, p. 205; Dézallier d'Argenville, Bibl. 183a, p. 211; *The Picture of London,* 1813, p. 324; [R. Smirke], Bibl. 358, p. 42; Waagen, Bibl. 384b, I, p. 346; Smith, No. 209; Cousin, Bibl. 456, p. 7; Magne, 1914, p. 198, No. 16; Blunt, Bibl. 972, p. 167; Davies, Bibl. 988a, p. 170, No. 39; Bertin-Mourot, Bibl. 1023, p. 49, No. XIX; Blunt, Bibl. 1026, pp. 7 f.; D. Panofsky, Bibl. 1046, p. 117 n. 18; Licht, p. 103; Mahon, Bibl. 1271, pp. 297 f.; Blunt, Bibl. 1357, pp. 494 ff.; Mahon, Bibl. 1367, pp. XI, 20 f., 29.

134. THE YOUTH OF BACCHUS. 135 × 168 cm.; about 10 cm. added at the top. Musée Condé, Chantilly (298).

HISTORY: Possibly John Purling sale, White, London, 16.ii.1801, lot 52. The Chantilly picture was bought by the Duc d'Aumale at the Northwick sale, Phillips, Cheltenham, 26 ff.vii.1859, lot 1094. Bequeathed with the remainder of the collection in 1897.

ENGRAVING: Published by Ciartres (Andresen, No. 373; Wildenstein, No. 133; Davies and Blunt, p. 214, No. 133). According to Andresen and Wildenstein the engraving is by Antoine Garnier, but the Northwick sale catalogue says the picture is engraved by Mariette.

NOTES: D. Wild (Bibl. 1185, p. 23) dates the picture to *c.* 1632; Mahon (Bibl. 1271, p. 298, and Bibl. 1367, pp. XI, 29) to 1629–30. In its present state the picture is very hard to judge, owing to the darkening effect of the bolus. In certain respects it is close to paintings like the National Gallery *Nurture of Bacchus* (No. 133), but the carefully calculated pyramidal composition and the statuesque nymphs indicate a later period and have even some connection with paintings of the last years of the 1630's, such as the Berlin *Nurture of Jupiter* (No. 162). On the whole it seems likely that the picture dates from about 1630–35. The satyr drinking from a horn appears in the same pose in the *Nymph with a Satyr drinking* in Moscow (No. 200).

BIBLIOGRAPHY: Smith, Nos. 220, 232; Friedlaender, 1914, p. 177; Grautoff, I, p. 103, II, No. 26; Magne, 1914, p. 198, No. 18; Bodkin, Bibl. 858, p. 180; Francastel, Bibl. 883, p. 151; Jamot, pp. 18, 20 ff., 64; Incisa della Rocchetta, Bibl. 1070, p. 41; Licht, p. 105; Wild, Bibl. 1185, p. 23; Mahon, Bibl. 1271, p. 298, and Bibl. 1367, pp. XI, 29.

135. BACCHUS-APOLLO. 98 × 73·5 cm. Nationalmuseum, Stockholm (2669).

HISTORY: Sir Andrew Fountaine; perhaps in his sale 1731–32, lot 75, as 'Bacchus and Ariadne'; if so, bt. in; sold by his descendant, Christie, London, 7.vii.1894, lot 36, bt. Holt; acquired by Langton Douglas in 1912 as from the Fountaine collection; Pearson collection, Paris; sold Berlin, 18.x.1927, lot 54; with Cassirer, Berlin. Acquired by the Museum in 1928.

DRAWING: Fitzwilliam Museum, Cambridge (*CR*, III, p. 22, No. 184; see below).

NOTES: For a full discussion of the iconography of the picture, see Panofsky (Bibl. 1273, *passim*, and Bibl. 1344, pp. 318 ff.), Blunt (Bibl. 1322, p. 437), and Costello (Bibl. 1360, pp. 137 ff.).

X-ray examination shows that the picture has been much altered. Panofsky (Bibl. 1273, *passim*) believes that the alterations were made by Poussin himself and that they were intended to introduce a change of iconography from Bacchus and Erigone to Bacchus-Apollo. Mahon (Bibl. 1367, pp. 9 ff.) puts forward the view that the changes are more likely to have been made by another hand and at a later date. It certainly seems to be the case that the lower right-hand corner of the picture has suffered; indeed the object hanging below the fruit which Bacchus touches with his right hand can, in my opinion, only be explained as the shaggy beard and chest of the goat, the rest of which has disappeared in later alterations. On the other hand I find it impossible to believe that all the alterations are later, and should follow Panofsky in thinking that Poussin introduced major changes, both formal and iconographical, during the actual execution of the work. I still feel some doubt, however, whether either the drawing or the painting in its first state represents the story of Bacchus and Erigone, and these doubts have been expressed with greater emphasis by Miss Jane Costello (*loc. cit.*).

Grautoff (II, No. 1) dated the picture to the Paris years, 1620–24, and was followed by Dr. Wild (Bibl. 1312, p. 157), but the Venetian handling and colour and the classical type of the principal figure rule this out. Mahon places the parts which he accepts as original to about 1626.

I have elsewhere (Bibl. 1322, p. 437) called attention to the fact that on the *verso* of the Cambridge drawing there is a study connected with the early drawing of the *Kingdom of Flora* (*CR*, III, p. 35, No. 214). The sheet also contains a further study of two figures which, I then suggested, might be connected with a *Massacre of the Innocents*, though it was not possible to relate it positively to either of the surviving versions. In fact, however, it is closely connected with a very similar fragmentary sketch on the *verso* of the Lille drawing for the Chantilly *Massacre*.

The evidence provided by these sketches has some bearing on the dating of the picture. The drawing for the *Kingdom of Flora* certainly dates from the early Roman years, probably about 1626, whereas the Chantilly *Massacre* is generally accepted as being painted about 1628–29. From the way in which the sketches on the *verso* of the Cambridge drawing are cut, one would tend to conclude that the drawing on the *recto* was done after those on the *verso*. The most probable solution seems to be that both *recto* and *verso* were made about 1626 and that Poussin did not develop the study for the *Massacre* into a painting till a year or two later.

BIBLIOGRAPHY: Waagen, Bibl. 384b, III, p. 430; Grautoff, I, p. 39, II, No. 1; Jamot, Bibl. 749, p. 91; Sirén, Bibl. 827, pp. 35 ff.; Grautoff, Bibl. 864, p. 325; Friedlaender, 1933, p. 322; Jamot, pp. 14 f., 48 f.; Licht, p. 70; Trapp, Bibl. 1181, pp. 235 f.; Blunt, Bibl. 1226, pp. 402 f., and Bibl. 1227, p. 165; *Exposition Poussin* (*Louvre*), No. 12; Mahon, Bibl. 1271, p. 296; Panofsky, Bibl. 1273; Waterhouse, Bibl. 1308, p. 291; Wild, Bibl. 1312, p. 157; Blunt, Bibl. 1322, p. 437; Ettlinger, Bibl. 1327, pp. 199 f.; Kauffmann, Bibl. 1332, p. 96, Bibl. 1333, p. 196, and Bibl. 1334, pp. 118 f.; Panofsky, Bibl. 1344, pp. 318 ff.; Costello, Bibl. 1360, pp. 137 ff.; Mahon, Bibl. 1367, pp. IX, 9 ff., 49, 86, 135 f.

BACCHANALS

136–138. *THE BACCHANALS FOR THE CHATEAU DE RICHELIEU*

HISTORY: On 19.v.1636 the Marchese Pompeo Frangipani wrote to Richelieu informing him that the Bishop of Albi, Gaspard de Daillon, had left Rome, carrying with him 'deux tableaux de Bacchanales que le peintre Poussin a déjà exécutés conformément à votre désir et intention' (Pintard, Bibl. 1278, p. 33). Daillon took the pictures to the Château de Richelieu in December, after having shown them to the Cardinal, apparently at Amiens (see below). These pictures were undoubtedly the *Triumph of Pan* and the *Triumph of Bacchus*, which are later recorded in the château and were replaced by copies (now in the museum of Tours, see below) when the originals were sold in the eighteenth century. The originals passed with the château and the whole estate to the Cardinal's great-nephew, Armand Jean de Vignerod du Plessis, Duc de Richelieu, and to his descendants. It is not known at what date they were sold, but the *Triumph of Pan* and the *Triumph of Bacchus* appeared in the Samuel Paris sale, Cock, London, 1741–42, Nos. 48, 49, and according to Vertue (Bibl. 132, XXII, pp. 105, 117) had been imported from France. Bt. Peter Delmé; Delmé sale, Christie, London, 13.ii.1790, lots 62, 63, bt. Lord Ashburnham; Ashburnham sale, Christie, London, 20.vii.1850, lots 63, 64. For the later histories see the entries for the individual pictures. For the question of the third painting executed for the Château de Richelieu, see the *Triumph of Silenus* (No. 138).

NOTES: Batiffol (Bibl. 897, p. 166) prints part of a letter from Daillon to Richelieu, which refers to his visit to the Château de Richelieu, but he does not quote what is, as far as the Poussins are concerned, the most important passage, which reads as follows: 'Monseigneur, Apres avoir pris congé de V. E. dans Amiens, ie m'en alloy au Lude, ou iay esté dans le lit six sepmaines, tourmanté de la plus grande incommodité du genouil qu'homme eut iamais, aussi tot que ma santé ma permis de me mettre en chemin pour Alby, ie lay faict, et pour satisfaire au Commandement que V. E. me fit d'apporter icy les deux tableaux du poussin, iy suis venu passer, ie les ay veus ceux de Monsieur de Mantoue, lesquels quoy que bons n'approchent point de la beauté, et de la perfection des deux qui iay apportes, Cela n'empeschera pas qu'ensemble ils ne rendent le Cabinet de la Chambre du Roy parfaictement beau'. (Archives des Affaires Etrangères, fonds français, 826, fol. 88r). This letter is undated. Batiffol places it late in December 1636, and the date 31.1. 1637 has been added to the manuscript by a later hand.

From this letter it can be deduced that the two *Triumphs* had been specifically commissioned from Poussin to complete the decoration of a room designed to contain the series of paintings from the studio of

Isabella d'Este in the palace at Mantua, which had been presented to Richelieu by the Duke of Mantua and which are described as being with the *Triumphs* in later accounts of the château. These are the *Parnassus* and the *Minerva driving out the Vices* by Mantegna, the *Allegory* and the *Kingdom of Comus* by Lorenzo Costa, and the *Combat of Love and Chastity* by Perugino, all of which were taken from Richelieu to the Louvre after the Revolution (cf. Bonnaffé, Bibl. 573, pp. 103 f.).

The earliest writer to describe the château, Elias Brackenhoffer, who visited it in 1644, does not mention either the Mantuan pictures or the Poussins in his description of the Cabinet du Roi (Bibl. 7, p. 225), but he often only picks out one or two objects in a room. Two years later Willem Schellinks and Lambert Doomer mention the two Mantegnas and three *Triumphs* by Poussin as being in the room (cf. Van den Berg, Bibl. 962, p. 16), and all the other accounts of the château written in the seventeenth and eighteenth centuries confirm the fact that the Cabinet du Roi contained three paintings by Poussin. Vignier's well-known account, written in 1676 (Bibl. 69a, pp. 165 f.), gives the fullest details, and it is confirmed by a short passage in Marot's *Magnifique Château de Richelieu* (Bibl. 51.1): 'Dessus le dit lambris il y a huit tableaux, deux d'André Mantaigne, un de Pietre Perusin, deux autres, et trois Bachanales du Poussin.' A detailed account, written in the middle of the eighteenth century—partly copied from Vignier but with additions and alterations—(cf. *Description*, Bibl. 188, pp. 222 ff.), shows that the general disposition of the room had at that time not been changed.

Unfortunately no plan of the first floor of the château exists, so that it is impossible to ascertain exactly how the pictures were arranged on the individual walls and in relation to the doors and windows. It is, however, clear, both from Vignier and from the eighteenth-century account of the château, that the order in which they were placed was as follows: Mantegna's *Parnassus*, followed by his *Minerva driving out the Vices*; then Costa's *Allegory* and the Perugino; next Poussin's *Triumph of Pan* and *Triumph of Bacchus*; these were followed by Costa's *Kingdom of Comus*, and the series was completed by Poussin's *Silenus*. It is, therefore, clear that the two *Triumphs* were disposed as a pair and that the *Silenus* was separated from them; the fact that it differs from them in format may well be explained by its position in a narrower wall-space. It is not clear, however, why all the Poussins should be so much smaller than the Mantegna canvases. The two *Triumphs* are roughly 30 cm. less in height and 50 cm. less in width, and even the *Silenus*, which is taller than the *Triumphs*, is still 15 cm. short of the Italian members of the series in height and 70 cm. narrower. The copies of the three Poussins at Tours have all been enlarged and would in their present state fit in with the Mantuan pictures.

The canvases were all set into panelling above a high dado. The latter was divided up into sections by ten figures of herm-caryatids in carved wood, coloured a dull gold. Between the caryatids were panels, some decorated with fleurs-de-lys on a blue ground, others with paintings depicting battles and triumphs of marine gods, no doubt an allusion to Richelieu's position of Grand Admiral of France. Above each of the caryatids, that is to say between the pictures themselves, stood ancient busts and statues. The ceiling was divided into panels, of which the central one, an oval, contained the *Apotheosis of Hercules*.

The dating of the pictures presents no problem. If they were despatched in May 1636, they must have been painted in the later part of 1635 and the first months of 1636. It is inconceivable that Poussin, at that stage of his career, would have kept so important a patron as Richelieu waiting longer than was absolutely necessary.

When the two pictures appeared at the Delmé sale in 1790, *The World* (Bibl. 294) reported that Delmé's father had paid £1100 for them and that Reynolds had offered £2000 for them. It also stated that Lord Ashburnham, who bought them at the sale, already had 'very fine' copies of them.

BIBLIOGRAPHY: Desmarets de Saint-Sorlin, Bibl. 19a, p. 95; La Fontaine, Bibl. 34a, p. 117; Chantelou, 1885, p. 64, and 1960, p. 124; Félibien, IV, p. 27; Marot, Bibl. 51.1; Bellori, p. 423; Vignier, Bibl. 69a, pp. 165 f.; Passeri, p. 327; Baldinucci, XVI, p. 102; Loménie de Brienne, p. 214; Florent Le Comte, III, p. 27; Vertue, Bibl. 132, XXII, pp. 105, 117; Dézallier, 1762, IV, p. 28; *Description du Château de Richelieu*, Bibl. 188, pp. 222 f.; Reynolds, Bibl. 235, p. 100; *World* and *Gazetteer*, Bibl. 294; Bonnaffé, Bibl. 573, p. 21; Friedlaender, 1914, pp. 66 f., 115; Magne, 1914, p. 95; Batiffol, Bibl. 897, pp. 166 f.; Van den Berg, Bibl. 962, p. 16; Davies, Bibl. 988a, pp. 173, 187 ff.; Jamot, pp. 53 ff.; Blunt, Bibl. 1086, p. 186, and Bibl. 1086a, p. 162; Licht, pp. 128 f.; Mahon, Bibl. 1268.1, p. 354, and Bibl. 1271, p. 303; Pintard, Bibl. 1278, pp. 31 ff.; Waterhouse, Bibl. 1308, p. 292; Mahon, Bibl. 1367, pp. XII, 95, 100 f., 104 f., 107.

136. THE TRIUMPH OF PAN. 134×145 cm. Simon Morrison, Sudeley Castle, England.

HISTORY: For the early history of the picture, see above. At the Ashburnham sale, Christie, London, 20.vii.1850, lot 64, it was bought by Hume for James Morrison; passed by descent to the present owner.

DRAWINGS: 1. Royal Library, Windsor Castle (*CR*, III, p. 24, No. 188).
2. Royal Library, Windsor Castle (*CR*, III, p. 24, No. 189).
3. Royal Library, Windsor Castle (*CR*, III, p. 24, No. 192).
4. Musée Bonnat, Bayonne (*CR*, III, p. 23, No. 186).
5. Musée Bonnat, Bayonne (*CR*, III, p. 24, No. 187).
6. Musée Bonnat, Bayonne (*CR*, III, p. 24, No. 190).
7. Musée Bonnat, Bayonne (*CR*, III, p. 24, No. 191).
8. Fleischauer collection (*CR*, III, p. 23, No. A 48).
9. Gabinetto dei Disegni, Florence (Santarelli 905 e; the *recto* is *CR*, III, p. 24, No. 193. The *verso* is not mentioned in *CR*).

COPIES: 1. Musée Fabrégat, Béziers. Traditionally attributed to Jacques Stella. From the collection of Mgr. de Saint-Simon, last bishop of Agde (cf. Thuillier, Bibl. 1299, p. 288).
2. Victoria and Albert Museum, London. Presented in 1867 by Captain Hans Busk.
3. Ecole des Beaux-Arts, Paris.
4. Musée des Beaux-Arts, Rheims (on deposit from the Louvre). Anon. sale, Christie, London, 22.vii.1910, lot 71, bt. Melcholovsky; Emile Bernard (Grautoff, II, No. 84); Paul Jamot (Royal Academy, London, Bibl. 879, No. 125); bequeathed by him to the Louvre (Jamot, pp. 7 ff.)
5. Musée des Beaux-Arts, Rouen. Attributed to Jacques Stella (cf. Thuillier, Bibl. 1299, p. 297).
6. Musée des Beaux-Arts, Tours. From the Château de Richelieu.
7. By Picasso, in the artist's collection (cf. A. Barr, *Picasso*, New York, 1946, p. 243).
8. Ashburnham sale, Christie, London, 20.vii.1850, lot 11 (perhaps the same as No. 4 above).
9. Paul Fréart de Chantelou in 1665 (Chantelou, 1885, p. 64, and 1960, p. 124).

NOTES: For a discussion of the picture, see text volume, pp. 137 ff. As indicated there, it is quite possible that the real subject is a Triumph of Priapus rather than one of Pan. Unfortunately the early sources only refer to it in general terms as a Bacchanal.

When the two *Triumphs* were sold at the Delmé sale in 1790, *The World* (Bibl. 294) stated that the collector Robert Udney had offered £1200 for the *Pan*.

BIBLIOGRAPHY: See above, p. 96, and Passeri, p. 327; Vertue, Bibl. 132, XXII, pp. 105, 117; *The World*, Bibl. 294; Buchanan, I, p. 153; Waagen, Bibl. 384b, III, p. 134, IV, p. 304; Smith, No. 212; Chennevières-Pointel, Bibl. 433, IV, p. 131; Friedlaender, 1914, p. 68; Grautoff, I, p. 156, II, No. 85; Magne, 1914, p. 199, No. 32; Batiffol, Bibl. 897, p. 166; Borenius, Bibl. 914, p. 63; *CR*, III, pp. 23 f.; Gombrich, Bibl. 959, p. 44; Blunt, Bibl. 975, p. 41, Nos. 199 *v*, 200, p. 46, No. 219 *v*; Davies, Bibl. 988a, pp. 173 ff.; Jamot, pp. 56 ff.; Godfrey, Bibl. 1057, p. 180; Blunt, Bibl. 1224, p. 57, and Bibl. 1226, p. 400; *Exposition Poussin (Louvre)*, No. 45; Mahon, Bibl. 1367, pp. 40, 89.

137. THE TRIUMPH OF BACCHUS. Original lost.

HISTORY: For the earlier history of the picture, see above. For the problems raised by existing versions, see the discussion below.

DRAWINGS: 1. Royal Library, Windsor Castle (*CR*, III, p. 23, No. 185). In *CR* it is stated that the connection with the painting is 'rather remote'. This is true, but the links are provided by the three following drawings, which were not known to the authors when *CR* III was published.
2. Gabinetto dei Disegni, Florence (905e *verso*).
3. Hermitage Museum, Leningrad (6995).
4. William Rockhill Nelson Gallery of Art, Kansas City (54-83).
5. T. Cottrell-Dormer collection, Rousham, Oxfordshire (cf. *Exposition Poussin (Louvre)*, No. 143). This drawing was discovered just before the Poussin exhibition and there catalogued as an original. Professor Jan van Gelder and other scholars have convincingly suggested that it is a copy by Jan de Bisschop.

COPIES: 1. Musée Fabrégat, Béziers. Traditionally attributed to Jacques Stella. From the collection of Mgr. de Saint-Simon, last bishop of Agde (cf. Thuillier, Bibl. 1299, p. 288).
2. Formerly Musée des Beaux-Arts, Calais (cf. Magne, 1914, p. 199, No. 33). Destroyed in 1940.
3. William Rockhill Nelson Gallery of Art, Kansas City. For the history of this picture, see below.
4. Victoria and Albert Museum, London. Given by Miss M. C. Trotter in 1862.
5. Formerly Musée Fourché, Orléans. Destroyed in the second World War.
6. Musée des Beaux-Arts, Poitiers (cf. Sandoz, Bibl. 1107, pp. 14 ff.). Said to come from a private collection in the town of Richelieu.
7. Musée des Beaux-Arts, Rouen. Attributed to Stella (cf. Thuillier, Bibl. 1299, p. 297; rep. *Actes*, I, Fig. 8).

8. Musée des Beaux-Arts, Tours. From the Château de Richelieu.
9. Cardinal Fesch collection (1841 catalogue, No. 1081; 27 × 30 inches).
10. Lord Ashburnham. According to *The World* (Bibl. 294), when Lord Ashburnham bought the two paintings at the Delmé sale, he already owned 'very fine' copies of them.
11. Paul Fréart de Chantelou in 1665 (Chantelou, 1885, p. 64, and 1960, p. 124).
12. A *Triumph of Bacchus* was in the Andrew Hay sale, London, 1741, second day, lot 43.
13. The painter Richard Cosway owned what was described as 'the finished sketch' for the *Triumph of Bacchus* (*The World*, Bibl. 294), but is more likely to have been a small copy.

NOTES: It has generally been assumed that the painting at Kansas City is the original, but as long ago as 1925, when the picture was shown at the French Landscape Exhibition at the Petit Palais, Paris, doubts were expressed by several scholars and were recorded in the Commemorative Catalogue (Bibl. 803, p. 135, No. 271) and by Jamot (pp. 64 f.) in an article on the exhibition. The objections to the picture were based on the feeling that it could not stand the comparison with the Jamot *Triumph of Pan*, which is itself now generally regarded as a copy. They would therefore have been even stronger if the original—the Morrison version (No. 136)—had been the standard of comparison.

The authenticity of the Kansas City picture has not, as far as I know, been otherwise challenged in print, but a careful inspection of it some years ago led me to feel that Jamot had been right in classing it as a copy. It is cold and mechanical in handling, and has nothing of the delicacy and sensitiveness of the Morrison picture. If it is in fact the picture painted for Richelieu, the only possible explanation would be that Poussin, anxious to produce the pictures ordered by the Cardinal as rapidly as possible, broke his normal rule and employed assistants in the execution of the *Bacchus*, while himself concentrating on the *Pan*. This would, however, have been taking a considerable risk, since there would have been plenty of people in Paris ready to point out to Richelieu the contrast between the two canvases, and to persuade him that only one of the two pictures was from the hand of Poussin himself; and Frangipani, as the agent through whom the commission was given, would have been equally exposed to criticism from his powerful patron.

The pedigree of the Kansas City picture is strongly in its favour. It was bought in 1932 as coming from the collection of the Hon. Geoffrey Howard, and as being therefore the picture bought by his ancestor, The Earl of Carlisle, at Lord Ashburnham's sale in 1850 (Christie, London, 20.vii.1850, lot 63). This provenance would, one might assume, link its history inseparably with that of the Morrison *Triumph of Pan*.

There are, however, certain points in the pedigree of the Richelieu pictures which may give rise to misgivings. First, nothing is known of the manner in which they were sold in the eighteenth century, beyond that it seems to have been somewhat secretive, since no contemporary reference to it is recorded. Given the fact that it was not uncommon for owners to sell pictures and replace them by copies, it is possible that the Duc de Richelieu may have disposed of one of the Bacchanals and replaced it by a copy, and then sold the resulting pair as being the two originals. Alternatively, an enterprising dealer may have bought the two originals, had two copies made, and then sold them in two pairs, each consisting of one original and one copy.

The whole problem is complicated by the fact, already mentioned, that according to a newspaper report Lord Ashburnham is said to have owned 'very fine' copies of the pictures as well as the originals. In the case of the *Triumph of Pan* this report is confirmed by the presence of a copy in the Ashburnham sale. One might be tempted to surmise that Lord Carlisle was fobbed off with a copy; but this hypothesis is made less plausible by the fact that Waagen, who saw the Carlisle picture at the 1857 Manchester exhibition, says of it (Bibl. 476.1, p. 23, No. 598): 'The most important picture here by this greatest master of the French school. Rich in the composition, of graceful motives, characteristic in the forms, clear in the colours, and carefully finished.' (This text states that the picture is referred to by Waagen in volume four of his *Art Treasures of Great Britain*, published in the same year as the exhibition, but this appears to be a mistake.)

On the whole, however, there are enough doubtful links in the pedigree of the Kansas City painting to make it possible that it may not be the original pair to the Morrison *Triumph of Pan*.

BIBLIOGRAPHY: See above, p. 96; the following items refer to either the original or the Kansas City version: Bellori, p. 423; Passeri, p. 327; Dézallier, 1745, II, p. 254, and 1762, IV, pp. 28, 38; Smith, No. 211; [G. S.], Bibl. 474, p. 56; Waagen, Bibl. 476.1, p. 23, No. 598; Grautoff, I, p. 156, II, No. 86; Hourticq, Bibl. 803, p. 135, No. 271; Jamot, pp. 64 f.; Godfrey, Bibl. 1057, p. 180; Sandoz, Bibl. 1107, p. 14.

138. THE TRIUMPH OF SILENUS. Original lost.

HISTORY: Painted for the Château de Richelieu (see above).

COPIES: 1. Musée Fabrégat, Béziers. Traditionally attributed to Jacques Stella. From the collection of Mgr. de Saint-Simon, last bishop of Agde (cf. Thuillier, Bibl. 1299, p. 288).

2. National Gallery, London (No. 42; 143.5 × 121 cm.). Perhaps in the collection of John Lock (Smith, No. 213; perhaps a mistake for William Lock of Norbury); John Purling sale, White, London, 17.ii.1801, lot 100, bt. Angerstein, or R. Walker sale, Christie, London, 5.iii.1803, lot 8, also said to be bt. Angerstein. In the Angerstein collection by 1809 (Davies, Bibl. 988a, p. 190). Bought with the whole Angerstein collection in 1824 (cf. Waagen, Bibl. 384b, I, p. 345; Smith, No. 213; Hazlitt, Bibl. 411, p. 15; Cousin, Bibl. 456, p. 7; Grautoff, I, p. 118, II, No. 50; Magne, 1914, p. 198, No. 26; Courthion, Bibl. 781, pp. 61 f.; Davies, Bibl. 988a, pp. 187 ff., No. 42; Jamot, pp. 56 ff.; Blunt, Bibl. 1038, p. 356).

3. Musée des Beaux-Arts, Tours. From the Château de Richelieu.

4. Paul Fréart de Chantelou in 1665 (Chantelou, 1885, pp. 84 f., and 1960, p. 125).

NOTES: The question whether this composition is the third of the Bacchanals painted for the Château de Richelieu has been exhaustively examined by Davies (Bibl. 988a, pp. 187 ff., No. 42). In the second edition of his catalogue he abandoned the ingenious but scarcely tenable hypothesis proposed in the first edition (Bibl. 988, pp. 40 ff., No. 42) that the *Silenus* was the composition painted by Pierre Dulin as a pastiche of Poussin to be added to a group of Bacchanals by the latter belonging to the Duc de Richelieu. In view of the general character of the picture, as we know it from the version in the National Gallery, London, and from the fact that a copy of it was one of the three pictures brought from Richelieu to Tours after the Revolution, there can be no doubt that it is the third of the compositions mentioned in the description of the Cabinet du Roi at Richelieu from 1646 onwards (Schellinks and Doomer, cf. Van den Berg, Bibl. 962, p. 16). The fact that the letters of Frangipani and Daillon about the transport of the first Bacchanals to Richelieu (Batiffol, Bibl. 897, p. 166, and Pintard, Bibl. 1278, p. 33) only refer to two paintings makes it clear that the *Silenus* was not part of the scheme as at first planned, but, since three paintings by Poussin are mentioned as early as 1646, and since the Cardinal's heir at his death in 1642 was a minor and is unlikely to have carried out extensive work on the château in his first years of ownership, it is reasonable to assume that the third picture was commissioned by the Cardinal and executed in his lifetime. This would be wholly in conformity with the style of the composition, which suggests a work of 1636 or slightly later.

The question of the other Bacchanals executed by Poussin for Cardinal Richelieu, also examined at length by Davies (*loc. cit.*), is complicated but does not essentially affect the problems raised by the three compositions connected with the château in Poitou.

The authenticity of the National Gallery painting has often been challenged. The arguments against it are fully formulated by Davies (*loc. cit.*), and are almost certainly justified. In particular it is probable that this version has been added to, since there are curiously blank and meaningless areas at the top and bottom of the composition.

BIBLIOGRAPHY: See above, p. 96.

139. THE ANDRIANS. 121 × 175 cm. Musée du Louvre, Paris (730).

HISTORY: Acquired by Louis XIV with the collection of the Duc de Richelieu in 1665 (Ferraton, Bibl. 1043, pp. 439, 444, 446). Possibly inherited by him from his great-uncle the Cardinal (see below).

DRAWING: Fogg Art Museum, Cambridge, Mass. (*CR*, III, p. 27, No. A 49).

ENGRAVING: By F. Ertinger (Andresen, No. 366; Wildenstein, No. 130). Dated 1685.

COPIES: 1. Musée Ingres, Montauban.

2. A copy of the left-hand group, combined with the putti on the extreme right, is in the collection of the Marquis of Cholmondeley at Houghton Hall, Norfolk. Perhaps the picture mentioned by Vertue (Bibl. 132, XXII, p. 108) as being in Lord Cholmondeley's house in Arlington Street.

3. Anon. sale, Christie, London, 5.vii.1926, lot 159 (36½ × 46½ inches).

4. Sir Anthony Mildmay sale, Christie, London, 28.vii.1933, lot 11 (Smith, No. 216; 45 × 66½ inches).

NOTES: The painting is generally called *La Bacchanale à la Joueuse de Luth*, but the subject is in fact the same as that of Titian's *Andrians* in the Prado (see text volume, p. 123). The picture is dated by Grautoff 1630–35 (II, No. 44), and by Mahon to the middle of the period running from the second half of 1629 to the beginning of 1631, that is to say presumably about the first half of 1630 (Bibl. 1367, pp. XI, 29). I should still adhere to the dating proposed in the catalogue of the Louvre exhibition (No. 30), namely 1631–33, since the sharpness of the forms brings the picture nearer than any of the other Bacchanals to the Dresden *Adoration* of 1633 (No. 44).

Stein (Bibl. 1079, p. 6) has pointed out the similarity of the sleeping figure on the left to Titian's various versions of *Danae* (cf. Tietze, *Titian*, Vienna and London, 1937, Pls. 179, 228), but an even closer model is the Mercury in the Bellini-Titian *Feast of the Gods* (text volume, Fig. 55).

There is no proof that the picture belonged to Cardinal Richelieu, but we know from the early sources (Bellori, p. 423; Félibien, IV, p. 27) that Poussin painted four Bacchanals for him, only three of which, those for the Château de Richelieu, are certainly identifiable. The Duc de Richelieu inherited a part of the Cardinal's possessions and it is therefore possible that this picture was among those that came to him in this way.

BIBLIOGRAPHY: P. de Champaigne, in Bibl. 55, p. 134; Piganiol de La Force, Bibl. 124, p. 123; Bailly, p. 302; Dézallier, 1745, II, p. 255, and 1762, IV, p. 39; Smith, No. 215; Friedlaender, 1914, pp. 50, 175; Grautoff, I, p. 112, II, No. 44; Magne, 1914, p. 198, No. 20; Jamot, p. 64; Ferraton, Bibl. 1043, pp. 439, 444, 446; Stein, Bibl. 1079, p. 6; Dorival, Bibl. 1088, p. 52; Licht, p. 106; Delbourgo and Petit, Bibl. 1243, pp. 40 ff.; *Exposition Poussin* (*Louvre*), No. 30; Mahon, Bibl. 1271, p. 297, and Bibl. 1367, pp. XI, 29, 53 f., 57 f., 61.

140. BACCHANAL IN FRONT OF A TEMPLE. Original lost.

HISTORY: Painted for 'Mr. du Fresne' (Félibien, IV, p. 146), probably Raphael Trichet du Fresne, the director of the royal printing press in Paris rather than de Fresne Hennequin, as was suggested in the catalogue of the Poussin exhibition in the Louvre (No. 98).

DRAWINGS: 1. Royal Library, Windsor Castle (*CR*, III, p. 26, No. 194).
2. Musée Condé, Chantilly (*CR*, III, p. 27, No. 195).

ENGRAVING: by Jean Mariette (Andresen, No. 367; Wildenstein, No. 131). Dated 1688.

COPIES: 1. Musée des Beaux-Arts, Besançon (209). Bequeathed by Jean Gigoux in 1892. A free variant.
2. Musée des Beaux-Arts, Caen (57). From the Mancel collection (104 × 150 cm.).
3. Musée des Beaux-Arts, Orléans. From the Frémont collection. Presented by Petit-Vaussin in 1888.
4. M. H. de Young Memorial Museum, San Francisco. Bt. from a dealer in Los Angeles, who stated that he had acquired it in England (*Exposition Poussin* (*Louvre*), No. 98; 74·5 × 101·5 cm.).
5. M. G. M. Bevan, Longstowe Hall, Cambridgeshire. Inherited from his uncle, R. G. Briscoe. Lent to the Burlington Fine Arts Club Exhibition, winter 1930–31 (No. 2, with dimensions wrongly given as 48 × 60 inches, which presumably included the frame). Offered for sale at Sotheby, London, 20.xi.1957, lot 107, bt. in.
6. Mme Cocquel-Trehu, Paris (87 × 115 cm.).
7. Maurice Helles, Château de Vieiza, Gironde (24 × 30 cm.).
8. Mme Labbé, Paris.
9. G. A. Morancé, Paris.
10. M. Souviron, Valenciennes (73·5 × 98·5 cm).
11. Fraula sale, de Vos, Brussels, 21.vii.1738, lot 59 (cf. Hoet, Bibl. 195, I, p. 523; 31 × 43 inches).
12. Marquis de Lassay sale, Paris, 22 ff.v.1775, lot 44 (3 × 4 feet). Presumably the *Bacchanale* mentioned by Dézallier d'Argenville (Bibl. 183b, p. 416) in the Hôtel de Lassay among the pictures which, he says, were acquired by the Marquis de Lassay, who died in 1738.
13. J. Bayley sale, Sotheby, London, 29 f.v.1865, second day, lot 83; with a false pedigree, which is in fact that of the National Gallery *Bacchanal with a herm of Pan* (No. 141).
14. Duguit sale, Bordeaux, 30.iv.1912, lot 31 (86 × 114 cm.). From the Aguado collection; exhibited at Le Millénaire Normand, 1911.
15. G. von Osmitz, C. E. Meyers and others sale, Lepke, Berlin, 11.ii.1913, lot 121 (81 × 100 cm.).
16. Anon. sale, Hôtel Drouot, Paris, 3.vi.1913, lot 52 (79 × 98 cm.).
17. Anon. sale, Christie, London, 10.iii.1939, lot 73 (31 × 40 inches). Bt. Roland, Browse and Delbanco; sold to a New York dealer.
18. Commander E. Culme-Seymour sale, Christie, London, 21.xi.1952, lot 13 (30 × 39 inches).
19. Formerly Walter P. Chrysler Jr. collection. According to the catalogue of his sale this picture came from the following collections: Earl of Liverpool; David Bevan (Smith, No. 217); Lady Lane, Carlton Hall, Suffolk; Kleinberger, New York (1940); Seligman sale, Parke-Bennett, New York, 23 f.i.1947, lot 241 (31½ × 39½ inches).
20. In the possession of Claudine Bouzonnet Stella in 1693–97 (cf. *Testament*, Bibl. 107, p. 40; *c.* 2 × 3 ft.).

NOTES: The composition can be identified as that painted for du Fresne on the basis of Félibien's description: 'l'on voit une femme enjouée, qui semble chanter et danser en touchant des castagnettes, pendant qu'un jeune homme joüe de la flûte' (IV. p. 146).

Of the many versions known of this composition four—those in the Morancé and Souviron collections, in the Duguit sale and in the de Young Memorial Museum—agree almost exactly with Mariette's engraving, in reverse, though all, except the Duguit picture, have slightly less space behind the piping boy than appears in the engraving. Six other versions—the Chrysler, Culme-Seymour, Osmitz, Cocquel-Trehu pictures, the one at the Hôtel Drouot in 1913, and that sold at Christie's in 1939—differ in having a curious superstructure over the entablature of the temple. One of these is probably the Bayley version, since the sale catalogue of that collection describes the scene as taking place 'in front of a noble pile of classic architecture, surmounted with a sarcophagus—the tomb of Adrian?' In fact there does not seem to be any classical prototype for this curious structure, which is not a sarcophagus but rather a sort of attic. The Orleans picture has the same feature, but the composition is considerably extended upwards and on the left by trees and sky. In the Briscoe version and in that sold at Sotheby in 1957 the temple is completed with a normal pediment. This is also the case with the Besançon picture, in which, however, the figures are very much altered.

It is not clear why this composition enjoyed such a great success, or why so many copies of it were made. If, however, I am right in supposing that the original was painted about 1650, that is to say much later than the other Bacchanals (see text volume, pp. 261 ff.), it would have enjoyed the unique privilege of being a gay subject but painted in Poussin's classical manner, which was more generally admired in the seventeenth century than his earlier Venetian style. Félibien (IV, p. 146) writes of it as follows: 'C'est un des tableaux où il a pris le plus de soin, et où il a suivi des proportions tirées des Statuës et des plus beaux bas-reliefs antiques'.

The question of dating is, however, a difficult one, since the drawings are undoubtedly much earlier than 1650. (My attempt to date the Chantilly drawing to 1645–50 (cf. *Exposition Poussin (Louvre)*, No. 98) was ingenious rather than plausible.) Mahon (Bibl. 1367, p. 119) suggests 1638–40, but I confess that I find the painting, as far as one can judge it from copies, nearer in style to, say, the Dublin *Holy Family* (No. 59) of 1649 than to the Wallace *Dance* (No. 121) or the Rouen *Venus and Aeneas* (No. 193).

BIBLIOGRAPHY: Félibien, IV, p. 146; Smith, No. 217; Grautoff, II, p. 258; *CR*, III, p. 26; Blunt, Bibl. 975, p. 40, No. 198, Bibl. 1224, p. 63, and Bibl. 1226, p. 400; Mahon, Bibl. 1367, p. 119.

141. BACCHANAL BEFORE A HERM. 100×142 cm. National Gallery, London (62).

HISTORY: Various traditions, almost certainly unreliable, state that the picture was painted for Cardinal Richelieu (Davies, Bibl. 988a, pp. 172 ff., No. 62), or that it came from the Colonna Palace (Nagler, Bibl. 397.1, XI, p. 562), or the Barberini Palace (see engraving by G. T. Doo, No. 2 below). Probably in the Basan collection (see anonymous engraving, No. 3 below). Randon de Boisset sale, Remy, Paris, 21.iii.1777, lot 165, with identifying description, bt. Lebrun. Comte de Vaudreuil (cf. Trumbull, Bibl. 249, p. 98); Vaudreuil sale, Lebrun, Paris, 27.xi.1787, lot 28, bt. Lebrun. Calonne sale, Skinner and Dyke, London, 28.iii.1795, lot 96, bt. Steer or Bryan, i.e. bt. in by Calonne's mortgagees (Buchanan, I, p. 218); exhibited at Bryan's gallery, 27 ff.iv.1795 (No. 134). According to Farington bt. by Hamilton (Davies, *loc. cit.*). Apparently sold by the Rev. Frederick Hamilton to Troward (Young, Bibl. 371.1, p. 19). William Troward sale, Phillips, London, 18.iv.1807, lot 10, bt. Lord Kinnaird (engraved in the Kinnaird collection, 1809, as from the 'Comte de Vergennes'); anon. (= Kinnaird) sale, Phillips, London, 21.v.1811, lot 13, bt. in (cf. Redford, Bibl. 601.1, I, p. 109); Lord Kinnaird sale, Phillips, London, 5.iii.1813, lot 86, bt. Delahante. Perhaps sold to the Rev. Thomas Basely (Whitley, Bibl. 829, p. 214). Thomas Hamlet (lent by him to the British Institution, 1816, No. 122). Purchased from him by the Gallery in 1826.

DRAWINGS: 1. Royal Library, Windsor Castle (*CR*, III, p. 27, No. 196).

2. Nationalmuseum, Stockholm (*CR*, III, p. 27, No. 197).

3. British Museum, London (*CR*, III, p. 27, No. 198).

ENGRAVINGS: 1. Attributed to Michel Dorigny by Robert-Dumesnil (Bibl. 398, IV, pp. 264 f.; Andresen, No. 369; Wildenstein, No. 132; Davies and Blunt, p. 214, No. 132). Wildenstein states, without giving any reason, that the engraving must have been made before *c.* 1650.

2. By G. T. Doo, 1834 (Andresen, No. 370).

3. Anon. Inscribed on the plate: *Le poussin inv.*, and in the margin: *Nic. Poussin del.* and *Ex Collect*. *Basan*. This inscription might lead to the conclusion that the engraving was after a drawing, but it corresponds sufficiently closely to the picture to justify the view that it is in fact based on it.

COPIES: 1. Musée des Beaux-Arts, Lyons (Thuillier, Bibl. 1299, p. 292).

2. Musée Municipal, Vire (Magne, 1914, p. 198, No. 27).

3. A copy of the two children on the left belongs to the Earl of Pembroke, Wilton House, Wiltshire. It is reproduced by Grautoff (II, No. 31) as an original. It has recently been restored to its original size by the removal of the later additions of canvas on all sides, except the bottom. At the same time the alterations that had been made to the hair of the right-hand child and the bird on a string, which was also of later date, were cleaned off. The result is that the picture is now very close indeed to Poussin and must have been painted under his direct supervision. It is close in character to the Stockholm drawing (see above, drawing No. 2).

NOTES: The dating of the picture presents difficulties. Grautoff (II, No. 83) placed it 1638–39; Friedlaender (1914, p. 67) 1635–40, and Mahon (Bibl. 1367, pp. XI, 92 ff.) 1633–34. One piece of evidence to be taken into consideration is the drawing at Windsor, which, *pace* Mahon, must date from the later 1620's, but it is unanimously agreed that the painting must be later than this. The colour and certain details, like the painting of the foliage and the garlands in the foreground, relate the painting to the last years of the 1630's; others, such as the richness of handling in the painting of flesh, suggest an earlier date. The relation of the picture to the National Gallery *Golden Calf* (No. 26) is of importance, but the arguments for placing one picture later or earlier than the other seem to be about equally balanced, and I should prefer not to go beyond a dating to the middle or later thirties.

BIBLIOGRAPHY: Trumbull, Bibl. 249, p. 98; Thiéry, Bibl. 289, II, p. 547; [R. Smirke], Bibl. 358, p. 37; Young, Bibl. 371.1, p. 19; Buchanan, I, pp. 96, 218; Waagen, Bibl. 384b, I, p. 344; Smith, No. 221; Nagler, Bibl. 397.1, XI, p. 562; Hazlitt, Bibl. 417, p. 198; Cousin, Bibl. 456, p. 7; Redford, Bibl. 601.1, I, p. 109; Friedlaender, 1914, p. 67; Grautoff, I, p. 155, II, No. 83; Magne, 1914, p. 198, No. 27; Courthion, Bibl. 781, p. 61; Whitley, Bibl. 829, p. 214; Blunt, Bibl. 975, p. 37, No. 174; Davies, Bibl. 988a, pp. 172 ff., No. 62; Jamot, p. 59; Blunt, Bibl. 1064, pp. 7 f.; Licht, p. 129; *Exposition Poussin (Louvre)*, No. 50; Mahon, Bibl. 1367, pp. XII, 81, 83, 86 f., 89, 92 ff.; Dempsey, Bibl. 1391, p. 117.

142. CAMILLUS AND THE SCHOOLMASTER OF FALERII. 252×268 cm. Musée du Louvre, Paris (725).

HISTORY: Commissioned by Louis Phélipeaux de la Vrillière in 1637 (Félibien, IV, p. 25). Passed by descent with his house to his great-grandson, the Marquis de la Vrillière et de Châteauneuf, who sold the hôtel to Raulin Rouillé, Sieur de Jouy, in 1705. Sold with the house by his widow in 1713 to the Comte de Toulouse. Passed by descent to the Duc de Penthièvre (cf. F. Laudet, *L'Hôtel de Toulouse*, Paris, 1932, pp. 2 ff.); confiscated in 1794 (*Les tableaux et objets d'art . . . au Muséum central*, Bibl. 305, p. 319) and transferred to the Louvre (Tuétey, Bibl. 295, II, p. 204).

DRAWINGS: 1. Dubaut collection, Paris. Formerly Charles Martine collection (cf. Dubaut, Bibl. 1053).
2. Royal Library, Windsor Castle (*CR*, II, p. 12, No. 123).

COPIES: 1. Musée d'Art et d'Histoire, Narbonne. Bequeathed by Maurice Peyre in 1859. A free variant.
2. A copy in tapestry was in the Palazzo dei Conservatori, Rome, in 1844 (cf. Melchiorri, Bibl. 408, p. 512).

NOTES: The story is told in Livy (V. 27), Plutarch (*Life of Camillus*, X) and Valerius Maximus (VI. 5.1).

The Louvre picture was painted for La Vrillière in 1637, according to Félibien. It was no doubt commissioned for the gallery of the hôtel built for this patron by François Mansart, where it hung in Félibien's time. The house was not begun till 1636, and the construction of the gallery was probably not complete in 1637, since it is now known from unpublished documents, discovered by Mr. Peter Smith, that the ceiling decoration by François Perrier was not painted till 1646; but it is certain that by 1637 La Vrillière had already planned the general decoration of the walls, which were to contain paintings of heroic subjects by the major artists working in Italy, for Malvasia (Bibl. 78, II, pp. 371, 373 f.) states that he commissioned the *Cato* from Guercino in that year.

Félibien (IV, p. 25) tells us that Poussin had painted a smaller version of the subject 'quelques années auparavant', and that at the time he wrote this belonged to Passart. In 1931 Friedlaender (Bibl. 853) published a painting from the Schaumburg-Lippe collection—then belonging to Prince Paul of Jugoslavia and now in a French private collection (No. 143)—as the missing Passart version. This view has been generally accepted, but there seem to be strong reasons for doubting the identification.

If the Schaumburg-Lippe picture is the Passart version, it would have to be several years earlier than

1637, that is to say about 1635 at the latest, but seen in the original it has all the marks of a painting belonging to the years 1638–40. The colour and handling are very close to the first series of Sacraments, particularly the greyish tonality of the whole and the cool yellows and peach colours in some of the boys' garments. The landscape background, peopled with little figures, is in the spirit of the *Manna* (No. 21), the Ellesmere-Sutherland *Moses striking the Rock* (No. 22), and the background of the 1638 *Finding of Moses* (No. 12). The heads of the boys are of the same type as those in the Louvre version of the subject, but they are also to be found in the *Baptism* from the first series of the Sacraments (No. 105) and the *St. Matthew* (No. 87), one painted during the Paris visit, the other probably shortly afterwards. On the other hand the painting has nothing in common with works of about 1635. Moreover, as will be seen later, the Louvre and Schaumburg-Lippe versions are both so closely connected with the two surviving drawings that one is forced to the conclusion that they must have been produced almost at the same moment.

Passart's composition is much more likely to be connected with the highly finished drawing in the British Museum (*CR*, II, p. 12, No. A 30; cf. text volume, Fig. 173). With its relatively small figures and its wide landscape this design would fit in well with the pictures of the mid-1630's. Further it is connected in its general composition with a *Continence of Scipio*, which formed one of the tapestries woven after the designs of Giulio Romano and his circle, in this case known to us through a drawing in the Louvre, and it was precisely in the mid-thirties that Poussin turned once more to Giulio Romano and his school for inspiration.

It seems possible, moreover, to work out a logical development which covers the two other surviving drawings and the two paintings.

If it is accepted that the British Museum drawing represents the Passart version, Poussin started with an oblong processional composition, similar in its general character to the *Crossing of the Red Sea* (No. 20). In the commission for La Vrillière Poussin was forced to condense this to an almost square design, since the panels of the gallery into which the canvas had to fit were of this format. The Dubaut sketch (No. 1 above), of which the underdrawing in chalk may be original, though the ink appears to be too feeble for Poussin, represents the artist's first attempt to fit the story into a square. The Windsor drawing (No. 2 above) is a variant of the Dubaut composition from Poussin's own hand. Like the former, it is for the Louvre painting and not the Schaumburg-Lippe version, for there is a line down the right-hand side of the sheet, which shows that the composition was always intended to be square and has not been cut on that side.

The principal groups connected with the story—the figure of Camillus seated in front of his tent surrounded by soldiers, and the schoolmaster being beaten by his pupils—appear in all three drawings and both paintings, but in the British Museum drawing additional figures are included: on the extreme right three children heading the procession, and further to the left three more, kneeling to thank Camillus for his generosity. The Dubaut and Windsor drawings are closely similar in general design, but there are differences which, though small, are interesting. The former contains right in the middle of the composition two children who repeat exactly in pose two of those leading the procession in the British Museum drawing. These disappear in the Windsor drawing, in which, however, another figure is introduced, that of a lictor unbinding the fasces in order to give the rods to the children. The Louvre painting follows the Windsor drawing fairly closely in the figure groups, except that the lictor is left out and on the right Poussin has added two soldiers and a third boy beating the schoolmaster. The Schaumburg-Lippe picture is wider in format than the Louvre version, and Poussin has filled the composition not by spreading out the groups but by reintroducing on the right the two children who were taken over from the British Museum drawing to the Dubaut study, though they are now placed in reverse order. At the same time he has moved the two soldiers, who in the Louvre version stand just behind the schoolmaster, to the right-hand edge of the canvas.

During the evolution of the design Poussin also introduced considerable variations in the background. The British Museum study shows a town with walls and a round tower, but in the Windsor drawing this is replaced by one with rectangular tower and walls, the main line of which slopes up to the right. In the Louvre painting Poussin pushes the tent so far to the left that it becomes a quite minor factor in the design, and returns to a landscape basically similar to that in the British Museum drawing (though without the two little pavilions which appear there, and of which one also occurs in the Windsor drawing). This introduces a rather surprising downward slope to the right, which the artist breaks by giving greater prominence to the lines of the standards, which now stand out against the landscape, and by introducing two vertically held spears. When in the Schaumburg-Lippe version Poussin spreads out the composition again, he once again gives prominence to the tent and shows the town in the form that it has in the Windsor drawing, combined with the large round tower that appeared in the British Museum version.

This seems the most logical sequence for the drawings and paintings, but even if the arrangement is partly hypothetical, it is important to emphasize that the Schaumburg-Lippe picture cannot be earlier than the Louvre version. If it was already in existence when Poussin came to paint the Louvre picture, there would have been no need for him to make either the Dubaut or the Windsor drawing, since all the elements that he uses in the Louvre picture would already have been available to him in La Vrillière's canvas, and, as we have seen, the Windsor drawing must have been made for the Louvre picture and not for the Schaumburg-Lippe version.

If the British Museum drawing derives in its general pattern from a model connected with Giulio Romano, the two paintings are close to a more famous and a more recent model, Domenichino's *Timoclea before Alexander*, now in the Louvre, which in Poussin's time was in the Villa Montalto, Rome. The general composition, the landscape and architecture, and even the pose of Camillus are all derived from this source.

BIBLIOGRAPHY: *Correspondance*, p. 4; Sauval, Bibl. 23, II, p. 230, III, p. 50, and Bibl. 23a, p. 150; Chantelou, 1885, pp. 226 f., and 1960, p. 131; Félibien, IV, p. 25; Brice, Bibl. 89a, I, p. 97, and Bibl. 89g, I, pp. 440 f.; Loménie de Brienne, pp. 214, 218; Florent Le Comte, III, p. 26; Antonini, Bibl. 160b, p. 166; Piganiol de La Force, Bibl. 173, III, p. 98; Dézallier, 1745, II, p. 255, and 1762, IV, p. 40; Dézallier d'Argenville, Bibl. 183, p. 100; Volkmann, Bibl. 290, I, p. 333; Tuétey, Bibl. 295, II, p. 204; *Les tableaux et objets d'art . . . au Muséum central*, Bibl. 305, p. 319; Smith, No. 174; Friedlaender, 1914, pp. 42, 115; Grautoff, I, p. 137, II, No. 69; Magne, 1914, pp. 94, 199, No. 37; Friedlaender, Bibl. 853; Jamot, p. 81; Licht, p. 117; Bardon, Bibl. 1218, pp. 128, 130; *Exposition Poussin (Louvre)*, No. 46; Mahon, Bibl. 1268.1, p. 354, Bibl. 1269, p. 261, and Bibl. 1271, p. 303; Thuillier, Bibl. 1296, p. 71, and Bibl. 1297, p. 41; Kauffmann, Bibl. 1332, p. 98; Mahon, Bibl. 1367, pp. 107, 128.

143. CAMILLUS AND THE SCHOOLMASTER OF FALERII. 81×133 cm. Private collection, Paris.

HISTORY: In the collection of the Fürsten zu Schaumburg-Lippe; listed in the inventory made of the collection by the painter Gumbrecht in 1738 (information kindly provided by the Fürstliche Hofkammer, Bückeburg). Sold Bückeburg, 3.iv.1929, bt. Rosenbaum, Frankfort; sold to Prince Paul of Jugoslavia (Friedlaender, Bibl. 853). Sold by him to Böhler, Munich, and by Böhler to Henry Lévy of Strasbourg in 1934. This is almost certainly the painting recorded in the following sales: J. Meijers sale, Rotterdam, 9.ix.1722, lot 1 (Hoet, Bibl. 195, I, p. 265; 40×54 inches); Cornelis Wittert van Valkenburg sale, Rotterdam, 11.iv.1731, lot 4 (Hoet, *op. cit.*, II, p. 366; same dimensions), presumably bt. in; van Valkenburg sale, Rotterdam, 7.x.1733, lot 14 (*ibid.*, p. 396).

DRAWINGS: See under No. 142.

NOTES: There are slight pentimenti in the drapery of one of the boys beating the schoolmaster.
    For a discussion of this painting, see No. 142.

BIBLIOGRAPHY: Smith, No. 175; Friedlaender, Bibl. 853; *CR*, II, p. 12; Blunt, Bibl. 975, p. 39; Mahon, Bibl. 1269, p. 261, Bibl. 1271, p. 303, and Bibl. 1367, p. 100.

144. CEPHALUS AND AURORA. 96·5×130·5 cm. National Gallery, London (65).

HISTORY: Probably in France by 1745 (cf. Dézallier, 1745, II, p. 254). Mme d'Hariague sale, Mariette, Paris, 14 ff.iv.1750, lot 19, with identifying description. Probably Peilhon sale, Remy, Paris, 16.v.1763, lot 57; John Knight collection by 1816 (lent by him in that year to the British Institution, No. 67); Knight sale, Phillips, London, 24.iii.1819, lot 139, bt. in; Knight sale, Phillips, London, 17.iii.1821, lot 45, bt. Cholmondeley (Redford, Bibl. 601.1, II, p. 281). Bequeathed to the Gallery by G. J. Cholmondeley in 1831.

NOTES: Davies (Bibl. 988a, p. 174, No. 65) notes various changes revealed by X-ray examination, particularly on the left, the most important of which is that there was originally a chariot, presumably that of Aurora, where the Pegasus and the recumbent female figure are now placed. The story is told by Ovid

(*Metamorphoses*, vii, 694 ff.). The particular incident represented by Poussin in this picture is the moment when Cephalus is rejecting the advances of Aurora. The device of showing a cupid holding up a portrait of Cephalus' wife, Procris, to remind him of his duty towards her is not mentioned by the poet, but, as has been pointed out by Davies (*loc. cit.*), it has a parallel in Rubens's Marie de Médicis series, where Hymen and Cupid bring the portrait of the princess to Henry IV when the marriage has been arranged (cf. A. Rosenberg, *P. P. Rubens*, Stuttgart and Leipzig, 1906, p. 237).

The iconography of the picture is somewhat puzzling. The figure asleep in the left foreground has been interpreted by Lavin (Bibl. 1101, p. 284) as Tithonus, Aurora's husband, who in certain versions of the story is said to have been asleep when Aurora crept away to join Cephalus, and who appears in a similar pose in Annibale Carracci's fresco of *Cephalus and Aurora* in the Galleria Farnese (*ibid.*, Pl. 39d); but he points out that the urn probably alludes to Oceanus, the site of the first loves of Aurora and Tithonus, according to the Homeric Hymn (V, 227). Davies (*loc. cit.*) rejects the identification with Tithonus, on the grounds that it is usual to represent him as a very old man; but at this stage of the story it would still be reasonable to suppose him to be a man of middle years. Lavin sees Procris in the figure lying at the foot of the tree on the left, but this seems extremely unlikely, since she was far away at the time. Davies suggests that she may be an earth goddess, which seems a plausible hypothesis, since she wears a wreath of flowers and corn. If this is so, Poussin may be referring not only to the cycle of day and night (see text volume, p. 122) but also to the sources of fertility, since Oceanus is according to most authorities (e.g. Cartari, pp. 206 ff.) the father of all the great rivers and the source of the fertility which comes from water. If Aurora is taken as standing for fire, there could also be an allusion to the four elements.

Poussin has probably followed Cartari (p. 76) in associating Pegasus with Aurora, but as Lavin has pointed out, the idea goes back to certain writers such as Lycophron and Tzetzes, whom Poussin seems to have used on other occasions.

Davies (*loc. cit.*) quoting Panofsky has suggested that the pose of Cephalus is connected with the Adam in Michelangelo's *Expulsion* on the ceiling of the Sistine Chapel (cf. Knapp, *Michelangelo*, Stuttgart, 1924, p. 26), but Mahon (Bibl. 992, p. 38, and Bibl. 1367, p. 47) points out that there is a much closer and more relevant similarity with the Bacchus in Titian's *Bacchus and Ariadne*.

Grautoff (II, No. 47) dates the picture 1630–35; Mahon (Bibl. 1367, p. XI) 1631–33. In view of the relative softness of the forms, compared to the crisp modelling of those in the *Kingdom of Flora* (No. 155), I should see the painting as before 1630 rather than after.

BIBLIOGRAPHY: Dézallier, 1745, II, p. 254; Waagen, Bibl. 384b, I, p. 345; Smith, No. 251; Hazlitt, Bibl. 417, pp. 100, 197; Cousin, Bibl. 456, p. 7; Friedlaender, 1914, p. 48; Grautoff, I, p. 115, II, No. 47; Magne, 1914, p. 199, No. 39; Hourticq, Bibl. 899, p. 120; Davies, Bibl. 988a, p. 174, No. 65; Mahon, Bibl. 992, p. 38; Blunt, Bibl. 1003, pp. 268, 269; Lavin, Bibl. 1101, pp. 284 ff.; Licht, p. 108; Walker, Bibl. 1145, p. 105; Mahon, Bibl. 1271, p. 299, and Bibl. 1367, pp. XI, 47, 57.

145. CEPHALUS AND AURORA. 79×152 cm. Sir William Worsley, Bart., Hovingham Hall, Yorkshire.

HISTORY: Probably in the possession of Cassiano dal Pozzo (de Cotte, Bibl. 98a, p. 203). William Worsley by 1770; by descent to the present owner.

DRAWING: British Museum, London (*CR*, III, p. 34, No. A 56). A copy after the painting.

COPIES: 1. Private collection, Malta (Sterling, Bibl. 1290, p. 272).
2. Anon. sale, Robinson and Fisher, London, 17.xi. 1938, lot 58.

NOTES: Both copies confirm the fact that the original has been cut at the top, probably by about 6 inches.

The composition is described in detail by Bellori (pp. 444 f.). It differs in essential features from the National Gallery picture (No. 144). In the Hovingham version the figure of Tithonus-Oceanus is pushed into the background, and there is no Ceres. As regards the chariot and horses, Poussin has here followed the Homeric Hymn in showing two horses, instead of the single Pegasus as in the National Gallery picture. Facing Cephalus and Aurora on the left stand two of the Horae, who, as Bellori explains, are reminding Aurora that it is time for her to be on her way. Below them sits Zephyr, who, according to Bellori, is present not because he is a morning wind but as the representative of Spring, the season of love.

Bellori also says that the swan who accompanies him is present because Zephyr incited it to sing. He gives no authority for this association and it seems more likely that the swan is shown here because it is regularly associated with the sun (cf. Cartari, p. 47) on account of its whiteness, which is a symbol of light.

Probably painted *c.* 1629–30.

BIBLIOGRAPHY: Bellori, pp. 444 f.; de Cotte, Bibl. 98, III, p. 153, and Bibl. 98a, p. 203; Friedlaender, 1914, p. 124; *CR*, III, p. 34; Davies, Bibl. 988a, p. 176, No. 65 n. 8; Blunt, Bibl. 1002, pp. 219, 269 f.; Bertin-Mourot, Bibl. 1023, p. 44, No. II; Sterling, Bibl. 1290, p. 272.

146. CLEOPATRA AND AUGUSTUS. 145×194.5 cm. National Gallery of Canada, Ottawa.

HISTORY: A nineteenth-century label on the stretcher states that the picture came from the Palazzo Barberini, Rome. It is not mentioned in the 1631 inventory, which is incomplete, nor in most of the later guide books, but it may be one of the 'due altri quadri, uno incontro all'altro, di Nicolò Pussino, che rappresentano diversi fatti della storia Romana' mentioned by Manazzale (Bibl. 308b, I, p. 143). English private collection; with Tomàs Harris, London, 1938 (Blunt, Bibl. 911, pp. 197 ff.); anon. (= Harris) sale, Sotheby, London, 21.vii.1948, lot 84, bt. in; bt. from Harris by the Gallery in 1952.

NOTES: A pentiment exists of the right foot of Cleopatra, which was originally painted pointing forward.

For the subject, see Blunt (Bibl. 911). The same theme was painted by Pietro da Cortona in a lunette in the Palazzo Pitti (cf. Briganti, Bibl. 1358, Pl. 210). The traditional attribution to Poussin is supported by many details. The group of women on the extreme left is like several to be found in the Marino drawings, such as *CR*, III, p. 10, No. 154, p. 11, No. 158, p. 13, No. 163, and corresponds in its general arrangement with one on the left of the *Triumph of David* at Dulwich (No. 33; cf. also the drawing *CR*, I, p. 14, No. 30). The head of the right-hand woman in the group on the left is almost identical with that of the left-hand mother in the Petit Palais *Massacre* (No. 66). The figures of soldiers in the portico on the right, which are derived ultimately from the reliefs on the column of Trajan, are like those in the early battle paintings (Nos. 29, 30). The man in the foreground on the right, derived from a relief on the Arch of Constantine (text volume, Fig. 61) and reminiscent of Ambroise Dubois (Fig. 16), recurs in the *Germanicus* (No. 156) and also in a rough sketch on the *verso* of an early drawing at Windsor (rep. Blunt, Bibl. 1227, Fig. 128). The brilliant painting of the armour and the rich orange-gold colour and creamy texture of Cleopatra's robe are typical of Poussin's handling of such passages in paintings of a slightly later period.

The combination of late Mannerist features with others typical of Poussin's painting in the later twenties points to his authorship, though the clumsiness of many parts leads to the view that this painting must be among the first works executed after the artist's arrival in Rome, probably in 1624–25.

The picture was rejected by Friedlaender (Bibl. 1056, p. 85) and by Thuillier (Bibl. 1180, p. 31), who ascribes it to Vuibert on the basis of a photograph and on a supposed similarity with a painting of the *Martyrdom of St. Cecilia* at Montpellier; the latter is probably not by Vuibert, and the similarity of the *Cleopatra* with it, visible in the photograph, is purely illusory. In the original, which is unusually large for Poussin, the free handling and the warm colour distinguish it completely from Vuibert's works.

The composition is influenced by Marcantonio's engraving of the *Queen of Sheba* after Giulio Romano (text volume, Fig. 60).

BIBLIOGRAPHY: Blunt, Bibl. 910, p. 1, and Bibl. 911, pp. 197 ff.; Bertin-Mourot, Bibl. 1023, p. 48, No. XVI; Friedlaender, Bibl. 1056, p. 85; Licht, p. 85; Thuillier, Bibl. 1180, p. 31; Bardon, Bibl. 1218, p. 129; Blunt, Bibl. 1227, p. 168.

147. CORIOLANUS. 112×198.5 cm. Strips have been added on three sides, but in the recent restoration these were folded back and are now concealed. The name Coriolanus, written on the tablet in the foreground, is a later addition, but the tablet itself is original. Hôtel-de-Ville, Les Andelys.

HISTORY: Belonged to the Marquis de Hauterive in 1685 (Félibien IV, p. 152; for the identity of this collector, see No. 100). Presumably the painting mentioned by Dézallier d'Argenville (Bibl. 183b, p. 186) as in the collection of M. Bouret, Fermier Général, in the rue Grange-Batelière. The picture at Les Andelys was confiscated by the State from the collection of Simon Charles Boutin in 1794 and sent to Les Andelys in 1802 (Thuillier, Bibl. 1297, p. 41); later hung in the Préfecture of the Eure at Evreux; returned to Les Andelys and hung in the town hall.

DRAWING: Royal Library, Windsor Castle (*CR*, II, p. 13, No. A 31). The pen drawing is certainly not by Poussin, but the chalk under-drawing may be from his hand.

ENGRAVINGS: 1. By E. Baudet (Andresen, No. 323; Wildenstein, No. 113; Davies and Blunt, p. 213, No. 113).
2. By Audran (Andresen, No. 322).
3. By B. Picart (Andresen, No. 324). Dated 1720.

4. Published by G. Billy (Andresen, No. 325).
5. By E. Kirkall (cf. Merchant, Bibl. 1105, p. 13).

COPY: A copy belonged to Claudine Bouzonnet Stella (*Testament*, Bibl. 107, p. 37). Wildenstein (*loc. cit.*) says that this is described in the Stella inventory as 'petit tableau exquis', but in fact the text reads 'exquise', which, as Sterling (Bibl. 1290, p. 272) has pointed out, means 'esquisse'.

NOTES: Grautoff (II, No. 68) dates the painting 1635–39; Mahon (Bibl. 1367, p. 134) to the middle forties. It is certainly not far from the second series of Sacraments, but I should tend to place it towards the end rather than in the middle of the forties.

BIBLIOGRAPHY: Félibien, IV, p. 152; Bellori, p. 450; *Testament*, Bibl. 107, p. 37; Loménie de Brienne, p. 224; Florent Le Comte, III, p. 31; Dézallier, 1745, II, p. 254, and 1762, IV, p. 39; 'Les tableaux . . . saisis . . .', Bibl. 305, p. 259; Fuseli, Bibl. 322, pp. 74, 144, 163; Smith, No. 173; Friedlaender, 1914, pp. 80, 126; Grautoff, I, p. 136, II, No. 68; Magne, 1914, p. 199, No. 44; Fried-laender, 1933, p. 325; Hourticq, Bibl. 899, p. 43; Blunt, Bibl. 975, p. 53, Bibl. 1086, p. 189, and Bibl. 1086a, p. 165; Licht, p. 117; Merchant, Bibl. 1105, p. 13; Bardon, Bibl. 1218, p. 128; Sterling, Bibl. 1290, p. 272; Thuillier, Bibl. 1297, p. 41; *Exposition Poussin (Rouen)*, No. 85; Mahon, Bibl. 1367, pp. 119, 134.

148. DIANA AND ACTAEON. 195 × 252 cm. Private collection, Paris.

HISTORY: Painted for the Château de Mornay (Charente-Maritime) probably in 1614 (Dupont, Bibl. 1248, pp. 241 ff.). Saved from a fire in 1947, and acquired by the present owner.

NOTES: In 1899 Ténaud (Bibl. 645) proposed to identify this painting and another of *Diana and Endymion* in the same gallery at Mornay (see below) with those mentioned by Bellori (p. 409), and Félibien (IV, p. 7) as having been painted for the 'jeune seigneur de Poitou', whom Poussin met in Paris. The identification has often been challenged, and Grautoff rejected it completely, on the grounds that the *Diana and Actaeon* is a copy after a composition by Josef Heintz, engraved by Sadeler (cf. text volume, Fig. 8). This is in itself no argument, since Poussin, at the age of twenty, would not have been above copying a composition by the celebrated artist who was the favourite painter of the Emperor Rudolf II.

The other painting in the gallery mentioned by Grautoff, *Diana contemplating Endymion*, now destroyed, was, as Dupont has shown (*op. cit.*, p. 242, and Fig. 293), a copy from an engraving after Abraham van Diepenbeeck and had no connection with Poussin.

BIBLIOGRAPHY: Félibien, IV, p. 7; Bellori, p. 409; La Moricière, Bibl. 643, pp. 112 ff.; Ténaud, Bibl. 645; J. P., Bibl. 649, pp. 28 f.; Dangibaud, Bibl. 691, p. 323; Grautoff, I, pp. 342 ff.; Jamot, Bibl. 749, p. 83, and Bibl. 1031, p. 9; Blunt, Bibl. 1086, p. 219 n. 180, and Bibl. 1086a, p. 272 note 182; Kauffmann, Bibl. 1203, p. 5; Dupont, Bibl. 1248, pp. 241 ff.

149. DIANA AND ENDYMION. 122 × 169 cm. The Detroit Institute of Arts, Detroit.

HISTORY: In the collection of Cardinal Mazarin by 1653 (Bibl. 20, p. 324, No. 269). Presumably passed to the Duc de Mazarin or Filippo Mancini. Perhaps John van Spangen sale, Ford, London, 12 ff.iii.1743, third day, lot 179, bt. Spencer, and John van Spangen sale, Cock and Langford, London, 10.ii.1748, lot 76 ('Diana, Endymion, Apollo, etc.'), bt. Blackwood. Perhaps Cardinal Fesch (1841 catalogue, No. 1772, described as 'école de Poussin', but the size agrees with the Mazarin inventory and with the Detroit version, and the description fits the Detroit painting); Fesch sale, George, Rome, 17 ff.iii.1845, part III, lot 408. The Detroit picture was bought from an English private collection by Cassirer, Berlin; bt. from him in 1922 by Julius Haas, Detroit; Mrs. Trent McMalt, Detroit; bt. by the Institute in 1936.

NOTES: The figure of Diana is related in its general character to those on Roman sarcophagus reliefs of Diana and Endymion (cf. Picard, Bibl. 1276), perhaps most closely to one formerly in the Giustiniani collection (*Galleria Giustiniana*, Rome, c. 1631, II, Pl. 110); but Poussin has invented a completely new composition, and the introduction of the chariot of Apollo in the sky has apparently no parallel in ancient art.

Grautoff (Bibl. 864, p. 331) cautiously dates the painting 1630–40; D. Wild (Bibl. 1312, p. 157), more precisely but not more convincingly, suggests c. 1625; Mahon (Bibl. 1367, p. XI) places it in the years 1631–33, a view with which I should concur.

BIBLIOGRAPHY: *Inventaire . . . Mazarin*, Bibl. 20, p. 324, No. 269; Comte de Cosnac, Bibl. 584, p. 318, No. 1099; Grautoff, Bibl. 864, p. 331; Valentiner, Bibl. 887, p. 96; anon., Bibl. 891, p. 317; Hourticq, Bibl. 899, p. 117; Friedlaender, Bibl. 947, p. 10, and Bibl. 964, p. 26; Bertin-Mourot, Bibl. 999, p. 78; Comstock, Bibl. 1007, p. 44; Bertin-Mourot, Bibl. 1023, p. 51, No. XXVII; Licht, pp. 108 f.; Bardon, Bibl. 1218, p. 126; *Exposition Poussin (Louvre)*, No. 26; Mahon, Bibl. 1268.1, pp. 352 ff., and Bibl. 1271, p. 300; Wild, Bibl. 1312, p. 157; *L'ideale classico (Bologna)*, No. 59; Mahon, Bibl. 1367, pp. XI, 55, 57, 78.

150. LANDSCAPE WITH DIOGENES. 160×221 cm. Musée du Louvre, Paris (741).

HISTORY: Painted for Lumague or Lumagne in 1648 (Félibien, IV, p. 59); Duc de Richelieu; bt. with his collection by Louis XIV in 1665 (Ferraton, Bibl. 1043, pp. 439, 446).

DRAWING: Musée Condé, Chantilly (*CR*, IV, p. 46, No. 280). For the upper left part of the landscape.

ENGRAVING: By E. Baudet (Andresen, No. 441; Wildenstein, No. 179).

COPIES: 1. Formerly in the Museum at Les Andelys (Magne, 1914, p. 200, No. 47). Destroyed in 1940.
2. Probably by Marco and Sebastiano Ricci, anon. sale, Christie, London, 24.x.1958, lot 155.
3. Lord St. Oswald, Nostell Priory, Yorkshire. A copy of part of the landscape in the form of a roundel (Grautoff, II, No. 145). Engraved in the manner of Châtillon (Andresen, No. 462; published by Van Meulen).

A painting formerly in the Earl de Grey collection and later in the Cook collection, Richmond, is based on the Louvre picture, but is upright in composition (cf. Brockwell, Bibl. 720, III, p. 51, No. 432); sold Sotheby, London, 25.vi.1958, lot 59. Attributed in the sale catalogue to Jean Lemaire, owing to a confusion with another picture in the same collection (Brockwell, *op. cit.*, III, p. 52, No. 433).
The following pictures mentioned in sale catalogues may be the Cook painting or copies of the Louvre composition:
1. Van Spangen sale, Cock and Langford, London, 10 ff.ii.1748, third day, lot 18.
2. General Plastow sale, Christie, London, 27 ff.vi.1791, lot 11.

NOTES: The picture was cleaned and lined in 1793 (Tuétey and Guiffrey, Bibl. 304, pp. 73, 314).

Félibien states that this painting was executed in 1648 for Lumague, a Genoese banker, who lived partly in Paris and partly in Lyons. This dating has recently been challenged by Mahon (Bibl. 1338, pp. 129 ff.), who wishes to place it with the second group of landscapes in the late 1650's, together with the *Polyphemus* (No. 175), which Félibien states was painted in 1649. Mahon rightly observes that in both these paintings nature has a luxuriance which is lacking in some members of the first group, such as the two Phocion landscapes, but is characteristic of almost all the second group. He also rightly points out that there is no proof that the Louvre painting is that made for Lumague, and that the description given by Félibien differs from the existing picture in one detail, since it says that Lumague's versions shows Diogenes breaking his bowl, whereas in the Louvre painting he has thrown it on the ground, where it is shown still intact. This detail is true, but is far from being a final argument against identifying the Louvre picture with that painted for Lumague.

Mahon's argument is mainly based on the view that all the landscapes of the years 1648 to 1651, except the *Diogenes* and the *Polyphemus*, are similar in style and general character, and these two, being different, must have been produced at another period. But, as I have tried to show in chapter IX of the text volume, there are wide differences within the group: The *Orpheus* (No. 170) is different from the Phocion pair; the *Pyramus and Thisbe* (No. 177) is totally unlike any others of the group; the *Storm* (No. 217) and the *Landscape with Buildings* in the Prado (No. 216) form a contrast with each other and with, say, the *Roman Road* (No. 210). It is, therefore, in my opinion wrong to see the *Diogenes* and the *Polyphemus* as two isolated exceptions in an otherwise uniform group; rather the contrary: in the landscapes of this period Poussin was trying various styles and changing his method according to the purpose that he had in mind.

Even on the question of the richness and grandeur of nature which links the two paintings under discussion with the later works I should not altogether agree with Mahon. Nature is treated with more love in the *Diogenes* than in the Phocion pair, but it does not have the almost clumsy grandeur to be found in the *Orion* (No. 169). In detail, moreover, the little figures in the middle distance of the *Polyphemus* are very close indeed to those in the boat in the *Man killed by a Snake* (No. 209) or in other paintings of the first group and unlike similarly placed figures in the later pictures. Both the *Polyphemus* and the *Diogenes* have an all-over green tonality, which is generally characteristic of the later group, but the colour is stronger and has not the earthy heaviness of the latter.

Mahon mentions the Chantilly drawing connected with the *Diogenes*, but sweeps it aside as not providing any relevant evidence. This does not seem to me quite justified. The drawing cannot, I think all would agree, be dated after *c.* 1650, and it was certainly used by Poussin in the painting, even if the connection between the two is not so exact that one can speak of it as a study for the painting. It would be very unlike Poussin to use in a painting a drawing which he made some ten years earlier, as would be the case if we are to accept Mahon's dating of the picture.

Moreover, the argument from the subject matter is important from two points of view. First, Diogenes would be an obvious hero for Poussin to choose in 1648, whereas there is no instance among the late works of his taking a philosopher as the theme for a landscape painting. Secondly, the theme would account for the one feature which, as Mahon points out, distinguishes the painting from other landscapes of the first group, that is to say, those painted in the years 1648–51. Poussin has tried to illustrate Diogenes' fundamental tenet that man should live according to nature, and for that very reason he has shown nature in a richer, more flourishing form than was appropriate, say, to the Phocion landscapes, which are severe and rational, like the hero whom they celebrate.

In short the stylistic and iconographic evidence is perfectly consistent with an early dating, and there is, in my opinion, no good reason for rejecting the statement of Félibien, supported by the evidence of the Chantilly drawing.

Mahon does his best to discredit Félibien as a source for dating Poussin's works. First he says that Félibien dates the *Man killed by a Snake* to the years 1651–52, whereas there is reason to think the correct date is 1648. This is not quite true. After assigning a number of pictures specifically to the individual years from 1647 to 1651, Félibien goes on: 'Ce fut encore dans le même temps qu'il peignit pour le même sieur Pointel deux grands paysages.' This rather vague phrasing is quite different from the precision of the preceding paragraphs and suggests that Félibien knew that his information on the dating of the Pointel pictures was not water-tight, and was scrupulously avoiding making a too definite statement.

Mr. Mahon does, it is true, convict Félibien of dating the Hermitage *Holy Family in Egypt* (No. 65) to 1659, when the correspondence tells a different story, but, as will be seen from the entry for that picture, although it was begun soon after 26.xii.1655, it was not finished till 24.xii.1657, and was certainly still not despatched by 15.iii.1658 and very probably not by 25.xi.1658. In the latter case it would not have reached Paris till early in 1659, and Félibien no doubt based his statement on its arrival, of which he would most probably have known immediately. In any case the error is trivial compared with that of mis-dating two pictures by about ten years.

BIBLIOGRAPHY: Chantelou, 1885, p. 234, and 1960, p. 132; Félibien, IV, p. 59; Florent Le Comte, III, p. 30; Bailly, p. 305; Dézallier, 1745, II, p. 254, and 1762, IV, p. 39; Gault de Saint-Germain, Pt. II, p. 38; Smith, No. 301: Gautier, Bibl. 575, pp. 64, 175; Friedlaender, 1914, pp. 96, 119; Grautoff, I, p. 253, II, No. 126; Magne, 1914, pp. 154, 192, 200, No. 47; Jamot, Bibl. 758, p. 158; Magnin, Bibl. 824, p. 55; Blunt, Bibl. 972, pp. 157, 162, and Bibl. 976, pp. 186, 189; Jamot, p. 38; Ferraton, Bibl. 1043, pp. 439, 446; Blunt, Bibl. 1086, p. 189, and Bibl. 1086a, p. 165; Dorival, Bibl. 1088, p. 51; Licht, p. 145; Royal Academy, London, Bibl. 1165, No. 110; *Exposition Poussin (Louvre)*, No. 82; Shearman, Bibl. 1285, p. 187; Kitson, Bibl. 1335, p. 158; Mahon, Bibl. 1338, pp. 129 ff.; *L'ideale classico (Bologna)*, No. 85; Mahon, Bibl. 1367, pp. XIV, 2, 121, 129.

151. ECHO AND NARCISSUS. 74×100 cm. Musée du Louvre, Paris (731).

HISTORY: Probably the picture bt. by Monconys in Rome in 1664 (Bibl. 35a, p. 118). Acquired by Louis XIV before 1683 (Bailly, p. 315).

ENGRAVING: By G. Audran (Andresen, No. 381; Wildenstein, No. 134; Davies and Blunt, p. 214, No. 134).

COPY: Formerly in the museum at Les Andelys (Magne, 1914, p. 200, No. 48). Destroyed in 1940.

A *Narcissus* by Poussin is recorded in the Andrew Fountaine sale, London, 1731/32, lot 58 (sold for £18 2s. od.), and what is probably the same picture re-appears in the Lord Halifax sale, London, 6 ff.iii.1739, third day, lot 81, described as 'A large and fine picture' (sold for £12 12s. od.). This cannot be the painting in Dresden, which was already in the Electoral collection by 1725 (see below, p. 175, R 77) and is unlikely to be the version engraved by Frey in 1749 (Andresen-Wildenstein, No. 382), which was presumably still in Rome at that time.

NOTES: If, as I believe, the other versions of the *Narcissus* attributed to Poussin—one in Dresden and one engraved by Frey—are not by him, there is a reasonable probability that the picture bought by Monconys is the one in the Louvre. Monconys records that on 29.v.1664 he called on Poussin 'qui reconnut et advoüa le tableau de *Nacisse* que j'avois de luy' (*loc. cit.*).

Examination by X-ray (see reproduction preceding p. 181 below) revealed the fact that under the present picture there are the remains of two other paintings. One of these represents a seated woman with a child on her knee, another in the bottom right-hand corner of the composition and a small group in the air above her. This is probably a *Rest on the Flight*, with the putti at the top gathering fruit to give to the Christ Child (cf. No. 63). In addition, however, the X-ray shows the head and part of the body of an almost life-size woman. Mme Hours (Bibl. 1256, pp. 6 ff.) interprets this as a figure lying down, with one arm raised above her head, but it could equally be read as a woman standing and holding up something in her right hand, perhaps a wine-cup (the hand itself is cut off by the edge of the canvas). In scale and general character the figure is not unlike that revealed by X-rays on the Ajaccio *Midas* (No. 166).

It was pointed out by Panofsky (Bibl. 815, pp. 267, 296) that the figure of Narcissus is similar to the dead Christ in a *Pietà* by Paris Bordone (text volume, Fig. 73), but Stein (Bibl. 1079, p. 7) has shown that it is also related to a figure in a fresco by Perino del Vaga in the Palazzo Doria in Genoa, which Poussin could have known through an engraving by a member of the school of Marcantonio.

The painting was dated by Grautoff (II, No. 3) 1623–26, and by Friedlaender (1914, p. 47) to the first half of the thirties. Mahon dates it in one place (Bibl. 1367, p. XI) 'between 1630–31' and later in the same article (pp. 25 f.) 'towards the end of 1630'. I should myself prefer to place it earlier, near the *Triumph of Flora* (No. 154) and the *Germanicus* (No. 156), that is to say, c. 1627.

BIBLIOGRAPHY: Monconys, Bibl. 35a, p. 118; Sand-rart, p. 258; Loménie de Brienne, p. 216; Bailly, p. 315; Dézallier, 1745, II, p. 255, and 1762, IV, p. 40; Gault de Saint-Germain, Pt. II, pp. 44 f.; Smith, No. 246; Friedlaender, 1914, pp. 47, 112; Grautoff, I, p. 41, II, No. 3; Magne, 1914, p. 200, No. 48; Panofsky, Bibl. 815, pp. 267, 296; Friedlaender, 1933, p. 323; Alpatov, Bibl. 882, pp. 5 ff.; Hour-ticq, Bibl. 899, p. 110; Blunt, Bibl. 972, p. 167; Mahon, Bibl. 992, p. 38; Jamot, pp. 12, 50, 72; D. Panofsky, Bibl. 1046, p. 114; Stein, Bibl. 1079, p. 6; Licht, p. 73; Berger, Bibl. 1113, p. 169; Bardon, Bibl. 1218, p. 126; Hours, Bibl. 1256, pp. 6 ff., and *Exposition Poussin* (*Louvre*), pp. 336 f.; *Exposition Poussin* (*Louvre*), No. 22; Mahon, Bibl. 1271, pp. 298 ff.; Chastel, Bibl. 1326; *Exposition Poussin* (*Rouen*), No. 75; *L'ideale classico* (*Bologna*), No. 56; Mahon, Bibl. 1367, pp. XI, 19, 21, 25 ff., 29, 132, 138.

152. THE TESTAMENT OF EUDAMIDAS. 110·5 × 138·5 cm. Nationalmuseum, Copenhagen (559).

HISTORY: Painted for Michel Passart (Bellori, p. 455); Froment de Veine before 1700 (engraved when in his possession by Jean Pesne (d. 1700); see engraving No. 1 below); Beauchamp, rue des Fossés-Mont-martre, Paris, c. 1757 (engraved when in his possession by Marcenay de Guy; see engraving No. 2 below, and also the gouache by him, copy No. 5 below). Bt. through Saly by Count Moltke in 1759; bt. from his descendant by the Museum in 1931.

DRAWINGS: 1. Ecole des Beaux-Arts, Paris (*CR*, II, p. 5, No. A 25). A copy either after the painting or after a lost drawing.
2. Musée des Beaux-Arts, Besançon (1206). From the Gigoux collection. Probably a copy after a lost original.

ENGRAVINGS: 1. By Jean Pesne (Andresen, No. 306; Wildenstein, No. 107; Davies and Blunt, p. 213, No. 107).
2. By A. de Marcenay de Guy (Andresen, No. 307). Since the inscription reads *A de Marcenay de ghuy p.bat et sculp.bat*, the engraving was presumably made after the gouache mentioned below (see copy No. 5).

COPIES: 1. Musée des Beaux-Arts, Besançon. Given by Jean Gigoux in 1880 (*Inventaire général...*, Bibl. 563, *Monuments Civils, Province*, V, p. 126).
2. Hermitage Museum, Leningrad. According to the 1916 museum catalogue bt. by the Emperor Alexander I in 1808 from the painter 'Caraffa', presumably Armand-Charles Caraffe, who was court painter to the Emperor from 1802 to 1812.
3. Musée Ingres, Montauban.
4. Dr. Neuhaus-Glaser, Biel-Bienne, Switzerland.
5. In gouache by Marcenay de Guy (cf. *Gravure*, Bibl. 206, p. 159).
6. Thomas Hollis collection (cf. Hollis, Bibl. 263, Pl. opp. p. 839). In oils on paper; engraved by Barto-lozzi (Andresen, No. 308); anon. sale, Christie, London, 3.v.1884, lot 106.
7. Lord Methuen, Corsham Court, Wiltshire. Oils on paper laid down on panel. 19 × 25 cm. (Smith, No. 165). Probably the same as copy No. 6.
8. Desmares collection, c. 1830–50 (cf. Bouchitté, Bibl. 478, p. 170).

9. According to Wildenstein (No. 107) versions of the composition were offered to the Louvre by Legrand on 25.ii.1851, and by the church of Chassenay on 20.vi.1855.

10. Rev. T. Mawkes; lent to the Manchester Art Treasures Exhibition in 1857 (No. 588); cf. [G. S.], Bibl. 474, p. 57.

11. Anon. sale, Nagus, Paris, 2 ff.vi.1779, lot 197 ('Le Testament de Damidas'), as school of Poussin.

12. Anon. sale, Christie, London, 9 ff.ii.1787, first day, lot 32.

13. Anon. sale, Christie, London, 29 f.xi.1791, lot 121, bt. for Strange.

14. Birckenstock sale, Artaria, Vienna, March 1811, lot 533.

15. Peyron sale, Regnault, Paris, 10 ff.vi.1816, lot 11 (39½ × 50½ inches).

16. J. E. Hope of Belmont sale, Christie, London, 20.xii.1929, lot 51.

17. Anon. sale, Robinson and Fisher, London, 9.ii.1939, lot 27, as Flemish school.

In addition three versions in sculpture exist:

1. Musée des Beaux-Arts, Besançon. By Luc Breton (cf. *Inventaire général* . . ., Bibl. 563, *Monuments Civils, Province*, V, p. 228).

2. Musée Historique, Lyons. In terracotta.

3. National Trust, Stourhead, Wiltshire. By Rysbrack.

NOTES: The story is told by Lucian (*Toxaris*, chap. 22), but it is possible that Poussin's attention may have been drawn to it by the fact that it is given at length by Montaigne (*Essais*, I, chap. xxviii; ed. A. Thibaudet and M. Rat, Paris, 1962, p. 189).

Dated by Grautoff (II, No. 112) 1644–48; by Friedlaender (1914, p. 82) near the *Extreme Unction* (No. 116) of the second series of Sacraments, that is to say, near the year 1644. Mahon (Bibl. 1367, p. 119) follows Friedlaender, but would tend to date the picture a shade earlier, 1643–44. I believe the picture to have been painted about the middle of the 1650's, near the Johnson *Baptism* (No. 72), the Munich *Adoration of the Shepherds* (No. 41), and the Louvre *Arcadian Shepherds* (No. 120).

BIBLIOGRAPHY: Bellori, p. 455; Loménie de Brienne, pp. 214, 218; Diderot, Bibl. 211, XII, p. 102; Bardon, I, p. 155; Guibal, 273, p. 40; Fuseli, Bibl. 322, pp. 75, 181 f.; Gault de Saint-Germain, Pt. II, pp. 46 f.; Smith, No. 165; Knowles, Bibl. 392, II, p. 220; Cousin, Bibl. 456, p. 17; Feuillet de Conches, Bibl. 460, p. 167; Bouchitté, Bibl. 478, pp. 169 ff.; Friedlaender, 1914, pp. 83, 126; Grautoff, I, p. 226, II, No. 112; Magne, 1914, p. 219, No. 342; Jamot, p. 81; Rocher-Jauneau, Bibl. 1120, pp. 57 ff.; Chastel, Bibl. 1238, p. 302; *Exposition Poussin (Louvre)*, No. 97; Seznec, Bibl. 1284, p. 345; Mahon, Bibl. 1367, p. 119.

153. THE RAPE OF EUROPA (Fragment). 100 × 80 cm. Cut down and badly damaged, with triangular insertions on the left of the canvas. M. Pierre Desprats, Cahors.

HISTORY: Painted for Pucques about 1650 (cf. below). The surviving fragment has been in the possession of the present owner's family for about eighty years.

DRAWINGS: 1. Gabinetto dei Disegni, Florence (*CR*, III, p. 14, No. 169).

2. Nationalmuseum, Stockholm. The whole composition on the *recto*, and two drawings for the principal group on the *verso* (*CR*, III, p. 14, Nos. 166–8).

NOTES: In a letter of 22.viii.1649 (*Correspondance*, p. 403) Poussin tells Chantelou that he will undertake to paint a *Europa* for a 'M. Pucques', since he is a friend of Chantelou. He adds: 'Le subiec est forbeau remply d'épisodes pour goutés. mais il y a beaucoup à faire, et la disposition requiert une toille de dix ou douze palme de longueur et au moins six de hauteur. et sur tout il faut que ledit Signeur face bonne municion de patiense. et tout yra bien.' There is a short reference to the commission again in a letter of 8.x.1649 (*Correspondance*, p. 408), but nothing further, so that it has generally been assumed that the painting itself was never executed.

The composition is known from the magnificent drawing at Stockholm (*CR*, III, p. 14, No. 166), of which the painting represents the right-hand third. Mahon (Bibl. 1338, p. 125 n. 17, and *L'ideale classico* (*Bologna*), pp. 208 ff.), basing himself on the similarity between certain figures in the drawing and those in the painting of *Orpheus and Eurydice* (No. 170) in the Louvre, has argued that the project for painting the *Europa* was abandoned and that the composition was transformed into the Louvre picture. The existence of the surviving fragment makes this hypothesis unnecessary. He further argued that the name Pucques, which is not otherwise recorded, is a misreading for Foucquet, but later abandoned this thesis.

In a recent article (Bibl. 1435, p. 137 n. 82) Mahon, basing himself on a photograph of the fragment, argues that so little of the original paint survives that it would be impossible to decide whether the painting was an original by Poussin or the work of a pasticheur. In spite of the extremely damaged condition of the painting, however, parts of it are sufficiently well preserved to show characteristics which conform exactly with Poussin's manner of painting. It has none of the marks either of a copy or of the work of a pasticheur.

The Stockholm drawing is important for the dating of the picture, because it is on the *verso* of a sheet made up of a series of drawings, joined together, which include two preliminary studies for the composition, one for a *Holy Family* (*CR*, I, p. 27, No. 52), and one for the *Moses striking the Rock*, painted for Stella in 1649 and now in the Hermitage (No. 23; *CR*, I, p. 13, No. 25). The last drawing confirms the dating of the whole *Europa* composition to about 1649–50, though, in view of what Poussin says in his two letters quoted above about being overworked, a little time may be allowed for the actual execution of the painting. The painting, however, follows the drawing so precisely that it must have been executed soon after it. This point is important, since the style of both drawing and painting would at first sight suggest a later date, and this is yet another example of the variety to be found in Poussin's landscape painting in the period around 1650, which makes it possible to accept Félibien's dating for works like the *Diogenes* (No. 150) and the *Polyphemus* (No. 175), which in some ways seems strange in this period.

BIBLIOGRAPHY: *Correspondance*, pp. 403 f., 408; Weng- ström and Hoppe, Bibl. 896, No. XV; *CR*, III, p. 14; Blunt, Bibl. 972, p. 165; *Exposition Poussin* (*Louvre*), No. 219; Mahon, Bibl. 1338, p. 125 n. 17; *L'ideale classico* (*Bologna*), pp. 208 ff.

154. THE TRIUMPH OF FLORA. 165 × 241 cm. Musée du Louvre, Paris (732).

HISTORY: According to Bellori (p. 442) painted for Cardinal Aluigi Omodei. Acquired by Louis XIV in 1684–85, perhaps as a gift, since there is no record of its purchase in the *Comptes des bâtiments*.

DRAWINGS: 1. Fitzwilliam Museum, Cambridge (*CR*, III, p. 36, No. A 59). Probably by an imitator.
2. Cooper Union, New York (1921–22–4). An early eighteenth-century copy after the painting.

ENGRAVINGS: 1. By M. Horthemels (Andresen, No. 390).
2. By E. Fessard (Andresen, No. 389). Dated 1770.

COPIES: 1. Musée de Tessé, Le Mans.
2. Musée des Beaux-Arts, Marseilles (394). Given by the State in 1819 (cf. Thuillier, Bibl. 1299, p. 293).
3. Musée du Louvre, Paris. Lent to the Ministry of the Interior 27.v.1819. Perhaps the picture mentioned as a copy in seventeenth-century inventories (cf. Bailly, p. 308).
4. University Art Museum, Princeton, New Jersey.
5. Pinacoteca Capitolina, Rome (cf. Ramdohr, Bibl. 287, I, p. 262; Burckhardt, Bibl. 465b, p. 990; Incisa della Rocchetta, Bibl. 1070, p. 37; Thuillier, Bibl. 1298, p. 265). Single figures from this version, which in the eighteenth century was considered an original, were engraved by Saint-Non in his *Fragments* (Bibl. 240; cf. Cayeux, Bibl. 1390.2, p. 343, No. 127c).
6. Robert Strange sale, Christie, London, 23.i.1819, lot 105.
7. Lord Northwick sale, Christie, Cheltenham, 27 ff. vii.1859, lot 180.

NOTES: Cardinal Omodei was only born in 1608, and it is generally agreed that the picture was painted in the late 1620's, so that it is not likely—though not altogether impossible—that he actually commissioned it. Bellori may have known that the picture was in his possession and concluded that he had originally ordered it. In 1655–56 Omodei was trying to sell his Poussins (cf. the Louvre *Rape of the Sabines*, No. 179), but the *Flora* was still in his possession in 1664 ([Bellori], Bibl. 36, p. 35).

Dated by Grautoff (II, No. 45) 1630–35; by Mahon (Bibl. 1367, p. X) to 1627, which seems to me appropriate.

BIBLIOGRAPHY: *Lettres à Nicolas Fouquet*, Bibl. 24a, p. 103; [Bellori], Bibl. 36, p. 35; Félibien, IV, p. 85; Bellori, p. 442; Piganiol de La Force, Bibl. 124, I, p. 150; Bailly, p. 308; Monicart, Bibl. 144, II, pp. 360 ff.; Guilbert, Bibl. 159, I, p. 118; Dézallier, 1745, II, p. 254, and 1762, IV, p. 39; Bardon, II, pp. 125 f.; Boyer d'Argens, Bibl. 231, p. 297; Smith, No. 243; Chatelain, Bibl. 667, p. 429; Friedlaender, 1914, pp. 49, 113; Grautoff, I, p. 113, II, No. 45; Magne, 1914, pp. 84, 203, No. 105; Francastel, Bibl. 883, p. 151; Hourticq, Bibl. 899, p. 130; Jamot, pp. 10, 13, 18 ff., 21, 24, 40, 43, 64, 84 f.; Licht, p. 114; Berger, Bibl. 1113, p. 163; Blunt, Bibl. 1167, p. 76; Bardon, Bibl. 1218, p. 125 n. 15; Blunt, Bibl. 1227, p. 174; *Exposition Poussin* (*Louvre*), No. 31; Mahon, Bibl. 1271, pp. 291, 296 f.; Thuillier, Bibl. 1295, p. 103; Wild, Bibl. 1312, p. 157; Mahon, Bibl. 1367, pp. X, 18, 32 f., 38, 53, 58, 61, 89, 134.

155. THE KINGDOM OF FLORA. 131×181 cm. Staatliche Gemäldegalerie, Dresden.

HISTORY: Painted in 1631 for Valguarnera (Costello, Bibl. 1052, pp. 272 ff., 275). Recorded in the collection of the Electors and later the Kings of Saxony from 1722.

DRAWINGS: 1. Royal Library, Windsor Castle (CR, III, p. 35, No. 214).

2. Royal Library, Windsor Castle (CR, III, p. 35, No. A 58). A studio drawing.

3. With Pollak, Paris, in 1947. A water-colour copy of the painting.

ENGRAVINGS: 1. By G. Audran (Andresen, No. 391; Wildenstein, No. 137; Davies and Blunt, p. 214, No. 137).

2. By J. Moyreau (in the Albertina; not listed by Andresen).

COPIES: 1. Musée des Beaux-Arts, Besançon. Bequeathed by Jean Gigoux in 1894. The figure of Ajax only. Engraved by an unknown artist (Andresen, No. 304).

2. By Antoine Fort-Bras (cf. de Loye, Bibl. 1267, p. 21).

3. Robert Strange sale, Christie, London, 20.ii.1772, lot 178 (50½×71 in.).

4. D'Abel sale, Stuttgart, 14.iv.1920, lot 59 (as Italian school, Parnassus).

NOTES: The dating of this picture has at different times given rise to various hypotheses, but, when it was shown at the Louvre exhibition in 1960 (No. 20), it was unanimously agreed that it must be the painting mentioned by Valguarnera at his trial in 1631, and that it can therefore be dated to the last months of 1630 and the beginning of 1631. Examination by X-ray made at the time of the exhibition made it clear that there were no alterations in the picture and that it was all executed at the same period.

The pergola and the herm of Priapus on the left of the composition seem to have been suggested to Poussin by an engraving by the Master L. D. after Primaticcio (rep. W. M. Ivins, 'French XVI century prints', Bulletin of the Metropolitan Museum of Art, New series, III, 1945–46, p. 128).

BIBLIOGRAPHY: Félibien, IV, p. 83; Bellori, p. 441; Sandrart, p. 258; Florent Le Comte, III, p. 33; Lairesse, Bibl. 129a, II, p. 75; Cambry, Bibl. 272a, p. 50; Smith, No. 269; Friedlaender, 1914, p. 114; Grautoff, I, pp. 15, 152, II, No. 82; Magne, 1914, pp. 84, 200, No. 50; Panofsky, Bibl. 893, p. 244; Hourticq, Bibl. 899, p. 130; Blunt, Bibl. 975, pp. 36, 47, and Bibl. 1026, pp. 4 ff.; Jamot, pp. 19, 24, 40, 85; Costello, Bibl. 1052, pp. 272 f., 275; Blunt, Bibl. 1086, pp. 186 f., and Bibl. 1086a, pp. 162 f.; Licht, p. 127; Blunt, Bibl. 1167, p. 76; Jack, Bibl. 1202, p. 212; Blunt, Bibl. 1226, p. 396, and Bibl. 1227, pp. 170, 174; Francastel, Bibl. 1251, p. 214; Exposition Poussin (Louvre), No. 20; Mahon, Bibl. 1271, pp. 291 ff., 298 f., Wild, Bibl. 1312, p. 157; Kauffmann, Bibl. 1332, p. 96; Mahon, Bibl. 1367, pp. XI, 3, 19, 23 ff., 28 ff., 39 f., 47, 53, 55 f., 63 f., 75, 84, 87 ff., 132, 135 f.; Kauffmann, Bibl. 1433; Spear, Bibl. 1438.

156. THE DEATH OF GERMANICUS. 146×195 cm. The Minneapolis Institute of Arts, Minneapolis.

HISTORY: Painted for Cardinal Francesco Barberini after his return from his legations abroad (Bellori, p. 413; Félibien, IV, p. 17). A payment of 60 scudi for the picture is recorded on 24.i.1628 (Bousquet, Bibl. 1231, pp. 3 f.). Passed by descent to the Princes of Palestrina and eventually to Prince Corsini; bt. from him in 1958 by Messrs. Wildenstein; bt. by the Minneapolis Institute of Arts in the same year.

DRAWINGS: 1. British Museum, London (CR, II, p. 15, No. 129).

2. Musée Condé, Chantilly (CR, II, p. 15, No. 130). Possibly made later than the painting as a preparation for an unexecuted second version.

3. Musée du Louvre, Paris (CR, II, p. 15, No. A 33).

ENGRAVINGS: 1. By G. Chasteau (Andresen, No. 327; Wildenstein, No. 115; Davies and Blunt, p. 214, No. 115). Dated 1663, with verses by Michel de Marolles.

2. Anonymous (Andresen, No. 328).

3. By J. J. Freidhof (Andresen, No. 330). Published in 1797.

COPIES: 1. Hermitage Museum, Leningrad (8630). Acquired in 1939 from the Hild collection (cf. Grautoff, II, No. 10).

2. Musée Gustave Moreau, Paris (cf. Grautoff, loc. cit.). By Moreau.

3. Colonel R. C. Parker, Browsholme, Lancashire. Said to have been bt. from the sale of Mrs. Chamberlain of Skipton, 9.xi.1848, lot 180, as a copy by Lebrun. Visible in a photograph of the room reproduced in Country Life, 13.vii.1935, p. 41.

4. Almazón collection, Madrid.

5. Sir Michael Culme-Seymour, Rockingham Castle, Leicestershire.

6. Private collection, Italy (1961).

7. Boyer d'Aguilles, Aix-en-Provence. Engraved by Coelemans (Andresen, No. 329; cf. Chennevières-Pointel, Bibl. 433, I, p. 143).

8. Lord Pomfret, Easton Neston, Northamptonshire. Seen there in 1732 by Vertue (Bibl. 132, XXIV, pp. 37 f.). Lord Pomfret sale, London, 1754, 2nd day,

lot 49, presumably bt. in; Lord Pomfret sale, London, 9 f.iii.1758, first day, lot 44. Said in the 1754 sale to be by Poussin and Pierre Mignard.

9. Formerly Sir Thomas Isham, Lamport Hall, Northamptonshire. Made by Giovanni Remigio in 1677–78 (cf. Burdon, Bibl. 1234, p. 6).

10. J. Richardson Senior, London (cf. Richardson, *Account*, p. 159). Richardson sale, Cock, London, 3 f.iii.1747, second day, lot 50, bt. Hervey. By Passeri.

11. André Charles Boulle. Destroyed by fire in 1720 (cf. Montaiglon, Bibl. 468, p. 343). Said to have been by Pierre Mignard.

12. Eudoxe Marcille, Paris (cf. Clément, Bibl. 516, p. 351). By Géricault.

13. Puccini family, Pistoia. Said to have been painted by Poussin and presented to the family out of gratitude for help given to him on his first journey to Italy (cf. Bousquet, Bibl. 1231, p. 2).

14. Lord Halifax sale, London, 6 ff.iii.1739, third day, lot 73.

15. Blackwood sale, London, 1756, lot 68.

16. Anon. sale, Prestage, London, 27.i.1767, lot 22.

17. Van Schorel sale, Antwerp, 7.vi.1774, lot 189 (36×53 inches).

18. Mme de la Haye sale, Remy, Paris, i.xii.1778, lot 53 (17×24 inches).

19. Anon. sale, Christie, London, 23.iv.1779, lot 62, bt. Devon.

20. Turner sale, Christie, London, 9 f.vi.1780, first day, lot 94, bt. Hart.

21. Alexander Stuart sale, Christie, London, 25 f.ii.1788, first day, lot 61.

22. Desmaret sale, Lebrun, Paris, 17.iii.1797, lot 25 (54×70 inches).

23. Sir Joshua Reynolds sale, Christie, London, 11 ff.iii.1798, second day, lot 90 (cf. [Borenius], Bibl. 977, p. 217, No. 90).

24. Anon. sale, Christie, London, 29 f.iv.1808, second day, lot 101.

25. Anon. sale, Christie, London, 16.iii.1819, lot 96, bt. Dyson.

26. Legrand sale, Paillet, Paris, 21.xi.1827, lot 72. From the collection of the Prince de Teingrie.

27. Anon. sale, Dowell, Edinburgh, 11.i.1896, lot 67.

NOTES: The subject is taken from Tacitus (*Ann.*, II, lxxi ff.).

According to Hunter (Bibl. 1201, p. 10) a close examination of the picture suggests that Poussin at first painted a landscape through the arch in the left background.

In the Barberini inventory of 1631 (Orbaan, Bibl. 746, p. 501; Pollak, Bibl. 832, I, p. 335) the dimensions are given as 6 by 8 palmi, i.e. 132×176 cm., that is to say considerably smaller than the existing canvas, but the size given in the inventory is probably only an approximation.

According to writers in the late eighteenth century the picture then appeared much damaged. Bottari in a note to Passeri (Passeri, p. 326) says that it was 'quasi perduto per l'umidità', and La Lande, who saw the picture in 1765–66, says that it has 'beaucoup changé' (Bibl. 224a, IV, p. 383). The damage must, however, have been purely to the varnish, since the picture is in fact in excellent condition.

As will be seen from the list given above, this was one of Poussin's most popular and most frequently copied compositions.

BIBLIOGRAPHY: Malvasia, Bibl. 30, p. 47; [Bellori], Bibl. 36, p. 10; Chantelou, 1885, p. 222, and 1960, p. 130; Félibien, II, pp. 345 f., III, pp. 221 f., IV, pp. 17, 82; Bellori, p. 413; Sirén, Bibl. 63, pp. 167 f., 171; Sandrart, p. 258; Passeri, p, 326; Baldinucci, XVI, p. 100; de Cotte, Bibl. 98, III, p. 154, and Bibl. 98a, p. 204; Deseine, Bibl. 101a, I, p. 193; Rossini, Bibl. 106, p. 57, and Bibl. 106e, p. 209; Loménie de Brienne, pp. 213, 218, 223; Rossi, Bibl. 114, pp. 351 f.; Florent Le Comte, III, p. 25; Pinaroli, Bibl. 123, II, p. 174; Lairesse, Bibl. 129a, II, p. 551; Caylus, Bibl. 133, p. 284; Wright, Bibl. 146, I, p. 291; Richardson, *Account*, pp. 159 ff.; Breval, Bibl. 151, II, p. 303; de Brosses, Bibl. 170a, II, p. 52; Keyssler, Bibl. 172, II, p. 49; Blainville, Bibl. 176, III, p. 85; Ficoroni, Bibl. 177.1, II, p. 53; Dézallier, 1745, II, pp. 249, 253, and 1762, I, p. 113, IV, pp. 27, 34, 38; Le Blanc, Bibl. 180, p. 150; Martinelli, Bibl. 186, p. 199; Bardon, II, p. 126; La Lande, Bibl. 224a, IV, p. 383; Northall, Bibl. 227, p. 319; Richard, Bibl. 229, IV, p. 68; La Roque, Bibl. 248, II, p. 245; [Weston], Bibl. 254, p. 140; Volkmann, Bibl. 257, II, p. 265; Magnan, Bibl. 260, I, p. 55; Canova, Bibl. 261, p. 105; Chiusole, Bibl. 269, p. 49; Cambry, Bibl. 272a, p. 20; Guibal, Bibl. 273, pp. 25, 38; Ramdohr, Bibl. 287, II, pp. 290 ff.; Martyn, Bibl. 296, p. 218; Starke, Bibl. 306, II, p. 33; Manazzale, Bibl. 308a, I, p. 110; Salmon, Bibl. 321, I, p. 199; Dalmazzoni, Bibl. 325a and b, p. 204; *Rome in the 19th century*, Bibl. 371, III, p. 23; Smith, No. 176; Friedlaender, 1914, pp. 33, 112, 142; Grautoff, I, p. 74, II, No. 10; Magne, 1914, pp. 12, 191, 201, No. 77; Orbaan, Bibl. 746, p. 501; Pollak, Bibl. 832, I, p. 335; Alpatov, Bibl. 882, p. 17; Francastel, Bibl. 883, p. 146; Blunt, Bibl. 911, pp. 197 ff., and Bibl. 1026, p. 4; Jamot, pp. 11, 83 f.; Licht, p. 85; Hunter, Bibl. 1201, p. 1; Bardon, Bibl. 1218, pp. 128, 130; Bousquet, Bibl. 1231, pp. 3 f.; Hazlehurst, Bibl. 1255, pp. 60 f.; Mahon, Bibl. 1271, pp. 290, 293, 295, 297; Waterhouse, Bibl. 1308, p. 294; Mahon, Bibl. 1367, pp. X, 19 ff., 26 ff., 38, 48, 52 f., 84, 86, 134, 136.

157. HANNIBAL CROSSING THE ALPS. 100×133 cm. Private collection, Paris.

HISTORY: Possibly painted for Cassiano dal Pozzo (see below). Nothing is known of the recent history of this picture beyond that it was said by the dealer from whom the present owner bought it to have come from England. It has on the stretcher a name which is hard to read, but which appears to read 'Mr. de Bonneville', perhaps the collector whose pictures were sold by Febvre, Paris, 7 f.vi.1844.

NOTES: The inventory of Cassiano dal Pozzo's collection, made in 1715, contained under Nos. 67, 68 'Due quadri d'elefanti da Imp.re uno di Pietro Testa e l'altro di Pussino' (Haskell and Rinehart, Bibl. 1254, p. 325). The word 'Imp.re' signifies a canvas of the size called *tela d'imperatore*, which is that of the first set of Sacraments mentioned in the same inventory. These are 95×119 cm., which corresponds closely enough with the size of the present painting.

From the inventory there is no means of deciding whether the present painting is the Testa or the Poussin, but other evidence is in favour of the latter hypothesis. In a letter to Cassiano dal Pozzo (*Correspondance*, p. 2) Poussin writes: 'Ho disegnato l'elefante, del quale (perchè m'è paruto che V. S. Illma n'aveva qualche desiderio) gliene farò un presente; essendo dipinto con un Annibale montato su, armato all'antica.' It is not clear whether Poussin is referring to both a painting and a drawing, since his use of *dipinto* might merely mean depicted, but the present painting undoubtedly represents Hannibal, since it shows in the background troops going through a mountain pass, and Poussin may well have been commissioned to paint a picture from the drawing.

The account of the Pozzo collection given in the papers of Robert de Cotte (Bibl. 98a, p. 203) mentions 'une bataille où il y a porus sur un éléphant' by Poussin. This might possibly refer to the same picture, though, if it does, the author has probably made a mistake—there are several in his account—for there is nothing in the picture to suggest that the soldiers represented are oriental, and the mountains visible in the background fit exactly with the subject of Hannibal.

The question of dating is difficult. In the catalogue of the Rouen exhibition (No. 94), which was held when the picture had just been discovered, I suggested 1629, but I agree with Mahon (Bibl. 1367, pp. 133 f.) that there are strong arguments against such a late dating. As he points out, the traditional placing of Poussin's letter referred to above in that year is based on unsound arguments, and the winter of 1626–27 is more plausible.

There is, however, as Mahon points out, a complication due to the fact that elephants were very rarely to be seen in Rome, and that there is no record of one having been available in Rome at the relevant time. Moreover, one was shown there in 1630, when it was engraved by Pietro Testa (cf. Petrucci, Bibl. 886.1, p. 409), and his engraving is strikingly close to the present painting. It does not, however, follow that either Poussin or Testa used the actual elephant shown in 1630 as a model for their compositions. Pozzo's collection contained a great many drawings of animals, now unfortunately scattered, and these would almost certainly have included representations of elephants. If this was the case, it is more than likely that Poussin would have used such a drawing as his source, and quite possible that Testa did the same when he came to engrave the elephant that he had actually seen, since to copy an existing drawing would have been far less trouble than to make careful drawings from life; and Testa certainly had access to Pozzo's collections (cf. Petrucci, *op. cit.* pp. 412 ff.).

The date 1626–27 therefore seems to be the most plausible suggestion, and this would be confirmed by the similarity in colour and handling to the Cherbourg *Pietà* (No. 81), which can be certainly placed in the years 1625–27, and the connection with the battle-pieces of 1625–26 (Nos. 29, 30) in the types and execution of the soldiers' heads and armour.

BIBLIOGRAPHY: *Correspondance*, p. 2; de Cotte, Bibl. 98a, p. 203; Haskell and Rinehart, Bibl. 1254, pp. 322, 325; Blunt, Bibl. 1323, p. 352; *Exposition Poussin (Rouen)*, No. 94; Mahon, Bibl. 1367, pp. IX, 133 f.

158. LANDSCAPE WITH HERCULES AND CACUS. 156·5×202 cm. Pushkin Museum, Moscow.

HISTORY: Bought by Diderot (together with the *Landscape with Polyphemus*, No. 175) in 1772 from the Marquis de Conflans for the Empress Catherine II of Russia (Tourneux, Bibl. 646, pp. 58, 428). Sent to Moscow from the Hermitage in 1930.

COPY: Anon. sale, Budapest, 26.xi.1928, lot 430 (without the figures of Hercules and Cacus).

NOTES: The subject is taken from Virgil (*Aeneid,* viii, 190 ff.).

It was for long assumed that, because this picture hung as a pair to the *Polyphemus*, it must have been painted at the same time, but in the catalogue of the Louvre exhibition (No. 108) I pointed out that there were strong reasons for thinking that the two pictures were not painted as pendants but had only been brought together at a later period, and further, that there were stylistic grounds for dating the *Hercules* to a later phase, *c.* 1655. In his article on Poussin's landscapes, published in *Art de France* (Bibl. 1338, pp. 126, 128) Mahon proposed an even later date, *c.* 1659–61, that is to say immediately before the Seasons. This seems to me not at all impossible, but I should not agree with Mahon's proposal to place the *Polyphemus* at about the same date (see No. 176).

BIBLIOGRAPHY: Smith, No. 307; Tourneux, Bibl. 646, pp. 58, 428; Grautoff, I, p. 257, II, No. 136; Magne, 1914, p. 217, No. 306; Blunt, Bibl. 972, pp. 157, 167; Jamot, pp. 38, 72; Dorival, Bibl. 1088, p. 51; Licht, p. 153; Bardon, Bibl. 1218, p. 130; *Exposition Poussin (Louvre)*, No. 108; Kitson, Bibl. 1335, p. 158; Mahon, Bibl. 1338, pp. 126, 128, and Bibl. 1367, pp. XIV, 2, 116, 121.

159. THE CHOICE OF HERCULES. 91×72 cm. The National Trust, Stourhead, Wiltshire.

HISTORY: Probably the picture mentioned by Félibien (IV, p. 152) and Loménie de Brienne (p. 224) as having belonged to the lawyer Richaumont and then to his son-in-law, the architect François Blondel (d. 1686), who is mentioned in the 1684 edition of Brice as owning pictures by Poussin, but without details (Bibl. 89, II, p. 196). Duke of Chandos sale, Cock, London, 7.v.1747, lot 119, bt. Sir Richard Hoare; passed by descent to Sir Henry Hoare, who gave Stourhead and its contents to the National Trust in 1947.

ENGRAVING: By Robert Strange (Andresen, No. 397). Dated 1759.

NOTES: Félibien (*loc. cit.*) and Loménie de Brienne (*loc. cit.*), who seems to be copying him, describe the Blondel picture as being 'des premières manières', whereas the present picture has all the marks of Poussin's style in about 1637. Either they are mistaken, or they are referring to a different painting, now lost.

BIBLIOGRAPHY: Félibien, IV, p. 152; Loménie de Brienne, p. 224; Florent Le Comte, III, p. 32; Walpole, Bibl. 192, p. 41; Waagen, Bibl. 384b, III, p. 172; Smith, No. 270; Friedlaender, 1914, p. 113; Grautoff, II, p. 258; Magne, 1914, p. 200, No. 59; Panofsky, Bibl. 841, pp. 140 ff.; Hourticq, Bibl. 899, p. 94; Blunt, Bibl. 1051, p. 70; *Exposition Poussin (Louvre)*, No. 49; Mahon, Bibl. 1271, p. 303; Rees Jones, Bibl. 1280, pp. 304 ff.; Waterhouse, Bibl. 1308, p. 292; *L'ideale classico (Bologna)*, No. 60; Mahon, Bibl. 1367, p. 82.

160. LANDSCAPE WITH JUNO, ARGUS AND IO. 120×195 cm. Staatliche Museen zu Berlin, Gemäldegalerie, Berlin.

HISTORY: Probably painted for the Marchese Vincenzo Giustiniani; in the inventory of his collection made in February 1638, after his death in December 1637 (Salerno, Bibl. 1282, p. 101, No. 133); bt. by the Kaiser-Friedrich-Museum with the Giustiniani collection in 1812.

NOTES: Rejected by Grautoff (II, pp. 260 f.). The evidence of the Giustiniani inventory is, however, almost final, and the picture is certainly an original by Poussin dating from about 1636–37 (cf. Blunt, Bibl. 1195, p. 389).

BIBLIOGRAPHY: Silos, Bibl. 61, p. 122, and Bibl. 61a, p. 158; de Cotte, Bibl. 98a, p. 204; *Verzeichniss . . .*, Bibl. 382, p. 43, No. 145; Grautoff, II, pp. 260 f., rep. on p. 272, owing to a confusion with a landscape in the Prado; Magne, 1914, p. 200, No. 62; Blunt, Bibl. 1195, p. 389; Salerno, Bibl. 1282, pp. 27, 101, No. 133; Thuillier, Bibl. 1298, p. 267; Kitson, Bibl. 1335, p. 145.

161. THE NURTURE OF JUPITER. 95×118 cm. Alleyn's College of God's Gift, Dulwich, London.

HISTORY: Blondel de Gagny by 1757 (Dézallier d'Argenville, Bibl. 183b, p. 279); Blondel de Gagny sale, Remy, Paris, 10.xii.1776, lot 94 (with description); Ogilvie sale, Christie, London, 6 ff.iii.1778, second day, lot 85 (as from the Blondel de Gagny collection), bt. Campbell. Desenfans by 1804 (Insurance list, at Dulwich College); at his death in 1807 bequeathed to Sir Francis Bourgeois, and by him in 1811 to the College.

COPIES: Two variants exist of the putto lying in the foreground:
1. Princess Pallavicini-Rospigliosi, Rome. In the 1708 inventory without the artist's name; in 1713 attributed to Poussin (cf. Zeri, Bibl. 1216, pp. 196 f., No. 341).

2. C. A. de Burlet, Basle. From the Ernst collection, Budapest (cf. Venturi, Bibl. 816, p. 250; Grautoff, Bibl. 864, p. 323; Friedlaender, 1933, p. 234, and Zeri, *loc. cit.*).

NOTES: The story is told by various ancient authors, but Poussin's most probable source is Callimachus (*Hymn to Zeus*, 49). The motive of the goat Amalthea actually suckling the infant Jupiter is taken from an engraving by Bonasone after Giulio Romano (Bartsch, XV, p. 142, No. 107). The general design and the pose of the nymph taking the honey from the tree are related to a medallion visible in a woodcut in the French edition of the *Hypnerotomachia*, published by Jean Martin in 1546 (cf. *Discours du Songe de Poliphile*, ed. B. Guégan, Paris, 1926, p. 25).

   Grautoff (II, No. 63) dates the picture 1633–35, Mahon (Bibl. 1367, pp. XII, 105) to 1635–36. Owing to the likeness to the *Pan and Syrinx* of 1637–38 (No. 172), as well as the Richelieu *Bacchanals* of 1635–36 (Nos. 136, 137), I should tend to place the *Jupiter* about 1636–37.

BIBLIOGRAPHY: Dézallier d'Argenville, Bibl. 183b, p. 279, and Bibl. 183d, p. 134; Waagen, Bibl. 384b, II, p. 347; Hazlitt, Bibl. 411, p. 33; Friedlaender, 1914, pp. 52, 183; Grautoff, I, p. 132, II, No. 63; Magne, 1914, p. 201, No. 66; Alfassa, Bibl. 776, p. 271; Royal Academy, London, Bibl. 879, No. 120; Francastel, Bibl. 883, pp. 146 f.; *CR*, III, p. 14; Blunt, Bibl. 1026, pp. 7 f.; Jamot, pp. 14, 50; Royal Academy, London, Bibl. 1048, No. 24; Blunt, Bibl. 1051, p. 70, Bibl. 1086, pp. 186 f., and Bibl. 1086a, pp. 162 f.; Zeri, Bibl. 1216, pp. 196 f.; *Exposition Poussin (Louvre)*, No. 48; Mahon, Bibl. 1271, p. 303; Kauffmann, Bibl. 1334, p. 114; Mahon, Bibl. 1338, p. 120, and Bibl. 1367, pp. XII, 105; Medley, Bibl. 1418, pp. 56 ff.

162. THE NURTURE OF JUPITER. 97×133 cm. Staatliche Museen, Museum Dahlem, Berlin.

HISTORY: Possibly belonged in the late seventeenth century to Simon d'Imbert, Aix-en-Provence, or to Alexander Colbenschlag, Lyons, since the engraving after the picture by Guillaume Chasteau (see No. 1 below) bears a dedication by the latter to the former. In the possession of Frederick the Great by 1786 (cf. Nicolai, Bibl. 283, II, p. 886, No. 53).

ENGRAVINGS: 1. By G. Chasteau (Andresen, No. 332; Wildenstein, No. 116; Davies and Blunt, p. 214, No. 116).
2. By E. Picart (Wildenstein, No. 116 bis; Davies and Blunt, p. 214, No. 116 bis).
3. By J. F. Bolt (Andresen, No. 333).

COPY: Dufourny sale, Delaroche, Paris, 22 ff.xi.1819, lot 80. The catalogue gives the title as *L'Education de Bacchus*, but refers to the engraving by Chasteau dedicated to Imbert.

NOTES: The Berlin painting differs from the Dulwich version (No. 161) in that in the former the goat is milked by a satyr and the child drinks from a gilt jug. Further, the nymph takes the honey from the hive, as in the Bonasone engraving mentioned under No. 161, and not from the tree trunk. The theme of a satyr milking a goat is common in Italian bronzes of the sixteenth century.

   Grautoff (II, No. 64) dates the picture 1633–36, but there is now general agreement (*Exposition Poussin (Louvre)*, No. 60; Mahon, Bibl. 1367, pp. XIII, 114) that it must have been executed later, just before the visit to Paris.

BIBLIOGRAPHY: Nicolai, Bibl. 283, II, p. 886, No. 53; Smith, No. 182; Friedlaender, 1914, p. 79; Grautoff, I, pp. 15, 132, II, No. 64; Magne, 1914, p. 201, No. 67; Francastel, Bibl. 883, pp. 146 f.; Blunt, Bibl. 1026, p. 8; *Exposition Poussin (Louvre)*, No. 60; Mahon, Bibl. 1271, p. 304, and Bibl. 1367, pp. XIII, 114.

163. MELEAGER AND ATALANTA HUNTING. 160×360 cm. Museo del Prado, Madrid (2320).

HISTORY: Probably Cassiano dal Pozzo (cf. Blunt, Bibl. 1426, p. 62). Spanish Royal Collection at Buen Retiro by 1701 (Museum catalogue).

DRAWING: Musée des Beaux-Arts, Besançon (1183). Probably a copy after a lost original.

ENGRAVING: An anonymous print is to be found in the Albertina, Vienna (formerly in the Hofbibliothek; Friedlaender, 1914, p. 129).

NOTES: A pair to the *Dance in honour of Priapus*, now at São Paulo (No. 176), which can be shown also to have been in the Spanish Royal Collection (cf. Blunt, *loc. cit.*). They probably correspond to the *Chasse* and the *Sacrifice* mentioned in the account of Pozzo's collection in the papers of Robert de Cotte.

The subject of the picture has sometimes (e.g. by Friedlaender, 1914, p. 129) been called *Dido and Aeneas*, but as Bardon (Bibl. 1218, p. 130) has pointed out, the details fit better with the account given by Ovid (*Metamorphoses*, viii, 298 ff.) of Meleager hunting with Atalanta than with Virgil's description (*Aeneid*, iv) of the scene at Carthage. In particular Atalanta's dress fits with Ovid's minute description in every detail save one, and this one can be explained. Ovid (line 319) says that Atalanta's hair was caught up in a knot, whereas Poussin has shown it falling over her shoulders; but he may well have done this to make her sex plain, since her hair is almost the only visible feature to show that she is a woman. Further, the cult figure of Diana, visible in the background, has a relevance in the story of Meleager, since she was to intervene in a vital way in the action by tearing the steel point off the spear hurled at the boar by Mopsus while it was in flight, with the result that the boar was not wounded but was goaded into fury (ll. 352 ff.) and attacked and killed many of Meleager's companions. A somewhat similar group of cult objects, but with a bear's head instead of a skull, appears in the drawing of *Venus and Adonis hunting* (text volume, Fig. 116), and again, but with a boar's head, in a drawing in the Musée Bonnat, Bayonne (*CR*, III, No. 228, Pl. 171). The tall urn on a column, decorated with a garland, appears in two studies for Bacchanals, one for the Richelieu *Triumph of Pan* (*CR*, III, No. 189 Pl. 148), the other for the *Bacchanal in front of a Temple* (*ibid.*, No. 195, Pl. 153). The presence of Pan in the right background is not easy to explain, but he may merely be included as the god of forests, since the whole of the hunt described by Ovid takes place in thick woods.

When it is first mentioned in the Spanish Royal inventory in 1701, the picture is simply described as 'original de Italia', but this phrase—or alternatively 'El Italiano'—seems to have been used for all the paintings at Buen Retiro which had been commissioned from Italy and does not imply an attribution to an Italian hand (cf. Blunt, Bibl. 1195, p. 389, note 6). In 1794 it was ascribed to Poussin (Museum catalogue).

The unusual size of the canvas and a certain dryness in the execution may give rise to some hesitation about the authenticity of the picture, but both it and its pendant are splendid designs, and the uncharacteristic features can be explained partly by the fact that Poussin was working on an unfamiliar scale, and partly perhaps on the hypothesis that he broke his normal rule and used assistants. Although Grautoff (II, No. 55) dates the picture 1632–36, this is almost certainly too early and both it and its pendant can be placed in the years just before the journey to Paris, a dating which would be confirmed by the many similarities which exist between the *Meleager* and the Louvre *Camillus* of 1637 (No. 142).

There is no information about the origin of the commission, and it is hard to believe that Pozzo would have ordered two such vast canvases for his house, which was not on a palatial scale. It may be tentatively suggested that they were painted for a patron who rejected them and perhaps bought partly out of kindness by Pozzo (the same may have happened in the case of the *St. Catherine* (No. 95), which is also unusually large and which does not seem to be directly connected with Pozzo's interests; cf. Blunt, Bibl. 1426, p. 62). Alternatively, was Poussin, alarmed at the prospect of working at the Louvre, trying out his hand at large-scale work?

BIBLIOGRAPHY: de Cotte, Bibl. 98, III, p. 153, and Bibl. 98a, p. 203; Mabilleau, Bibl. 635, p. 310; Moschetti, Bibl. 706, pp. 373 f.; Friedlaender, 1914, p. 129; Grautoff, I, p. 121, II, No. 55; Magne, 1914, p. 199, No. 41; Friedlaender, Bibl. 726, p. 233; Jamot, p. 37; Bardon, Bibl. 1218, p. 130; Rinehart, Bibl. 1281, p. 29; Blunt, Bibl. 1426, p. 62.

164. MERCURY, HERSE AND AGLAURUS. 53×77 cm. Ecole Nationale Supérieure des Beaux-Arts, Paris (69).

HISTORY: E. Gatteaux; bequeathed to the school by him in 1881 (Bouleau-Rabaud, Bibl. 1229, p. 255).

NOTES: The subject is taken from Ovid (*Metamorphoses*, ii, 814 ff.).

The picture was severely damaged in a fire which occurred in Gatteaux's house in the rue de Lille in March 1871 during the Commune. The middle area of the painting is now almost entirely repainted, but the parts which are reasonably well preserved, notably the figure of Mercury and the drapery of Aglaurus, who lies at his feet, are clearly from the hand of Poussin himself.

The picture has been little mentioned in recent literature, and few suggestions have been made about its dating. Mahon (Bibl. 1367, p. 29), while making every reservation on account of the damaged condition of the picture, tentatively proposes the middle of the period which runs from the second half of 1629 to the middle of 1631. In my view it is probably earlier, perhaps even as early as the *Triumph of Flora* (No. 154), that is to say *c.* 1627.

BIBLIOGRAPHY: Duplessis, Bibl. 526, p. 347; Muntz, Bibl. 612, p. 285; Chennevières-Pointel, Bibl. 629, p. 125; Magne, 1914, p. 201, No. 75; Hourticq, Bibl. 899, pp. 143 ff.; Bertin-Mourot, Bibl. 1023, p. 50, No. XXII; Bardon, Bibl. 1218, p. 130; Bouleau-Rabaud, Bibl. 1229, pp. 255 ff.; Mahon, Bibl. 1367, pp. 19 f., 26, 29.

165. MIDAS WASHING AT THE SOURCE OF THE PACTOLUS. 97.5×72.5 cm. The Metropolitan Museum of Art, New York.

HISTORY: Cardinal Camillo Massimi; on his death bequeathed to his brother, Fabio Camillo Massimi (Orbaan, Bibl. 746, p. 521). Possibly Donjeux sale, Lebrun, Paris, 29.iv.1793, lot 312. Probably Solirène sale, Henry, Paris, 5 ff.v.1829, lot 118, presumably bt. in; bt. from Solirène by J. Smith in 1836 (Smith, No. 248). The Metropolitan picture was acquired in 1871. According to Sterling (Bibl. 1122, pp. 68 ff.) it came from the collections of the Earl of Shaftesbury and Count Cornet, Brussels.

COPIES: 1. A copy with some variants and greatly enlarged in height belongs to Prince Massimi, Rome, and is accompanied by a similarly enlarged copy of the *Arcadian Shepherds* (No. 119), to which the original was a pair.

2. A very good early copy was on the London art market in 1938 and again in 1963. It varies from the Metropolitan painting in that, instead of the two putti in the foreground, it has a single putto, lying asleep and holding a cornucopia.

The following pictures mentioned in the eighteenth and early nineteenth centuries may possibly be connected either with the Metropolitan picture or with copy No. 2 referred to above:

1. The inventory of the collection of the artist J. F. Chantereau, made after his death in 1757, includes 'une esquisse de Poussin représentant un *Fleuve*' (Guiffrey, Bibl. 581, II, p. 246).

2. Marquis of Lansdowne sale, Coxe, London, 19 f. iii.1806, first day, lot 58; 'A repose of River Gods'. The pair to it, *Venus and Cupid, with a Man offering Fruit* (No. 188), is described as 'being evidently painted at a time when he was contemplating and felt the colouring of the Venetian School'.

NOTES: The Donjeux picture is not given any title but is described as follows: 'Une composition de quatre figures dans un paysage; celle qui se distingue principalement représente un homme endormi et vu de dos.' The size is 35×26 inches.

The picture in the Solirène sale, though entitled *Faunes endormis*, is described in detail, with a reference to two putti, so that it can certainly be identified with the Metropolitan composition, with which its dimensions also agree (36×26 inches).

The subject is identified by the reference in the Massimi inventory (Orbaan, *loc. cit.*), where it is listed as a pair to the *Arcadian Shepherds* (No. 119). It is taken from Ovid (*Metamorphoses*, xi, 134 ff.). Grautoff (II, No. 38) puts the painting among the works of 1630–35; Mahon (Bibl. 1367, p. 29) places it early in the phase beginning in the middle of 1629 and ending early in 1631. I should propose *c.* 1629–30 (cf. No. 119).

BIBLIOGRAPHY: Smith, No. 248; Grautoff, I, p. 108, II, No. 38; Orbaan, Bibl. 746, p. 521; Blunt, Bibl. 912, pp. 96 ff.; Friedlaender, Bibl. 964, pp. 21 ff.; Blunt, Bibl. 1086, p. 185, and Bibl. 1086a, p. 161; Licht, pp. 113, 123; Sterling, Bibl. 1122, pp. 68 ff.; Blunt, Bibl. 1167, p. 79; Hunter, Bibl. 1201, p. 12; Panofsky, Bibl. 1273, pp. 45 ff.; Mahon, Bibl. 1367, p. 29.

166. MIDAS AT THE SOURCE OF THE PACTOLUS. 50×66 cm. Musée Fesch, Ajaccio, Corsica.

HISTORY: Stefano Roccatagliata; Valguarnera (Blunt, Bibl. 1167, pp. 76 ff.); Cardinal Fesch; bequeathed by him to the museum in 1839.

NOTES: The attribution to Poussin was originally suggested, on the basis of a photograph, by Professor Roberto Longhi.

At the trial of Valguarnera in 1631 the dealer Roccatagliata stated that he had sold the Sicilian 'un quadrettino d'un Rè Mida con altra figurina ignuda... di Monsù Posin', a description which would exactly fit the Ajaccio picture (see Blunt, *loc. cit.*). The painting can therefore be dated before 1631. Mahon (Bibl. 1367, p. 29) places it in the middle of the period beginning in the second half of 1629 and ending at the beginning of 1631. Without wishing to be so precise, I should suggest a dating to *c.* 1629–30.

Examination by X-rays has shown that Poussin used for this painting a fragment of a much larger canvas, on which the life-size head and shoulders of a woman are visible (see text volume, Fig. 71). The head in the radiograph would not immediately suggest that it was by Poussin, but it is difficult to suppose that he would have used a canvas already painted on by another artist, and there are certain analogies between the head and that of the mother in the Chantilly *Massacre* (No. 67).

BIBLIOGRAPHY: Costello, Bibl. 1052, pp. 271, 273, 278; Blunt, Bibl. 1166, p. 9, Bibl. 1167, pp. 76 f., and Bibl. 1227, p. 165; Hours, Bibl. 1256, pp. 10 ff.; *Exposition Poussin (Louvre)*, No. 16; Mahon, Bibl. 1271, pp. 290, 298; Thuillier, Bibl. 1298, p. 286; Mahon, Bibl. 1367, p. 29.

167. THE TRIUMPH OF NEPTUNE. 114·5×146·5 cm. Philadelphia Museum of Art, Philadelphia, Pa.

HISTORY: Presumably the *Triumph of Neptune* described by Bellori (p. 423) and Félibien (IV, p. 27) and stated by them to have been painted for Cardinal Richelieu. Since the picture was not among those sold by the Duc de Richelieu to Louis XIV in 1665 (cf. Ferraton, Bibl. 1043), it presumably passed to the Cardinal's other heir, the Duchesse d'Aiguillon, who appears to have sold pictures in order to get money for her works of piety. Fromont de Brevannes by 1700 (engraved when in his possession by J. Pesne, who died in 1700). Possibly the *Vénus triomphante sur les mers* mentioned by Brice in 1713 (Bibl. 89d, II, p. 163) at the Hôtel de Bretonvilliers. This picture was no doubt removed—and probably sold—in 1719, when the Hôtel de Bretonvilliers was taken over for the offices of the Fermiers Généraux (cf. Piganiol de La Force, Bibl. 173, I, p. 347, who speaks in the past tense of the picture having been there). The Philadelphia picture belonged in 1755 to Louis Antoine Crozat, Baron de Thiers (*Catalogue*, Bibl. 200, p. 55), who in 1750 had inherited from his elder brother, Louis François Crozat, Marquis du Châtel, the collection formed by their uncle, Pierre Crozat, who died in 1740 (cf. Clément de Ris, Bibl. 553, pp. 183 ff.). In 1771 it was sold with the whole Crozat de Thiers collection of paintings to the Empress Catherine II of Russia. Sold by the Russian government about 1930 and acquired by the museum in 1932.

DRAWING: Sir Anthony Blunt, London (*CR*, III, p. 34, No. 213).

ENGRAVINGS: 1. By Jean Pesne (Andresen, No. 385; Davies and Blunt, p. 221).
2. By Pieter Schenk (In the Albertina; not listed by Andresen).

COPIES: 1. Arturo Edwards, Santiago, Chile (exhibited Sala Chile, Museo de Bellas Artes, Santiago, August 1948, No. 42). Perhaps the same as Nos. 3 and 4 below.
2. R. Hamilton sale, Foster, London, 15.iii. 1832, lot 315.
3. Sir Francis Lloyd sale, Ludlow, Briscoe and Hughes, at Aston Hall, Birmingham, 5.vii.1923, lot 955. According to Smith (No. 238) this had belonged to Thomas Walker and passed by descent to Sir Eliah Harvey, and in his day belonged to William Lloyd. In the sale catalogue the picture is called 'Italian school' and is described as follows: 'The Marine Venus riding on a dolphin chariot, attended by Neptune, sea nymphs and flying cupids.' 46×60 inches.
4. Ehrhardt Gallery, Berlin, in 1928 (cf. Grautoff, Bibl. 830, p. 104, and Bibl. 864, p. 331). 117×153 cm.

NOTES: The subject of this picture has given rise to much discussion. In the Crozat catalogue of 1755 (Bibl. 200, p. 55) it is called a *Galatea*, a title which was still retained by Grautoff (II, No. 87). This is manifestly wrong, but it means that both Loménie de Brienne (p. 214) and Florent Le Comte (III, p. 27) may be referring to the Philadelphia picture when they talk of a *Galatée*.

More recently Sommer (Bibl. 1348) proposed that the Philadelphia painting represented a *Triumph of Venus* or, more precisely, a *Venus Anadyomene*. His thesis was attacked by Levey (Bibl. 1397), but in an article in the *Journal of the Warburg and Courtauld Institutes* Charles Dempsey (Bibl. 1430) supports Sommer's hypothesis.

It seems probable that Poussin was planning a *Birth of Venus* at the same time that he was preparing the *Neptune*. Three drawings exist (*CR*, III, p. 29, Nos. 203–5) which certainly represent the former subject, but which have several features in common with the Philadelphia composition, notably the cupid on a dolphin and the couples of sea-gods and nymphs. These drawings being in a technique unusual for Poussin—black chalk only—cannot be precisely dated, but they appear to belong, like the Philadelphia picture, to the second half of the 1630's. One of these drawings, moreover, *CR*, No. 204, is on the *verso* of a study which is said in *CR* (No. 216) to be for a *Triumph of Galatea*, but which could equally well be for a *Birth of Venus*.

The most plausible solution seems to be that Poussin was playing at one and the same time with various related themes—a Triumph of Neptune and Amphitrite, a Birth of Venus, and possibly also a Triumph of Galatea—and that the painting which finally emerged, though actually representing Neptune and Amphitrite, retained echoes of the other subjects. Such overlapping of motives would not be unusual in Poussin's mythological paintings.

The existence of the *Vénus Marine* at the Hôtel de Bretonvilliers and the fact that it may actually well be the Philadelphia picture suggests that early collectors may have confused the two subjects and the confusion seems to have continued till the present century, since a copy of the Philadelphia painting was sold in 1923 as a *Marine Venus* (see above, copy No. 3). It is worth noting that Poussin made a drawing which certainly represents the *Birth of Venus* (*CR*, III, p. 29, No. 205), but this appears to have been made at a later date.

The picture was dated 1635–36 by Grautoff (II, No. 87). In the catalogue of the Louvre exhibition (No. 47) I suggested *c.* 1637, but I should now agree with Mahon (Bibl. 1367, p. XII) in placing it in 1635–36 with the Richelieu Bacchanals.

BIBLIOGRAPHY: Félibien, IV, p. 27; Bellori, p. 423; Sandrart, p. 258; Passeri, p. 327; Baldinucci, XVI, p. 102; Brice, Bibl. 89d, II, p. 163; Loménie de Brienne, p. 214; Florent Le Comte, III, p. 27; Piganiol de La Force, Bibl. 173, I, p. 347; Dézallier, 1745, II, p. 254, and 1762, IV, pp. 28, 38, 39; Dézallier d'Argenville, Bibl. 183b, p. 136; *Catalogue . . . du Cabinet de M. Crozat*, Bibl. 200, p. 55; Dulaure, Bibl. 278a, II, p. 75; Smith, No. 237; Friedlaender, 1914, pp. 68, 116; Grautoff, I, p. 159, II, No. 87; Magne, 1914, pp. 95, 203, No. 106; Hourticq, Bibl. 899, p. 142; Jamot, pp. 55 ff., 66, 85; Stein, Bibl. 1079, p. 8; Licht, pp. 128 f.; *Philadelphia Museum of Art Bulletin*, Bibl. 1142, pp 1 f.; *Exposition Poussin (Louvre)*, No. 47; Mahon, Bibl. 1271, p. 303; Pintard, Bibl. 1278, pp. 31, 34; Kauffmann, Bibl. 1332, p. 96; Sommer, Bibl. 1348, pp. 323 ff.; Mahon, Bibl. 1367, pp. XII, 40, 100, 105; Levey, Bibl. 1397; Dempsey, Bibl. 1430.

168. NUMA POMPILIUS AND THE NYMPH EGERIA. 75×100 cm. Musée Condé, Chantilly.

HISTORY: Probably painted for Cassiano dal Pozzo; almost certainly Lethières sale, Paillet, Paris, 29.xi.1829, lot 13, as from the 'Boca Paduli' collection (i.e. the Palazzo Boccapaduli, Rome). Bt. by the Duc d'Aumale from the Reiset collection.

NOTES: The story of Numa Pompilius and Egeria is told by many ancient writers, including Plutarch (*Life of Numa*, iv), but as Bardon (Bibl. 1218, p. 125 note 15) has pointed out, the authors who refer to the sacred grove which the nymph Egeria tended are Livy (I, 21, 3) and Juvenal (3, 13).

Although doubted by Friedlaender (1933, p. 324) and rejected by D. Wild (Bibl. 1185, p. 15)—probably on account of its damaged state and the difficulty of seeing it in a good light—the quality of the picture and its probable provenance from the Pozzo collection put its authenticity beyond doubt. It is dated by Grautoff (II, No. 35) 1630–35, a dating which might be qualified to one between 1631 and 1633.

BIBLIOGRAPHY: Grautoff, II, No. 35; Magne, 1914, p. 201, No. 80; Friedlaender, 1933, p. 324; Jamot, p. 48; Wild, Bibl. 1185, p. 15; Bardon, Bibl. 1218, p. 125 n. 15; Blunt, Bibl. 1426, p. 61.

169. LANDSCAPE WITH ORION. 119×183 cm. The Metropolitan Museum of Art, New York.

HISTORY: Painted for Passart (Bellori, p. 455; Félibien, IV, p. 66) in 1658 (Félibien, *loc. cit.*). Pierre de Beauchamp, Maître des Ballets du Roi (d. after 1698) by 1687 (Brice, Bibl. 89a, I, p. 51). Andrew Hay sale, London, 15 f.ii.1745, second day, lot 46, bt. Duke of Rutland; Duke of Rutland sale, London, 1758, lot 60, bt. J. Reynolds; Calonne sale, Skinner and Dyke, London, 23 ff.iii.1795, fourth day, lot 98, as from the Reynolds collection, bt. Bryan (i.e. bt. in by Calonne's mortgagees); Bryan pictures for sale by private treaty, 27.iv.1795, lot 135; Desenfans; sale of pictures bt. by him for the King of Poland, Skinner and Dyke, London, 18.iii.1802, lot 172; Philip Panné sale, Christie, London, 26 ff.iii.1819, first day, lot 63, bt. Bonnemaison; probably sold by him to the Rev. John Sanford, who lent it to the British Institution in 1821 (No. 15); bequeathed to his son-in-law, Lord Methuen; sold by his son in or shortly before 1924; bt. by Durlacher, London, in 1924 (Burroughs, Bibl. 769, p. 103); bt. by the museum in the same year.

NOTES: For a discussion of the subject of this picture, see text volume, pp. 315 f.

BIBLIOGRAPHY: Félibien, IV, p. 66; Bellori, p. 455; Brice, Bibl. 89a, I, p. 51; Loménie de Brienne, p. 222; Florent Le Comte, III, p. 32; Desenfans, Bibl. 323, I, p. 123; Buchanan, I, p. 254; Waagen, Bibl. 384b, IV, p. 396; Smith, No. 324; Hazlitt, Bibl. 417, pp. 190 ff.; *Catalogue of pictures . . . of the Rev. John Sanford*, Bibl. 428, p. 9; Friedlaender, 1914, p. 124; Grautoff, II, p. 259; Magne, 1914, pp. 155, 202, No. 87; Borroughs, Bibl. 769, pp. 103 f.; Whitley, Bibl. 829, p. 32; Borenius, Bibl. 850, p. 207; Friedlaender, 1933, p. 326; Blunt, Bibl. 972, p. 165; Gombrich, Bibl. 974, pp. 37 ff.; Bertin-Mourot, Bibl. 1023, p. 54, No. XXXVIII; D. Panofsky, Bibl. 1046, pp. 112 ff.; Blunt, Bibl. 1050, p. 40, Bibl. 1086, p. 194, and Bibl. 1086a, p. 170; Licht, p. 171; Blunt, Bibl. 1223, p. xxvii; *Exposition Poussin (Louvre)*, No. 113; Kauffmann, Bibl. 1334, p. 114; Mahon, Bibl. 1338, p. 125; Friedlaender, Bibl. 1365, pp. 254 f.; Mahon, Bibl. 1367, pp. 121, 129.

170. LANDSCAPE WITH ORPHEUS AND EURYDICE. 120×200 cm. Musée du Louvre, Paris (740).

HISTORY: Bt. by Branjon for Louis XIV in 1685 (*Comptes des bâtiments*, II, pp. 586, 664).

DRAWING: British Museum, London (*CR*, IV, p. 47, No. 284).

ENGRAVINGS: 1. By E. Baudet (Andresen, No. 443; Wildenstein, No. 181; Davies and Blunt, p. 215, No. 181).
2. By Desaulx and Bovinet (Andresen, No. 443a).

COPIES: 1. Musée Municipal, Brest (Magne, 1914, p. 202, No. 88). Destroyed in the Second World War.
2. Lord Methuen, Corsham Court, Wiltshire.
3. Leuchtenberg collection.
4. Lethières sale, Paillet, Paris, 24 ff.xi.1829, lot 12 ('Semblable à celui du musée'). Said to have belonged in the lifetime of the artist to the Valenti family in Rome.

NOTES: Grautoff (II, No. 155) proposed to identify the picture with the landscape which Félibien (IV, p. 66) tells us was painted by Poussin in 1659 for Charles Lebrun, but stylistically this is quite impossible and, since Félibien does not specify the subject of Lebrun's landscape, there is no reason to connect it with the *Orpheus* (cf. the *Landscape with two Nymphs and a Snake*, No. 208). As was pointed out in the catalogue of the Louvre exhibition (No. 93), the drawing in the British Museum connected with the painting (see above) is on the *verso* of a study for a *Holy Family*, which can be dated to 1650, and the painting was no doubt executed at about the same period. Mahon (Bibl. 1338, pp. 125, 127, 131) agrees with this dating.

BIBLIOGRAPHY: *Comptes des bâtiments*, II, pp. 586, 664; Bailly, p. 314; Dézallier, 1745, II, p. 255, and 1762, IV, p. 40; Cambry, Bibl. 272a, p. 45; Gault de Saint Germain, Pt. II, pp. 13 f.; Smith, No. 302; Gautier, Bibl. 575, p. 175; Friedlaender, 1914, pp. 97, 124; Grautoff, I, p. 282, II, No. 155; Magne, 1914, pp. 156, 202, No. 88; Alfassa, Bibl. 776, p. 274; Finberg, Bibl. 934, p. 89; Blunt, Bibl. 972, pp. 157, 165; Jamot, pp. 71 f.; Dorival, Bibl. 1088, p. 46; Licht, p. 178; *Exposition Poussin (Louvre)*, No. 93; Shearman, Bibl. 1285, pp. 186 f.; Friedlaender, Bibl. 1329, pp. 155 ff.; Mahon, Bibl. 1338, pp. 125, 127, 131; *L'ideale classico (Bologna)*, No. 81; Mahon, Bibl. 1367, p. 117.

171. PAN AND SYRINX. 106·5×82 cm. Staatliche Gemäldegalerie, Dresden (718).

HISTORY: Painted about 1637 for the painter Nicolas Guillaume La Fleur (Félibien, IV, p. 25), who died in Paris in 1663 (cf. Thieme-Becker, VIII, p. 578). The picture belonged later to the Chevalier de Lorraine, in whose collection it is recorded by Félibien in 1685 (*loc. cit.*), by Brice in 1687 (Bibl. 89b, I, p. 110) and by

Florent Le Comte in 1700 (III, p. 26). In fact it had probably passed before 1695 into the possession of Etienne Texier de Hautefeuille, called the Commandant or the Bailli de Hautefeuille, Ambassador of the Order of Malta to the French court, since Loménie de Brienne (pp. 214, 218) says of the picture that it is 'présentement dans le Cabinet du Bailly de Hautefeuille qui l'a eu du Ch^{lier} de Lorraine'. According to Saint-Simon (Bonnaffé, Bibl. 583, p. 136) Hautefeuille, who died in 1703, left all his pictures to the Knights of Malta, who presumably sold them. The Dresden picture was bought by Augustus III of Saxony from the Dubreuil collection, Paris, through his agent de Brais in 1742 (Gallery catalogue).

ENGRAVING: Andresen (No. 359) wrongly states that an engraving of this subject by B. Picart, dated 1724 and inscribed: *N. Poussin pinxit* (rep. Andresen-Wildenstein, p. 175, No. 359), is after the Dresden picture. In fact it is after a quite different composition, which may be connected with a picture that passed through two English sales in 1791 (Dalton sale, Christie, London, 9 ff.iv.1791, lot 27, and Jacob Hemett sale, Christie, London, 16 f.vi.1791, second day, lot 84) and was described in each case as 'A river god with Pan and Syrinx'.

NOTES: The subject is from Ovid (*Metamorphoses*, i, 689 ff.).

Poussin refers to this picture in a letter to Jacques Stella, of which the original is lost but parts of which are quoted by Félibien and Loménie de Brienne (*loc. cit.*). In the passage quoted by the latter Poussin writes: 'Je me suis plû à peindre le sujet de la fable de Pan et de Syringue que j'envoye à M. de la Fleur mon confrère. Si j'ay jamais fait quelque chose de bien je croy que c'est dans la manière dont ce sujet est traité. Je l'ay peint avec amour et tendresse. Le sujet le vouloit ainsi.' Little is known of La Fleur, but Florent Le Comte, writing of Poussin (*loc. cit.*), refers to him and Jacques Stella as 'deux de ses plus intimes amis'. Félibien refers to La Fleur as *Peintre*, but his few surviving works are in fact all engravings. He was in Rome in 1638 (cf. Thieme-Becker, *loc. cit.*), but went to Paris in 1644, when Poussin writes to Chantelou to thank him for the welcome he had given to La Fleur (*Correspondance*, p. 271).

Félibien (*loc. cit.*) implies a date of *c.* 1637 for the picture. Mahon (Bibl. 1367, p. 105) hesitates between 1636–37 and 1637–38.

BIBLIOGRAPHY: Félibien, IV, p. 25; Brice, Bibl. 89b, I, p. 110; Loménie de Brienne, pp. 214, 218; Florent Le Comte, III, p. 26; Smith, No. 234; Friedlaender, 1914, pp. 56, 115; Grautoff, I, pp. 15, 133, II, No. 66; Magne, 1914, pp. 93, 202, No. 90; Hourticq, Bibl. 899, p. 142; Mahon, Bibl. 1271, p. 303, and Bibl. 1367, p. 105.

172. PHAETHON BEGGING THE CHARIOT OF APOLLO. 122×153 cm. Staatliche Museen, Museum Dahlem, Berlin.

HISTORY: Jean Michel Picart in 1674 (see below). Recorded in the Neues Palais, Potsdam, in 1773 (Oesterreich, Bibl. 242.1, p. 35, No. 89).

ENGRAVINGS: 1. By Nicolas Pérelle (Andresen, No. 388; Wildenstein, No. 136; Davies and Blunt, p. 214, No. 136).
2. By Cesare Fantetti (Andresen, No. 387).

COPIES: 1. Anon. sale, Langford, London, 26 ff.iii. 1778, third day, lot 54, with detailed description and claiming a provenance from the Palazzo Borghese and the collection of Cardinal de Polignac. Later, in December 1795, exhibited with pictures offered for sale by S. Pawson (No. 38) with the same provenance.
2. Dupille de Saint-Séverin sale, Joullain, Paris, 21.ii. 1785, lot 231.
3. Grautoff (II, No. 81) mentions a replica or copy belonging to 'M. Wilkins in London', but as he gives no further details it has not been possible to identify this picture.

NOTES: The *Procès-verbaux* of the Academy of Painting in Paris record that on 30.vi.1674 'Monsieur *Picar* Peintre, c'est présanté, aportant à la Compagnie un tableau de la grandeur de 4 piez 9 pouse large, 3 piez 9 p. de haut, représentant comme Faëton demande a son perre Apolon la conduite de son char, lequel Apolon est acompagné de 4 Saison de l'anée, priant l'Académie de juger si elle le trouve original ou coppié. L'Académie ayant examiné led. tableau, l'Académie l'a reconu et jugé original de la main du *Poussain* et aresté qu'il sera deslivré coppie du présan acte au dit sieur *Picard*, qu'il l'a instamant demandé, pour luy servir selon qu'il avisera bon estre' (Bibl. 13, II, p. 29). The 'Picar' in question must be the Flemish landscape and flower painter Jean Michel Picart, who settled in Paris about 1640 and died there in 1682. According to Thieme-Becker (XXVI, p. 575) he was a dealer as well as a painter.

The subject is taken from Ovid (*Metamorphoses*, ii, 19 ff.). Poussin has followed the text closely in showing the four Seasons surrounding Apollo. The poet further tells us that 'To right and left stood Day and Month and Year and Century and the hours set at equal distances'. Here the painter has followed him less closely, but the Hours are seen harnessing the horses to the chariot of Apollo and the Year is represented by the circle of the Zodiac. The remaining elements may be regarded as all subsumed under the figure of Father Time, who stands on the left behind the crouching old man who symbolizes Winter.

The picture was dated 1633–38 by Grautoff (II, No. 81), 1631–33 by Mahon (Bibl. 1367, p. XI). I should myself place it about 1633–35.

BIBLIOGRAPHY: Montaiglon, Bibl. 13, II, p. 29; Sandrart, pp. 258, 261; Tuétey, Bibl. 295, II, p. 21; Lazzarini, Bibl. 332, I, pp. 161 f.; Smith, No. 242; Friedlaender, 1914, pp. 48, 127, 167; Grautoff, I, pp. 15, 152, II, No. 81; Magne, 1914, p. 202, No. 94; Panofsky, Bibl. 893, p. 243; Hourticq, Bibl. 899, p. 127; Bardon, Bibl. 1218, p. 130; *Exposition Poussin (Louvre)*, No. 40; Mahon, Bibl. 1271, p. 299; Thuillier, Bibl. 1296, p. 76; Kauffmann, Bibl. 1332, p. 97; *L'ideale classico (Bologna)*, No. 58; Mahon, Bibl. 1367, pp. XI, 55 f.

173. LANDSCAPE WITH THE BODY OF PHOCION CARRIED OUT OF ATHENS.
114×175 cm. The Earl of Plymouth, Oakly Park, Shropshire.

HISTORY: Painted with its pendant in the collection of the Earl of Derby (No. 174) for Cérisier in 1648 (Félibien, IV, p. 59); still in his possession in 1665 (Chantelou, 1885, p. 90, and 1960, p. 127). Pierre de Beauchamp (d. after 1698), Maître des Ballets du Roi (cf. Bonnaffé, Bibl. 583, p. 15) by 1687 (Brice, Bibl. 89a, I, p. 51). In the collection of Denis Moreau in 1702 (Charlotte, Duchesse d'Orléans, Bibl. 125, I, pp. 261 f.). Passed by descent to the Nyert family (Davies, Bibl. 988a, pp. 180 f.). Recorded in the inventory of Louis de Nyert, Marquis de Gambias, taken at his death in 1736 (Rambaud, Bibl. 1420, I, p. 584). Two pictures corresponding to the Plymouth and Derby paintings appeared in the Samuel Dickenson sale, Christie, London, 11 f. iii.1774, second day, lots 78, 79, bt. Beauvais. It is possible that the Plymouth picture was bought at this sale, since it is first recorded in the inventory of Lord Clive's possessions made after his death in November 1774. He was, however, ill and preoccupied during the last years of his life and may not have been interested in buying paintings. It is perhaps more likely that he acquired the picture through Strange, who bought paintings from the Nyert family about this time (cf. No. 209) and from whom Lord Clive bought a *Holy Family* attributed to Leonardo (now at Oakly Park as Luini) (Strange sale, Christie, London, 6. iii.1773, lot 113). The *Phocion* passed by descent to the present owner.

ENGRAVINGS: 1. By E. Baudet (Andresen, No. 446; Wildenstein, No. 185; Davies and Blunt, p. 215, No. 185). Dated 1684.
2. By S. Vallée (Andresen, No. 446a).

COPIES: 1. Musée Municipal, Arras (cf. Thuillier, Bibl. 1299, p. 287).
2. Musée du Louvre, Paris. From a private collection in Guernsey, sold anonymously, Foster, London, about 1920, bt. by Mason and Phillips; sold by them to the Louvre (cf. Dezarrois, Bibl. 755; Jamot, Bibl. 758, pp. 158 ff.; Grautoff, Bibl. 864, p. 324; Blunt, Bibl. 972, p. 156, and Jamot, pp. 73 ff.).
3. Countess of Seafield, Scotland. A variant in which the body of Phocion is replaced by a man, which, as has been pointed out verbally by Miss Montagu, is taken from Lebrun's *Entry of Alexander into Babylon*.
4. Philip Johnson, New York.
5. Lord St. Oswald, Nostell Priory, Yorkshire.
6. Private collection (cf. Brown, Bibl. 725).
7. Pozzo collection, Rome (cf. Richardson, *Account*, pp. 186 f., and Keyssler, Bibl. 172a, II, p. 401).
8. Cardinal Fesch sale, George, Rome, 17 ff.iii.1845, Part II, lot 412.
9. Anon. sale, Christie, London, 22.vi.1925, lot 37.

NOTES: For a discussion of this picture, see text volume, pp. 165 ff.

BIBLIOGRAPHY: Chantelou, 1885, p. 90, and 1960, p. 127; Félibien, IV, pp. 59, 148; Brice, Bibl. 89a, I, p. 51, and Bibl. 89b, I, pp. 168 f.; Loménie de Brienne, p. 215; Florent Le Comte, III, p. 30; Fénelon, Bibl. 121a, XIX, p. 336, and Bibl. 121b, p. 225; Charlotte, Duchesse d'Orléans, Bibl. 125, I, pp. 261 f.; Winckelmann, Bibl. 203, I, p. 238; Smith, No. 300; Friedlaender, 1914, p. 119; Grautoff, II, p. 259; Magne, 1914, pp. 161, 217, No. 318; Bodkin, Bibl. 778, p. 322; Courthion, Bibl. 781, pp. 61 ff.; Francastel, Bibl. 883, p. 154; Blunt, Bibl. 972, pp. 156 ff.; Davies, Bibl. 988a, pp. 180 f.; Bertin-Mourot, Bibl. 1023, p. 53, No. XXXVI; Clark, Bibl. 1040, pp. 67 f.; Watson, Bibl. 1047, pp. 14, 18; Blunt, Bibl. 1050, p. 39, Bibl. 1086, pp. 189, 192, and Bibl. 1086a, pp. 165, 168; Licht, p. 151; Blunt, Bibl. 1226, p. 400; *Exposition Poussin (Louvre)*, No. 80; Waterhouse, Bibl. 1308, p. 295; Kauffmann, Bibl. 1332, p. 97; Mahon, Bibl. 1338, pp. 122, 125, 127, 129 ff.; *L'ideale classico (Bologna)*, No. 75; Mahon, Bibl. 1367, p. 129.

174. THE ASHES OF PHOCION COLLECTED BY HIS WIDOW. 116×176 cm. The Earl of Derby, Knowsley Hall, Lancashire.

HISTORY: Painted with its pendant, No. 173, for Cérisier in 1648 (Félibien, IV, p. 59); still in his possession in 1665 (Chantelou, 1885, p. 90, and 1960, p. 127). The Derby picture was not, like its pendant, bt. by Beauchamp and Moreau, since the version owned by the latter is recorded as a copy in the inventory after death of Louis de Nyert, Marquis de Gambais, to whom his collection passed (cf. Davies, Bibl. 988a, pp. 180 f., and Rambaud, Bibl. 1420, I, p. 584). If Dickenson bought the Nyert pair (cf. No. 173), then his version of this composition must have been a copy and the Knowsley picture must have a different provenance. Bought by the 9th Earl of Derby in 1782.

DRAWING: Musée des Beaux-Arts, Besançon (CR, IV, p. 51, No. A 139). A copy after the painting or after a lost drawing.

ENGRAVINGS: 1. By E. Baudet (Andresen, No. 447; Wildenstein, No. 184; Davies and Blunt, p. 215, No. 184).
2. By S. Vallée (Andresen, No. 447a).
3. By Jazet (Andresen, No. 447b).

COPIES: 1. Holburne of Menstrie Museum, Bath (No. 140, as Patel).
2. The Hon. Mrs. Marten, Crichel House, Dorset.
3. Lord St. Oswald, Nostell Priory, Yorkshire.
4. Cardinal Fesch sale, George, Rome, 17 ff.iii.1845, Part II, lot 413.
5. Anon. sale, Robinson and Fisher, London, 1.xii.1938, lot 170.

NOTES: For a discussion of this picture, see text volume, pp. 165 ff.

BIBLIOGRAPHY: Chantelou, 1885, p. 90, and 1960, p. 127; Félibien, IV, p. 59; Loménie de Brienne, p. 215; Florent Le Comte, III, p. 30; Charlotte, Duchesse d'Orléans, Bibl. 125, I, pp. 261 f.; Smith, No. 321; Friedlaender, 1914, p. 119; Grautoff, I, p. 255, II, No. 129; Magne, 1914, pp. 155, 217, No. 319; Jamot, Bibl. 758, p. 158; Bodkin, Bibl. 778, p. 322; Petit Palais, Paris, Bibl. 795, p. 135, No. 269; Royal Academy, London, Bibl. 879, No. 127; Blunt, Bibl. 972, pp. 157 f.; Davies, Bibl. 988a, p. 181; Jamot, pp. 45, 68, 74; Clark, Bibl. 1040, pp. 67 f.; Watson, Bibl. 1047, p. 14; Blunt, Bibl. 1086, p. 192, and Bibl. 1086a, p. 168; Licht, p. 151; Exposition Poussin (Louvre), No. 81; Kitson, Bibl. 1335, pp. 143, 154; Mahon, Bibl. 1338, pp. 122, 125, 127, 129 ff.; L'ideale classico (Bologna), No. 76; Mahon, Bibl. 1367, p. 129.

175. LANDSCAPE WITH POLYPHEMUS. 150×198 cm. Hermitage Museum, Leningrad (1186).

HISTORY: Painted in 1649 for Pointel (Félibien, IV, p. 59). Bt. by Diderot, with No. 158, from the collection of the Marquis de Conflans in 1772 for the Empress Catherine II of Russia (cf. Tourneux, Bibl. 646, pp. 58, 428).

ENGRAVING: By E. Baudet (Andresen, No. 440; Wildenstein, No. 178).

COPIES: 1. Prado Museum, Madrid (2322).
2. Formerly Captain E. G. Spencer-Churchill, Northwick Park, Gloucestershire (Lord Berwick sale, Phillips, London, 6 f.vi.1825, lot 164; John Webb sale, Phillips, London, 10 ff.vi.1829, lot 70, bt. Lord Northwick).
3. Paul Alfassa, Paris (till 1946).
4. Trouard sale, Paillet, Paris, 22.ii.1779, lot 10 (39× 54 inches).
5. Isaac Pittar sale, Phillips, London, 19.iv.1842, lot 63. As from Lord Radstock's collection, but not traceable in either of his sales.
6. Anon. sale, Christie, London, 24.vii.1936, lot 49.
7. Earl of Derby sale, Christie, London, 26.vii.1940, lot 32, bt. Adams.
8. Anon. sale, Christie, London, 3.v.1946, lot 127, bt. Condamine (41×54 inches).

NOTES: Félibien (loc. cit.) states that the Polyphemus was painted for Pointel in 1649. Mr. Mahon (Bibl. 1338, pp. 126 ff.) has recently challenged this dating and wishes to put the picture about ten years later. For my general reasons for not accepting his conclusions, see the entry for the Diogenes (No. 150). The case of the Polyphemus presents a puzzling problem, particularly if, as seems reasonable, a very late dating to about 1660 is accepted for the Hercules and Cacus (No. 158), since it would be curious for Poussin to have painted two pendants at a distance of more than ten years. On the other hand it is by no means certain that the two pictures were originally painted as a pair. They are not found together till their purchase by Catherine the Great in 1772; they are markedly different in style, and their themes are not apparently related to each other. I should prefer to accept the hypothesis that they were painted at widely separated dates rather than reject Félibien's statement, which, it seems to me, is supported by the evidence of style.

BIBLIOGRAPHY: Félibien, IV, p. 59; Loménie de Brienne, p. 215; Florent Le Comte, III, p. 30; Smith, No. 306; Leslie, Bibl. 413a, pp. 297, 314; Hazlitt, Bibl. 417, p. 196; Tourneux, Bibl. 646, pp. 58, 428; Friedlaender, 1914, pp. 120, 250; Grautoff, I, p. 255, II, No. 135; Magne, 1914, pp. 155, 217, No. 307; Blunt, Bibl. 972, pp. 157, 161, 167; Jamot, pp. 49, 72 f.; Dorival, Bibl. 1088, p. 50; Licht, p. 153; Du Colombier, Bibl. 1246, p. 55; Goertz, Bibl. 1253; *Exposition Poussin* (*Louvre*), No. 89; Kitson, Bibl. 1335, pp. 156, 158; Mahon, Bibl. 1338, pp. 126 ff., and Bibl. 1367, pp. XIV, 2, 18, 116 f., 121.

176. DANCE IN HONOUR OF PRIAPUS. 167×376 cm. Museu de Arte, São Paulo.

HISTORY: Probably Cassiano dal Pozzo collection (Blunt, Bibl. 1426, p. 62). Spanish Royal Collection by 1701 (see below). Lord Beaumont sale, Foster, London, 25.iii.1896, lot 80. Sir Herbert Cook (Brockwell, Bibl. 720, III, p. 47, No. 428). By descent to Sir Francis Cook; sold by him *c.* 1950.

NOTES: Probably a pair to the *Meleager and Atalanta hunting* in the Prado (No. 163; q.v.). The fact that the São Paulo picture was at one time in the Spanish Royal Collection is established by a late eighteenth-century drawing after the picture by Manuel de la Cruz, discovered in the Lisbon Museum by Mrs. Henri Frankfort, with an inscription which specifically states that the original was in the Royal Palace in Madrid (cf. Blunt, *loc. cit.*). It was presumably looted from the palace during the Peninsular War.

For a discussion of the subject, see text volume, pp. 143 f.

In a recent article (Bibl. 1329, pp. 153 ff.) Professor Walter Friedlaender has suggested that the painting represents the story of Hymenaeus as told by Cartari, who took it from Servius. There is, however, one grave difficulty in accepting this explanation. Servius explicitly states that the ceremony which Hymenaeus attended disguised as a girl was the mystery of Demeter at Eleusis, whereas, as Friedlaender himself points out, the god worshipped in the painting is Priapus.

The picture was dated by Grautoff (II, No. 72) 1638–40, which is probably a little late. Like its pendant (No. 163), it was probably painted 1637–38.

BIBLIOGRAPHY: De Cotte, Bibl. 98a, p. 202; Ponz, Bibl. 238a, p. 527; Cumberland, Bibl. 285.1, p. 57; Brockwell, Bibl. 720, III, p. 47, No. 428; Grautoff, I, p. 149, II, No. 72; Magne, 1914, p. 200, No. 46; Pilon, Bibl. 752, p. 31; Friedlaender, 1933, p. 325; Emmerling, Bibl. 933, p. 40; Licht, p. 117; Blunt, Bibl. 1224, pp. 62 ff.; Haskell and Rinehart, Bibl. 1254, p. 324; Friedlaender, Bibl. 1329, p. 153 ff.; Blunt, Bibl. 1426, p. 62.

177. LANDSCAPE WITH PYRAMUS AND THISBE. 192·5×273·5 cm. Staedelsches Kunstinstitut, Frankfurt am Main.

HISTORY: Painted for Cassiano dal Pozzo in or shortly before 1651 (*Correspondance*, p. 424). Sir William Morice, Werrington, Devonshire, by 1750 (Pocock, Bibl. 187, p. 134); engraved by Vivares and Chatelin while in his possession; by inheritance to his cousin, Humphrey Morice (seen at his villa at Chiswick by Horace Walpole in 1781; Bibl. 192, p. 77). Bt. with the whole of the Morice collection by Lord Ashburnham in 1786 (Reynolds, Bibl. 281, p. 150); Ashburnham sale, Christie, London, 20.vii.1850, lot 82. With Max Rothschild, London, in 1923; with Asti, Paris, in 1926. Bt. by the museum from J. Böhler in 1931.

DRAWING: Musée Bonnat, Bayonne (*CR*, III, p. 42, No. 225).

COPY: Lord Mount Edgcumbe sale, Christie, London, 27.vi.1958, lot 50. In gouache.

ENGRAVING: By Vivares and Chatelin (Andresen, No. 453). Dated 1769.

NOTES: For a discussion of this painting, see text volume pp. 295 f.

BIBLIOGRAPHY: *Correspondance*, p. 424; Félibien, IV, p. 160; Bellori, p. 455; Sirén, Bibl. 63, p. 187; de Cotte, Bibl. 98, III, p. 153, and Bibl. 98a, p. 203; Caylus, Bibl. 133, p. 297; Dézallier, 1745, II, p. 254, and 1762, IV, p. 39; Pocock, Bibl. 187, p. 134; Walpole, Bibl. 192, p. 77; Reynolds, Bibl. 281, p. 150; Smith, No. 304; Friedlaender, 1914, p. 122; Grautoff, II, p. 259; Magne, 1914, pp. 154, 217, No. 308; Fry, Bibl. 761, p. 53; Grautoff, Bibl. 864, p. 330; Blunt, Bibl. 972, pp. 157, 168; Bertin-Mourot, Bibl. 1023, p. 53, No. XXXVII; Bialostocki, Bibl. 1098, pp. 131 ff.; Licht, p. 161; Haskell and Rinehart, Bibl. 1254, pp. 322, 325; Rinehart, Bibl. 1281, pp. 24, 27, 28; Mahon, Bibl. 1338, p. 125, and Bibl. 1367, p. 120.

178. THE SAVING OF THE INFANT PYRRHUS. 116×160 cm. Musée du Louvre, Paris (726).

HISTORY: Duc de Richelieu; bt. with his whole collection by Louis XIV in 1665 (Ferraton, Bibl. 1043, pp. 439, 446).

DRAWINGS: 1 and 2. Royal Library, Windsor Castle (CR, II, p. 6, Nos. 108, 109).

ENGRAVINGS: 1. By G. Audran (Andresen, No. 310; Wildenstein, No. 109).
2. By G. Chasteau (Andresen, No. 311; Wildenstein, No. 110).
3. Published by Chéreau (Andresen, No. 312).

COPIES: 1. Musée Ingres, Montauban.
2. Nationalmuseum, Stockholm.
3. George Walter Vincent Smith Art Museum, Springfield, Mass.

4. Private collection, Kingston, Jamaica.
5. With Ebeling, Leipzig (cf. Grautoff, Bibl. 864, p. 331).
6. A. J. M. Kunst, Utrecht. 118×160 cm.
7. Anon. sale, Christie, London, 3.iv.1776, lot 33.
8. Anon. sale, Bertels, London, 26 ff.v.1783, third day, lot 73.
9. Girodet-Trioson sale, Pérignon, Paris, 11.iv.1825, lot 435, 44×52 inches.
10. Lord Darnley sale, Christie, London, 1.v.1925, lot 59 (cf. Waagen, Bibl. 384b, III, p. 25).

NOTES: The subject is taken from Plutarch, *Life of Pyrrhus*, ii.

The two left-hand figures in the foreground, one throwing a stone and the other a spear, are connected with two of the illustrations to Leonardo's *Trattato* (cf. CR, IV, p. 30, No. 253).

The painting was dated by Grautoff (II, No. 57) 1633–36; in the catalogue of the Louvre exhibition (No. 54) I proposed 1637–38. Mahon (Bibl. 1367) agrees with this suggestion.

The composition was freely imitated by G. B. Castiglione in a drawing in the Royal Library, Windsor Castle (Blunt, Bibl. 1099, p. 34, No. 76).

BIBLIOGRAPHY: Montaiglon, Bibl. 13, II, p. 162; *Comptes des bâtiments*, I, p. 927; Félibien, IV, p. 82; *Mémoires inédits*, I, p. 314; Loménie de Brienne, pp. 211, 214; Perrault, Bibl. 113, I, p. 90; Florent Le Comte, I, p. 202; Piganiol de La Force, Bibl. 124, I, p. 123; Bailly, p. 301; Thornhill, Bibl. 140, p. 3; Dézallier, 1745, II, p. 255, and 1762, IV, p. 39; Bardon, I, p. 225, II, p. 126; Mengs, Bibl. 264a, p. 118, and Bibl. 264b, p. 235; Cambry, Bibl. 272a, p. 48; Tuétey, Bibl. 295, II, p. 162; Fuseli, Bibl. 322, p. 74; Gault de Saint-Germain, Pt. II, p. 50; Smith, No. 166; Friedlaender, 1914, pp. 41, 125; Grautoff, I, p. 126, II, No. 57; Magne, 1914, pp. 98, 191; Blunt, Bibl. 975, p. 39, No. 189; Jamot, p. 14; Ferraton, Bibl. 1043, pp. 439, 446; Blunt, Bibl. 1086, p. 186, and Bibl. 1086a, p. 162; Licht, p. 114; Bialostocki, Bibl. 1221, p. 138; Hours, Bibl. 1256, pp. 26 f.; *Exposition Poussin (Louvre)*, No. 54; Mahon, Bibl. 1271, pp. 303 f.; Rinehart, Bibl. 1281, p. 27; Waterhouse, Bibl. 1308, p. 288; *Exposition Poussin (Rouen)*, No. 79; *L'ideale classico (Bologna)*, No. 63; Mahon, Bibl. 1367, pp. XIII, 103.

179. THE RAPE OF THE SABINES. 159×206 cm. Musée du Louvre, Paris (724).

HISTORY: Painted for Cardinal Aluigi Omodei (Bellori, p. 24), who was trying to sell it in 1655 (Fouquet, Bibl. 24a, p. 103). Almost certainly sent as a gift to Louis XIV from Rome in 1685 (Fouquet, *op. cit.* p. 103 note 2). Recorded in the inventory of the Royal Collection made by Lebrun at an undetermined date within a few years of 1683.

DRAWINGS: 1. The Chatsworth Settlement, Derbyshire (CR, II, p. 9, No. 114).
2. Gabinetto dei Disegni, Florence (CR, II, p. 9, No. 115).
3. Royal Library, Windsor Castle (CR, II, p. 9, No. 116).
4. Musée des Beaux-Arts, Besançon. From the Gigoux collection. Probably a copy after a lost original.

ENGRAVING: By E. Baudet (Andresen, No. 316; Wildenstein, No. 112).

COPIES: 1. Formerly in the Henri Rouart collection. By E. Degas (cf. P. A. Lemoisne, *Degas et son oeuvre*, 1946, II, No. 273).
2. With Lory, Paris, in about 1935; said to have been sold to Hugo von Grundherr, London. Differs from the Louvre picture in that Romulus is seated.

The inventory of André Le Nôtre, made after his death in 1700, contained a picture of this subject said to be a copy after Poussin, but there is no means of determining whether it was after the Louvre or the Metropolitan version.

NOTES: The story is told by Livy (I, ix), Plutarch (*Life of Romulus*, XIV) and Virgil (*Aeneid*, viii. 1 ff.). Poussin follows Plutarch most closely.

Grautoff (II, Nos. 70, 71) dates both the Louvre and the Metropolitan versions 1637–39; Mahon (Bibl. 1367, pp. XII, 92 ff., 99 ff.) places the Metropolitan picture (No. 180) much earlier, in 1634–35, and the Louvre version 1637–38. I still maintain the view which I proposed in the catalogue of the Louvre exhibition (No. 41), namely *c.* 1635 for the Louvre version, near the *Golden Calf* (No. 26) and the *Red Sea* (No. 20), and *c.* 1637 for the Metropolitan painting, near paintings such as the *Pan and Syrinx* (No. 171).

Both versions contain many quotations from earlier works, such as Gian Bologna's famous group in the Loggia dei Lanzi, the Lodovisi *Gaul*, and Titian's *Marchese del Vasto addressing his troops.*

BIBLIOGRAPHY: Fouquet, Bibl. 24a, p. 103; Félibien, IV, p. 24; Bellori, p. 449; Florent Le Comte, III, p. 26; Bailly, pp. 306 ff.; [C. Saugrain], Bibl. 138a, I, p. 93; Guilbert, Bibl. 159, I, p. 117; Dézallier, 1745, II, p. 254, and 1762, IV, p. 39; Dézallier d'Argenville, Bibl. 183a, p. 345; Boyer d'Argens, Bibl. 231, p. 297; La Roque, Bibl. 248, I, p. 143; Gault de Saint-Germain, Pt. II, pp. 7 ff.; Smith, No. 170; Bouchitté, Bibl. 478, p. 401; Duranty, Bibl. 554, p. 281; Friedlaender, 1914, pp. 37, 114; Grautoff, I, p. 139, II, No. 70; Magne, 1914, pp. 94, 200, No. 53; Courthion, Bibl. 781, pp. 59 ff.; Francastel, Bibl. 883, p. 154; Blunt, Bibl. 972, p. 162, and Bibl. 975, p. 39; Costello, Bibl. 1008, pp. 197 ff.; Jamot, pp. 20, 63; Blunt, Bibl. 1086, p. 186, and Bibl. 1086a, p. 162; Licht, p. 117; Bardon, Bibl. 1218, pp. 128 f.; Delbourgo and Petit, Bibl. 1243, pp. 42 f.; Hazlehurst, Bibl. 1255, p. 60; Hours, Bibl. 1256, pp. 24 f.; *Exposition Poussin* (*Louvre*), No. 41; Mahon, Bibl. 1271, p. 304; Rinehart, Bibl. 1281, p. 27; Thuillier, Bibl. 1295, p. 103; *Exposition Poussin* (*Rouen*), No. 78; Mahon, Bibl. 1367, pp. XII, 92 ff., 101, 128; Du Colombier, Bibl. 1413, pp. 81 ff.

180. THE RAPE OF THE SABINES. 154×206 cm. The Metropolitan Museum of Art, New York.

HISTORY: Probably the picture which belonged to the Duchesse d'Aiguillon and later to Jean Néret de La Ravoye (Brice, Bibl. 89b, I, p. 273), which Florent Le Comte (III, p. 26) and Guilbert (Bibl. 159, I, p. 117) wrongly identify with the Louvre version. The Duchesse d'Aiguillon almost certainly inherited the picture, with all her other possessions, from her uncle, Cardinal Richelieu, who probably received it as a gift, perhaps from Cardinal Francesco Barberini. Perhaps later belonged to Bénigne de Ragois de Bretonvilliers, as a picture of this subject is mentioned in the Hôtel de Bretonvilliers by Brice in 1698 (Bibl. 89b, I, p. 273) and in 1713 (Bibl. 89d, II, p. 163), by which time the Louvre version was already in the Royal Collection. The pictures in the Hôtel de Bretonvilliers were removed and probably sold when it was taken over as offices for the Fermiers Généraux in 1719 (cf. Piganiol de La Force, Bibl. 173, I, p. 347). The Metropolitan picture belonged to Henry Hoare of Stourhead, Wiltshire, by 1762 (Walpole, Bibl. 192, p. 41). Passed by descent to Sir Henry Hoare; Hoare sale, Christie, London, 2.vi.1883, lot 63, bt. Lesser; Sir Francis Cook; by descent to his grandson; bt. from him by Knoedler in 1946; bt. by the museum the same year.

DRAWING: Royal Library, Windsor Castle (*CR*, II, p. 10, No. 117).

ENGRAVING: By J. Audran (Andresen, No. 315; Wildenstein, No. 111; Davies and Blunt, p. 213, No. 111).

COPIES: 1. Comte R. de Montméja, Château de Rouffillac, Dordogne. 153×172 cm.

2. Anon. (= Archdeacon Cambridge) sale, Christie, London, 11.v.1824, lot 87, bt. in. From the collection of Richard Owen Cambridge of Twickenham (d. 1802).
3. Earl of Ducie sale, Christie, London, 17.vi.1949, lot 135. Said to be by Stella; if so, probably the copy mentioned in the inventory of Claudine Bouzonnet Stella in 1697 (*Testament*, Bibl. 107, p. 37).
4. Anon. sale, Christie, London, 24.vii.1959, lot 167.

NOTES: For the subject and the dating, see No. 179.

BIBLIOGRAPHY: Brice, Bibl. 89b, I, p. 273, and Bibl. 89d, II, p. 163; Florent Le Comte, III, p. 26; Guilbert, Bibl. 159, I, p. 117; Walpole, Bibl. 192, p. 41; Dulaure, Bibl. 278a, II, p. 75; Hoare, Bibl. 361, p. 16; Waagen, Bibl. 384b, III, p. 172; Smith, No. 169; Bonnaffé, Bibl. 573, pp. 109, 111; Brockwell, Bibl. 720, III, No. 430; Friedlaender, 1914, pp. 37, 117; Grautoff, I, p. 139, II, No. 71; Magne, 1914, p. 200, No. 54; Royal Academy, London, Bibl. 879, p. 34, No. 122; Blunt, Bibl. 972, p. 162, and Bibl. 975, p. 39; Costello, Bibl. 1008, pp. 197 ff.; Blunt, Bibl. 1086, p. 186, and Bibl. 1086a, p. 162; Licht, p. 117; Sterling, Bibl. 1122, pp. 70 f.; Bardon, Bibl. 1218, pp. 128 f.; *Exposition Poussin* (*Louvre*), No. 51; Mahon, Bibl. 1268.1, p. 354, Bibl. 1271, pp. 300, 303, and Bibl. 1367, pp. XII, 40, 92 f., 95, 99 ff., 128; Du Colombier, Bibl. 1413, pp. 81 ff.

181. THE CONTINENCE OF SCIPIO. 116×150 cm. Pushkin Museum, Moscow.

HISTORY: C. J. B. Fleuriau, Comte de Morville (Walpole, Bibl. 319, II, p. 276), who died in 1732 (Water-house, Bibl. 1308, p. 290); Sir Robert Walpole by 1741 (engraved by Dubosc in that year as in his collection; see engraving No. 1 below); bt. with the Walpole collection by the Empress Catherine II of Russia in 1779 (Hermitage catalogue); sent to Moscow in 1930.

DRAWING: Musée Condé, Chantilly (CR, II, p. 13, No. 125).

ENGRAVINGS: 1. By C. Dubosc (Andresen, No. 321; Andresen-Wildenstein, No. 321). Dated 1741.
2. By F. Legat (Andresen, No. 322). Dated 1784.

COPIES: 1. A copy by John Smibert was taken by him to Boston in 1728 (Whitley, Bibl. 828, I, p. 67).

2. A copy was made by Ranelagh Barrett in 1742 (Vertue, Bibl. 132, XXII, p. 112).
3. Hourmouzios collection, London, in 1958. Perhaps the same as anon. sale, Robinson and Fisher, London, 25.v.1939, lot 24.

NOTES: The story is told by Livy (XXVI, 50), Plutarch (Moralia, 196 B), and Valerius Maximus (iv.3.1.).
Grautoff (II, No. 107) dated the picture to 1643 on the basis of a reference in letters written by Poussin from Paris to Cardinal Francesco Barberini to a drawing of a subject connected with Scipio. Poussin is in fact, however, almost certainly referring to the subject of Scipio and the Pirates, of which drawings from this period exist (CR, II, pp. 15 f., Nos. 126–8 and A 32). In the catalogue of the Poussin exhibition at Rouen (under No. 85) I suggested that the Scipio might have been painted as a pair to the Coriolanus (No. 147), and that both might date from 1648–49. Mahon (Bibl. 1367, pp. 119, 134) believes that this dating is too late, and, in spite of the connections with the Judgment of Solomon of 1649 (No. 35), this may well be the case, and his proposal to date the picture soon after Poussin's return to Rome, that is to say c. 1643–45, may be correct. Since, however, I have not seen the picture for many years, I should prefer to be cautious. If the earlier dating is accepted, it would, in my view, mean abandoning the theory that the Scipio and the Coriolanus were painted as pair, but, though iconographically tempting, the link is not stylistically compelling.

BIBLIOGRAPHY: Vertue, Bibl. 132, XXX, pp. 175, 195; Walpole, Bibl. 319, II, pp. 274 ff., 285, IV, pp. 103 f.; Le Breton, Bibl. 339, p. 394; Smith, No. 171; Friedlaender, 1914, pp. 80, 117; Grautoff, I, p. 222, II, No. 107; Magne, 1914, p. 199, No. 43; Waterhouse, Bibl. 1308, p. 290; Exposition Poussin (Rouen), p. 44; Mahon, Bibl. 1367, pp. 119, 134.

182. THESEUS FINDING HIS FATHER'S ARMS. 98×134 cm. Musée Condé, Chantilly (300).

HISTORY: John Knight by 1816 (lent to the British Institution, No. 59); J. Knight sale, Phillips, London, 17.iii.1821, lot 39, presumably bt. in; J. Knight sale, Phillips, London, 24.v.1839, lot 20; E. Higginson sale, Christie, London, 6.vi.1846, lot 195 (as from the Knight collection), presumably bt. in; E. Higginson sale, Christie, London, 16.vi.1860, lot 30, bt. Cooper, presumably for Nieuwenhuys for the Duc d'Aumale (cf. museum catalogue); bequeathed by the Duc d'Aumale to the Musée Condé.

ENGRAVING: Attributed to either Remy Vuibert or Pierre Lemaire (Andresen, No. 305; Wildenstein, No. 106; Davies and Blunt, p. 213, No. 106).

COPIES: 1. Galleria degli Uffizi, Florence (1004). Bt. in Paris in 1792 (cf. Boyer, Bibl. 1127, p. 26; Smith, No. 64; Grautoff, II, No. 76; Beaucamp, Bibl. 931, I, pp. 116 ff.; Jamot, pp. 52 f.; Thuillier, Bibl. 1298, p. 276).
2. Musée Fabre, Montpellier (713). By F. Demarais.
3. With Wildenstein, New York (1958). Probably the picture with Tomàs Harris, London, in 1950. This is presumably also the painting in the Chavagnac sale, George, Paris, 20.vi.1854, lot 43, in the Liel sale, Paillet, Paris, 23 f.iv.1869, lot 73 (102×130 cm.), and the Norton sale, London, 15.i.1869, lot

781, since this cannot be either the Chantilly or the Uffizi version. It is probably also the picture exhibited in the rue de Choiseul in 1865 (Lagrange, Bibl. 512·1, p. 486).
4. A painting of this subject was offered to du Tillot in Mariette's time (Bibl. 157, IV, p. 204), who presumably bought it, since Fragonard made a drawing of it in 1761, when he saw it in du Tillot's collection in Parma. (The drawing was in the Mrs. Hubert Chanler of Geneseo, New York, sale, Sotheby, 10.vi.1959, lot 17, Vol. III, No. 5, as from the collection of the late Hon. Irwin Laughlin, Washington, D.C.). The picture was later sold in the Marquis de Félino (= du Tillot) sale, Paillet, Paris, 27.iii.1775, lot 40 (36×49 inches), and in the

9

Lambert sale, Lebrun, Paris, 27.iii.1787, lot 155 (as from the Félino sale, with the same dimensions). It was presumably the du Tillot version that was offered to Louis XVI in 1775 (cf. Angiviller, Bibl. 276, p. 48), and it can probably be identified with either the Chantilly or the Uffizi version.

Paintings of this subject, attributed to Poussin, are recorded in the following sales:

1. Newton and others, by private contract, 125, Pall Mall, London, 8.iv.1788, No. 147.
2. Anon. sale, Christie, London, 6.iii.1801, lot 89.
3. Martin sale, Paillet, Paris, 5.iv.1802, lot 145.
4. Anon. sale, Christie, London, 16.vi.1821, lot 51; from the Rev. W. Hamilton collection, bt. Tringham.

NOTES: The subject is taken from Plutarch (*Life of Theseus*, vi). The idea of painting the theme may have been inspired by the account in Pausanias (Bk. I, *Attica*, XXVII, 8) of a relief on the Acropolis representing the subject, which was all of bronze, except the rock, which was of marble.

Mariette (Bibl. 157, IV, p. 204) says that the architecture in the picture is by Jean Lemaire, who was a specialist in the painting of ruins and a close friend of Poussin. This would be in conformity with what is known of Lemaire's painting (cf. Blunt, Bibl. 963 and 1196), but contrary to Poussin's general principle of not employing assistants. It is, however, possible that in this case, as in the *Dance in Honour of Priapus* (No. 176), there may have been some special reason which compelled him to adopt this course.

Grautoff (II, No. 75) dates this picture *c.* 1638 because of the similarity of Aethra and her attendant with Pharaoh's daughter and her maiden in the *Finding of Moses* of 1638 in the Louvre (No. 12), but, as far as can be judged from the present uncleaned condition of the picture, its colour is too warm for that phase and it should probably be placed a year or two earlier.

BIBLIOGRAPHY: Mariette, Bibl. 157, IV, p. 204; Smith, No. 164; Friedlaender, 1914, pp. 57, 192; Grautoff, II, No. 75; Magne, 1914, p. 203, No. 102; Friedlaender, 1933, p. 325; Francastel, Bibl. 883, p. 154; Jamot, pp. 25, 52 f., 62 f.; Wild, Bibl. 1185, p. 18; Bardon, Bibl. 1218, p. 129; Sterling, Bibl. 1290, p. 267; Rinehart, Bibl. 1346, p. 46.

183. MARS AND VENUS. 155 × 213.5 cm. Museum of Fine Arts, Boston, Mass.

HISTORY: Probably Cassiano dal Pozzo (see below). Almost certainly Furness sale, 4.ii.1758, lot 55, as *Venus and Adonis*, bt. the 1st Earl Harcourt; by descent to the 2nd Viscount Harcourt; bt. from him by the museum in 1940.

DRAWINGS: 1. Musée du Louvre, Paris (*CR*, III, p. 30, No. 206).
2. Royal Library, Windsor Castle (*CR*, III, p. 30, No. A 50). A very skilful early copy of No. 1.

ENGRAVING: By Fabrizio Chiari (Andresen, No. 349; Wildenstein, No. 122). Dated 1635. After the Louvre drawing. This and the *Venus and Mercury* (see No.184), dated 1636, are much the earliest engravings after Poussin.

NOTES: The account of the Pozzo collection among Robert de Cotte's papers (Bibl. 98a, p. 203) mentions a 'mars et venus'. No picture with this title appears in Ghezzi's list of the collection made in 1715, but the painting might be one of those simply described as Bacchanals.

Grautoff (II, No. 32) dated the picture 1630–35. In my view both the drawing and the painting point to an earlier date, just before 1630.

Thuillier (Bibl. 1350, p. 346) believes that Chiari's engraving is after a lost picture of the subject, but there seems every reason to think that it is after the Louvre drawing. The Windsor copy after the latter is an alarming example of how skilfully Poussin's early drawings were sometimes imitated.

BIBLIOGRAPHY: De Cotte, Bibl. 98, III, p. 153, and Bibl. 98a, p. 203; *Harcourt Papers*, Bibl. 201, III, p. 233; Waagen, Bibl. 384b, IV, p. 350; Smith, No. 197; Friedlaender, 1914, p. 129; Grautoff, I, p. 103, II, No. 32; Borenius, Bibl. 914, pp. 54 f.; Waterhouse, Bibl. 926, p. 4; Cunningham, Bibl. 946, p. 55; Friedlaender, Bibl. 958, pp. 17 ff.; Blunt, Bibl. 975, p. 37, and Bibl. 1002, p. 219; Licht, p. 107; Hunter, Bibl. 1201, p. 12; Blunt, Bibl. 1227, p. 167; Rinehart, Bibl. 1281, pp. 28 f.; Thuillier, Bibl. 1350, p. 346; Mahon, Bibl. 1367, p. 20.

184. VENUS AND MERCURY. Right-hand part: 78×85 cm. Alleyn's College of God's Gift, Dulwich, London (481). Left-hand part: 57×51 cm., with a band of 5 cm. added on the right. Musée du Louvre, Paris (733).

HISTORY: Almost certainly the picture in the Lankrinck sale, Smith and Bassett, London, 11.i.1693, lot 309 (Borenius, Bibl. 978, p. 32); in the J. Meijers sale, Willis, Rotterdam, 9.ix.1722, lot 2, 38×54 inches (cf. Hoet, Bibl. 195, I, p. 265), and in the Elector of Cologne sale, Paris, 1764, lot 52 (3½×4 ft.), bt. Basan. It was probably at this stage that the picture was cut in two, since the right-hand part from now onwards appears in English collections, whereas the left-hand section seems never to have left France.

Right-hand part: Anon. ('A gentleman gone abroad, 20 Portman Square', Christie, London, 11.ii.1778, lot 22, bt. Lebrun; later with Desenfans; bequeathed by him at his death in 1807 with his whole collection to Sir Francis Bourgeois, and by him to the college in 1811.

Left-hand part: Probably Duc de Penthièvre; if so, seized with his other possessions in 1794; entered in the museum records as 'ancienne collection', which generally means from the collection of an *émigré* (*Exposition Poussin* (*Louvre*), No. 36).

DRAWING: Musée du Louvre, Paris (*CR*, III, p. 30, No. 208).

ENGRAVING: By Fabrizio Chiari (Andresen, No. 348; Wildenstein, No. 121). Dated 1636. After the Louvre drawing. This and Chiari's engraving of *Mars and Venus* (see No. 183) are the two earliest engravings made after Poussin.

COPIES OF THE WHOLE COMPOSITION: 1. Musée des Beaux-Arts, Lille (618; cf. Thuillier, Bibl. 1299, p. 292).

2. Museo Comunale, Prato. Oval; in reverse, and therefore probably after the engraving.

3. Cottini-Copian collection (cf. Coutil, Bibl. 775, II, p. 11, without further details).

4. Anon. sale, Christie, London, 10.iv.1959, lot 65 (as Testa; in reverse).

COPY AFTER THE LEFT-HAND PART ONLY: H. Jannot, Paris.

NOTES: The Louvre fragment has a strip of about 5 cm. added on the right, but if this is imagined to be removed, the two fragments fit together, though there is not visible—either to the naked eye or under X-ray—any single object that runs from one canvas to the other. The top left-hand corner, with an area of sky and branches, is missing and was no doubt destroyed when the canvas was cut in two.

The Louvre picture is dated by Grautoff (II, No. 27) 1630–35; Mahon dates both parts to a point near the middle of the period which runs from the second half of 1629 to the beginning of 1631, presumably to about the middle of 1630. Noehles (Bibl. 1419, p. 93) suggests 1630, or slightly earlier. My own feeling would be that the appropriate dating would be somewhat earlier, perhaps about 1627–29.

BIBLIOGRAPHY FOR THE WHOLE COMPOSITION: Friedlaender, 1914, pp. 45, 129; Grautoff, II, p. 257; Magne, 1914, p. 201, No. 71; Borenius, Bibl. 978, p. 32; Blunt, Bibl. 1026, p. 4; Mahon, Bibl. 1271, p. 297; Panofsky, Bibl. 1273, p. 42; Kauffmann, Bibl. 1332, p. 97; Mahon, Bibl. 1367, pp. 28 ff., 53, 79; Noehles, Bibl. 1419, p. 93.

BIBLIOGRAPHY FOR RIGHT-HAND PART: Smith, No. 196; *Exposition Poussin* (*Louvre*), No. 35; Mahon, Bibl. 1367, pp. XI, 19 ff., 24, 26.

BIBLIOGRAPHY FOR LEFT-HAND PART: Grautoff, I, p. 103, II, No. 27; Magne, 1914, p. 215, No. 283; Jamot, pp. 15 ff., 40, 51; *Exposition Poussin* (*Louvre*), No. 36; Thuillier, Bibl. 1297, p. 41.

185. VENUS AND ADONIS. 75×99 cm. Rhode Island School of Design, Providence, Rhode Island.

HISTORY: A painting of this subject was in the collection of Zacharie de Raousset, Comte de Boulbon, at Aix-en-Provence in 1739 (cf. Boyer, Bibl. 1428, p. 100). This cannot be the Caen painting, which was already in the French Royal Collection, and it is therefore quite likely to be the Rhode Island picture. Earl Waldegrave sale, Prestage, London, 19.xi.1763, lot 25 (probably bought in Paris between 1730 and 1740, when Lord Waldegrave was Ambassador to Louis XV; cf. Waterhouse, Bibl. 1308, p. 291). Sir Joshua Reynolds by 1766 (engraved as in his possession by Earlom in that year). Lord Carrington by 1842 (Smith, Supplement, No. 7). Passed by descent to the 6th Lord Carrington; Carrington sale, Christie, London, 4.v.1951, lot 85, bt. Agnew; bt. by the gallery in 1954.

ENGRAVINGS: 1. By R. Earlom (Andresen, No. 342; Andresen-Wildenstein, No. 342).

2. By W. Baillie (Andresen, No. 426; Andresen-Wildenstein, No. 426). The putti on the left-hand side only.

NOTES: A picture hardly mentioned in recent literature on Poussin and very much damaged, but clearly original. Probably to be dated soon after 1630.

BIBLIOGRAPHY: Smith, No. 189, and Supplement, No. 7; Grautoff, II, p. 257; Davidson, Bibl. 1156, pp. 9 ff.; Blunt, Bibl. 1167, pp. 82, 85; Waterhouse, Bibl. 1308, p. 291; Boyer, Bibl. 1428, p. 100.

186. VENUS WITH THE DEAD ADONIS. 57×128 cm. Musée des Beaux-Arts, Caen.

HISTORY: Listed in the inventory of the French Royal Collection drawn up soon after 1683 (Bailly, p. 314). Sent to Caen in 1804.

ENGRAVING: By Baquoy (Andresen, No. 347; Andresen-Wildenstein, No. 347).

NOTES: Grautoff (II, No. 34) dated the painting 1630–35; Mahon to the middle of the period running from the second half of 1629 to the beginning of 1631, that is to say presumably about the middle of 1630. I should suggest c. 1630.

BIBLIOGRAPHY: Loménie de Brienne, p. 216; Bailly, p. 314; Dézallier, 1745, II, p. 255, and 1762, IV, p. 40; Smith, No. 195; Chennevières-Pointel, Bibl. 443, p. 28; Friedlaender, 1914, p. 127; Grautoff, I, p. 105, II, No. 34; Magne, 1914, p. 201, No. 76; Schneider, Bibl. 739, p. 369; Petit Palais, Paris, Bibl. 795, p. 136, No. 278; Benoist, Bibl. 849, pp. 71 f.; Brière, Bibl. 851, p. 209; Hourticq, Bibl. 899, p. 113; Friedlaender, Bibl. 948, p. 11; Jamot, p. 51; Blunt, Bibl. 1086, p. 186, and Bibl. 1086a, p. 162; Licht, p. 108; Blunt, Bibl. 1166, p. 5, and Bibl. 1226, p. 402; *Exposition Poussin (Louvre)*, No. 25; Mahon, Bibl. 1271, p. 297; Thuillier, Bibl. 1297, p. 41; Mahon, Bibl. 1367, p. 29.

187. VENUS AND CUPID. Original lost.

HISTORY: Possibly Cassiano dal Pozzo (see below). According to the Triqueti manuscript list of Poussin's works (Bibl. 440, p. 4, and Bibl. 441, p. 103) a painting corresponding to the engraving (see below) belonged in his day (i.e. c. 1850) to 'M. de la Salle', presumably the collector His de la Salle.

ENGRAVINGS: 1. By E. Baudet (Andresen, No. 351; Wildenstein, No. 123). Inscribed: *Romae 1665.*   2. By R. Hecquet (Andresen, No. 352).

NOTES: Since Baudet's engraving was made in Rome, the original was presumably there in 1665. It may, therefore, have been the *Venus* recorded as belonging to Pozzo in the account of the collection among the papers of Robert de Cotte (Bibl. 98a, p. 203). In the absence of the original it is impossible to propose a precise dating, but from the engraving it is safe to conclude that it must have been executed in the 1630's.

BIBLIOGRAPHY: De Cotte, Bibl. 98a, p. 203; Smith, No. 199; Triqueti, Bibl. 440, p. 48, and Bibl. 441, p. 103; Friedlaender, 1914, p. 128; Grautoff, II, p. 257; Wild, Bibl. 1184, p. 168.

188. VENUS AND CUPID, WITH A MAN OFFERING FRUIT. 75×63.5 cm. Messrs. Wildenstein, New York.

HISTORY: Almost certainly the picture which appeared in the following sales in the eighteenth century: Vassal de Saint-Hubert, Rémy, Paris, 17.i.1774, lot 65 ('un satyre qui apporte des fruits à sa femme que l'amour embrasse'; 29×24 inches); Prince de Conti sale, Remy, Paris, 8 ff.iv.1777, lot 533 ('Vénus assise sur une draperie d'écarlate; elle embrasse un Amour: un homme couronné de feuilles de vignes lui apporte des fruits'; dimensions given as 23×29 inches, but these may have been transposed); Dupille de Saint-Séverin sale, Hayot, Paris, 21 ff.ii.1785, lot 228 ('Vénus nue et assise par terre, elle embrasse l'Amour; un homme debout lui présente des fleurs'; 29×25½ inches); anon. (= Lenglier) sale, Lebrun, Paris, 24 ff.iv.1786, lot 113 (detailed description, which fits the Wildenstein picture, but the dimensions are given as in the Conti sale); Marquis of Lansdowne sale, Coxe, London, 19.iii.1806, lot 59; Earl of Darnley sale, Christie, London, 1.v.1925, lot 61 (as from the Lansdowne collection), bt. Colnaghi; Major O. E. Kay, London; sold through Mrs. Drey, London, to Messrs. Wildenstein in 1958.

NOTES: It is not certain whether the female figure is Venus or simply a nymph, but the action of Cupid in embracing her supports the hypothesis that it is the goddess. Probably to be dated just after 1630. The male figure may be Vertumnus (see below, p. 155).

BIBLIOGRAPHY: Waagen, Bibl. 384b, III, p. 25; Smith, No. 233.

189. VENUS SPIED ON BY SHEPHERDS. 71×96 cm. Staatliche Gemäldegalerie, Dresden (721).

HISTORY: Bought for the Electoral Collection through Leplat in Paris before 1722, when it is recorded in the Dresden inventory.

DRAWING: Gabinetto Nazionale dei Disegni, Rome. A copy after the painting.

COPIES: 1. Akademie der bildenden Künste, Vienna. From the Lamberg collection, where it was listed as an original by Castiglione.
2. Formerly with Dowdeswell, London.

NOTES: The picture is often described as 'A Nymph spied on by Shepherds', and this may be correct; but the two winged putti with their bows and arrows suggest a mythological subject. Moreover, in a painting similar in general character in the Brunswick museum (488), tentatively attributed to Domenichino, the principal figure is certainly Venus, since the doves, sacred to the goddess, appear on the wall behind the sleeping figure. Poussin is certainly credited with painting this subject, since Loménie de Brienne (p. 214) tells a melancholy story of mutilating a painting of this type, which belonged to him, in the supposed interests of morality.

Accepted by Grautoff (II, No. 23) and dated 1630–31. I have not seen the original for many years, but from my memory and from good reproductions its authenticity does not appear above suspicion. In particular the heads of the shepherds on the right seem unlike Poussin in type and handling. It might be argued that they are repainted, but they appear in almost identical form in the copy in Vienna.

BIBLIOGRAPHY: Friedlaender, 1914, pp. 44, 157; Grautoff, I, pp. 15, 100, II, No. 23; Magne, 1914, pp. 192, 203, No. 110; Hourticq, Bibl. 899, p. 145; Mahon, Bibl. 992, p. 38; Jamot, pp. 18, 40, 64; Walker, Bibl. 1145, p. 105.

190. VENUS BRINGING ARMS TO AENEAS. 108×133 cm. Art Gallery of Toronto, Ontario.

HISTORY: According to the inscription on the engraving made by Francesco Aquila (active 1690–1740), the painting belonged at the time to the Principe di Cellamare at Naples. This would have been either Domenico Giudice (d. 1718), or his son Antonio (d. 1733). It is possible that the painting may have been commissioned by Nicolas Giudice, father of Domenico, who was created Principe di Cellamare in 1631 (cf. Blunt, Bibl. 1167, p. 84). Passed by descent to the Duchessa di Cellamare, who had the picture in Rome about 1785–87 (cf. Hoare, Bibl. 280, I, pp. 76 f.). The Toronto picture had a label on the frame which said it had come from the collection of the Duke of Lucca; Duke of Lucca sale, Phillips, London, 5.vi.1841, lot 24; Arthur Ledger, Sheffield; sold by him in 1945 to a dealer in Sheffield; bt. from him by H. Barnes, Glasgow, who sold the picture to the gallery in 1948.

ENGRAVINGS: 1. By Francesco Aquila (Andresen, No. 354; Wildenstein, No. 125).
2. By Ignazio Pavon (Andresen, No. 355).
3. Mezzotint by Frederick Kerseboom (cf. Waterhouse, Bibl. 1308, pp. 286 f.; rep. Fig. 251).

COPIES: Paintings of this subject in the Jacob Kirckman sale, Christie, London, 9.ii.1793, lot 5, and in the D. Girou de Buzereingues sale, Chevallier, Paris, 26.ii.1892, may be connected with either the Toronto or the Rouen picture (No. 191).

NOTES: The subject is taken from Virgil (Aeneid, viii, 597 ff., and x, 835 ff.).

In the catalogue of the Louvre exhibition (No. 44) I proposed a date of c. 1636, which still seems to me reasonable; Mahon (Bibl. 1367) proposes c. 1637.

BIBLIOGRAPHY: Hoare, Bibl. 280, I, pp. 76 f.; Smith, No. 201; Grautoff, II, p. 257; Magne, 1914, p. 204, No. 121; Art Gallery of Toronto, Annual Report, Bibl. 1108, p. 16; Hubbard, Bibl. 1131, p. 152; Blunt, Bibl. 1166, p. 5, and Bibl. 1167, pp. 83 f., 86; Exposition Poussin (Louvre), No. 44; Mahon, Bibl. 1271, p. 303; Sterling, Bibl. 1290, p. 270; Waterhouse, Bibl. 1308, pp. 286 f.; Mahon, Bibl. 1367, pp. XIII, 104, 109, 128.

191. VENUS BRINGING ARMS TO AENEAS. 105×142 cm. Musée des Beaux-Arts, Rouen.

HISTORY: Painted in 1639, and later belonged to Antoine Bouzonnet Stella (Félibien, IV, p. 151); bequeathed to his niece, Claudine Bouzonnet Stella, and by the latter to her niece, Anne Molandier (Testament, Bibl. 107, pp. 19, 43). Probably Prince de Carignan sale, Pailly, Paris, 30.vii.1742, lot 33 (the dimensions are given as 58×72 inches, but they may include the frame); Robit sale, Paillet, Paris, 11.v.1801, lot

89, bt. Bryan; sold by him to Sir Simon Clarke (Buchanan, II, p. 58); Clarke sale, Christie, London, 9.v.1840, lot 103 (as from the Carignan and Robit collections), bt. Nieuwenhuys; Lord Northwick by 1854 (Waagen, Bibl. 384b, III, p. 205); Northwick sale, Phillips, Cheltenham, 26 ff.vii.1859, tenth day, lot 991 (as from the Carignan, Robit and Clarke collections), bt. Nieuwenhuys; Van Cuyck sale, Escribe, Paris, 7.ii.1866, lot 49 (as from the Carignan, Robit, Clarke and Northwick collections), bt. by the Rouen museum.

DRAWING: Private collection (with Alisteir Mathews, Bournemouth, 1960). Shows slight variations from the picture and may be a copy of a lost drawing by Poussin.

ENGRAVING: By N. Loir (Andresen, No. 353; Wildenstein, No. 124).

COPY: Victoria and Albert Museum, London. From the Dolgorouki collection (rep. Friedlaender, 1914, p. 182).

NOTES: It is evident on grounds of style that Félibien's date of 1639 must apply to the Rouen and not the Toronto version.

BIBLIOGRAPHY: Félibien, IV, p. 151; Bellori, p. 446; *Testament*, Bibl. 107, pp. 19, 43; Florent Le Comte, III, p. 31; Dézallier, 1745, II, p. 254; Buchanan, II, pp. 58, 66; Waagen, Bibl. 384b, III, p. 205; Smith, No. 200, and Supplement, No. 6; Burty, Bibl. 486, p. 56; Friedlaender, 1914, pp. 52, 116, 182; Grautoff, I, p. 134, II, No. 67; Magne, 1914, p. 203, Nos. 119, 120; Coutil, Bibl. 775, II, p. 16; Royal Academy, London, Bibl. 1165, No. 119; Blunt, Bibl. 1167, p. 84; Bardon, Bibl. 1218, p. 125; *Exposition Poussin (Louvre)*, No. 59; Mahon, Bibl. 1271, p. 304; Sterling, Bibl. 1290, p. 270; *Exposition Poussin (Rouen)*, No. 82; Mahon, Bibl. 1367, pp. XIII, 110, 114, 128.

192. PUTTI WITH A CHARIOT AND GOATS. Tempera on linen. 56×76·5 cm. Incisa della Rocchetta collection, Rome.

HISTORY: In the collection of Cardinal Flavio Chigi at his death in 1693 (cf. Rossini, Bibl. 106, p. 44); mentioned in the manuscript inventory of the Cardinal (information from Marchese Giovanni Incisa della Rocchetta); passed by descent to the late Marchesa Eleonora Incisa della Rocchetta, *nata* Chigi.

ENGRAVING: By Saint-Non after a drawing by Fragonard (Andresen, No. 427; Andresen-Wildenstein, No. 427; Cayeux, Bibl. 1390.2, p. 341, No. 116). Dated 1772.

NOTES: Almost certainly, with No. 193, the 'scherzi e baccanali à guazzo' which, according to Bellori (p. 412), Poussin made in his early years in Rome, based on his study of Titian's *Feast of Venus* (see text volume Fig. 56). Bellori states that these pictures were executed before the return to Rome of Cardinal Francesco Barberini, which occurred in December 1626, so the picture can with almost complete certainty be dated to that year.

Vasi (Bibl. 298c, I, p. 11) refers to 'tre puttini del Pussino', which presumably means three pictures of little putti. It is possible, therefore, that a third member of the series is lost.

BIBLIOGRAPHY: Bellori, p. 412; Rossini, Bibl. 106, p. 44; La Lande, Bibl. 224a, IV, p. 508; Volkmann, Bibl. 257, II, p. 310; Magnan, Bibl. 260, II, col. 10; Ramdohr, Bibl. 287, III, p. 105; Vasi, Bibl. 298c, I, p. 11; Laouriens, Bibl. 356, p. 398; Incisa della Rocchetta, Bibl. 1070, pp. 38 ff.; *Exposition Poussin (Louvre)*, No. 5; Thuillier, Bibl. 1298, pp. 274 f.; *Exposition Poussin (Rouen)*, No. 55; Mahon, Bibl. 1367, p. IX; Noehles, Bibl. 1419, pp. 90 ff.

193. PUTTI WITH GOATS AND MASKS. Tempera on linen. 74·5×85·5 cm. Incisa della Rocchetta collection, Rome.

HISTORY: See No. 192.

ENGRAVING: By Saint-Non after a drawing by Fragonard (Andresen, No. 428; Andresen-Wildenstein, No. 428; Cayeux, Bibl. 1390.2, p. 342, No. 124). Dated 1772.

COPY: Schönborn collection, Pommersfelden. Background changed and format altered to an upright shape.

NOTES: Kauffman (Bibl. 1332, p. 96) has pointed out that one of the children is taken from an engraving by Beatrizet (Bartsch, No. 40).

BIBLIOGRAPHY: See No. 192, and *Exposition Poussin (Louvre)*, No. 6; Kauffmann, Bibl. 1332, p. 96.

194. PUTTI FIGHTING ON GOATS (Fragment). 35·5 × 40·5 cm. Michael Kroyer, London.

HISTORY: Archdeacon Cambridge sale, Christie, London, 11.v.1824, lot 68; bt. shortly before the Second World War by Christopher Norris. Mrs. Pascal (formerly Mrs. Norris) sale, Sotheby, London, 23.v.1951, lot 45, bt. Calman; bt. from Calman by the present owner.

DRAWING: Ecole Nationale Supérieure des Beaux-Arts, Paris (*CR*, III, p. 44, No. 232).

NOTES: The drawing shows that the complete composition included on the left two nymphs, one seated, the other standing, the latter of whom holds up two wreaths for the winner of the fight (cf. *Venus and Mercury*, No. 184).

An X-ray photograph (see reproduction preceding p. 181 below) shows almost the whole of the standing nymph and part of an arm and a leg of the seated nymph. Both figures differ slightly in pose from their counterparts in the drawing: the seated girl stretches out one hand towards the combatants, and the standing one holds her right hand down instead of upwards. The rock filling the top right-hand corner does not show in the X-ray photograph and may have been painted in later to cover a rather large damage.

Both painting and drawing suggest a date of about 1629–30.

BIBLIOGRAPHY: *CR*, III, p. 44; *Exposition Poussin* (*Louvre*), No. 21; Mahon, Bibl. 1271, pp. 297 f.; Kauffmann, Bibl. 1332, p. 97; Mahon, Bibl. 1367, pp. 29, 86.

195. FOUR PUTTI AND TWO DOGS. 67 × 51 cm. Hermitage Museum, Leningrad (1196).

HISTORY: Almost certainly belonged to Cardinal Mazarin (see below); presumably passed at his death either to Hortense Mancini, wife of the Duc de la Meilleraye, who became Duc de Mazarin, or to Filippo Mancini (cf. Cosnac, Bibl. 584, pp. 271 ff.). Before the mid-1690's belonged to Etienne Texier de Hautefeuille, called the Commandant or the Bailli de Hautefeuille (Loménie de Brienne, p. 216), who was Ambassador of the Order of Malta to the Court of France, and at his death in 1703 left his pictures to the Knights of Malta, who presumably sold them (Bonnaffé, Bibl. 583, p. 136). Belonged in 1775 to Louis Antoine Crozat, Baron de Thiers (*Catalogue*, Bibl. 200, pp. 7 f.), who in 1750 had inherited from his elder brother, Louis François, Marquis du Châtel, the collection formed by their uncle, Pierre Crozat (d. 1740). Bt. with all the pictures of the Crozat collection in 1771 by the Empress Catherine II of Russia.

ENGRAVINGS: 1. Anonymous, late eighteenth century (in the Albertina; not listed by Andresen).
2. According to Coutil (Bibl. 775, II, p. 7), there is an engraving after this composition by 'Van Outen', presumably the G. Van Houten who executed an engraving after a composition of *Alexander sacrific-* *ing at the Tomb of Achilles*, wrongly ascribed to Poussin (Andresen, No. 313; Andresen-Wildenstein, No. 313), but no such print is mentioned by Andresen and it does not appear to be traceable elsewhere.

NOTES: In the 1653 inventory of Mazarin's possessions (Bibl. 20, p. 303) the picture is described as 'Quatre enfans tous nuds avec deux chiens, plus que petit, sans bordure. Pussino'. The entry in the 1661 inventory is almost identical, but gives the dimensions as 24 × 18 inches, which corresponds fairly closely with those of the Hermitage canvas. Loménie de Brienne's note (*loc. cit.*) reads as follows: 'J'ai vu chez le commandant de Hautefeuille *les 4. ages* ou *les 4. saisons* qu'avoit le cardinal Mazarin représentés sous la figure de 4. Enfants. C'est une très belle chose (?), mais ce tableau commence à se gaster, n'ayant pas esté si bien conservé.' It is unlikely that Brienne's interpretation of the composition is correct, and the painting is probably a fragment of a larger canvas representing a hunting scene, perhaps with Venus and Adonis.

I have not seen the painting for many years, but my impression from memory and from a good photograph is that it is a damaged and incomplete original, a hypothesis which would be strengthened by Brienne's comment about its state on the one hand and its provenance from the Mazarin collection on the other.

Probably to be dated 1630–33.

BIBLIOGRAPHY: *Inventaire . . . Mazarin*, Bibl. 20, p. 303; Loménie de Brienne, p. 216; Dézallier d'Argenville, Bibl. 183b, p. 119; *Catalogue du . . . Cabinet Crozat*, Bibl. 200, pp. 7 f.; Cosnac, Bibl. 584, p. 293, No. 934; Friedlaender, 1914, p. 128; Magne, 1914, p. 197, No. 6; Coutil, Bibl. 775, II, p. 7; Friedlaender, 1933, p. 324; Mahon, Bibl. 1268.1, p. 352.

196. PUTTI PLAYING. 95 × 72 cm. Hermitage Museum, Leningrad (1187).

HISTORY: Possibly the *Bachanale de petits enfants* which Monconys bought on 31.v.1664 from *le sculpteur du Pape* (Bibl. 35a, p. 118). This may be Bernini's assistant Carlo Matteo, who seems to have owned the *Plague of Ashdod* (cf. Blunt, Bibl. 1426, p. 67). Probably the *petite Baccanale de petits enfans* which is recorded by Le Maire (Bibl. 91, III, p. 265) as belonging to Colbert de Seignelay in 1685. Presumably passed to his brother and nephew. The Hermitage picture belonged in 1755 to Crozat de Thiers (*Catalogue*, Bibl. 200, p. 41, with dimensions 34 × 26 inches). Presumably inherited in 1750 from his elder brother Marquis du Châtel, who had inherited the collection formed by his uncle, Pierre Crozat (d. 1740). Bt. with all the pictures of the Crozat collection in 1771 by the Empress Catherine II of Russia.

COPY: Hermitage Museum, Leningrad (depot). Possibly from the Dupille de Saint-Séverin sale, Hayot, Paris, 21 ff.ii.1785, lot 226 (with dimensions 3 ft. × 2 ft. 3 inches).

NOTES: Probably dates from *c.* 1630–33.

BIBLIOGRAPHY: Monconys, Bibl. 35a, p. 118; Le Maire, Bibl. 91, III, p. 265; Dézallier d'Argenville, Bibl. 183b, p. 133; *Catalogue du ... Cabinet Crozet*. Bibl. 200, p. 41; Magne, 1914, p. 215, No. 275; Blunt, Bibl. 1426, p. 67.

197. PUTTI PLAYING WITH LEOPARDS (Fragment). 64 × 76 cm. Oval. The surviving part of the original canvas, which is roughly diamond-shaped, has been extended on all sides, except the top left, to form an oval. Private collection, France.

HISTORY: Almost certainly belonged to William Hastings in 1837 (lent by him to the British Institution in that year; cf. Smith, Supplement, No. 3). W. Anthony sale, Christie, London, 3 ff.ii.1871, lot 170 (stencil on stretcher), bt. Money.

DRAWING: Royal Library, Windsor Castle (CR, III, p. 21, No. 181). For the connection, see below.

NOTES: The painting is much damaged and repainted. The rock in the upper right area goes over the added canvas without change of brushwork and must be completely a later addition.

The painting shows two putti playing with two leopards, one of which rubs its head affectionately against the other. The left-hand putto holds a torch, while the other puts a bit in the mouth of one of the leopards. The theme is obviously *Omnia vincit amor*, a subject much loved by Poussin but usually treated through the variant symbolism of *Amor vincit Panem* (cf. CR, III, p. 32, Nos. 209, 210).

The fragment is related to a drawing at Windsor (see above), which represents a marriage scene and shows in the lower left-hand corner a putto playing with a leopard, which has much the same pose as that in the painting. The drawing is too rough for the action to be certainly identified, but the putto seems to be putting a bit in the animal's mouth.

This composition, of which a more finished drawing, also at Windsor (CR, III, p. 21, No. 182), is known, has been identified as the *Marriage of Bacchus and Ariadne*, and also simply as a marriage scene in the antique manner. On the whole the latter seems more likely, since the Bacchic dance visible in the background of the rougher drawing could be introduced into a painting representing a marriage other than that of Bacchus, and the presence of the second woman sitting next to the weeping bride would not be explicable in a *Bacchus and Ariadne*. This group, and indeed the whole composition, would on the other hand fit exactly with the type of marriage scene known in ancient paintings and bas-reliefs, of which the most famous was the fresco, *The Aldobrandini Wedding*, now in the Vatican, but in Poussin's day in the Vigna Aldobrandini (cf. text volume Fig. 112). Several of these ancient compositions were engraved in P. S. Bartoli's *Admiranda romanarum antiquitatum, ac veteris sculpturae vestigia ...* Rome, 1693, where they are given the title of *Nova Nupta*.

In the inventory of the pictures having belonged to Cassiano dal Pozzo, made in 1715 (Haskell and Rinehart, Bibl. 1254, p. 324) there appears under No. 42 a painting of this subject by Poussin (for the reading of the missing word, see *ibid.* p. 321; since the publication of the article Mrs. Rinehart has looked at the manuscript again and confirmed my conjecture). It seems therefore possible that the present painting is a fragment of the picture mentioned in Pozzo's collection (cf. Blunt, Bibl. 1426, pp. 62 f.).

The style of the drawings and of the fragment would confirm this hypothesis, since it suggests a date about 1630–33, when Poussin was working largely for Pozzo and his circle.

The attribution of the fragment to Poussin is rejected by Mahon (Bibl. 1367, pp. 132 f.).

BIBLIOGRAPHY: Smith, Supplement, No. 3; Haskell and Rinehart, Bibl. 1254, p. 324; Blunt, Bibl. 1323, p. 352; Mahon, Bibl. 1367, pp. 132 f.; Blunt, Bibl. 1426, pp. 62 f.

198. NYMPH, SATYR, FAUN AND CUPIDS. 96.5 × 75.5 cm. Staatliche Gemäldegalerie, Kassel (459).

HISTORY: Listed in the inventory of Landgraf William of Hesse in 1749. According to the gallery catalogue perhaps from the C. W. van Valkenburg sale, Willis, Rotterdam, 11.iv.1731, lot 5 (cf. Hoet, Bibl. 195, I, p. 366).

DRAWING: British Museum, London (CR, III, p. 44 No. 229).

ENGRAVING: By M. Blot (Andresen, No. 380).

COPIES: 1. Musée Bonnat, Bayonne (cf. Guiffrey, Bibl. 763).
2. Château de Fontaine-Henri, Normandy.
3. Probably anon. sale, Banqueting Hall, London, 2.vi.1684, lot 167 (cf. Waterhouse, Bibl. 1308, p. 285).
4. Probably Alexander Voet sale, Antwerp, 1689, lot 100 (cf. Denucé, Bibl. 862, p. 311).
5. Probably Jean-Baptiste Anthoine sale, Antwerp, 1691, lot 168 (ibid. p. 360).
6. Marquis de Lassay sale, Paris, 22 ff.v.1775, lot 45 (dimensions 3 ft. × 2 ft. 4 inches; price 25 livres).
7. John Blackwood (engraved as in his possession by P. T. Tassaert in 1769 (Andresen, No. 379; Andresen-Wildenstein, No. 379); Marquis of Lansdowne; Earl of Darnley (cf. Waagen, Bibl. 384b, III, p. 25); Earl of Darnley sale, Christie, London, 1.v.1925, lot 60, bt. Colonel Swinfen-Brown; Swinfen-Brown sale, Christie, London, 10.xii.1948, lot 114; anon. sale, Christie, London, 20.vii.1956, lot 50.
8. In the Dublin art trade about 1914 (cf. Grautoff, II, No. 51).

NOTES: Dated by Grautoff (II, No. 51) 1632–36; probably later than most of Poussin's small upright compositions of this kind, c. 1635.

BIBLIOGRAPHY: Hoet, Bibl. 195, I, p. 366; Smith, No. 225; Friedlaender, 1914, p. 46; Grautoff, I, p. 119, II, No. 51; Magne, 1914, p. 199, No. 30; Licht, p. 105; Thuillier, Bibl. 1297, p. 43; Mahon, Bibl. 1367, p. 86.

199. NYMPH RIDING A GOAT. 72 × 56 cm. Hermitage Museum, Leningrad (1178).

HISTORY: Probably the picture bt. in Rome by the Abbate Flavio Ruffo for his brother, Antonio Ruffo, Duca di Bagnara, Messina, in 1647, and certified by Poussin as an original (cf. Blunt, Bibl. 1167, p. 85). Probably either Président Crozat de Tugny sale, Delatour, Paris, June 1751, lot 33 (with description and dimensions 28 × 21 inches), or Dufourny sale, Delaroche, Paris, 22 ff.xi.1819, lot 92 (said to have been bt. from Giovanni Pezzi in Rome about 1800). The Hermitage picture was bt. from Korsakov in St. Petersburg in 1822 (Museum catalogue, 1958, correcting a different provenance given in previous editions).

DRAWING: Albertina, Vienna (CR, III, p. 44, No. 230).

ENGRAVINGS: 1. By A. Geiger (Andresen, No. 377). Dated 1801.
2. By M. A. de Homo (Andresen, No. 378).

COPIES: 1. Akademie der bildenden Künste, Vienna (931). From the Lamberg collection.
2. Anon. sale, Sotheby, London, 24.ii.1965, lot 112 (as Albani).

NOTES: Probably even later than the Kassel picture (No. 198), about 1636.

BIBLIOGRAPHY: Dézallier d'Argenville, Bibl. 183b, p. 130; Smith, No. 226; Grautoff, I, p. 120, II, No. 52; Magne, 1914, p. 202, No. 82; Du Colombier, Bibl. 1054, p. 95; Licht, p. 105; Blunt, Bibl. 1167, p. 85; Thuillier, Bibl. 1295, p. 122.

200. NYMPH WITH A SATYR DRINKING. 77×62 cm. Pushkin Museum, Moscow.

HISTORY: Possibly the picture seen by Evelyn in the collection of the Comte de Liancourt in 1644 (Bibl. 8b, II, p. 113). Jean-Baptiste Boyer d'Aguilles, Aix-en-Provence, before 1705 (engraved by J. Coelemans in that year for the catalogue of Boyer's collection); Louis Lanthier, Aix-en-Provence (d. 1737; cf. Vallery-Radot, Bibl. 806). Belonged in 1755 to Louis Antoine Crozat, Baron de Thiers (*Catalogue*, Bibl. 200, pp. 36 f.); presumably inherited in 1750 from his elder brother, Louis François, Marquis du Châtel, who had inherited the collection formed by their uncle, Pierre Crozat (d. 1740). Bt. with the Crozat collection in 1771 by the Empress Catherine II of Russia (Hermitage catalogue (1916), No. 1401). Sent to Moscow in 1930.

ENGRAVING: B. J. Coelemans (Andresen, No. 376; Andresen-Wildenstein, No. 376). Dated 1705; for the catalogue of the Boyer d'Aguilles collection, Aix-en-Provence.

COPIES: 1. Musée des Beaux-Arts, Besançon (210). From the Gigoux collection.
2. National Gallery, Dublin (2519). Perhaps Robert Strange sale, Christie, London, 7.ii.1771, lot 20, bt. Stephenson. Duke of Sutherland by 1836 (cf. Passavant, Bibl. 399, I, p. 144); Duke of Sutherland sale, Christie, London, 11.vii.1913, lot 35, bt. Martin for Sir Hugh Lane; bequeathed by him to the gallery in 1916 (cf. Bodkin, Bibl. 858, p. 179).
3. Museo del Prado, Madrid (2318). Said to have been bt. by Philip V in 1724 from the heirs of Carlo Maratta (museum catalogue), but the picture does not fit with the description given in the inventory of Maratta's collection (Galli, Bibl. 818, XXIII, p. 60, No. 145; cf. also Ponz, Bibl. 238a, p. 895, paragraph 59; Grautoff, II, No. 53; Hourticq and others, Bibl. 803, p. 134, No. 265).
4. Martin sale, Paillet, Paris, 5.iv.1802, lot 148 (24× 17 inches).

NOTES: The provenance of the Moscow picture from the Boyer d'Aguilles collection can be established by the Coelemans engraving, which corresponds precisely with it and differs clearly from all the other known versions.

As with all Poussin's compositions of this type, it is uncertain whether the artist is merely depicting a group of sylvan figures, or whether there is some precise mythological reference. In some instances (e.g. No. 188) the female figure seems to be Venus, but here this is unlikely to be the case, as there would be no precedent for her to be depicted holding the flask of wine. In the Dublin version the copyist has added in the background a bent stick and pipes hanging on a tree, perhaps to indicate that the goat-footed figure is Pan and not merely a satyr.

The figure of the satyr kneeling and drinking is also to be found in the *Youth of Bacchus* at Chantilly (No. 134), though here he drinks from a horn instead of a golden wine-pot and does not have a cupid to help him in the process. Moreover, the young Bacchus in this picture makes almost the same gesture as the nymph in the Hermitage composition, as if ordering the satyr to drink.

Dated by Grautoff (II, No. 54) 1632–36; I would propose 1633–35.

BIBLIOGRAPHY: Evelyn, Bibl. 8b, II, p. 113, and Bibl. 8c, p. 74; Mariette, Bibl. 177.2, p. 14, No. IV; Dézallier d'Argenville, Bibl. 183b, p. 130; *Catalogue du . . . Cabinet Crozat*, Bibl. 200, pp. 36 f.; Smith, No. 228; Chennevières-Pointel, Bibl. 433, I, p. 143; Friedlaender, 1914, p. 46; Grautoff, II, No. 54; Magne, 1914, p. 198, No. 24; Vallery-Radot, Bibl. 806, pp. 31 ff., and Bibl. 807, p. 52; Bodkin, Bibl. 858, p. 179; Friedlaender, 1933, p. 324; Licht, p. 105.

201. THE FEAST OF THE GODS. 171·5×189 cm. Copy after the painting by Bellini and Titian, now in the National Gallery of Art, Washington, D.C. National Gallery of Scotland, Edinburgh (458).

HISTORY: Perhaps Charles Jarvis sale, London, 12.iii.1739, lot 128. W. Coningham sale, Christie, London, 9.vi.1849, lot 4. Sir Charles Eastlake; presented by him to the gallery in 1862–63. On loan to the National Gallery, London, from 1921 to 1927.

NOTES: A copy of Titian's *Andrians* (Prado) in the National Gallery of Scotland (368) was attributed to Poussin by Grautoff (II, No. 22), probably owing to a confusion with the present picture. Another version of the *Andrians*, regarded by some as a product of the studio of Titian, was attributed to Poussin by Holmes (Bibl. 838, p. 287), but from the reproduction this does not seem very probable. The picture in question was sold at Sotheby, London, 21.v.1935, lot 23.

A copy of the *Feast of the Gods* in the Castel S. Angelo, Rome, also attributed to Poussin, is in my opinion not by him.

The attribution of the Edinburgh picture to Poussin is rejected by Mahon (Bibl. 1271, p. 290), Kauffmann (Bibl. 1332, p. 97) and D. Wild (Bibl. 1312, p. 159), but in spite of their views I feel no doubt about its authenticity. It should, however, in my opinion be placed not in the 1620's, when, according to Bellori, Poussin began to study the Aldobrandini *Bacchanals*, since the handling is not like that of the artist at that period, but about 1635.

BIBLIOGRAPHY: Waagen, Bibl. 384b, II, p. 266; Alfassa, Bibl. 776, p. 271; Gamba, Bibl. 898, p. 171; Mahon, Bibl. 992, p. 38; Bertin-Mourot, Bibl. 1023, p. 54, No. XXXIX; Clark, Bibl. 1040, p. 67; Licht, p. 78; Walker, Bibl. 1145, pp. 62, 106; *Exposition Poussin* (*Louvre*), No. 28; Mahon, Bibl. 1271, p. 290; Wild, Bibl. 1312, p. 159; Kauffmann, Bibl. 1332, p. 97; Mahon, Bibl. 1367, p. 52.

201–a. WOMEN BATHING. See L. 117 on p. 166 below.

202. RINALDO AND ARMIDA. 80×107 cm. Alleyn's College of God's Gift, Dulwich, London.

HISTORY: Possibly anon. sale, Christie, London, 29.iv.1788, lot 88; Noël Desenfans by 1804 (Insurance List at Dulwich College); bequeathed at his death in 1807 to Sir Francis Bourgeois, and by him to the College in 1811.

ENGRAVINGS: 1. By G. Audran (Andresen, No. 412; Wildenstein, No. 166; Davies and Blunt, p. 215, No. 166. 2. By P. Dupin (Andresen, No. 413). Dated 1722.

NOTES: The subject is taken from Tasso's *Gerusalemme Liberata* (XIV, 65 ff.).

Rejected by Grautoff (I, p. 109, II, p. 264), but accepted by all other writers on Poussin.

Friedlaender (1914, p. 51) dates the picture to the second half of the 1630's, but this is almost certainly too late. In my paper to the Poussin Colloque (Bibl. 1227, p. 167) I placed it before 1630, near the Chantilly *Massacre* (No. 67) and the *St. Erasmus* (No. 97), i.e. *c*. 1628–29. In the catalogue of the Louvre exhibition (No. 14) I suggested *c*. 1630, which I now believe is too late. Mahon (Bibl. 1367) places it in 'the period, including the whole of 1628 and something over the first half of 1629'.

An X-ray photograph of this picture shows that Poussin had turned round and re-used a canvas on which he had painted a composition which may have represented a related subject. It shows a man asleep or dying, supported by a putto, while on the right a woman stretches out a hand towards him. Behind both figures are visible dark masses, which might be either trees or architectural features (see reproduction preceding p. 181 below). This composition could not represent the moment shown in the picture visible to the eye, since the woman is clearly not about to stab the man, but it might be connected with the next incident in the story, when Armida orders her attendants to carry Rinaldo to her chariot (see No. 204). If this is the case, the rather hard lines of the dark band behind the female figure could be explained as showing the column which is mentioned by Tasso in his account of this story, and which appears, though more distantly, in No. 204.

BIBLIOGRAPHY: Gault de Saint-Germain, Pt. II, pp. 47 f.; Smith, No. 286; Friedlaender, 1914, pp. 51, 115; Grautoff, I, p. 109, II, p. 264; Magne, 1914, p. 218, No. 329; Friedlaender, Bibl. 726, p. 231; Rouchès, Bibl. 752.1, II, p. 201; Hourticq, Bibl. 899, pp. 84, 93 f.; *CR*, II, p. 21; Waterhouse, Bibl. 1022, p. 161; Blunt, Bibl. 1026, p. 7, Bibl. 1086, p. 185, Bibl. 1086a, p. 161, Bibl. 1222, p. 331, and Bibl. 1227, p. 167; *Exposition Poussin (Louvre)*, No. 14; Mahon, Bibl. 1271, p. 297; Lee, Bibl. 1336, p. 347; Mahon, Bibl. 1367, pp. X f., 23 ff., 29, 57, 59, 78.

203. RINALDO AND ARMIDA. 95×133 cm. Pushkin Museum, Moscow.

HISTORY: Acquired by the Empress Catherine II of Russia (Hermitage catalogue (1916), No. 1407). Sent to Moscow in 1930.

NOTES: Dated by Grautoff (II, No. 40) 1630–35, but perhaps nearer the middle than the beginning of the decade.

BIBLIOGRAPHY: Smith, No. 287; Friedlaender, 1914, pp. 51, 115; Grautoff, I, p. 109, II, No. 40; Magne, 1914, p. 218, No. 331; Rouchès, Bibl. 752.1, II, p. 201; Hourticq, Bibl. 899, pp. 95, 174; *CR*, II, p. 21; Lee, Bibl. 1336, p. 347.

204. ARMIDA CARRYING OFF RINALDO. 122×151 cm. Staatliche Museen zu Berlin, Gemäldegalerie, Berlin (486).

HISTORY: Painted for Jacques Stella *c.* 1637; about 1685 belonged to Joachim de Seiglière de Boisfranc (Félibien, IV, p. 25). Probably Pasquier sale, Remy, Paris, 10.iii.1755, lot 14 (as engraved by Chasteau, with dimensions 3 ft. 7½ inches × 4 ft. 6½ inches). The Berlin picture was recorded in the Neues Palais, Potsdam, in 1773 (cf. Oesterreich, Bibl. 242.1, p. 32, No. 75).

DRAWINGS: 1. and 2. Musée du Louvre, Paris (*CR*, III, p. 21, No. 142, and p. 22, No. 144).
3. and 4. Royal Library, Windsor Castle (*CR*, III, p. 22, Nos. 143, A 39).

ENGRAVINGS: 1. By G. Chasteau (Andresen, No. 409; Wildenstein, No. 164).
2. By P. Simonneau (Andresen, No. 410).
3. By C. Massé (Andresen, No. 411; Wildenstein, No. 165). After drawing No. 2 above.

COPIES: 1. T. Laurent, Paris (114×144 cm.).
2. Comte R. de Montméja, Château de Roufillac, Dordogne.
3. Formerly Pearson collection, Paris; later Galerie Barbazanges, Paris. Friedlaender (1914, p. 115) says that this is the best surviving version and suggests that it might be the original, but this seems unlikely (cf. Notes, below).
4. Anon. sale, Robinson and Fisher, London, 23.iii. 1939, lot 32; later on the Paris art market.

NOTES: I have not seen the Berlin painting, but from a good photograph it appears to be of much better quality than the other known versions, and, in spite of the fact that it has always been regarded as a copy (cf. Friedlaender, p. 115; Grautoff, II, p. 261), there does not seem to be any reason to doubt that it is the original. Of all the known versions it is the only one to agree in almost every detail with the engravings by Chasteau and Simonneau (Nos. 1 and 2 above). The ex-Pearson version (No. 3 above) is close to the engravings in the disposition of the figures, but differs markedly from them in the treatment of the trees, and furthermore it is lifeless and mechanical in the handling of the foliage. In the other two copies the arrangement of the trees is entirely different. The slight hardness apparent in the Berlin picture is perfectly in accordance with Poussin's style in 1637, and the fact that the group of the river god and two nymphs on the right is based on the engraving of the *Judgment of Paris* by Marcantonio after Raphael (Bartsch XIV, p. 197, No. 245) would also fit with that phase in his art. The arrangement of the crossing trees on the left and the general disposition of the landscape are close to the Louvre *St. John baptising the People* (No. 69).

The painting represents the phase of the story immediately after that depicted in Nos. 202 and 203, when Armida orders her attendants to carry the sleeping Rinaldo to her chariot (*Gerusalemme liberata*, XIV, 68 ff.). The column in the background is specifically mentioned by Tasso (*ibid.*, IV, 57). The two knights beside it, one standing and one sitting, apparently in an attitude of mourning, are not immediately explicable on Tasso's text, but they may be a slightly anachronistic allusion to the two warriors who were in due course to come and save Rinaldo from the enchantments of Armida.

BIBLIOGRAPHY: *Correspondance*, p. 3; Tristan L'Hermite, Bibl. 12a, p. 81; Chantelou, 1885, p. 228, and 1960, p. 132; Félibien, IV, p. 25; Bellori, p. 447; Loménie de Brienne, p. 218; Florent Le Comte, III, p. 26; Oesterreich, Bibl. 242.1, p. 32, No. 75; Smith, No. 288; Friedlaender, 1914, p. 115; Grautoff, I, p. 139, II, p. 261; Magne, 1914, pp. 94, 218, No. 330; Rouchès, Bibl. 752.1, II, p. 201; *CR*, II, p. 21; Blunt, Bibl. 975, pp. 41, 47; Lee, Bibl. 1336, p. 347; Mahon, Bibl. 1367, p. 107.

205. THE COMPANIONS OF RINALDO. 119×101 cm. Countess Stephanie Harrach, Vienna.

HISTORY: Cassiano dal Pozzo (see below).

NOTES: On the stretcher is an old label with the inscription:

> Carolus et Hubertus
> Tassus cec. Rinaldum
> liberaturi
> Poussinus Roma.

The subject is taken from Tasso's *Gerusalemme Liberata* (XV, 45 ff.).

The account of Pozzo's collection among the papers of Robert de Cotte mentions a painting 'representant les deux chevalier qui vond délivrer Renaud des enchantements darmide' (Bibl. 98a, p. 203), a description which fits precisely with the Harrach painting.

The boat is taken from a Roman relief in Venice, engraved by the Master of the Die (cf. Kauffmann, Bibl. 1334, p. 113).

Grautoff dates the picture 1630–35 (II, No. 41); Mahon (Bibl. 1367, p. 53) to 1630–33. I should see it as slightly later, c. 1633–35.

BIBLIOGRAPHY: De Cotte, Bibl. 98, III, p. 152, and Bibl. 98a, p. 203; Grautoff, I, p. 110, II, No. 41; Hourticq, Bibl. 899, p. 97; *Exposition Poussin (Louvre)*, No. 32; Rinehart, Bibl. 1281, p. 28; Kauffmann, Bibl. 1334, p. 113; Lee, Bibl. 1336, p. 347; Mahon, Bibl. 1367, pp. XI, 53, 55.

206. TANCRED AND ERMINIA. 98×147 cm. Hermitage Museum, Leningrad (1189).

HISTORY: Bt. by the Empress Catherine II of Russia from the painter Abel (no doubt the miniaturist Ernst August Abel) in Paris in 1766 (museum catalogue).

NOTES: Dated by Grautoff (II, No. 39) 1630–35, and by Mahon (Bibl. 1367) to 1631. The dating of 1635, which I proposed in the catalogue of the Louvre exhibition (No. 42) now seems to me too late, and I should suggest c. 1631–33.

BIBLIOGRAPHY: Le Breton, Bibl. 339, p. 394; Smith, No. 290; Grautoff, I, p. 108, II, No. 39; Magne, 1914, p. 219, No. 339; Rouchès, Bibl. 752.1, II, p. 201; Hourticq, Bibl. 899, p. 84, 98 f.; Bodkin, Bibl. 932, pp. 254 f.; Licht, p. 110; Blunt, Bibl. 1226, p. 400; Jullian, Bibl. 1261, p. 230; *Exposition Poussin (Louvre)*, No. 42; Mahon, Bibl. 1271, p. 299, and Bibl. 1367, pp. 28 f.

207. TANCRED AND ERMINIA. 75×100 cm. The Barber Institute of Fine Arts, Birmingham.

HISTORY: Bt. by Sir James Thornhill in Paris in 1717 (Richardson, Bibl. 239a, pp. 192 ff.); Sir James Thornhill sale, Cock, London, 25.ii.1734, lot 98, bt. W. Lock (engraved while in his possession by J. Van der Gucht, see below); sold by his son to Earl Poullett, from whose descendant it was bt. in 1938 by the Institute through Frank Sabin.

ENGRAVING: By J. Van der Gucht (Andresen, No. 414; Andresen-Wildenstein, No. 414; and cf. Walpole, Bibl. 319, IV, p. 107).

COPIES: 1. Prince Paul of Jugoslavia.
2. Commander E. Culme-Seymour, Edinburgh.

NOTES: In the catalogue of the Louvre exhibition (No. 53) I proposed a date of about 1637–38. Mahon (Bibl. 1 67, p. XII) suggests 1633–34.

BIBLIOGRAPHY: Vertue, Bibl. 132, XXII, p. 74; Richardson, Bibl. 143, p. 75; Dézallier, 1745, II, pp. 227 ff.; Richardson, Bibl. 239a, pp. 192 ff.; Graham, Bibl. 365, No. 83; Smith, No. 290; Bodkin, Bibl. 932, pp. 253 ff.; Richardson, Bibl. 967, pp. 134, 136, 207; Massignon, Bibl. 1017, p. 35; Bertin-Mourot, Bibl. 1023, p. 51, No. XXVIII; Davis, Bibl. 1242, p. 468; *Exposition Poussin (Louvre)*, No. 53; Mahon, Bibl. 1271, p. 300; Waterhouse, Bibl. 1308, p. 289; Mahon, Bibl. 1367, pp. XII, 83.

LANDSCAPES

208. LANDSCAPE WITH TWO NYMPHS AND A SNAKE. 118×179 cm. Musée Condé, Chantilly (302).

HISTORY: Probably painted for Charles Lebrun in 1659 (Mahon, Bibl. 1338, pp. 125 f.). Radziwill collection; Reiset collection; bt. from him by the Duc d'Aumale (museum catalogue).

ENGRAVING: By L. de Châtillon (Andresen, No. 455; Wildenstein, No. 187).
COPY: Bruce-Binney, Pewsey, Wiltshire. From the Lord Radstock sale, Christie, London, 12.v.1826, lot 56; Marquis of Ailesbury (Smith, No. 328). In this picture the snake is not visible, perhaps because of damage.

NOTES: The attribution of the picture to Poussin is rejected by D. Wild (Bibl. 1185, pp. 23 ff.), but is accepted by all other writers. Mahon (Bibl. 1338, pp. 125 ff.) has convincingly suggested that the Chantilly picture may be the landscape mentioned by Félibien (IV, p. 66) as having been painted for Lebrun in 1659.

BIBLIOGRAPHY: Félibien, IV, p. 66; Loménie de Brienne, p. 222; Smith, No. 311; Friedlaender, 1914, pp. 100, 261; Grautoff, I, p. 282, II, No. 154; Magne, 1914, p. 216, No. 303; Blunt, Bibl. 972, p. 165; Licht, pp. 135, 175; Wild, Bibl. 1185, pp. 23 ff.; Mahon, Bibl. 1338, pp. 125 ff., and Bibl. 1367, p. 121.

209. LANDSCAPE WITH A MAN KILLED BY A SNAKE. 119.5×198.5 cm. National Gallery, London (5763).

HISTORY: Painted for Pointel (Félibien, IV, p. 63) probably in 1648 (see below). After his death, which probably took place between 1657 and 1662, bt. by Duplessis-Rambouillet; in 1685 belonged to Denis Moreau (Félibien, op. cit.). Passed by descent to the Nyert family. Bt. from them early in, or shortly before, 1773 by Robert Strange (see below). Strange sale, Christie, London, 6.iii.1773, lot 113, bt. by Sir Watkin Williams-Wynn, 4th Bart.; bt. in 1947 from the 8th Bart. through Horace Buttery.

DRAWINGS: 1. Musée du Louvre, Paris (CR, IV, p. 47, No. 281).
2. Musée des Beaux-Arts, Dijon (CR, IV, p. 47, No. 282).
3. Musée Bonnat, Bayonne (CR, IV, p. 47, No. 283).

ENGRAVING: By E. Baudet (Andresen, No. 442; Wildenstein, No. 180).

COPIES: 1. Musée Magnin, Dijon (806). Bt. at the Haro sale in 1912 (cf. Magnin, Bibl. II, 764, pp. 30 ff.; 100 × 173 cm.).
2. John Hutton, Glasgow.
3. Mrs. Pascal, London. A small copy, probably after the engraving, attributed to Richard Wilson.
4. Lord Northwick in 1846 (Visits, Bibl. 427, pp. 251 ff.).
5. Dufourny sale, Delaroche, Paris, 22 ff.xi.1819, lot 88 (22 × 30 inches).

Paintings of this subject were offered to the Louvre, Paris, by Ozon in 1850 and by Hunes in 1865 (Wildenstein, No. 180).

NOTES: The National Gallery picture was discovered and published by Waterhouse (Bibl. 942). Watson (Bibl. 1047) added the entry from the Strange sale catalogue, and Davies much new material in his entry for the National Gallery Catalogue (Bibl. 988a, pp. 179 ff., No. 5763).
The entry from the Strange sale catalogue is of such importance that it is worth quoting in full:
113 *An historical landscape,*
The scene of this picture represents a prospect of the antient City of Terracina, in the kingdom of Naples. It was in the neighbourhood of this city, in the morass of Pontius, that the catastrophe which gave rise to the subject of this picture, happened, in the year 1641. For a more particular description of it, see that beautiful dialogue which Fenelon, archbishop of Cambray, subjoined to his life of Mignard, supposes between Poussin and Leonardo da Vinci, upon the propriety and excellence of painting, and in which this picture is cited as an example.
Félibien, in his life of Poussin, in mentioning several pictures he had painted for Pointel, says: 'Ce fut encore dans le même temps qu'il fit pour le même Pointel deux grands paisages: dans l'un il i a un homme

mort et entouré d'un serpent, et un autre homme effragé qui s'enfuit. Ce tableau que M. de Plessis Rambouillet, acheta apres la mort du Sieur Pointel, est presentement dans le cabinet de Monsieur Moreau premier valet de Garderobe du Roi, il doit être regardé comme un des plus beaux paisages que le Poussin ait fait.' Since the death of Moreau this picture has been in the collection of Monsieur des Niert first valet de chambre to the king, from whose family it was lately purchased. Mr. Demaso has in his custody a series of letters wrote by the hand of Poussin to several of his friends, and amongst others is one to the above Pointel, dated from Rome the last of August 1648, and wherein he gives him advice of his having finished the above picture, &c. These circumstances, it is presumed, will certify the authenticity of it beyond a doubt.

The Demaso in question is almost certainly a member of the Lyons family of Demaso or Demasso, one of whom was the mother of Jacques Stella.

The statement in the catalogue that the picture was finished in 1648 must be regarded as correct, since the authority of the lost letter to Pointel carries great weight. It is true that Félibien's reference to the picture (IV, p. 63) suggests a later date, about 1651, but his formulation of the statement is vaguer than is usual with this author. The reference comes after a passage about a painting executed in 1651, but the words *le même temps* as compared with *la même année* suggest that the writer was not quite as certain of his facts as he normally was.

The indication of the theme illustrated in the painting is supported by the evidence of the inscription on the engraving by Baudet, which ends as follows: 'L'on tient que le Poussin peignit ce tableau à l'occasion d'un accident semblable qui arriva de son temps aux environs de Rome.' For a discussion of the precise subject, see text volume, pp. 286 ff.

The relation of the drawings to the painting has been analysed by Shearman (Bibl. 1285, pp. 184 ff.).
For the problem of the copy said to have belonged to Cassiano dal Pozzo, see No. 215 below.

BIBLIOGRAPHY: Félibien, III, p. 204, IV, pp. 63, 150; Florent Le Comte, III, p. 31; Charlotte, Duchesse d'Orléans, Bibl. 125, I, pp. 261 f.; Fénelon, in Bibl. 156, pp. 224 ff.; Walpole, Bibl. 162, VIII, p. 253; Diderot, Bibl. 211, XI, pp. 161 f., 280 f.; Burney, Bibl. 233, I, pp. 204 f.; Gault de Saint-Germain, Pt. II, pp. 34 f.; Smith, No. 308; Leslie, Bibl. 413a, p. 297; Friedlaender, 1914, p. 122; Grautoff, II, p. 259; Bodkin, Bibl. 778, p. 322; Waterhouse, Bibl. 942, pp. 102 f.; Blunt, Bibl. 972, pp. 157, 161; Davies, Bibl. 988a, pp. 179 ff., No. 5763; Bertin-Mourot, Bibl. 1023, p. 53, No. XXXVI; Jamot, p. 68; Watson, Bibl. 1047, pp. 14 ff.; Tervarent, Bibl. 1082, p. 343; Dorival, Bibl. 1088, p. 51; Licht, p. 163; *Exposition Poussin (Louvre)*, No. 83; Shearman, Bibl. 1285, pp. 184 ff.; Waterhouse, Bibl. 1308, p. 293; Mahon, Bibl. 1338, pp. 125, 127 ff.; Tervarant, Bibl. 1349.1, pp. 9 ff.; *L'ideale classico (Bologna)*, No. 74; Mahon, Bibl. 1367, pp. 127, 129.

210. LANDSCAPE WITH A ROMAN ROAD. 78×99 cm. Alleyn's College of God's Gift, Dulwich, London (203).

HISTORY: Painted in 1648; in 1685 belonged to the Chevalier de Lorraine (Félibien, IV, p. 59). The Dulwich picture belonged to Noël Desenfans, who at his death in 1807 bequeathed it to Sir Francis Bourgeois; bequeathed by him to the College in 1811.

ENGRAVINGS: 1. By E. Baudet (Andresen, No. 444; Wildenstein, No. 183).
2. By J. L. Allais (Andresen, No. 444a).
3. By S. Vallée (Andresen, No. 444b).

COPIES: 1. Musée des Beaux-Arts, Valence.
2. Sir Anthony Blunt, London. Anon. (= Executors of Miss de Burgh) sale, Christie, London, 23.vi.1939, lot 141, bt. Long (= bt. in); bt. by the present owner from the Executors.
3. Robert Lutyens, London. From the collection of Sir Hugh Lane.

4. In the possession of Claudine Bouzonnet Stella in 1697 (*Testament*, Bibl. 107, p. 40).
5. Anon. sale, Lebrun, Paris, 3.xii.1782, lot 80, bt. Homont (12×15 inches).
6. Donjeux sale, Lebrun, Paris, 29.iv.1793, lot 422.
7. De Frey sale, Charpentier, Paris, 12.vii.1933, lot 31.
8. Earl of Crawford and Balcarres sale, Christie, London, 11.x.1946, lot 107, bt. Singer (24×29 inches). A variant attributed to Millet.

NOTES: The Dulwich painting is much damaged, but such parts of it as are reasonably well preserved are of good enough quality to justify the belief that it is the original.

An examination of the picture by X-ray produced surprising results, for it is clear that Poussin has turned on its side and re-used a canvas on which he had already begun another composition. Further, the figures visible in the X-ray photograph correspond precisely with the three left-hand figures in the *Moses trampling on Pharaoh's Crown* in the Louvre (No. 15). Nothing is visible on the rest of the canvas in the X-ray photograph. See reproduction preceding p. 181.

There is no other instance known of Poussin re-using a canvas at such a late stage in his career, and none at any date of his repeating a group so precisely. Some special circumstances must have led him to take this course.

A possible explanation is that he began the *Moses* and that, when only just begun, the canvas was damaged on the right. Poussin may then have abandoned it, painted the *Moses* on a fresh canvas, and later have cut down the damaged canvas to use it for the smaller landscape. The width of the Dulwich picture—99 cm.—is 7 cm. greater than the height of the *Moses*, but the latter may well have lost a little at the top, so that the dimensions may once have corresponded.

An alternative hypothesis would be that both the lower and the upper paintings are copies, and that the copyist, having begun to paint the *Moses*, changed his mind, cut down the canvas and copied the landscape; but the quality of the painting visible to the naked eye makes this the less plausible theory.

The discovery of the fragment under the landscape has some bearing on the dating of the Louvre *Moses*, since, although the damaged canvas may have lain in Poussin's studio for many years, it is not likely to have done so. The new evidence would tend to support Mahon's view that the Louvre version is later than the Woburn picture (No. 16) and nearer to 1648, the date of the landscape.

The *Landscape with a Roman Road* was apparently painted as a pair to the *Landscape with a Man washing his feet at a Fountain* (see next number).

BIBLIOGRAPHY: Félibien, IV, p. 59; *Testament*, Bibl. 107, p. 40; Florent Le Comte, III, p. 30; Waagen, Bibl. 384b, II, p. 348; Smith, No. 310; Hazlitt, Bibl. 411, p. 34; Friedlaender, 1914, p. 119; Magne, 1914, p. 216, No. 292; Blunt, Bibl. 1026, p. 8; Clark, Bibl. 1040, p. 66 n. 1; *Exposition Poussin (Louvre)*, No. 84; Kauffmann, Bibl. 1332, p. 99.

211. LANDSCAPE WITH A MAN WASHING HIS FEET AT A FOUNTAIN. 74.5 × 100 cm. National Gallery, London (40).

HISTORY: In Sir George Beaumont's collection by 1787 (when engraved by Pether, see below); given by him to the Gallery in 1826.

ENGRAVINGS: 1. By E. Baudet (Andresen, No. 445; Wildenstein, No. 182; Davies and Blunt, p. 215, No. 182).
2. By S. Vallée (Andresen, No. 445a).
3. By W. Pether (Andresen, No. 445b). Dated 1787.

COPIES: 1. Auckland City Art Gallery, New Zealand. Anon. sale, Christie, London, 21.xii.1951, lot 108 (as Bourdon).
2. Musée des Beaux-Arts, Nîmes.
3. Countess of Seafield, Scotland.
4. Private collection, Texas.

5. With Böhler, Munich, before 1934 (as Millet).
6. With de Beer, London, 1946.
7. Anon. sale, Sotheby, London, 8.iii.1950, lot 65 (as Orizonte), bt. Jeudwine.
8. Anon. sale, Christie, London, 16.vii.1954, lot 270 (as Bourdon). The lower left-hand part of the composition only.

A copy after Poussin, described as 'un paysage: sur le devant est un Tombeau', which belonged to Claudine Bouzonnet Stella (*Testament*, Bibl. 107, p. 40) may have been a version of this composition.

NOTES: The National Gallery picture has in recent years been regarded as a copy, but Mr. Michael Levey has recently suggested verbally that it is the original, and a careful examination of the picture confirms this view. The painting of the landscape is of very high quality, and the only part to leave a feeling of doubt is the handling of the two figures in the right foreground, which is surprisingly coarse. This area may, however, have been damaged and restored.

The picture was almost certainly painted as a pair to the *Roman Road* (No. 210), to which it corresponds in general character and in dimensions. Both were engraved by Baudet in a series of four landscapes, of which the other two are the Phocion pair (Nos. 173, 174). This has led to the National Gallery painting being called *Phocion* in early editions of the National Gallery catalogue. It is presumably of the same date as the *Roman Road*, that is to say 1648.

BIBLIOGRAPHY: Montaiglon, Bibl. 13, II, p. 278; Leslie, Bibl. 413a, pp. 84, 297; Smith, No. 309; Grautoff, I, p. 254, II, No. 127; Magne, 1914, p. 217, No. 317; Blunt, Bibl. 972, p. 157; Davies, Bibl. 988a, p. 182, No. 40.

212. LANDSCAPE WITH A WOMAN WASHING HER FEET. 114·5 × 175 cm. National
Gallery of Canada, Ottawa (4587).

HISTORY: Painted in 1650, perhaps for Passart, to whom it belonged (Félibien, IV, p. 62). The Ottawa
picture was probably in the James Fenton sale, Christie, London, 26 ff.ii.1880, lot 120 (cf. Smith, No. 312).
Earl Howe by 1885 (lent by him to the Royal Academy winter exhibition in that year, No. 163); Earl
Howe sale, Trollope, London, 21.vii.1920, lot 99. With Duits, London, 1929; with Durlacher, London,
1930; bt. H. S. Southam, Ottawa; presented to the Gallery in 1944.

DRAWING: Royal Library, Windsor Castle (*CR*, IV, p. 54). A copy after the painting.

ENGRAVING: Attributed to Châtillon (Andresen, No. 456; Wildenstein, No. 188; Davies and Blunt, p. 215, No. 188).

COPIES: 1. Musée Condé, Chantilly. French private collection before the Revolution; left with the restorer Hacquin when the owner emigrated; Reiset collection (Chennevières-Pointel, Bibl. 433, III, p. 151); bt. by the Duc d'Aumale (Grautoff, II, No. 143, and Bibl. 864, p. 337).
2. Musée des Beaux-Arts, Rheims. Bequeathed by Paul Jamot (cf. Hourticq and others, Bibl. 803, p.

136, No. 282; Grautoff, Bibl. 864, p. 337; Jamot, p. 69).
3. In the Pozzo collection (cf. Richardson, *Account*, p. 186; de Brosses, Bibl. 170a, II, p. 455).
4. Felice Maragliane, Genoa, in the early nineteenth century (2 ft. 3 inches × 4 ft.). Mentioned in a manuscript catalogue of the collection among the papers at Attingham Hall, Shropshire.
5. Bt. by Norbert Fischmann, Munich, in 1932 from an English collection (Grautoff, Bibl. 864, p. 367); anon. (=Fischmann) sale, Christie, London, 16.iv.1937, lot 90, presumably bt. in; with Fischmann, London, in 1944.

NOTES: For a discussion of the subject, see text volume pp. 292 f.

BIBLIOGRAPHY: Félibien, IV, p. 62; Smith, No. 312; Friedlaender, 1914, pp. 121, 128; Magne, 1914, p. 216, No. 300; Friedlaender, Bibl. 947, pp. 14, 24; Blunt, Bibl. 972, p. 157; Hubbard, Bibl. 1011, p. 223; Bertin-Mourot, Bibl. 1023, p. 52, No. XXXIV; Licht, pp. 135, 160; Hubbard, Bibl. 1131, p. 100; Bertin-Mourot, Bibl. 1165.1, p. 366; Wild, Bibl. 1185, pp. 15 f.; *Exposition Poussin (Louvre)*, No. 91; Mahon, Bibl. 1338, p. 125, and Bibl. 1367, p. 118.

213. LANDSCAPE WITH A BOY DRINKING FROM A STREAM. 63 × 78 cm. Private
collection. On loan to the National Gallery, London.

HISTORY: Cassiano dal Pozzo; by descent to the Boccapaduli family (see below); Lord Grenville, Dropmore House, Berkshire; by descent to the Fortescue family; sold at Dropmore in 1939, bt. Tomàs Harris; bt. from him by Sir George Leon; bequeathed to his widow, later Mrs. Parrington; presumably sold by her to R. F. Heathcoat Amory; sold by his executors, Sotheby, London, 27.vi.1962, lot 88, bt. by the present owner.

NOTES: The picture and its pair, No. 214, can be traced to the Pozzo collection by the labels and seals on the back, which prove that in 1739 they were given by Cosimo Antonio dal Pozzo to his daughter, Maria Laura, who had married Pietro Paolo Boccapaduli (cf. Blunt, Bibl. 976, p. 186).

When I first published these landscapes (*loc. cit.*), I proposed a date of about 1644–46. I now believe them to be a little earlier, among the first works executed by the artist after his return to Rome at the end of 1642, that is to say probably in 1643–44. Mahon (Bibl. 1338, p. 120, and Bibl. 1367, p. XIII, and *L'ideale classico* (Bologna), Nos. 64, 65) dates them 1638–40, but seeing them at Bologna before the opening of the exhibition next to the *St. Matthew* (No. 87) and also next to the *Manna* (No. 21) and the *Finding of Moses* (No. 12) I was confirmed in my view that they were nearer in date to the former than to the latter.

BIBLIOGRAPHY: Blunt, Bibl. 972, p. 156, and Bibl. 976, p. 186; Bertin-Mourot, Bibl. 1023, p. 52, No. XXXI; Dorival, Bibl. 1088, p. 51; Licht, p. 135; Rinehart, Bibl. 1281, pp. 28, 29; Mahon, Bibl. 1338, p. 120; *L'ideale classico* (Bologna), Nos. 64, 65; Mahon, Bibl. 1367, p. XIII.

214. LANDSCAPE WITH TRAVELLERS RESTING. 63 × 78 cm. Private collection. On
loan to the National Gallery, London.

HISTORY: See No. 213.

NOTES: See No. 213.

BIBLIOGRAPHY: See No. 213, and Bertin-Mourot, Bibl. 1023, p. 52, No. XXX.

215. LANDSCAPE WITH A MAN PURSUED BY A SNAKE. 65×76 cm. Sir Anthony Blunt, London.

HISTORY: Probably Cassiano dal Pozzo (see below). Possibly Marquis of Bute sale, Christie, London, 7 f.vi.1822, lot 80 ('A bold and fine landscape with a figure angling'). The present picture was bt. by Duncan Grant in Paris soon after 1920; bt. from him by the present owner, 1964.

NOTES: Richardson (*Account*, p. 186) mentions among Poussin's paintings in the Pozzo collection: 'The Landskip where the man flies from the serpent.' This has generally been taken to be a copy of the National Gallery *Landscape with a Man killed by a Serpent* (No. 209), but the description given by the Président de Brosses (Bibl. 170a, II, p. 455) of what must evidently be the same picture makes this explanation not altogether convincing, for he calls it 'l'Homme poursuivi par un serpent'. This description would, on the other hand, exactly fit the present picture. The provenance from Pozzo is confirmed by the fact that the picture is very close in style and almost identical in its dimensions with the two landscapes which certainly belonged to him (Nos. 213, 214).

Poussin seems here to have been experimenting with the theme of fear, which he developed more fully in the National Gallery landscape.

BIBLIOGRAPHY: Richardson, *Account*, p. 186; de Brosses, Bibl. 170a, II, p. 455; Blunt, Bibl. 1426, pp. 63 f., 74.

216. LANDSCAPE WITH BUILDINGS. 120×187 cm. Museo del Prado, Madrid (2310).

HISTORY: Recorded in the collection of Philip V at La Granja in 1746.

ENGRAVING: Attributed to Châtillon (Andresen, No. 459; Wildenstein, No. 191).

NOTES: Attributed to Gaspard Dughet by D. Wild (Bibl. 1184, p. 168). Accepted by all other writers on Poussin.

Dated by Grautoff (II, No. 128) 1645–50; *c.* 1651 by Sterling (*Exposition Poussin (Louvre)*, p. 264), followed by Mahon (Bibl. 1367, pp. XIV, 120). Sterling plausibly suggests that the Prado picture may be the composition mentioned by Félibien (IV, p. 63) as having been painted for Pointel as a pair to the *Storm* (No. 217) of 1651.

BIBLIOGRAPHY: Smith, No. 314; Friedlaender, 1914, p. 255; Grautoff, I, p. 254, II, No. 128; Magne, 1914, p. 216, No. 301; Blunt, Bibl. 972, p. 157; Wild, Bibl. 1184, p. 168, and Bibl. 1185, p. 25; *Exposition Poussin (Louvre)*, pp. 264 f.; Mahon, Bibl. 1338, pp. 125, 127, and Bibl. 1367, pp. XIV, 120.

217. LANDSCAPE WITH A STORM. Original lost.

HISTORY: Painted for Pointel in 1651, with a pair representing 'un tems calme et serein', which cannot be identified with certainty (but see No. 216); in 1685 belonged to Bay, a merchant of Lyons (Félibien, IV, p. 63).

ENGRAVING: Attributed to Châtillon (Andresen, No. 457; Wildenstein, No. 189).

COPIES: 1. A version appeared in the sale of Fürst Adolph zu Schaumburg-Lippe, Helbig, Munich, 1930, lot 236, attributed to Gaspard Dughet.
2. In the possession of Claudine Bouzonnet Stella in 1697 (*Testament*, Bibl. 107, p. 40).

Pictures recorded in the following sales may be connected with the Pointel composition:

1. J. B. de Troy sale, Remy, Paris, 9.iv.1764, lot 81 (33×48 inches).
2. Anon. sale, Christie, London, 28 ff.iii.1771, second day, lot 52 (18×28 inches).
3. Anon. (=Vigné) sale, Remy, Paris, 1.iv.1773, lot 79 (36×48 inches; cf. Beaumont, Bibl. 627, p. 644).
4. Bragge sale, Langford, London, 5 ff.ii.1778, third day, lot 66.
5. Bonnemaison sale, Lebrun, Paris, 15.vii.1802, lot 113.
6. Anon. sale, Christie, London, 7.vi.1829, lot 54.

BIBLIOGRAPHY: Félibien, III, pp. 54 f., IV, p. 63; Loménie de Brienne, pp. 215, 221; Florent Le Comte, III, p. 31; Le Blanc, Bibl. 180, p. 158; Smith, No. 315; Beaumont, Bibl. 627, p. 644; Friedlaender, 1914, p. 122; Grautoff, II, p. 259; Magne, 1914, p. 216, No. 299, p. 217, No. 321; Wild, Bibl. 1184, p. 168 (as a fragment).

SCULPTURE

218. Copy of the SLEEPING ARIADNE. Wax. Height 29 cm.; length 55 cm.; depth 20 cm. Musée du Louvre, Paris.

HISTORY: The wax was bt. by the collector Gatteaux in 1855 at the sale of Duchesne, keeper of the Cabinet des Estampes at the Bibliothèque Nationale (Paris, 25.v.1855, lot 168). It was supposed to have been bt. by an ancestor of his from a collateral descendant of Paul Fréart de Chantelou (cf. Charageat, Bibl. 1087, p. 36). If this tradition is sound, the wax was no doubt obtained by Chantelou direct from the artist.

NOTES: Since no comparable works by the artist exist, there is no basis for a stylistic comparison which might confirm the attribution or throw doubt on it, but the quality of the wax is so high that there is no reason whatsoever to doubt that it is from the hand of Poussin himself.

For the same reason the question of dating is difficult. It is at first sight tempting to associate the model with the statement of Bellori (p. 412) that Poussin made wax models after Titian in the years immediately after his arrival in Rome, but the grandeur of the figure and the clarity and sharpness of the draperies point to a later period. There is no reason to think that Poussin did not go on making wax models beyond his early years—indeed we know that he used the medium for the little figures from which he painted his compositions—and the *Ariadne* may well have been modelled in the 1640's or even 1650's.

In Poussin's time the celebrated Roman statue in the Vatican (rep. Charageat, *loc. cit.*), of which the wax is a copy, was generally believed to be a Cleopatra, and the name of Ariadne was only attached to it later.

BIBLIOGRAPHY: Duplessis, Bibl. 526, pp. 341 f.; Schneider, Bibl. 688, p. 251; Brinckmann, Bibl. 768, III, p. 5; Jamot, Bibl. 989, p. 22 note 4; Charageat, Bibl. 1087, pp. 34 ff.; Licht, p. 102; Bouleau-Rabaud, Bibl. 1229, p. 256.

THE MARBLE HERMS FROM VAUX-LE-VICOMTE, NOW IN THE GARDENS OF VERSAILLES

In 1655 the Surintendant Nicolas Fouquet sent his brother, the Abbé Louis Fouquet, to Rome, partly for political reasons and partly to collect works of art for the houses that he was building and decorating. On 27 December the Abbé wrote to his brother from Rome as follows about Poussin: 'M. Poussin . . . vous fera faire des Termes admirables; ce seront des statues qui vaudront celles de l'antiquité. Jusques' à présent on a travaillé aux modèles, aptitudes, etc.' (*Lettres de Fouquet*, Bibl. 24a, p. 104). On 29 February the following year he wrote again: 'Vos Termes l'occuperont bien encore deux mois' (*ibid.*). We have no further information about the completion or the despatch of the statues, but the fact that Poussin actually designed such a series of herms for Fouquet is confirmed by Bellori, who writes as follows.

Diceva che la pittura, e la scoltura erano un' arte sola d'imitatione, dipendenti dal disegno, non in altro differenti che nel modo; benche la prima per la finta apparenza più artificiosa. E ben lo diede à vedere nelle statue de' Termini, per la Villa, che faceva Monsiù Fochet: lavorò di sua mano li modelli di creta grandi quanto le statue al naturale, eseguite da diversi Scultori, in casa de' quali io lo viddi più volte lavorare di stecco la creta, e modellare con facilità grande. Non mancava certamente à lui altro che la pratica del marmo, per essere ottimo Scultore, havendo tutta l'arte e chi vedrà in Francia queste statue, autenticherà la fede, poi che sono trà le megliori delle moderne. Rappresentò li varij Genij de' fiori, e de' frutti della terra in figure di huomini, e di donne con tutto il petto humano sopra Termini, overo herme, che dovevano disporsi ne' viali del giardino. Evvi il Dio Pane con la sampogna pastorale, coronato di pino con un ramo in mano, il Dio Fauno ridente inghirlandato d' ellera il petto, Pallade cinto l'elmo d'ulivo, col ramo nella destra, e'l serpente: Cerere, Bacco con le spiche, e l'uve, et altre, ninfe, e numi, con seni di fiori, e di frutti, e corna d'abbondanza in contrasegno della fertile, e delitiosa villa. Con queste disegnò due vasi all' antica, grandi circa quattro palmi, con li manichi avvolti in serpenti, che fece lavorare, et eseguire di marmo Africano antico' (pp. 436 f.).

Bellori already knew Poussin personally by 1655–56, and we must therefore accept his evidence as proving the somewhat surprising fact that the artist actually made full-size models for the herms commissioned by Fouquet.

There is nothing in the Abbé Fouquet's letters or in Bellori's account to show for which of Fouquet's houses the herms were commissioned, but, if, as is generally believed (cf. Cordey, Bibl. 770.1, p. 15), he had begun building at Vaux-le-Vicomte in 1656, it is probable that they were originally planned for this château, on which Fouquet was to lavish all his efforts and of which the gardens were to be the chief splendour.

In any case they were certainly at Vaux by 1661, when the Surintendant was arrested, and they can be traced from there to their present location at Versailles in the Quinconces du Nord et du Midi, formerly the Bosquets du Dauphin et de la Girandole, on either side of the Tapis Vert.

After the arrest of Fouquet various inventories were made of his possessions, one of which, drawn up at Vaux on 17 July 1665, contains the following items.

> Item dans le grand parterre dix termes demy corps avec leurs bras et attribus, de marbre blanc moderne de six pieds et demi de hault, prisez six cens livres piece, font ensemble . . . . VI^M l.t.
>
> Plus un autre terme de la mesme suitte encore enquaissé estant dans l'un des passages du chasteau, prisé six cens livres cy. . . . . VI^c l.t.
>
> Item deux autre terme de pareille grandeur demy corps avec les bras, de marbre blanc moderne posez a costé de la gerbe au dessus de la grande cascade, prisez quatre cens cinquante livres piece font neuf cens livres cy. . . . . .IX^c l.t.
>
> (Bonnaffé, Bibl. 572, p. 70.)

From this we learn that in 1665 there were ten herms, standing on the *grand parterre*, and one more of the same series in the château, still not unpacked. They were valued at 600 livres apiece. In addition, standing above the Grande Cascade, there were two more herms of the same size, but valued at 450 livres. These must either have been of inferior quality compared with the main series, or damaged and therefore valued at a lower price.

Eighteen years later Louis XIV bought eleven herms from Fouquet's son, the Comte de Vaux. The *Comptes des bâtiments* (II, pp. 328, 463) show that they were transported from Vaux to Versailles in December 1683 and paid for in 1684.

The first record of the herms at Versailles is supplied by the engravings in Simon Thomassin's *Recüeil des Figures, Groupes, Thermes, Fontaines, Vases et autres Ornemens tels qu'ils se voyent a prese.^t dans le Château et Parc de Versailles* (Bibl. 109), published without date, but based on drawings made in 1689, as the author tells us in the dedicatory epistle to the King. Thomassin reproduces thirteen herms which he attributes to Poussin and which can be identified with existing herms in the two Quinconces at Versailles as follows, though in several cases his titles can be shown to be incorrect:

Hercule (Thomassin, Pl. 179, No. 220 below); Minerve (*ibid.*, Pl. 180, No. 225 below); Vertumne (*ibid.*, Pl. 181, cf. No. 221 below); Pomone (*ibid.*, Pl. 182, No. 226 below); Morphée (*ibid.*, Pl. 183, No. 223 below); Flore (*ibid.*, Pl. 184, No. 227 below); Un Moissonneur (*ibid.*, Pl. 185, No. 229 below); La Libéralité (*ibid.*, Pl. 186, No. 228 below); Pan (*ibid.*, Pl. 187, No. 222 below); Bacchante (*ibid.*, Pl. 188, see p. 157 below); Faune (*ibid.*, Pl. 189, No. 219 below); Flore (*ibid.*, Pl. 190, No. 224 below); Bacchus (*ibid.*, Pl. 191, No. 230 below).

For reasons that are not apparent Thomassin does not reproduce the Ceres (No. 231 below), which is, however, recorded in the guide books from 1701 onwards and appears in fact to have formed part of the series as originally set up in the two Bosquets between 1683 and 1689.

In 1701 Piganiol de La Force in the first edition of his *Nouvelle description . . . de Versailles et de Marly* (Bibl. 124, II, pp. 282 f., 314 f.) names fourteen herms in the two Bosquets. In the Bosquet de la Girandole, now the Quinconce du Midi, he lists the following: Minerve; Morphée; La Jeunesse (by elimination this must be Thomassin's Moissonneur); Femme qui tient des raisins (Thomassin's Bacchante); Pomone; Jeune homme qui tient une massue (Thomassin's Vertumne); Flore; Hercule; and in the Bosquet du Dauphin, now the Quinconce du Nord, he gives the remainder: L'Abondance (Thomassin's Libéralité); Faune; Cerès; Bacchus; Un Satyre (Thomassin's Pan); Flore.

Curiously enough in later editions, from 1713 onwards, this list is different and incomplete; there is no mention of the Minerva or of 'La Jeunesse' in the Bosquet de la Girandole, and the Faunus is omitted in the account of the Bosquet du Dauphin (cf. Bibl. 124a, II, pp. 141, 168). Since, however, they still stand in the positions described in the 1701 edition, it seems likely that this is simply a mistake on the author's part. All the editions of Piganiol also mention two herms of Summer and Winter by Théodon, which then stood one in each of the Bosquets, whereas now they are both in the Quinconce du Nord. They are both engraved by Thomassin as after Théodon.

A. N. Dézallier d'Argenville in his *Voyage Pittoresque des environs de Paris* (Bibl. 200.1, pp. 97 and 103) gives a slightly different list of titles for the herms. In the Bosquet de la Girandole he mentions Priapus, Pomona, Flora, Hercules and Morpheus, and in the Bosquet du Dauphin Isis, Abundance, Faunus, and two herms representing Satyrs. In addition he mentions the Flora and Bacchus, but describes them as antique. His identifications are so confused that they do not help us to a clearer understanding of the statues.

Some idea of how the herms looked can be gained from a poor engraving of the Bosquet de la Girandole, published by Mariette. This shows four of them standing against a tall trellis, which would have supplied the background so sadly lacking in the present arrangement, where they stand completely isolated and can be viewed from all sides. In the engraving the trellis in the foreground has been made lower to clear the view into the Bosquet, but this is no doubt simply a device of the engraver. The alteration of the setting took place in the years 1774–76, when the Bosquets were transformed into Quinconces and the fountains abolished (cf. Dulaure, Bibl. 282, II, p. 292, and P. Verlet, *Versailles*, Paris, 1961, p. 635).

The first problem that needs to be examined is that there are now fourteen herms, all attributed to Poussin by Piganiol in 1701 and thirteen of them engraved as after Poussin by Thomassin, whereas according to the documents Louis XIV only bought eleven herms from Vaux-le-Vicomte, presumably but not certainly the eleven listed as belonging to the same series in 1665.

At this stage of the argument it will be convenient to continue to refer to the statues by the titles given to them by Thomassin, though in several instances he can be shown to have been mistaken. Ten of the herms are similar in general conception—though, as will be seen, they vary in execution—and have identical shafts and bases, and it is reasonable to assume that they form the bulk of the set acquired by Louis XIV from Vaux-le-Vicomte. They are the following: Faunus (No. 219); Hercules (No. 220); Vertumnus (No. 221); Pan (No. 222); Morpheus (No. 223); the two of Flora (Nos. 224, 227); Minerva (No. 225); Pomona (No. 226); Liberality (No. 228). The obvious solution to the problem would be to look for one more herm to complete the series, but this solution will not work because the ten do not include two—Bacchus (No. 230) and Ceres (No. 231)—which are mentioned by Bellori as among those designed by Poussin, and of which herms exist at Versailles, though of different types. We are forced, therefore, to look for a different solution.

One of the herms, the Bacchante can be immediately ruled out as not belonging to the original series. Not only does it have a different base, but its style is entirely alien to that of the main series. It is conceived in a mode of rhetoric unthinkable in either Rome or France in the 1650's, but perfectly in accordance with the art of Versailles in the 1680's, though it is a particularly feeble and clumsy example of this style. Moreover, it would not fit with Bellori's statement that the herms represented deities connected with gardens.

The problem of the Bacchus (No. 230), the Ceres (No. 231) and the Moissonneur (No. 229) is more complicated. At first sight their general appearance is so clumsy and unsatisfactory that, taking into account the fact that they have bases and shafts of designs different from the first ten, it would seem obvious that they should be dismissed out of hand; but a close examination shows that in each case the head is of a different marble from the rest and of far higher quality. Moreover, in style the heads correspond to those of the main series. The Moissonneur is close to the Vertumnus; the Bacchus, so strangely feminine, is like the two Floras, and the Ceres wears a wreath composed of ears of corn which have the stylized simplicity of Pan's pine-needles.

The base of the Moissonneur corresponds with that of the Bacchante, and since the treatment of the drapery is also similar, the statue—except for the head—is probably from the same hand. In the case of the Bacchus the figure grows awkwardly out of the shaft, the action of pouring wine from the jug into the bowl is unconvincing, and the action of the snake unaccountable. Furthermore Bellori describes the Bacchus as being accompanied by grapes, which is not here the case. In the Ceres the head does not fit the torso, and the drapery is slovenly in treatment. It seems possible, therefore, that heads from Poussin's herms for Vaux were acquired by Louis XIV and made up so as to complete the series.

It is true that the accounts speak only of the transport of complete herms, but it is not impossible that fragments of others may have been acquired by the king. The gardens of Vaux-le-Vicomte were badly neglected after the arrest of Fouquet, and it is more than likely that the statues suffered considerably during the twenty-two years which intervened before the herms were bought by Louis XIV. Several of those which are still complete—particularly No. 226—have in fact been seriously broken and repaired, though it is impossible to tell whether this damage occurred before or after their arrival at Versailles. It may well be, therefore, that some were so much damaged that only the heads could be saved and that new torsos and shafts were made for them. Among the sources of such fragments may have been the two herms mentioned in the inventory of 1665 as standing beside fountains above the big cascade.

Even if this hypothesis is accepted, however, there remains the problem that on the above showing there would be ten complete herms and three heads, all of which appear to belong to the series brought from Vaux, whereas the accounts only mention a total of eleven herms. For this no positive solution can be offered, but it is not inconceivable that, after the eleven herms were transported to Versailles, some further fragments were brought from Vaux, perhaps in the same waggon as other objects, such as trees or tanks of carp, which at various times were carried from Vaux to Versailles. A single head would probably have been considered of so little importance that its purchase and its transport might not be individually recorded in the *Comptes des bâtiments*.

It is not easy to distinguish the various herms originally at Vaux. There are two sets of herms still *in situ*: a huge series of Janus-headed herms in coarse *grès* on the grille to the right and left of the main entrance, and another set, eight foot in height, now eleven in number but obviously planned to be twelve, which stand against a clipped hedge along the right-hand side of the garden as one comes from the château. The inventory of 1665 (Bonnaffé, *op. cit.*, p. 69) records four herms in this position, together with a statue of Flora in the semi-circle which breaks the line of the hedge in the middle, and the present number has probably been made up by moving across the parterre six of the herms which according to the inventory stood against the opposite hedge along the left-hand side of the garden, together with two more recorded in an unspecified position.

The herms which are assumed to be those now at Versailles are described as being 'dans le grand parterre' (Bonnaffe, *op. cit.* p. 70). This parterre is composed of two parts separated by a circular fountain. The upper part, nearer to the château, consists of two large *broderie* beds, and the lower part of two lawns surrounding fountains. These lawns are rectangular in shape, but their two edges facing the central path of the garden are set back at the corners. An early engraving by Pérelle (see illustration facing p. 153) shows herms at each corner of the low wall surrounding these lawns on the sides facing the central path, making twelve in all. The herms are too small in the engraving to be identified with certainty, but it is reasonable to suppose that they are the set designed by Poussin.

Stylistically the complete herms and heads which have been singled out as probably belonging to the original series brought from Vaux to Versailles fall into two main groups. The first is markedly Baroque, whereas the second is much more classical. To the first belong the Pan, the Morpheus, the Faunus, and the Hercules. These are free in movement, vigorous in modelling, naturalistic and deeply cut in the detail of flowers and fruit, and varied in the treatment of texture. In fact they conform in execution to an idiom current among the less extreme Baroque sculptors active in Rome at this time. The freedom of execution, however, does no more than veil the fundamental classicism of the series, for each herm is strictly designed so as to present three main views, one frontal and one from each side. The remaining herms are completely classical not only in their main design but in their regular features, in the disposition of their hair, lightly and delicately carved, and in the severity of the drapery. It is easy to understand why Louis Fouquet should have said that the herms would equal in quality the statues of Antiquity, and why Bellori should have so warmly praised them as being 'among the best modern statues', for they embodied those principles of classicism which he had for so long supported against the protagonists of the full Baroque.

In the present state of our knowledge it would be difficult to suggest a name for the sculptor of either group—even assuming that each is the work of a single hand, which is far from certain—but it seems likely that the author of the Baroque group was Italian, perhaps a sculptor attached to the circle of the 'moderate' Algardi rather than a member of Bernini's studio, though it is worth remembering that one of the latter, Carlo Matteo, almost certainly owned at least one painting by Poussin (see No. 32).

The iconography of the herms presents a number of problems. In many cases the titles given by Thomassin are entirely convincing: Pan, Faunus, Hercules, Pomona, Minerva, Bacchus, and Ceres bear their traditional attributes and their identification is easy. Thomassin is probably also correct in giving the name of Liberalité to No. 228, since the attributes held by the figure correspond exactly to those given to the virtue by Cesare Ripa, *Iconologia overo descrittione di diverse imagini cavate dall' antichità . . .*, Rome, 1603, p. 291. On the other hand Piganiol de La Force is not far wrong when he calls the statue Abundance, for the liberality ascribed to the patron would be based on the abundance of his fields and gardens.

In other instances, however, the titles given to the herms by Thomassin cannot be accepted. The most disquieting feature of his identifications is that he gives the name of Flora to two statues (Nos. 224, 227). As will be seen later, it is not inconceivable that the series should contain more than one herm of the same deity, but with the Flora there is no need to make such a hypothesis, since the figure of No. 227, who holds roses only, is much more likely to be Venus, to whom this flower was sacred (cf. Cartari, p. 434). The deity presented in No. 224 carries a garland of mixed flowers, which is appropriate to Flora.

The most obviously incorrect of Thomassin's titles is his Vertumnus. The figure carries a club, a cornucopia, and a lion's skin, of which the mask hangs down at the back. The conclusion is therefore inescapable that he is Hercules, who normally carries the first two attributes and who was frequently shown in Antiquity with the cornucopia, because, according to one account, the cornucopia was the horn of Achelous, which was broken off during the combat with Hercules (cf. text volume, p. 152).

It may seem gratuitous to eliminate a second Flora and then introduce a second Hercules, but it is not impossible that this particular deity would have been represented twice in a single series. Hercules was the god most closely associated by the ancients with gardens, primarily because of his connection with the garden of the Hesperides, but also in his capacity as a protector of men against evil forces (cf. Pierre Grimal, *Les Jardins romains*, Paris, 1943, pp. 79 ff., 340 ff.). The two herms from Vaux emphasize these two aspects of the god; in one he is shown holding the apples of the Hesperides in his left hand and across the front of the shaft is twined the dead body of the dragon which guarded the tree on which they grew; in the other the club and the cornucopia allude to Hercules' function as a protector of men. As will be seen later, Poussin probably had a particular precedent in mind when he made this duplication.

The herm described by Thomassin as Morpheus (No. 223) cannot in fact represent that deity, who would have to carry poppies as his attribute. In fact the statue corresponds in all major respects to the figure of Priapus, the god of gardens, as described by Cartari (p. 357). According to this authority Priapus should be shown 'in forma di huomo con barba, e chioma rabbuffatta'. Admittedly he should be shown naked and with his particular attribute prominent, but it is not surprising that in seventeenth-century France these details should have been suppressed. The artist does, however, follow Cartari (p. 358) in another feature. He writes of Priapus: 'Lo vestirono alle volte anchora con un panno, ch'ei teneva raccolto con mano, e portava nel grembo frutti di ogni sorte.' Admittedly in the herm at Versailles the fruit consists only of figs, but they are appropriate to the god, since they are a symbol of lechery and the phallus carried at the ceremonies of Priapus was made from the wood of the fig tree (cf. Horace, *Satires*, Bk. I, Satire 8, 1, quoted by Cartari, *loc. cit.*). It is quite possible that Priapus was not thought a suitable deity to be displayed in royal gardens, and his name may have been changed to Morpheus for reasons of modesty. Some slight support for the identification of this herm as Priapus is provided by Dézallier d'Argenville's account of the series (*op. cit.*), as he mentions this god as one of those represented, but his evidence is not of much value, since he also mentions Morpheus. Indeed it seems more likely that he meant to identify the Pan as the representation of Priapus.

It is worth noticing that the so-called Morpheus is very close to a statue of Vertumnus engraved by Montfaucon (*Antiquity explained*, London, 1721, Supplement, Pl. opp. p. 93), which in his day stood in Colbert's park at Sceaux. The statue seems to have disappeared, and from the engraving it might well be a forgery rather than a genuine work of ancient Roman art, but it was evidently accepted in the seventeenth century, and Poussin may have intended his herm to have an allusion to Vertumnus, as it would be surprising for a series of herms to include Pomona but not Vertumnus; on the other hand it must be remembered that the series may never have been completed.

The most difficult herm to identify is the one called by Thomassin *Un Moissonneur* (No. 229) and by Piganiol de La Force *La Jeunesse*. The former title is evidently wrong, because, although the sculptor who made the lower part of the statue gave the figure a miniature sickle to hold, the head—the only original part—is crowned with a wreath composed of laurel at the back and a five-petalled flower, not clearly identifiable, in the front. The laurel would suggest Apollo and the flower might be an allusion to Hyacinthus.

If the identifications proposed above are accepted, all the herms belonging to the original series can be related to the theme defined by Bellori: 'Rappresentò li varii Genii de' fiori, e de' frutti della terra.' Some

Pan (Cat. No. 222).

Hercules (Cat. No. 220).

Hercules (Cat. No. 220). Detail of Lion's skin.

Pan (Cat. No. 222). Detail of hand and fir cones.

Pan (Cat. No. 222).   Detail of head.

Faunus (Cat. No. 219).

Priapus (Cat. No. 223).

Flora (Cat. No. 224).   Venus (Cat. No. 227).

Flora (Cat. No. 224).   Detail of head.

Minerva (Cat. No. 225).

Pomona (Cat. No. 226).

Minerva (Cat. No. 225).   Detail of head.

Hercules (Cat. No. 221).

Liberality (Cat. No. 228).

Liberality (Cat. No. 228).   Detail of head.

Apollo (?) (Cat. No. 229).   Bacchus (Cat. No. 230).

Bacchus (Cat. No. 230).   Upper part.

A Bacchante.

Ceres (Cat. No. 231).

Ceres (Cat. No. 231). Upper part.

Hercules (Cat. No. 220).

Engraving by S. Thomassin.

Venus (Flora) (Cat. No. 227).

Engraving by S. Thomassin.

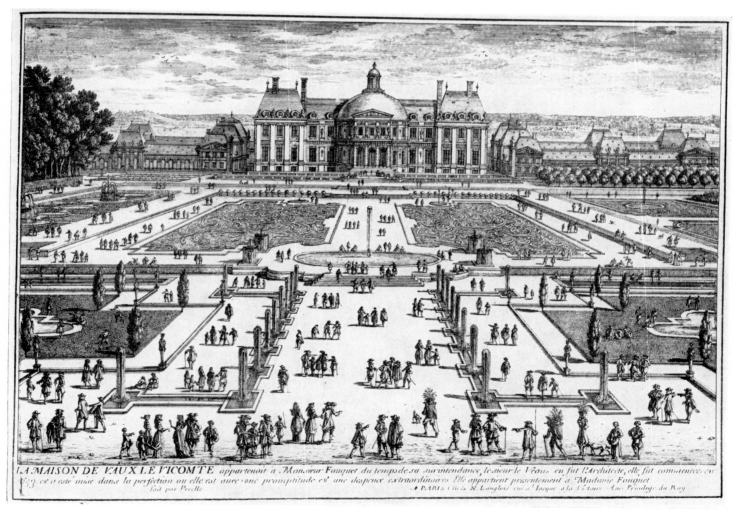

Vaux-le-Vicomte.   Engraving by Pérelle, probably between 1661 and 1670.

By courtesy of the Master and Fellows of Magdalene College, Cambridge.

of the series—Liberality, Pomona, Flora—would have a general allusion to the fertility of gardens and fields; others would be associated with a particular plant or tree; Priapus with figs, Faunus with ivy, Pan with the pine, Ceres with corn, Bacchus with the vine, Minerva with the olive, Venus with the rose, Hercules with the apples. If the so-called Moissonneur is in fact Apollo, he may belong to the first group and play the part of the sun, the source of fertility and plant life, or he may be specifically associated with the flower that appears in his wreath. Faunus may also play a double part; in the statue he is cinctured with ivy, but he was venerated by the Romans as a god of agriculture in general.

Faced with the for him quite unusual commission to design a series of sculptured herms, Poussin seems to have done what one would have expected him to do: he turned to Antiquity for his models. He seems to have found two sources, one carved and one written, which gave him the inspiration that he sought; and there is reason to believe that in his mind the two sources were connected.

In the 1650's there was in Rome one—and apparently only one—famous series of ancient herms used to decorate a garden, that in the Villa Ludovisi, which ornamented the Piazza in front of the Casino del l'Aurora (the sculptures in both the Cesi and the Pio da Carpi gardens, which included herms, had been scattered by the 1630's, some items passing to Cardinal Ludovisi (cf. Christian Hülsen, *Römische Antikengärten des XVI. Jahrhunderts*, Heidelberg, 1917, pp. 1 ff., 34 ff. According to the inventory of the collection drawn up in 1633 there were eight such herms. Two have disappeared, but the remaining six are now in the Museo delle Terme (cf. T. Schreiber, *Die antiken Bildwerke der Villa Ludovisi in Rom*, Leipzig, 1880, Nos. 1, 3, 8, 55, 60, 62; four of the herms are catalogued and reproduced in E. Paribeni, *Museo Nazionale Romano, Sculture Greche del V secolo*, Rome, 1953, Nos. 9, 34, 35, 104). Unlike the normal type of herm, which consists simply of a head set on a shaft, the Ludovisi series are all half-length figures. The male effigies grow into the shaft at the groin, whereas the female are equipped with drapery which covers the greater part of the shaft. In this respect Poussin follows the Ludovisi series, though in most of his male figures the join between human and architectural forms is covered with drapery or an animal's skin.

It is of interest to notice that the Ludovisi series includes a Hercules carrying the cornucopia (Paribeni, *op. cit.*, No. 35), and another herm (*ibid.*, No. 34) which, though usually regarded as representing Theseus, has been more plausibly identified by some scholars as a second Hercules. Unfortunately the 1633 inventory does not give specific names to the herms and we have, therefore, no means of knowing whether this particular herm was taken in Poussin's time to represent Hercules or Theseus, but there can be no question that he studied it when he was preparing his own series, for its style is reflected in the conception and modelling of both the herms which appear to represent Hercules.

In other herms Poussin made use of different classical models—the Minerva is related to statues of the goddess then in the Ludovisi and Giustiniani collections; and Faunus seems to be based on a bust in the latter collection—but the inspiration for the series as a whole must have been the cycle that Poussin saw in the gardens of the Villa Ludovisi, of which, it is important to notice, four at least go back to Greek originals of the fifth century B.C.

According to Paribeni (*op. cit.*, No. 9) it was for long maintained that the Ludovisi herms had belonged to Cicero and that they were the actual herms of which he speaks with such enthusiasm in his letters to Atticus (I, 1, 4 and 10) as ornaments of the gymnasium in his villa at Tusculum. This supposed connection would have been enough to give the statues a peculiar significance for Poussin and would have singled them out for him as the ideal models for his own series. It is indeed probable that in planning the herms for Vaux Poussin was attempting to recreate the sort of sculpture cycle which he imagined might have adorned an ancient Roman villa, more specifically that of Cicero at Tusculum.

At first sight it is difficult to see any connection between the herms and Poussin's painting, but in fact the statues represent the very gods and goddesses of fertility, fruit and gardens that appear with such striking frequency in the master's paintings and drawings, and, although it is unlikely that Poussin intended any hidden meanings in composing this series of herms, he would have felt at home in modelling Flora, Ceres, and Pomona, or Hercules and Priapus.

An interest in ancient gardens and their decoration can be traced back to an early phase in Poussin's work. The *Kingdom of Flora* of 1631 (No. 155) not only shows all the heroes and heroines of Ovid's stories who were transformed into flowers but represents them in a setting which corresponds to the current conception of an ancient garden: on the right the pergola, on the left the statue of Priapus and the fountain springing from a grotto; many of these elements are taken from an engraving of a garden after Primaticcio. A number of the themes included in the *Kingdom of Flora* occur in other early paintings by Poussin. The type of herm seen in the *Flora* is also to be found in one of the Chigi Children's Bacchanals

(No. 193), the National Gallery *Bacchanal before a Herm* (No. 141), and the Morrison *Triumph of Pan* (No. 136). The connection with horticulture is even more evident in the preparatory drawings for the *Triumph*: two show putti in the process of gathering grapes for the vintage (*CR*, III, pp. 24 ff., Nos. 187, 193), and another (*ibid.*, No. 192) shows the scene under a vine trellis. The São Paulo *Dance in honour of Priapus* (No. 176) is a more explicit statement of the artist's interest in gardens, and the theme is taken up again in the *Bacchanal in front of a Temple* (No. 140), executed, I believe, in the 1650's, that is to say, at a date not far removed from the planning of the herms. There are indeed close resemblances between the painting and the series of statues: the satyr in the *Bacchanal* is very close in type to the herm of Pan; the young votaries of Bacchus are strikingly like the Faunus, and the seated and dancing Bacchantes recall, not the Bacchante among the Versailles herms but the Flora or the Venus. In short the herms are not nearly as eccentric as one would at first sight suppose in the work of Poussin, but are evidence of an interest which was apparent in the artist's work from the 1620's.

It is not easy to imagine Poussin consenting—particularly in his later years—to make designs and models which were to be executed by others in a medium strange to him, but the evidence that he did so is overwhelming, and in many of the statues—the Pan, the Faunus, the Flora, and the Venus—the sculptors succeeded to a remarkable extent in capturing his spirit and infusing it into the marble. It is perhaps not unreasonable to be reminded of the aged Renoir giving the young sculptor Guino such precise guidance that the bronzes produced as a result of their collaboration are rightly regarded as typical and important examples of Renoir's own late style.

GENERAL BIBLIOGRAPHY: *Lettres de Louis Fouquet*, Bibl. 24a, p. 104; *Comptes des bâtiments*, II, pp. 328, 463; Bellori, pp. 436 f.; Thomassin, Bibl. 109, Pls. 179 ff.; Piganiol de La Force, Bibl. 124, II, pp. 282 f., 314 f.; Dézallier, 1762, IV, pp. 32 f.; Dézallier d'Argenville, Bibl. 200.1, pp. 97, 103; Dulaure, Bibl. 282, II, pp. 292 f.; Bonnaffé, Bibl. 572, pp. 69 f.; Nolhac, Bibl. 716.1, pp. 107 f.; Francastel, Bibl. 839.1, p. 243; Puvis de Chavannes, Bibl. 878.1, pp. 141 ff., and Bibl. 886, pp. 93 ff.; Coural, Bibl. 1240.

In the following catalogue entries the heights given refer to the herms alone, without the tall pedestals on which they stand. The measurement of six-and-a-half feet given in the inventory of 1665 corresponds roughly to the height of the actual herms and proves that the pedestals (which measure about 75 cm.) were made after the statues reached Versailles. The herms themselves stand on bases which are approximately 33 cm. wide by 25 cm. deep. Where the names given by Thomassin do not agree with what I believe to be the correct titles, they are given in brackets after the true name.

219. FAUNUS. Marble. Height: 201 cm. Versailles, Quinconce du Nord.

NOTES: The tip of the bent stick, the first finger of the right hand, and the end of the lion's skin are repaired.

Very close to Pan (No. 222) in its movement and in the rough cutting of the animal's skin.

Poussin has based his Faunus on an ancient bust of the same subject formerly in the Giustiniani collection (*Galleria Giustiniana*, Rome, *c.* 1640, I, Pl. 48).

BIBLIOGRAPHY: See above, and Thomassin, Bibl. 109, Pl. 189; Coural, Bibl. 1240, Fig. 3.

220. HERCULES. Marble. Height: 205 cm. Versailles, Quinconce du Midi.

NOTES: Two areas of the shaft and the ends of the tails of snake and lion's skin are repaired. The left hand holding the apples is of different marble and may possibly be a fragment of an ancient statue.

Thomassin's engraving shows drapery hanging between the two arms of the hero, where at present the serpent is coiled, but this must be a mistake. There are no signs of recutting, and the head of the serpent, which hangs against the lion's skin, is clearly original.

Poussin no doubt had in mind as a model for this herm the famous bronze statue now in the Capitoline Museum, which was discovered in the pontificate of Sixtus IV.

BIBLIOGRAPHY: See above, and Thomassin, Bibl. 109, Pl. 179; Coural, Bibl. 1240, Fig. 5.

221. HERCULES (VERTUMNUS). Marble. Height: 213 cm. Versailles, Quinconce du Midi.

NOTES: The tip of the nose is repaired, and there are several cracks on the back and the stomach.

Thomassin gives the name of Vertumnus to this herm, but it must in fact represent Hercules.

Based in type and modelling on the so-called Theseus of the Ludovisi collection; iconographically more closely connected with the Hercules of the same series.

BIBLIOGRAPHY: See above, and Thomassin, Bibl. 109, Pl. 181; Coural, Bibl. 1240, Fig. 8.

222. PAN. Marble. Height: 206 cm. Versailles, Quinconce du Nord.

NOTES: The bottom left-hand part of the shaft is repaired.

The head of the leopard's (or lioness') skin is visible at the back of the statue. The hair, with its wreath of pine-needles, is deeply cut, as is the bunch of pine-needles which the god holds with his left hand.

The form of the pine-wreath is close to that shown in the statue of Vertumnus from Sceaux illustrated in Montfaucon, which Poussin may also have used as a model for the Priapus.

BIBLIOGRAPHY: See above, and Thomassin, Bibl. 109, Pl. 187; Coural, Bibl. 1240, Fig. 1.

223. PRIAPUS (MORPHEUS). Marble. Height: 210 cm. Versailles, Quinconce du Midi.

NOTES: The bottom left-hand part of the base is new and there are small repairs in the drapery.

Figs and fig-leaves compose the wreath worn by the god and also fill the drapery which he holds up before him.

BIBLIOGRAPHY: See above, and Thomassin, Bibl. 109, Pl. 183; Coural, Bibl. 1240, Fig. 7.

224. FLORA. Marble. Height: 216 cm. Versailles, Quinconce du Midi.

NOTES: The tip of the nose, the fingers of the right hand, and small parts of the drapery are repaired.

The statue is very similar in style to No. 227, though with deeper cutting in the wreath and the flowers which the goddess holds.

BIBLIOGRAPHY: See above, and Thomassin, Bibl. 109, Pl. 190; Coural, Bibl. 1240, Fig. 12.

225. MINERVA. Marble. Height: 240 cm. Versailles, Quinconce du Midi.

NOTES: The owl on the helmet has been broken off but appears to belong to the rest of the statue. The nose is repaired; the right arm has been broken and rejoined, and the third and fourth fingers of the right hand, together with part of the middle finger and of the palm, are new.

The statue is taller than the others and may have been intended as a centrepiece and therefore given bigger scale to dominate its neighbours.

Bellori says that the goddess holds the olive-branch in her right hand, whereas in fact it is in her left.

Poussin may have had in mind as a model the Minerva in the Giustiniani collection (cf. *Galleria Giustiniana*, Rome, *c.* 1640, II, Pl. 3).

BIBLIOGRAPHY: See above, and Thomassin, Bibl. 109, Pl. 180; Coural, Bibl. 1240, Fig. 4.

226. POMONA. Marble. Height: 211 cm. Versailles, Quinconce du Midi.

NOTES: The statue has been broken in two pieces on a line running from the left shoulder across the breast and through the right elbow. There are further repairs on the back, the left shoulder-blade, the left forearm, and in the drapery.

The statue belongs to the classical group, though there is deep drilling in the fruit which the figure holds.

BIBLIOGRAPHY: See above, and Thomassin, Bibl. 109, Pl. 182; Coural, Bibl. 1240, Fig. 6.

11*

227. VENUS (FLORA). Marble. Height: 214 cm. Versailles, Quinconce du Nord.

NOTES: The head has been broken off, but appears to belong to the lower part. The neck has been repaired, and there are two repairs to the upper part of the shaft. A bad crack, but not a complete break, runs through the lower part of the back and the right thigh of the goddess. The end of the drapery on her left side is repaired. The goddess holds roses in both hands and the wreath that she wears consists of the same flowers.

Thomassin (Pl. 184) shows the goddess carrying a small rod in her right hand, but there is no sign of reworking on this part of the statue and it seems likely that, as with the Hercules, the engraver has been inaccurate.

For the identification of the herm as Venus, see above, p. 152. The statue is, surprisingly enough, described by Dézallier d'Argenville (Bibl. 200.1, p. 97) as ancient.

BIBLIOGRAPHY: See above, and Thomassin, Bibl. 109, Pl. 184; Dézallier d'Argenville, Bibl. 200.1, p. 97; Coural, Bibl. 1240, Fig. 9.

228. LIBERALITY. Marble. Height: 206 cm. Versailles, Quinconce du Nord.

NOTES: The bottom of the base is repaired at the back. There are also small repairs to the right forearm and the drapery.

Very close in style to the Flora (No. 224). The head and hair are lightly cut, but there is heavy drilling in the fruit which fills the cornucopia.

The head is based on a Greek type of the fourth century B.C. Iconographically the herm is close to Liberality as described and illustrated in Ripa (op. cit., p. 291).

BIBLIOGRAPHY: See above, and Thomassin, Bibl. 109, Pl. 186; Coural, Bibl. 1240, Fig. 2.

229. APOLLO (?) (UN MOISSONNEUR). Marble. Height: 204 cm. Versailles, Quinconce du Midi.

NOTES: The shaft and base are similar to those of the Bacchante, which certainly does not form part of the original series. One element of the moulding has been broken off, and there are small repairs to the drapery and the sickle.

The drapery suggests that this part of the statue is by the same hand as the Bacchante.

The head, however, which is in a different marble, is of finer quality and very similar in style to 221. It is impossible to identify it with any of the herms mentioned by Bellori, as can be done for the Bacchus and Ceres, but its similarity to other members of the Vaux series is sufficiently close to suggest that it has the same origin.

BIBLIOGRAPHY: See above, and Thomassin, Bibl. 109, Pl. 185; Coural, Bibl. 1240, Fig. 13.

230. BACCHUS. Marble. Height: 210 cm. Versailles, Quinconce du Nord.

NOTES: The right elbow is broken and repaired. The head is in a different marble from the rest of the statue. The shaft differs from those of the main series, but is almost identical with that of the Ceres; the torso and arms are feeble in conception and modelling, and the action is almost meaningless. The whole of the body and shaft must in fact be replacements. The head, on the other hand, is close in style to the classical group above, and since Bellori specifically mentions a Bacchus, it is reasonable to suppose that the head originally belonged to one of the series, though it should be noticed that it is exceptionally feminine in type, even for a youthful Bacchus. Bellori's account (see above, p. 148) is not quite clear, but he appears to mean that Bacchus was shown with grapes and Ceres with ears of corn. The head of the present statue is actually crowned with ivy, but the figure may well have held a bunch of grapes.

Like No. 227 this statue is described by Dézallier d'Argenville (Bibl. 200.1, p. 97) as ancient.

BIBLIOGRAPHY: See above, and Thomassin, Bibl. 109, Pl. 191; Dézallier d'Argenville, Bibl. 200.1, p. 97; Coural, Bibl. 1240, Fig. 10.

231. CERES. Marble. Height: 205 cm. Versailles, Quinconce du Nord.

NOTES: The shaft and base are almost identical with those of the Bacchus and differ from those of the main series.

As with the Bacchus (No. 230), only the head is original (the tip of the nose is repaired). The rest of the figure is clumsy and does not fit the head even in scale. The head is crowned with ears of corn, which would agree with Bellori's description. In form they are like the clusters of pine-needles on the wreath worn by Pan (No. 222).

This statue is not engraved by Thomassin. It is described by Dézallier d'Argenville (Bibl. 200.1, p. 97) as Isis.

BIBLIOGRAPHY: See above, and Dézallier d'Argenville, Bibl. 200.1, p. 97; Coural, Bibl. 1240, Fig. 11.

A BACCHANTE. Marble. Height: 219 cm. Versailles, Quinconce du Midi.

NOTES: The base is a pair to that of the Moissonneur (No. 229). The head has been broken off, but is in the same marble as the rest of the statue and apparently belongs to it. The shaft has been broken in two pieces and mended.

For the grounds on which the connection of the statue with the Vaux series must be rejected, see above.

BIBLIOGRAPHY: See above, and Thomassin, Bibl. 109, Pl. 188; Coural, Bibl. 1240, Fig. 14.

EARLY RECORDS OF PAINTINGS ATTRIBUTED TO POUSSIN

The following pages contain all the records known to me of paintings attributed to Poussin in early sources, printed or manuscript. Almost all of these works are now untraceable, but a certain number of them survive, rejected by general consent as genuine works by Poussin and in some cases attributed to other painters.

In principle I have taken as an upper limit the date 1715, that is to say fifty years after Poussin's death, but in a few instances I have gone slightly beyond this when the record referred to a collection formed at an earlier date. In the case of engravings I have taken roughly the same date limit.

I have included references which do not give the subject of the painting in question, since it may on occasion be useful to know that a particular collector owned works by Poussin, even if we cannot at present identify them.

OLD TESTAMENT

L1. THE CALLING OF ABRAHAM
The inventory of Joannes Philippus Happart, drawn up in Antwerp in 1686, contains a *Roepinge van Abraham, van Poesyn* (Denucé, Bibl. 862, p. 334).

L2. THE SACRIFICE OF NOAH
A painting of this subject is mentioned by Félibien (IV, p. 152) as belonging to F. Blondel, who had inherited it from his uncle, Richaumont, the mathematical tutor to the Dauphin. Félibien next names the *Choice of Hercules* (Cat. No. 159) and adds the words: 'des premières manières'. Presumably, but not quite certainly, this phrase is meant to apply to both pictures. The Richaumont-Blondel picture is probably the one which Brice mentions in 1752 (Bibl. 89g, I, p. 473) as in the Hôtel d'Epernon, which had been owned by Charles Jean-Baptiste Fleuriau, Comte de Morville, who died in 1732. It may also be the picture recorded among the goods seized from the Marquis de Vintimille in 1795 (Bibl. 305, p. 334), of which the size is given as 23 × 35 inches.

L3.
The de Cotte papers mention *Un Sacrifice de noë au sortir de larche* in Pozzo's collection (Bibl. 98a, p. 203), which may possibly be the painting now at Tatton Hall (see below, R7), which, however, in my opinion is not by Poussin (cf. Blunt, Bibl. 1357, pp. 489 f.).

L4. SAMSON
The Barberini inventory of 1631 contains *un Sansone, che sta a sedere, con un mano che l'appoggia ad una guancia, con una pelle di leone e la mascella di cavallo* (Orbaan, Bibl. 746, p. 511).

L5. SAMSON DESTROYING THE TEMPLE OF DAGON
A painting described as *Sansone quando rompe le Colonne del Tempio*, attributed to Poussin, is mentioned as in the Palazzo Rospigliosi by Rossini in 1693 (Bibl. 106, p. 66), with a pair representing a *Triumph of David* (cf. also Pinaroli, Bibl. 123, II, p. 53). Both pictures are mentioned again in the 1700 and 1704 editions of the *Mercurio*, but in the 1776 edition (Bibl. 106c, II, p. 125) the name of Poussin disappears and the pictures are attributed to Domenichino. The *Samson* is still in the Palazzo Rospigliosi-Pallavicini and is now attributed to the circle of the Carracci (cf. Zeri, Bibl. 1216, p. 80, No. 117), but the *David* is no longer traceable.

L6. THE TRIUMPH OF DAVID
See previous item.

L7. THE JUDGMENT OF SOLOMON
The Robert de Cotte papers (Bibl. 98a, p. 204) mention a *jugement de Salomon* by Poussin in the Palazzo Giustiniani. In 1700 Pinaroli (Bibl. 123, I, p. 140) gives a more detailed description of it as follows: *Il quadro con una prospettiva, ove è espresso il primo giuditio di Salomone.* This confirms Thuillier's suggestion (Bibl. 98a, p. 204, note 8) that the Giustiniani picture is the one engraved by Agricola (Andresen-Wildenstein, No. 86). In Andresen's day this was in the Belvedere, Vienna, and it appears in nineteenth-century catalogues of the Imperial collection under the name of Jacques Stella, having been bought as a Poussin in 1795, a date at which the Giustiniani were beginning to sell their pictures (cf. E. von Engerth, *Kunsthistorische Sammlungen des allerhöchsten Kaiserhauses*, Vienna, 1884, I, p. 468). No *Judgment of Solomon* attributed to Poussin went with the bulk of the Giustiniani collection to Berlin in 1812.
The picture is presumably identical with the one mentioned in the 1638 Giustiniani inventory (Salerno, Bibl. 1282, p. 97, No. 95), where it is ascribed to *Monsù Remigio,* no doubt Remy Vuibert. There is every reason to think that this attribution is correct.

L8. A PROPHET
Félibien (IV, p. 11) mentions a painting of a prophet executed by Poussin in his first years in Rome, for which he was paid eight francs, whereas another artist received four écus for copying it.

L9. THE CAPTURE OF JERUSALEM BY TITUS
Painted for Cardinal Francesco Barberini (Bellori, p. 413) and paid for on 13.ii.1626 (Bousquet, Bibl. 1231,

p. 3). Given away by the Cardinal soon afterwards (Bellori, *loc. cit.*), probably to Cardinal Richelieu, since in Félibien's time it belonged to his niece, the Duchesse d'Aiguillon, who sold it to Sainctot (Félibien, IV, p. 18). Loménie de Brienne, writing in 1693–95 (p. 215), speaks of it as *chez Mad? la marquise d'Aligre*, and this is confirmed by a list made in 1697 of pictures belonging to François Quesnel but pledged to Mme d'Aligre, at her house in the rue St. Guillaume. These pictures were recovered by Quesnel in 1698 (cf. Bibl. 618, pp. 92, 94). Florent Le Comte, who states (III, p. 25) that the picture still belonged to Sainctot, was probably simply copying Félibien. Probably Carignan sale, Poilly, Paris, 1742, 54×72 inches.

Some idea of the composition is probably supplied by an engraving after a lost drawing, formerly in the Gatteaux collection (*CR*, II, p. 18, No. A 37). See also text volume, p. 62, Fig. 59, and note 20.

There is a remote possibility that the lost *Capture of Jerusalem* may be connected with a picture in the collection of Didot de Saint-Marc in 1811 (Bibl. 343.1, No. 169). It is true that the catalogue of this collection describes it as a *Massacre of the Innocents*, but it goes on to say that it was painted about 1628 for Cardinal Francesco Barberini, who gave it to 'Prince Eschenberg', the form which Félibien gives to the name of Eggenberg, the actual recipient of the *Capture*. This suggests that the picture may be the *Capture of Jerusalem*, and this is confirmed by the description given of it, which states that there are about eighty figures, including a soldier on a rearing horse, and that the background consists of a pilastered palace decorated with ancient statues, behind which appear fortifications and mountains. It is said to have been brought back to France forty years previously by a French ambassador, from whom it was bought by Lebrun. Its size is given as 5⅓×3¾ feet, though it is not clear which is length and which is height.

NEW TESTAMENT

L10. THE NATIVITY
On his visit to Paris in 1665 Bernini was shown *une Nativité* by Poussin in the Hôtel de la Vrillière (cf. Chantelou, 1960, p. 131).

L11.
Pinaroli (Bibl. 123, I, p. 138) mentions *La Nascità di Christo* by Poussin in the Palazzo Giustiniani.

L12. THE ADORATION OF THE KINGS
A picture of this subject is mentioned by La Lande (Bibl. 224a, VII, p. 86) in the Palazzo della Torre, Naples. La Lande did not visit Italy till 1765–66, but the greater part of the della Torre collection was inherited from Cardinal Ascanio Filomarino, Archbishop of Naples, who owned several works by Poussin during the artist's lifetime (cf. Blunt, Bibl. 1167, p. 83).

L13.
A tradition, which goes back to Bruzen de La Martinière's *Grand Dictionnaire* of 1738 (cf. Thuillier,

Bibl. 1297, p. 37), records a picture of this subject, 18×12 feet, in the church of St. Germain, Triel, which had been given by the Pope to Queen Christina of Sweden and by her to Poiltenet, a native of Triel, who had given it to the church. It was still there at the time of the Revolution, but is no longer traceable.

THE MADONNA
L14.
The Robert de Cotte papers (Bibl. 98a, p. 203) mention *une vierge* in the Palazzo Giustiniani. This also appears in the 1693 edition of Rossini's *Mercurio Errante* (Bibl. 106, p. 42).

L15.
In 1700 Pinaroli (Bibl. 123, II, p. 174) mentions in the Palazzo Barberini *un quadro tondo con Maria Vergine, e il Bambino Giesù*. It is also mentioned in 1740–41 by Keyssler (Bibl. 172, II, p. 345). It may possibly be the painting now in the Musée du Berry at Bourges, which was in an anonymous sale at Sotheby, London, 18.v.1938, lot 115 (see below, R26).

L16.
A picture described as *La Madonna con il Bambino in Seno in boscareggio* appears in the 1713 Rospigliosi inventory, with dimensions of 4×6 palmi (cf. Zeri, Bibl. 1216, p. 324, No. 625).

L17.
The Robert de Cotte papers (Bibl. 98a, p. 203) mention in the Pozzo collection *une Vierge*, which is no doubt identical with No. 4 of the Ghezzi inventory: *Quadro da 4 pal. con Madonna Putto e S. Giuseppe* (Bibl. 1254, pp. 320, 324) and with the *Sainte Famille* seen by Caylus in 1714–15 (Bibl. 133, p. 297). The only known painting showing these three figures is the Detroit picture (Cat. No. 46), but the size does not agree.

L18.
A Madonna with two other figures is recorded in an anonymous sale at the Banqueting House, London, 2.vi.1684, lot 1 (cf. Waterhouse, Bibl. 1308, p. 288).

L19.
An inventory drawn up in 1688 of the pictures belonging to Don Giuliano Colonna, Principe di Galatro, lists *una Madonna, che siede sotto un albero; S. Gio. e puttini, che scherzono*, 2×3 palmi (cf. Blunt, Bibl. 1167, p. 84).

L20.
Sublet de Noyers seems to have asked Poussin to paint a *Vierge* in 1642 (*Correspondance*, p. 134), but the project does not seem to have been carried out.

L21.
In 1685 Evelyn records seeing at Lord Newport's house *a Christo in gremio by Pussine, an admirable piece*. This is probably a Madonna and Child rather than a Pietà (cf. Waterhouse, Bibl. 1308, p. 286).

THE HOLY FAMILY
L22.
The inventory of pictures belonging to Paolo Falconieri, drawn up before 1721, contains a *Quadro della Madonna e S. Elisabetta con Ntro Sig. re e S. Gio. Batta, e S. Giuseppe*. For its probable identity, see Blunt, Bibl. 1426, p. 70.

L23.
Magne (1914, p. 214, note 1) refers to a *Holy Family* sold in 1694 by Floris Escot of Lyons to the painter Dominique Lapierre of the same city.

L24. Brice in his 1713 edition (Bibl. 89d, II, p. 191) mentions a picture in the collection of Raoul Pierre de la Porte, in the rue de Seine, which he describes as follows: 'Un autre du même sujet (the Holy Family), où Saint-Joseph est appuyé sur un tronc d'arbre aussi avec un fond d'architecture et de païsage.' This does not seem to be identifiable with any of the known paintings.

L25. THE PURIFICATION OF THE VIRGIN
Sublet de Noyers seems in 1642 to have asked Poussin to paint a picture of this subject (*Correspondance*, p. 134), but the project does not appear to have been carried out.

L26. CHRIST BESIDE THE SEA OF GALILEE
A painting described as *Cristo quando mangiò appresso al mare con paese e pesci, e uno che tira la rete e altri che portano pesci*, 2 braccia in width, belonged to Lelio Boscoli, in the Casa Boscoli, Parma, in 1690 (cf. Campori, Bibl. 525.1, p. 383, No. XXIX).

L27. CHRIST AND THE CANAANITE WOMAN
Mentioned in the list of pictures belonging to Sir Francis Child in 1706 (cf. *Historical Manuscripts Commission*, eighth report, Pt. I, p. 100b). Richardson (Bibl. 149, p. 8) mentions a picture of this subject in the French Royal collection, but this seems to be due to a confusion, probably with *The Woman taken in Adultery* (Cat. No. 76).

L28. CHRIST DRIVING THE TRADERS OUT OF THE TEMPLE
Recorded in the manuscript inventory of the Alcazar at Madrid, drawn up in 1666 (Archivo General de Palacio, Seccion administrativa, Lagajo No. 38). Mentioned by Justi (Bibl. 599a, p. 349).

L29. THE LAST SUPPER
Recorded in the manuscript inventory of pictures in the Alcazar at Madrid in 1666 (Archivo General de Palacio, Seccion administrativa, Legajo No. 38).

L30. THE AGONY IN THE GARDEN
Sandrart (p. 258) lists a painting of *Christus im Oelgarten von dem Engel gestärket*, no doubt the picture in Pozzo's collection mentioned by various writers. Robert de Cotte (Bibl. 98a, p. 203) gives no details about it, but the Ghezzi inventory (Haskell and Rinehart, Bibl. 1254, pp. 321, 325, No. 49) states that it was on copper. Tessin says that it was 'treflich gemahlet mit dem rothen glantz herum' (cf. Sirén, Bibl. 63, p. 187). The painting was no doubt based on the drawing at Windsor (*CR*, I, p. 33, No. 64) and may have been the model for a Poussinesque composition in the writer's possession (cf. Blunt, Bibl. 1426, pp. 72f.). In the eighteenth century Pozzo's picture was pledged with the *Sacraments* to the Marchese del Buffalo (see Cat. Nos. 105–11).

L31. THE DESCENT FROM THE CROSS
and another unspecified subject.
Félibien (IV, p. 7) states that on his return from Poitou Poussin painted two pictures for the Capuchins of Blois. This statement is repeated by Perrault (Bibl. 113, I, p. 89). A document of 1795 (cf. Montaiglon, Bibl. 564.1, p. 314) identifies the subject of one of these as a Descent from the Cross. At the Revolution it was moved to the village of Oisly, and in 1795 back to Blois. As Montaiglon (*loc. cit.*) and Magne (1928, p. 54) point out, the evidence that Poussin actually executed these paintings is very uncertain, the greatest difficulty being that the Capuchins had left Blois after the assassination of Henry III in 1588 and did not return till 1623. Loménie de Brienne (p. 212) refers to one picture painted for the Capuchins of Blois, but says he has not seen it. His comment is of little importance, since he is only annotating Félibien.

L32. NOLI ME TANGERE
Félibien (IV, p. 63) tells us that in 1653 Poussin painted for Pointel a picture which he describes as *Notre Seigneur en Jardinier, et la Magdeleine à ses pieds*. The composition has generally been connected with a picture in the Prado (2306), engraved by Pietro del Po (Andresen, No. 212). Friedlaender (1914, p. 122) and Grautoff (II, p. 269) consider this to be a copy of a lost original, while Mrs. Wild (Bibl. 1383, pp. 240 f.) believes it to be the original. In my view it is more likely to be a pastiche by Pietro del Po (cf. Bibl. 1226, p. 401). Loménie de Brienne (pp. 215, 218, 221) mentions the picture three times, and on the last occasion comments: *peu de chose*. Florent Le Comte (III, p. 31) lists it without comment. Whitley (Bibl. 829, p. 129) records a *Magdalen* by Poussin, sold in August 1807 by William Beckford with the contents of his father's house at Fonthill. It was bought by Jeffrey for 210 guineas and must therefore have been a painting of some importance, perhaps the missing Pointel painting.

L33. PENTECOST
In a manuscript history of the monastery of Saint-Victor, Paris, said to have been composed about 1685, Philippe Goureau says that he commissioned a painting of this subject to be made after one by Poussin (cf. Thuillier, Bibl. 1295, p. 189).

THE VIRGIN AND SAINTS

L34. THE IMMACULATE CONCEPTION
A picture of *La Concetione della Madonna* was commissioned from Poussin by Marcantonio Borghese, Principe di Sulmona L, in 1628 and sent to Spain (cf. Paola della Pergola, Bibl. 1129, p. 67).

L35. THE ASSUMPTION
The Giustiniani inventory of 1638 (cf. Salerno, Bibl. 1282, p. 97, No. 96) lists *Un quadro dell' Assuntione della Beata Vergine, con un gruppo d'Angeli Putti, che la portano*. The size is given as 6×4 palmi (134×88 cm.) and the writer adds: *si crede di mano di Nicolo Pussin Pittor francese*.

Salerno (*loc. cit.*) identifies this with the picture now in the National Gallery, Washington (Cat. No. 93), but there are good reasons to suppose that this really came from the Palazzo Soderini. The Giustiniani picture is the subject of a Latin poem by Silos, published in his *Pinacotheca* of 1673 (Bibl. 61a, p. 158).

L36. A picture described as the *Assunta con angeli da testa de Pussin* is given as item 98 in the Ghezzi inventory of Pozzo's pictures (Bibl. 1254, pp. 322, 325). It is no doubt identical with the painting described by La Lande (Bibl. 224a, V, p. 293) as follows: *Une assomption de la Vierge portée dans le ciel par les Anges, au son du violon.*

L37. THE CRUCIFIXION OF ST. ANDREW
A picture of *Saint André crucifié, et plusieurs figures de Spectateurs*, $3\frac{1}{2} \times 2\frac{2}{3}$ feet, is recorded in the collection of the Elector Palatine, Düsseldorf, probably in 1725 (cf. Kasch, Bibl. 150.1, No. 236). This is probably the painting engraved in the 1778 Düsseldorf catalogue (Bibl. 260.1, No. 124) as by Annibale Carracci.

L38. ST. JOHN THE BAPTIST
A half-length picture of this subject was commissioned from Poussin by Marcantonio Borghese, Principe di Sulmona, in 1628 and sent to Spain (cf. Paola della Pergola, Bibl. 1129, p. 67).

L39. ST. JOHN THE EVANGELIST
A half-length picture of this subject was commissioned from Poussin by Marcantonio Borghese, Principe di Sulmona, in 1628 and sent to Spain (cf. Paola della Pergola, Bibl. 1129, p. 67).

L40. MARY MAGDALEN IN THE DESERT
A picture of *Die heilige Magdalena in der Wüsten* is mentioned by Sandrart (p. 258) but by no other writer. It is possible that Sandrart may be confusing the subject with St. Mary of Egypt in the Wilderness, of which Poussin made a drawing, now at Windsor (*CR*, IV, p. 44, No. 275), from which it is possible that he made a painting for Philip IV of Spain (cf. Blunt, Bibl. 1195, p. 390; cf. also L47, *St. Mary of Egypt*).

L41. MARY MAGDALEN
In 1710 the Farnese family bought from C. A. Canopi *una batalia di mano di Nicolò Pusino et una Madalena figura intiera* (cf. Filangieri, Bibl. 652.1, p. 287). The *Battle* is probably the picture in the Vatican (Cat. No. 31), but the *Magdalen* is not now traceable. It is not even quite clear from the entry whether it is by Poussin.

L42. THE CONVERSION OF ST. PAUL
In his letters to Chantelou between 1649 and 1658 Poussin often refers to the Conversion of St. Paul as the subject of a painting projected for his friend in Paris. In October 1649 (*Correspondance*, p. 409) he talks of starting on it in the winter. In another letter, of which only a rough draft exists but which must date from towards the end of 1650 (*CR*, I, pp. 28 f.), he acknowledges a payment from Chantelou for a picture

of *St. Paul*, which appears to be the *Conversion* referred to in the earlier letters. (It obviously cannot refer to Chantelou's *Ecstacy of St. Paul,* which had been painted seven years earlier.) In spite, therefore, of what is said in *CR*, I, p. 35, it seems almost certain that Poussin did execute a *Conversion of St. Paul* for Chantelou in 1649–50. It is possible, however, that he may have given it away, because it is not mentioned in the account which he gives of his collection when he showed it to Bernini.

Between 1655 and 1658 the subject is again mentioned in letters to Chantelou (*Correspondance*, pp. 438, 442–7, 449). In December 1657 Poussin promises to begin the painting in the New Year; in March 1658 he has found the design for it, but in November 1658 he writes that he has made a fresh sketch based on a completely new concept. After this the subject is not mentioned again and the projected second painting does not seem to have been carried out.

For the drawings connected with this subject, see *CR*, I, pp. 36 f. The original of No. A 15 has now been rediscovered and is in an English private collection.

L43. ST. CATHERINE
Sir James Thornhill's manuscript diary for his visit to Paris in 1717 (Bibl. 140, p. 1) contains a note: 'A Landsk. of N. Poussin and a St. Catherine engᵣ of Boit for Mᵣ Walker.' Boit is presumably the Swedish enamel painter, Carl Boit, who had worked in England till 1710 or 1712, when he moved to Paris, but it is not known that he did engraving. Thornhill's note is obscure, and it is not clear to what painting he is referring. It is conceivable that the St. Catherine may be the *Mystic Marriage of St. Catherine* (Cat. No. 95). It is not known who Mr. Walker is.

L44. ST. CHARLES BORROMEO AND ST. FRANCIS
According to Bernier's *Histoire de Blois* of 1682 (Bibl. 86a, p. 186) Poussin designed two stained-glass windows of these saints in the choir of the church of the Capuchins at Blois, but there is no other evidence to confirm his assertion.

L45. THE MIRACLES OF ST. IGNATIUS AND ST. FRANCIS XAVIER
Bellori (p. 410) and Félibien (IV, p. 8) state that Poussin executed six large tempera paintings in six days for the celebrations organized by the Jesuits in honour of the Canonization of St. Ignatius and St. Francis Xavier. In the middle of the eighteenth century four of them were still preserved in the Jesuit College of Louis le Grand (cf. Brice, Bibl. 89g, III, p. 78, and Dézallier d'Argenville, Bibl. 183, p. 195). Dézallier d'Argenville gives the subjects of these four as follows: *S. Ignace en extase, un Soleil couchant où ce Saint ecrit ses méditations, S. Ignace et S. François Xavier auxquels Notre Seigneur et la Vierge apparoissent, et S. Xavier persécuté par les démons* (cf. Thuillier, Bibl. 1297, pp. 32 f.).

In the 1713 edition Brice (Bibl. 89d, II, p. 349) only mentions one composition, but his description is worth quoting in full:

> 'Dans les sales interieures on voit . . . un fort beau paysage de *Nicolas Poussin*.
>
> Un des premiers ouvrages de *Poussin*, dont la maniere est fort differente de celle qu'il a suivie depuis. Le coloris en est fort vif, & on y remarque beaucoup de feu; mais il n'y paroît aucune correction dans le dessein. C'est une Vierge qui apparoît à saint Ignace.'

L46. THE MARTYRDOM OF ST. LAWRENCE

Recorded in the manuscript inventory of the Alcazar at Madrid, drawn up in 1666 (Archivo General de Palacio, Seccion administrativa, Legajo Nos. 38, 301) with dimensions $9 \times 7\frac{1}{2}$ feet. Mentioned by Justi (Bibl. 599a, p. 349).

L47. ST. MARY OF EGYPT

Brice (Bibl. 89b, II, pp. 260 f.) mentions as by Poussin *Sainte Marie Egyptienne, qu'il peignit avant que d'entreprendre le voyage d'Italie* in a chapel of Notre-Dame, Paris. Thuillier (Bibl. 1297, p. 32) points out that the picture is not mentioned by other writers and suggests that either the picture has disappeared or, more probably, that Brice was referring to a painting of the same subject in Notre-Dame by Lubin Baugin, which was engraved by Du Flos.

CLASSICAL SUBJECTS

L48. ALEXANDER AND HIS PHYSICIAN

An inventory of the pictures lent from the Palazzo Falconieri to an exhibition at S. Salvatore in Lauro in 1717 includes *Alessandro Magno in letto che beve il veleno*, with size 4 palmi (manuscript in the Museo di Roma, kindly communicated by Mr. Francis Haskell). The subject is not known to have been painted by Poussin but was represented in a lost painting by Le Sueur (cf. Blunt, Bibl. 1426, p. 70).

L49. APOLLO AND MARSYAS

A painting of *La Contesa di Marsia et Apollo con un altra figura* is mentioned in the inventory of Carlo II Gonzaga, Duke of Mantua, in 1665 (cf. d'Arco, Bibl. 473, II, p. 184).

BACCHANALS

L50. BACCHANALS FOR THE CHATEAU DE CHEVERNY

Félibien (IV, p. 7) and Bernier (Bibl. 86, p. 89) both state that Poussin painted some *Bacchanals* at the Château de Cheverny on his return from Poitou. Félibien, in his *Mémoires pour servir à l'histoire des Maisons Royalles* (Bibl. 81a, p. 185) adds that the *Bacchanals* were in *un ancien Cabinet ou une espèce de loge ouverte des deux costez* and that they were already much damaged.

L51. BACCHANALS FOR RICHELIEU

The *Bacchanals* for the Château de Richelieu are discussed under catalogue Nos. 136–8, but it seems likely that Poussin painted at least one more for the Cardinal, perhaps for Rueil or for the Palais Cardinal. One may be *The Andrians* (Cat. No. 139), but it is possible that another is lost. For a full discussion of this problem, see Davies, Bibl. 988a, pp. 187 ff.

L52. BACCHANALS FOR POZZO

The Robert de Cotte papers (Bibl. 98a, p. 203) mention in all four *Bacchanals* in Pozzo's collection but give no details. The Ghezzi inventory (Bibl. 1254, pp. 321, 325) lists the following items:

No. 23. *Baccanale da 8 e 4.*
No. 47. *Un Baccanale grande da 9 e 6.*
No. 58. *Il Baccanale da Imp.re*
No. 59. *Altro Baccanale di Venere da Imp.re*
No. 66. *Il Baccanale grande da 9, e 12.*

A *Bacchanal* is also mentioned as No. 54. Ghezzi does not name the author, but this picture, listed together with a perspective, comes immediately after one ascribed to Poussin and it is possible that the attribution is meant to cover all three works.

One of the *Bacchanals* mentioned above is no doubt the picture described by Richardson (*Account*, p. 186) as follows: *Bacchus and Ariadne, Bacchus stands upon his Chariot, and Ariadne lies down, he looks with great tenderness towards her*, and by Keyssler (Bibl. 172a, II, p. 401) as *Bacchus and Ariadne*.

Bacchanals without any further specification are recorded in the following contexts:

L53. The inventory of Marie Chaudron, wife of Léonard Hugot, made in Paris in 1655 (cf. Wildenstein, No. 133).

L54. Anonymous sale, Banqueting House, London, 2.vi.1684, lot 93 (cf. Waterhouse, Bibl. 1308, p. 285).

L55. The inventory of the Maréchal d'Humières, drawn up after his death in 1694 (cf. *Inventaire . . .*, Bibl. 108.1, p. 93, No. 342). A copy of a *Bacchanal* appears in the same list (*ibid.*, p. 94, No. 360).

L56. *Un baccanale lungo un braccio gagliardo, con tre figure* appears in the inventory of the Gonzaga collection, Mantua, made in *c.* 1700 (cf. d'Arco, Bibl. 473, II, p. 187).

L57. The inventory of the Princesse des Ursins, made in Rome in 1713, mentions a *Bacchanal*, with size given as *toile d'empereur* (cf. *Les Tableaux . . .*, Bibl. 132.1, p. 33).

L58. *Un Bacco, che preme l'uva e un Satiro mezze figure grandi al naturale* occurs in the inventory of Carlo Maratta, taken in 1713 (cf. Galli, Bibl. 818, XXIII, p. 60, No. 145). Mentioned in the list of pictures sold by Maratta's heirs to the King of Spain in 1722 (cf. *Nota delli quadri*, Bibl. 549, p. 143, and Battisti, Bibl. 1218.1, p. 88).

L59. CALLISTO

In a letter written to Ruffo in 1665 Abraham Bruegel refers to a painting by Poussin of *Callisbo*, presumably a mistake for *Callisto*, 4×6 palmi. This may have been a painting of Jupiter and Callisto or Diana and Callisto. If the former, it cannot be the Philadelphia picture (see below, p. 175, R83), as the size does not agree (cf. Blunt, Bibl. 1167, p. 86).

L60. CAMILLUS AND THE SCHOOLMASTER OF FALERII

According to Félibien (IV, p. 25) painted a few years before 1637 and later in the possession of Passart (cf. Cat. No. 142).

L61. DANAË

According to Félibien (IV, p. 151) a picture of *Danaé couchée sur un lit* belonged to 'le sieur Stella aux Galeries du Louvre'. This is probably a slip for Claudine Bouzonnet Stella, since both Jacques Stella and Antoine Bouzonnet Stella were dead when this volume of the *Entretiens* was published. Stella had bequeathed his pictures to his niece, Claudine, but the *Danaë* does not appear in the inventories of her possessions made in 1693 and 1697 (Bibl. 107). The picture is also mentioned by Loménie de Brienne (p. 214) and by Florent Le Comte (III, p. 31). It probably belonged later to Crozat de Thiers and was bought with his collection by the Empress Catherine II of Russia, but it is not traceable in the Imperial collection after 1797 (cf. Ernst, Bibl. 1055, p. 86).

L62. FLORA AND ZEPHYR

Félibien (IV, p. 20) mentions a painting of the *amours de Flore et de Zephir* among works painted about 1630, and Florent Le Comte (III, p. 25) repeats his note. No painting is known, but the original may have been connected with a drawing in the Louvre (*CR*, III, p. 36, No. A 60).

L63. HERCULES CARRYING OFF DEIANIRA

Félibien (IV, pp. 26 f.) records that in about 1637 Poussin painted a picture of this subject for Jacques Stella. Later it belonged to Chantelou (cf. Chantelou, 1885, p. 64, and 1960, p. 124; and Florent Le Comte, III, p. 27). Drawings of the subject which are almost certainly for the lost picture are preserved at Windsor (*CR*, III, p. 38, No. 218), the Louvre (*ibid.*, No. 219) and the Uffizi (*ibid.*, No. A 63, probably a copy). An engraving by G. Audran exists after the Louvre drawing (Andresen, No. 398; Wildenstein, No. 158). The format of the lost painting cannot at present be exactly determined. The Windsor drawing shows a broad composition with Hercules carrying off Deianira on the left, and on the right a group of figures offering the cornucopia to Ceres. The other drawings only show the left-hand part of the composition, and it seems likely that Poussin reduced it to the upright format, since on the Windsor drawing he made a line cutting the design in two at a point corresponding fairly accurately to the edge of the engraved composition.

Bernini expressed the greatest admiration for Chantelou's picture when he saw it in Paris in 1665 (cf. Chantelou, *loc. cit.*).

L64. THE DEATH OF LEANDER

Georges de Scudéry devotes a poem in his *Cabinet* (Bibl. 10a, p. 76) to a picture by Poussin entitled *Léandre mort entre les bras des néréides*. Many of his poems, however, seem to be based on fantasy, and it is by no means certain that Poussin ever executed such a work.

L65. MEDEA

Bellori (p. 449) gives a detailed description of a composition representing Medea killing her children. This corresponds closely to a finished drawing at Windsor (*CR*, III, p. 40, No. A 64), which may be the source of his description (cf. *La Tintura della Rosa*, below, L73, and *La Tintura del Corallo*, below, L72).

L66. NARCISSUS

Félibien (IV, p. 152) mentions a picture of *Narcisse qui se regarde dans une fontaine* said to be *de la première manière*. He cannot be referring to the Louvre picture, which shows Narcissus lying dead on the river bank. It has generally been thought that his description refers to the Dresden painting, but this, in my opinion, is not by Poussin (cf. Bibl. 1324, pp. 457 ff.). Sandrart (p. 258) also mentions a *Narcissus*, but gives no details about it.

L67. LA NOVA NUPTA

A painting of this subject, described as *bislungo*, is listed as No. 42 in the Ghezzi inventory of the Pozzo collection (Bibl. 1254, pp. 321, 324). It is presumably the same as the copy of the Aldobrandini Wedding mentioned by Richardson (*Account*, p. 189), but there is evidence that Poussin at any rate projected a composition of his own on this theme (cf. Blunt, Bibl. 1426, pp. 62 f.).

L68. LANDSCAPE WITH ORPHEUS

Recorded in the Sacchetti inventory of 1688. See below, R 90.

L69. PAN AND SYRINX

A picture of this subject is recorded in the collection of Antonio Ruffo, Duca di Bagnara, about the middle of the seventeenth century. In some inventories it is ascribed to Poussin, but in others to an unknown artist (cf. Blunt, Bibl. 1167, p. 85).

L70. THE MARRIAGE OF PELEUS AND THETIS

In a letter written to Cassiano dal Pozzo from Paris on 4.iv.1642 (*Correspondance*, p. 127) Poussin says he likes the subject of the Marriage of Peleus and Thetis which Pozzo has proposed for a painting. This does not, however, seem to have been executed. The *Acis and Galatea* in Dublin (Cat. No. 128) has been called *Peleus and Thetis*, but this is incorrect, and in any case the picture must have been painted many years before 1641.

L71. A SIBYL
Una mezza figura . . . che rappresenta una sibilla con candela in mano et un libro al naturale is listed in the inventory of Carlo Maratta, taken in 1713 (cf. Galli, Bibl. 818, XXIII, p. 60, No. 210).

L72. LA TINTURA DEL CORALLO
Bellori (p. 443) describes a composition of this name, which corresponds exactly to a finished drawing at Windsor (*CR*, III, p. 42, No. A 66). No painting by Poussin of this subject is known, but Bourdon executed a free variant of it, now in Munich. It is probable that Bellori based his description on the drawing (cf. *Medea*, above, p. L65, and *La Tintura della Rosa*, next item and text volume, p. 120, Fig. 115).

L73. LA TINTURA DELLA ROSA
Bellori (p. 443) gives a detailed description of a composition which corresponds to a finished drawing at Windsor (*CR*, III, p. 31, No. A 51; cf. text volume, Fig. 116), so closely indeed that he seems actually to be describing the drawing itself. If this is so, it is possible that no painting was executed (cf. *Medea*, above, L65, *La Tintura del Corallo*, previous item and text volume, p. 120).

VENUS

L74. *Une Vénus* is recorded in the inventory of the studio of Claude Vignon, made 29.vii.1643 (cf. Wildenstein, Bibl. 1163.1, p. 191, and Thuillier, Bibl. 1296, p. 73).

L75. *Un quadro istoriato di Monsù Posini con una Venere* was on sale in Brescia in 1687 (cf. Campori, Bibl. 525.1, p. 335, No. xxvii).

L76. The Robert de Cotte papers (Bibl. 98a, p. 203) mention *une Venus* in Pozzo's collection. The Ghezzi inventory of 1715 (Bibl. 1254, p. 325) lists a *Baccanale di Venere*. La Roque, who was in Rome between 1775 and 1778 speaks of *Vénus et Adonis; grand paysage de Nicolas Poussin* (Bibl. 248, II, p. 320), and Manazzale in 1794 gives *un paysage avec des figures représentant Vénus et Adonis* (Bibl. 308, II, p. 95). The last two authors are undoubtedly referring to the picture now at Montpellier (see below, R105), which is not actually by the artist, and which does not seem to be identical with that mentioned in the earlier accounts.

L77. MARS AND VENUS
Mentioned in the inventories of the French Royal collection since *c.* 1683 (cf. Bailly, p. 312) and still in the Louvre (727), but rightly rejected by all modern writers on Poussin.

L77a. The inventory of the collection of the Baron de Valbelle-Saint-Symphorien, drawn up in 1656, includes the following item: 'Vénus qui arme Mars, par le Poucin; un pied sept pouces de haut sur un pied trois pouces de large' (cf. Albanès, Bibl. 626.1, p. 555). In a later inventory, dating from 1720, it is said to be on

paper (cf. Boyer, Bibl. 1428, p. 103). From its size it is likely to be an oil sketch on paper rather than a drawing.

L78. *Venus avec plusieurs Cupidons et Mars en l'air dans un chariot, long de travers* is listed in Mazarin's inventory of 1653 (Bibl. 20, p. 299, No. 56), but not recorded in his inventory of 1661, which has a *Venus* by Camassei in its place (cf. Cosnac, Bibl. 584, p. 288, No. 914). This may be the same picture under a different and probably more accurate attribution.

L79. VENUS AND ADONIS
A painting of *Venere e Adone con 4 puttini* is recorded in the collection of Antonio Ruffo, Duca di Bagnara, at Messina, before 1649 (cf. Blunt, Bibl. 1167, p. 85). Its size is given as 3½ × 5 palmi.

L80. VENUS SPIED ON BY SHEPHERDS AND GUARDED BY THREE CUPIDS
Loménie de Brienne (pp. 211, 214, 223) refers several times to a picture of this subject which he owned. According to his account he cut the picture in half and had the surviving fragment repainted for reasons of modesty.

L81. VENUS AND SATYRS
A painting of this subject is mentioned in an inventory of pictures belonging to Paolo Falconieri, made by Giuseppe Ghezzi (cf. Blunt, Bibl. 1426, p. 70). For a discussion of its possible identity, see below, R113.

L82. QUEEN ZENOBIA
The Rospigliosi inventory of 1713 mentions *Una donna svenuta in braccio ad altre due Donne con altre figure con una figura d'un fiume opera dell' ultima maniera del Pusino* (Zeri, Bibl. 1216, p. 307, No. 233). This corresponds to a composition of the *Finding of Queen Zenobia* (cf. Blunt, Bibl. 1426, p. 66) known in drawings and paintings (for the drawings see *CR*, II, pp. 16 ff., Nos. 131–133, A34–36. Of these No. 133 is probably neither an original by Poussin nor a copy of a lost original). It is closely connected with a painting in the Hermitage and with one engraved in the 1819 Dufourny sale catalogue as by Dufresnoy (this version is reproduced in *CR*, II, Fig. 15, where it is wrongly identified as the Hermitage version). When I saw the Hermitage painting many years ago, I did not think it was by Poussin, but it has since been published as such by V. K. Guerz ("Tableau inédit de N. Poussin 'Zénobie Sauvée par les Bergers'", *Transactions of the Hermitage Museum, West European Art*, VI, 1961, pp. 274 ff.), and, when this catalogue was already in page proof, Dr. J. Shearman, who had recently examined the painting, assured me that he was convinced that it was an original by Poussin, though in many parts unfinished.

A picture of this subject is recorded as belonging to the painter Quesnel and as being in pledge to Mme d'Aligre in 1697 (cf. Grouchy, Bibl. 618, p. 91). This cannot be the Rospigliosi picture, which was still in Rome in 1713, but it may be the Dufourny version.

L83. NYMPH, SATYRS AND PUTTI
An inventory, drawn up in 1688 of pictures belonging to Don Giuliano Colonna, Principe di Galastro, lists *una donna nuda, con satiri e puttini, che scherzano* as a copy after Poussin, with dimensions 7×6 palmi. The previous picture in the inventory, of an almost identical subject, is said to be *alla maniera di Monzù Pussino* (cf. Blunt, Bibl. 1167, p. 84).

L84. A SATYR
A picture of this subject belonged to Jean de la Fourcade in Lyons in the second half of the seventeenth century (cf. Bonnaffé, Bibl. 583, p. 151).

L85.
Un Satirino istoriato was for sale at an unspecified place at an uncertain date in the seventeenth century (cf. Campori, Bibl. 525.1, p. 452, Nos. XL–XLVIII).

L86. A HERMAPHRODITE
A picture of this subject belonged in the late seventeenth century to Laurent le Tessier de Montarsy (Bonnaffé, Bibl. 583, p. 223). It is probably the picture properly called *Jupiter and Antiope* (see below, R82).

L87. NYMPH, SHEPHERD AND PUTTI
Un pastore che si trastulla con una pastorella, e molti puttini che li fanno sopra Ghirlanda di fiori con bell. mo paese, with dimensions 2×1¾ bracci, is listed in the inventory of Andrea and Lorenzo del Rosso, Florence, made in November 1689 (cf. Gualandi, Bibl. 99, II, p. 115).

CHILDREN'S BACCHANALS

L88. *Un quadro d'Amorini* belonged to the painter Nicolas Regnier in Venice between 1634 and 1639 (cf. Waterhouse, Bibl. 1083.1, p. 21, No. 7).

L89. In 1664 Monconys (cf. Bibl. 35a, p. 118) records buying a *Baccanale de petits enfans* for 600 écus from *le sculpteur du Pape*, who may be Carlo Matteo, the sculptor who probably owned the *Plague at Ashdod* (Cat. No. 32). The picture is probably the same as that owned by Seignelay in 1685 (cf. Lemaire, Bibl. 91, III, p. 265), and may be the canvas now in the Hermitage (No. 1411; cf. Blunt, Bibl. 1426, p. 67).

L90. The inventory of pictures in the Ducal Palace at Mantua, drawn up in 1665, includes *un scerzo di Putini* (Luzio, Bibl. 714, p. 316). It reappears in the inventory of *c.* 1700, with size 1½ bracci (cf. d'Arco, Bibl. 473, II, p. 188).

PUTTI
L91. A picture of *Twee Kindeken* is recorded in the inventory of Erasmus Quellinus, made in 1678 (cf. Denucé, Bibl. 862, p. 284).

L92. A picture of *Due Putti nudi abbracciati in tela da mezza testa*, said to be a copy after Poussin, was in the 1713 Rospigliosi inventory (cf. Zeri, Bibl. 1216, p. 322, No. 572).

L93. A SACRIFICE
A picture of this subject is mentioned in the Robert de Cotte papers as in Pozzo's collection (Bibl. 98a, p. 202). Probably, but not quite certainly, the *Dance in honour of Priapus* at São Paulo (Cat. No. 176).

L94. A HUNTING SCENE
A picture of *une chasse* is mentioned in the Robert de Cotte papers as in Pozzo's collection (Bibl. 98a, p. 203). Probably, but not certainly, the *Meleager and Atalanta* now in the Prado (Cat. No. 163). It is possible, however, that Poussin painted another picture of a hunt, because a drawing in the Louvre, which in the Catalogue Raisonné (II, p. 11, No. 120) it was suggested represents *Metius Curtius*, is in fact a fragment of a larger composition representing a hunt, of which another version in the Hermitage (No. 5133) will be published in volume V of the Catalogue of the Drawings.

L95. A RIVER GOD WITH GODDESSES
Un fleuve avec des deesses is listed in the inventory of François Mansart, taken in 1666 (cf. Fleury, Bibl. 1130.1, p. 243). Possibly identical with L.117.

L96. COPY OF THE BARBERINI (PORTLAND) VASE
Mentioned by Edward Wright in the Pozzo collection (Bibl. 146, I, pp. 292, 319). It is no doubt identical with No. 41 in the Ghezzi inventory (Bibl. 1254, pp. 321, 324): *Un sopraporta rappresentante un Cameo di Chiaro e scuro*.

L97. COPIES AFTER TITIAN'S *FEAST OF VENUS*
Bellori (p. 412) and Félibien (IV, p. 12) both state that with his friend Duquesnoy Poussin studied the *Feast of Venus* by Titian, now in the Prado (text volume, Fig. 56), copied it and made wax models after the putti. For a copy by Poussin of the *Feast of the Gods* from the same series, see Cat. No. 201.

TASSO

L98. CLORINDA
Richardson (*Account*, p. 8) mentions a *Clorinda coming to the Shepherds, from Tasso* in the French Royal collection, but this is probably due to a confusion with a work by another artist.

LANDSCAPES

L99. VIEW OF GROTTAFERRATA
A painting described as *La veduta di Grotta Ferrata* is given as No. 51 in the Ghezzi inventory of Pozzo's pictures (cf. Blunt, Bibl. 1426, p. 62).

L100. THE ARCH OF CONSTANTINE
A picture of this subject *with figures frome Monsr. Possino* belonged to Robert Harpur in 1677 (cf. Burdon, Bibl. 1234, p. 12).

L101. *Un paese grande abozzato di mano di Monsù Pousiin* was recorded in Poussin's studio at his death (cf. Boyer, Bibl. 42, p. 148).

L102. On his visit to Paris in 1665 Bernini was shown *trois petits paysages* in the house of Cérisier (cf. Chantelou, 1960, p. 127), which cannot at present be identified.

L103. The inventory of Cardinal Camillo Massimi's possessions made after his death in 1677 contains *un paese*, with dimensions 4×5 palmi (cf. Orbaan, Bibl. 746, p. 517).

L104. *UN TEMS CALME ET SEREIN*
Félibien (IV, p. 63) mentions such a picture as a pair to the *Storm* (Cat. No. 217, q.v.).

L105. The Robert de Cotte papers (Bibl. 98a, p. 203) mention *neuf petits paysages* in the Pozzo collection. The Ghezzi inventory (Bibl. 1254, pp. 320 ff., 324 ff.) lists the following unspecified landscapes:

Nos. 4, 5, 7, 8   of 4 palmi
Nos. 18, 19   of 7×5 palmi
Nos. 33, 34   of 4 palmi, with figures
Nos. 48, 139   *in tela di testa*
No. 83   *in tela da Imp.re*

These no doubt included Cat. Nos. 213, 214, 215, and probably Nos. 94 and 168.

L106. The Robert de Cotte papers (Bibl. 98a, p. 205) mention in the Palazzo Barberini a *paisage du Poussin où il y a des pescheurs*.

L107. A *Landskip* is recorded in an anonymous sale, Banqueting House, London, 2.vi.1684, lot 111.

L108. A *Paysage avec de petites figures, première manière* is listed in the inventory of the Duc de Créqui's pictures, made at his death in 1687 (cf. Magne, Bibl. 936, p. 186).

L109. *Un altro quadro con architettura di portico e colonnato antico con la Piramide di Curio ed una nicchia con le statua, con una figura a sedere su le ruine, altra in atto di seppelire un morto postolo in terra, con bel paese*, with dimensions 5×7¾ palmi, is listed in the collection of Queen Christina of Sweden, Rome, c. 1689 (cf. Campori, Bibl. 525.1, p. 356, No. XXVIII). Mentioned later in the collection of Don Livio Odescalchi (cf. Montaiglon and Guiffrey, Bibl. 45, IV, pp. 360, 367). Almost certainly a painting by Jean Lemaire, recorded in a drawing in the Albertina, Vienna (cf. Blunt, Bibl. 1196, p. 443, and Bibl. 1426, p. 69).

L110. A *lanskip, by Nicolas Poussin* was sold at the *Auctio Davisiana . . . consisting of the collections of Cardinal Antonio Barberini, Sir James Palmer, &c.*, E. Davis and E. Millington, London, 23.xi.1691, lot 11.

The inventory of Claudine Bouzonnet Stella's pictures, drawn up in 1697, lists landscapes by Poussin as follows:

L111. *un tableau de 3 pied en longueur: un paysage, il y a un bois, première maniere.*

L112. *un tableau de 3 pied en longueur, il y a des cailloux* (cf. *Testament*, Bibl. 107, p. 39, Nos. 125, 126).

L113. *Deux petit Paysage d'un pied chacun, coppié après le Poussin* (ibid., p. 41, No. 143).

L114. *Due Paesi . . . con figurine* are mentioned in the inventory of Carlo Maratta, taken in 1713 (cf. Galli, Bibl. 818, XXIII, p. 60, No. 166). Mentioned in the list of pictures sold in 1722 by the artist's heirs to the King of Spain (cf. *Nota delli quadri . . .*, Bibl. 549, p. 129, Nos. 153, 165, and Battisti, Bibl. 1218.1, p. 88).

L115. In 1708 the Marchese Ruspoli owned a landscape described as *Paese grande di Nicolò Pusino con le figure di Stendardo* (i.e. Pieter van Bloemen), cf. *Paesisti e Vedutisti* (Bibl. 1137.1) p. 42.

L116. *Une perspective* is mentioned in the Robert de Cotte papers (Bibl. 98a, p. 203) as in Pozzo's collection. This is not clearly identifiable in Ghezzi's inventory, but under No. 53 (Bibl. 1254, p. 325) he mentions *una prospettiva*, without naming the artist, and as the previous picture is listed as by Poussin, it is possible that the *prospettiva* is also his. On the other hand the author of the de Cotte papers may be referring to the perspective by Jean Lemaire, mentioned by Ghezzi under No. 92.

MISCELLANEOUS SUBJECTS

L117. WOMEN BATHING
Félibien records (IV, p. 24) that Poussin painted for the Duc de Créqui *Un bain de femmes* which in his day belonged to Jacques Stella. It passed by inheritance to Claudine Bouzonnet Stella, and at her death in 1697 to her cousin, Claudine Perichon of Lyons (Testament, Bibl. 107, p. 15). The statement in Brice (Bibl. 89b, I, pp. 44 f.) that the picture belonged to the painter Bain seems to be due to a confusion, but the Créqui picture is mentioned by Florent Le Comte (III, p. 26).

Créqui's painting has generally been identified with the composition known from an engraving by E. Jeaurat (Andresen-Wildenstein, No. 384), a view which I have hitherto challenged, on the grounds that the types in the engraving are unlike Poussin's figures (cf. Bibl. 1357, p. 493). When this catalogue was in page-proof, however, a painting was discovered and acquired by Professor George Zarnecki (110.5 × 81 cm) which corresponds in reverse with the engraving and which, though a ruin, appears to be an original by Poussin and certainly rehabilitates the composition. It has the characteristics of a work of 1637–38, which would be in conformity with the fact that Félibien mentions it with the paintings of the 1630's. The painting has none of the un-Poussinesque heaviness which marks the engraving, but is elegant in its forms, recalling the *Pan and Syrinx* of 1637.

In its present form the composition is somewhat unbalanced, with unexplained movements leading out of the design on the right, and the picture may possibly have been cut on this side (if so, before 1708, when the engraving was made). In this case it may be connected with a drawing at Windsor (*CR*, III, p. 43, No. 227), on which a similar group on nymphs appears on the left and the cut-off figure of a river-god can be seen at the right. Another drawing (*CR*, III, p. 46, No. 236) may possibly be connected with the right-hand half of the composition. In this form it would correspond to L95.

LI18. PAINTINGS OF BIRDS

The Ghezzi inventory of the Pozzo collection lists the following items (Bibl. 1254, pp. 320, 324 ff.):

No. 12	*Quadro grande da 7 e cinque rappresentante uno Struzzo*
Nos. 90, 91	*Due ucelli da Imp.re*
No. 113	*Una testa d'un Aquila piccola*
Nos. 118, 119	*Due uccelli da Imp.re . . . grandi assai*
No. 124	*Un' altro ucello sopra porto quadrato*
No. 134	*Un' Aquila dipinta in carta*

None of these paintings can now be identified, but it is possible that drawings or water-colours of birds by Poussin may have been included in Pozzo's volumes devoted to ornithology, formerly at Windsor, but now broken up.

UNIDENTIFIED SUBJECTS

LI19. A PAINTING FOR THE CHAPEL IN THE CHÂTEAU DE FONTAINEBLEAU

In a letter written to Carlo Antonio dal Pozzo from Paris on 6.i.1641 (*Correspondance*, p. 41) Poussin says he has been commissioned to paint a large picture for the chapel at Fontainebleau. In the event it does not seem to have been executed, though Florent Le Comte (III, p. 27) mentions it in his list of Poussin's work.

LI20. In 1650 Evelyn records seeing a painting by Poussin in the house of 'Linclere', i.e. Lintlaër, who was in charge of the pump at the Samaritaine (Bibl. 8c, p. 85).

LI21. In 1663 Monconys saw two unspecified paintings by Poussin belonging to M. d'Aminvilliers in The Hague (Bibl. 35, II, p. 136), and another belonging to M. Lamoureux in the same city (*ibid.*).

LI22. On 21.v.1664 Monconys acquired a painting by Poussin, together with some by other artists, in exchange for a precious stone (*ibid.*, II, p. 452).

LI23. On 3.vi.1664 Monconys (*ibid.*, II, p. 465, and Bibl. 35a, p. 119) records having bought a painting by Poussin from M. Salviati which was acknowledged by the artist as an original when Monconys showed it to him. Salviati is presumably Monsignor Salviati, who

attended Poussin's funeral (see *Correspondance*, p. 481, and a letter from the Abbé Nicaise, published by Georges Wildenstein, Bibl. 1385, p. 566).

LI24. Tessin, on his visit to Paris in 1687-88 (Sirén, Bibl. 63, p. 107) mentions unspecified paintings by Poussin in the collection of 'Bourdeloux', nephew of 'Père Bourdeloux'. This is Claude de Bourdaloue (cf. Bonnaffé, Bibl. 583, p. 38).

LI25. The sale of pictures belonging to Cardinal Antonio Barberini, Sir James Palmer, &c., E. Davis and E. Millington, London, 23.xii.1691, contained as lot 67 *A Sketch* by Poussin.

LI26. The inventory of Guillaume Potteau, drawn up in Antwerp in 1692, includes *Een Schetse, van Nicolo Poussin* (cf. Denucé, Bibl. 862, p. 369). It is unfortunately not clear whether in this case the word *Schetse* means a drawing or an oil sketch.

LI27. In the 1692 edition of the *Notizie del bello . . . della Città di Napoli* (Bibl. 105, *Giornata Quarta*, p. 59) Celano refers to pictures by Poussin belonging to two brothers, Carlo and Francesco Garofalo.

LI28. Rossini, in the 1693 edition of the *Mercurio Errante* (Bibl. 106, p. 48) mentions *un bellissimo quadro di figure di Nicolò Possini* in the Palazzo Colonna. This is probably the version of the *Plague at Ashdod* now in the National Gallery, London (cf. Cat. No. 32, Copy No. 1).

LI29. In the 1706 edition of his guide to Paris (Bibl. 89c, II, p. 354), Brice lists unspecified paintings by Poussin belonging to the painter Antoine Benoist. One of these may be the *Annunciation* now in Munich (see Cat. No. 39).

LI30. In the 1713 edition of Brice (Bibl. 89d, II, p. 191) the author describes the pictures belonging to Raoul Pierre de la Porte in the rue de Seine. After naming the most important Poussins, he adds *quelques autres du même maître*.

LI31. The Ghezzi inventory of Pozzo's collection (Bibl. 1254, p. 325) lists as Nos. 60 and 61 *L'Historia di Rachele, et il compagno da Imp.re*. For the *Rachel*, see Cat. No. 9; the subject of the companion painting cannot be determined. Nos. 80, 81, 85 and 86 are also of unspecified subjects. No. 136 is simply described as *Ottangoo*.

LI32. Sir James Thornhill, in the diary of his visit to Paris in 1717 (Bibl. 140, p. 5), notes: 'Mr. Hubert sends Mr. Hays . . . a figr. of Poussin.' It is not known who Mr. Hays is, but Mr. Hubert reappears on p. 7 as 'Marchand jouailler sur le Quay des Morfondus à Paris', which was on the north side of the Ile de la Cité.

LI33. Bequeathed by the Doge Nicolò Sagredo to Cardinal Basadonna *il quadro di Puccin, ch'è . . . nella Camera dove dormo* (Archivio di Stato, Venice, 1168, I, 137).

SCULPTURE AND ARCHITECTURE

L134. MARBLE VASES

Bellori (p. 437) states that, in addition to the Herms, Poussin designed for Fouquet *due vasi all' antica, grandi circa quattro palmi, con le manichi avvolti in serpenti, che fece lavorare, et esseguire di marmo Africano antico.* These are no longer at Vaux-le-Vicomte and do not seem to have gone to Versailles with the Herms. They are, moreover, not mentioned in the inventories of house and garden at Vaux, made after the disgrace of the Superintendent.

L135. DESIGN FOR A COAT-OF-ARMS FOR SUBLET DE NOYERS

In two letters written in 1641 (*Correspondance*, pp. 65, 79, 80) Poussin refers to making designs for a relief of the arms of Sublet de Noyers for the Noviciat des Jésuites, but it is not clear whether the work was ever carried out. The church is destroyed.

L136. WORK FOR THE ORANGERY AT THE LUXEMBOURG

In a letter of 4.ix.1642 Sublet de Noyers refers to *les desseins que Mons. le Poussin a projettés pour l'Orengerie de Luxembourg,* and gives instructions that they shall be carried out (cf. Thuillier, Bibl. 1295, p. 66). Nothing is, however, known of this project.

L137. DESIGNS FOR DECORATION IN THE HOUSE OF SUBLET DE NOYERS

In several letters written in 1641 (*Correspondance*, pp. 81, 88 f., 91) Poussin refers to the decoration of a room in Sublet de Noyers's house in Paris. He seems mainly to have been concerned with modifying the designs of the architect, but may also have produced projects of his own.

L138. DECORATION FOR THE QUARAN-TORE AT THE ORATORIO DEL PADRE GARAVITA, Rome

According to Passeri (p. 331) Poussin designed this decoration before going to Paris in 1640. He adds that the Oratory was at that time inside the Collegio Romano, and as it was rebuilt on its present site in the via Garavita in 1633, the decoration must have been executed before that year.

PAINTINGS WRONGLY ATTRIBUTED TO POUSSIN

The following list includes all the compositions reputably attributed to Poussin which I believe not to be by him. The limits for such a list are difficult to define, as it would clearly be impossible to include every picture attributed to Poussin by optimistic collectors, engravers, or auctioneers. Generally speaking, I have only included compositions recorded in seventeenth-century engravings and paintings ascribed to Poussin by scholars since 1914, the year in which Friedlaender, Grautoff, and Magne published their monographs. I have, however, added pictures listed by Smith in cases where they are still traceable and where it was possible to give some fairly positive information about them. I have not included paintings rejected by Grautoff, unless they were included by some other recent writer as genuine. Where possible I have suggested alternative attributions, but in many cases it is hard to say more than that the picture in question is not by Poussin himself. I have not included the many eighteenth and early nineteenth-century engravings which are said to be after Poussin, but which have no connection with him. They are listed by Andresen, and many of them are reproduced by Wildenstein in his article on Andresen (Bibl. 500a).

It would obviously have been desirable to reproduce the paintings listed below, because it would be useful to have available in a series of reproductions paintings which I reject but which have been accepted in the past, and some of which other scholars undoubtedly will wish to put back into the canon of Poussin's works now or in the future. The practical difficulties would, however, as I know from my own experience, have been insuperable, since I have on occasion been refused permission, both by private owners and public galleries, to reproduce in articles paintings which I wanted to discuss and to attribute to specific followers of Poussin. In fact, however, almost every item in the following list of rejected works is available in reproduction in a book, an article, or an engraving.

PORTRAITS

R1. PORTRAIT OF POUSSIN. Sir William Worsley, Bt., Hovingham Hall, Yorkshire.
This portrait, which almost certainly represents Poussin, is traditionally ascribed to him, but it is more likely to be by Bernini (cf. Blunt, Bibl. 1426, p. 61).

R2. SUPPOSED PORTRAIT OF POUSSIN. The Marquis of Bute, Mount Stuart, Rothesay, Isle of Bute, Scotland.
Smith, No. 3; Dorival, Bibl. 1009, p. 42. Engraved by Patch in 1769, when in the collection of Sir Horace Mann in Florence (Andresen, No. XVI). Certainly neither of nor by Poussin.

R3. PORTRAIT OF FRANCESCO BARBERINI.
Known from the engraving by Vouillemont in the 1640 edition of Barberini's *Documenti d'Amore* (Andresen, No. 434); rightly rejected by Wildenstein (p. 354, No. VII). The attribution to Poussin is based on the inscription *Nic. Pucci inu.*, *Pucci* having been taken as a poor Italianization of Poussin. Davies and Blunt (p. 216, No. VII), however, point out that Baglione, writing only two years later, attributes the design to a *Niccolò Pucci* not otherwise recorded.

R4. PORTRAIT OF FRANÇOIS DUQUESNOY. The Toledo Museum of Art, Toledo, Ohio. Formerly The Earl of Desborough, Panshanger, England.
Listed by Magne (1914, p. 218, No. 327) as Poussin, but now attributed to Jacques Blanchard.

R5. PORTRAIT OF CARDINAL GIULIO ROSPIGLIOSI. Galleria Nazionale, Rome.
Almost certainly by Giovanni Maria Morandi (cf. Zerner, Bibl. 1354, pp. 66 f.).
A small version of the head and shoulders only in the Musée Fabre, Montpellier, is a studio copy (cf. Grautoff, II, p. 275, and Zerner, *loc. cit.*).

OLD TESTAMENT

R6. THE FLOOD. Formerly Town Hall, Les Andelys, Normandy. Destroyed in 1940.
Published by Hourticq (Bibl. 899, p. 47) as by Poussin, but by the Italian imitator who painted the pendant of the *Sacrifice of Noah* (see R9 below).

R7. THE SACRIFICE OF NOAH. National Trust, Tatton Hall, Cheshire.
The picture belonged to Cardinal Corsini when it was engraved by Frey (cf. Wildenstein, No. 5) and was bought about 1800 by Wilbraham Egerton, from whom it passed by inheritance to Lord Egerton, who

bequeathed it with Tatton Hall to the National Trust. In spite of its history I believe it to be by an imitator who also painted a picture of the same subject in the possession of Mr. Francis Jekyll, and also probably a *Feast of Bacchus* engraved by J. H. Lips in 1786 (Andresen-Wildenstein, No. 368; wrongly stated to be in the Hermitage). For a discussion of the picture, see Blunt Bibl. 1357, pp. 489 f.

R8. No painting known.
Engraved by Cossin (Wildenstein, No. 6), who died in 1704, but in spite of this the composition is obviously not by Poussin. When first doubting it (Bibl. 1357, p. 490), I suggested that the original might be by a French artist of the late seventeenth century, but Mr. R. E. Spear (Bibl. 1422, p. 234) later pointed out that the engraving was connected with a painting at Chatsworth by Sacchi or the young Maratta. The latter attribution seems to be the most likely. Miss Ann Sutherland, who is completing a monograph on Sacchi, is of opinion that the painting is not by this artist, and Dr. Eckhard Schaar has kindly called my attention to a drawing at Düsseldorf (FP 9651), closely connected with the painting and in his opinion by the young Maratta.

R9. Formerly Town Hall, Les Andelys, Normandy. Destroyed in 1940.
Published by Hourticq (Bibl. 899, p. 45) as by Poussin, but by an Italian imitator. A pair to the *Flood* (see above, R 6).

R10. REBECCA AND ELIEZER. Musée de Tessé, Le Mans.
Rightly rejected by Grautoff (II, p. 265), but published by Hourticq (Bibl. 899, p. 59) as by Poussin.

R11. JACOB AND LABAN.
No painting known.
Engraving published by Mariette (Wildenstein, No. 8). The composition appears to be by a French artist of the late seventeenth century.

R12. JOSEPH'S STEWARD FINDING THE CUP IN THE SACK OF BENJAMIN. National Gallery of Ireland, Dublin.
Smith, No. 10; from the Miltown collection. By a French artist of about 1700 near Antoine Coypel.

R13. MOSES STRIKING THE ROCK. Musée du Louvre, Paris.
Presented by Mrs. Pearson in 1947 and published by T. Bertin-Mourot as by Poussin (Bibl. 998, pp. 56 ff.). Certainly by Lebrun. Included in the Lebrun exhibition at Versailles in 1963, but not in the catalogue.

R14. Comte de Rohan-Chabot, Paris.
Published by Hourticq (Bibl. 899, pp. 166 f.). Apparently by a French imitator of the late seventeenth century.

R15. THE TRIUMPH OF DAVID. Galleria Nazionale, Rome.
Certainly not by Poussin; probably by a Roman Contemporary.

R16. BATHSHEBA. Duke of Bedford, Woburn Abbey, Bedfordshire.
Smith, No. 41; Grautoff, II, No. 58.
Possibly Seger Tierens sale, The Hague, 23 ff.vii.1743, lot 27, with dimensions 41×60 inches, which may include the frame (cf. Hoet, Bibl. 195, II, p. 98). Probably in the La Roque sale, Gersaint, Paris, April 1745, lot 17, and Cressent sale, 15.i.1749, lot 86, with dimensions 39×57 inches (cf. Ballot, Bibl. 737.1, p. 189, No. 85).
It is said by Smith—and later scholars have followed him—to have belonged to the Duke of Orleans in 1749, but there does not seem to be any evidence to support this assertion and the picture is not mentioned in the very full list of the duke's paintings published in that year in Dézallier d'Argenville's *Voyage Pittoresque de Paris*. It was in the Robit collection and was bought there by Bryan, who brought it to England. Buchanan, who records this fact (II, p. 58), does not give the name of the owner and it may therefore not have been sold immediately. It was, however, presumably bought by the Duke of Bedford before 1827, since it appeared in the anon. (= Duke of Bedford) sale, Christie, London, 30.vi.1827, lot 99, when it was bought in. It appeared again in a further sale of the same kind at Christie's, 6.vi.1829, lot 53, and was again bought in. It was exhibited with a selection of the Bedford pictures at the Scottish Royal Academy and the Royal Academy in London in 1950 (No. 72).
The attribution to Poussin has often given rise to doubts. In 1933 Friedlaender, in his Thieme-Becker article (p. 324), was hesitant; in 1960 Thuillier ascribed it to Charles Mellin (Bibl. 1296, p. 82). I myself believe it to be by the 'Hovingham Master' (cf. Bibl. 1324, pp. 457 f.).

R17. JONAH AND THE WHALE. Royal Collection, Windsor Castle.
Smith, No. 43; Grautoff, II, p. 267. Engraved by Vivares (Andresen, No. 449). Certainly by Gaspard Dughet.

R18. THE DISOBEDIENT PROPHET. Musée des Beaux-Arts, Le Havre.
Grautoff (II, No. 144) published this painting as a *Landscape with Pyramus* and attributed it to Poussin. In the exhibition of the *Age of Louis XIV* it was left without certain attribution (Bibl. 1165, p. 67, No. 116), but it must in fact be a late work by Gaspard Dughet (cf. Sutton, Bibl. 1377, p. 300).

NEW TESTAMENT

R19. THE NATIVITY. Alte Pinakothek, Munich (617).
Published by D. Wild as an original (Bibl. 1383, pp. 235 f.), but in my opinion by an imitator, perhaps Pietro del Po (cf. Blunt, Bibl. 1226, pp. 400 f.).

R20. THE ADORATION OF THE SHEP-
HERDS.
No painting known.
Known from an anonymous engraving published by
Quenaut (Wildenstein, No. 34). A composition made
up by the engraver from elements taken from different
designs by Poussin (cf. Davies and Blunt, p. 209, No.
34, and Blunt, Bibl. 1357, p. 489).

R21. No painting known.
Known from an anonymous engraving (cf. Blunt, Bibl.
1357, pp. 488 f.) made up of elements taken from two
compositions by Poussin.

R22. No painting known.
Known from an engraving by Hainzelmann (Wildenstein, No. 36). Attributed by Zani, no doubt rightly,
to Simon Guillebault (cf. Blunt, Bibl. 1357, p. 489).

R23. THE ADORATION OF THE MAGI.
No painting known.
Known from an engraving by P. Picault (Andresen,
No. 113). This is presumably Pierre Picault, who died
in 1711, but, in spite of its early date and the inscription
N. Poussin pinx, the engraving seems to be after a
painting by a Roman artist such as Giacinto Gimig-
nani rather than one by Poussin.

R24. THE HOLY FAMILY.
No painting known.
Engraved by E. Picart (Wildenstein, No. 46). A
pastiche in the manner of Poussin.

R25. No painting known.
Engraving published by Poilly (Wildenstein, No. 47
and No. XI). The composition is probably by a French
follower of the later seventeenth century.

R26. THE VIRGIN, CHRIST AND ST. JOHN.
Musée du Berry, Bourges.
Probably by the 'Master of the Clumsy Children' (cf.
Blunt, Bibl. 1357, p. 497).

R27. THE HOLY FAMILY.
No painting known.
Known from an engraving published by G. Vallet,
inscribed Iao. Poussin in. (Andresen, No. 125). Rightly
rejected by Wildenstein (p. 347, No. I).

R28. THE HOLY FAMILY WITH ST. JOHN
AND ST. ELIZABETH.
Listed by Smith, No. 84, as coming from the Lenglier
collection. Perhaps the painting now in the Hermitage
Museum, Leningrad (cf. Blunt, Bibl. 1357, p. 497).

R29. THE HOLY FAMILY WITH ST.
JOHN AND TWO ANGELS.
No painting known.
A drawing by Fragonard of such a composition is
inscribed du Poussin Palais du Duc Torre a Naples (Mrs.
Hubert Chanter of Geneseo, New York, sale, Sotheby,
London, 10.vi.1959, lot 17).
No such picture is mentioned in the various accounts
of the della Torre collection, and, even allowing for the

liberties which Fragonard normally takes with his
originals, the composition and types seem impossible
for Poussin. The picture suggests rather an Italian
artist of the early seventeenth century, probably a
follower of the Carracci.

R30. THE VIRGIN AND CHILD WITH
ST. JOHN AND PUTTI. National Museum,
Budapest (577).
The picture was in the Bevilacqua sale, Sangiorgi,
Venice, 15 ff.x.1900, lot 149; it was bought by the
Museum from F. Ongania, Venice, in 1957, with
supposed provenance from the Principessa della
Cisterna, said to be a relation of the Pozzo family (cf.
Takács, Bibl. 1213, pp. 39 ff., and Bibl. 1291, pp.
259 ff.).
The canvas is oval, 58×75 cm. As far as I can judge
from a photograph, the painting is too sweet and too
soft for Poussin. It may be by the 'Master of the
Clumsy Children' (cf. Blunt, Bibl. 1357, p. 497, note
56).

R31. THE HOLY FAMILY WITH ST. JOHN,
ST. ELIZABETH AND PUTTI. Hermitage
Museum, Leningrad.
Probably by the 'Master of the Clumsy Children' (cf.
Blunt, Bibl. 1357, p. 497).

R32. THE FLIGHT INTO EGYPT.
No painting known.
Known from an engraving by Macret after a drawing
by Fragonard taken from a painting in the Palazzo
della Torre, Naples (Andresen, No. 150; Andresen-
Wildenstein, No. 150). No painting corresponding to
this engraving is known, and given the extreme freedom with which Fragonard and the engravers after
him treated their originals, it is difficult to speculate
what the painting may have been like and, therefore,
to express even a tentative judgment about its authenticity (cf. Blunt, Bibl. 1167, p. 83). A picture of this
subject in the Palazzo della Torre is mentioned by La
Lande (Bibl. 224a, VII, p. 57).

R33. THE REST ON THE FLIGHT INTO
EGYPT.
No painting known.
Known from an engraving by Claudine Bouzonnet
Stella (Andresen, No. 151). Weigert (Bibl. 945, II, p.
81, No. 14) points out that the robe of the Virgin is
inscribed J. Stella in., so that the design can confidently
be ascribed to this artist (cf. Wildenstein, p. 349, No.
III, and Davies and Blunt, p. 216, No. III).

R34. THE PRESENTATION OF CHRIST
IN THE TEMPLE.
No painting known.
Known from an engraving, possibly by Pietro del Po
(Andresen, No. 142), rightly rejected by Wildenstein
(p. 348, No. II; cf. also Davies and Blunt, p. 216, No.
II). Thuillier (Bibl. 1296, p. 82) convincingly attributes
the design to Mellin.

R35. CHRIST AND THE WOMAN TAKEN
   IN ADULTERY. Formerly Major Kincaid-
   Lennox, Downton Castle, Shropshire.
Inherited from Richard Payne-Knight (1750-1824);
sold at Sotheby, London, 26.vi.1957, lot 25. First
published by Waterhouse (Bibl. 1096, p. 306) as probably by Poussin, an attribution which I at first accepted
(Blunt, Bibl. 1227, p. 168). Having studied the picture
more closely, however, I now feel confident that it
cannot be by Poussin. It is difficult to propose an
alternative attribution, but the picture has many
affinities with the *Shepherds' Dream* in the Palazzo
Colonna (Grautoff, II, p. 281), for which the name of
Testa has been suggested.

R36. CHRIST HEALING THE SICK.
No painting known.
Known from an engraving published by Bonnart
(Wildenstein, No. 60), which is dated 1687 (Davies and
Blunt, p. 211, No. 60). Certainly not a composition by
Poussin.

R37. ECCE HOMO.
No painting known.
Known from an engraving attributed to Pietro del Po
(Andresen, No. 199), rightly rejected by Wildenstein
(p. 351, No. V).

R38. THE FLAGELLATION.
No painting known.
Known from an anonymous engraving, inscribed
N. Poussin pinx. In fact after a composition by Jacques
Stella (cf. Thuillier, Bibl. 1296, pp. 112 f.).

R39. THE LAMENTATION OVER THE
   DEAD CHRIST. Royal Collection, Hampton
   Court Palace, England.
Listed by Magne (1914, p. 210, No. 211) as a Poussin,
but apparently by an Italian artist of the late seventeenth
century.

R40. Sir Anthony Blunt, London.
Engraved by Pietro del Po (Wildenstein, No. 71). The
painting may perhaps also be by him (cf. Blunt, Bibl.
1226, p. 401). An almost identical version was on the
London art market in about 1961.

R41. NOLI ME TANGERE. Museo del Prado,
   Madrid (2306).
Grautoff, II, p. 269. By an imitator, perhaps Pietro del
Po (see above, L32).

R42. THE DEATH OF THE VIRGIN. St.
   Etienne-du-Mont, Paris.
Hourticq (Bibl. 899, p. 194) tried unsuccessfully to
prove that this is the missing picture for Notre-Dame.
In fact it is by a seventeenth-century Roman artist,
near Sacchi or the young Maratta (cf. Hourticq, Bibl.
813.1, pp. 167 ff., and Dacier, Bibl. 812, pp. 165 ff.).

R43. ST. JOHN THE BAPTIST. Musée des
   Augustins, Toulouse.
The attribution to Poussin was strongly supported by
Jamot (pp. 28 ff.), but the painting is undoubtedly a
work of Sébastien Bourdon.

R44. ST. PAUL.
No painting known.
Known from an engraving published by E. Gantrel
(Wildenstein, p. 353, No. VI; Davies and Blunt, p. 216,
No. VI). D. Wild (Bibl. 1384, pp. 313 f.) has con-
vincingly shown that the engraving is after a design
by J. B. de Champaigne.

R45. PAUL AND BARNABAS BEFORE
   SERGIUS PAULUS.
No painting known.
Known from an engraving published by E. Gantrel
(Wildenstein, No. 76). The composition is certainly
not by Poussin.

R46. PAUL AND SILAS.
No painting known.
Known from an engraving by Jean Lepautre, who
died in 1682 (Wildenstein, No. 77; Davies and Blunt,
p. 212, No. 77). In spite of the early date of this
engraving the composition cannot be by Poussin. It is
closer to works by Le Sueur, such as the story of Sts.
Protasius and Gervasius.

R47. THE MARTYRDOM OF ST. STEPHEN.
   Church of St. Etienne, Caen.
Published as a Poussin by Hourticq (Bibl. 899, pp.
188 ff.). Probably by Romanelli.

R48. THE INCREDULITY OF ST. THOMAS.
No painting known.
Known from an engraving published by G. Audran
(Wildenstein, No. 73; Davies and Blunt, p. 211. No.
73). A composition made up of the figures from the
Ordination belonging to the second series of Sacraments, against a setting taken from the *Eucharist* of the
same series. Only the figure of Christ has been invented
by the engraver.

SAINTS

R49. THE MARTYRDOM OF ST.
   BARTHOLOMEW.
No painting known.
Known from an engraving by Jean Couvay, who died
in 1675 (Wildenstein, No. 85). This is exactly based on
a large drawing in the Gabinetto dei Disegni, Rome
(FN 9920), 54·6 × 35·3 cm.) which is a variation on
Poussin's *Martyrdom of St. Erasmus* (Cat. No. 97). The
drawing may, like the engraving, be by Couvay.
A painting of poor quality of the same composition
appeared in the Kann sale, American Art Association,
New York, 7.i.1927, lot 70, as from the collection of
Cardinal Fesch.

R50. THE MARTYRDOM OF ST. CECILIA.
   Musée Fabre, Montpellier.
Rejected by all modern writers except Magne, who
lists it (1914, p. 211, No. 219). Attributed by Longhi
(Bibl. 835.1, pp. 88 ff.) and Salerno (Bibl. 1138.1, p. 32)

to Antonio Carracci, and by Thuillier (Bibl. 1180, pp. 22 ff.) to Remy Vuibert. The former attribution seems the more convincing.

R51. ST. DENIS CROWNED BY AN ANGEL. Musée des Beaux-Arts, Rouen.

From St. Germain-l'Auxerrois, Paris; confiscated in 1793, and recorded at that time as a copy after Poussin (Thuillier, Bibl. 1297, p. 33). Exhibited at Rouen in 1961 (*Exposition Poussin (Rouen)*, No. 42).
The attribution of this picture presents problems, but it cannot in my opinion be by Poussin (cf. Blunt, Bibl. 1323, p. 352).

R52. ST. DENIS TERRIFYING HIS EXECUTIONERS. Abbaye de Notre-Dame de Melleray, Loire Atlantique.

From the Abbey of St. Denis (cf. Thuillier, Bibl. 1297, pp. 33 f.). Exhibited at Rouen in 1961 (*Exposition Poussin (Rouen)*, No. 93), with a tentative attribution to Poussin. This cannot, however, really be maintained (cf. Blunt, Bibl. 1323, p. 352). This picture may even be Italian and has certain affinities with the works of Alessandro Turchi.

R53. ST. NORBERT. Alte Pinakothek, Munich (468).

Listed by Magne (1914, p. 214, No. 269) as a Poussin, but actually by Walter Damery (cf. Helbig, Bibl. 673.1, I, pp. 59 f.).

R54. TITLE-PAGE TO THE IMITATIO CHRISTI.

No painting known.
The engraving by Claude Mellan is traditionally said to be after Poussin (Wildenstein, No. 170), but is actually after Jacques Stella (cf. Thuillier, Bibl. 1296, pp. 103 f.).

ALLEGORY

R55. TIME SAVING TRUTH FROM ENVY AND DISCORD. Musée des Beaux-Arts, Lille (616).

Published by Grautoff (II, No. 105) as an original sketch. The picture has been generally and rightly regarded as a variant by an artist of the early nineteenth century, perhaps Géricault (cf. *Exposition Poussin (Rouen)*, p. 53, No. 103).

R56. THE DANCE OF THE FOUR SEASONS.

No painting known.
Known from an engraving by J. J. Avril, dated 1779 (Andresen-Wildenstein, No. 393), and listed by Smith, No. 274, from the engraving. Certainly not by Poussin. Pictures of this subject occur in various sales (e.g. Cardinal Antonio Barberini, etc., Davis and Millington, London, 23.xi.1691, lot 84) and collections,

but in many cases they are in fact copies of *A Dance to the Music of Time* (Cat. No. 121).
A picture entitled simply *Les Quatre Saisons* by Poussin is mentioned in the list of those belonging to Quesnel in pledge to Mme d'Aligre in 1697 (cf. Grouchy, Bibl. 618, pp. 92ff.).
The iconography of the picture is unusual, since the Seasons are represented by four deities—Venus, Bacchus, Mercury and Cupid—who dance to the music of Apollo.

R57. VANITAS. Galleria Spada, Rome (123).

Attributed by Zeri (Bibl. 1109.1, p. 133, No. 123) to Testa, but earlier regarded as a copy after Poussin. Almost certainly by Andrea Podestà (cf. Blunt, Bibl. 1166, p. 15).

R58. AMOR VINCIT OMNIA. The Cleveland Museum of Art, Cleveland, Ohio.

This picture was included in the Poussin exhibition (*Exposition Poussin (Louvre)*, No. 53), but at once aroused grave doubts (cf. Blunt, Bibl. 1226, p. 400). A drawing for the painting in the Lugt collection was published by Schaar (Bibl. 1347, pp. 184 ff.), who attributes both painting and drawing to Mola. The pedigree of the picture, as given in the Poussin exhibition catalogue, can be slightly amplified, since it appeared in the Erle-Drax sale, Christie, London, 19.ii.1910, lot 105.

R59. Hermitage Museum, Leningrad (1403).

Rightly rejected by Grautoff (II, p. 278), this picture must be by the 'Hovingham Master', though I did not realize this when I put his *oeuvre* together. What may be this picture or a copy of it appeared in the F. Verwyck sale, London, 1690, lot 166.

R60. Present whereabouts unknown.

Listed by Smith (No. 241) and Magne (1914, p. 215, No. 274) as by Poussin. A version of this composition was in the J. C. Gregory sale, Sotheby, London, 26.vi.1957, lot 57. It appeared to be by Testa.

CLASSICAL SUBJECTS

R61. ACHILLES AMONG THE DAUGHTERS OF LYCOMEDES. Musée du Louvre, Paris (3130).

Given by Paul Jamot in 1920 and published by him in that year (Bibl. 744). The attribution to Poussin has not been accepted by later scholars, except Fry, who discusses the picture in *Transformations* (Bibl. 801, pp. 18 ff.). It may be by Nicolas Colombel.

R62. APOLLO AND DIANA HUNTING. Herzog Anton-Ulrich Museum, Brunswick, Germany.

Probably by the 'Hovingham Master' (cf. Blunt, Bibl. 1324, p. 457).

R63. ARCAS AND CALLISTO. The Westminster Estates (at present with Lord Robert
Grosvenor, Ely Lodge, Iniskillen, Co. Fermanagh,
Northern Ireland).
Grautoff, II, p. 266. Presumably the picture in the
Dupille de Saint-Séverin sale, Joullain, Paris, 21 ff.ii.
1785, lot 227 (with detailed description; dimensions
2×3 ft.) and Collet sale, Lebrun, Paris, 14.v.1787, lot
273. Bought by Earl Grosvenor with the Ellis Agar
collection; passed by inheritance to the Dukes of
Westminster. Certainly by J. F. Millet.

R64. THE NURTURE OF BACCHUS. Musée
du Louvre, Paris (729).
Smith, No. 206; Grautoff, I, No. 25. Engraved by
Pool (Wildenstein, No. 129). In spite of its provenance
from the collection of Louis XIV this painting is
probably not by Poussin. I have elsewhere suggested
an attribution to the 'Master of the Clumsy Children'
(cf. Blunt, Bibl. 1357, pp. 494 f.). The picture is a
variant of one in the National Gallery, London (Cat.
No. 133).

R65. THE EDUCATION OF BACCHUS. Nat-
ional Gallery of Ireland, Dublin (800; there called
The Youth of Romulus).
Bodkin (Bibl. 858, pp. 174 f.) quotes Friedlaender as
suggesting François Duquesnoy as the author of their
picture. Since Duquesnoy was a sculptor, the name
intended was no doubt Charles Alphonse Dufresnoy.
In fact the picture appears to be by Jean Lemaire (cf.
Blunt, Bibl. 963, p. 242).

R66. BACCHUS AND ARIADNE. Museo del
Prado, Madrid (2312).
This picture (Grautoff, II, No. 49, and Dorival, Bibl.
1028, pp. 27 ff.) was in the Spanish royal collection by
1746 and may possibly have been the picture sold at the
Banqueting House, Whitehall, London, 2.vi.1684, lot
93 (in a sale which also included a *Parnassus*, perhaps
the Prado picture of that title, Cat. No. 129). In the
early nineteenth century the *Bacchus and Ariadne* was
ascribed to Castiglione, an attribution which is not
correct but contains an element of truth. In my opinion
it is very close to the *Amor vincit omnia* at Cleveland
(see above, R58; cf. Blunt, Bibl. 1226, p. 400). Mahon
(Bibl. 1367, pp. X, 17 f.) accepts the painting as an
original and dates it to 1627.

R67. Hermitage Museum, Leningrad.
This painting comes from the Stroganoff collection
and was engraved in the eighteenth century by Beauvais (Andresen-Wildenstein, No. 365). In my opinion,
however, it is by the 'Master of the Clumsy Children'
(cf. Blunt, Bibl. 1357, p. 497).

R68. Private collection, France.
This picture, first published as a Poussin by Grautoff
(Bibl. 864, pp. 323 ff.) and reproduced by Dorival
(Bibl. 1028, p. 28), is based on a drawing in the Ecole
des Beaux-Arts, reproduced by Dorival (*loc. cit.*).
Neither painting nor drawing can be by Poussin. In

CR, III, p. 22, No. B23, the name Dufresnoy was proposed as the possible author of both painting and drawing, but I should now incline to think that Nicolas
Chapron is a more likely candidate. The following
paintings of this subject are recorded: Richardson
mentions one in the Pozzo collection (see above,
L51); one is listed in the inventory of Cardinal de
Polignac's collection in 1738 (with dimensions 17×
19½ inches; cf. Bibl. 169.1, p. 268, No. 98), and three
are recorded in sales: Geminiani sale, Cock, London,
21.iv.1725, lot 10; Bryan sale, Coxe, London, 7 ff.v.
1804, third day, lot 17, and Allan Gilmore sale,
Phillips, London, 2.v.1843, lot 53.

R69. BACCHANAL.
Present whereabouts unknown.
Radstock sale, Christie, London, 12 f.v.1826, 2nd day,
lot 17, as from the collection of the Duc de Valentinois.
Later Frederick Cavendish-Bentinck; lent by him to
the Grafton Galleries in 1911 (cf. Fry, Bibl. 703.1,
p. 167). Sold Sotheby, London, 15.xii.1948, lot 109, as
Castiglione.
This picture is in my opinion by the 'Heytesbury
Master' (see below, R112).

R70. Herzog Anton-Ulrich Museum, Brunswick,
Germany (512).
Grautoff (II, p. 262) rightly rejects this picture, which
appears to be by the 'Heytesbury Master' (see below,
R112).

R71. Rouart collection, Paris.
From the Emile Péreire collection (cf. Bürger, Bibl.
508, pp. 193, 203). Listed by Magne (1914, p. 178, No.
19) as by Poussin, but in fact by an artist nearer to
Castiglione.

R72. LANDSCAPE WITH DIANA ASLEEP.
Museo del Prado, Madrid (2319).
Rightly rejected by Grautoff (II, p. 272), but repro-
duced by Magne (1914, Pl. opp. p. 182). Near to the
'Silver Birch Master', i.e. the early Gaspard Dughet.

R73. DIANA AND ENDYMION.
Formerly in the Château de Mornay (cf. *Diana and
Actaeon*, Cat. No. 148). Destroyed by a fire in 1947.
Described by Grautoff (I, p. 343) as *Diana and Orion*.
Dupont (Bibl. 1248, p. 242) points out that the picture
is a copy of an engraving after a design by Diepenbeeck.

R74. DIDO AND AENEAS. The Toledo Museum
of Art, Toledo, Ohio.
Smith, No. 289; Grautoff, II, No. 60. Both Smith and
Grautoff describe the composition as *Rinaldo and
Armida*; Lee (Bibl. 1091, p. 159) suggest the *Toilet of
Venus*; but Sterling (*Exposition Poussin (Louvre)*, p. 41,
No. 1) is undoubtedly right in identifying the subject
as Dido and Aeneas.
At the Poussin exhibition in 1960 the attribution of the
picture to Poussin gave rise to serious doubts, and I
later proposed that it was a work by the 'Hovingham
Master' (Bibl. 1324, pp. 457 ff.).

R75. Musée des Beaux-Arts, Besançon (213).
In the museum catalogue the picture is called *Le Bois sacré*. Probably by the 'Hovingham Master' (cf. Blunt, Bibl. 1324, p. 457).

R76. DIDO AND AENEAS TAKING RE-FUGE IN THE CAVE. National Gallery, London (95).
Listed by Smith (No. 330) as Poussin, but in fact by Gaspard Dughet.

R77. ECHO AND NARCISSUS. Staatliche Ge-mäldegalerie, Dresden.
Grautoff, I, No. 2. Attributed to the 'Hovingham Master' (cf. Blunt, Bibl. 1324, pp. 457 f.).

R78. HERCULES CROWNED BY MINERVA. Galerie Heim, Paris.
This picture is listed by Smith (No. 268) as by Poussin and as belonging to the Marquis of Bute. His description corresponds, however, almost exactly to a painting by La Hyre belonging to Heim, Paris, except that the width should be 3 ft. 9½ inches, instead of 4 ft. 9½ inches, and that the personifications of the continents are male and not female.

R79. THE HORATII. Museo del Prado, Madrid (2315).
Also called *A gladiatorial Combat*. Rightly rejected by Grautoff (II, p. 271), but reproduced by Magne (1914, Pl. opp. p. 166). By an artist near Testa.

R80. THE NURTURE OF JUPITER.
This picture is known in two versions, one in the National Gallery of Art, Washington (reproduced Blunt, Bibl. 1324, p. 459), the other belonging to Mr. George Tait, Malibu, California (reproduced Bertin-Mourot, Bibl. 1024, p. 92). Both are in my opinion by the 'Hovingham Master', as is also the drawing of the subject in Stockholm (*CR*, III, p. 13, No. 165).

R81. Private collection, Paris.
Landon, No. 165; Smith, No. 208 (who wrongly identifies it with the Dulwich picture, Cat. No. 161). The composition appears to be by an early and close imitator of Poussin.

R82. JUPITER AND ANTIOPE.
This composition is known in several versions, one in the Zorn Museum, Mora, Sweden, one in an English private collection, and one formerly in the Breslau Museum but now apparently destroyed. It was engraved by B. Picart in 1693 under the title *Hermaphrodite* (Wildenstein, No. 238). The composition is certainly not by Poussin, but is probably by the 'Hovingham Master' (cf. Blunt, Bibl. 1324, p. 458).

R83. JUPITER AND CALLISTO. Philadelphia Museum of Art, Philadelphia, Pa.
Smith, No. 183; Grautoff, II, No. 61.
The Philadelphia picture, which was bequeathed to the Museum by Mrs. Carol Tyson in 1963, was bought from Wildenstein, who had it from the Baron de la Tournelle. It is almost certainly the picture with the following pedigree: F. X. Geminiani, Rome, 1752, when engraved by Frey; brought to Paris in 1752 (cf. Guibal, Bibl. 273, p. 54, and Bouchitté, Bibl. 478, p. 347); Holbach sale, Paris, 16.iii.1789 (49×64 inches; as engraved by Frey and Daullé); Donjeux sale, Paris, 29.iv.1793, lot 31 (as from the Holbach sale); probably the painting in the Lebrun Gallery (Saint-Victor, Bibl. 449, p. 56); probably in the Fesch collection; Moret sale, Paris, 28 f.iv.1859 (as from the Fesch collection), bt. Mesteil (cf. Coutil, Bibl. 775, I, p. 2); sold Paris, 18.iv.1868, bt. Baron Clary; sold Paris, 2.v.1872, lot 27 (190×225 cm.; as from the Mesteil sale).
Other pictures of this subject are recorded as follows:
1. Count von Plattenberg und Wittem sale, Amster-dam, 2.iv.1738, lot 17 (cf. Hoet, Bibl. 195, I, p. 496; 58×70 inches).
2. Van Zwieten sale, The Hague, 12.iv.1741, lot 13 (*ibid.*, II, p. 11; 48×68 inches; perhaps the same as the last, though the dimensions do not agree).
3. Pier Francesco Grimaldi, Genoa (cf. Ratti, Bibl. 228a, I, p. 137).
A small version of the Philadelphia picture belonged till a few years ago to M. de la Caillerie, Parthenay, Deux-Sèvres, but is said to have been recently on the London art market.
Some doubts have been expressed verbally about the authenticity of the Philadelphia picture, but those who were sceptical have generally suggested that it was a copy of a lost original. The hard quality of the painting, the mechanical treatment of the foliage, and the cold colouring all confirm the view that the painting cannot be from the hand of Poussin himself, but it is more than doubtful if even the design is his. Even in the eight-eenth century Diderot (Bibl. 211, X, p. 497), who must have known the picture when it belonged to his friend Holbach, commented on the fact that it contains a breach of the unity of time, since Callisto appears twice, once in the foreground being embraced by Jupiter disguised as Diana, and once in the back-ground being dragged along by the jealous Juno. This is a feature which is never found in works certainly by Poussin (but see *Midas before Bacchus*, below, R89) and would be contrary to his way of think-ing. The work in fact shows all the characteristics of the paintings which have been ascribed to Karel Philips Spierincks (cf. Blunt, Bibl. 1225, pp. 308 ff.) and it can be attributed to him with a considerable degree of confidence.

R84. LEDA. Sir William Worsley, Bt., Hovingham Hall, Yorkshire.
Engraved by Louis de Châtillon (Wildenstein, No. 117). This and its pair, the *Toilet of Venus* (see below, R102) are the works around which I have attempted to group the personality of the 'Hovingham Master' (cf. Blunt, Bibl. 1324, pp. 454 ff.).

R85. Musée Condé, Chantilly (299).
Rightly rejected by Grautoff (II, p. 262), but repro-duced by Magne (1914, Pl. opp. p. 86).

R86. MARS AND RHEA SILVIA. Musée du Louvre, Paris (728).

Rejected by all modern critics except Magne, who lists it (1914, p. 27, No. 72).

R87. MERCURY, HERSE AND AGLAURUS. Sir Francis Cook, London.

Also described as *Classical Scene*. Rightly rejected by Grautoff (II, p. 280), but listed and reproduced by Magne (1914, p. 219, No. 337, and Pl. opp. p. 18). Attributed to Jean Lemaire (cf. Blunt, Bibl. 963, p. 245).

R88. LANDSCAPE WITH MERCURY AND ARGUS.

No painting known.

Known from an engraving by G. Volpato (Andresen-Wildenstein, No. 451). From the engraving the composition seems more likely to be by Dughet, but it is worth noting that in 1780 Volpato bought a landscape attributed to Poussin from the Marchese Boccapaduli (letter to Earl Cowper, dated 26.ii.1780 among the Cowper papers in the Hertfordshire County Record Office, kindly brought to my notice by Mr. Francis Watson).

R89. MIDAS BEFORE BACCHUS. Alte Pinakothek, Munich (528).

Smith, No. 272; Grautoff, II, No. 56.

First recorded in the Electoral collection in 1781. Copies are known in the museum at Burgos, the Musée Magnin at Dijon, and in an anon. sale, Christie, London, 30.v.1958, lot 162.

The picture has hung since the eighteenth century as a pair to the *Apollo and Daphne* (Cat. No. 130), but there is no evidence to show that they were painted as pendants, and it is significant that, whereas the *Apollo* was engraved in the seventeenth century, the *Midas* was not engraved till the nineteenth century (by Piloty; Andresen, No. 375).

The attribution to Poussin has never been challenged but is, I think, wrong for the following reasons.

First, the picture contains a breach of the unity of time, in that Midas appears in the foreground kneeling before Bacchus and again in the distance on the right washing in the Pactolus. There is no example of such an illogical arrangement in any work certainly by Poussin (but see the *Jupiter and Callisto* above, R83) and it is altogether contrary to his principles.

Secondly, there is no instance in Poussin's work of the sort of confused designing which occurs in the middle of the present picture, where the two satyrs behind the principal figures are so disposed that it is hard to know their exact position in space, and Bacchus seems at first sight to be sticking his left hand into the open mouth of the seated satyr, who is in fact well behind him.

Thirdly, the actual paint is thin and chalky, with a quality not to be paralleled in genuine works of Poussin; on the other hand the picture does not look like a copy.

It would be difficult to propose an alternative attribution, but certain parts of the picture, such as the sleeping Silenus and the two satyrs, have affinities with the group of works which I should tentatively ascribe to the 'Heytesbury Master' (see below, p. 178, R112).

R90. LANDSCAPE WITH ORPHEUS. Pinacoteca Capitolina, Rome.

From the Sacchetti collection (cf. Grautoff, I, p. 441, and Thuillier, Bibl. 1298, p. 266). Shown in the exhibition *I Francesi a Roma*, Palazzo Braschi, Rome, 1961, No. 258.

In the 1688 inventory of the Sacchetti collection it is described as follows: 'di Raffaellino et il Paese di Nicolò Pussino.' 'Raffaellino' is Giovanni Maria Bottalla, who was a pupil of Pietro da Cortona and died in 1644 (cf. Thieme-Becker, *ad vocem*). The painting bears no resemblance to his few known works (e.g. the *Jacob and Esau*, also in the Capitoline Museum), and the landscape has nothing to do with Poussin. Both figures and landscape are, however, identical in style with a painting of *Juno and Argus* in the Galleria Nazionale, Rome. In 1950 I ascribed this painting to the 'Silver Birch Master' (Bibl. 1051, p. 70), but I now believe it must be taken away from him. The landscape suggests that the artist might be a Fleming working in Rome. Another work possibly by the same hand is the *Pan and Syrinx*, also in the Galleria Nazionale, Rome.

R91. ORPHEUS AND EURYDICE. Metropolitan Museum of Art, New York.

Now universally regarded as by an imitator, but listed by Smith (No. 303) and Magne (1914, p. 202, No. 89) as an original (cf. CR, IV, pp. 52 f.).

R92. THE TRIUMPH OF OVID. Galleria Nazionale, Rome.

Published by Thuillier (Bibl. 1298, p. 266) with hesitant support for the old attribution to Poussin, which, however, cannot be maintained.

R93. PERSEUS AND PHINEUS. National Gallery, London (99).

Listed as a Poussin by Smith (No. 285, and Supplement, p. 801) and Magne (1914, p. 202, No. 95), but generally accepted as by Berthollet Flémalle (cf. Daniel and Jamot, Bibl. 861, pp. 191 ff.).

R94. THE MARRIAGE OF PIRITHOUS. National Gallery of Canada, Ottawa.

Listed by Magne (1914, p. 201, No. 69) as by Poussin, but in fact by Lebrun and connected with the gallery at the Hôtel Lambert (cf. Blunt, Bibl. 971, pp. 186 ff.).

R95. THE PLAGUE AT ATHENS. Sir Francis Cook, London.

Rightly rejected by Grautoff (II, p. 280), but reproduced by Magne (1914, Pl. opp. p. 20). Now attributed to Sweerts (cf. Longhi, Bibl. 880, pp. 271 ff.).

R96. THE PLAGUE AT MARSEILLES. Graf Czernin, Vienna.

Listed by Magne (1914, p. 202, No. 93) as by Poussin. The subject is in fact Tobit burying the dead, and the picture has been attributed to Andrea di Lione (cf. Blunt, Bibl. 943, pp. 142 ff.).

R97. THE RAPE OF PROSERPINE. Formerly Alexandre Benois collection, St. Petersburg.

Shown at an exhibition entitled *Les anciennes écoles de peinture dans les palais et collections privées russes* held in St. Petersburg in 1909.

Grautoff (II, p. 279) gives no verdict on the picture, which he had not seen, but from the reproduction it seems to be by Gaspard Dughet or J. F. Millet.

A picture of this subject is recorded in an anon. sale, Christie, London, 26 f.v.1780, second day, lot 14.

R98. PSYCHE AND HER FATHER CONSULTING THE ORACLE OF APOLLO. Herzog Anton-Ulrich Museum, Brunswick, Germany.

Smith, No. 219. Probably by the 'Hovingham Master' (cf. Blunt, Bibl. 1324, p. 457).

R99. PYRAMUS AND THISBE. Musée Thomas Henry, Cherbourg.

Rightly rejected by Grautoff (II, p. 115), but published by Hourticq as by Poussin (Bibl. 899, p. 115).

R100. Present whereabouts unknown.

First published by Grautoff (Bibl. 864, pp. 330 ff.) and reproduced by Bertin-Mourot (Bibl. 1023, No. XXIII). The picture, which in 1932 was in Berlin, was on the London art market in 1949. It may be by the same hand as the picture of the same subject in the Musée Henry, Cherbourg (see above).

R101. THE DRUNKEN SILENUS. Museo del Prado, Madrid (2321).

Listed by Magne as by Poussin (1914, p. 198, No. 25), but rightly identified by Grautoff (II, p. 273) as Neapolitan and probably a copy after Giordano.

R102. THE TOILET OF VENUS. Sir William Worsley, Bt., Hovingham Hall, Yorkshire.

A pair to the *Leda* (see above, R84) and like it by the 'Hovingham Master' (cf. Blunt, Bibl. 1324, pp. 454 ff.). Another version of the *Venus* was in the Westenberg sale, Lepke, Berlin, 27.x.1908.

R103. THE TRIUMPH OF VENUS. The Chatsworth Settlement, Chatsworth, Derbyshire.

Rightly rejected by Grautoff (II, p. 265), but reproduced by Magne (1914, Pl. opp. p. 198).

R104. MARS AND VENUS. Musée du Louvre, Paris (727).

In the French Royal collection by 1683 (cf. Bailly, p. 312). In spite of this provenance, however, the picture has been generally recognized as not being by Poussin (e.g. by Grautoff, II, p. 276). In my opinion it is by the 'Hovingham Master' (cf. Blunt, Bibl. 1324, p. 457). This picture was particularly admired by Ruskin (Bibl. 420, XII, p. 453).

R105. VENUS AND ADONIS. Musée Fabre, Montpellier (455).

Grautoff (II, p. 275) gives no decision on the picture, owing to the difficulty of seeing it (cf. Thuillier, Bibl. 1299, pp. 293 f., who is also cautious).

The seals on the back of the canvas, and a label reading *di casa Boccapadule*, prove that the painting came from the Palazzo Boccapaduli, but it cannot be certainly identified with any picture in the early accounts of the Pozzo collection. It must be the *Vénus et Adonis; grand paysage* mentioned by La Roque, who was in Rome between 1775 and 1778 (Bibl. 248, II, p. 320), and the *Paysage avec des figures représentant Vénus et Adonis* given by Manazzale in 1794 (Bibl. 308, II, p. 95). In spite of its provenance, however, I do not believe the picture to be by Poussin. It seems to be by a very skilful imitator, close to Testa (cf. Royal Academy, *The Age of Louis XIV*, Bibl. 1165, p. 73, No. 129, and Blunt, Bibl. 1166, pp. 10 ff.).

R106. Known from an engraving by Pool (Andresen-Wildenstein, No. 346) and a small oil painting in the Clerk of Penicuik collection, Penicuik, Scotland. The composition cannot be by Poussin, though the figure of Venus is almost exactly taken from the *Venus and Mercury* (Cat. No. 184).

R107. Several versions are known of this picture, of which the best is probably that in the collection of Sir Francis Cook (cf. Blunt, Bibl. 1357, pp. 494 f.).

Smith (No. 193) and Grautoff (II, No. 33) catalogue the Wilbraham version as an original, but the design belongs to the group which I attribute to the 'Master of the Clumsy Children' (*loc. cit.*). T. Bertin-Mourot (Bibl. 1023, Nos. XVII and XVIII) illustrates both the ex-Wilbraham (later Smith College, Northampton, Mass.) and the Cook versions. The Cook version is described as *Localisation inconnue*, owing to the fact that on the Anderson photograph of it is wrongly stated to be in the Prado.

R108. The Chatsworth Settlement, Chatsworth, Derbyshire.

By an artist influenced by both Poussin and Vouet (cf. Blunt, Bibl. 1357, p. 493).

R109. CHILDREN PLAYING. Calouste Gulbenkian Foundation, Lisbon.

Smith, No. 292; Grautoff, II, No. 28. Engraved by Avice (Wildenstein, No. 168).

The picture has the following pedigree: Nyert sale, Musier, Paris, 30.iii.1772, lot 2; Randon de Boisset sale, Remy, Paris, 27.ii.1777, lot 166; Ellis Agar by 1778, where it was engraved by Baillie as in his collection (Andresen-Wildenstein, No. 424); bt. with the Ellis Agar collection by Earl Grosvenor; passed by inheritance to the Dukes of Westminster; sold Christie, London, 9.vii.1924, lot 39, bt. Colnaghi.

In spite of its provenance the picture cannot be from the hand of Poussin. I have elsewhere proposed an attribution to the 'Master of the Clumsy Children' (cf. Bibl. 1357, pp. 493 f.).

R110. Prince Liechtenstein, Vaduz, Liechtenstein. Grautoff, II, No. 30. Probably by the 'Heytesbury Master' (see below, R112).

R111. TWO CHILDREN. The Earl of Pembroke and Montgomery, Wilton House, Wiltshire.
Grautoff, II, No. 31. A very fine early copy after two figures in the *Bacchanal before a Herm* in the National Gallery, London (Cat. No. 141), *q.v.*

R112. NYMPH SURPRISED BY SATYRS. Present whereabouts unknown.
The picture, formerly in the collection of Lord Heytesbury, was published in 1933 by Borenius (Bibl. 872, p. 3). I have never seen the original, but it is clear from the reproduction that it cannot be by Poussin. It can, however, be related to a group of paintings which I propose to put under the heading of the 'Heytesbury Master'. This artist seems to have been a specialist in the painting of Bacchanals characterized by obscenely grinning satyrs and nymphs either drunk or asleep, which show affinities with figures to be found in the paintings of Carpioni (see Pilo, Bibl. 1345.1, Figs. 91, 100, 107, 110). His most important work is perhaps the *Bacchanal* which formerly belonged to Frederick Cavendish-Bentinck (see above, R69), but he seems also to be responsible for the following works, all Bacchanals: Herzog Anton-Ulrich Museum, Brunswick (512; Smith, No. 218; see above, R70); A. Rosner collection, Tel Aviv; N. Klotz collection, Colombes, Seine; a composition known in two versions, a small one formerly in the Yarborough collection (sold Christie, London, 12.vii.1929, lot 73) and now belonging to Professor Richard Ellis, Edinburgh, the other, slightly larger, in an American private collection. The latter is probably the painting recorded in the Panné sale, Christie, London, 26 ff.iii.1819, 1st day, lot 61.
This artist may also be credited with the Liechtenstein *Children playing* (see above, R110) and a drawing in the Louvre of two sleeping nymphs surprised by a satyr (No. 14244).

R113. Another composition of this subject is known in three versions: two, almost identical versions, in the Kunsthaus, Zurich and the collection of Dr. Kurt Thalberg in the same city (cf. engraving by Daullé, Andresen-Wildenstein, No. 357), and a variant in the National Gallery, London.
The Kunsthaus version was shown at the Poussin exhibition (*Exposition Poussin (Louvre)*, No. 34), but immediately aroused doubts and cannot in fact be by the artist. The Thalberg version (Bertin-Mourot, Bibl. 1023, No. XX) is less sensitive and is probably a copy of the Kunsthaus picture with small variations.
The National Gallery picture (91; cf. Grautoff, II, No. 24, and Davies, Bibl. 988a, p. 183) seems to be by a later hand.

The Kunsthaus picture may possibly be the one mentioned in inventories of the Falconieri collection (cf. Blunt, Bibl. 1426, p. 70).

R114. NYMPHS, SATYRS AND CUPIDS. Royal Collection, Hampton Court Palace, England.
Grautoff, II, p. 267. Engraved by Pool (Wildenstein, No. 128). First recorded in the collection of Charles II as by *Carlo Fellippo*, i.e. Karel Philips Spierincks (cf. Blunt, Bibl. 1225, pp. 308 ff.).

R115. NYMPHS AND PUTTI. Musée des Beaux-Arts, Besançon (211).
Probably by the 'Hovingham Master' (cf. Blunt, Bibl. 1324, p. 457).

R116. PASTORAL SCENE. Musée des Beaux-Arts, Marseilles.
By an imitator, probably the hand responsible for a drawing of the Finding of Romulus in the Worcester Art Museum, Mass. and another pastoral scene in a private collection (cf. Blunt, Bibl. 1166, p. 12).

R117. COPY OF THE *ALDOBRANDINI WEDDING*. Palazzo Doria, Rome.
Grautoff, II, No. 7. There is a tradition going back to the early eighteenth century that this copy is by Poussin, but its quality is so low that this cannot be the case (cf. Blunt, Bibl. 1426, pp. 62 f.).
Another copy in the Musée des Beaux-Arts, Chartres, has also been ascribed to Poussin, but it dates from the late eighteenth century (cf. Thuillier, Bibl. 1298, p. 272, and Bibl. 1299, p. 288).

R118. COPY AFTER TITIAN'S *ANDRIANS*.
National Gallery of Scotland, Edinburgh.
Published by Grautoff (II, No. 22) as by Poussin, owing to a confusion with the copy of the *Feast of the Gods* (Cat. No. 201).

LANDSCAPES

R119. LANDSCAPE WITH ARCADIAN SHEPHERDS. Walker Art Gallery, Liverpool.
Accepted by Grautoff (II, No. 36), who wrongly states that the picture belonged to Roscoe. According to the catalogue of the Gallery it was probably bought by the Liverpool Royal Institution in 1842. Also accepted by Jamot (Bibl. 788, pp. 82 f.), but apparently by the same hand as the *Amor vincit omnia* at Cleveland (see above, p. 173, R58).

R120–121. TWO LANDSCAPES WITH FIGURES.
Present whereabouts unknown.
Listed by Smith (Nos. 334, 335). Both were on the London art market in the 1930's (for one cf. Blunt, Bibl. 1166, p. 11, Fig. 12).

R122. LANDSCAPE WITH A RECLINING NYMPH. Pendant to R.123.

R123. LANDSCAPE WITH A NYMPH RIDING A GOAT. Formerly Metropolitan Museum of Art, New York (92.14.1 and 2).
Grautoff, II, Nos. 37 and 46. The attribution to the 'Silver Birch Master' (Blunt, Bibl. 1051, p. 70) has been generally accepted, and this notional artist has now been identified by Dr. John Shearman as the young Gaspard Dughet (cf. Blunt, Bibl. 1195, p. 390, note 9).

R124–129. LANDSCAPES. Museo del Prado, Madrid (2305, 2307, 2308, 2310, 2316, 2323).
All listed by Magne (1914, Nos. 309, 310, 313, 314, 333, 334) as by Poussin. No. 2305 is probably by the 'Silver Birch Master' (cf. Blunt, Bibl. 1051, pp. 69 ff.), i.e. the early Gaspard Dughet. Nos. 2307, 2308, 2310, 2316 and 2323 are probably by Jean Lemaire (cf. Blunt, Bibl. 963, pp. 241 ff.).

R130. Musée Condé, Chantilly.
Grautoff (II, No. 142) is the only writer on Poussin to ascribe to him this picture, which is clearly a work of Gaspar Dughet.

R131. Formerly Blumenthal Gallery, Berlin.
Published by Grautoff (Bibl. 864, p. 334). Certainly not by Poussin, perhaps by Millet.

R132. THE LAKE OF BOLSENA.
Formerly (1925) J. de Beruete, Madrid (Smith, No. 341). Lord Radstock sale, Phillips, London, 19.iv.1823, lot 69, bt. in; Lord Radstock sale, Christie, London, 12.v.1826, lot 35; N. Bailie (Smith, *loc. cit.*); Lord Northwick (Waagen, Bibl. 384b, III, p. 205, No. 5); Northwick sale, Cheltenham, 26 ff.vii.1859, 5th day, lot 424, bt. J. Drax.
Published as a Poussin by Jamot (Bibl. 788, p. 112), who regards a very similar picture, then in the May collection, Paris, as a copy by Gaspard Dughet. In fact both are probably late works by Gaspard.

R133. Oskar Reinhart Institute, Winterthur.
Listed by Smith (No. 340), published by Friedlaender (1914, p. 253) and later by Grautoff (Bibl. 864, p. 338) and Bertin-Mourot (Bibl. 1023, No. XXXII). Mahon (Bibl. 1338, p. 119) accepts it as an original and dates it *c.* 1637, but in spite of its quality I believe that it is an exceptionally fine work of Gaspard Dughet.

R134–135. The Chatsworth Settlement, Chatsworth, Derbyshire.
Listed by Smith (Nos. 326, 327). Apparently by Gaspard Dughet.

R136–137. The Marquis of Bute, Mount Stuart, Rothesay, Isle of Bute, Scotland.
Listed by Smith (Nos. 332, 333). In the manner of Gaspard Dughet.

R138. Prince Liechtenstein, Vaduz, Liechtenstein.
Listed by Magne (1914, p. 217, No. 305) and reproduced as by Poussin by P. Marois (Bibl. 1104, Pl. 44). Probably by an imitator of Gaspard Dughet.

R139. National Gallery, London (2619).
Listed twice by Magne (1914, p. 201, No. 65, and p. 217, No. 320) as by Poussin. More recently attributed to the 'Silver Birch Master' (cf. Blunt, Bibl. 1051, pp. 69 ff.), i.e. the early Gaspard Dughet.

MISCELLANEOUS

R140. WOMEN BEFORE A TOMB. Musée Magnin, Dijon (261).
Certainly not by Poussin. The picture has been ascribed to C. A. Dufresnoy (cf. Demonts, Bibl. 781.1, p. 175), but it has also affinities with the work of Jean Lemaire.

R141. FIGURE STUDIES.
Wildenstein (No. 237) includes in his list of seventeenth-century engravings after Poussin a set by Benedikt Winckler after single figures purporting to come from compositions by Poussin. This artist lived from *c.* 1727 to 1797, and the figure of Noah reproduced by Wildenstein, though connected with figures in several compositions by Poussin (e.g. the *Adoration of the Magi*, Cat. No. 24), does not correspond exactly to any one figure. I have not seen the other engravings of the series.

REFERENCE ILLUSTRATIONS
TO THE CATALOGUE OF
POUSSIN'S PAINTINGS

1

2

3

4

5

6

7

8

9

10

11

12

13

14

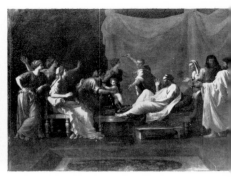

15

16

17

18

19

20

21

22

23

24

25

26

27

28

29

30

31

32

33

34

35

36

37

38

39

40

41

42

43

44

45

46

47

48

49

50

51

52

53

54

55

56

57

58

59

60

61

62

63

64

65

66

67

68

69

70

71

72

73

4

75

76

77

78

79

80

81

82

83

84

85

86

87

88

89

90

91

92

93

94

95

96

97

98

99

100

01

102

103

104

105

106

107

108

109

110

112

113

114

115

116

117

118

119

120

121

122

123

124

125

126

127

128

129

130

131

132

133

134

135

136

137

138

139

140

141

142

143

144

145

146

147

148

149

150

151

152

153

154

155

156

157

158

159

160

161

162

163

164

165

166

167

168

169

170

171

172

174 175

176 177

178 179 180

181 182 183

184   185

186   187   188

189   190   191

192   193   194

195 196 197 198

199 200 201

202 203 204

205 206 207

208

209

210

211

212

213

214

215

216

217

L. 117

218

Putti fighting on Goats (Cat. No. 194). X-ray photograph showing parts of the figures of two nymphs on the left.

Echo and Narcissus (Cat. No. 151). X-ray photograph showing a seated woman with children, possibly a 'Madonna and Child with putti', and also the almost life-size head and arm of a woman.

The Virgin protecting the city of Spoleto (Cat. No. 94). X-ray photograph showing the figure of a reclining nymph. The figure of the Virgin Mary is visible upside down at the bottom of the picture.

Rinaldo and Armida (Cat. No. 202).   X-ray photograph showing the figure of a dead or wounded man attended by a putto,
possibly part of a composition representing the same subject as the picture now visible.

Landscape with a Roman Road (Cat. No. 210).   X-ray photograph showing on the left three figures identical with those in the left-hand group of Poussin's painting of *Moses trampling on Pharaoh's Crown* in the Louvre (Cat. No. 15).

BIBLIOGRAPHY

The following bibliography contains in principle the books and articles known to me which refer to Poussin. Of necessity it cannot be complete, partly because there are undoubtedly sources that have escaped me, and partly because some lower limit of importance had to be drawn. It would obviously have been useless to include, for instance, every newspaper article referring to the Poussin exhibition in the Louvre in 1960, and it may well be that I have gone rather further than was sensible in adding such items to the bibliography.

Catalogues of public museums and galleries have not generally been included, since, where a connection with a particular gallery is indicated, it is assumed that the reader will refer to the catalogue if he wishes. Exceptions have been made for a few catalogues, such as Martin Davies's catalogue of the French pictures in the National Gallery, London, which make a vital contribution to our knowledge of the pictures concerned, particularly of their histories.

At the suggestion of the Bollingen Foundation, who were originally to have published this bibliography, it has been arranged in chronological order. This has the advantage that the reader can see at a glance the ebb and flow of interest in Poussin. It has the disadvantage that, if one knows the author of a book but not the date of its publication, it cannot be traced immediately in the bibliography, but this defect is remedied by the alphabetical index of authors appended to the bibliography.

The chronological arrangement has involved a certain number of arbitrary decisions as regards the placing of items, but generally speaking they have been put in the chronological sequence at the point where they seem to belong most happily; that is to say, inventories or early accounts of collections have generally been placed at the date at which they were made, even if they were not published till much later, and early diaries covering long periods have been put under the year in which Poussin is first mentioned. In every case cross-reference is made at the date of publication.

With a work such as the monograph on Poussin, to which this bibliography is a kind of supplement, the process of gestation has been lengthy—the bibliography was first completed in 1961 and gradually expanded—and it is inevitable that changes should have been made after the numbering was settled, with the result that certain numbers have been left blank; books which came to my notice at a later stage have been given numbers with decimal points.

This bibliography only contains books which mention Poussin and not the many other works which are referred to in the text volume, but which are only concerned with the background to Poussin's art.

In view of the enormous number of books listed below it may help a student of Poussin to have some indication of the most important sources for Poussin's life and of some of the most important recent works dealing with the artist.

The essential sources are the artist's own letters (Bibl. 3) and the biographies by Bellori (Bibl. 56) and Félibien (Bibl. 44), both of whom knew Poussin and were able to base their accounts on first-hand information. Some further details can be gleaned from Mancini (Bibl. 1), who wrote his biography a few years after Poussin's arrival in Rome, and from Sandrart (Bibl. 67), who knew him during the years he himself spent in Rome, which he left in 1635. Passeri's biography (Bibl. 75) is mainly based on Bellori's Life, but differs from it in one or two particulars. Chantelou's diary of Bernini's visit to Paris in 1665 (Bibl. 41) is important as recording the reactions of the great sculptor to paintings by Poussin which he saw in Paris.

No important biography of Poussin was written during the eighteenth century, but Dézallier d'Argenville (Bibl. 178) supplies some information about the location of pictures in the middle of the century. Otherwise books listed under eighteenth-century dates consist mainly of guide books or works by those who travelled to France and Italy and recorded paintings by Poussin that they saw.

The nineteenth century saw the publication of two basic catalogues: Smith's (Bibl. 390) of the paintings, and Andresen's (Bibl. 500) of the engravings after Poussin, but very little else published in this period is more than of incidental interest, though Hazlitt's descriptions of Poussin's paintings (Bibl. 411, 417) are well worth reading as examples of art criticism.

Desjardins's short monograph (Bibl. 656), published in 1903, marks a turning point in Poussin studies, although it is now superseded by later research. The year 1914 saw the publication of Walter Fried-laender's sensitive and penetrating essay (Bibl. 722), Emile Magne's biography (Bibl. 724), and Grautoff's two volumes (Bibl. 723), of which the second contains a catalogue of works known to him. Many of his attributions and much of his dating would not now be generally acceptable, but his was a pioneer work.

Since about 1930 publications on Poussin have appeared at an increased rate. Friedlaender's article in Thieme-Becker (Bibl. 875), published in 1933, adds much factual matter to his earlier essay. The first volume of the catalogue raisonné of the drawings (Bibl. 944) appeared in 1939; three more volumes have already appeared, and a fifth is in preparation. A number of articles published by Paul Jamot during the 1930's were reprinted in a collective volume in 1948 (Bibl. 1031).

Since the war important articles have appeared either in journals, like the Burlington Magazine, the Journal of the Warburg and Courtauld Institutes, the Gazette des Beaux-Arts, and the Revue des Arts, or in collected volumes, such as the Bulletin de la Société Poussin (1947–50) and the Actes of the Colloque Nicolas Poussin, published in 1960.

The exhibition of Poussin's works held at the Louvre in 1960 was made the occasion for an extensive catalogue (Bibl. 1266) and aroused considerable controversy over questions of chronology. Denis Mahon's views are set out in his 'Poussiniana' (Bibl. 1367), which appeared in a special Poussin number of the Gazette des Beaux-Arts for July-August 1962.

The study of Poussin's iconography was sparked off by Professor Gombrich's article on the *Orion* (Bibl. 974) and followed up by the present writer's, also published in 1944 (Bibl. 972). It has since been carried still further by Professor Panofsky (Bibl. 1273) and Dr. Sauerländer (Bibl. 1140).

In 1966 Professor Walter Friedlaender published a further book on Poussin, which is undoubtedly the most valuable general treatment of Poussin's work in the English language.

LIST OF ABBREVIATIONS USED IN THE BIBLIOGRAPHY

AA	L'Art et les Artistes	JWCI	Journal of the Warburg and Courtauld Institutes
AAF	Archives de l'Art français	MP	Magasin Pittoresque
AB	Art Bulletin	MSHP	Mémoires de la Société de l'Histoire de Paris
Actes	Actes du Colloque International Nicolas Poussin	NAAF	Nouvelles Archives de l'Art français . . .
AF	Art de France	RA	Revue des Arts
AN	Art News	RAAM	Revue de l'Art ancien et moderne
AQ	Art Quarterly	RKW	Repertorium für Kunstwissenschaft
BM	Burlington Magazine	RSBAD	Réunion des Sociétés des Beaux-Arts des Départe-ments
BSHAF	Bulletin de la Société de l'Histoire de l'Art français	RUA	Revue Universelle des Arts
BSP	Bulletin de la Société Poussin	ZBK	Zeitschrift für bildende Kunst
GBA	Gazette des Beaux-Arts	ZKG	Zeitschrift für Kunstgeschichte
IS	Italian Studies	ZKW	Zeitschrift für Kunstwissenschaft
JWI	Journal of the Warburg Institute		

BIBLIOGRAPHY

1627–1628

1 Mancini, Giulio, *Considerazioni sulla pittura*, ed. Adriana Marucchi and Luigi Salerno (Accademia Nazionale dei Lincei), Rome, 1956–57. 2 vols.
1a Life of Poussin reprinted in J. Thuillier, 'Pour un "Corpus Pussinianum" ', *Actes*, II, 1960, p. 52.

1638

2 Salomon, R. 'An unknown letter of Nicolas Poussin', *JWI*, I, 1937, pp. 79 ff.

1639–

3 Poussin, Nicolas, *Collection des lettres de Nicolas Poussin*, ed. Quatremère de Quincy, Paris, 1824.
3a *Correspondance de Nicolas Poussin*, ed. Ch. Jouanny, Paris 1911.
3b *Lettres de Poussin*, ed. P. du Colombier, Paris, 1929.
3c 'Nicolas Poussin. Lettre communiquée par M. Chambry', *AAF*, 1852–53, pp. 225 ff.
3d 'Nicolas Poussin. Lettre au Cavalier del Pozzo communiquée par M. Antoine-Augustin Renouard', *AAF*, 1853–55, pp. 1 f.
3e *Nicolas Poussin. Lettres et propos sur l'art*, ed. Anthony Blunt, Paris, 1964.

1642

4 Baglione, Giovanni, *Le vite de' pittori, scultori et architetti. Dal Pontificato di Gregorio XIII del 1572. In fino a' tempi di Papa Urbano Ottavo nel 1642*, Rome, 1642.
4a Facsimile. Ed. Valerio Mariano, Rome, 1935.
4b Passage referring to Nicolas Poussin reprinted in J. Thuillier, 'Pour un "Corpus Pussinianum" ', *Actes*, II, 1960, p. 69.

1643

5 *Basilica in honorem S Francisci Xaverii . . . descripta*, Paris, 1643.
5a Parts reprinted in J. Thuillier, 'Pour un "Corpus Pussinianum" ', *Actes*, II, 1960, pp. 69 ff.
6 Bosse, Abraham, *La Pratique du trait à preuves de M. Desargues*, Paris, 1643.
6a Parts reprinted in J. Thuillier, 'Pour un "Corpus Pussinianum" ', *Actes*, II, 1960, p. 73.

1643–1644

7 Brackenhoffer, Elias. *Voyage en France, 1643–1644*, tr. from the German by H. Lehr, Paris, 1925.

1644

8 Evelyn, John, *Memoirs, illustrative of the life and writings of John Evelyn, Esq. F. R. S. . . . comprising his diary from the year 1641 to 1705–1706, and a selection of his familiar letters . . . The whole now first published from the original MSS.*, ed. William Bray, London, 1818. 2 vols.

8a *The Diary of John Evelyn*, ed. Austin Dobson, London 1906. 3 vols.
8b *The Diary of John Evelyn*, ed. E. S. de Beer, Oxford, 1955. 6 vols.
8c Relevant passages reprinted in J. Thuillier, 'Pour un "Corpus Pussinianum" ', *Actes*, II, 1960, pp. 74, 85, 190.

1646

9 Ferrari, Giovanni Battista, *Hesperides sive de Malorum aureorum cultura et usu libri quatuor*, Rome, 1646.
10 Scudéry, Georges de, *Le Cabinet de Mr de Scudéry*, Paris, 1646.
10a Relevant parts reprinted in J. Thuillier, 'Pour un "Corpus Pussinianum" ', *Actes*, II, 1960, pp. 75 ff.

1647–1649

11 Félibien, André, Manuscripts concerning his visit to Italy (Bibliothèque de Chartres, MSS. 15–19), ed. by Yves Delaporte, 'André Félibien en Italie, 1647–49', *GBA*, 1958, I, pp. 193 ff.
11a Parts reprinted in J. Thuillier, 'Pour un "Corpus Pussinianum" ', *Actes*, II, 1960, pp. 79 ff.

1648

12 Tristan L'Hermite, François, *Les vers héroiques du Sieur Tristan l'Hermite*, Paris, 1648.
12a Parts reprinted in J. Thuillier, 'Pour un "Corpus Pussinianum" ', *Actes*, II, pp. 81 f.

1648–1793

13 *Académie Royale de peinture et de sculpture, Procès-verbaux*, ed. Anatole de Montaiglon, Paris, 1875–1909. 11 vols.

1649

14 Bosse, Abraham, *Sentimens sur la Distinction des Diverses Manieres de Peinture, Dessein et Graveure, et des Originaux d'avec leurs Copies*, Paris, 1649.
14a Parts reprinted in J. Thuillier, 'Pour un "Corpus Pussinianum" ', *Actes*, II, 1960, pp. 82 ff.
15 Pader, Hilaire, *Traicté de la Proportion naturelle et artificielle des choses*, Toulouse, 1649. (Partial tr. of G. P. Lomazzo, *Trattato dell' Arte della Pittura*, Milan, 1584.)
15a Parts reprinted in J. Thuillier, 'Pour un "Corpus Pussinianum" ', *Actes*, II, 1960, pp. 84 f.

1650

16 Fréart de Chambray, Roland, *Parallèle de l'architecture antique et de la moderne*, Paris, 1650.
16a *A parallel of the Antient Architecture with the Modern*, tr. John Evelyn, London, 1664.
16b Parts reprinted in J. Thuillier, 'Pour un "Corpus Pussinianum" ', *Actes*, II, 1960, pp. 86 f.

1651

17 Leonardo da Vinci, *Traitté de la Peinture de Leonard de Vinci donné au public et traduit d'Italien en François*, tr. Roland Fréart de Chambray, Paris, 1651.

17a *Trattato della pittura*, Paris, 1651.

17b Parts reprinted in J. Thuillier, 'Pour un "Corpus Pussinianum" ', *Actes*, II, 1960, pp. 87 ff.

1652

18 Berthod, Sieur, *La Ville de Paris en vers burlesque*, Paris, 1652.

18a Parts reprinted in J. Thuillier, 'Pour un "Corpus Pussinianum" ', *Actes*, II, 1960, pp. 93 ff.

1653

19 Desmarets de Saint-Sorlin, Jean, *Les Promenades de Richelieu ou les vertus chrétiennes*, Paris, 1653.

19a Parts reprinted in J. Thuillier, 'Pour un "Corpus Pussinianum" ', *Actes*, II, 1960, pp. 95 ff.

20 *Inventaire de tous les meubles du Cardinal Mazarin*, London, 1861.

21 Pader, Hilaire, *La peinture parlante*, Toulouse, 1653.

21a Parts reprinted in Chennevières-Pointel, *Recherches*, IV, pp. 91 ff. See No. 433.

21b Parts reprinted in J. Thuillier, 'Pour un "Corpus Pussinianum" ', *Actes*, II, 1960, pp. 97 ff.

22 Saint-Amant, Marc Antoine Gérard de, *Moyse sauvé, idylle héroïque*, Paris, 1653.

22a Parts reprinted in J. Thuillier, 'Pour un "Corpus Pussinianum" ', *Actes*, II, 1960, pp. 96 f.

c. 1655

23 Sauval, Henri, *Histoire et recherches des antiquités de la Ville de Paris*, Paris, 1724. 3 vols.

23a Parts reprinted in J. Thuillier, 'Pour un "Corpus Pussinianum" ', *Actes*, II, 1960, pp. 147 ff.

1655–1656

24 'Nicolas Poussin. Lettres de Louis Fouquet à son frère Nicolas Fouquet', ed. Ernest de Buchère de Lépinois and Anatole de Montaiglon, *AAF*, 1862, pp. 267 ff.

24a Parts reprinted in J. Thuillier, 'Pour un "Corpus Pussinianum" ', *Actes*, II, 1960, pp. 102 ff.

1656–1657

25 Symonds, Richard, *Diary*. Unpublished MSS. in the British Museum (MSS. Egerton, 1635, 1636).

1657

25.1 La Salle, His de, 'Lettre de Bouzonnet-Stella au Poussin', *AAF*, 1853–55, pp. 366 ff.

26 Scanelli, Francesco, *Il Microcosmo della pittura, overo trattato diviso in due libri*, Cesena, 1657.

26a Parts reprinted in J. Thuillier, 'Pour un "Corpus Pussinianum" ', *Actes*, II, 1960, pp. 107 f.

1657–1659

27 Coulanges, M. de, *Relations de mon voyage d'Allemagne et d'Italie ez années mil six cens cinquante sept et cinquante huit*. Manuscript in the Bibliothèque Nationale, Paris (MS. fr. 8994). Parts printed in J. Thuillier, 'Pour un "Corpus Pussinianum" ', *Actes*, II, 1960, pp. 108 f.

1658

28 Pader, Hilaire, *Songe énigmatique sur la peinture universelle*, Toulouse, 1658.

28a Parts reprinted in Chennevières-Pointel, *Recherches*, IV, pp. 134 ff. See No. 433.

1659

28.1 Chassant, Alphonse, and Bordeaux, Raymond, 'Voeux d'une religieuse des Andelys, présumée soeur de Nicolas Poussin', *AAF*, 1855–56, pp. 40 f.

c. 1660

29 *Les choses les plus remarquables de Paris*, Paris, n.d.

29a Reprinted by Paulin Paris in his ed. of *Le Voyage de Lister . . .*, see No. 115a.

29b Parts reprinted in J. Thuillier, 'Pour un "Corpus Pussinianum" ', *Actes*, II, 1960, p. 110.

c. 1660–1675

30 Malvasia, Carlo Cesare, *Vite di Pittori Bolognesi*, ed. Adriana Arfelli, Florence, 1961.

1662

31 Bie, Cornelis de, *Het Gulden Cabinet van de edele vry Schilder-Const*, Antwerp, 1662.

31a Part reprinted in J. Thuillier, 'Pour un "Corpus Pussinianum" ' *Actes*, II, 1960, p. 115.

32 Fréart de Chambray, Roland, *Idée de la Perfection de la Peinture*, Paris, 1662.

32a *An idea of the Perfection of Painting*, tr. by John Evelyn, London, 1668.

32b Parts reprinted in J. Thuillier, 'Pour un "Corpus Pussinianum" ', *Actes*, II, 1960, pp. 110 ff.

33 Loménie, Louis Henri, Comte de Brienne, *Ludovicus Henricus Lomenius Briennae comes . . . de Pinacotheca sua*, Paris, 1662.

33a Part reprinted in J. Thuillier, 'Pour un "Corpus Pussinianum" ', *Actes*, II, 1960, p. 115.

1663

34 La Fontaine, Jean de, *Oeuvres*, ed. Henri Régnier, Paris, 1883–97. 12 vols.

34.1 Skippon, Philip, *An account of a journey made thro' part of the Low-Countries, Germany, Italy and France*, in *A Collection of voyages and travels*, ed. A. and J. Churchill, VI, London, 1732.

1663–1664

35 Monconys, Balthasar de, *Journal des Voyages*, Lyons, 1665–66. 3 vols.

35a Parts reprinted in J. Thuillier, 'Pour un "Corpus Pussinianum" ', *Actes*, II, 1960, pp. 116 ff.

1664

36 [Bellori, Giovanni Pietro] *Nota delli musei, librerie, galerie, et ornamenti di statue e pitture, ne' palazzi, nelle case, e ne' giardini di Roma*, Rome, 1664.

37 Dati, Carlo Roberto, *Delle lodi del Commendatore Cassiano dal Pozzo*, Florence, 1664.

Fréart de Chambray, Roland, *Parallèle . . .*, see No. 17a.

c. 1664

38 Rosa, Salvator, *Satire*, Amsterdam, n.d. (*c.* 1664).

38a Reprinted in his *Poesie e lettere*, ed. G. A. Cesareo, Naples, 1892. 2 vols.

1664–1715

39 Guiffrey, Jules, *Comptes des bâtiments du roi sous le règne de Louis XIV* (Collection des documents inédits sur l'histoire de France publiés par les soins du Ministre de l'Instruction Publique, troisième série, Archéologie), Paris, 1881–1901. 5 vols.

1665

40 Bosse, Abraham, *Traité des Pratiques Géometrales et Perspectives enseignées dans l'Académie Royale de la Peinture et Sculpture*, Paris, 1665.

40a Parts reprinted in J. Thuillier, 'Pour un "Corpus Pussinianum" ', *Actes*, II, 1960, pp. 121 f.

41 Fréart de Chantelou, Paul, *Journal du voyage du Cavalier Bernin en France*, ed. Ludovic Lalanne, *GBA*, 1877–84.

41a Reprint in one volume, Paris, 1885.

41b *Tagebuch des Herrn von Chantelou über die Reise des Cavaliere Bernini nach Frankreich*, tr. W. H. Rose, Munich, 1919.

41c Reprint of original text, Paris, 1930.

41d *Bernini in Francia*, tr. Stefano Bottari, Rome, 1946.

41e Parts reprinted in J. Thuillier, 'Pour un "Corpus Pussinianum" ', *Actes*, II, 1960, pp. 123 ff. All references to 1885 ed.

1665–1666

Monconys, Balthasar de, *Journal des voyages*, see No. 35.

1665–

42 Boyer, Ferdinand, 'Les Inventaires après décès de Nicolas Poussin et de Claude Lorrain', *BSHAF*, 1928, pp. 143 ff.

1666

43 Marolles, Michel de, *Catalogue de livres d'estampes et de figures en taille douce, avec un dénombrement des pièces qui y sont contenues fait à Paris en l'année 1666*, Paris, 1666.

43a Parts reprinted in J. Thuillier, "Pour un "Corpus Pussinianum" ', *Actes*, II, 1960, pp. 139 f.

1666–1688

44 Félibien, André, *Entretiens sur les vies et sur les ouvrages des plus excellens peintres anciens et modernes*, Paris, 1666–88. 5 vols.
The *Entretien* containing the life of Poussin first appeared in the last volume published in 1688.

44a 2nd edition, Paris, 1685–88. 2 vols.

44b Reprint, London, 1705. 5 vols.

44c Reprinted. Trévoux, 1725. 6 vols., of which the last two contain the *Conférences* (see No. 47); the *Idée du Peintre parfait* by Roger de Piles (see No. 118), and various works by J. F. Félibien, son of André, and Mlle Catherine Perrot.

44d *Entretien sur la vie et les ouvrages de Nicolas Poussin*, Geneva, 1947. (A reprint of the 9th *Entretien*.)
All references to the 1725 ed.

1666–1793

45 Montaiglon, Anatole de, and Guiffrey, Jules, *Correspondance des Directeurs de l'Académie de France à Rome avec les Surintendants des Bâtiments 1666–1793*, Paris, 1887–1912. 18 vols.

1667

46 Bosse, Abraham, *Le Peintre converty aux precises et universelles regles de son art*, Paris, 1667.

46a Ed. R. A. Weigert, Paris, 1964.

46b Parts reprinted in J. Thuillier, 'Pour un "Corpus Pussinianum" ', *Actes*, II, 1960, pp. 91 f., 138 f.

47 *Conférences de l'Académie Royale de Peinture et de Sculpture pendant l'année 1667*, Paris, 1667.

47a Reprinted in H. Jouin, *Conférences . . .*, see No. 580.1.

47b Parts reprinted in J. Thuillier, 'Pour un "Corpus Pussinianum" ', *Actes*, II, 1960, pp. 141 ff.

48 Dufresnoy, Charles Alphonse, *De arte graphica*, Paris, 1667.

48a *L'art de peinture, traduit en français, avec des remarques nécessaires et très amples*, with notes by Roger de Piles (in Latin and French), Paris, 1673.

48b *The Art of Painting*, tr. and preface by John Dryden, London, 1695.

c. 1667

49 Bosse, Abraham, *Différentes manières de dessiner et de peindre* (Paris), *c.* 1667.

1668

Fréart de Chambray, Roland, *Idée de la perfection . . .*, see No. 32a.

1669

50 Le Blond de la Tour, Sieur, *Lettre à un de ses amis touchant la peinture*, Bordeaux, 1669.

50a Section about Poussin reprinted in *RUA*, XIX, 1864, pp. 247 f.

50b Parts reprinted in J. Thuillier, *Actes*, II, 1960, pp. 145 ff.

1670

51 Lassels, Richard, *The Voyage of Italy*, ed. S. Wilson, Paris and London, 1670. 2 vols.

c. 1670

51.1 Marot, Jean, *Le Magnifique chasteau de Richelieu* n.p. [1670?].

1671

52 Barri, Giacomo, *Viaggio pittoresco, in cui si notano tutte le pitture famose . . . che si conservano in qualsivoglia città dell' Italia*, Venice, 1671.

52a *A Painter's voyage of Italy*, tr. by W. Lodge, London, 1679.

53 Bouhours, Père Dominique, *Entretiens d'Ariste et d'Eugène*, Paris, 1671.

54 Episcopius, J. (Bisschop, Jan de), *Paradigmata graphices variorum artificium, voor-beelden der tekenkonst van verscheyde meesters*, The Hague, 1671.

1671–

55 Fontaine, André, *Conférences inédites de l'Académie Royale de Peinture et de Sculpture d'après les manuscrits des archives de l'Ecole des Beaux-Arts*, Paris (1903).

1672

56 Bellori, Giovanni Pietro, *Le Vite de' pittori, scultori et architetti moderni . . .*, Rome, 1672.

56a 2nd ed., Rome, 1728.

56b Reprint, Pisa, 1821. 3 vols.

56c Facsimile ed., Rome, 1931.

56d *La vie de Nicolas Poussin*, tr. by Georges Rémond, Geneva, 1947.

All references to the 1672 ed.

57 Marolles, Michel de, *Catalogue de livres d'estampes et de figures en taille douce . . . fait à Paris en l'année 1672*. Paris, 1672.

57a Part reprinted in J. Thuillier, 'Pour un "Corpus Pussinianum" ', *Actes*, II, 1960, p. 140 note 16.

58 Seignelay, Marquis de, 'Relation du voyage du Marquis de Seignelay en Italie', *GBA*, 1865, I, pp. 176 ff., 357 ff., 445 ff.

c. 1672

59 Bellori, Giovanni Pietro, *Vite di Guido Reni, Andrea Sacchi e Carlo Maratti trascritte dipl. dal manoscritto M. S. 2506 della Biblioteca Municipale di Rouen*, ed. M. Piacentini, Rome, 1942.

1673

Dufresnoy, Charles Alphonse, *De arte graphica*, see No. 48a.

60 Piles, Roger de, *Dialogue sur le coloris*, Paris, 1673.

60a *Dialogue upon colouring*, tr. by John Ozell, London, 1711.

60b Parts reprinted in J. Thuillier, 'Pour un "Corpus Pussinianum" ', *Actes*, II, 1960, pp. 153 f.
Reprinted in 1740, wrongly ascribed to Noël Coypel (cf. anon., 'Sentiments de Noël Coypel et d'Oudry sur le coloris', *RUA*, XV, 1862, pp. 319 ff.).

61 Silos, Johannes Michael, *Pinacotheca, sive Romana pictura et sculptura libri duo*, Rome, 1673.

61a Parts reprinted in J. Thuillier, 'Pour un "Corpus Pussinianum" ', *Actes*, II, 1960, pp. 158 f.

62 Spon, Jacob, *Recherches des antiquités et curiosités de la ville de Lyon*, Lyons, 1673.

62a Parts reprinted in J. Thuillier, 'Pour un "Corpus Pussinianum" ' *Actes*, II, 1960, pp. 189 f.

1673–1688

63 Sirén, Osvald, *Nicodemus Tessin d. y:s Studieresor,* Stockholm, 1914.

1674

64 Scaramuccia, Luigi, *Le Finezze de' pennelli Italiani*, Pavia, 1674.

64a Parts reprinted in J. Thuillier, 'Pour un "Corpus Pussinianum" ', *Actes*, II, 1960, pp. 159 f.

65 Titi, Filippo, *Studio di pittura, scoltura et architettura nelle chiese di Roma*, Rome, 1674.

65a *Ammaestramente utile e curioso di pittura, scultura ed architettura nelle chiese di Roma*, Rome, 1686.

65b *Nuovo studio di pittura, scoltura et architettura nelle chiese di Roma*, Rome, 1708.

65c *Nuovo studio di pittura scoltura et architettura nelle chiese di Roma*, Rome, 1721.

65d *Descrizione delle pittura, sculture ed architettura esposte al pubblico in Roma*, Rome, 1763.

1675–1676

66 Spon, Jacob, and Wheler, George, *Voyage d'Italie, de Dalmatie, de Grèce, et du Levant, fait aux années 1675 et 1676*, Amsterdam, 1679. 2 vols.

1675–1679

67 Sandrart, Joachim von, *Teutsche Academie der edlen Bau-, Bild- und Mahlerey-Künste*, Nuremberg, 1675–79.

67a Latin ed., Nuremberg, 1683.

67b Ed. A. R. Peltzer, Munich, 1925.

67c Parts reprinted in J. Thuillier, 'Pour un "Corpus Pussinianum" ', *Actes*, II, 1960, pp. 60 ff.
All references to the 1925 ed.

c. 1675–1680

68 Arnauld, Abbé Antoine, *Mémoires de M l' Abbé Arnauld contenant quelques anecdotes de la Cour de France depuis 1634 jusqu'à 1675*, Amsterdam, 1756.

68a Reprinted in C. B. Petitot, *Collection complète des mémoires relatifs à l'histoire de France*, 2ᵉ série, XXXIV, Paris, 1824.

1676

69 Vignier, Jacques, *Le Chasteau de Richelieu ou l'histoire des dieux et des héros de l'antiquité*, Saumur, 1676.
69a Parts reprinted in J. Thuillier, 'Pour un "Corpus Pussinianum"', *Actes*, II, 1960, pp. 165 f.

1676–1677

70 *Le Banquet des Curieux*, Paris, n.d.
70a Reprinted by Paul Lacroix, *RUA*, IV, 1856, pp. 47 ff.
70b Parts reprinted in J. Thuillier, 'Pour un "Corpus Pussinianum"', *Actes*, II, 1960, pp. 170 f.
71 *Response au Banquet des Curieux*, Paris, n.d.
71a Parts reprinted in J. Thuillier, 'Pour un "Corpus Pussinianum"', *Actes*, II, 1960, pp. 171 f.

Before 1677

72 Marolles, Michel de, *Le livre des peintres et graveurs*, n.p., n.d.
72a Ed. Georges Duplessis, Paris, 1872.
72b Parts reprinted in J. Thuillier, 'Pour un "Corpus Pussinianum"', *Actes*, II, 1960, pp. 176 f.

1677

73 Félibien, André, *Tableaux du Cabinet du Roy, statues et bustes antiques des maisons royales*, Paris, 1677.
73a Parts reprinted in J. Thuillier, 'Pour un "Corpus Pussinianum"', *Actes*, II, 1960, p. 176.
74 Piles, Roger de, *Conversations sur la connaissance de la peinture*, Paris, 1677.
74a Parts reprinted in J. Thuillier, 'Pour un "Corpus Pussinianum"', *Actes*, II, 1960, pp. 168 ff.

Before 1678

75 Passeri, Giambattista, *Vite de' pittori, scultori ed architetti che anno lavorato in Roma, morti del 1641 fino al 1673*, Rome, 1772.
75a German tr. by Bianconi, Leipzig, 1786.
75b *Die Künstlerbiographien von Giovanni Battista Passeri*, ed. Jacob Hess, Leipzig-Vienna, 1934.
75c Parts reprinted in J. Thuillier, 'Pour un "Corpus Pussinianum"', *Actes*, II, 1960, p. 177.
All references to the 1934 ed.

1678

76 'Dessins, estampes et statues de la succession de Nicolas Poussin (1678)." Communication by Léopold Delisle, *AAF*, XI, 1858–60, pp. 241 ff.
77 *Le songe d'Ariste à Philandre sur les différentes opinions concernant la peinture*, Paris [1678?].
77a Reprinted in *RUA*, IV, 1856, pp. 232 ff. (ed. P. Lacroix).
77b Parts reprinted in J. Thuillier, 'Pour un "Corpus Pussinianum"', *Actes*, II, 1960, pp. 172 ff.

1678

78 Malvasia, Carlo Cesare, *Felsina pittrice. Vite de' pittori Bolognesi*, Bologna, 1678. 2 vols.
78a Ed. Giampietro Zanotti, Bologna, 1841. 2 vols.
78b Parts reprinted in J. Thuillier, 'Pour un "Corpus Pussinianum"', *Actes*, II, 1960, pp. 177 f.

1679

Barri, Giacomo, *A Painter's voyage of Italy*, see No. 52a.
79 [Félibien, André], *Noms des peintres les plus célèbres et les plus connus anciens et modernes*, Paris, 1679.
79a Parts reprinted in J. Thuillier, 'Pour un "Corpus Pussinianum"', *Actes*, II, 1960, p. 179.
Spon, Jacob, and Wheler, George, *Voyage d'Italie*, see No. 66.

1680

80 Testelin, Henri, *Sentimens des plus habiles peintres sur la pratique de la peinture et sculpture*, Paris, 1680.

1681

81 Félibien, André, *Mémoires pour servir à l'histoire des maisons royalles et bastimens de France*, ed. A. de Montaiglon, Paris, 1874.
81a Parts reprinted in J. Thuillier, 'Pour un "Corpus Pussinianum"', *Actes*, II, 1960, p. 185.
82 Huguetan, Jean, *Voyage d'Italie curieux et nouveau*, Lyons, 1681.
83 Piles, Roger de, *Dissertation sur les ouvrages des plus fameux peintres avec la vie de Rubens*, Paris, 1681.
84 Restout, Jacques, *La Réforme de la peinture*, Caen, 1681.
84a Parts reprinted in J. Thuillier, 'Pour un "Corpus Pussinianum"', *Actes*, II, 1960, pp. 183 f.

1681–1728

85 Baldinucci, Filippo, *Notizie de' professori del disegno da Cimabue in quà*, Florence, 1681–1728. 6 vols.
85a *Notizie dei professori ... Edizione accresciuta di annotazioni da Domenico Maria Manni*, Florence, 1767–73. 21 vols.
85b *Notizie dei professori ...*, ed. F. Ranalli, Florence, 1845–47. 5 vols.
85c Parts reprinted in J. Thuillier, 'Pour un "Corpus Pussinianum"', *Actes*, II, 1960, pp. 226 f.

1682

86 Bernier, Jean, *Histoire de Blois*, Paris, 1682.
86a Parts reprinted in J. Thuillier, 'Pour un "Corpus Pussinianum"', *Actes*, II, 1960, pp. 185 f.
87 'Sur l'Etablissement de l'Académie Royale de Peinture et de Sculpture et sur Mᵣ Colbert', *Nouveau Mercure Galant*, November 1682, p. 13.

1682–1684

88 Loménie, Louis Henri, Comte de Brienne, *Mémoires de Messire Louis-Henry de Loménie, Comte de Brienne*, ed. Paul Bonnefon, Paris, 1916.

1683

Sandrart, Joachim von, *Teutsche Academie . . .*, see No. 67a.

1684

89 Brice, Germain, *Description nouvelle de ce qu'il y a de plus remarquable dans la ville de Paris*, Paris, 1684. 2 vols.
89a 2nd ed., Paris, 1687. 2 vols.
89b 3rd ed., Paris, 1698. 2 vols.
89c 5th ed., Paris, 1706. 2 vols.
89d 6th ed., Paris, 1713. 2 vols.
89e 7th ed., Paris, 1717. 3 vols.
89f 8th ed., Paris, 1725. 4 vols.
89g 9th ed., posthumous ed. by P. J. Mariette, Paris, 1752. 4 vols.
89h Parts reprinted in J. Thuillier, 'Pour un "Corpus Pussinianum" ', *Actes*, II, 1960, pp. 187 ff.
90 Piles, Roger de, *Les premiers éléments de la peinture pratique*, Paris, 1684.

1685

91 Le Maire, C., *Paris ancien et nouveau*, Paris, 1685. 3 vols.
91a Parts reprinted in J. Thuillier, 'Pour un "Corpus Pussinianum" ', *Actes*, II, pp. 191 f.

1685–1688

Félibien, André, *Entretiens . . .*, see no. 44a.

1686

92 Baldinucci, Filippo, *Cominciamento e progresso dell' arte dell' intagliare in rame . . .*, Florence, 1686.
92a Parts reprinted in J. Thuillier, 'Pour un "Corpus Pussinianum" ' *Actes*, II, 1960, pp. 195 f.
93 'Gravure', *Mercure Galant*, June, 1686, p. 272.
Titi, Filippo, *Ammaestramente . . . di pittura . . .*, see No. 65a.

1687

Brice, Germain, *Nouvelle Description . . .*, see No. 89a.
94 Catherinot, Nicolas, *Traité de la peinture*, Bourges, 1687.
94a Ed. M. Faucheux, *RUA*, X, 1859, pp. 178 ff.; XI, 1860, pp. 271 ff.
94b Parts reprinted in J. Thuillier, 'Pour un "Corpus Pussinianum" ', *Actes*, II, 1960, p. 196.

1687–1689

95 Mabillon, Jean, and Germain, Michel, *Museum Italicum sive collectio veterum scriptorum ex bibliothecis Italices eruta*, Paris, 1687–89, 2 vols.
95 2nd ed., Paris, 1724.

1688

96 Callières, François de, *Histoire poétique de la guerre nouvellement déclarée entre les anciens et les modernes*, Paris, 1688.
96a Parts reprinted in J. Thuillier, 'Pour un "Corpus Pussinianum" ', *Actes*, II, 1960, pp. 201 f.

1688–1696

97 Perrault, Charles, *Parallèle des anciens et des modernes en ce qui regarde les arts et les sciences*, Paris, 1688–96.

1689 (?)

98 Cotte, Robert de, *Mémoire*. MS. faisant partie des Papiers de Cotte, Bibliothèque Nationale, Paris, MS. Frs 9447, fol. 210–13. Published by P. de Chennevières-Pointel, see No. 433.
98a Parts reprinted in J. Thuillier, 'Pour un "Corpus Pussinianum" ', *Actes*, II, 1960, pp. 202 ff.

1689

99 [Gualandi, M. A.], "Quadreria dì Andrea Lorenzo del Rosso in Firenze a dì 2 novembre 1689', *Memorie Originali Italiane risguardanti le Belle Arti*, II, 1841, p. 115.

1690

100 [Bordelon, Abbé Laurent], *Remarques ou réflexions critiques, morales et historiques*, Paris, 1690.
101 Deseine, François, *Description de la ville de Rome . . .*, Lyons, 1690. 4 vols.
101a *Rome moderne . . .*, Leyden, 1713. 4 vols.

c. 1690

102 *Mémoires Inédits sur la vie et les ouvrages des membres de l'Académie Royale de Peinture et de Sculpture*, ed. Louis Dussieux and others, Paris, 1854. 2 vols.
102a Reprint, Paris, 1887. 2 vols.
102b Parts reprinted in J. Thuillier, 'Pour un "Corpus Pussinianum" ', *Actes*, II, 1960, pp. 207 f.

1691

103 Patin, Caroline Catherine, *Tabellae selectae ac explicatae*, Padua, 1691.
103a *Pitture scelte e dichiarate*, Cologne, 1691.

1692

104 Bromley, William, *Remarks in the Grand Tour of France and Italy. Lately Perform'd by a person of quality, in the year 1691*, London, 1692.
105 Celano, Carlo, *Notizie del bello, dell' antico, e del curioso della Città di Napoli*, Naples, 1692. 10 vols.
105a Another ed., Naples, 1792.

1693

106 Rossini, Pietro, *Il Mercurio errante delle grandezze di Roma, tanto antiche, che moderne*, Rome, 1693.
106a Rome, 1700.
106b Rome, 1750, 2 vols.
106c Rome, 1776.
106d Rome, 1789.
106e Parts reprinted in J. Thuillier, 'Pour un "Corpus Pussinianum" ', *Actes*, II, 1960, pp. 208 f.

107 'Testament et inventaire des biens, tableaux, dessins, planches de cuivre, bijoux, etc., de Claudine Bouzonnet Stella rédigés et écrits par elle-même. 1693–1697', ed. Jules Guiffrey, *NAAF*, 1877, pp. 1 ff.

1693–1695

108 Loménie, Louis Henri, Comte de Brienne, *Discours sur les ouvrages des plus excellens peintres anciens et nouveaux avec un traité de la peinture composé et imaginé par Mre L. H. de L. C. de B. Reclus* (MS. Bibliothèque Nationale, Anc. Saint-Germain 16986), published in J. Thuillier, 'Pour un "Corpus Pussinianum" ', *Actes*, II, 1960, pp. 210 ff. (An incomplete transcript is given by L. Hourticq, see No. 669.)

1694

108.1 'Inventaire des biens du Maréchal d'Humières', ed. Jules Guiffrey, *NAAF*, 1899, pp. 59 ff.

109 Thomassin, Simon, *Recueil des statues, groupes, fontaines, termes, vases, etc., du Château et Parc de Versailles*, Paris, 1694.

1695

109.1 Bellori, Giovanni Pietro, *Descrizzione delle imagini dipinte da Rafaelle d'Urbino*, Rome, 1695.

110 Dryden, John, *A Parallel of Poetry and Painting,* London, 1695.
Dufresnoy, Charles Alphonse, *De arte graphica*, see No. 48b.

1696

111 Bonanni, Filippo, *Numismata summorum pontificum*, Rome, 1696.

c. 1696

112 Perrault, Charles, *Mémoires*, Avignon, 1759.
112a Reprinted in *Œuvres choisies de Ch. Perrault*, ed. Collin de Plancy, Paris, 1826.
112b Ed. Paul Lacroix, Paris, 1878.
112c *Mémoires de ma vie par Charles Perrault. Voyage à Bordeaux (1669) par Claude Perrault*, ed. Paul Bonnefon, Paris, 1909.
112d Parts reprinted in J. Thuillier, 'Pour un "Corpus Pussinianum" ', *Actes*, II, 1960, p. 119.

1696–1700

113 Perrault, Charles, *Les Hommes illustres qui ont paru en France pendant ce siècle*, Paris, 1696–1700. 2 vols.
113a Parts reprinted in J. Thuillier, 'Pour un "Corpus Pussinianum" ', *Actes*, II, 1960, pp. 227 f.

1697

114 Rossi, Michelangelo and Pier Vincenzo, *Descrizione di Roma moderna*, Rome, 1697. Other editions quoted:
114a Rome, 1707.
114b Rome, 1727.

1698

Brice, Germain, *Nouvelle Description . . .*, see No. 89b.
115 Lister, Martin, *A Journey to Paris in 1698*, London, 1699.
115a *Le Voyage de Lister à Paris en MDCXCVIII*, tr. by Paulin Paris, Paris, 1873.
116 Monier, Pierre, *Histoire des Arts qui ont rapport au dessein*, Paris, 1698.
116a English tr., London, 1699.
116b Reprint of original, Paris, 1705.
116c Parts reprinted in J. Thuillier, "Pour un "Corpus Pussinianum" ', *Actes*, II, 1960, p. 228.

1699

117 Du Puy du Grez, Bernard, *Traité sur la peinture pour en apprendre la théorie et se perfectionner dans la pratique*, Toulouse, 1699.
117a Parts reprinted in J. Thuillier, 'Pour un "Corpus Pussinianum" ', *Actes*, II, 1960, pp. 234 ff.
Lister, Martin, *A Journey to Paris*, see No. 115.
Monier, Pierre, *Histoire des Arts . . .*, see No. 116a.
118 Piles, Roger de, *Abrégé de la vie des peintres . . . et un Traité du Peintre parfait . . .*, Paris, 1699.
118a *The Art of painting and the lives of the painters*, English tr., London, 1706.
118b Parts reprinted in J. Thuillier, 'Pour un "Corpus Pussinianum" ', *Actes*, II, 1960, pp. 229 ff.

1699–1700

119 Florent Le Comte, *Cabinet des singularitez d'architecture, peinture, sculpture et graveure*, Paris, 1699–1700. 3 vols.
119a 2nd ed., Brussels, 1702. 3 vols.
119b Parts reprinted in J. Thuillier, 'Pour un "Corpus Pussinianum" ', *Actes*, II, 1960, pp. 232 ff.
All references to the 1702 ed.
120 Vigneul de Marville (pseudonym of Bonaventure d'Argonne), *Mélanges d'histoire et de littérature*, Rouen, 1699–1700. 3 Vols.
120a Reprinted in *Ana*, t. 6–7, ed. C. Garnier, Amsterdam, 1799.
120b Parts reprinted in J. Thuillier, 'Pour un "Corpus Pussinianum" ', *Actes*, II, 1960, pp. 336 f.

1700

121 Fénelon, François de Salignac de la Mothe, *Dialogues sur la Peinture*, first published in Monville, Abbé de, *La Vie de Pierre Mignard*, Paris, 1730, see No. 156.
121a Reprinted in *Œuvres*, Versailles and Paris, 1820–30. 23 vols.
121b Parts reprinted in J. Thuillier, 'Pour un "Corpus, Pussinianum" ', *Actes*, II, 1960, pp. 225 f.
122 Parrino, Domenico Antonio, *Napoli città nobilissima*, Naples, 1700. 2 vols.
122a 2nd ed., Naples, 1725.
123 Pinaroli, Giacomo, *Trattato delle cose più memorabili di Roma*, Rome, 1700. 2 vols.
123a With French tr., Rome, 1725. 3 vols.
Rossini, Pietro, *Il Mercurio errante . . .*, see No. 106a.

1701

124 Piganiol de La Force, Jean Aymar, *Nouvelle description de Versailles et de Marly*, Paris, 1701.

124a 5th ed., Paris, 1724. 2 vols. Later editions only show the movements of paintings within the Royal collection and are therefore not quoted.

1702

Florent Le Comte, *Cabinet des singularitez . . .*, see No. 119a.

125 Orléans, Charlotte, Duchesse d', *Correspondance de Madame la Duchesse d'Orléans*, ed. Ernest Jaeglé, Paris, 1890. 2 vols.

1704

126 Orlandi, Pellegrino Antonio, *L'Abecedario Pittorico*, Bologna, 1704. The biography of Poussin is repeated unchanged in the later editions.

1705

127 Baraton, *Poésies diverses*, Paris, 1705.
Félibien, André, *Entretiens . . .*, see No. 44b.
Monier, Pierre, *Histoire des Arts . . .*, see No. 116b.

1706

Brice, Germain, *Nouvelle Description . . . .*, see No. 89c.
Piles, Roger de, *Abrégé . . .*, see No. 118a.

128 [Rogissart, Sieur de], and [Havard, Abbé], *Les Délices de l'Italie*, Leiden, 1706. 3 vols.

128a 2nd ed., Paris, 1707. 4 vols.

1707

129 Lairesse, Gérard de, *Het Groot Schilderboek*, Amsterdam, 1707.

129a *Le Grand Livre des peintres*, tr. by Hendrik Jansen, Paris, 1787. 2 vols.
[Rogissart, Sieur de] and [Havard, Abbé], *Les Délices de l'Italie . . .*, see No. 128a.
Rossi, Michelangelo and Pier Vincenzo, *Descrizione . . .*, see No. 114a.

1708

130 Piles, Roger de, *Cours de peinture par principes*, Paris, 1708.

130a *The Principles of Painting . . ., translated by a painter*, London, 1743.
Titi, Filippo, *Nuovo studio di pittura . . .*, see No. 65b.

1709–1710

131 Bailly, Nicolas, *Inventaire des tableaux du Roy rédigé en 1709 et 1710*, ed. Fernand Engerand, Paris, 1899.

1709–1756

132 Vertue, George, *Notebooks*, ed. Sir Henry Hake and others, *Walpole Society*, Vols. XVIII, XX, XXII, XXIV, XXVI, XXIX, XXX, Oxford, 1929–55.

1711

Piles, Roger de, *Dialogue upon colouring*, see No. 60a.

1713

Brice, Germain, *Nouvelle Description . . .*, see No. 89d.
Deseine, François, *Rome moderne . . .*, see No. 101a.

132.1 'Les Tableaux de la Princesse des Ursins à Rome', ed. Ferdinand Boyer, *BSHAF*, 1931, pp. 29 ff.

1714–1715

133 Caylus, Anne Claude Philippe, Comte de, *Voyage d'Italie*, ed. Amilda A. Pons, Paris, 1914.

1715

134 Guérin, Nicolas, *Description de l'Académie Royale des arts de peinture et de sculpture*, Paris, 1715.

134a Reprinted in N. Guérin and A. N. Dézallier d'Argenville, *Description de l'Académie Royale de Peinture et de Sculpture*, 1715–81, ed. Anatole de Montaiglon, Paris, 1893.

135 Richardson, Jonathan, *An essay on the theory of painting*, London, 1715.

1715–1724

136 Palomino de Castro y Velasco, Antonio, *El Museo Pictorico y escala óptica*, Madrid, 1715–24. 3 vols.

136a *Histoire abrégée des plus fameux peintres, sculpteurs et architectes espagnols*, Paris, 1749. Translation of No. 136.

1716

137 Gayot de Pitaval, François, *Heures perdues et divertissantes*, Amsterdam, 1716.

138 L.R. [Saugrain, Claude], *Les Curiositez de Paris*, Paris, 1716.

138a 2nd ed., Paris, 1733. 2 vols.

1716–1717

139 Dubois de Saint-Gelais, Louis François, *Histoire journalière de Paris*, Paris, 1885.

1717

Brice, Germain, *Nouvelle Description . . .*, see No. 89e.

140 Thornhill, Sir James, Sketchbook and note book of a visit to Paris in 1717. Manuscript belonging to the Victoria and Albert Museum, London.

1718

141 Piganiol de La Force, Jean Aymar, *Nouvelle description de la France*, Paris, 1718. 6 vols.

141a 2nd ed., Paris, 1742. 8 vols.

141b 3rd ed., Paris, 1753–54. 13 vols.

1719

142 Du Bos, Abbé Jean Baptiste, *Réflexions critiques sur la poésie et sur la peinture*, Paris, 1719. 2 vols.
143 Richardson, Jonathan, *Two discourses*, London, 1719.

1720

144 Monicart, Jean Baptiste de, *Versailles immortalisée*, Paris, 1720. 2 vols.

c. 1720

145 Susinno, Francesco, *Le vite de' pittori Messinesi*, ed. V. Martinelli, Florence, 1960.

1720–1722

146 Wright, Edward, *Some observations made in travelling through France, Italy, &c., in the years 1720, 1721, and 1722*, London, 1730. 2 vols.

1721

147 Coypel, Antoine, *Discours prononcez dans les Conférences de l'Académie Royale de Peinture et de Sculpture*, Paris, 1721.
Titi, Filippo, *Nuovo studio di pittura . . .*, see No. 65c.

1722

148 'Catalogue imprimé d'un cabinet de tableaux rares et curieux (David Amoury)', *Mercure*, May 1722, p. 128.
149 Richardson, Jonathan, *An account of the statues, bas-reliefs, drawings and pictures in Italy, France, etc.*, London, 1722.

1724

Mabillon, Jean, and Germain, Michel, *Museum Italicum . . .*, see No. 95a.
Piganiol de La Force, Jean Aymar, *Nouvelle description de Versailles . . .*, see No. 124a.
Sauval, Henri, *Histoire et recherches . . .*, see No. 23.

1725

Brice, Germain, *Nouvelle description . . .*, see No. 89 f.
Félibien, André, *Entretiens . . .*, see No. 44c.
Parrino, Domenico Antonio, *Napoli città nobilissima*, see No. 122a.
Pinaroli, Giacomo, *Trattato*, see No. 123a.
150 Roisecco, Gregorio, *Roma ampliata e rinnovata*, Rome, 1725.
150a Rome, 1752.

c. 1725

150.1 Kasch, G. J., *Designation exacte des Peintures . . . de son Altesse Ser^me Electorale Palatine à Düsseldorf*, Düsseldorf, ? 1725.

1726

151 Breval, Jean Durant de, *Remarks on several parts of Europe*, London, 1726. 2 vols.

1726–1739

152 Bruzen de la Martinière, Antoine Augustin, *Le grand dictionnaire géographique et critique*, La Haye, 1726–39. 9 vols.

1727

153 Dubois de Saint-Gelais, Louis François, *Description des tableaux du Palais Royal*, Paris, 1727.
Rossi, Michelangelo and Pier Vincenzo, *Descrizione . . .* see No. 114b.

1728

Bellori, Giovanni Pietro, *Le Vite . . .*, see No. 56a.
153.1 'Catalogue des tableaux de Charles Tardif', ed. Jules Guiffrey, *NAAF*, 1899, pp. 227 ff.
154 Richardson, Jonathan, *Traité de la peinture*, Amsterdam, 1728. 3 vols.

1730

155 Caylus, Anne Claude Philippe, Comte de, *Recueil de testes de caractère et de charges*, Paris, 1730.
156 Monville, Abbé de, *La vie de Pierre Mignard, Premier Peintre du Roy, avec le Poème de Molière sur les peintures du Val de Grâce et deux Dialogues de M. de Fénelon*, Paris, 1730.
Wright, Edward, *Some observations . . .*, see No. 146.

c. 1730

157 Mariette, Pierre Jean, *Abecedario . . .*, ed. Ph. de Chennevières-Pointel and A. de Montaiglon, *AAF*, 1851–60. 6 vols.

1730–1736

158 Pascoli, Lione, *Vite de' pittori, scultori, et architetti moderni*, Rome, 1730–36. 2 vols.

1731

159 Guilbert, Abbé Pierre, *Description historique des château, bourg et forest de Fontainebleau*, Paris, 1731. 2 vols.

1732

160 Antonini, Abbé Annibale, *Mémorial de Paris et ses environs*, Paris, 1732.
160a 4th ed., Paris, 1749. 2 vols.
160b *Description de Paris: Où l'on rend compte des palais, des édifices publics, des bibliothèques, des manufactures, et des tableaux qui y méritent l'attention des étrangers* (in French and English), Paris, 1763.
Skippon, Philip, *An account of a journey . . .*, see No. 34.1.

1732–1749

161 Moréri, Louis, *Le grand dictionnaire historique*, Paris, 1732–49. 10 vols.
Reprints the life from R. de Piles, *Abrégé de la vie des peintres*, see No. 118.

1732–1797

162 Walpole, Horace, Earl of Orford, *Letters*, ed. Paget Toynbee, Oxford, 1903–15. 16 vols. Supplement, London, 1918. 2 vols.
162a *Horace Walpole's Correspondence*, ed. W. S. Lewis, New Haven, 1937– .

1733

L.R. [Saugrain, Claude], *Les Curiositez . . .*, see No. 138a.
163 Sempill, The Hon. ——, *Diaries*. Manuscript in the possession of Lord Sempill, Craigievar Castle, Aberdeen.
164 Voltaire, François Marie Arouet de, *Le temple du Goût*, Rouen, 1733.

1735

165 'Abrégé de l'éloge historique de Bernard Picart, dessinateur et graveur', *Mercure de France*, December 1735, pp. 2804 ff.
166 Dolce, Ludovico, *Dialogue sur la peinture*, Paris, 1735. Tr. of *L'Aretino*, Venice, 1557, with preface by L. Vleughels.
167 Review of Picart's *Impostures Innocentes*, *Mercure de France*, October, 1735, pp. 2193 ff.

1736

168 Marsy, Abbé François Marie de, *Pictura, Carmen*, Paris, 1736.

1738

169 'Estampes nouvelles', *Mercure de France*, January 1738, pp. 1603 ff.
169.1 'Inventaire du mobilier et des collections antiques et modernes du Cardinal de Polignac', ed. Jules Guiffrey, *NAAF*, 1899, pp. 252 ff.

1739

170 Brosses, Charles, Comte de, *Lettres historiques et critiques sur l'Italie*, Paris, 1799.
170a *Lettres familières sur l'Italie*, ed. Yvonne Bézard, Paris, 1931. 2 vols.

1740

171 Turnbull, George, *A Treatise on ancient painting*, London, 1740.

1740–1741

172 Keyssler, Johann Georg, *Neueste Reisen durch Teutschland, Böhmen, Ungarn, die Schweitz, Italien und Lothringen*, Hanover, 1740–41. 2 vols.
172a English tr., London, 1760, 4 vols.

1742

173 Piganiol de La Force, Jean Aymar, *Description de Paris, de Versailles, de Marly, de Meudon, de Saint-Cloud, de Fontainebleau, et de toutes les autres belles maisons et châteaux des environs de Paris*, Paris, 1742. 8 vols.
173a Other ed. quoted, Paris, 1765. 10 vols.
Piganiol de La Force, *Nouvelle description*, see No. 141a.
174 Walpole, Horace, Earl of Orford, *A Sermon on painting preached before the Earl of Orford, at Houghton, 1742*, in *Aedes Walpolianae*, see No. 175.
175a Reprinted in H. Walpole, *Works*, II, pp. 253 ff., see No. 319.

1742–1743

175 Walpole, Horace, Earl of Orford, *Aedes Walpolianae: or, a description of the collection of pictures at Houghton-Hall in Norfolk, the seat of the Right Honorable Sir Robert Walpole, Earl of Orford*, London, 1747.
175a Reprinted in H. Walpole, *Works*, II, pp. 253 ff., see No. 319.

1743

Piles, Roger de, *The Principles of painting*, see No. 130a.

1743–1745

176 Blainville, — de, *Travels through Holland, Germany, Switzerland, and other parts of Europe; but especially Italy*, tr. by G. Turnbull and W. Guthrie, London, 1743–45. 3 vols.

1743–1747

177 Posse, Hans, 'Die Briefe des Grafen Francesco Algarotti an den sächsischen Hof und seine Bilderkäufe für die Dresdner Gemäldegalerie 1743-1747', *Jahrbuch der preussischen Kunstsammlungen*, LII, Beiheft, 1931, pp. 12 ff.

1744

177.1 Ficoroni, Francesco de', *Le singolarità di Roma moderna*, Book II: *Le vestigia, e rarita di Roma antica*, Rome, 1744.
177.2 [Mariette, Pierre Jean] *Recueil d'estampes d'après les tableaux des peintres les plus célèbres*, Paris, 1744.

1745

178 Dézallier d'Argenville, Antoine Joseph, *Abrégé de la vie des plus fameux peintres, avec leurs portraits gravés en taille-douce, les indications de leurs principaux ouvrages, quelques réflections sur leurs caractères, et la manière de*

connoître les desseins et les tableaux des grands maîtres, Paris, 1745. 3 vols.

178a 2nd ed., Paris, 1762. 4 vols.

179 Roisecco, Gregorio, *Roma antica e moderna*, Rome, 1745. 3 vols.

179a 2nd ed., Rome, 1750. 3 vols.

1747

180 Le Blanc, Abbé Jean Bernard, *Lettre sur l'exposition . . . de l'année 1747*, Paris, 1747.

Walpole, Horace, Earl of Orford, *Aedes Walpolianae . . .*, see No. 175.

1747-1750

181 Caylus, Anne Claude Philippe, Comte de, *Vies d'artistes du XVIIe siècle*, Paris, 1910.

1748

182 Le Cerf de La Viéville, J. P., *Eloge des Normands*, Paris, 1748.

1749

Antonini, Abbé Annibal, *Mémorial de Paris . . .*, see No. 160a.

183 Dézallier d'Argenville, Antoine Nicolas, *Voyage Pittoresque de Paris*, Paris, 1749.

183a 2nd ed., Paris, 1752.

183b 3rd ed., Paris, 1757.

183c 4th ed., Paris, 1765.

183d 5th ed., Paris, 1770.

183e 6th ed., Paris, 1778.

Palomino de Castro y Velasco, Antonio, *Histoire abrégée . . .*, see No. 136a.

1750

184 Gougenot, Abbé Louis (?), 'L'Exposition des tableaux du roi au Luxembourg en 1750', *BSHAF*, 1909, p. 179.

185 Mariette, Pierre Jean, *Traité des Pierres gravées*, Paris, 1750. 2 vols.

186 Martinelli, Fioravante, *Roma ricercata nel suo sito con tutte le curiosità, che in essa si ritrovano, tanto antiche, come moderne . . .*, Rome, 1750.

186a *Roma ricercata nel suo sito . . .*, Rome, 1769.

187 Pocock, Richard, *The Travels through England of Dr. Richard Pocock*, ed. J. J. Cartwright, London, 1888.

Roisecco, Gregoria, *Roma antica e moderna*, see No. 179a.

Rossini, Pietro, *Il Mercurio errante . . .*, see No. 106b.

c. 1750

188 'Description du château de Richelieu par un anonyme du milieu du 18ème siècle', ed. Charles de Grandmaison, *NAAF*, 1882, pp. 211 ff.

1751

189 Smollett, Tobias, *The Adventures of Peregrine Pickle*, London, 1751. 4 vols.

190 Voltaire, François Marie Arouet de, *Le siècle de Louis XIV*, Paris, 1751.

1751-1764

191 Marigny, Abel François Poisson, Marquis de, 'Correspondance de M. de Marigny avec Coypel, Lépicié et Cochin', Ed. M. Furcy-Raynaud, *NAAF*, 1903 (publ. 1904).

See also No. 219.

1751-1784

192 Walpole, Horace, Earl of Orford, 'Horace Walpole's Journals of visits to Country Seats', ed. Paget Toynbee, *The Walpole Society*, XVI, 1927-28, pp. 9 ff.

1752

193 *Réflexions Critiques sur les différentes écoles de peinture*, Paris, 1752.

Brice, Germain, *Nouvelle Description . . .*, see No. 89g.

Dézallier d'Argenville, Antoine Nicolas, *Voyage Pittoresque . . .*, see No. 183a.

194 Lépicié, Bernard, *Vies des Premiers Peintres du Roi depuis M. Le Brun jusqu'à présent*, Paris, 1752. 2 vols.

1752-1770

195 Hoet, Gerard, *Catalogus of Naamlyst van Schilderyen met derzelven Pryzen*. The Hague, 1752-70. 3 vols.

1753

196 Hogarth, William, *The Analysis of Beauty. Written with a view of fixing the fluctuating ideas of taste*, London, 1753.

1753-1754

Piganiol de La Force, Jean Aymar, *Nouvelle description . . .*, see No. 141b.

1754

197 Bottari, Giovanni Gaetano, *Dialoghi sopra le tre artidel disegno*, Lucca, 1754.

198 'Découverte importante', *Mercure de France*, December 1754, pp. 152 ff.

1754-1768

199 Bottari, Giovanni Gaetano, *Raccolta di lettere sulla pittura, scultura ed architettura*, Rome, 1754-68. 6 vols.

199a Bottari, Giovanni, and Ticozzi, Stefano, *Raccolta di lettere sulla pittura, scultura ed architettura scritte da' più celebri personnagi dei secoli XV, XVI e XVII*, Milan, 1822-25. 8 vols.

1755

200 *Catalogue des tableaux du Cabinet de M. Crozat, Baron de Thiers*, Paris, 1755.

200.1 Dézallier d'Argenville, Antoine Nicolas. *Voyage Pittoresque des environs de Paris*, Paris, 1755.

201 *The Harcourt Papers*, ed. Edward William Harcourt, London, 1880–1905. 14 vols.

202 Monaldini, Venantius, *Risposta alle reflessioni critiche . . . del Sig. Marchese d'Argens*, Rome, 1755.

1755–1768

203 Winckelmann, Johann Joachim, *Kleine Schriften und Briefe*, Leipzig, 1925.

1755–1779

204 Saint-Aubin, Gabriel de, *Catalogues de ventes et livrets de Salons . . . illustrés par Gabriel de Saint-Aubin*, Ed. Emile Dacier, Paris, 1909–21. 11 catalogues in 6 vols.

1756

205 Bernéty, Dom. Antoine Joseph, *Dictionnaire portatif de peinture*, Paris, 1756.

1757

Dézallier d'Argenville, Antoine Nicolas, *Voyage pittoresque . . .*, see No. 183b.

206 'Gravure', *Mercure de France*, November 1757, p. 159.

1758

207 Cochin, Charles Nicolas, *Voyage d'Italie*, Paris, 1758. 3 vols.

1759

208 'Gravure', *Mercure de France*, March 1759, p. 194.

209 Lacombe, Jacques, *Dictionnaire portatif des Beaux-Arts*, Paris, 1759.

210 Le Fèvre, Antoine Martial, *Description des curiosités des églises de Paris*, Paris, 1759.

Perrault, Charles, *Mémoires . . .*, see No. 112.

1759–1781

211 Diderot, Denis, *Oeuvres complètes*, ed. J. Assézat and Maurice Tourneux, Paris, 1875–77. 20 vols.

1760

Keyssler, Johann Georg, *Neueste Reisen*, see No. 172a.

212 Watelet, Claude Henri, *L'Art de peindre. Poëme avec des réflexions sur les différentes parties de la peinture*, Paris, 1760.

1761

213 'Catalogue des estampes de feu Gérard Audran', *Mercure de France*, July 1761, pp. 168 ff.

214 Dodsley, R. and J., *London and its environs described*, London, 1761. 6 vols.

1762

Dézallier d'Argenville, Antoine Joseph, *Abrégé . . .*, see No. 178a.

215 Hagedorn, Christian Ludwig von, *Betrachtungen über die Mahlerey*, Leipzig, 1762.

215a *Réflexions sur la peinture*, tr. by M. Huber, Leipzig, 1775. 2 vols.

Roisecco, Gregorio, *Roma ampliata . . .*, see No. 150a.

1763

Antonini, Abbé Annibale, *Description de Paris . . .*, see No. 160b.

216 Aubert, Marcel, 'Un guide de Notre Dame illustré par Gabriel de Saint-Aubin', *Société d'Iconographie Parisienne*, III, 1910, pp. 1 ff.; IV, 1911, p. 8.

217 [Maihows, Dr.], *Voyage en France, en Italie et aux Isles de l'Archipel . . .*, tr. Philippe Florent de Puisieux, Paris, 1763, 4 vols.

218 M. C. P. G., *Description historique des curiosités de l'église (de Notre Dame) de Paris*, Paris, 1763.

Titi, Filippo, *Descrizione delle pitture . . .*, see No. 65d.

1764

218.1 Oesterreich, Mathias, *Description de la Gallerie et du Cabinet du Roi à Sans-Souci*, Potsdam, 1764.

1764–1773

219 Marigny, Abel François Poisson, Marquis de, 'Correspondance de M. de Marigny avec Coypel, Lépicié et Cochin', ed. M. Furcy-Raynaud, *NAAF*, 1904 (publ. 1905).

See also No. 191.

1765

220 Bardon, Michel François Dandré, *Traité de peinture*, Paris, 1765. 2 vols.

Dézallier d'Argenville, Antoine Nicolas, *Voyage pittoresque . . .*, see No. 183c.

221 Méry, Abbé, *La théologie des peintres*, Paris, 1765.

Piganiol de La Force, Jean Aymar, *Description de Paris . . .*, see No. 173a.

222 Raguenet, François de, *Observations nouvelles sur les ouvrages de peinture, de sculpture et d'architecture qui se voyent à Rome, et aux environs*, London, 1765.

223 Raguenet, François de, *L'Education du jeune Comte D. B.*, London, 1765.

1765–1766

224 La Lande, Joseph Jérôme Le Français de, *Voyage d'un François en Italie fait dans les années 1765–66*, Venice and Paris, 1769. 8 vols.

224a *Voyage en Italie*, Paris, 1786. 8 vols.

1765–1775

225 Walpole, Horace, Earl of Orford, *Paris Journals*, in *Horace Walpole's Correspondence*, ed. W. S. Lewis, VII, pp. 255 ff., see No. 162a.

1766

226 Martyn, Thomas, *The English Connoisseur, containing an account of whatever is curious in painting, sculpture, &c. in the palaces and seats . . . of England*, London, 1766. 2 vols.
227 Northall, John, *Travels through Italy*, London, 1766.
228 Ratti, Carlo Giuseppe, *Istruzione di quanto può vedersi di più bello in Genova*, Genoa, 1766.
228a 2nd ed., Genoa, 1780. 2 vols.
229 Richard, Abbé Jérôme, *Description historique et critique de l'Italie*, Dijon and Paris, 1766. 6 vols.
230 Venuti, Ridolfino, *Accurata e succinta descrizione topografica e istorica di Roma moderna*, Rome, 1766. 2 vols.
230a 2nd ed., Rome, 1767. 4 vols.
230b 3rd ed., Rome, 1824. 2 pts.

1767

Venuti, Ridolfino, *Accurata . . . descrizione . . .* see No. 230a.

1767–1773

Baldinucci, Filippo, *Notizie . . .*, see No. 85a.

1767–1778

230.1 Réau, Louis, *Correspondance de Falconet avec Catherine II, 1767–1778*, Paris, 1921.

1768

231 Boyer d'Argens, Jean Baptiste, *Examen critique des différentes écoles de peinture*, Berlin, 1768.
232 Orbessan, Anne Marie d'Agnan, Marquis d', *Mélanges historiques, critiques, de physique, de littérature et de poésie*, Paris, 1768. 3 vols.

1768–1778

233 Burney, Fanny, *The early diary of Fanny Burney*, ed A. R. Ellis, London, 1889. 2 vols.

1769

La Lande, Joseph Jérôme Le Français de, *Voyage . . .*, see No. 224.
Martinelli, Fioravante, *Roma ricercata . . .*, see No. 186a.
234 Le Mierre, Antoine Marin, *La Peinture, poëme en trois chants*, Paris, 1769.

1769–1790

235 Reynolds, Sir Joshua, *The Discourses of Sir Joshua Reynolds*, Oxford, 1907.
235a Ed. Robert R. Wark, San Marino, California, 1959.

1770

Dézallier d'Argenville, Antoine Nicolas, *Voyage pittoresque . . .*, see No. 183d.
Hoet, Gerard, *Catalogus of Naamlyst . . .*, see No. 195.

1771

236 [Molé, Guillaume François Roger] *Observations historiques et critiques sur les erreurs des peintres, sculpteurs et dessinateurs dans la représentation des sujets tirés de l'histoire sainte*, Paris, 1771. 2 vols.
237 Laugier, Abbé Marc Antoine, *Manière de bien juger des ouvrages de peinture*, Paris, 1771.

1772

Passeri, Giovanni Battista, *Vite de' pittori*, see No. 75.
238 Ponz, Antonio, *Viaje de España*, Madrid, 1772–94. 18 vols.
238a *Viaje de España. Seguido de los dos tomos del Viaje fuera de España*, Madrid, 1947.
239 Richardson, Jonathan, *The works of Jonathan Richardson, containing I, The theory of painting. II, Essay on the art of criticism. III, The science of a connoisseur*, Strawberry Hill, 1772.
239a Reprinted in 1792.
240 Saint-Non, Abbé Jean Claude Richard de, *Fragments choisis dans les peintures et les tableaux les plus intéressants des palais et églises de l'Italie*, Paris, 1772.

1773

241 'Arts, Gravures', *Mercure de France*, January 1773, II, p. 182.
242 Keate, George, *The Monument in Arcadia*, London, 1773.
242.1 Oesterreich, Mathias, *Description de tout l'intérieur des deux palais de Sans-Souci, de ceux de Potsdam, et de Charlottenburg . . .*, Potsdam, 1773.

1773–1774

243 Bergeret and Fragonard. *Journal inédit d'un voyage en Italie 1773–1774*, ed. M. Tornézy, Paris, 1895.

1773–1782

244 Angiviller, Charles Claude Labillarderie, Comte d', 'Correspondance de M. d'Angiviller avec Pierre', *NAAF*, ed. M. Furcy-Raynaud, 1905 (publ. 1906). See also No. 276.

1774

245 Walpole, Horace, Earl of Orford, *A Description of the Villa of Mr. Horace Walpole at Strawberry-Hill near Twickenham, Middlesex*, London, 1774.
245a Reprinted in H. Walpole, *Works*, II, pp. 393 ff. (see No. 319).

1774–1796

246 Grimm, Friedrich Melchior, Baron von, 'Corres-
    pondance artistique de Grimm avec Catherine II',
    ed. Louis Réau, *NAAF*, 1932, pp. 1 ff.

1775

246.1 Courajod, Louis, 'Documents sur la vente du cabinet
    de Mariette', *NAAF*, 1872, pp. 346 ff.
    Hagedorn, Christian Ludwig von, *Betrachtungen über die
    Mahlerey*, see No. 215a.

247 Sulzer, Johann Georg, *Allgemeine Theorie der schönen
    Künste*, Leipzig, 1775.

1775–1778

248 La Roque, M. de, *Voyage d'un amateur des arts en Flandre,
    dans les Pays-Bas, en Hollande, en France, en Savoye, en
    Italie, en Suisse, fait dans les années 1775–1776–1777–
    1778*, Amsterdam, 1783. 4 vols.

1775–1780

249 Trumbull, John, *The autobiography of Col. John Trumbull*,
    ed. Theodore Sizer, New Haven, 1953.

1775–1785

250 Courtepée, Claude, and Béguillet, Edmé, *Description
    générale et particulière du duché de Bourgogne*, Dijon, 1775–
    85. 7 vols.

1776

251 Nougaret, Pierre Jean Baptiste, *Anecdotes des Beaux-
    Arts, contenant tout ce que la peinture, la sculpture, la
    gravure, l'architecture, la littérature, la musique, etc., et la vie
    des artistes, offrent de plus curieux . . .*, Paris, 1776. 2 vols.

252 Papillon de La Ferté, Denis Pierre Jean, *Extrait des
    différens ouvrages publiés sur la vie des peintres*, Paris, 1776.
    2 vols.
    Rossini, Pietro, *Il Mercurio errante . . .*, see No. 106c.

253 'Suite de l'extrait des différens ouvrages publiés sur la
    vie des peintres par M. D. L. F. A. (= Papillon de la
    Ferté)', *Mercure de France*, August 1776, pp. 69 ff.

254 [Weston, S.], *Viaggiana: or detached remarks on the
    buildings, pictures, statues, inscriptions, etc., of ancient and
    modern Rome*, London, 1776.

1777

255 [Pidenzat de Mairobert, Mathieu Francis], 'Lettre sur
    l'Académie Royale de Sculpture et de Peinture et sur
    le Salon de 1777', *RUA*, XIX, 1864, p. 177.

256 *Lettres pittoresques à l'occasion des tableaux exposés au
    Salon de 1777*, Paris, n.d.

256.1 Vasi, Giuseppe, *Itinerario istruttivo . . .*, Rome, 1777.

1777–1778

257 Volkmann, Johann Jakob, *Historisch-kritische Nach-
    richten von Italien . . .*, Leipzig, 1777–78. 3 vols.
    (First published, Leipzig, 1770).

1778

Dézallier d'Argenville, Antoine Nicolas, *Voyage pittor-
    esque . . . .*, see No. 183e.

258 [Hayley, William], *A poetical epistle to an eminent
    painter*, London, 1778.

259 Lescallier, Antoine, *Poème sur la peinture en sept chants*,
    London, 1778.

260 Magnan, Dominique, *La Ville de Rome*, Rome, 1778.
    4 vols.

260.1 Pigage, Nicolas de, *La Galerie Electorale de Düsseldorf
    ou Catalogue raisonné et figuré de ses tableaux*, Basle, 1778.

1779–1780

261 Canova, Antonio, Marchese, *I quaderni di viaggio (1779–
    1780)*, ed. E. Bassi, Venice and Rome, 1959.

1780(?)

262 *A rhapsody on antique rings, written in Rome*, Rome,
    1780(?).

1780

263 Hollis, Thomas, *Memoirs*, London, 1780.

264 Mengs, Anton Raphael, *Opere*, Parma, 1780. 2 vols.

264a Reprint, Rome, 1787.

264b *Oeuvres*, tr. by Hendrik Jansen, Paris, 1786.

264c English tr. by the Chev. Don J. N. d'Azara, London,
    1796. 2 Vols.

264.1 Ratti, Carlo Giuseppe, *Descrizione delle pitture . . .
    dello stato Ligure*, Genoa, 1780.
    Ratti, Carlo Giuseppe, *Istruzione . . .*, see No. 228a.

c. 1780

265 Descriptions des tableaux de divers maîtres des écoles
    d'Italie, de Flandre, d'Hollande, de France, d'Espagne
    &c. [= Catalogue of the Baudouin collection]. Biblio-
    thèque de l'Institut d'Art et d'Archéologie, Paris, MS.
    44.

1781

266 *Description des beautés de Gênes et de ses environs*, Genoa,
    1781.

1781–1785

267 Saint-Non, Abbé Jean Claude Richard de, *Voyage
    pittoresque ou description des royaumes de Naples et de
    Sicile*, Paris, 1781–85. 5 vols.

1782

268 *An essay on landscape painting*, London, 1782.

269 Chiusole, Adamo Conte, *Itinerario delle pitture, sculture
    ed architetture più rare di Roma*, Vicenza, 1782.

270 Delille, Jacques, *Les jardins ou l'art d'embellir les paysages*,
    Paris, 1782.

270.1 Pellengo, Giuseppe Antonio, *Libri di figura d'Anni-
    bale Caracci . . . di Nicola Poussin Normano, . . . copiatti*

da me Giuppe Anto. Pellengo nell' anno 1782, (?) Turin, 1782.

271 Pimarta, T., *Itinerario delle pitture, sculture ed architetture ... d'Italia*, Vicenza, 1782.

1783

272 Cambry, Jacques de, *Essai sur la vie et sur les tableaux de Poussin*, Rome and Paris, 1783.

272a 2nd ed., Paris, 1799.

273 Guibal, Nicolas, *Eloge de Nicolas Poussin*, Paris, 1783.

274 La Blanchery, H. de, *Essai d'un tableau historique des peintres français*, Paris, 1783.

La Roque, M. de, *Voyage d'un amateur* . . ., see No. 248.

275 Review of J. de Cambry's *Essai sur la vie et sur les tableaux de Poussin, Mercure de France*, Nov. 1783, pp. 31 ff. See No. 272.

1783–1785

276 Angiviller, Charles Claude Labillarderie, Comte d', 'Correspondance de M. Angiviller avec Pierre', ed. M. Furcy-Raynaud, *NAAF*, 1906 (publ. 1907). See also No. 244.

1784

277 Review of Nicolas Guibal's *Eloge de Nicolas Poussin, Mercure de France*, March 1784, pp. 45 ff. See No. 273.

1785

278 Dulaure, Jacques Antoine, *Nouvelle description des curiosités de Paris*, Paris, 1785. 2 Parts.

278a 2nd ed., Paris, 1787–88. 2 vols.

279 Volkmann, Johann Jakob, *Neueste Reisen durch Spanien*, Leipzig, 1785. 2 vols.

1785–1787

280 Hoare, Sir Richard Colt, *Recollections abroad during the years 1785, 1786, 1787*, Bath, 1815. 4 vols.

Lairesse, Gérard de, *Het Groot Schilderboek*, see No. 129a.

1785–1791

281 Reynolds, Sir Joshua, *Letters of Sir Joshua Reynolds*, coll. and ed. by Frederick Whiley Hilles, Cambridge, 1929.

1786

282 Dulaure, Jacques Antoine. *Nouvelle Description des Environs de Paris*. Paris, 1786. 2 vols.

La Lande, Joseph Jérôme Le Français de, *Voyage* . . ., see No. 224a.

Mengs, Anton Raphael, *Opere*, see No. 264b.

283 Nicolai, Christoph Friedrich, *Beschreibung der königlichen Residenzstädte Berlin und Potsdam*, Berlin, 1786. 3 vols.

Passeri, Giambattista, *Vite* . . ., see No. 75a.

284 Prunetti, Michel Angelo, *Saggio pittorico*, Rome, 1786.

1786–1803

285 Couché, J., Fontenai and Croze-Magnan, *La Galerie du Palais-Royal, gravéeé d'après les tableaux des différentes écoles qui la composent, par J. C., avec une description de chaque tableau par de Fontenai*, Paris, 1786–1808. 3 vols.

1787

285.1 Cumberland, Richard, *An accurate and descriptive catalogue of the several paintings in the King of Spain's palace at Madrid; with some account of the pictures at Buen Retiro*, London, 1787.

Dulaure, Jacques Antoine, *Nouvelle description* . . ., see No. 278a.

Mengs, Anton Raphael, *Opere*, see No. 264a.

286 Newspaper reports on the arrival of the 'Sacraments': in the *World* (23.ii., 30.v.1787); in the *St. James's Chronicle* (8.v.1787).

287 Ramdohr, Friedrich Wilhelm Basilius von, *Ueber Malerei und Bildhauerarbeit in Rom*, Leipzig, 1787. 3 vols.

1787–1788

Dulaure, Jacques Antoine, *Nouvelle description* . . ., see No. 278a.

288 Newspaper reports of a lawsuit between Noël Desenfans and Benjamin Vandergucht: in *The World* (23.v., 8.vi. and 13.vi.1787; 30.iv., 10.v. 1788); in the *London Chronicle* (9.vi.1787); in the *Morning Herald* (11.vi., 12.vi. and 18.vi.1787); in the *Morning Chronicle* (29.iv.1788); in the *Gazetteer* (29.iv.1788).

289 Thiéry, Luc Vincent, *Guide des amateurs et des étrangers voyageurs à Paris*, Paris, 1787–88. 3 vols.

290 Volkmann, Johann Jakob, *Neueste Reisen durch Frankreich*, Leipzig, 1787–88. 3 vols.

1788–1789

291 Sigismondo, Giuseppe, *Descrizione della città di Napoli*, Naples, 1788–89. 3 vols.

1789

292 Lanzi, Luigi, *Storia pittorica dell' Italia dal risorgimento delle belle arti fin presso al fine del XVIII secolo*, Bassano, 1789.

Rossini, Pietro, *Il Mercurio errante* . . ., see No. 106d.

1790

293 Murville, Pierre Nicolas de, *Le paysage de Poussin ou mes illusions*, Paris, 1790.

294 Newspaper reports of the Delmé sale: in the *World* (15.ii.1790); in the *Morning Herald* (16.ii.1790); in the *Gazetteer* (17.ii.1790).

1790–1794

295 Tuétey, Louis, 'Procés-verbaux de la Commission des Monuments 1790–94', *NAAF*, 1901–2. 2 vols.

1791

296 Martyn, Thomas, *A Tour through Italy*, London, 1791.

297 Quatremère de Quincy, Antoine, *Considérations sur les arts du dessin en France, suivies d'un plan de l'Académie*, Paris, 1791.

298 Vasi, Mariano, *Itinerario istruttivo di Roma ossia descrizione generale delle opere più insigni di pittura, scultura e architettura e di tutti i monumenti si antichi e moderni di quest' alma città, e parte delle sue adjacenze*, Rome, 1791. 2 vols.

298a *Itinerario istruttivo*, Rome, 1794. 2 vols.

298b *Itinerario istruttivo*, Rome, 1804. 2 vols.

298c *Itinerario istruttivo . . .*, Rome, 1814. 2 vols.

298d *Itinerario istruttivo . . .*, Rome, 1816. 2 vols.

298e Vasi, Mariano, and Nibby, Antonio, *Itinerario istruttivo di Roma . . .*, Rome, 1818. 2 vols. Also 1819. 2 vols.

298f Vasi, Mariano, and Nibby, Antonio, *Itinerario istruttivo . . .* Rome, 1820. 2 vols.

1791–1794

299 Algarotti, Count Francesco, *Opere del Conte Algarotti*, Venice, 1791–94. 17 vols.

1792

300 'Catalogue of the pictures at Amisfield', *Archaeologia Scotica*, 1792, pp. 77 ff.
 Celano, Carlo, *Notizie . . . di Napoli*, see No. 105a.

301 Galanti, Giuseppe Maria, *Breve descrizione della città di Napoli e del suo contorno*, Naples, 1792.

302 Ramdohr, Friedrich Wilhelm Basilius von, *Studien zur Kenntnis der schönen Natur, der schönen Künste, der Sitten und Staatsverfassung auf einer Reise nach Dänemark*. Hanover, 1792.
 Richardson, Jonathan, *The works . . .*, see No. 239a.

303 Watelet, Claude Henri, *Dictionnaire des arts de peinture, sculpture et gravure*, Paris, 1792. 5 vols.

1792–1793

304 Tuétey, Alexandre, and Guiffrey, Jean, 'La commission du muséum et la création du Musée du Louvre', *NAAF*, 1909.

1792–1796

305 'Les tableaux et objets d'art saisis chez les émigrés et condamnés et envoyés au muséum central', ed. M. Furcy-Raynaud, *NAAF*, 1912.

1792–1798

306 Starke, Mariana, *Letters from Italy between the years 1792 and 1798, containing a view of the Revolution in that country, from the capture of Nice by the French Republic to the expulsion of Pius VI*, London, 1800. 2 vols.

1793–1795

307 Bromley, Robert Anthony, *A philosophical and critical history of the Fine Arts*, London, 1793–95. 2 vols.

1794

308 Manazzale, Andrea, *Rome et ses environs*, Florence, 1794. 2 vols.

308a *Rome et ses environs. Dernière édition augmentée et corrigée par l'antiquaire André Manazzale*, Rome, 1802. 2 vols.

308b *Itinéraire instructif de Rome et ses environs*, Rome, 1816. 2 vols.

308c *Itinerario di Roma e dei suoi contorni*, Rome, 1817. 2 vols.

309 Newspaper report of a 'Bacchanalian Fête' on view at the European Museum, St. James's Square: in the *Morning Chronicle* (19.iv.1794).

310 Stolberg, Count Friedrich Leopold, *Reise in Deutschland, der Schweiz, Italien und Sicilien*, Königsberg, 1794. 4 vols.

310a *Travels through Germany, Switzerland, Italy and Sicily*, tr. by T. Holcroft, London, 1796–97. 4 vols.
 Vasi, Mariano, *Itinerario istruttivo . . .*, see No. 298a.

311 Zani, Pietro, *Enciclopedia metodica delle belle arti*, Parma, 1794. 8 vols.

311a 2nd ed., Parma, 1817–28. 28 vols.

1794–1798

312 Price, Uvedale, *An essay on the picturesque as compared with the sublime and the beautiful; and on the use of studying pictures for the purpose of improving real landscape*, London, 1794–98. 2 vols.

1796

313 Fortia de Piles, Comte Alphonse, *Voyage de deux français en Allemagne, Danemarc, Suède, Russie et Pologne*, Paris, 1796. 4 vols.
 Mengs, Anton Raphael, *Opere*, see No. 264c.

1796–1797

Stolberg, Count Friedrich Leopold, *Travels . . .*, see No. 310a.

1796–1814

314 Blumer, Marie Louise, 'Catalogue des peintures transportées d'Italie en France de 1796–1814', *BSHAF*, 1936, pp. 244 ff., 333.

1797

315 *Description of Nuneham-Courtnay*, London, 1797.

316 Milizia, Francesco, *Dizionario delle belle arti del disegno*, Bassano, 1797. 2 vols.

317 Venturi, Giovanni Battista, *Essai sur les ouvrages physico-mathématiques de Léonard da Vinci, avec les fragments tirés de ses manuscrits apportés de l'Italie*, Paris, 1797.

1798

318 Newspaper report of the 'Image de la vie humaine' to be sold at the European Museum, St. James's Square: in the *Morning Post* (2.iv.1798).

319 Walpole, Horace, Earl of Orford, *The works of Horace Walpole, Earl of Orford*, ed. R. Berry, London, 1798. 5 vols.

1799

Brosses, Charles Comte de, *Lettres historiques . . .*, see No. 170.
Cambry, Jacques de, *Essai sur la vie . . . de Poussin*, see No. 272a.
Vigneul de Marville, *Mélanges d'histoire . . .*, see No. 120a.

1800

320 Legrand, Jacques Guillaume, 'Projet de monument pour le Poussin', *Journal du Département de l'Oise*, 6.viii.1800.
321 Salmon, J. *An historical description of ancient and modern Rome*, London, 1800. 2 vols.
Starke, Mariana, *Letters . . .*, see No. 306.

1801-1810

322 Fuseli, Henry, *Lectures on painting, delivered at the Royal Academy*, London, 1820.

1802

323 Desenfans, Noël, *A descriptive catalogue (with remarks and anecdotes never before published in English) of some pictures, of the different schools, purchased for His Majesty the late King of Poland . . .*, London, 1802. 2 vols.
Manazzale, Andrea, *Rome et ses environs*, see No. 308a.

1802-1803

324 Forsyth, Joseph, *Remarks on antiquities, arts and letters during an excursion in Italy in the years 1802 and 1803*, London, 1813.

1803

325 Dalmazzoni, Angelo, *The antiquarian or the guide for foreigners to go the rounds of the antiquities of Rome*, Rome, 1803.
325a French tr., Rome, 1804.
325b Italian tr., Rome, 1804.

1803-1817

326 Landon, Charles Paul, *Vies et œuvres des peintres les plus célèbres de toutes les écoles*, Paris, 1803-17. 25 vols.

1804

Dalmazzoni, Angelo, *The antiquarian . . .*, see Nos. 325a and b.
Vasi, Mariano, *Itinerario istruttivo . . .*, see No. 298b.

1804-1863

327 Delacroix, Eugène, *Correspondance générale*, ed. André Joubin, Paris, 1935-38. 5 vols.

1805

328 Lecarpentier, Charles Jacques François, *Eloge historique du Poussin*, Rouen, 1805.
329 Newspaper report of a 'Bacchanalian Fête' to be sold: in the *Morning Post* (3.iv.1805).

1806

330 Gault de Saint-Germain, Pierre Marie, *Vie de Nicolas Poussin*, Paris, 1806.
331 Huet, Paul, *Les anténors modernes ou voyage de Christine et de Casimir en France, pendant le règne de Louis XIV*, Paris, 1806. 3 vols.
332 Lazzarini, Canonico Gio. Andrea, *Opere*, Pesaro, 1806. 2 vols.

1807

333 Drechsler, *Collection d'estampes d'après quelques tableaux de la galerie de S. E. M. le Comte de Stroganof*, Petersburg, 1807.
334 Haron, Jean Baptiste Philippe, *Appel pour une souscription et description du monument élevé à la mémoire de Nicolas Poussin*, n.p., 1807.
335 Opie, John, *Lectures on painting, delivered at the Royal Academy of Arts; with a letter on the proposal for a public memorial of the naval glory of Great Britain*, London, 1809.
336 Taillasson, Jan Joseph, *Observations sur quelques grands peintres*, Paris, 1807.

1808

337 Gault de Saint-Germain, Pierre Marie, *Les trois siècles de la peinture en France . . .*, Paris, 1808.

1808-1846

337.1 Haydon, Benjamin Robert, *The Diaries of Benjamin Robert Haydon*, ed. W. B. Pope, Cambridge, Mass., 1960-63. 5 vols.

1809

338 Barry, James, *The works of James Barry*, London, 1809. 2 vols.
339 Le Breton, 'La Galerie de l'Hermitage', *Mercure de France*, May 1809, pp. 394 ff.
Opie, John, *Lectures on painting . . .*, see No. 335.
340 Ruault, Nicolas, *Eloge de Nicolas Poussin*, Paris, 1809.

1810

341 Sobry, J. F., *Poétique des arts*, Paris, 1810.

1810-1811

341.1 Simond, Louis, *Journal of a Tour and Residence in Great Britain during the years 1810 and 1811*, Edinburgh, 1815. 2 vols.
341.1a 2nd ed., Edinburgh, 1817.

1810-1829

342 Tischbein, Wilhelm, *Aus meinem Leben*, ed. Lothar Brieger, Berlin, 1922.

1811

343　Castellan, L., *Vie de Poussin*, Paris, 1811.
343a　Reprinted in London, 1813.
343.1　*Description des Tableaux capitaux de la Galerie de Mr Didot-Saint-Marc*, Paris, 1811.
344　Neumayr, Antonio, *Memoria storico-critica sopra la pittura*, Padua, 1811.

1812

345　Chamberlaine, John, *Original designs of the most celebrated masters of the Bolognese, Roman, Florentine and Venetian schools* (in Windsor Castle), London, 1812.
346　'Gravures', *Mercure de France*, March 1812, p. 479.
347　Landon, Charles Paul, *Galerie Giustiniani*. (Les Annales du musée et de l'école des Beaux-Arts. Seconde collection. Partie ancienne, vol. 1.) Paris, 1812.

1813

Castellan, L., *Vie de Poussin*, see No. 343a.
348　Andrée, Eugène, 'Eloge du Poussin', *Magasin Encyclopédique*, VI, 1813, p. 47.
Forsyth, Joseph, *Remarks on antiquities . . .*, see No. 324.
349　La Rochefoucauld-Liancourt, Marquis de, *Notice historique sur l'arrondissement des Andelys*, Paris, 1813.
350　Séroux d'Agincourt, J. B. L. G., 'Lettre de M. d'Agincourt, addressée de Rome à Monsieur Castellan, le – Décembre 1813' (sic), *AAF*, 1851–52, pp. 142 ff.

1814

351　Hoare, Sir Richard Colt, *Two studies from Nicolas Poussin from a painting in the possession of Sir R. C. H.*, London, 1814.
352　Lavallée, Joseph, and Filhol, Antoine Michel, *Galerie du Muséum de France*, Paris, 1814. 10 vols.
Vasi, Mariano, *Itinerario istruttivo . . .*, see No. 298c.

1815

353　Chateaubriand, François René, Vicomte de, *Souvenirs d'Italie, d'Angleterre et d'Amérique*, London, 1815. 2 vols.
Hoare, Sir Richard Colt, *Recollections abroad . . .*, see No. 280.
354　Romanelli, Domenico, *Napoli antica e moderna*, Naples, 1815. 3 vols.
Simond, Louis, *Journal of a Tour . . .*, see No. 341.1.

1816

355　Hazlitt, William, 'The catalogue raisonné of the British Institution', *The Examiner*, 3.xi.1816.
355a　Reprinted in *Criticisms on Art*, pp. 99 ff. (see No. 417).
355b　Reprinted in *The collected works of William Hazlitt*, London, 1903, IX, pp. 311 ff. (see No. 655).
356　Laouriens, G., *Tableau de Rome vers la fin de 1814*, Brussels, 1816.
Manazzale, Andrea, *Itinéraire instructif de Rome . . .*, see No. 308b.

357　Newspaper reports on paintings lost in the fire at Belvoir Castle:
in the *Morning Chronicle* (1.xi.1816);
in the *Morning Post* (1 and 4.xii.1816).
358　[Smirke, R.], *A Catalogue rasionné of the pictures now exhibiting in Pall Mall*, London, 1816. 2 vols.
Vasi, Mariano, *Itinerario istruttivo . . .*, see No. 298d.

1817

359　Jay, L. J., *Recueil de lettres sur la peinture, la sculpture et l'architecture . . ., publiées à Rome par Bottari en 1754, traduites et augmentées*, Paris, 1817.
Manazzale, Andrea, *Itinerario di Roma . . .*, see No. 308c.
Simond, Louis, *Journal of a Tour . . .*, see No. 341.1a.
360　Stendhal (Henri Beyle), *Histoire de la peinture en Italie*, Paris, 1817. 2 vols.

1817–1828

Zani, Pietro Abbate, *Enciclopedia metodica . . .*, see No. 311a.

1818

361　Hoare, Sir Richard Colt, *A description of the house and gardens at Stourhead*, n.p., 1818.
Evelyn, John, *Memoirs*, see No. 8.
362　Ticozzi, Stefano, *Dizionario dei pittori dal rinnovamento delle belle arti fino al 1800*, Milan, 1818. 2 vols.
Vasi, Mariano, and Nibby, Antonio, *Itinerario istruttivo . . .*, see No. 298e.

1818–1865

363　Boyer d'Agen, Auguste Jean, *Ingres d'après une correspondance inédite*, Paris, 1909.

1819

364　Destouches, P. E., *Epître à Nicolas Poussin, par un jeune peintre*, Paris, 1819.
Vasi, Mariano, and Nibby, Antonio, *Itinerario istruttivo . . .*, see No. 298e.

1820

Fuseli, Henry, *Lectures on painting . . .*, see No. 322.
365　Graham, Maria (afterwards Lady Callcott) *Memoirs of the life of Nicolas Poussin*, London, 1820.
Vasi, Mariano, and Nibby, Antonio, *Itinerario istruttivo . . .*, see No. 298f.

c. 1820

366　Andrée, Eugène, *Observations sur le caractère des ouvrages du Poussin, communiquées à l'Institut*, Paris, n.d.

1820–1830

Fénelon, François de Salignac de la Mothe, *Dialogues des Morts*, see No. 121a.

1821

Bellori, Giovanni Pietro, *Le Vite . . .*, see No. 56b.

367 Lecarpentier, Charles Jacques François, *Galerie des peintres célèbres*, Paris, 1821. 2 vols.

368 Young, John, *A catalogue of the pictures at Grosvenor House*, London, 1821.

1821–1822

369 Hazlitt, William, 'On a landscape of Nicolas Poussin', *Table Talk; or Original Essays*, London, 1821–22. 2 vols.

369a Reprinted in *Criticisms on Art*, pp. 190 ff. (see No. 417).

369b Reprinted in *The collected works of William Hazlitt*, London, 1903, VI, pp. 168 ff. (see No. 655).

1822

370 Deperthes, Jean Baptiste, *Histoire de l'art du paysage depuis la Renaissance des beaux-arts jusqu'au dix-huitième siècle*, Paris, 1822.

371 *Rome in the nineteenth century*, Edinburgh, 1822. 3 vols.

371.1 Young, John, *A Catalogue of pictures at Leigh Court, near Bristol; the seat of Philip John Miles, Esq., M.P.*, London, 1822.

1822–1825

Bottari, Giovanni, and Ticozzi, Stefano, *Raccolta di Lettere . . .*, see No. 199a.

1822–1863

372 Delacroix, Eugène, *Journal de Eugène Delacroix . . . nouvelle édition publiée d'après le manuscrit original*, ed. André Joubin, Paris, 1932. 3 vols.

1823

373 Gence, Jean Baptiste Modeste, Life of Poussin, *Biographie Universelle ancienne et moderne . . . ouvrage . . . redigé par une société de gens de lettres*, XXXV, 1823, pp. 560 ff.

373a Reprinted *Notice sur le Poussin*, Paris, 1825.

374 Missirini, Melchior, *Memorie per servire alla storia della romana Accademia di S. Luca*, Rome, 1823.

1823–1832

375 Eckermann, Johann Peter, *Gespräche mit Goethe*, Leipzig and Magdeburg, 1836–48.

1824

Arnauld, Abbé Antoine, *Mémoires . . .*, see No. 68a.

376 Buchanan, William, *Memoirs of paintings with a chronological history of the importation of pictures by the great masters into England since the French Revolution*, London, 1824. 2 vols.

377 Hazlitt, William, *Sketches of the principal picture-galleries in England with a criticism on 'Mariage à la Mode'*, London, 1824.

377a Reprinted in *Criticisms on Art*, London, 1843, pp. 1 ff. (see No. 411).

377b Reprinted in *The collected works of William Hazlitt*, London, 1903, IX, pp. 7 ff. (see No. 655).

378 [Patmore, Peter George], *British galleries of art*, London, 1824.

Poussin, Nicolas, *Lettres . . .*, see No. 3.

Venuti, Ridolfino, *Accurata . . . descrizione . . .*, see No. 230b.

378.1 Westmacott, C. M., *British Galleries of painting and sculpture, comprising a general historical and critical catalogue*, London, 1824.

379 Z. [Hazlitt, William], 'Fine Arts', Supplement to the *Encyclopaedia Britannica*, 1824, I, pp. 549 ff.

379a Reprinted in *Criticisms on Art*, pp. 155 ff. (see No. 411).

379b Reprinted in *The collected works of William Hazlitt*, London, 1903, IX, pp. 377 ff. (see No. 655).

1825

Gence, Jean Baptiste Modeste, *Notice sur le Poussin*, see No. 373a.

1826

380 Hazlitt, William, *The Plain Speaker: Opinions on books, men and things*, London, 1826. 2 vols.

380a Reprinted in *The collected works of William Hazlitt*, London, 1903, VII, pp. 5 ff. (see No. 655).

381 Hazlitt, William, *Notes on a journey through France and Italy*, London, 1826.

381a Reprinted in *The collected works of William Hazlitt*, London, 1903, IX, pp. 89 ff. (see No. 655).

Perrault, Charles, *Mémoires de Charles Perrault . . .*, see No. 112a.

382 *Verzeichniss der ehemals zu der Giustinianischen, jetzt zu den königlichen Sammlungen gehörigen Gemälde*, Berlin, 1826.

1827

383 Nibby, Antonio, *Itinerario istruttivo di Roma e delle sue vicinanze*, Rome, 1827. 2 vols.

383a *Itinerario di Roma e delle sue vicinanze . . .*, 4th ed., Rome, 1838. 2 vols.

1827–1828

384 Waagen, Gustav Friedrich, *Kunstwerke und Künstler in England und Paris*, Berlin, 1827–39. 3 vols.

384a *Works of art and artists in England*, tr. by H. E. Lloyd, London, 1838. 3 vols.

384b *Art Treasures in Great Britain*, tr. by Lady Eastlake, London, 1854–57. 3 vols. and Suppl.

384c Graves, Algernon, *Summary of and index to Waagen*, London, 1912.

1829

385 Denon, Baron Vivant, *Monuments des arts du dessin . . .*, Paris, 1829. 4 vols.

386 Girodet-Trioson, Anne Louis, *Oeuvres posthumes*, Paris, 1829. 2 vols.
387 Paillot de Montabert, Jacques Nicolas, *Traité complet de la peinture*, Paris, 1829. 9 vols.
388 *Poussin, Brunel et Les Andelys, Ode*, Rouen, 1829.
389 Roussel-Desfresches, Louis François, *Les Andelys, Nicolas Poussin et M. de Chateaubriand*, Rouen, 1829.

1829–1842

390 Smith, John, *A catalogue raisonné of the works of the most eminent Dutch, Flemish and French painters*, London, 1829–42. 9 vols.

1831

391 Balzac, Honoré de, *Le chef d'œuvre inconnu*, Paris, 1831.
392 Knowles, John, *The life and writings of Henry Fuseli*, London, 1831. 3 vols.

1833

393 La Rochefoucauld-Liancourt, Marquis de, *Histoire de l'arrondissement des Andelys*, Les Andelys, 1833.
394 'Nicolas Poussin', *MP*, I, 1833, pp. 35 f.

1833–1834

394.1 Cunningham, Allan, *The Cabinet Gallery of Pictures . . . which adorn Great Britain*, London, 1833–34. 2 vols.

1834

395 Busoni, Philippe, 'Poussin', *L'Artiste*, VII, 1834, pp. 49 ff.
396 'Mort du Poussin, par M. Granet', *MP*, II, 1834, pp. 137 f.

1835

397 Lottin de Laval, René Victorien, 'Nicolas Poussin', *Mémoires de la Société académique des sciences, arts et belles-lettres de Falaise*, 1835, pp. 106 ff.

1835–1851

397.1 Nagler, G. K. *Neues allgemeines Künstler-Lexicon, oder Nachrichten von dem Leben und den Werken der Maler, Bildhauer, Baumeister . . . etc.*, Munich, 1835–51. 21 vols.

1835–1871

398 Robert-Dumesnil, A. P. F., *Le peintre-graveur français . . . suite au peintre-graveur de M. Bartsch*, Paris, 1835–71. 11 vols.

1836

399 Passavant, Johann David, *Tour of a German artist in England with notices of private galleries and remarks on the state of art*, London, 1836. 2 vols.

1836–1848

Eckermann, Johann Peter, *Gespräche mit Goethe*, see No. 375.

1838

401 Duchesne, Jean, 'Notice sur Nicolas Poussin', *Recueil de la Société Libre de l'Eure*, IX, Evreux, 1838.
402 Miel de Lacombe, *Essai physiognomonique sur le Poussin*, Paris, 1838.
Nibby, Antonio, *Itinerario di Roma . . .*, see No. 383a.
Waagen, Gustav Friedrich, *Works of art . . . in England*, see No. 384a.

1838–1840

403 Mennechet, Edouard, *Le Plutarque français, vies des hommes et femmes illustres de la France avec leurs portraits en pied*, Paris, 1838–40. 8 vols.

1839

404 Laviron, Gabriel, 'Nicolas Poussin' *L'Artiste*, I, 1839, pp. 55 ff., 71 ff., 89 ff., 101 ff.
405 'Le Testament d'Eudamidas', *MP*, VII, 1839, pp. 385 f.

1839–1847

406 Rosini, Giovanni, *Storia della pittura Italiana*, Pisa, 1839–47. 7 vols.

1840

407 'Les Bergers d'Arcadie', *MP*, VIII, 1840, pp. 9 f.
408 Melchiorri, Giuseppe, *Guida metodica di Roma e suoi contorni*, Rome, 1840.

1841

409 'Cabinets de tableaux et autres collections artistiques de la ville d'Aix', *Mémorial d'Aix*, 13.vi.1841.
410 Eller, Irvin, *The history of Belvoir Castle*, London, 1841.
[Gualandi, M. A.], 'Quadreria di Andrea Lorenzo del Rosso . . .' see No. 99.
Malvasia, Carlo Cesare, *Felsina pittrice . . .*, see No. 78a.

1843

411 Hazlitt, William, *Criticisms on art: and sketches of the picture galleries of England*, London, 1843.
412 Jacquemart, A., *Les Sept Sacrements, d'après Nicolas Poussin*, Paris, 1843.
413 Leslie, Charles Robert, *Memoirs of the life of John Constable*, London, 1843.
413a Ed. J. Mayne, London, 1951.
All references to the 1951 ed.
414 Raoul-Rochette, Désiré, *Discours sur Nicolas Poussin*, Paris, 1843.

1843–1860

415 Ruskin, John, *Modern painters*, London, 1843–60. 5 vols.
415a Reprinted in *Works*, ed. E. T. Cook and A. Wedderburn, London, 1903–12, vols, III–VII (see No. 662). All references to the 1903–12 ed.

1844

416 Fontenais, Alexis de, *Biographie des peintres les plus célèbres*, Paris, 1844.

417 Hazlitt, William, *Criticisms on art, with catalogues of the principal galleries of England*, 2nd series, London, 1844.

417.1 Jameson, Anna, 'The collection of Lord Francis Egerton, known as the Bridgewater Gallery', *Companion to the most celebrated Private Collections of Art in London*, London, 1844, pp. 77 ff.

418 Mitford, J., Notebooks. Unpublished MS. in the British Museum (Add. MS. 32566).

1844–1845

419 Lenoir, Alexandre, 'Catalogue historique et critique des peintures et tableaux réunis au dépôt national des Monuments Français', *Bulletin archéologique publié par le comité historique des arts et monuments*, III, 1844–45, pp. 276 ff.

1844–1854

420 Ruskin, John, *Notes on the Louvre* (first published in *Works*, ed. 1903–12, vol. XII, pp. 448 ff.; see No. 662). All references to the 1903–12 ed.

1845

421 Blanc, Charles, *Histoire des peintres français*, Paris, 1845.
422 'Le Déluge', *MP*, XIII, 1845, pp. 177 f.

1845–1846

423 Delaistre, Louis, 'Notice bibliographique sur N. Poussin', *Annales de la Société Libre des Beaux-Arts*, 1845–46, pp. 142 ff.

424 'Vente de la Galerie Fesch à Rome', *Cabinet de l'Amateur*, IV, 1845–46, pp. 138 ff., 279 ff.

1845–1847

Baldinucci, Filippo, *Notizie dei Professori . . .*, see No. 85b.

1846

425 'Les effets de la terreur', *MP*, XIV, 1846, pp. 20 f.
426 'Moïse sauvé des eaux', *MP*, XIV, 1846, pp. 186 ff.
427 'Visits to private galleries, No. XV. The collection of the Rt. Hon. Lord Northwick, Thirlestane House, Cheltenham', *The Art Union*, VIII, 1846, pp. 251 ff.

1847

428 *Catalogue raisonné of pictures the property of Rev. John Sanford*, London, 1847.
429 Gisors, Alphonse de, *Le Palais du Luxembourg*, Paris, 1847.
430 La Boullaye, Ferdinand de, *Corneille chez Poussin*, Paris, 1847.
431 'Polyphème', *MP*, XV, 1847, pp. 57 f.

1847–1850

432 Duplat, 'Dissertation sur le tableau de Nicolas Poussin connu sous le nom de "Diogène" ', *Annales de la Société Libre des Beaux-Arts*, XVII, 1847–50, pp. 44 ff.

1847–1862

433 Chennevières-Pointel, Charles Philippe de, *Recherches sur la vie et les ouvrages de quelques peintres provinciaux de l'ancienne France*, Paris, 1847–62. 4 vols.

1848

434 'Phocion. Tableaux de Poussin', *MP*, XVI, 1848, pp. 145 f.

1849

435 Chateaubriand, Francois René, Vicomte de, *Mémoires d'outre-tombe*, Paris, 1849. 12 vols.
436 Vitet, Louis, *Eustache Lesueur. Sa vie et ses oeuvres*, Paris 1849.

1849–1876

437 Blanc, Charles, *Histoire des peintres de toutes les écoles, Ecole française*, Paris, 1849–76. 14 vols.

1850

438 Clément, Charles, 'Nicolas Poussin', *Revue des Deux Mondes*, 2nd nouvelle pér., 15.ii.1850, V, pp. 696 ff.
439 Montaiglon, Anatole de, *Les peintures de Jean Mosnier*, Paris, 1850.

c. 1850

440 Triqueti, Baron Henri de, Catalogue de l'œuvre de Poussin. MS. in the Ecole des Beaux-Arts, Paris (440).

c. 1850

441 Triqueti, Baron Henri de, Répertoire de l'œuvre de N. Poussin. MS. in the Ecole des Beaux-Arts, Paris (346).

1850–1888

442 Le Blanc, Charles, *Manuel de l'amateur d'estampes*, Paris, 1850–88.

1851

443 Chennevières-Pointel, Charles Philippe de, *Inauguration de la statue de N. Poussin aux Andelys*, Argentan, 1851.
444 Chennevières-Pointel, Charles Philippe de, *Observations sur le musée de Caen*, Argentan, 1851.
445 Crémieu, Edouard, *Poussin et son monument*, Evreux, 1851.
446 Mouton, B., *Vie de Nicolas Poussin*, Les Andelys, 1851.
447 Poucet, *Vie de Nicolas Poussin*, Les Andelys, 1851.
448 Ruskin, John, *Pre-Raphaelitism*, London, 1851.

448a Reprinted in *Works*, ed. 1903–12, vol. XII, pp. 338 ff. (see No. 662).
All references to the 1903–12 ed.
449 Saint-Victor, Paul de, 'La Galerie Lebrun. Collection de M. George', *L'Artiste*, 5th series, VI, 1851, pp. 38 ff., 54 ff., 65 ff.

1851–1852

450 [Chennevières, Philippe de], 'Documents inédits relatifs à l'histoire des arts en France. Nicolas Poussin', *AAF*, Paris, 1851–52, pp. 1 ff.
450a Parts reprinted in J. Thuillier, 'Pour un "Corpus Pussinianum"', *Actes*, II, 1960, pp. 51 f., 133 f.
Séroux d'Agincourt, J. B. L. G., 'Lettre . . . à Monsieur Castellan', see No. 350.

1851–1860

Mariette, Pierre Jean, *Abecedario . . .*, see No. 157.

1852

451 Guizot, François, *Etudes sur les beaux-arts*, Paris, 1852.

1852–1853

Chambry, M., 'Nicolas Poussin. Lettre . . .', see No. 3c.

1853

452 Cousin, Jean Victor, 'De l'art français au XVIIᵉ siècle', *Revue des Deux Mondes*, 2nd series, II, 1853, pp. 865 ff.
453 Delacroix, Eugène, 'Le Poussin', *Moniteur Universel*, 26, 29, 30.vi.1853.
453a Reprinted in *Oeuvres Littéraires*, Paris, 1923, II, pp. 57 ff.
454 Dumesnil, Jules, *Histoire des plus célèbres amateurs italiens et de leurs relations avec les artistes*, Paris, 1853.
455 Eméric-David, Toussaint Bernard, *Vie des artistes*, Paris, 1853.

1853–1855

456 Cousin, Jean Victor, 'De divers tableaux du Poussin qui sont en Angleterre et particulièrement de L'Inspiration du Poète', *AAF*, 1853–55, pp. 3 ff.
La Salle, His de, 'Lettre de Bouzonnet-Stella . . .', see No. 25.1.
Renouard, Antoine Augustin, 'Nicolas Poussin, Lettre au Cavalier del Pozzo', see No. 3d.

1853–1856

457 Guhl, Ernst, *Künstlerbriefe*, Berlin, 1853–56. 2 vols.
457a 2nd ed., ed. by A. Rosenberg, Berlin, 1880. 2 vols.
457b ed. by H. Uhde-Bernays, Dresden, 1926. 2 vols.

1854

458 Cousin, Jean Victor, *Du vrai, du beau, du bien*, Paris, 1854.

459 Delaborde, Henri, Vicomte, 'De la peinture française et de son histoire', *Revue des Deux Mondes*, 1854, pp. 1109 ff.
460 Feuillet de Conches, Félix Sébastien, *Léopold Robert. Sa vie, ses oeuvres et sa correspondance*, Paris, 1854.
461 Houssaye, Arsène, *Histoire de l'art en France: recueil raisonné et annoté de tout ce qui a été écrit et imprimé sur la peinture, la sculpture, etc., par Poussin, Félibien, Mignard, etc.*, première série, Paris, 1854.
Mémoires inédits . . ., see No. 102.
462 'Pyrame et Thisbe', *MP*, XXII, 1854, p. 216.

1854–1857

Waagen, Gustav Friedrich, *Art treasures in Great Britain*, see No. 384b.

1854–1870

463 Bartsch, Adam, *Le peintre graveur*, Leipzig, 1854–70. 21 vols.

1855

464 Aline, Alphonse, *Notice en vers sur le Poussin*, Andelys, 1855.
465 Burckhardt, Jacob, *Der Cicerone: eine Anleitung zum Genuss der Kunstwerke Italiens*, Basle, 1855.
465a *The Cicerone: an art guide to painting in Italy for the use of travellers and students*, tr. by A. H. Clough, London, 1873.
465b Reprint of original ed., Leipzig, 1924.
All references to the 1924 ed.
466 C. R., 'Le traité de la peinture de Léonard de Vinci illustré par Poussin', *Bulletin du Bibliophile Belge*, XI, 1855, pp. 387 ff.
467 Stirling-Maxwell, Sir William, *Velázquez and his works*, London, 1855.

1855–1856

Chassant, A. and Bordeaux, R., 'Voeux d'une religieuse des Andelys', see No. 28.1.
468 Montaiglon, Anatole de, 'Documents sur Pierre et André-Charles Boulle, ébénistes de Louis XIII et de Louis XIV', *AAF*, 1855–56, pp. 321 ff.

1856

469 [Desperets, A.], 'Dessin inédit du Poussin', *MP*, XXIV, 1856, pp. 195 f.
470 Dussieux, Louis Etienne, *Les artistes français à l'étranger*, Paris, 1856.
Le banquet des curieux, see No. 70a.
Le songe d'Ariste à Philandre . . ., see No. 77a.
471 'Une lettre de Nicolas Poussin', *MP*, XXIV, 1856, pp. 337 f.

1856–1858

472 Dumesnil, Jules, *Histoire des plus célèbres amateurs français, et de leurs relations avec les artistes*, Paris, 1856–58. 3 vols.

1857

473 D'Arco, Carlo, *Delle belle arti e degli artefici di Mantova*, Mantua, 1857, 2 vols.

474 [G. S.], *A Handbook to the paintings by ancient masters in the Art Treasures Exhibition*. Being a reprint of critical notices originally published in the *Manchester Guardian*, London, 1857.

475 Planche, Gustave, 'Le paysage et les paysagistes: Ruysdael, Claude Lorrain et Nicolas Poussin', *Revue des Deux Mondes*, 15.vi.1857, pp. 756 ff.

475.1 Rou, J., *Mémoires inédits et opuscules*, Paris, 1857.

476 Taine, Hippolyte A., *Les philosophes français du XIXᵉ siècle*, Paris, 1857.

476.1 Waagen, Gustav Friedrich, *A Walk through the Art-Treasures Exhibition at Manchester*, London, 1857.

1857–1860

477 Leroy, Alphonse, *Collection de dessins originaux des grands maîtres*, Paris, 1857-60.

1858

478 Bouchitté, Henri, *Le Poussin, sa vie et son oeuvre, suivi d'une notice sur la vie et les ouvrages de Philippe de Champagne et de Champagne le Neveu*, Paris, 1858.

479 Duplessis, Georges, 'Comment les graveurs ont interpreté les oeuvres de Nicolas Poussin', *RUA*, VIII, pp. 6 ff.

480 Mantz, Paul, 'Un nouveau livre sur le Poussin', *L'Artiste*, IV, 1858, pp. 39 ff.

1858–1860

'Dessins, . . . de Nicolas Poussin', see No. 76.

1859

481 Arnauldet, Thomas, 'Nicolas Poussin et ses détracteurs', *GBA*, 1859, III, pp. 348 ff.

482 Benoit, Arthur, 'Le peintre Poussin commentateur d'un verset du Prophète Isaïe', *Bulletin de la Société des Antiquaires de France*, Paris, 1859, p. 142.

483 Clément de Ris, Louis, Comte, *Le Musée royal de Madrid*, Paris, 1859.

484 Delpit, J., 'Etablissement de l'Académie de Peinture et de Sculpture de Bordeaux', *RUA*, IX, 1859, pp. 49 ff.

485 'Documents pour servir à l'histoire des Musées du Louvre', *RUA*, IX, 1859, pp. 504 ff.; X, 1859, pp. 33 ff.

486 Burty, P., 'Mouvement des arts et de la curiosité. Vente de la collection de Lord Northwick à Thirlestane House', *GBA*, 1859, II, pp. 52 ff.

487 Lagrange, Léon, 'L'atelier d'Overbeck', *GBA*, 1859, I, pp. 321 ff.

488 Lemonnier, Henry, 'Documents relatifs à Nicolas Poussin', *Annuaire de la Société Philotechnique*, Paris, 1859, pp. 178 ff.

489 Tonnellé, Alfred, *Fragments sur l'art et la philosophie suivis de notes et pensées diverses recueillies dans les papiers de A. T.*, ed. G. A. Heinrich, Tours, 1859.

1859–1860

Catherinot, Nicolas, *Traité . . .*, see No. 94a.

1860

490 Bürger, W. (= Thoré, Et. Jos. Th.), 'Exposition de tableaux de l'école française', *GBA*, 1860, III, pp. 257 ff.

491 Dumesnil, Jules, *Histoire des plus célèbres amateurs étrangers . . . et de leurs relations avec les artistes*, Paris, 1860.

492 Gandar, Eugène, 'Souvenirs de la jeunesse de Nicolas Poussin aux Andelys', *GBA*, 1860, I, pp. 65 ff.

493 Mantz, Paul, 'Le cabinet de M. A. Dumont à Cambrai', *GBA*, 1860, IV, pp. 303 ff.

494 Renouvier, Jules, 'Le Musée de Montpellier', *GBA*, 1860, I, pp. 7 ff.

495 Renouvier, Jules, 'Communication sur Nicolas Poussin', *GBA*, 1860, III, p. 123.

1860–1866

496 Blanc, Charles, 'Grammaire des arts du dessin', *GBA*, 1860, II, p. 14; 1862, I, pp. 245 ff.; 1865, II, p. 67; 1866, II, pp. 124 ff., 234 ff.

1861

496.1 Azeglio, Roberto d', 'Sulla maniera di Niccolò Pussino', *Studi sulle Arti del Disegno*, II, 1861, p. 182.

497 'Claude Lorrain, Poussin et le Guaspre dans la Campagne Romaine', *MP*, XXIX, 1861, pp. 228 ff. *Inventaire . . . du Cardinal Mazarin*, see No. 20.

498 Lévêque, Charles, *La science du beau étudiée dans ses applications et dans son histoire*, Paris, 1861. 2 vols.

499 Vitet, Louis, *L'Académie Royale de Peinture et de Sculpture. Etude historique*, Paris, 1861.

1862

499.1 Didron, Albert, 'Les vitraux du Grand Andely', *Annales Archéologiques*, XXII, 1862, p. 260. 'Nicolas Poussin'. Lettres de Louis Fouquet . . .', see No. 24.

1863

500 Andresen, A., *Nicolas Poussin, Verzeichniss der nach seinen Gemälden gefertigten gleichzeitigen und späteren Kupferstiche*, Leipzig, 1863.

500a Abridged French tr. by G. Wildenstein in *GBA*, 1962, II, pp. 139 ff.

501 Chesneau, E., 'Le réalisme et l'esprit français dans l'art', *Revue des Deux Mondes*, XLVI, 1.vii.1863, pp. 218 ff.

502 Montaiglon, Anatole de, 'Documents pour servir à l'histoire des musées du Louvre et incidemment d'un des premiers tableaux du Poussin', *RUA*, XVIII, 1863, pp. 156 ff.

1863–1864

503 Brossard de Ruville, *Histoire de la ville des Andelis et de ses dépendances*, Les Andelys, 1863–64.

504 Parthey, Gustav, *Deutscher Bildersaal*, Berlin, 1863–64. 2 vols.

505 Woodward, Bernard Bolingbroke, and Triqueti, Baron Henri, 'Catalogue of the drawings by Nicolas Poussin in the Royal Collection, Windsor Castle', *Fine Arts Quarterly Review*, I, 1863, pp. 263 ff.; II, 1864, pp. 175 ff.; III, 1864, pp. 105 ff.

1863–1865

506 Lejeune, Théodore, *Guide théorique et pratique de l'amateur de tableaux*, Paris, 1863–65. 3 vols.

1864

507 Becker, Wolfgang, *Kunst und Künstler des XVII. Jahrhunderts*, Leipzig, 1864.

508 Bürger, W. (= Thoré, Et. Jos. Th.), 'Les cabinets d'amateurs à Paris. Galerie de MM. Péreire', *GBA*, 1864, I, pp. 193 ff.

509 Fillon, Benjamin, 'Dans quel château du Poitou Nicolas Poussin a-t-il séjourné quelque temps, au commence, ment du règne de Louis XIII?', *Congrès Archéologique de France*, XXXIe Session (Fontenay), Paris, 1864 (publ. 1865), pp. 228 f.

510 Gautier, Théophile, Houssaye, Arsène, and Saint-Victor, Paul de, *Les dieux et les demi-dieux de la peinture-* Paris, 1864.

Le Blond de la Tour, Sieur, *Lettre . . .*, see No. 50a.
'Lettre sur l'Académie Royale . . . et sur le Salon de 1777', see No. 255.

511 Waagen, Gustav Friedrich, *Die Gemäldesammlung in der Kaiserlichen Ermitage zu St. Petersburg*, Munich, 1864.

1865

512 Clément, Charles, 'Nicolas Poussin', *Etudes sur les Beaux-Arts en France*, Paris, 1865.

512.1 Lagrange, Léon, 'Bulletin Mensuel, April 1865', *GBA*, 1865, II, pp. 485 ff.

Seignelay, Marquis de, 'Relation du Voyage . . .', see No. 58.

1866

513 Taine, Hippolyte A., *Voyage en Italie*, Paris, 1866. 2 vols.

1866–1867

514 Waagen, Gustav Friedrich, *Die vornehmsten Kunstdenkmäler in Wien*, Vienna, 1866–67. 2 vols.

1867

515 Chardon, Henri, *Amateurs d'art et collectionneurs manceaux du XVIIe siècle. Les Frères Fréart de Chantelou*, Le Mans, 1867.

516 Clément, Charles, 'Catalogue de l'œuvre de Géricault', *GBA*, 1867, II, pp. 272 ff., 351 ff.

517 Couture, Thomas, *Méthode et entretiens d'atelier*, Paris, 1867.

518 Grandsart, Antoinette, *Le Corrège, suivi de notices sur Nicolas Poussin, Pergolèse, Charles de Steuben*, Lille and Paris, 1867.

519 Jal, Auguste, *Dictionnaire critique de biographie et d'histoire, errata et supplément pour tous les dictionnaires historiques d'après des documents authentiques inédits*, Paris, 1867.

520 Taine, Hippolyte A., *De l'idéal dans l'art*, Paris, 1867.

1868

521 Banville, Théodore de, 'Nicolas Poussin', *L'Artiste*, XXXVIII, 4, 1868, pp. 139 ff.

522 Charpillon, *Dictionnaire historique de toutes les communes du département de l'Eure*, Rouen, 1868. 2 vols.

523 Galichon, Emile, 'Un dessin du Poussin: Bacchus et Ariane', *GBA*, 1868, I, pp. 276 ff.

524 Pillon, P., *Nicolas Poussin. Etude biographique*, Lille and Paris, 1868.

524.1 Roy, Elie, 'Le sentiment de la nature dans l'art français. Les paysagistes contemporains et disciples du Poussin', *L'Artiste*, XXXVIII, 2, 1868, pp. 353 ff.

1869

525 Joly, Alexandre, 'Le Poussin et l'art en 1868', *L'Artiste*, XXIX, 1, 1869, pp. 397 ff.

1870

525.1 Campori, G. *Raccolta di cataloghi ed inventarii inediti . . .*, Modena, 1870.

526 Duplessis, Georges, 'Le cabinet de M. Gatteaux', *GBA*, 1870, II, pp. 341 ff.

527 Woodward, B., *Specimens of the drawings of ten Masters*, London, 1870.

1871

528 Suchet, Dr., *Un tableau de Nicolas Poussin*, Paris, 1871.

1872

Courajod, Louis, 'Documents sur la vente . . . Mariette', see No. 246.1.

529 'Esquisses du Poussin', *MP*, XL, 1872, pp. 234 f.

530 Jordan, Max, *Untersuchungen über das Malerbuch des Leonardo da Vinci*, Leipzig, 1872.

531 'L'art du peintre selon quelques lettres du Poussin', *L'Artiste*, N.S. II (2), 1872, pp. 35 ff.

531.1 Le Roy, P., 'Jehan Poucin, Maçon de Vernon (1437)', *NAAF*, 1872, pp. 134 ff.

Marolles, Michel de, *Le livre des peintres . . .*, see No. 72a.

532 Pattison, Mrs. Mark, 'Nicolas Poussin', *Fortnightly Review*, XVII, 1872, pp. 472 ff.

1873

533 Bonnaffé, Edmond, *Les collectionneurs de l'ancienne France*, Paris, 1873.
Burckhardt, Jacob, *The Cicerone . . .*, see No. 465a.
534 'Enterrement d'un génie', *MP*, XLI, 1873, p. 304.
Lister, Martin, *Le Voyage de Lister . . .*, see No. 115a.

1873–1875

535 Dramard, E., 'Etudes sur le Poussin', *Recueil des travaux de la Société Libre de l'Eure*, 4th series, II, 1873–75, pp. 19 ff.

1874

536 Duplessis, Georges, *Les ventes de tableaux, dessins, estampes et objets d'art au XVIIᵉ et au XVIIIᵉ siècle*, Paris, 1874.
Félibien, André, *Mémoires . . .*, see No. 81.
537 Gautier, Théophile, *Portraits contemporains*, Paris, 1874.
538 Gonse, Louis, 'Musée de Lille. Le musée de peinture: école française', *GBA*, 1874, I, pp. 138 ff.
539 Lücke, Heinrich, 'Die neuen Erwerbungen der Berliner Gemäldegalerie: Die Landschaft von Nicolas Poussin', *ZBK*, IX, 1874, pp. 446 ff.
540 Lumbroso, Giacomo, 'Notizie sulla vita di Cassiano dal Pozzo', *Miscellanea di Storia Italiana*, XV, 1874, pp. 129 ff.
540a Published separately, Turin, 1875.
541 Mantz, Paul, 'Exposition en faveur de l'œuvre des Alsaciens et Lorrains', *GBA*, 1874, I, pp. 97 ff.
542 Tardieu, Charles, 'La collection W. Wilson', *GBA*, 1874, I, pp. 41 ff.

1875

543 Adeline, Jules, *Les Andelys. La statue de N. Poussin et les autres monuments*, Rouen, 1875. (Extract from *Bulletin de la Société des Amis des sciences naturelles de Rouen*.)
544 Chéravay, Etienne, 'Nicolas Poussin. Le tableau de la Cène conservé au musée du Louvre', *Revue des Documents Historiques*, II, 1875, pp. 91 f.
545 Dramard, E., *Etudes sur le Poussin*, Evreux, 1875.
Lumbroso, Giacomo, 'Notizie sulla vita . . . dal Pozzo', see No. 540a.

1875–1877

Diderot, Denis, *Oeuvres . . .*, see No. 211.

1875–1880

546 Legay, C., 'Testament de Nicolas Poussin', *Bulletin de la Société de l'Histoire de Normandie*, 1875–80, pp. 148 ff.

1875–1909

Académie Royale . . . Procès-verbaux, see No. 13.

1876

547 Carutti, Domenico, 'Di un nostro maggiore, ossia di Cassiano dal Pozzo il Giovane', *Atti della Reale Accademia dei Lincei*, serie seconda, III, Pt. 3, 1876, pp. 17 ff.
548 Ludwig, Heinrich, *Ueber die Grundsätze der Oelmalerei und das Verfahren der klassischen Meister*, Leipzig, 1876.
549 'Nota delli quadri, che si ritrovano nella casa del Maratta per la Maestá di Filippo Quinto', *Revista de Archivos Biblioteca y Museo*, VI, 1876, pp. 128 ff., 143 ff.
550 Robert, U., and Montaiglon, Anatole de, 'Quittances de peintres, sculpteurs et architectes français 1535–1711 . . .', *NAAF*, 1876, p. 32.

1877

551 Berger, Georges, 'Le Poussin. Cours donné à l'Ecole Nationale des Beaux-Arts', *L'Art*, XI, 1877, pp. 73 ff.
552 Bougot, André, *Essai sur la critique d'art ses principes—sa méthode—son histoire en France*, Paris, 1877.
553 Clément de Ris, Louis, Comte, *Les amateurs d'art d'autrefois*, Paris, 1877.
554 Duranty, 'Promenades au Louvre. Remarques sur le geste dans quelques tableaux', *GBA*, 1877, I, pp. 281 ff.
'Testament et inventaire . . . de Claudine Bouzonnet Stella . . .', see No. 107.

1877–1884

Fréart de Chantelou, Paul, *Journal*, see No. 41.

1878

555 A. D., 'Nicolas Poussin', *L'Intermédiaire*, XI, 1878, pp. 399 f.
556 E. G. P., 'Nicolas Poussin', *L'Intermédiaire*, XI, 1878, p. 316.
557 Ménard, René, *La mythologie dans l'art ancien et moderne*, Paris, 1878.
Perrault, Charles, *Mémoires de Charles Perrault . . .*, see No. 112b.
558 Reiset, 'Une visite aux musées de Londres en 1876. La National Gallery', *GBA*, 1878, I, pp. 305 ff.
559 Ward, C. A., 'Nicolas Poussin', *L'Intermédiaire*, XI, 1878, p. 260.

1879

560 Berger, Georges, *L'Ecole française de peinture*, Paris, 1879.
561 Chennevières-Pointel, Charles Philippe de, 'Les dessins des maîtres anciens', *GBA*, 1879, II, pp. 126 ff.
562 Jolibois, Emile, 'L'Histoire des Beaux-Arts à Toulouse', *RSBAD*, 1879, pp. 50 ff.

1879–

563 *Inventaire général des richesses d'art de la France*, Paris, 1879– .

1880

564 Clément de Ris, Louis, Comte, 'Le Musée imperial de l'Ermitage', *GBA*, 1880, I, pp. 262 ff.
Guhl, Ernst, *Künstlerbriefe*, see No. 457a.

1880–1881

564.1 Montaiglon, Anatole de, 'Nicolas Poussin. La descente de Croix des Capucins de Blois', *NAAF*, 1880–81, pp. 314 f.

1880–1905

The Harcourt papers, see No. 201.

1881

565 Bonnaffé, Edmond, 'Les amateurs de l'ancienne France. Le surintendant Foucquet', *L'Art*, XXVII, 1881, pp. 122 ff.
566 Both de Tauzia, Vicomte, *Notice des dessins de la collection His de la Salle exposés au Louvre*, Paris, 1881.
567 Lafenestre, Georges, 'Le château de Chantilly et ses collections', *GBA*, 1881, II, pp. 315 ff.
568 Sensier, Alfred, *La vie et l'oeuvre de J. F. Millet*, Paris, 1881.
568a *Jean-François Millet, peasant and painter*, tr. by H. de Kay, London, 1881.
569 'Un dessin allégorique du Poussin', *MP*, XLIX, 1881, pp. 1 f.
570 Woermann, Karl, 'Die Provinzial-Galerien Frankreichs, 2. Caen', *ZBK*, XVI, 1881, pp. 114 ff.
571 Woermann, Karl, 'Die Provinzial-Galerien Frankreichs, 8. Marseille', *ZBK*, XVI, 1881, pp. 324 ff.

1881–1901

Guiffrey, Jules, *Comptes des bâtiments . . .*, see No. 39.

1882

572 Bonnaffé, Edmond, *Le Surintendant Foucquet*, Paris, 1882.
573 Bonnaffé, Edmond, 'Notes sur les collections des Richelieu', *GBA*, 1882, II, pp. 5 ff., 96, 112, 205 ff.
'Description du château de Richelieu', see No. 188.
574 Ephrussi, Charles, 'Les dessins de la collection His de la Salle', *GBA*, 1882, II, pp. 486 ff.
575 Gautier, Théophile, *Guide de l'amateur au Musée du Louvre*, Paris, 1882.
576 Gonse, Louis, 'Exposition de maîtres anciens à la Royal Academy de Londres', *GBA*, 1882, I, pp. 288 ff.
577 Krantz, Emile, *Essai sur l'esthétique de Descartes*, Paris, 1882.

1883

578 Brunetière, Fernand, 'La critique d'art au XVIIᵉ siècle', *Revue des Deux Mondes*, 3ᵉ pér., LVIII, 1.vii. 1883, pp. 207 ff.
579 Carutti, Domenico, *Breve storia della Accademia dei Lincei*, Rome, 1883.

580 'Chronique', *Revue de l'art Chrétien*, XXXIII, 1883, p. 615.
580.1 Jouin, Henry. *Conférences de l'Académie royale de peinture et de sculpture*. Paris, 1883.

1883–1884

581 Guiffrey, Jules, 'Scellés et inventaires d'artistes', *NAAF*, 1883 and 1884.

1883–1897

La Fontaine, Jean de, *Oeuvres*, see No. 34.

1884

582 Besneray, Marie de, *Les grandes époques de la peinture, Le Poussin, Ruysdaël, Claude Lorrain*, Paris, 1884.
583 Bonnaffé, Edmond, *Dictionnaire des amateurs français au XVIIᵉ siècle*, Paris, 1884.
584 Cosnac, G. J., Comte de, *Les richesses d'art du Palais Mazarin*, Paris, 1884.
585 Pardiac, Jean Baptiste, 'L'orthodoxie dans les Beaux-Arts', *Revue de l'Art Chrétien*, 3rd series, II, 1884, pp. 291 ff.
586 Pattison, Mrs. Mark, *Claude Lorrain, sa vie et ses oeuvres*, Paris, 1884.

1885

Dubois de Saint-Gelais, *Histoire journalière . . .*, see No. 139.
587 Ferrero, G., *Composizioni di Raffael, Pusino, Domenichino, etc.*, Rome, 1885.
Fréart de Chantelou, Paul, *Journal*, see No. 41a.
588 Müntz, Emile, and Molinier, Emile, 'Le château de Fontainebleau', *MSHP*, XII, 1885, pp. 255 ff.
589 'Un groupe de Nicolas Poussin', *MP*, LIII, 1885, pp. 128 ff.

1886

590 Arnaud, Jean, *L'Académie de Saint-Luc à Rome*, Rome, 1886.
591 Bertolotti, Antonio, *Artisti francesi in Roma nei secoli XV, XVI, XVII. Ricerche e studi negli archivi romani*, Mantua, 1886.
592 Chennevières-Pointel, Philippe de, 'Artistes Normands', *NAAF*, 1886, p. 343.
593 Rouaix, Paul, 'La Dulwich College Gallery', *GBA*, 1886, I, pp. 233 ff.

1887

594 Ferrand, 'Un tableau de Poussin', *L'Intermédiaire*, XX, 1887, p. 199.
595 L. G., 'Un tableau de Poussin', *L'Intermédiaire*, XX, 1887, p. 426.
Mémoires inédits . . ., see No. 102a.
596 Vesme, Alessandro de, 'Sull' acquisto fatto da Carlo Emanuele III Re de Sardegna della quadreria del Principe Eugenio di Savoia', *Miscellanea di Storia Italiana*, XXV, 1887, pp. 163 ff.

1887–1912

Montaiglon, Anatole de, and Guiffrey, Jules, *Correspondance des Directeurs de l'Académie de France . . .*, see No. 45.

1888

597 Ferrand, 'Où sont les papiers de Nicolas Poussin?', *L'Intermédiaire*, XXI, 1888, p. 108.

598 Guiffrey, J. J., 'Le plafond du Poussin du Musée du Louvre', *NAAF, Revue*, 1888, p. 188.

599 Justi, Carl, *Diego Velasquez und sein Jahrhundert*, Bonn, 1888.

599a *Diego Velasquez and his times*, tr. by A. H. Keane, London, 1889.

600 Montaiglon, Anatole de, 'Jean Jouvenet', *NAAF*, 1888, pp. 118 f.

601 Pattison, Mrs. Mark, *Art in the modern state*, London, 1888.

Pocock, Richard, *Travels through England*, see No. 187.

601.1 Redford, George, *Art Sales. A history of sales of pictures and other works of art*, London, 1888. 2 vols.

602 Th. D., 'Où sont les papiers de Nicolas Poussin?', *L'Intermédiaire*, XXI, 1888, p. 182.

1889

Burney, Fanny, *The early diary . . .*, see No. 233.

603 Chennevières-Pointel, Philippe de, 'Eustache Restout', *NAAF*, 1889, pp. 87 ff.

604 Fitzgerald, Edward, *Letters and literary remains of Edward Fitzgerald*, ed. W. A. Wright, London, 1889. 3 vols.

605 Janitschek, Hubert, *Geschichte der deutschen Kunst; Malerei*, Berlin, 1889.

606 Jouin, Henry, *Charles Le Brun et les arts sous Louis XIV*, Paris, 1889.

Justi, Carl, *Diego Velasquez . . .*, see No. 599a.

607 Portalis, Baron Roger, *Honoré Fragonard, sa vie et son œuvre*, Paris, 1889.

608 Stranahan, C., *A history of French painting from its earliest to its latest practice: including an account of the French academy of painting, its salons, schools of instruction and regulations*, London, 1889.

1890

609 Mesnard, L., *Essais de critique d'art*, Paris, 1890.

Orléans, Charlotte, Duchesse d', *Correspondance . . .*, see No. 125.

610 Stein, Henri, 'Etat des objets d'art placés dans les monuments religieux et civils de Paris au début de la Révolution', *NAAF Review*, 1890, pp. 27 ff.

611 Swarte, Victor de, 'Les financiers amateurs d'art', *RSBAD*, 1890, pp. 108 ff.

1890–1891

612 Muntz, Eugène, 'Le Musée de l'Ecole des Beaux-Arts', *GBA*, 1890, II, pp. 282 ff.; 1891, I, pp. 41 ff.

613 Jameson, Mrs. (Anna), *Legends of the monastic Orders as represented in the fine arts*, London, 1891.

1892

615 Arréat, Lucien, *Psychologie du peintre*, Paris, 1892.

616 Esthènes, J., 'Un tableau de Poussin à determiner', *L'Intermédiaire*, XXV, 1892, p. 211.

617 Gachot, E., *Le Poussin à Rome*, Evreux, 1892.

618 Grouchy, Vicomte de, 'Inventaires des tableaux de François Quesnel', *NAAF*, 1892, pp. 90 ff.

Rosa, Salvator, *Poesie e lettere*, see No. 38a.

619 Valmy, Edmond, 'Nicolas Poussin en Poitou', *L'Intermédiaire*, XXVI, 1892, p. 51.

620 Valmy, Edmond, 'Le premier protecteur de Nicolas Poussin', *L'Intermédiaire*, XXVI, 1892, p. 326.

1893

621 Beani, Gaetano, *Clemente IX, Giulio Rospigliosi Pistoiese, Notizie Storiche*, Prato, 1893.

622 Boislisle, A. de, 'Paul Scarron et Françoise d'Aubigné', *Revue des Questions Historiques*, LIV, 1893, pp. 86 ff., 389 ff.

623 Germain, Alphonse, *De Poussin et des bases de l'art figuratif*, Paris, 1893.

Guérin, Nicolas, and Dézallier d'Argenville, Antoine Nicolas, *Descriptions de l'Académie . . .*, see No. 134a.

624 Lemonnier, Henry, *L'art français au temps de Richelieu et de Mazarin*, Paris, 1893.

625 Ludwig, Heinrich, *Die Technik der Oelmalerei*, Leipzig, 1893.

626 Morsolin, B., 'Nicolas Poussin et le covolo de Costazza dans le Vicentin', *L'Art*, LIV, 1893, pp. 137 ff., 215 ff.

1894

626.1 Albanès, Abbé, *Manuscrits de la Bibliothèque d'Aix*, in *Catalogue général des manuscrits des Bibliothèques publiques de France. Départements*, XVI, Paris, 1894.

627 Beaumont, Charles, Comte de, 'Pierre Vigné, architecte du roi', *RSBAD*, 1894, pp. 610 ff.

628 Bouyer, Raymond, *Le paysage dans l'art*, Paris, 1894. Reprinted from *L'Artiste*.

629 Chennevières-Pointel, Charles Philippe de, *Essais sur l'histoire de la peinture française*, Paris, 1894.

629.1 Ginoux, Charles, 'Artistes de Toulon', *NAAF* 1894, pp. 193 ff.

630 Le Vasseur, Gustave, *Un souvenir de l'inauguration de la statue de Poussin en 1851*, Caen, 1894.

631 Seidel, Paul, 'Friedrich der Grosse als Sammler', *Jahrbuch der preussischen Kunstsammlungen*, XV, 1894, pp. 81 ff.

1894–1902

632 Venturi, Adolfo, *Le Gallerie nazionali italiane*, Rome, 1894–1902. 5 vols.

For relevant articles, see No. 652.1.

1895

Bergeret and Fragonard, *Journal . . .*, see No. 243.

633 Bernardin, Napoléon Maurice, *Un précurseur de Racine Tristan l'Hermite, Sieur du Solier, 1601–1655. Sa famille, sa vie, ses oeuvres*, Paris, 1895.

634 Courajod, Louis, *Ecole du Louvre: Les origines de l'art moderne—L'art au XVIIe siècle. L'école académique*, Paris, 1895.

634.1 Estrée, Paul d', 'Une académie bachique au XVIIe siècle', *Revue d'histoire littéraire de la France*, II, 1895, pp. 491 ff.

635 Mabilleau, L., 'La peinture française au musée de Madrid', *GBA*, 1895, I, pp. 299 ff.

1896

636 Bourgeois, Emile, *Le grand siècle: Louis XIV, les arts et les artistes*, Paris, 1896.

1896–1909

637 Spemann, Wilhelm, *Das Museum*, Berlin and Stuttgart, 1896–1909. 11 vols.

1897

638 Granberg, Olof, *La galerie de tableaux de la reine Christine de Suède*, Stockholm, 1897.

639 Schmarsow, August, *Barock und Rokoko*, Leipzig, 1897.

1898

640 Denio, Elizabeth, *Nicolas Poussin, Leben und Werke*, Berlin, 1898.

640a English tr., London, 1899.

641 Justi, Carl, *Winckelmann und seine Zeitgenossen*, Leipzig, 1898.

642 Nietzsche, Friedrich, *Menschliches Allzumenschliches, Part II: Der Wanderer und sein Schatten*, Leipzig, 1898.

1899

Bailly, Nicolas, *Inventaire* . . ., see No. 131.
'Catalogue des tableaux de Charles Tardif', see No. 153.1.
Denio, Elizabeth, *Nicolas Poussin* . . ., see No. 640a.
'Inventaire . . . du Cardinal de Polignac', see No. 169.1.
'Inventaire . . . du Maréchal d'Humières', see No. 108.1.

643 La Moricière, 'Assassinat de MM. de l'Isle et Marlonge', *Revue de la Saintonge et de l'Aunis*, XIX, 1899, p. 112.

644 Nielsen, C. V., *Nicolas Poussin og den franske Kunsts Forhold til Perspektiven et Afsnit af Perspektivens Historie*, Copenhagen, 1899.

645 Ténaud, E., 'Nicolas Poussin au château de Mornay', *Gaulois du Dimanche*, 21–22.x.1899.

646 Tourneux, Maurice, *Diderot et Catherine II*, Paris, 1899.

1899–1901

647 Graves, Algernon, and Cronin, William Vine, *A history of the works of Sir Joshua Reynolds*, London, 1899–1901. 4 vols.

1900

648 Canavazzi, C., *Papa Clemente IX poeta*, Modena, 1900.

648.1 Champier, Victor, and Sandoz, G. R., *Le Palais-Royal* . . ., Paris, 1900. 2 vols.

649 J. P. 'Nicolas Poussin en Saintonge', *Revue de la Saintonge et de l'Aunis*, XX, 1900, pp. 28 f.

1901

650 Lanoe, Georges, and Brice, Tristan, *Histoire de l'école française de paysage de Poussin à Millet*, Paris, 1901.

650.1 Lapauze, Henri, *Les dessins de J. A. D. Ingres au musée de Montauban*, Paris, 1901.

651 Vitry, Paul, *De C. A. Dufresnoy pictoris poemate quod 'De Arte graphica' inscribitur*, Paris, 1901.

1901–1902

Tuétey, Louis, 'Procès-verbaux . . .', see No. 295.

1902

652 Advielle, Victor, *Recherches sur Nicolas Poussin*, Paris, 1902.

652.1 Filangieri di Candida, A., 'La Galleria Nazionale di Napoli (Documenti e Ricerche)', *Le Gallerie nazionali italiane: Notizie e Documenti*, ed. A. Venturi, V, 1902, pp. 208 ff.

653 Mithouard, Adrien, 'Du héros chez Poussin,' *L'Occident*, II, 1902, pp. 179 ff.

654 Popp, Hermann, *Maleraesthetik*, Strasbourg, 1902.

1902–1906

655 Hazlitt, William, *The collected works of William Hazlitt*, ed. A. R. Waller and A. Glover, London, 1902–6. 13 vols.

1903

656 Desjardins, Paul, *Poussin*, Paris (1903).
Fontaine, André, *Conférences inédites* . . ., see No. 55.

657 Fontaine, André, *Essai sur le principe et les lois de la critique d'art*, Paris, 1903.

658 Lange, Julius, *Die menschliche Gestalt in der Geschichte der Kunst*, Strasbourg, 1903.
Marigny, Abel François Poisson, Marquis de, 'Correspondance . . .', see No. 191.

659 Meier-Graefe, Julius, 'Von Poussin bis Maurice Denis', *Die Zeit*, XXXIV, 1903, pp. 57 ff.

660 Michel, Emile, 'La collection Dutuit. Tableaux et dessins', *GBA*, 1903, I, pp. 19 ff., 228 ff.

661 Veuclin, E., 'Artistes français admirateurs effectifs de Nicolas Poussin en Normandie (1700–1851)', *RSBAD*, XXVII, 1903, pp. 232 ff.

1903–1912

662 Ruskin, John, *Works*, ed. E. T. Cook and A. Wedderburn, London, 1903–12. 39 vols.
All references are to this edition.

1903–1915

Walpole, Horace, Earl of Orford, *Letters*, see No. 162.

1903–1923

663 Fenaille, Maurice, *État général des tapisseries de la manu-facture des Gobelins, depuis son origine jusqu'à nos jours 1600–1900*, Paris, 1903–23. 6 vols.

1904

664 Bertrand, Louis, 'L'Art français à Rome', *RDM*, I, 1904, pp. 354 ff., 597 ff.

665 Desjardins, Paul, *La Méthode des classiques français: Corneille, Poussin, Pascal*, Paris, 1904.

666 Foerster, R., 'Philostrats Gemälde in der Renaissance', *Jahrbuch der preussischen Kunstsammlungen*, XXV, 1904, pp. 15 ff.

Marigny, Abel François Poisson, Marquis de, 'Corres-pondance . . . avec Coypel . . .', see No. 219.

1905

Angiviller, Charles Claude Labillarderie, Comte d', 'Correspondance . . . avec Pierre', see No. 244.

667 Chatelain, Urbanus Victor, *Le Surintendant Nicolas Foucquet, protecteur des lettres, des arts et des sciences*, Paris, 1905.

668 Cook, Herbert, 'La collection de Sir Frederick Cook à Richmond', *Les Arts*, August, 1905, pp. 1 ff.

669 Hourticq, Louis, 'Un amateur de curiosités sous Louis XIV, Louis Henri de Loménie, Comte de Brienne', *GBA*, 1905, I, pp. 57 ff., 237 ff., 326 ff.

670 Magne, Emile, *Scarron et son milieu*, Paris, 1905.

670a 2nd ed., Paris, 1924.

671 Marcel, Pierre, *La peinture française au début du dix-huitième siècle 1690–1721*, Paris (1905).

1905–1906

672 Alexandre, Arsène, 'The pantomime and expression in the paintings of Nicolas Poussin', *Magazine of Fine Arts*, I, 1905–6, pp. 175 ff.

1906

Angiviller, Charles Claude Labillarderie, Comte d', 'Correspondance . . . avec Pierre', see Nos. 244 and 276.

Evelyn, John, *The Diary*, see No. 8a.

1906–1909

673 Bosseboeuf, V. L., 'Une famille de peintres du Blésois, les Mosnier; documents sur les arts en Blésois', *RSBAD*, 1906, pp. 241 ff.; 1909, pp. 52 ff.

1906–1911

673.1 Helbig, Jules. *L'Art Mosan depuis l'introduction du christianisme jusqu'à la fin du XVIIIe siècle*. Brussels, 1906–11. 2 vols.

1907

Angiviller, Charles Claude Labillarderie, Comte d', 'Correspondance . . . avec Pierre', see Nos. 244 and 276.

674 Lechevallier-Chevignard, E., 'La publication des lettres de Poussin', *BSHAF*, 1907, pp. 13 ff.

Reynolds, Sir Joshua, *The discourses . . .*, see No. 235.

675 Tarbel, Jean, 'Le grand peintre français Nicolas Poussin', *Le Correspondant*, 10.viii.1907, p. 544.

1908

676 Dorbec, Prosper, 'La tradition classique dans le pay-sage au milieu du XIXe siècle', *RAAM*, XXIV, 1908, pp. 259 ff., 357 ff.

677 Fontaine, André, 'L'esthétique janséniste', *RAAM*, XXIV, 1908, pp. 141 ff.

677.1 Riegl, Alois, *Die Entstehung der Barockkunst in Rom*, Vienna, 1908.

678 Vauxelles, Louis, 'La collection de M. P. Gallimard', *Les Arts*, September 1908, pp. 1 ff.

679 Waetzoldt, Wilhelm, *Die Kunst des Porträts*, Leipzig, 1908.

1909

Bosseboeuf, V. L., 'Une famille de peintres du Blésois . . .', see No. 673.

Boyer d'Agen, Auguste Jean, *Ingres d'après une corres-pondance . . .*, see No. 363.

679.1 Demonts, Louis, 'Dessins français des cabinets d'Allemagne', *BSHAF*, 1909, pp. 259 ff.

680 Fontaine, André, *Les doctrines d'art en France: peintres, amateurs, critiques. De Poussin à Diderot*, Paris, 1909.

681 Fontaine, André, 'Félibien et les Poussinistes', *Bulletin de l'Institut général physiologique*, August and September 1909.

682 Giolli, Raffaello, 'Un quadro del Poussin', *Vita d'Arte*, 1909, pp. 25 ff.

Gougenot, Abbé Louis (?), 'L'Exposition . . . au Luxembourg en 1750', see No. 184.

683 Jamot, Paul, 'Un tableau inconnu de Poussin', *BSHAF*, 1909, p. 179.

684 La Farge, John, *The higher life in art*, London, 1909.

685 Lapauze, Henri, 'Une vie de Poussin annotée par Ingres', *Revue de Paris*, 15.xii.1909, pp. 864 ff.

Perrault, Charles and Claude, *Mémoires de ma vie . . .*, see No. 112c.

686 Pilon, Edmond, 'Poussin aux Andelys', *Revue Politique et Littéraire. Revue Bleue*, XLVII (2), 1909, pp. 329 ff.

687 Rouart, Louis, 'Un tableau de Poussin', *BSHAF*, 1909, pp. 92 ff.

688 Schneider, René, 'La première édition des lettres de Nicolas Poussin', *BSHAF*, 1909, pp. 251 ff.

689 Serra, Luigi, *Domenico Zampieri detto il Domenichino*, Rome, 1909.

690 Tietze, Hans, Review of André Fontaine, *Les doctrines d'art en France de Poussin à Diderot*, *Kunstgeschichtliche Anzeigen*, 1909, pp. 67 ff.

Tuétey, Alexandre, and Guiffrey, Jean, 'La commis-sion . . . du Louvre', see No. 304.

1909–1921

Saint-Aubin, Gabriel de, *Catalogues de ventes . . .*, see No. 204.

1910

Caylus, Anne Claude Philippe, Comte de, *Vies d'artistes . . .*, see No. 181.
691 Dangibaud, Charles, 'Nicolas Poussin est-il venu en Saintonge?', *Revue de la Saintonge et de l'Aunis*, XXX, 1910, p. 323.
692 Fontaine, André, *Les collections de l'Académie Royale de Peinture et de Sculpture*, Paris, 1910.
693 Marcel, Pierre, *Charles Le Brun*, Paris (1910?).
694 Meier-Graefe, Julius, *Spanische Reise*, Berlin, 1910.
695 Schaller, E., *Figurenbild und Landschaft. Beiträge zur Vorgeschichte der Landschaftsmalerei*, Stuttgart, 1910.

1910–1911

Aubert, Marcel, 'Un guide de Notre Dame . . .', see No. 216.

1911

696 Grautoff, Otto, 'Handzeichnungen aus dem Louvre', *Kunst und Künstler*, IX, 1911, pp. 532 ff.
697 Guiffrey, Jules, 'Testament et inventaire après décès de André Le Nostre', *BSHAF*, 1911, pp. 217 ff.
698 Jamot, Paul, 'L'Inspiration du Poète par Nicolas Poussin', *GBA*, 1911, II, pp. 177 ff.
699 Lemonnier, Henry, *L'art français au temps de Louis XIV*, Paris, 1911.
700 Leprieur, Paul, 'L'Inspiration du Poète', *RAAM*, XXX, 1911, p. 161.
701 Pilon, Edmond, 'La danse dans l'œuvre de Poussin, de Watteau et de Corot', *Revue Bleue*, XLIX, 1911, p. 78.
702 Pilon, Edmond, 'Le décor français du Poussin', *La Licorne*, I (1), 1911, pp. 9 ff.
Poussin, Nicolas, *Correspondance . . .*, see No. 3a.
703 Rodin, Auguste, *L'art. Entretiens réunis par Gsell*, Paris, 1911.

1911–1912

703.1 Fry, Roger. 'Exhibition of Old Masters at the Grafton Galleries', *BM*, XX, 1911–12, pp. 66 ff., 161 ff.

1911–1917

703.2 Orbaan, J. A. F., and Hoogewerff, G. J., *Bescheiden in Italië omtrent Nederlandsche Kunstenaars en Geleerden*, The Hague, 1911–17. 3 vols.

1912

704 Gramm, Joseph, *Die ideale Landschaft*, Freiburg, 1912.
Graves, Algernon, *Summary . . . to Waagen*, see No. 384c.
705 Hautecoeur, Louis, *Rome et la Renaissance de l'antiquité à la fin du XVIIIe siècle*, Paris, 1912.
705.1 Jouanny, Charles, 'Lyon dans la correspondance de Poussin', *Revue d'Histoire de Lyon*, 1912, pp. 223 ff. 'Les tableaux . . . saisis', see No. 305.
706 Moschetti, Andrea, 'Dell' influsso del Marino sulla formazione artistica di Nicolas Poussin', *Atti del Congresso internazionale di storia dell' Arte*, Rome 1912, (published 1922), pp. 356 ff.
707 Posse, Hans, 'Einige Gemälde des römischen Malers Andrea Sacchi', *Mitteilungen aus den sächsischen Kunstsammlungen*, III, 1912, pp. 49 ff.
708 Rivière, J., 'Poussin et la peinture contemporaine', *L'Art Décoratif*, XXVII, 1912, pp. 133 ff.
709 Thiébault-Sisson, F., 'Un chef-d'œuvre du Poussin. L'Inspiration du Poète', *Les Arts Revue Mensuelle des Musées, Collections, Expositions*, January 1912, pp. 20 ff.

1913

710 Demonts, Louis, 'Essai sur la formation de Simon Vouet en Italie 1612–1627', *BSHAF*, 1913, p. 309.
711 Fontaine, André, 'Les derniers jours de Poussin . . .', *Mélanges Lemonnier (NAAF)*, 1913, pp. 201 ff.
712 Gillet, Louis, *La peinture. XVIIe et XVIIIe siècles*, Paris, 1913.
713 Lemonnier, Henry, *L'art moderne*, Paris, 1913.
714 Luzio, Alessandro, *La galleria dei Gonzaga venduta all' Inghilterra nel 1627–28: documenti degli archivi di Mantova e Londra*, Milan, 1913.
715 Magne, Emile, 'Le voyage de Nicolas Poussin en France', *RAAM*, XXXIV, 1913, pp. 214 ff., 287 ff.
716 Milliet, Jean Paul, 'Claude Mellan', *L'Art Décoratif*, XV (2), 1913, pp. 73 ff.
716.1 Nolhac, Pierre de, *Les Jardins de Versailles*, Paris, 1913.
717 Rouchès, Gabriel, *La peinture bolonaise à la fin du XVIe siècle*, Paris, 1913.
718 Stryenski, Casimir, *La galerie du Régent Philippe, Duc d'Orléans*, Paris, 1913.

1913–1914

719 Frimmel, Theodor von, *Lexikon der Wiener Gemäldesammlungen*, Munich, 1913–14. 2 vols.

1913–1915

720 Brockwell, Maurice W., *Catalogue of the paintings at Doughty House*, London, 1913–15. 3 vols.

1914

Caylus, Anne Claude Philippe, Comte de, *Voyage d'Italie*, see No. 133.
721 Fontaine, André, *Académiciens d'autrefois*, Paris, 1914.
722 Friedlaender, Walter, *Nicolas Poussin. Die Entwicklung seiner Kunst*, Munich, 1914.
723 Grautoff, Otto, *Nicolas Poussin: sein Werk und sein Leben*, Munich, 1914. 2 vols.
724 Magne, Emile, *Nicolas Poussin, premier peintre du roi, 1594–1665*, Brussels and Paris, 1914.
724a New ed., Paris, 1928.
Sirén, Osvald, *Nicodemus Tessin . . .*, see No. 63.

1915

725 Brown, John, 'Unidentified painting', *Connoisseur*, XLIII, 1915, pp. 95 f.

726 Friedlaender, Walter, Review of A. Moschetti, *Dell'influsso del Marino sulla formazione artistica di Nicolas Poussin*, RKW, XXXVII, 1915, pp. 230 ff.

727 Whitley, William T., *Thomas Gainsborough*, London, 1915.

1916

728 Lemonnier, Henry, 'Sur deux volumes de dessins attribués à Poussin ou Errard', *AAF*, VIII, 1916, pp. 110 ff.

Loménie, Comte de Brienne, Louis Henri, *Mémoires . . .*, see No. 88.

729 Lowinsky, Victor, 'Raum und Geschehen in Poussin's Kunst', *Zeitschrift für Aesthetik und allgemeine Kunstwissenschaft*, XI, 1916, pp. 36 ff.

729.1 Marcel, Pierre, 'La correspondance de Charles Le Brun . . .', *Mélanges offerts à Jules Guiffrey*, Paris, 1916, pp. 170 ff.

730 Ruffo, Vincenzo, 'La Galleria Ruffo nel secolo XVII in Messina', *Bollettino d'Arte*, X, 1916, pp. 21 ff., 95 ff.

730a Parts reprinted by P. du Colombier, *BSP*, III, 1950, p. 95.

730b Parts reprinted in J. Thuillier, 'Pour un "Corpus Pussinianum" ', *Actes*, II, 1960, pp. 109, 116, 122.

1917

731 Colvin, Sidney, *John Keats, his life and poetry, his friends, his critics and after-fame*, London, 1917.

732 Fraenger, Wilhelm, *Die Bild-Analysen des Roland Fréart de Chambray*, Heidelberg, 1917.

733 Fry, Roger, 'Pictures lent to the National Gallery', *BM*, XXX, 1917, pp. 198 ff.

734 Lavallée, Pierre, 'La collection de dessins de l'Ecole des Beaux-Arts. Dessins français', *GBA*, 1917, pp. 417 ff.

735 Stein, Wilhelm, *Die Erneuerung der heroischen Landschaft nach 1800*, Strasbourg, 1917.

736 Waldmann, Emil, 'Poussin und wir', *Kunst und Künstler*, XV, 1917, pp. 595 ff.

1918

737 Jamot, Paul, 'Un tableau de Nicolas Poussin au musée de Toulouse', *GBA*, 1918, pp. 345 ff.

Walpole, Horace, Earl of Orford, *Letters*, see No. 162.

1919

737.1 Ballot, M. J., 'Charles Cressent, sculpteur, ébéniste, collectionneur', *AAF*, 1919, p. 189.

Fréart de Chantelou, Paul, *Journal*, see No. 41b.

738 Johnstone, J., 'An early picture by Nicolas Poussin', *BM*, XXXV, 1919, p. 91.

729 Schneider, René, 'La mort d'Adonis de Nicolas Poussin au musée de Caen', *GBA*, 1919, pp. 369 ff.

740 Steinmann, Ernst, 'Das Schicksal der Kreuzlegende des Daniello Volterra', *Monatshefte für Kunstwissenschaft*, XII, 1919, pp. 193 ff.

1919–1920

741 Jamot, Paul, 'Poussin et l'Italie', *AA*, n.s., I, 1919–20, pp. 313 ff.

1920

743 Fraenger, Wilhelm, 'Zur Geschichte der Kunstkritik . . .', *RKW*, XLII, 1920, pp. 48 f.

744 Jamot, Paul, 'Un tableau inconnu de Poussin', *BSHAF*, 1920, pp. 195 ff.

745 Muther, R., *Geschichte der Malerei*, Leipzig, 1920. 3 vols.

746 Orbaan, J. A. F., *Documenti sul barocco in Roma*, Rome, 1920.

1920–1921

747 Martine, Charles, 'Le retour de Nicolas Poussin', *AA*, n.s., II, 1920–21, pp. 131 ff.

1921

748 Hourticq, Louis, *De Poussin à Watteau*, Paris, 1921.

749 Jamot, Paul, 'Etudes sur Nicolas Poussin', *GBA*, 1921, II, pp. 81 ff.

750 Joubin, A., 'Sur les oeuvres de Poussin au musée de Montpellier', *Actes du Congrès de l'Histoire de l'Art*, Paris, 1921 (publ. 1924), II, (1), pp. 338 ff.

751 Martine, Charles, and Marotte, Léon, *Nicolas Poussin, cinquante reproductions de Léon Marotte avec un catalogue par Charles Martine*, Paris, 1921.

752 Pilon, Edmond, 'La Danse dans l'oeuvre de Poussin, de Watteau et de Corot', *Revue de Genève*, 13.ii.1921, pp. 27 ff.

Réau, Louis, *Correspondance de Falconet . . .*, see No. 230.1.

752.1 Rouchès, Gabriel, 'L'interprétation du "Roland furieux" et de la "Jérusalem délivrée" dans les arts plastiques', *Etudes Italiennes*, III, 1921, pp. 129 ff., 193 ff.

753 Tatlock, Robert Rattray, 'Poussin and Claude', *BM*, XXXVIII, 1921, p. 3.

1921–1922

754 Lemonnier, Henry, *La peinture et la gravure en France pendant la première moitié du XVIIe siècle*, in André Michel, *Histoire de l'Art*, Paris, 1921–22, VI, ch. V, pp. 230 ff.

1922

755 Dezarrois, Eugène, 'Un nouveau Poussin au Louvre: Le Corps de Phocion emporté hors d'Athènes', *RAAM*, XLI, 1922, p. 82.

756 Duportal, Jeanne, 'Les "Hespérides" du P. Ferrari et Nicolas Poussin', *RAAM*, XLI, 1922, pp. 311 ff.

757 Friedlaender, Walter, 'Die Stellung Nicolas Poussins innerhalb der römischen Barockmalerei des 17. Jahrhunderts', *Atti del Congresso internazionale di Storia dell'Arte*, Rome, 1912 [published 1922], pp. 352 ff.

758 Jamot, Paul, 'Poussin's two pictures of the story of Phocion', *BM*, XL, 1922, pp. 158 ff.

759 Krohn, M., *Frankrigs og Danmarks kunstneriske Forbindelse i det 18. Aarhundrede*, Copenhagen, 1922.

760 Lhote, André, 'Les dessins de Nicolas Poussin', *Feuillets d'Art*, II, 1922, pp. 181 f.

Moschetti, Andrea, 'Dell' influsso del Marino . . .', see No. 706.

Tischbein, Wilhelm, *Aus meinem Leben*, see No. 342.

1923

Delacroix, Eugène, 'Le Poussin', see No. 453a.

761 Fry, Roger, '*Pyramus and Thisbe* by Nicolas Poussin', *BM*, XLIII, 1923, p. 53.

762 Gerstenberg, Kurt, *Die ideale Landschaftsmalerei: Ihre Begründung und Vollendung in Rom*, Halle, 1923.

763 Guiffrey, Jean, 'Le Musée Bonnat à Bayonne', *Beaux-Arts*, 1.viii.1923.

764 Magnin, Jeanne, *Un cabinet d'amateur Parisien en 1922*, Dijon, 1923. 2 vols.

766 Rouchès, Gabriel, *Eustache Le Sueur*, Paris, 1923.

767 Sutro, Esther, *Nicolas Poussin*, London, 1923.

1923–1925

768 Brinckmann, A. E., *Barock-Bozzetti*, Frankfort, 1923–25. 4 vols.

1924

Burckhardt, Jacob, *Der Cicerone* . . ., see No. 465b.

769 Burroughs, Bryson, 'Two pictures by Poussin', *Bulletin of the Metropolitan Museum of Art*, XIX, 1924, pp. 100 ff.

770 Bouyer, Raymond, 'L'art français au musée de l'Ermitage', *Renaissance de l'Art français*, VII, 1924, pp. 6293 ff.

770.1 Cordey, Jean, *Vaux-le-Vicomte*, Paris, 1924.

Joubin, André, 'Sur les oeuvres de Poussin', see No. 750.

Magne, Emile, *Scarron et son milieu*, see No. 670a.

771 Mirot, Léon, *Roger de Piles, peintre, amateur, critique, membre de l'Académie de Peinture (1635–1709)*, Paris, 1924.

772 Panofsky, Erwin, *Idea. Ein Beitrag zur Begriffsgeschichte der Kunsttheorie*, Berlin, 1924.

772a 2nd ed., Berlin, 1960.

773 Schneider, René, 'Des sources ignorées . . . de l'art de Poussin', *Mélanges Bertaux*, 1924, pp. 46 ff.

1924–1925

774 Grautoff, Otto, 'Französische Museumskunst', *Kunstwanderer*, 1924–25, pp. 105 ff.

1924–1934

775 Coutil, Léon, *Nicolas Poussin*, Les Andelys, 1924–34. 2 vols.

1925

776 Alfassa, Paul, 'Poussin et le paysage', *GBA*, 1925, I, pp. 265 ff.

777 Bodkin, Thomas, 'Exhibition of French Landscapes in Paris: I—From Poussin to Corot', *BM*, XLVII, 1925, pp. 3 ff.

778 Bodkin, Thomas, 'Poussin's two pictures of the story of Phocion', *BM*, XLVI, 1925, pp. 322 ff.

779 Borenius, Tancred, 'The Roccatagliata Madonna of Nicolas Poussin', *Art in America*, XIII, 1925, pp. 92 ff.

Brackenhoffer, Elias, *Voyage en France* . . ., see No. 7.

780 Brillant, Maurice, 'L'Esprit du paysage français de Poussin à Corot', *Le Correspondant*, 25.vi.1925.

781 Courthion, Pierre, 'Le Poussin, créateur de rythmes', *Belvedere*, VIII, 1925, pp. 59 ff.

781.1 Demonts, Louis, 'Deux peintres de la première moitié du XVIIe siècle: Jacques Blanchard et Charles-Alphonse Dufresnoy, *GBA*, 1925, II, pp. 162 ff.

782 Dorner, Alexander, 'Hannover. Provinzialmuseum', *Kunstchronik*, N.F., XXXV, 1925, p. 233.

783 Friedlaender, Walter, 'Eine neu aufgetauchte Zeichnung zu der Komposition Nicolas Poussins "Moses treibt die Hirten vom Brunnen" ', *Belvedere Forum*, VII, 1925, p. 65.

784 Fry, Roger, 'Exhibition of French Landscape in Paris: II—Claude and Poussin', *BM*, XLVII, 1925, pp. 10 ff.

785 Gronkowski, Camille, 'Regard sur une exposition prochaine, le paysage français de Poussin à Corot', *Renaissance de l'Art français*, VIII, 1925, pp. 55 ff.

786 Guey, F., 'Sur un Poussin du musée de Rouen', *BSHAF*, 1925, p. 31.

787 Hourticq, Louis, 'L'Exposition du paysage français de Poussin à Corot', *RAAM*, XLVIII, 1925, pp. 3 ff.

788 Jamot, Paul, 'Nouvelles études sur Poussin à propos de l'exposition du Petit Palais', *GBA*, 1925, II, pp. 73 ff.

789 Jamot, Paul, 'Sur quelques tableaux de Poussin', *BSHAF*, 1925, pp. 166 f.

790 Lemonnier, Henry, 'A propos des neuf Poussins du Musée Condé', *BSHAF*, 1925, p. 31.

791 Lemonnier, Henry, 'Les sources des *Bergers d'Arcadie*', *RAAM*, XLVII, 1925, pp. 273 ff.

792 Leporini, Heinrich, *Die Stilentwicklung der Handzeichnung. XIV. bis XVIII. Jahrhundert*, Vienna and Leipzig (1925).

793 Levallet, Mlle G., 'Notes inédites sur la collection de Choiseul', *BSHAF*, 1925, pp. 201 ff.

794 Manwaring, Elizabeth Wheeler, *Italian landscape in 18th century England*, London, 1925.

794.1 Peltzer, R. A. 'Sandrart-Studien', *Münchner Jahrbuch der bildenden Kunst*, II, 1925, pp. 103 ff.

795 *Petit Palais, Paris: Le paysage français*, Paris, 1925.

796 Posse, Hans, *Der römische Maler Andrea Sacchi*, Leipzig, 1925.

Sandrart, Joachim von, *Teutsche Academie* . . ., see No. 67b.

797 Vaudoyer, Jean Louis, 'Le voluptueux Poussin', *L'Art Vivant*, 15.ii.1925, p. 10.

Winckelmann, Johann Joachim, *Kleine Schriften* . . ., see No. 203.

1925–1926

798 Fosca, François, 'La méthode de Poussin', *AA*, N.S., XII, 1925–26, pp. 1 ff.

1926

799 Benoist, Luc, 'La collection Paul Jamot', *L'Amour de l'Art*, VII, 1926, pp. 165 ff.

800 Courthion, Pierre, 'La collection Oscar Reinhart', *L'Amour de l'Art*, VII, 1926, pp. 3 ff.

801 Fry, Roger, *Transformations*, London, 1926.
Guhl, Ernst, *Künstlerbriefe*, see No. 457b.

802 Hendy, Philip, 'Nicolas Poussin. Some pictures in the National Gallery and at Hertford House', *Apollo*, III, 1926, p. 217.

803 Hourticq, Louis, and others, *Le paysage français de Poussin à Corot à l'exposition du Petit Palais (Mai-Juin, 1925). Etudes et catalogue par L. H., Emile Dacier, Georges Wildenstein, Raymond Bouyer, Paul Jamot, Gaston Brière. Préface par Etienne Bricon*, Paris, 1926.

804 Milliken, William, 'The landscape with nymphs and satyrs by Nicolas Poussin', *Bulletin of the Cleveland Museum of Art*, XIII, 1926, p. 86.

805 Réau, Louis, *L'Art français aux Etats-Unis*, Paris, 1926.

806 Vallery-Radot, Jean, 'Note sur un tableau de Poussin: le "Satyre buvant" du musée de l'Ermitage', *BSHAF*, 1926, pp. 31 ff.

807 Vallery-Radot, Jean, 'Sur un tableau de Poussin, le "Satyre buvant" du musée de l'Ermitage' *Beaux-Arts*, IV, 1926, p. 52.

1926–1927

808 Dimier, Louis, *Histoire de la peinture française du retour de Vouet à la mort de Lebrun 1627 à 1690*, Paris and Brussels, 1926–27. 2 vols.

809 Friedlaender, Walter, '*Achilles auf Skyros* von Nicolas Poussin', *ZBK*, LX, 1926–27, pp. 141 ff.

810 Henkel, M. D., 'Illustrierte Ausgaben von Ovids Metamorphosen im XV., XVI. und XVII. Jahrhundert', *Vorträge der Bibliothek Warburg, 1926–27*, Leipzig and Berlin, 1930.

1927

811 Dacier, Emile, 'Discours', *BSHAF*, 1927, p. 82.

812 Dacier, Emile, 'Un document probant sur la "Mort de la Vierge" de Poussin', *BSHAF*, 1927, pp. 165 ff.

813 Dorner, Alexander, *Meisterwerke aus dem Provinzialmuseum Hannover*, Hanover, 1927.

813.1 Hourticq, Louis, 'Sur un tableau perdu de la jeunesse de Poussin', *BSHAF*, 1927, pp. 162 f., 167 ff.

814 Hussey, Christopher, *The Picturesque. Studies in a point of view*, London and New York, 1927.

815 Panofsky, Erwin, 'Imago pietatis', *Festschrift für Max Friedlaender*, Leipzig, 1927, pp. 267 ff.

816 Venturi, Adolfo, 'La biblioteca di Sir Robert Witt', *L'Arte*, XXX, 1927, p. 250.

817 Wechsler, Eduard, *Esprit und Geist*, Bielefeld and Leipzig, 1927.

1927–1928

818 Galli, R., 'I tesori d'arte di un pittore del seicento', *Archiginnasio*, XXII, 1927, pp. 217 ff.; XXIII, 1928, pp. 59 ff.
Walpole, Horace, Earl of Orford, *Journals of visits to country seats*, see No. 192.

1928

819 Aynard, Jacques, *Nicolas Poussin*, Paris, 1928.

819.1 Borenius, Tancred, 'An Exhibition of Poussin and Claude drawings', *Old Master Drawings*, III, 1928, pp. 17 ff.
Boyer, Ferdinand, 'Les Inventaires . . . de Nicolas Poussin', see No. 42.

820 Ernst, Serge, 'L'exposition de peinture française des XVIIe et XVIIIe siècle au musée de l'Hermitage, à Petrograd', *GBA*, 1928, I, pp. 163 ff.

821 Glück, Gustav, and Haberditzl, F. M., *Die Handzeichnungen von Rubens*, Berlin, 1928.

822 Grautoff, Otto, and Pevsner, Nikolaus, *Die Barockmalerei in den romanischen Ländern*, Wildpark, 1928.

823 Heil, Walter, 'The Edgar B. Whitcomb collection in Detroit', *Art in America*, XVI, 1928, p. 55.
Magne, Emile, *Nicolas Poussin*, see No. 724a.

824 Magnin, Jeanne, *Le paysage français*, Paris, 1928.

825 O'Sullivan-Köhling, Ilse, *Shelley und die bildende Kunst*, Halle, 1928.

826 Réau, Louis, 'Catalogue de l'art français dans les musées Russes', *BSHAF*, 1928, pp. 167 ff.

826a Reprinted, Paris, 1929.

827 Sirén, Osvald, 'Nyförvärvade och deponerade gamla mästare i Nationalmuseum, IV: Poussins Bacchus och Erigone', *Nationalmusei Årsbok*, X, 1928, pp. 35 ff.

828 Whitley, William T., *Artists and their friends in England, 1700–1799*, London, 1928. 2 vols.

829 Whitley, William T., *Art in England 1800–1820*, Cambridge, 1928.

1928–1929

830 Grautoff, Otto, 'Neu aufgefundene Werke von Nicolas Poussin', *Kunstwanderer*, 1928–29, pp. 104 ff.

831 Troendle, H., 'Das Erbe Poussins', *Kunst und Künstler*, XXVII, 1928–29, pp. 425 ff.

1928–1938

832 Pollak, Otto, *Kunsttätigkeit unter Urban VIII.*, Vienna, 1928–38. 2 vols.

832a Parts reprinted in J. Thuillier, 'Pour un "Corpus Pussinianum" ', *Actes,* II, 1960, pp. 52 f.

1929

833 Courthion, Pierre, *Nicolas Poussin*, Paris, 1929.

834 Friedlaender, Walter, 'The Massimi Poussin drawings at Windsor', *BM*, LIV, 1929, pp. 116 ff., 252 ff.

835 La Tourette, Gilles de, *Nicolas Poussin*, Paris, 1929.

835.1 Longhi, Roberto, *Precisioni nelle Gallerie Italiane; Galleria Borghese*, Rome, 1929.

Poussin, Nicolas, *Lettres de Poussin*, see No. 3b.

Réau, Louis, 'Catalogue de l'art français dans les musées Russes', see No. 826a.

Reynolds, Sir Joshua, *Letters . . .*, see No. 281.

836 Singleton, Esther, *Old World masters in New World collections*, New York, 1929.

837 Sjöblom, Axel, 'En målning av Nicolas Poussin i den Svenska Konstmarknaden', *Konstrevy*, 1929, p. 29.

1929–1955

Vertue, George, *Notebooks*, see No. 132.

1930

838 'A Bacchanal and the problem of its authorship', *Apollo*, XII, 1930, pp. 285 ff.

839 Dodgson, Campbell, *Drawings by French masters of the XVII–XIX centuries*, London, 1930.

839.1 Francastel, Pierre, *La Sculpture de Versailles. Essai sur les origines et l'évolution du goût français classique*, Paris, 1930.

Fréart de Chantelou, Paul, *Journal*, see No. 41c.

840 Friedlaender, Walter, *Hauptströmungen der französischen Malerei von David bis Cézanne—I, von David bis Delacroix*, Bielefeld and Leipzig, 1930.

840a *David to Delacroix*, tr. R. Goldwater, Cambridge, Mass., 1952.

Henkel, M. D., 'Illustrierte Ausgaben von Ovids Metamorphosen . . .', see No. 810.

841 Panofsky, Erwin, *Herkules am Scheidewege, Studien der Bibliothek Warburg*, Leipzig and Berlin, 1930, pp. 140 ff.

842 Posse, Hans, '*Johannes auf Patmos*, ein wiedergefundenes Gemälde des Nicolas Poussin', *Pantheon*, V, 1930, p. 62.

843 Rich, Daniel Catton, 'Poussin and Cézanne, comparison of "St. John on Patmos" and "L'Estaque"', *Bulletin of the Art Institute of Chicago*, XXIV, 1930, pp. 113 ff.

844 *Sammlung Schloss Rohoncz*, Munich, 1930. 2 vols.

845 Valentiner, Wilhelm R., *Unknown Masterpieces*, London, 1930.

846 Weisbach, Werner, 'Et in Arcadia ego. Ein Beitrag zur Interpretation antiker Vorstellungen in der Kunst des 17. Jahrhunderts', *Die Antike*, VI, 1930.

c. 1930

847 Lieure, J., *L'Ecole française de gravure. XVIIᵉ siècle*, Paris, n.d.

1931

848 Bell, Clive, *An account of French painting*, London, 1931.

Bellori, Giovanni Pietro, *Le Vite . . .*, see No. 56c.

849 Benoist, Luc, 'La *Mort d'Adonis* par Nicolas Poussin', *Bulletin des Musées de France*, 1931, pp. 71 ff.

850 Borenius, Tancred, 'A great Poussin in the Metropolitan Museum', *BM*, LIX, 1931, pp. 206 f.

850.1 Boyer, Ferdinand. 'Documents d'Archives romaines et florentines sur Le Valentin, Le Poussin et Le Lorrain', *BSHAF*, 1931, pp. 233 ff.

1931

851 Brière, Gaston, 'L'Exposition des chefs-d'œuvre des musées de Province', *BSHAF*, 1931, pp. 189 ff.

Brosses, Charles Comte de, *Lettres familières . . .*, see No. 17oa.

852 Colombier, Pierre du, *Poussin*, Paris, 1931.

853 Friedlaender, Walter, 'Le Maître d'Ecole de Faléries châtié de sa trahison', *GBA*, 1931, II, pp. 52 ff.

854 Friedlaender, Walter, 'Zeichnungen Nicolas Poussins in der Albertina', *Belvedere*, II, 1931, pp. 56 ff.

855 Jamot, Paul, 'French painting', *BM*, LIX, 1931, pp. 257 ff.

'Les Tableaux de la Princesse des Ursins', see No. 132.1.

855.1 *Palais des Beaux-Arts, Valenciennes, Catalogue illustré et annoté des œuvres exposées au Palais des Beaux-Arts de la ville de Valenciennes*, Valenciennes, 1931. 2 vols.

Posse, Hans, 'Die Briefe des Grafen . . . Algarotti . . .', see No. 177.

856 Underwood, Eric Gordon, *A short history of French painting*, London, 1931.

1931–1932

857 Reiners, Heribert, 'Ein unbekanntes Bild von Poussin?', *Der Kunstwanderer*, XIII, 1931–32, pp. 43 ff.

1932

858 Bodkin, Thomas, 'Nicolas Poussin in the National Gallery, Dublin', *BM*, LX, 1932, pp. 174 ff.

859 Chambers, Frank P., *The history of taste. An account of the revolutions of art criticism and theory in Europe*, New York, 1932.

860 Clutton-Brock, Alan, *An introduction to French painting*, London, 1932.

861 Daniel, Augustus, and Jamot, Paul, 'Poussin and Berthollet Flémalle', *BM*, LX, 1932, pp. 191 ff.

Delacroix, Eugène, *Journal . . .*, see No. 372.

862 Denucé, Jan, *The Antwerp art galleries, inventories of the art-collections in Antwerp in the 16th and 17th centuries*, Antwerp, 1932.

863 Fry, Roger, *Characteristics of French art*, London, 1932.

864 Grautoff, Otto, 'Nouveaux tableaux de Nicolas Poussin', *GBA*, 1932, I, pp. 323 ff.

Grimm, Friedrich Melchior, Baron von, 'Correspondance . . . avec Catherine II', see No. 246.

865 Mâle, Emile, *L'Art religieux après le Concile de Trente. Etude sur l'iconographie de la fin du XVIᵉ siècle, du XVIIᵉ, siècle: Italie, France, Espagne, Flandres*, Paris, 1932.

866 Romney-Towndrow, Kenneth, 'Poussin and Berthollet Flémalle', *BM*, LX, 1932, pp. 314 f.

866.1 Rosenthal, E., 'Poussin-Studie', *Die Gabe. Dichtungen und Aufsätze Wilhelm Hausenstein zugeeignet*, Munich, 1932, pp. 79 ff.

867 *Royal Academy, London: French art, 1200–1900*, 1932. For *Commemorative Catalogue*, see No. 879.

868 Stechow, Wolfgang, *Apollo und Daphne*, Leipzig and Berlin, 1932.

869 Weisbach, Werner, *Französische Malerei des XVII. Jahrhunderts*, Berlin, 1932.

1933

870 Alfassa, Paul, 'L'origine de la lettre de Poussin sur les modes d'après un travail récent', *BSHAF*, 1933, pp. 125 ff.

871 Alpatov, Mikhail W. (Michel), 'Das Selbstbildnis Poussins im Louvre', *Kunstwissenschaftliche Forschungen*, II, 1933, pp. 113 ff.

872 Borenius, Tancred, 'An unrecorded Poussin', *BM*, LXIII, 1933, pp. 2 f.

873 Dumolin, Maurice, *Le château de Bussy-Rabutin*, Paris, 1933.

874 Fels, Marthe de, *Poussin*, Paris, 1933.

875 Friedlaender, Walter, 'Nicolas Poussin', in Ulrich Thieme and Felix Becker, *Allgemeines Lexikon der bildenden Künstler*, Leipzig, 1908–50, XXVII, pp. 321 ff.

876 Gibson, William, 'Nicolas Poussin (1593–1665)', *Old Master Drawings*, VIII, 1933, p. 25.

877 Klingsor, Tristan, 'Les dessins de Poussin à Chantilly', *Beaux-Arts*, 14.vii.1933, p. 2.

878 Malo, Henri, *Cent-deux dessins de Nicolas Poussin*, Paris, 1933.

878.1 Puvis de Chavannes, Henri. 'Conséquences des révisions d'attributions de Versailles. Les Termes de Poussin?', *RAAM*, LXIV, 1933, pp. 141 ff.

879 *Royal Academy, 1932: Commemorative Catalogue of the exhibition of French art, 1200–1900, Royal Academy of Arts, London, January-March 1932*, Oxford and London, 1933.

1934

880 Longhi, Roberto, 'Zu Michiel Sweerts', *Oud-Holland*, LI, 1934, pp. 271 ff.

Passeri, Giambattista, *Die Künstlerbiographien . . .*, see No. 75b.

881 Sterling, Charles, *Les peintres de la réalité en France au XVIIe siècle* (catalogue), Orangerie, Paris, 1934.

1935

882 Alpatov, Mikhail W. (Michel), 'Poussin problems', *AB*, XVII, 1935, pp. 5 ff.

Baglione, Giovanni, *Le Vite . . .*, see No. 4a.

882.1 Buscaroli, Rezio, 'Diffusione ed evoluzione dei principii Leonardeschi e Veneziani nelle regioni Italiane', *La Pittura di Paesaggio in Italia*, Bologna, 1935, XIII, pp. 199 ff.

883 Francastel, Pierre, 'Poussin et le milieu romain de son temps', *Revue de l'Art*, LXVIII, 1935, pp. 145 ff.

884 Gillet, Louis, *La peinture de Poussin à David*, Paris, 1935.

885 Marignon, Robert de, 'Les sept Sacraments "convertis en sept autres histoires" par Nicolas Poussin', *Revue des Questions Historiques*, LXIII, 1935, pp. 73 ff.

886 Puvis de Chavannes, Henri, 'Nicolas Poussin et la sculpture: le problème des termes de Versailles', *RAAM*, LXVIII, 1935, pp. 93 ff.

1935–1936

886.1 Petrucci, Alfredo, 'Originalità del Lucchesino', *Bollettino d'Arte*, XXIX, 1935–36, pp. 409 ff.

887 Valentiner, Wilhelm R., 'Selene and Endymion by Poussin', *Bulletin of the Detroit Institute of Arts*, XV, 1935–36, pp. 96 ff.

1935–1938

Delacroix, Eugène, *Correspondance . . .*, see No. 327.

1936

888 Barazzetti, S., 'Sublet de Noyers, surintendant des bâtiments du roi', *Beaux-Arts*, 10.iv.1936, p. 2.

Blumer, M. L., 'Catalogue des peintures transportées . . .', see No. 314.

889 Elling, Christian, 'Bendix Le Coffre', *Kunstmuseets Årsskrift*, XXIII, 1936, pp. 1 ff.

890 Hilles, Frederick Whiley, *The literary career of Sir Joshua Reynolds*, Cambridge, 1936.

891 'Un nouveau Poussin à l'Institute of Arts: Séléné et Endymion', *Revue de l'Art*, LXIX, 1936, pp. 316 f.

892 *Palais des Beaux-Arts, Brussels: Les plus beaux dessins français du Musée du Louvre, 1936–37.* (Catalogue) Brussels, 1936.

893 Panofsky, Erwin, '*Et in Arcadia Ego*', *Philosophy and History. Essays presented to E. Cassirer*, Oxford, 1936, pp. 223 ff.

894 Saxl, Fritz, 'Veritas filia temporis', *Philosophy and History. Essays presented to E. Cassirer*, Oxford, 1936, pp. 212 ff.

895 Schapiro, Meyer, 'The new Viennese School', *AB*, XVIII, 1936, pp. 258 f.

896 Wengström, Gunnar, and Hoppe, Ragnar, *Collection de dessins du Musée National, Stockholm. II, Nicolas Poussin*, Malmö, 1936.

1937

897 Batiffol, Louis, *Autour de Richelieu*, Paris, 1937.

897.1 Bush, Douglas, *Mythology and the Romantic Tradition in English Poetry*, Cambridge, Mass., 1937.

898 Gamba, Carlo, *Giovanni Bellini*, Milan, 1937.

899 Hourticq, Louis, *La jeunesse de Poussin*, Paris, 1937.

900 Huisman, Georges, *Chefs-d'œuvre de l'art français*, Paris, 1937. 2 vols.

901 Klein, Jerome, 'An analysis of Poussin's *Et in Arcadia Ego*', *AB*, XIX, 1937, pp. 314 ff.

902 Lemordant, J., 'Les origines de N. Poussin', *AA*, XXXIV, 1937, pp. 181 ff.

903 *Palais National des Arts, Paris: Chefs d'œuvre de l'art français*, Paris, 1937.

Salomon, Richard, 'An unknown letter by Nicolas Poussin', see No. 2.

904 Waterhouse, Ellis K., *Italian baroque painting* (Cantor Lectures of the Royal Society of Arts), London, 1937.

905 Weisbach, Werner, '*Et in Arcadia Ego*', *GBA*, 1937, II, pp. 287 ff.

1937–1938

906 Blunt, Anthony, 'The "Hypnerotomachia Poliphili" in 17th century France', *JWI*, I, 1937–38, pp. 117 ff.

907 Blunt, Anthony, 'Poussin's notes on painting', *JWI*, I, 1937–38, pp. 344 ff.
908 Mitchell, Charles, 'Poussin's *Flight into Egypt*', *JWI*, I, 1937–38, pp. 340 ff.
909 Wittkower, Rudolf, 'Chance, Time and Virtue', *JWI*, I, 1937–38, pp. 315 ff.

1937–

Walpole, Horace, Earl of Orford, *Correspondence*, see No. 162a.
Walpole, Horace, Earl of Orford, *Paris Journals*, see No. 225.

1938

910 Blunt, Anthony, 'A Bristol. Une exposition d'art français du XVIIe siècle', *Beaux-Arts*, 25.xi.1938, p. 1.
911 Blunt, Anthony, 'A newly discovered Poussin', *Apollo*, XXVII, 1938, pp. 197 ff.
912 Blunt, Anthony, 'Poussin's "Et in Arcadia Ego" ', *AB*, XX, 1938, pp. 96 ff.
913 Blunt, Anthony, 'The Royal Academy exhibition of seventeenth-century art', *Apollo*, XXVII, 1938, pp. 3 ff.
914 Borenius, Tancred, 'The French school at Burlington House', *BM*, LXXII, 1938, pp. 54 ff.
915 Brieger, Peter, 'French classic painting', *AB*, XX, 1938, pp. 339 ff.
916 Denis, Maurice, 'Poussin et notre temps', *L'Amour de l'Art*, XIX, 1938, pp. 185 ff.
917 Jamot, Paul, 'Sur la naissance du paysage dans l'art moderne, du paysage abstrait au paysage humaniste', *GBA*, 1938, I, pp. 233 ff.
918 Lord, Douglas (= Cooper, Douglas), 'Une exposition d'art français du XVIIe siècle à Bristol', *L'Amour de l'Art*, XIX, 1938, p. 394.
919 Lossky, Boris, 'Œuvres d'art françaises en Yougoslavie', *BSHAF*, 1938, pp. 175 ff.
920 Niclausse, Juliette, *Le Musée des Gobelins 1938; notices critiques*, Paris, 1938.
921 Panofsky, Erwin, '*Et in Arcadia Ego*, et le tombeau parlant', *GBA*, 1938, I, pp. 305 f.
922 Praz, Mario, 'Milton and Poussin', *Seventeenth Century Studies presented to Sir Herbert Grierson*, ed. Dover Wilson, Oxford, 1938.
923 Praz, Mario, 'Milton e Poussin alla scuola dell' Italia', *Romana*, XI, 1938, pp. 30 ff.
924 Senior, Elizabeth, 'A sheet of studies by Nicolas Poussin', *British Museum Quarterly*, XII, 1938, pp. 51 ff.
925 Vasič, Paul, 'Nikola Pusen u Pismima', *Umetnichki Pregled*, XI, Belgrade, 1938, pp. 346 ff.
925.1 Vasič, Paul, 'N. Poussin Kod nas', *Umetnichki Preglad*, No. 5, Belgrade, 1938.
926 Waterhouse, Ellis K., 'Seventeenth-century art in Europe at Burlington House—The paintings', *BM*, LXXII, 1938, pp. 3 ff.

1938–1939

927 Blunt, Anthony, 'Blake's "Ancient of Days". The symbolism of the compasses', *JWI*, II, 1938–39, pp. 53 ff.
928 Blunt, Anthony, 'An echo of the "Paragone" in Shakespeare', *JWI*, II, 1938–39, pp. 260 ff.
929 Blunt, Anthony, 'The triclinium in religious art', *JWI*, II, 1938–39, pp. 271 ff.
930 Wittkower, Rudolf, 'Eagle and serpent. A study in the migration of symbols', *JWI*, II, 1938–39, pp. 293 ff.

1939

931 Beaucamp, Fernand, *Le peintre lillois, Jean Baptiste Wicar*, Lille, 1939. 2 vols.
932 Bodkin, Thomas, 'A re-discovered picture by Nicolas Poussin', *BM*, LXXIV, 1939, pp. 252 ff.
933 Emmerling, Sophie Charlotte, *Antikenverwendung und Antikenstudium bei Nicolas Poussin*, Würzburg, 1939.
933.1 Ernst, Serge, 'Les dessins de Poussin à l'Académie de Venise', *BSHAF*, 1939, p. 222.
934 Finberg, Alexander J., *The life of J. M. W. Turner*, Oxford, 1939.
935 Lossky, Boris, 'Œuvres d'art françaises en Bulgarie, Bohème, Moravie et Slovaquie', *BSHAF*, 1939, pp. 121 ff.
936 Magne, Emile, *Images de Paris sous Louis XIV*, Paris, 1939.
937 'Poussin, Schlafende Venus von Satyren belauscht' *Jahresbericht der Zürcher Kunstgesellschaft*, 1939, pp. 31 ff.
938 Raschke, M., 'Nicolas Poussin, Schlafende Venus von Hirten belauscht', *Kunst*, LXXXI, 1939, pp. 18 f.
939 Rice, J. V., *Gabriel Naudé, 1600–1653*, Baltimore and London, 1939.
940 Rouchès, Gabriel, *Musée du Louvre. Collection de reproductions de dessins publiés sous la direction de Gabriel Rouchès. I: Nicolas Poussin*, Paris, 1939.
941 Stechow, Wolfgang, 'Catalogue of the woodcuts of Ludolph Buesinck', *Print Collector's Quarterly*, XXVI, 1939, pp. 349 ff.
942 Waterhouse, Ellis, K., 'Nicolas Poussin's *Landscape with the Snake*', *BM*, LXXIV, 1939, pp. 102 f.

1939–1940

943 Blunt, Anthony, 'A Poussin-Castiglione problem: classicism and the picturesque in seventeenth-century Rome', *JWCI*, III, 1939–40, pp. 142 ff.

1939–

944 Friedlaender, Walter, and Blunt, Anthony, *The drawings of Nicolas Poussin, a catalogue raisonné*, London, 1939– .
Four volumes published. Publication continuing.

945 Weigert, Roger Armand, *Bibliothèque Nationale. Inventaire du fonds français. Graveurs du XVIIᵉ siècle*, Paris, 1939– .

1940

946 Cunningham, Charles, 'Poussin's *Mars and Venus*', *Bulletin of the Museum of Fine Arts, Boston*, XXXVIII, 1940, pp. 55 ff.

947 Friedlaender, Walter, 'America's first Poussin show', *AN*, XXXVIII, 1940, pp. 1 ff.

948 Friedlaender, Walter, '*Venus and Adonis* by Nicolas Poussin', *Bulletin of the Smith College Museum of Art, Northampton*, XXI, 1940, pp. 3 ff.

949 Lee, Rensselaer, 'Ut pictura poesis: The Humanist theory of painting', *AB*, XXII, 1940, pp. 197 ff.

950 Seznec, Jean, *La survivance des dieux antiques*, London, 1940.

950a *The survival of the pagan gods*, tr. B. F. Sessions, London, 1953.

1941

951 Du Colombier, Pierre, *Le style Henry IV–Louis XIII* Paris, 1941.

952 Goertz, W., '*Moïse frappant le rocher* du Poussin et le problème des sujets héroïques dans l'art classique', *Musée de l'Hermitage, Travaux du Département de l'art européen*, II, 1941, pp. 149 ff.

953 Pierson, William, The drawings of Rubens and Poussin after the antique. Thesis presented at the Institute of Fine Arts, New York University, May 1941 (not published).

1942

Bellori, Giovanni Pietro, *Vite di Guido Reni . . .*, see No. 59.

954 Blunden, Edmund, 'Romantic poetry and the fine arts', *Proceedings of the British Academy*, XXVIII, 1942, pp., 101 ff.

955 Christoffel, Ulrich, *Poussin und Claude Lorrain*, Munich, 1942.

956 Comstock, Helen, 'The Connoisseur in America. Loan exhibition of Old Masters', *The Connoisseur*, CIX, 1942, pp. 143 f.

957 Dorival, Bernard, *La peinture française*, Paris, 1942. 2 vols.

958 Friedlaender, Walter, 'Iconographical studies of Poussin's works in American public collections—I: The Northampton *Venus and Adonis* and the Boston *Venus and Mars*', *GBA*, 1942, II, pp. 17 ff.

959 Gombrich, Ernst H., 'Reynold's theory and practice of imitation', *BM*, LXXX–LXXXI, 1942, pp. 40 ff.

960 Hautecoeur, Louis, *Littérature et peinture en France du XVIIᵉ au XXᵉ siècle*, Paris, 1942.

961 Peyre, H., *Le classicisme français*, New York, 1942.

962 Van den Berg, H. M., 'Willem Schellinks en Lambert Doomer in Frankrijk', *Oudheidkundig Jaarboek*, XI, 1942, pp. 1 ff.

1943

963 Blunt, Anthony, 'Jean Lemaire: painter of architectural fantasies', *BM*, LXXXIII, 1943, pp. 241 ff.

964 Friedlaender, Walter, 'Iconographical studies of Poussin's works in American public collections—II: The Metropolitan Museum of Art's *King Midas . . .* and the Detroit Institute of Art's *Endymion kneeling before Luna*', *GBA*, 1943, I, pp. 21 ff.

965 Jamot, Paul, *Introduction à l'histoire de la peinture*, Paris, 1943.

966 Pintard, René, *Le libertinage érudit*, Paris, 1943.

967 Richardson, John, 'Sir James Thornhill's collection', *BM*, LXXXIII, 1943, pp. 134 ff.

968 Rudrauf, Lucien, *L'Annonciation, étude d'un thème plastique et de ses variations en peinture et en sculpture*, Paris, 1943.

1943–1945

969 Donahue, Kenneth, ' "The ingenious Bellori". A biographical study', *Marsyas*, III, 1943–45 (publ. 1946), pp. 107 ff.

1943–1957

970 Hautecoeur, Louis, *Histoire de l'architecture classique en France*, Paris, 1943–57. 9 vols.

1944

971 Blunt, Anthony, 'The early works of Charles Le Brun', *BM*, LXXXV, 1944, pp. 165 ff., 186 ff.

972 Blunt, Anthony, 'The heroic and the ideal landscape of Nicolas Poussin', *JWCI*, VII, 1944, pp. 154 ff.

973 [Borenius, Tancred], 'The history of Poussin's *Orion*; a postscript', *BM*, LXXXIV, 1944, p. 51.

974 Gombrich, Ernst H., 'The subject of Poussin's *Orion*', *BM*, LXXXIV, 1944, pp. 37 ff.

1945

975 Blunt, Anthony, *The French drawings in the collection of His Majesty The King at Windsor Castle*, Oxford and London, 1945.

976 Blunt, Anthony, 'Two newly discovered landscapes by Nicolas Poussin', *BM*, LXXXVII, 1945, pp. 186 ff.

977 [Borenius, Tancred], 'Sir Joshua Reynolds' collection of pictures', *BM*, LXXXVII, 1945, pp. 133 f., 211 ff., 263 ff.

978 Borenius, Tancred, 'P. H. Lankrink's collection', *BM*, LXXXVI, 1945, pp. 29 ff.

979 Christoffel, Ulrich, *Von Poussin zu Ingres und Delacroix: Betrachtungen uber die französische Malerei*, Zurich (1945).

980 Gide, André, *Poussin*, Paris, 1945.

981 *Palais Pitti, Florence: La peinture française à Florence*, Florence (1945). *Preface*: Bernard Berenson.

1945–1946

982 Lens, A. de, 'Une statuette de cire attribuée à Nicolas Poussin', *BSHAF*, 1945–46, pp. 98 ff.

1946

983 Barr, Alfred, *Picasso: fifty years of his art*, New York, 1946.

984 Bazin, Germain, 'Poussin vu par André Gide', *L'Amour de l'Art*, N.S. IX, 1946, p. 55.

985 Bertin-Mourot, Thérèse, 'Les bacchanales du château de Richelieu', *Beaux-Arts*, 31.v.1946.

986 Bertin-Mourot, Thérèse, 'Réflexions sur quelques tableaux de Poussin', *L'Amour de l'Art*, N.S. IX, 1946, pp. 55 f.

987 Blunt, Anthony, 'French seventeenth century art', *BM*, LXXXVIII, 1946, p. 203.

988 Davies, Martin, *National Gallery catalogue: French school*, London, 1946.

988a 2nd ed., London, 1957.

Donahue, Kenneth, ' "The ingenious Bellori" ...', see No. 969.

Fréart de Chantelou, Paul, *Journal*, see No. 41d.

989 Jamot, Paul, 'The *Concert* by Nicolas Poussin', *AQ*, IX, 1, 1946, pp. 18 ff.

990 Lemoisne, Paul André, *Degas et son oeuvre*, Paris, 1946–48. 4 vols.

991 Leroy, Alfred, *Evolution de la peinture française des origines à nos jours*, Paris (1946).

992 Mahon, Denis, 'Nicolas Poussin and Venetian painting', *BM*, LXXXVIII, 1946, pp. 15 ff., 37 ff.

993 Mauricheau-Beaupré, Charles, *L'art au XVIIme siècle en France; première période 1594–1661*, Paris, 1946.

994 Volskaja, V., *Poussin*, Moscow, 1946. (In Russian.)

995 *Wildenstein, New York: French painting of the time of Louis XIII and Louis XIV*, New York, 1946. *Introduction* and *Summary of French painting under Louis XIII*: C. Sterling; *Discourse on the Grande Manière*: W. Friedlaender.

1947

996 Adhémar, Jean, 'La dernière commande de Poussin', *BSP*, I, 1947, p. 50.

997 Anikieva, V. N., 'De l'idée au tableau (N. Poussin)', *Travaux de l'Académie des Beaux-Arts*, Moscow and Leningrad, I, 1947, pp. 67 ff.

Bellori, Giovanni Pietro, *La vie de Nicolas Poussin*, see No. 56d.

998 Bertin-Mourot, Thérèse, 'Moïse frappant le rocher', *BSP*, I, 1947, p. 56 ff.

999 Bertin-Mourot, Thérèse, 'Notes et documents', *BSP*, I, 1947, pp. 72 ff.

1000 Blunt, Anthony, 'The "Annunciation" by Nicolas Poussin', *BSP*, I, 1947, pp. 18 ff.

1001 Blunt, Anthony, 'French seventeenth-century painting at Messrs. Wildenstein', *BM*, LXXXIX, 1947, pp. 160 ff.

1002 Blunt, Anthony, 'Poussin Studies I: Self-Portraits', *BM*, LXXXIX, 1947, pp. 219 ff.

1003 Blunt, Anthony, 'Poussin Studies II: Three early works', *BM*, LXXXIX, 1947, pp. 266 ff.

1004 Blunt, Anthony, 'Two exhibitions of 17th century art', *The Listener*, XXXVIII, 1947, pp. 55 ff.

1005 Bromehead, Cyril E. N., 'A geological museum of the early seventeenth century', *Quarterly Journal of the Geological Society of London*, CIII, 1947, pp. 65 ff.

1006 Christoffel, Ulrich, *Das Buch der Maler*, Baden-Baden, 1947.

1007 Comstock, Helen, 'The Connoisseur in America', *The Connoisseur*, CXX, 1947, p. 44.

1008 Costello, Jane, 'The "Rape of the Sabine Women" by Nicolas Poussin', *Bulletin of the Metropolitan Museum of Art*, V, 1947, pp. 197 ff.

1009 Dorival, Bernard, 'Les autoportraits de Poussin', *BSP*, I, 1947, pp. 39 ff.

1010 Du Colombier, Pierre, 'L'année 1658', *BSP*, I, 1947, pp. 29 ff.

Félibien, André, *Entretiens . . .*, see No. 44d.

1011 Hubbard, Robert H., 'The recent acquisitions of the National Gallery of Canada', *AQ*, X, 1947, pp. 222 f.

1012 Huyghe, René, 'Poussin hors de ses limites', *BSP*, I, 1947, pp. 5 ff.

1013 La Tourette, Gilles de, 'La critique morphologique et Nicolas Poussin', *BSP*, I, 1947, p. 53.

1014 Loisy, J., 'Gide et Poussin', *Arts*, 11.iv.1947, p. 1.

1015 McLanathan, Richard B. K., '*Achilles on Skyros* by Nicolas Poussin', *Bulletin of the Museum of Fine Arts*, Boston, XLV, 1947, pp. 1 ff.

1016 Mahon, Denis, *Studies in seicento art and theory*, London (1947).

1017 Massignon, Louis, 'L'Amour courtois de l'Islam dans la *Gerusalemme Liberata* du Tasse: A propos d'un tableau de Poussin', *BSP*, I, 1947, pp. 35 ff.

1018 Moussali, Ulysse, 'Philippe de Champagne; Nicolas Poussin', *Arts*, 4.v.1947, p. 1.

Ponz, Antonio, *Viaje de Espana*, see No. 238a.

1019 Régamey, P. R., 'La signification religieuse de *L'Annonciation* de Poussin', *BSP*, I, 1947, pp. 27 f.

1020 Sayce, R., 'Saint-Amand and Poussin', *French Studies*, I, 1947, pp. 241 ff.

1020.1 Vanbeselaere, W., 'De Diogenes van Poussin', *Nieuw Vlaamsch Tijdschrift*, I, 1947, pp. 1103 ff.

1021 Weigert, Roger Armand, 'Deux marchés inédits, pour le tombeau de Richelieu (1646–1650)', *BSP*, I, 1947, p. 67.

1947–1948

1022 Waterhouse, Ellis K., 'Tasso and the visual arts', *IS*, III, 1947–48, pp. 146 ff.

1948

1023 Bertin-Mourot, Thérèse, 'Addenda au catalogue de Grautoff depuis 1914', *BSP*, II, 1948, pp. 43 ff.

1024 Bertin-Mourot, Thérèse, 'Notes et documents', *BSP*, II, 1948, pp. 88, 91 f.

1025 Blunt, Anthony, 'The Dulwich pictures: Nicolas Poussin', *Leeds Art Calendar*, spring 1948, pp. 11 ff.; summer 1948, pp. 12 ff.

1026 Blunt, Anthony, 'Poussin Studies III: The Poussins at Dulwich', *BM*, XC, 1948, pp. 4 ff.

1026.1 Burckhardt, Jacob, and Wölfflin, Heinrich, *Briefwechsel und andere Dokumente ihrer Begegnung, 1882–1897*, ed. Joseph Gantner, Basle, 1948.

1027 *Cincinnati Art Museum: Nicolas Poussin and Peter Paul Rubens*, Cincinnati, 1948. *Introduction*: P. R. Adams.

1028 Dorival, Bernard, 'Une Bacchanale de Poussin à Madrid', *BSP*, II, 1948, pp. 27 ff.

1029 Dorival, Bernard, 'Du nouveau sur Poussin', *Arts*, 18.vi.1948, p. 1.

1030 Greig, T. P., 'The auction rooms', *The Connoisseur*, CXXII, 1948, p. 65.

1031 Jamot, Paul, *Connaissance de Poussin*, Paris, 1948.

1032 Lavallée, Monique, 'Poussin et Vouet', *BSP*, II, 1948, pp. 90 f.

1033 Lavallée, Pierre, *Le dessin français*, Paris, 1948.

1034 Longhi, Roberto, 'La Santa Margherita della Pinacoteca di Torino', *BSP*, II, 1948, pp. 5 ff.

1035 Rudrauf, Lucien, 'Une *Annonciation* de Nicolas Poussin', *BSP*, II, 1948, pp. 8 ff.

1036 Taylor, Francis, *The taste of angels*, Boston, 1948.

1949

1037 *Bibliothèque Nationale, Paris: Nicolas Poussin; peintures, dessins et gravures. Exposition organisée avec le concours de la Société Poussin et la participation du Musée du Louvre*, Paris, July–September 1949.

1038 Blunt, Anthony, 'Nicolas Poussin', *BM*, XCI, 1949, pp. 355 ff.

1039 Champigneulle, B., *Le règne de Louis XIII*, Paris, 1949.

1040 Clark, Sir Kenneth, *Landscape into art*, London, 1949.

1041 Denucé, Jan, *Na Peter Pauwel Rubens*, Antwerp and The Hague, 1949.

1042 Du Colombier, Pierre, 'Nicolas Poussin, ancêtre toujours vivant', *L'Epoque*, 8.iv.1949.

1043 Ferraton, Claude, 'La collection du Duc de Richelieu au Musée du Louvre', *GBA*, 1949, I, pp. 437 ff.

1044 Kleiner, Gerhard, 'Die Inspiration des Dichters', *Kunstwerk und Deutung*, V, 1949, pp. 13 ff.

1045 Moussali, Ulysse, 'Genèse de l'*Inspiration du Poète* de Nicolas Poussin', *Arts*, 8.iv.1949, p. 1.

1046 Panofsky, Dora, '*Narcissus and Echo*; notes on Poussin's *Birth of Bacchus* in the Fogg Museum of Art', *AB*, XXXI, 1949, pp. 112 ff.

1047 Watson, Francis, 'A new Poussin for the National Gallery', *BM*, XCI, 1949, pp. 14 ff.

1949–1950

1048 *Royal Academy, London: Landscape in French Art, 1500–1700*, London, 1949–50.

1950

1049 Adhémar, Jean, 'Fénelon paysagiste', *BSP*, III, 1950, pp. 73 f.

1050 Blunt, Anthony, 'Poussin Studies IV: Two rediscovered late works', *BM*, XCII, 1950, pp. 38 ff.

1051 Blunt, Anthony, 'Poussin Studies V: "The Silver Birch Master" ', *BM*, XCII, 1950, pp. 69 ff.

1052 Costello, Jane, 'The twelve pictures "ordered by Velasquez" and the trial of Valguarnera', *JWCI*, XIII, 1950, pp. 237 ff.

1052a Parts reprinted in J. Thuillier, 'Pour un "Corpus Pussinianum" ', *Actes*, II, 1960, pp. 54 ff.

1053 Dubaut, Pierre, 'Deux dessins inédits', *BSP*, III, 1950, pp. 88, 95.

1054 Du Colombier, Pierre, 'Notes et documents', *BSP*, III, 1950, p. 95.

1055 Ernst, Serge, 'Un tableau disparu de Poussin: Danaë', *BSP*, III, 1950, p. 86.

1056 Friedlaender, Walter, Review of Paul Jamot, *Connaissance de Poussin*, and *Bulletin de la Société Poussin* I and II, *AB*, XXXII, 1950, pp. 83 ff.

1057 Godfrey, F. M., 'Baccanale e giardino d'amore', *The Connoisseur*, CXXVI, 1950, pp. 175 ff.

1058 Gombrich, Ernst H., 'The Sala dei Venti in the Palazzo del Tè', *JWCI*, XIII, 1950, pp. 189 ff.

1059 Koch, Robert, 'A landscape by Nicolas Poussin', *Princeton Museums Record*, IX, No. 1, 1950, pp. 17 ff.

1059.1 Löhneysen, W. von, 'Entstehung und Ausbildung der Landschaft bei Poussin'. *Schüler-Festschrift zum 50. Geburtstag von Prof. Dr. Heinz Rudolf Rosemann*, Göttingen, 1950, pp. 191 ff.

1060 Panofsky, Erwin, 'Poussin's "Apollo and Daphne" in the Louvre', *BSP*, III, 1950, pp. 27 ff.

Ruffo, Vincenzo, 'La Galleria Ruffo . . .', see No. 730a.

1061 Waterhouse, Ellis, K., 'Exhibition at Edinburgh of pictures from Woburn Abbey', *BM*, XCII, 1950, pp. 53 ff.

1062 Weigert, Roger Armand, 'Poussin et l'art de la tapisserie: Les Sacrements et l'histoire de Moïse', *BSP*, III, 1950, pp. 79 ff.

c. 1950

1063 Vergnet-Ruiz, Jean, *Musée du Louvre: Les peintures de Nicolas Poussin*, Paris, n.d.

1951

1064 Blunt, Anthony, *Nicolas Poussin: The Adoration of the Golden Calf*, London, 1951.

1065 Blunt, Anthony, 'Poussin Studies VI: Poussin's decoration of the Long Gallery in the Louvre', *BM*, XCIII, 1951, pp. 369 ff.

1066 Bousquet, Jacques. Recherches sur le séjour des artistes français à Rome au XVIIe siècle. (Thesis, Ecole du Louvre), Paris, 1951.

1067 Frankfurter, A. M., 'Holy family on the steps, *ca.* 1648, Kress collection', *Art News Annual*, XXI, 1951, pp. 116 f.

1068 Godfrey, F. M., 'South European representations of the Baptism', *Apollo*, LIII, 1951, pp. 92 ff.

1069 Griseri, A., 'Annotazioni ad alcuni disegni inediti di Nicolas Poussin', *Commentari*, II, 1951, pp. 106 ff.

1070 Incisa della Rocchetta, Marchese Giovanni, 'I "Baccanali Chigi" di Nicolas Poussin', *Paragone*, II, 15, 1951, 36 ff.

Leslie, Charles Robert, *Memoirs of the life of John Constable*, see No. 413a.

1071 Longhi, Roberto, 'Volti della Roma Caravaggesca', *Paragone*, II, No. 21, 1951, p. 38.

1071.1 Stewart, William McCausland, 'Charles Le Brun et
       Jean Racine; contacts et points de rencontre', *Atti del
       Quinto Congresso Internazionale di Lingue et Letterature
       moderne*, Florence 1951 (published 1955), pp. 213 ff.

1952

1072 Bland, D. S., 'Poussin and English literature', *Cam-
     bridge Journal*, VI, 1952, pp. 102 ff.

1073 Blunt, Anthony, 'Philippe de Champaigne at the
     Orangerie', *BM*, XCIV, 1952, pp. 172 ff.

1074 Bousquet, Jacques, 'Documents sur le séjour de Simon
     Vouet à Rome', *Mélanges d'Archéologie et d'Histoire
     publiés par l'Ecole française de Rome*, Rome, 1952.
     Friedlaender, Walter, *David to Delacroix*, see No. 840a.

1075 Ivanoff, Nicola, 'Il concetto dello stile nel Poussin e
     in Marco Boschini', *Commentari* III, 1952, pp. 51 ff.

1076 Ladoué, Pierre, 'La scène de l'Annonciation vue par
     les peintres', *GBA*, 1952, I, pp. 351 ff.

1077 Löhneysen, H. von, 'Die ikonographischen und
     geistesgeschichtlichen Voraussetzungen der "Sieben
     Sakramente" des Nicolas Poussin', *Zeitschrift für Reli-
     gions- und Geistesgeschichte*, IV, 2, 1952, pp. 133 ff.

1078 Simon, K. E., 'Le portrait de Poussin, peint par lui-
     même dans la galerie de Berlin', *Arts*, 29.x.1952, p. 2.

1079 Stein, Meir, 'Notes on the Italian sources of Nicolas
     Poussin', *Konsthistorisk Tidskrift*, 1952, pp. 5 ff.

1080 Sterling, Charles, *La nature morte de l'antiquité à nos
     jours*, Paris, 1952.

1080a Second edition, Paris, 1959.

1081 Sypher, Wylie, 'Late-baroque image: Poussin and
     Racine', *Magazine of Art*, XLV, 1952, pp. 209 ff.

1082 Tervarent, Guy de, 'Le véritable sujet du *Paysage au
     Serpent* de Poussin à la National Gallery de Londres',
     GBA, 1952, II, pp. 343 ff.

1083 Tolnay, Charles de, 'Le portrait de Poussin par lui-
     même au Musée du Louvre', *GBA*, 1952, II, pp. 109 ff.

1083.1 Waterhouse, Ellis K. 'Paintings from Venice for
       17th-century England', *IS*, VII, 1952, p. 21.

1952–1953

1084 Bishop, Morchard, 'The natural history of Arcadia',
     The Cornhill Magazine, CLXVI, 1952–53, pp. 81 ff.

1953

1085 Bialostocki, Jan, *Poussin i teoria klasycyzmu*, Warsaw,
     1953.

1086 Blunt, Anthony, *Art and Architecture in France, 1500–
     1700*, London, 1953.

1086a 2nd ed., London, 1957.

1087 Charageat, Marguerite, 'L'Ariane endormie, cire de
     Nicolas Poussin', *RA*, III, 1953, pp. 34 ff.

1088 Dorival, Bernard, 'Expression littéraire et expression
     picturale du sentiment de la nature au XVIIe siècle
     français', *RA*, III, 1953, pp. 44 ff.

1089 Francis, Henry, 'The "Flight into Egypt" by Nicolas
     Poussin', *Bulletin of the Cleveland Museum of Art*, XL,
     1953, pp. 211 ff.

1090 Ladendorf, Heinz, *Antikenstudium und Antikenkopie
     in der neueren Kunst*, Berlin, 1953.

1091 Lee, Rensselaer, Review of W. Friedlaender and A.
     Blunt, *The drawings of Nicolas Poussin* (see No. 944), *AB*,
     XXXV, 1953, pp. 158 f.

1092 Dr. P., 'Poussins Selbstbildnis', *Weltkunst*, XXIII,
     1953, p. 9.
     Seznec, Jean, *The survival of the pagan gods . . .*, see No.
     950a.

1093 Steinitz, Kate Trauman, 'Poussin, illustrator of
     Leonardo da Vinci and the problem of replicas in
     Poussin's studio', *AQ*, XVI, 1953, pp. 40 ff.

1094 Sterling, Charles, 'Quelques œuvres inédites des
     peintres Millereau, Lallemand, Vignon, Sacquespée et
     Simon François', *BSHAF*, 1953, p. 105.

1095 Stuttmann, Ferdinand, *Kunstschätze in Hannover*, Hano-
     ver, 1953.
     Trumbull, John, *The autobiography of . . . Trumbull*, see
     No. 249.

1096 Waterhouse, Ellis K., 'Some notes on the exhibition
     of *Works of Art from Midland Houses* at Birmingham',
     BM, XCV, 1953, pp. 305 ff.

1954

1097 Bassoli, F., 'Un singolare giudizio del Poussin sul
     "Trattato della Pittura" di Leonardo da Vinci', *Raccolta
     Vinciana*, XVII, 1954, pp. 157 ff.

1098 Bialostocki, Jan, 'Une idée de Léonard réalisée par
     Poussin', *RA*, IV, 1954, pp. 131 ff.

1099 Blunt, Anthony, *The drawings of G. B. Castiglione and
     Stefano della Bella at Windsor Castle*, London, 1954.

1100 Crozet, René, *La vie artistique en France au XVIIe
     siècle (1598–1661). Les artistes et la société*, Paris, 1954.

1100.1 Hussey, Christopher, 'A classical landscape park',
       Country Life, CXV, 1954, pp. 1126 ff.

1101 Lavin, Irving, 'Cephalus and Procris', *JWCI*, XVII,
     1954, pp. 260 ff.

1102 Licht, Fred Stephen, *Die Entwicklung der Landschaft in
     den Werken von Nicolas Poussin*, Basle and Stuttgart,
     1954.

1103 Marabottini, Alessandro, 'Novità sul Lucchesino. I
     Il percorso artistico.—II. Il "Trattato di pittura" e i
     disegni', *Commentari*, V, 1954, pp. 116 ff.

1104 Marois, Pierre, *Poussin*, Paris, n.d.

1105 Merchant, W. M., 'A Poussin "Coriolanus" in Rowe's
     1709 Shakespeare', *Bulletin of the John Rylands Library,
     Manchester*, XXXVII, 1954, pp. 13 ff.

1106 Pariset, François Georges, 'Georges Lallemant émule
     de Jacques de Bellange', *GBA*, 1954, II, pp. 299 ff.

1107 Sandoz, Marc, 'Autour de Poussin: Une version
     ancienne retrouvée du *Triomphe de Bacchus*', *Dibutade*, I,
     1954, pp. 14 ff.

1108 'Two acquisitions from the R. W. Leonard Memorial
     Fund', *Art Gallery of Toronto, Annual Report*, 1954, p.
     16.

1109 Zeitler, Rudolf, *Klassizismus und Utopia*, Uppsala,
     1954.

1109.1 Zeri, Federico, *La Galleria Spada in Roma*, Florence,
       1954.

1954–1955

1110 *City Art Gallery, Leeds: Paintings from Chatsworth House*, Leeds, 1954–55.

1111 'Poussin's Roccatagliata Madonna', *Bulletin of the Detroit Institute of Arts*, XXXIV, 1954–55, pp. 12 f.

1954–1958

1112 Quarré, Pierre, 'Les noms tracés sur les statues du portail de la Chartreuse de Champmol', *Mémoires de la Commission des Antiquités du département de la Côte-d'Or*, XXIV, 1954–58, pp. 187 ff.

1955

1113 Berger, Klaus, 'Poussin's style and the 19th century', *GBA*, 1955, I, pp. 161 ff., 192 ff.

1114 Bousquet, Jacques, 'Un rival inconnu de Poussin: Charles Mellin dit Le Lorrain (1597–1649)', *Annales de l'Est*, 1955, pp. 12 f.

1114a Parts reprinted in J. Thuillier, 'Pour un "Corpus Pussinianum"', *Actes,* II, 1960, pp. 53 f.

1115 Costello, Jane, 'Poussin's drawings for Marino and the new Classicism: I—Ovid's *Metamorphoses*', *JWCI*, XVIII, 1955, pp. 296 ff.

Evelyn, John, *The Diary*, see No. 8b.

1116 Grohn, H. W., *Staatliche Museen zu Berlin. Gemälde-galerie*, Berlin, 1955.

1117 Huyghe, René, *Dialogue avec le visible*, Paris, 1955.

1118 Kauffmann, George, 'Unbekannte Zeichnungen von Poussin', *Wallraf-Richartz Jahrbuch*, XVII, 1955, pp. 230 ff.

1119 Lucas, John, 'Picasso as a copyist', *AN*, LIV, 1955, pp. 36 f.

McCausland Stewart, William, 'Charles Le Brun et Jean Racine', see No. 1071.1.

1120 Rocher-Jauneau, Madeleine, 'Deux reliefs en terre-cuite au Musée Historique de Lyon', *Bulletin des Musées Lyonnais*, IV, 1955, pp. 55 ff.

1121 Sandoz, Marc, 'Autour de Poussin (II). Peintures diverses au Musée des Beaux-Arts de Poitiers', *Dibutade*, II, 1955, pp. 15 ff.

1122 Sterling, Charles, *A catalogue of French paintings XV–XVIII centuries*, Metropolitan Museum of Art, New York, 1955.

1123 Sterling, Charles, *La peinture française au XVIIe siècle*, Paris, 1955.

1124 *Wildenstein Gallery, London: Artists in 17th century Rome. Catalogue*: Denis Mahon and Denys Sutton, London, 1955.

Wildenstein, Georges, 'Les graveurs de Poussin . . .', see No. 1186.

1125 Wittkower, Rudolf, *Gian Lorenzo Bernini*, London, 1955.

1956

1126 Bardon, Henry, 'A propos d'un dessin de Nicolas Poussin', *Latomus*, Brussels, 1956.

1127 Boyer, Ferdinand, 'Les relations artistiques entre la France et la Toscane de 1792 à 1796', *Revue des Etudes Italiennes*, 1956, pp. 23 ff.

1128 Clark, Sir Kenneth, *The Nude. A study in ideal form*, New York and London, 1956.

1129 Della Pergola, Paola, 'Appunti. Due documenti in cerca di referimento', *Paragone*, VII, No. 83, 1956, pp. 66 f.

1130 D'Otrange-Mastai, M. L., 'Nicolas Poussin and the Barberini tapestries: The Apollo series', *Apollo*, LXIII, 1956, pp. 171 ff.

1130.1 Fleury, Marie Antoinette, 'Les Dispositions testamentaires et l'inventaire après décès de François Mansart', *BSHAF*, 1956, pp. 228 ff.

1131 Hubbard, Robert, *European paintings in Canadian collections: Earlier schools*, Toronto, 1956.

1132 Kamenskaya, T., 'Dva peizadjnik risunka Pussena v sobpanii Ermitadja', *Soobshchenija Gosudarstvennogo Ermitadja*, I, 1956, pp. 49 ff.

1133 Kamenskaya, T., 'K voprosu o rukopisi "Traktata o zivopisi" Leonardo da Vinci i jeje illustrcjach v sobranii Ermitaza, Trudy Gosudarstvennogo Ermitaza, I', *Zapadnoevropejskoe iskusstvo*, I, 1956, pp. 49 ff. For summary in English, see No. 1151.

1134 *Kunsthaus, Zürich: Unbekannte Schönheit* (catalogue), Zurich, 1956.

1135 Le Gall, J., 'Tiberina: Le ponte Rotto et le ponte Molle, dessins', *Revue Archéologique*, 6th series, XLVII, 1956, pp. 34 ff.

1136 Lindahl, Göran, 'Poussintolkningar', *Konstrevy*, XXXII, 1956, pp. 92 ff.

1137 Miles, Hamish, The transitional period in French painting, *ca.* 1580–*ca.* 1630. Thesis, Oxford University, 1956.

1137.1 *Palazzo Barberini, Rome: Paesisti e Vedutisti a Roma nel '600 e nel '700*. Rome, 1956. *Catalogue*: Nolfo di Carpegna; *Introduction*: Emilio Lavagnino.

1956

1138 Pigler, Andreas, *Barockthemen: Eine Auswahl von Verzeichnissen zur Ikonographie des 17. und 18. Jahrhunderts*, Budapest and Berlin, 1956. 2 vols.

1138.1 Salerno, Luigi. 'L'Opera di Antonio Carracci', *Bollettino d'Arte*, XLI, 1956, pp. 30 ff.

1139 Sandoz, Marc, 'Autour de Poussin (III). Peintures diverses au Musée des Beaux-Arts de Poitiers', *Dibutade*, III, 1956, pp. 7 ff.

1140 Sauerländer, Willibald, 'Die Jahreszeiten. Ein Beitrag zur allegorischen Landschaft beim späten Poussin', *Münchner Jahrbuch der bildenden Kunst*, Dritte Folge, VII, 1956, pp. 169 ff.

1141 Schlenoff, Norman, *Ingres: ses sources littéraires*, Paris, 1956. 2 vols.

1142 'The "Triumph of Neptune and Amphitrite" by Nicolas Poussin', *Philadelphia Museum of Art Bulletin*, LII, 1956, pp. 1 f.

1143 Vanuxem, Jacques, 'Mondaye dans l'art de son temps', *Art de Basse Normandie*, 1956.

1144 Vermeule, Cornelius, 'The dal Pozzo-Albani drawings of classical antiquities, notes on their content and arrangement', *AB*, XXXVIII, 1956, pp. 31 ff.

1145 Walker, John, *Bellini and Titian at Ferrara*, London, 1956.

1956–1957

Mancini, Giulio, *Considerazioni . . .*, see No. 1.

1957

1146 Alazard, Jean, *Nicolas Poussin 1594–1665*, Milan, 1957.

1147 Argan, Giulio Carlo, 'Il Tasso e le arti figurative', *Torquato Tasso*, ed. by the Comitato per le Celebrazioni di Torquato Tasso Ferrara 1954, Milan, 1957, pp. 209 ff.

1148 Bardon, Henry, 'Ovide et le Grand Roi', *Les Etudes Classiques*, 1957, pp. 401 ff.

1149 Bardon, Henry, 'Souvenirs latins', *Latomus*, XXVIII, 1957, pp. 88 ff.

1150 Bertin-Mourot, Thérèse, *Supplément à l'addenda au catalogue de Grautoff paru dans le second cahier . . . du Bulletin de la Société Poussin, 'Poussin inconnu'*, Paris, 1957.

1151 Bialostocki, Jan, 'Recent research: Russia II', *BM*, XCIX, 1957, p. 425.

Blunt, Anthony, *Art and architecture in France*, see No. 1086a.

1152 Blunt, Anthony, 'The Précieux and French art', *Fritz Saxl 1890–1948. A volume of Memorial Essays from his friends in England*, London, 1957, pp. 326 ff.

1154 Chastel, André, 'L'art et le sentiment de la mort au XVIIe siècle', *Bulletin de la Société d'Etude du XVIIe siècle*, XXXVI–XXXVII, 1957, pp. 287 ff.

1155 Comstock, Helen, 'The Virginia Museum purchases French masters' (Connoisseur in America), *The Connoisseur*, CXL, 1957, pp. 71 f.

1156 Davidson, Bernice F., 'A tragic legend illustrated', *Bulletin of the Rhode Island School of Design*, XLIII, 1957, pp. 9 ff.

Davies, Martin, *National Gallery . . . French school*, see No. 988a.

1157 Hess, Jacob, 'Un nuovo manoscritto delle vite di G. B. Passeri', *Commentari*, VIII, 1957, pp. 262 ff.

1158 Lossky, Boris, 'Le peintre Charles Mellin dit le Lorrain et les Musées de Tours', *BSHAF*, 1956, pp. 50 ff.

1159 Sterling, Charles, *Musée de l'Ermitage, la peinture française de Poussin à nos jours*, Paris, 1957.

1160 Tapié, Victor L., *Baroque et classicisme*, Paris, 1957.

1161 Thuillier, Jacques, 'Polémiques autour de Michel-Ange au XVIIe siècle', *Bulletin de la Société d'Etude du XVIIe siècle*, XXXVI–XXXVII, 1957, pp. 353 ff.

1162 Voss, Hermann, 'Die Flucht nach Aegypten', *Saggi e Memorie di Storia dell' Arte*, I, 1957, pp. 47 f.

1163 Wildenstein, Georges, 'A propos de l'inventaire Hesselin', *GBA*, 1957, I, p. 111.

1163.1 Wildenstein, Georges, 'Deux Inventaires de l'atelier de Claude Vignon', *GBA*, 1957, I, pp. 183 ff.

1164 Wildenstein, Georges, 'L'inventaire de Louis Hesselin (1662)', *GBA*, 1957, I, pp. 57 ff.

1957–1958

1165 *Royal Academy, London: The age of Louis XIV*. *Foreword*: Jean Vergnet-Ruiz; *Introduction*: Anthony Blunt; *Catalogue*: Michel Laclotte, London, 1957–58.

1958

1165.1 Bertin-Mourot, Thérèse, 'La Vierge sur des degrés', *GBA*, 1958, I, p. 366.

1166 Blunt, Anthony, 'Poussin dans les musées de province', *RA*, VIII, 1958, pp. 5 ff.

1167 Blunt, Anthony, 'Poussin Studies VII: Poussin in Neapolitan and Sicilian collections', *BM*, C, 1958, pp. 76 ff.

Delaporte, Chanoine, 'André Félibien en Italie . . .', see No. 11.

1168 Ettlinger, Leopold, 'Naturalism and rhetoric', *Listener*, 30.i.1958, p. 193.

1169 Fleming, John, 'Cardinal Albani's drawings at Windsor—their purchase by James Adam for George III', *The Connoisseur*, CXLII, 1958, pp. 164 ff.

1170 Gelder, Jan van, *De Schilderkunst van Jan Vermeer*, Utrecht, 1958.

1171 Glasser, Hannelore, 'Reappearance of a lost Poussin', *Virginia Museum of Fine Arts Bulletin*, XVIII, No. 9, 1958.

1172 Hartt, Frederick, *Giulio Romano*, New Haven, Conn., 1958. 2 vols.

1173 Hoffmann, Edith, 'Current and forthcoming exhibitions (Paintings of Old Masters from the Wadsworth Atheneum, Hartford, Conn.)', *BM*, C, 1958, p. 105.

1173.1 Imdahl, Max, 'Raumstellung und Raumwirkung: zu verwandten Landschaftsbildern von Domenichino, C. Lorrain & J. F. von Bloemen', *Festschrift M. Wackernagel zum 75. Geburtstag*, Cologne, 1958.

1174 Laclotte, Michel, *Le XVIIe siècle français. Chefs-d'œuvre des musées de Province*, Paris, 1958.

1175 Messerer, Wilhelm, 'Zwei Wirkungen von Antonio Carracci's Sintflutbild', *Kunstchronik*, XI, 1958, p. 248.

1176 Milliken, Wilhelm, 'Moses sweetening the Waters of Marah', *The Baltimore Museum of Art News*, XXII, 1, 1958, pp. 3 ff.

1177 'Le Musée des Beaux-Arts en 1957', *Bulletin du Musée Hongrois des Beaux-Arts*, XII, 1958, pp. 77 ff.

1178 *The National Gallery, July 1956–June 1958*, London, 1958.

1179 Steinitz, Kate Trauman, *Leonardo da Vinci's Trattato della Pittura. Treatise on painting. A bibliography of the printed editions 1651–1956 based on the complete collection in The Elmer Belt Library of Vinciana, preceded by a study of its sources and illustrations*, Copenhagen, 1958.

1180 Thuillier, Jacques, 'Pour un peintre oublié: Rémy Vuibert', *Paragone*, XCVII, No. 97, 1958, pp. 22 ff.

1181 Trapp, J. B., 'The Owl's Ivy and the Poet's Bays', *JWCI*, XXI, 1958, pp. 227 ff.

1182 Vanuxem, Jacques, 'Les Jésuites et la peinture au XVIIe siècle à Paris', *RA*, VIII, 1958, pp. 85 ff.

1183 Vermeule, Cornelius, 'Aspects of scientific archaeology in the seventeenth century', *Proceedings of the American Philosophical Society*, CII, 2, 1958, pp. 193 ff.

1184 Wild, Doris, Review of Georges Wildenstein's *Les graveurs de Poussin au XVIIe siècle*, *Kunstchronik*, XI, 1958, pp. 165 ff.

1185 Wild, Doris, 'Les tableaux de Poussin à Chantilly', *GBA*, 1958, I, pp. 15 ff.

1186 Wildenstein, Georges, 'Les graveurs de Poussin au XVIIe siècle', *GBA*, 1955, II, pp. 73 ff. (Actually published in 1958, with date 1955 on title-page; also published in 1958 as a separate volume with different pagination.)

1187 Wilenski, Reginald, *Poussin*, London, 1958.

1958–1959

1188 Mongan, Agnes, '*The Infant Bacchus entrusted to the Nymphs* by Poussin', *Fogg Art Museum Annual Report*, 1958–59, pp. 29 ff.

1959

1189 Aulanier, Christiane, 'Le temps soustrait la Vérité aux atteintes de la discorde et de l'envie', *NAAF*, XXII, 1959, pp. 80 ff.

1190 Badt, Kurt, 'Das 17. Jahrhundert in der französischen Malerei', *Kunstchronik*, XII, 1959, pp. 121 ff.

1191 Berger, John, 'Poussin at Dulwich', *New Statesman*, 4.iv.1959, p. 472.

1192 Bertin-Mourot, Thérèse, '*Poussin inconnu*: Certitudes et incertitudes à propos de la "*Vierge assise sur des degrés*"', Paris, 1959.

1193 Bialostocki, Jan, *Pięć Wieków myśli o Sztuce*, Warsaw, 1959.

1194 Blunt, Anthony, 'The leadership of Poussin: The artist's pictures come to America', *AN*, January 1959, pp. 37 f.

1195 Blunt, Anthony, 'Poussin Studies VIII: A series of anchorite subjects commissioned by Philip V from Poussin, Claude, and others', *BM*, CI, 1959, pp. 389 ff.

1196 Blunt, Anthony, 'Poussin Studies IX: Additions to the work of Jean Lemaire', *BM*, CI, 1959, pp. 440 ff.
Canova, Antonio, Marchese, *I Quaderni di viaggio . . .*, see No. 261.

1197 Chastel, André, 'Nicolas Poussin et l'art français', *Médecine de France*, No. 106, 1959, pp. 17 ff.

1198 Du Bouchet, André, 'The leadership of Poussin: The artist his own demigod', *AN*, January 1959, pp. 35 f.

1199 Friedlaender, Walter, 'The leadership of Poussin: The artist engraved for posterity', *AN*, January 1959, pp. 37 f.

1200 Gaudibert, Pierre, 'Poussin et le Néo-Stoïcisme', *Europe*, 1959, p. 27.

1201 Hunter, Sam, 'Poussin's *Death of Germanicus*', *The Minneapolis Institute of Arts Bulletin*, XLVIII, 1, 1959, pp. 1 ff.

1202 Jack, Ian, 'The realm of Flora in Keats and Poussin', *The Times Literary Supplement*, 10.iv.1959, p. 212.

1203 Kauffmann, George, 'Colloque Poussin', *Kunstchronik*, XII, 1959, pp. 3 ff.

1204 Kauffmann, George, 'Vasari-Poussin', *Mitteilungen des Kunsthistorischen Instituts in Florenz*, VIII, 1959, pp. 252 ff.

1205 *Kunstmuseum, Berne: Das 17. Jahrhundert in der französischen Malerei*, Berne, 1959.

1206 *Minneapolis Institute of Arts, Minnesota: Nicolas Poussin 1594–1665, a loan exhibition organized by the Minneapolis Institute of Arts in collaboration with the Toledo Museum of Arts*, Minneapolis, 1959. *Introductions*: Anthony Blunt and Walter Friedlaender.

1207 Pirotta, L., 'Due mancati presidenti dell' Accademia di S. Luca', *Strenna dei Romanisti, Natale di Roma*, Rome, 1959, pp. 264 ff.

1208 Praz, Mario, *Gusto neoclassico*, 2nd ed., Naples (1959).
Reynolds, Sir Joshua, *The Discourses . . .*, see No. 235a.

1209 Richards, Louise, 'Italian landscape, a drawing by Poussin', *Bulletin of the Cleveland Museum of Art*, XLVI, 1959, pp. 171 f.

1210 Roberts, George and Mary, *Triumph on Fairmount: Fiske Kimball and the Philadelphia Museum of Art*, Philadelphia and New York, 1959.

1211 Sichel, P., 'A la recherche de Poussin', *Europe*, April 1959, p. 63.
Sterling, Charles, *La nature morte . . .*, see No. 1080a.

1213 Takács, Marianne, 'Un tableau de Nicolas Poussin au Musée des Beaux-Arts', *Bulletin du Musée Hongrois des Beaux-Arts*, XV, 1959, pp. 39 ff.
Toledo Museum of Art, Ohio: Nicolas Poussin 1594–1665, see No. 1206.

1214 Vaughan, Malcolm, 'Poussin in America', *The Connoisseur* (ed. America), CXLIII, 1959, pp. 123 ff.

1215 Wild, Doris, 'Nicolas Poussin. Von den Schlachtenbildern zum sterbenden Germanikus', *Actes du XIXe Congrès International d'Histoire de l'Art Paris 8–13 Septembre 1958*, Paris, 1959, pp. 448 ff.

1216 Zeri, Federico, *La galleria Pallavicini*, Florence, 1959.

1960

1217 Alpatov, Mikhail W. (Michel), 'Poussin peintre d'histoire', *Actes*, I, 1960, pp. 189 ff.

1218 Bardon, Henry. 'Poussin et la littérature latine', *Actes*, I, 1960, pp. 123 ff.

1218.1 Battisti, Eugenio, 'Postille documentarie su artisti italiani a Madrid e sulla collezione Maratta', *Arte antica e moderna*, IX, 1960, pp. 77 ff.

1219 Bean, Jacob, 'Le séjour pathétique de Poussin à Paris', *Connaissance des Arts*, May 1960, pp. 66 ff.

1220 Berne-Joffroy, André, 'Poussin et nous', *Jardin des Arts*, No. 67, May 1960, pp. 1 ff.

1220a Italian tr., *Paragone*, XIII, No. 155, 1962, pp. 52 ff.

1221 Bialostocki, Jan, 'Poussin et le "Traité de la Peinture" de Léonard', *Actes*, I, 1960, pp. 133 ff.

1222 Blunt, Anthony, 'Colloque Nicolas Poussin', *BM*, CII, 1960, pp. 330 ff.

1223 Blunt, Anthony, 'Etat présent des études sur Poussin', *Actes*, I, 1960, pp. XX ff.

1224 Blunt, Anthony, 'Poussin et les cérémonies religieuses antiques', *RA*, X, 1960, pp. 56 ff.

1225 Blunt, Anthony, 'Poussin Studies X: Karel Philips Spierincks, the first imitator of Poussin's *Bacchanals*', *BM* (Special issue), CII, 1960, pp. 308 ff.

1226 Blunt, Anthony, 'Poussin Studies XI: Some addenda to the Poussin number', *BM*, CII, 1960, pp. 396 ff., 489.

1227 Blunt, Anthony, 'La première période romaine de Poussin', *Actes*, I, 1960, pp. 163 ff.

1228 Blunt, Anthony, and Cooke, H. L., *The Roman drawings at Windsor Castle*, London, 1960.

1229 Bouleau-Rabaud, Wanda, 'Le "Mercure et Hersé" de l'Ecole Nationale Supérieure des Beaux-Arts', *Actes*, II, 1960, pp. 255 ff.

1230 Bousquet, Jacques, 'Chronologie du séjour romain de Poussin et de sa famille d'après les archives romaines', *Actes*, II, 1960, pp. 1 ff.

1231 Bousquet, Jacques, 'Les relations de Poussin avec le milieu romain', *Actes*, I, 1960, pp. 1 f.

1232 Briganti, Giuliano, 'L'altare di Sant' Erasmo, Poussin e il Cortona', *Paragone*, XI, No. 123, 1960, pp. 16 ff.

1233 Brugnoli, Maria Vittoria, 'La mostra del Poussin al Louvre', *Bollettino d'Arte*, IV, 1960, pp. 373 ff.

1234 Burdon, G., 'Sir Thomas Isham, an English collector in Rome in 1677-8', *IS*, XV, 1960, pp. 1 ff.

1235 Champris, Pierre de, *Picasso, ombre et soleil*, Paris, 1960.

1236 Chastel, André, 'Un fragment inédit de Poussin', *Actes*, II, 1960, p. 239.

1237 Chastel, André, ' "Monsù Poussino", peintre français', *Le Monde*, 13.v.1960, p. 8.

1238 Chastel, André, 'Poussin et la postérité', *Actes*, I, 1960, pp. 297 ff.

1240 Coural, Jean, 'Les termes de Poussin à Versailles', *RA*, X, 1960, pp. 19 ff.

1241 Damiron, Suzanne, 'Un inventaire manuscrit de l'oeuvre gravé de Poussin (XVIIIe siècle)', *Actes*, II, 1960, pp. 11 ff.

1242 Davis, Frank, '18th-century homage to Nicolas Poussin', *The Illustrated London News*, 19.iii.1960, p. 468.

1243 Delbourgo, Suzy, and Petit, Jean, 'Application de l'analyse microscopique et chimique à quelques tableaux de Poussin', *Bulletin du Laboratoire du Musée du Louvre*, V, 1960, pp. 41 ff.

1244 Dorival, Bernard, 'Poussin et Philippe de Champaigne', *Actes*, I, 1960, pp. 57 ff.

1245 Du Colombier, Pierre, 'Les deux aspects du XVIIe siècle', *Revue Française*, May 1960, pp. 51 ff.

1246 Du Colombier, Pierre, 'Poussin et Claude Lorrain', *Actes*, I, 1960, pp. 47 ff.

1247 Du Colombier, Pierre, 'The Poussin exhibition', *BM*, CII, 1960, pp. 282 ff.

1248 Dupont, Jacques, 'La "Diane surprise par Actéon" du château de Mornay', *Actes*, II, 1960, pp. 241 ff.

1249 Ecalle, Martine, 'Le "Massacre des Innocents" du Petit-Palais. Dossier d'un tableau', *Actes*, II, 1960, pp. 247 ff.

1250 França, J. A., 'Poussin/1960', *Colóquio Revista de Artes e Letras*, XI, 1960, pp. 25 ff.

1251 Francastel, Pierre, 'Les paysages composés chez Poussin: Académisme et classicisme', *Actes*, I, 1960, pp. 201 ff.

1252 Gnudi, Cesare, 'Poussin et le panorama du classicisme romain', *Actes*, I, 1960, pp. 233 ff.

1253 Goertz, W., *Nicolas Poussin: Landscape with Polyphemus*, Leningrad, Hermitage, 1960. (Pamphlet in Russian.)

1254 Haskell, Francis, and Rinehart, Sheila, 'The dal Pozzo collection, some new evidence', *BM* (Special issue), CII, 1960, pp. 318 ff.

1255 Hazlehurst, F. Hamilton, 'The artistic evolution of David's *Oath*', *AB*, XLII, 1960, pp. 59 ff.

1256 Hours, Madeleine, 'Nicolas Poussin: Etude radiographique au Laboratoire du Musée du Louvre', *Bulletin du Laboratoire du Musée du Louvre*, V, 1960, pp. 3 ff.

1257 'Inaccessible Poussins', *The Connoisseur*, August 1960, pp. 43 ff.

1258 Isarlo, Georges, 'La grande exposition du Musée du Louvre; Poussin et ses problèmes', *Combat*, 13.vi.1960 (Art), p. 1.

1259 Isarlo, Georges, *La peinture en France au XVIIe siècle*, Paris, 1960.

1260 Jamot, Paul, *Petit discours sur l'art français*, Paris (1960).

1261 Jullian, René, 'Poussin et le Caravagisme', *Actes*, I, 1960, pp. 225 f.

1262 Kauffmann, Georg, *Poussin-Studien*, Berlin, 1960.

1263 Kauffmann, Georg, 'La "Sainte famille à l'escalier" et le problème des proportions dans l'œuvre de Poussin', *Actes*, I, 1960, pp. 141 ff.

1264 Kitson, Michael, 'The "Altieri Claudes" and Virgil', *BM*, CII, 1960, pp. 312 ff.

1265 Lapique, Charles, 'Actualité de Poussin', *Actes*, I, 1960, pp. XIII ff.

1266 *Louvre, Paris: Exposition Nicolas Poussin*. *Préface*: Germain Bazin; *Catalogue*: Sir Anthony Blunt; *Biographie*: Charles Sterling; *Documents de Laboratoire*: Madeleine Hours, Paris, 1960.
All references are to the second, corrected edition.

1267 Loye, Georges de, 'Le trompe-l'oeil d'Antoine Fort-Bas', *RA*, X, 1960, pp. 19 ff.

1268 MacGreevy, Thomas, *Nicolas Poussin*, Dublin, 1960.

1268.1 Mahon, Denis, 'Mazarin and Poussin', *BM*, CII, 1960, pp. 352 ff.

1269 Mahon, Denis, 'Poussin au carrefour des années trente', *Actes*, I, 1960, pp. 237 ff.

1270 Mahon, Denis, 'Poussin's development: questions of method', *BM*, CII, 1960, pp. 455 f.

1271 Mahon, Denis, 'Poussin's early development: An alternative hypothesis', *BM*, CII, 1960, pp. 288 ff.

1272 Moulin, J., 'Rencontre de Poussin et de Quentin Varin aux Andelys', *Nouvelles de l'Eure (Les Andelys Patrie de Nicolas Poussin)*, V, 1960, pp. 22 f.
Panofsky, Erwin, *Idea . . .*, see No. 772a.

1273 Panofsky, Erwin, *A mythological painting by Poussin in the Nationalmuseum Stockholm*, Stockholm, 1960.

1274 Pariset, François Georges, 'Les natures mortes chez Poussin', *Actes*, I, 1960, pp. 215 ff.

1275 Perrault, I., 'Nicolas Poussin pictor Andeliensis' *Nouvelles de l'Eure (Les Andelys Patrie de Nicolas Poussin)*, V, 1960, pp. 24 ff.

1276 Picard, Charles, 'Poussin et les sarcophages latins de Rome', *Actes*, I, 1960, pp. 117 ff.

1277 Pintard, René, 'Le nouveau jugement de Salomon de

Poussin, son copiste et le Cardinal Barberini', *Actes*, II, 1960, pp. 45 ff.

1278 Pintard, René, 'Rencontres avec Poussin', *Actes*, I, 1960, pp. 31 ff.

1278.1 Plumb, J. H., *Sir Robert Walpole. The King's Minister*, London, 1960.

1279 'Poussin au Louvre', *RA*, X, 1960, pp. 55 ff.

1280 Rees Jones, Stephen, 'Notes on radiographs of five paintings by Poussin', *BM*, CII, 1960, pp. 304 ff.

1280.1 Reff, Theodore, 'Cézanne and Poussin', *JWCI*, XXIII, 1960, pp. 150 ff.

1281 Rinehart, Sheila, 'Poussin et la famille dal Pozzo', *Actes*, I, 1960, pp. 19 ff.

1282 Salerno, Luigi, 'The picture gallery of Vincenzo Giustiniani', *BM*, CII, 1960, pp. 21 ff., 93 ff., 135 ff.

1283 Sandoz, Marc, 'Note sur deux tableaux poussinesques du Musée de Poitiers', *Actes*, II, 1960, pp. 279 ff.

1284 Seznec, Jean, 'Le "Musée" de Diderot', *GBA*, 1960, I, pp. 343 ff.

1285 Shearman, John, 'Les dessins de paysages de Poussin', *Actes*, I, 1960, pp. 179 ff.

1286 Shearman, John, 'Gaspard, not Nicolas', *BM*, CII, 1960, pp. 326 ff.

1287 Soria, Martin S., 'Andrea de Leone, master of the bucolic scene', *AQ*, XVIII, 1960, pp. 23 ff.

1288 Steinitz, Kate Trauman, 'Bibliography never ends . . . Addenda to "Leonardo da Vinci's Trattato della Pittura, Treatise on Painting". A Bibliography (Copenhagen, Munksgaard, 1958)', *Raccolta Vinciana*, XVIII, 1960, pp. 97 ff.

1289 Sterling, Charles, 'Une peinture pour la délectation', *Arts*, 11.v.1960.

1290 Sterling, Charles, 'Quelques imitateurs et copistes de Poussin', *Actes*, I, 1960, pp. 265 ff.

Susinno, Francesco, *Le vite de' pittori . . .*, see No. 145.

1291 Takács, Marianne, 'Une "Sainte Famille" au Musée des Beaux-Arts de Budapest', *Actes*, II, 1960, pp. 259 ff.

1292 Tervarent, Guy de, 'Sur deux frises d'inspiration antique', *GBA*, 1960, I, pp. 307 ff.

1293 Thomé, J. R., 'Les dessins de Nicolas Poussin', *Le Courrier Graphique*, May 1960, pp. 19 ff.

1294 Thuillier, Jacques, 'Note sur les tableaux "Poussinesques" des églises de France', *Actes*, II, 1960, pp. 301 ff.

1295 Thuillier, Jacques, 'Pour un "Corpus Pussinianum" ', *Actes*, II, 1960, pp. 49 ff.
   See also Nos.: 1a, 4b, 5a, 6a, 8c, 10a, 11a, 12a, 14a, 15a, 16b, 17b, 18a, 19a, 21b, 22a, 23a, 24a, 26a, 27, 29b, 31a, 32b, 33a, 34a, 35a, 40a, 41e, 43a, 46b, 47b, 50b, 57a, 60b, 61a, 62a, 64a, 67c, 69a, 70b, 71a, 72b, 73a, 74a, 75c, 77b, 78b, 79a, 81a, 84a, 85c, 86a, 89h, 91a, 92a, 94b, 96a, 98a, 102b, 106e, 108, 112d, 113a, 116c,, 117a, 118b, 119b, 120b, 121b, 450a, 730b, 832a, 1052a 1114a.

1296 Thuillier, Jacques, 'Poussin et ses premiers compagnons français à Rome', *Actes*, I, 1960, pp. 71 ff.

1297 Thuillier, Jacques, 'Tableaux attribués à Poussin dans les archives révolutionnaires', *Actes*, II, 1960, pp. 27 ff.

1298 Thuillier, Jacques, 'Tableaux attribués à Poussin dans les galeries italiennes', *Actes*, II, 1960, pp. 263 ff.

1299 Thuillier, Jacques, 'Tableaux "Poussinesques" dans les musées de Province français', *Actes*, II, 1960, pp. 285 ff.

1300 Thuillier, Jacques, 'The three faces of Nicolas Poussin', *Art News*, 1960, pp. 32 ff.

1301 Valsecchi, Marco, 'Nicolas Poussin depingeva il paese dell'anima', *L'Illustrazione Italiana*, LXXXVII, 8, 1960, pp. 60 ff.

1302 Vanuxem, Jacques, 'Les "Tableaux Sacrés" de Richeome et l'iconographie de l'Eucharistie chez Poussin', *Actes*, I, 1960, pp. 151 ff.

1303 Venturi, Lionello, 'Il pennello revoluzionario', *L'Espresso*, 7.viii.1960.

1304 Vermeule, Cornelius, 'The dal Pozzo-Albani drawings of classical antiquities in the British Museum', *Transactions of the American Philosophical Society*, new series, L, Pt. 5, 1960.

1304.1 Veronesi, Giulia, 'Nicolas Poussin al Louvre', *Emporium*, CXXXII, 1960, pp. 99 ff.

1305 Virch, Claus, 'The Walter C. Baker collection of master drawings', *The Metropolitan Museum of Art Bulletin*, XVIII, 1960, pp. 309 ff.

1306 Volpi, Mischi Romana de, 'Nicolas Poussin', *Arte Figurativa*, VIII, 1960, pp. 16 ff.

1307 Wallace, Richard, W., '*Venus at the Fountain* and *The Judgment of Paris*. Notes on two late Poussin drawings in the Louvre', *GBA*, 1960, I, pp. 11 ff.

1308 Waterhouse, Ellis K., 'Poussin et l'Angleterre jusqu' en 1744', *Actes*, I, 1960, pp. 283 ff.

1309 Weigert, Roger Armand, 'La gravure et la renommée de Poussin', *Actes*, I, 1960, pp. 277 ff.

1310 Wild, Doris, 'Die Poussin-Ausstellung in Paris', *Neue Zürcher Zeitung*, 30 and 31.v.1960.

1311 Wild, Doris, 'Poussins Selbstbildnisse', *Neue Zürcher Zeitung*, 12.vi.1960.

1312 Wild, Doris, 'Poussin-Studien zum ersten Jahrzehnt in Rom', *Pantheon*, XVIII, No. 3, 1960, pp. 157 ff.

1960–1961

1313 Milhaud, G., 'Poussin ressuscité', *La Nouvell Critique*, December 1960, pp. 87 ff.; January 1961, pp. 108 ff.

1960–1963

Haydon, Benjamin, Robert, *The Diaries . . .*, see No. 337.1.

1961

1314 Ackerman, Gerald, 'Gian Battista Marino's contribution to seicento art theory', *AB*, XLIII, 1961, pp. 326 ff.

1315 Agnew, Geoffrey, 'Poussin's "Et in Arcadia Ego" ', *The Listener*, 17.viii.1961, pp. 248 f.

1316 'Artist in a classical landscape', *The Times Literary Supplement*, 12.v.1961, p. 288.

1317 'Beauty in Arcadia', *The Listener*, 17.viii.1961, p. 232.

1318 Bialostocki, Jan, 'Georg Kauffmann, *Poussin-Studien*', *AB*, XLIII, 1961, pp. 68 ff.

1319 Bialostocki, Jan, 'Das Modusproblem in den bildenden Künsten', *ZKG*, XXIV, 1961, pp. 128 ff.

1320 *Bibliothèque Nationale, Paris: Mazarin homme d'état ee collectionneur 1602–1661. Exposition organisée pour le troisième centenaire de sa mort.* Prefaces: J. Cain and J. Vallery-Radot; *Introduction*: R. A. Weigart, Paris, 1961.

1321 Bjurström, Per, *Giacomo Torelli and baroque stage design*, Stockholm, 1961.

1322 Blunt, Anthony, 'A mythological painting by Poussin', *BM*, CIII, 1961, p. 437.

1323 Blunt, Anthony, 'Poussin and his circle at Rouen', *BM*, CIII, 1961, pp. 351 ff.

1324 Blunt, Anthony, 'Poussin Studies XII: The Hovingham Master', *BM*, CIII, 1961, pp. 454 ff.

1325 Brody, Jules, 'Platonisme et classicisme', *Saggi e ricerche di letteratura francese*, II, 1961, pp. 7 ff.

1326 Chastel, André, 'Poussin au Musée de Rouen', *Le Monde*, 5.v.1961.

1327 Ettlinger, Leopold, 'Georg Kauffmann, *Poussin-Studien* und Erwin Panofsky, *A mythological painting by Poussin in the Nationalmuseum Stockholm*', *Kunstchronik*, XIV, 1961, pp. 196 ff.

1328 Francastel, Pierre, 'Lumière et invention chez Poussin', *AF*, I, 1961, pp. 349 f.

1329 Friedlaender, Walter, 'Hymenaea', *De Artibus Opuscula XL. Essays in Honour of Erwin Panofsky*, I, New York, 1961, pp. 153 ff.

1330 Held, Julius S., 'Flora, goddess and courtesan', *De Artibus Opuscula XL. Essays in Honour of Erwin Panofsky*, I, New York, 1961, pp. 201 ff.

1331 Jaquillard, P., 'Actualité de Poussin. II. Evénements Poussiniens récents', *Versailles*, No. 6, 1961, pp. 23 f.

1332 Kauffmann, Georg, 'Beobachtungen in der Pariser Poussin-Ausstellung', *Kunstchronik*, XIV, 1961, pp. 83 ff.

1333 Kauffmann, Georg, 'Die Poussin-Literatur 1940–1960', *ZKG*, XXIV, 1961, pp. 188 ff.

1334 Kauffmann, Georg, 'Poussins letztes Werk', *ZKG*, XXIV, 1961, pp. 101 ff.

1335 Kitson, Michael, 'The relationship between Claude and Poussin in landscape', *ZKG*, XXIV, 1961, pp. 142 ff.

1336 Lee, Rensselaer, 'Armida's abandonment. A study in Tasso iconography before 1700', *De Artibus Opuscula XL. Essays in Honour of Erwin Panofsky*, I, New York, 1961, pp. 335 ff.

1337 Mahon, Denis, 'Poussin's "Et in Arcadia Ego" ', *The Listener*, 24.viii.1961, p. 281.

1338 Mahon, Denis, 'Réflexions sur les paysages de Poussin', *AF*, I, 1961, pp. 119 ff.
Malvasia, Carlo Cesare, *Vite di pittori Bolognesi*, see No. 30.

1338.1 Martin, John Rupert, 'Portraits of Poussin and Rubens in works by Daniel Seghers', *Bulletin du Musée National de Varsovie*, II, 3, 1961, pp. 67 ff.

1339 Montagu, Jennifer, 'The "Institution of the Eucharist" by Charles Le Brun', *JWCI*, XXIV, 1961, pp. 309 ff.

1340 Morassi, Antonio, 'Francesco Simonini, ein Schlachtenmaler des Settecento', *Pantheon*, XIX, No. 1, 1961, pp. 1 ff.

1341 *Musée des Beaux-Arts de Rouen: Exposition Nicolas Poussin et son temps. Catalogue*: P. Rosenberg; *Introduction*: Sir Anthony Blunt; *Poussin et son Temps*: J. Thuillier; *Documents de Laboratoire*: Madeleine Hours, Rouen, 1961.

1342 Nersesov, N., *Nikola Poussin . . .*, Moscow, 1961.

1343 *Palazzo Braschi, Rome: I Francesi a Roma. Residenti e viaggiatori nella Città Eterna dal rinascimento agli inizi del Romanticismo*, Rome, March-July 1961.

1344 Panofsky, Erwin, 'A mythological painting by Poussin', *BM*, CIII, 1961, pp. 318 ff.

1345 Pietrangeli, Carlo, *Villa Paolina*, Florence, 1961.

1345.1 Pilo, Giuseppe Maria, *Carpioni*, Venice, 1961.

1346 Rinehart, Sheila, 'Cassiano dal Pozzo (1588–1657): Some unknown letters', *IS*, XVI, 1961, pp. 35 ff.

1347 Schaar, Eckhard, 'Eine Poussin-Mola Frage', *ZKG*, XXIV, 1961, pp. 184 ff.

1348 Sommer, Frank H., 'Poussin's "Triumph of Neptune and Amphitrite" : A re-identification', *JWCI*, XXIV, 1961, pp. 323 ff.

1349 Sterling, Charles, 'Les peintres Jean et Jacques Blanchard', *AF*, I, 1961, pp. 77 ff.

1349.1 Tervarent, Guy de, 'De la méthode iconologique', *Académie Royale de Belgique (Classe des Beaux-Arts) Mémoires*, XII, 1961.

1350 Thuillier, Jacques, 'L'année Poussin', *AF*, I, 1961, pp. 336 ff.

1352 Voss, Hermann, 'Neues zum Werk von Remy Vuibert', *ZKG*, XXIV, 1961, pp. 177 ff.

1353 Wild, Doris, 'Actualités de Poussin: I. Les termes de Nicolas Poussin dans le parc de Versailles', *Versailles*, No. 6, 1961.

1354 Zerner, Henri, 'On the portrait of Giulio Rospigliosi, and its attribution to Poussin', *BM*, CIII, 1961, pp. 66 f.

1961–1962

1354.1 Bean, Jacob, 'The Drawings collection', *The Metropolitan Museum of Art Bulletin*, XX, 1961–62, pp. 157 ff.

1962

1355 Adhémar, Jean, 'Note sur les addenda et corrigenda qui suivent', *GBA*, 1962, II, pp. 203 f.

1356 Adhémar, Hélène, 'Alexandre au tombeau d'Achille', *GBA*, 1962, II, p. 315.
Andresen, A., *Verzeichniss . . .*, see No. 500a.

1357 Blunt, Anthony, 'Poussin Studies XIII: Early falsifications of Poussin', *BM*, CIV, pp. 486 ff.

1358 Briganti, Giulio, *Pietro da Cortona o della pittura barocca*, Florence, 1962.

1359 Cattaui, Georges, 'Reflections on Poussin (Review), *Apollo*, LXXVI, 1962, pp. 645 ff.

1360 Costello, Jane, 'Erwin Panofsky, *A mythological painting by Poussin in the Nationalmuseum Stockholm*' (Review), *AB*, XLIV, 1962, pp. 137 ff.

1361 Crelly, William R., *The Painting of Simon Vouet*, New Haven, 1962.

1362 Cummings, Frederick, 'Poussin, Haydon, and the Judgement of Solomon', *BM*, CIV, 1962, pp. 146 ff.

1363 Davies, Martin, and Blunt, Anthony, 'Some corrections and additions to M. Wildenstein's "Graveurs de Poussin au XVIIe siècle"', *GBA*, 1962, II, pp. 205 ff.

1364 Fleming, John, *Robert Adam and his circle in Edinburgh and Rome*, London, 1962.

1365 Friedlaender, Walter, 'Poussin's old age', *GBA*, 1962, II, pp. 249 ff.

1366 Jaffé, Michael, 'The Lunettes and after: Bologna 1962', *BM*, CIV, 1962, pp. 410 ff.

1366.1 Kamenskaya, Tatiana, 'Le Manuscrit du "Traité de la Peinture" de Léonard de Vinci au Musée de l'Ermitage', *Raccolta Vinciana*, XIX, 1962, pp. 255 ff.

1367 Mahon, Denis, 'Poussiniana. Afterthoughts arising from the exhibition', *GBA*, 1962, II, pp. 1 ff.
Also published as a separate volume with the same pagination and an introduction, Paris, New York and London, 1962.

1368 Montagu, Jennifer, 'The church decoration of Nicodemus Tessin the Younger', *Konsthistorisk Tidskrift*, I, 1962, pp. 1 ff.

1369 *Palazzo dell' Archiginnasio, Bologna: L'Ideale classico del seicento in Italia e la pittura di Paesaggio*, Bologna, 1962. *Introduction*: Cesare Gnudi; Section on *Gaspard Dughet*: Francesco Arcangeli; Section on *Claude Lorrain*: Michael Kitson; Section on *Nicholas Poussin*: Denis Mahon; Sections on *Algardi* and *Du Quesnoy*: Amalia Mezzetti.
All references are to the 2nd revised edition.

1370 'Perspectives du XVIIe siècle', *AF*, II, 1962, pp. 252 ff.

1371 Reff, Theodore, 'Cézanne's Bather with outstretched arms', *GBA*, 1962, I, pp. 173 ff.

1372 Röthlisberger, Marcel, 'Les dessins de Claude Lorrain à sujets rares', *GBA*, 1962, I, pp. 153 ff.

1373 Schnapper, Antoine, 'De Nicolas Loir à Jean Jouvenet. Quelques traces de Poussin dans le troisième tiers du XVIIe siècle', *La Revue du Louvre et des Musées de France*, XII, 1962, pp. 115 ff.

1374 Schneider, Pierre, 'Poussin: ou le voir et le savoir', *GBA*, 1962, II, pp. 265 ff.

1375 Simpson, Joyce G., *Le Tasse et la littérature et l'art baroques en France*, Paris, 1962.

1376 Sutton, Denys, 'The classical ideal—an exhibition at Bologna', *Apollo*, LXXVI, 1962, pp. 164 ff.

1377 Sutton, Denys, 'Gaspard Dughet: some aspects of his art', *GBA*, 1962, II, pp. 269 ff.

1378 Ternois, Daniel, 'Sur quelques tableaux de la collection d'Ingres', *AF*, II, 1962, pp. 207 ff.

1379 Tolnay, Charles de, 'Poussin, Michel-Ange et Raphael', *AF*, II, 1962, pp. 260 ff.

1380 Vitzthum, Walter, 'Poussin illustrateur des "Documenti d'Amore"', *AF*, II, 1962, pp. 262 ff.

1381 Vitzthum, Walter, and Thuillier, Jacques, 'Un nouveau dessin de Poussin pour Marino?', *AF*, II, 1962, p. 265.

1382 Voss, Hermann, 'L'Ideale classico del seicento in Italia e la pittura di paesaggio', *Kunstchronik*, XV, 1962, pp. 339 ff.

1382.1 Wallace, Richard W., 'The later version of Poussin's Achilles in Scyros', *Studies in the Renaissance*, IX, 1962, pp. 322 ff.

1383 Wild, Doris, '*L'Adoration des Bergers* de Poussin à Munich et ses tableaux religieux des années cinquante', *GBA*, 1962, II, pp. 223 ff.

1384 Wild, Doris, 'Au sujet de la gravure anonyme: "Un saint ou un ermite se préparant à écrire" G. W. Sup. VI', *GBA*, 1962, II, pp. 313 f.
Wildenstein, Georges, 'Catalogue des graveurs de Poussin...', see No. 500a.

1385 Wildenstein, Georges, 'Note sur l'Abbé Nicaise et quelques-uns de ses amis romains', *GBA*, 1962, II, pp. 565 ff.

1386 Wildenstein, Georges, 'Préface', *GBA*, 1962, II, pp. 1 ff.

1387 Wind, Edgar, 'Une copie de la gravure de Claude Mellan pour l'Horace de 1642 utilisée comme frontispice pour un Juvénal', *GBA*, 1962, II, p. 316.

1963

1388 Andersen, Wayne V., 'A Cézanne drawing after Couture', *Master Drawings*, I, 1963, pp. 44 ff.

1389 Baer, Curtis O., 'An Essay on Poussin', *The Journal of Aesthetics and Art Criticism*, XXI, 3, 1963.

1390 Blunt, Anthony, 'Baroque and Antiquity: Introduction', *Studies in Western Art, III. Latin and American Art, and the Baroque period in Europe* (Acts of the Twentieth International Congress of the History of Art), Princeton, N.J., 1963, pp. 3 ff.

1390.1 Châtelet, Albert, and Thuillier, Jacques, *La Peinture française de Fouquet à Poussin*, Geneva, 1963.

1390.2 Cayeux, Jean de, 'Introduction au catalogue critique des *Griffonis* de Saint-Non', *BSHAF*, 1963, pp. 297 ff.

1391 Dempsey, Charles G., 'Poussin and Egypt', *AB*, XLV, 1963, pp. 109 ff.

1392 Haskell, Francis, *Patrons and Painters. A study in the relations between Italian art and society in the age of the baroque*, London, 1963.

1393 Held, Julius S., 'The early appreciation of drawings', *Studies in Western Art, III. Latin and American Art, and the Baroque period in Europe* (Acts of the Twentieth International Congress of the History of Art), Princeton, N.J., 1963, pp. 72 ff.

1394 Kamenskaya, Tatiana, 'Fragment inédit d'une lettre de Poussin au Musée de l'Ermitage', *GBA*, 1963, II, pp. 345 ff.

1395 Kauffmann, Georg, 'Peruzzis Musenreigen', *Mitteilungen des Kunsthistorischen Institutes in Florenz*, XI, 1963, pp. 55 ff.

1396 Lee, Rensselaer W., 'Van Dyck, Tasso and the Antique', *Studies in Western Art, III. Latin and American Art, and the Baroque period in Europe* (Acts of the Twentieth International Congress of the History of Art), Princeton, N.J., 1963, pp. 12 ff.

1397 Levey, Michael, 'Poussin's "Neptune and Amphitrite" at Philadelphia: A re-identification rejected', *JWCI*, XXVI, 1963, pp. 359 f.

1398 Menz, Henner, 'Ein Dresdener Poussin-Bild in Bologna. Zur Ausstellung "Der Klassizismus des 17.

Jahrhunderts in Italien und die Landschaftsmalerei" ', *Dresdener Kunstblätter. Monatsschrift der Staatlichen Kunstsammlungen*, I, 1963, pp. 2 ff.

1398.1 Mirollo, James V. *The Poet of the Marvelous: Giambattista Marino*, New York and London, 1963.

1399 Reff, Theodore, 'Cézanne et Poussin', *AF*, III, 1963, pp. 302 ff.

1399.1 Rowland, Benjamin Jr., *The classical tradition in western art*, Cambridge, Mass., 1963.

1399.2 Salerno, Luigi, *Salvator Rosa*, Milan, 1963.

1400 Thuillier, Jacques, 'Gaspard Dughet, le "Guaspre" Poussin', *AF*, III, 1963, pp. 247 ff.

1401 Vasconcelos, Flórido de, 'A notável colecçao de desenhos italianos da Escola Superior de Belas-Artes de Porto', *Colóquio. Revista de Artes e Letras*, XXII, 1963, pp. 11 ff.

1402 *Château de Versailles: Charles Le Brun, 1619–1690, peintre et dessinateur. Preface, Catalogue of Paintings, and Biography*: Jacques Thuillier. *Catalogue of Drawings*: Jennifer Montagu. Versailles, 1963.

1403 Vitzthum, Walter, 'Pietro da Cortona', *BM*, CV, 1963, pp. 213 ff.

1404 Waddingham, Malcolm R., 'The Dughet problem', *Paragone*, XIV, No. 161, 1963, pp. 37 ff.

1405 Wittkower, Rudolf, 'The role of classical models in Bernini's and Poussin's preparatory work', *Studies in Western Art, III. Latin and American Art, and the Baroque period in Europe* (Acts of the Twentieth International Congress of the History of Art), Princeton, N.J., 1963, pp. 41 ff.

1406 Ziff, Jerrold, ' "Backgrounds, Introduction of architecture and landscape": A lecture by J. M. W. Turner', *JWCI*, XXVI, 1963, pp. 124 ff.

1963–1964

1407 Zeitler, Rudolf, *Poussinstudien*, Uppsala, 1963–64. 2 vols.

1964

1408 Barocchi, Paola, 'Ricorsi italiani nei trattatisti d'arte francesi del Seicento', in *Il Mito del Classicismo del Seicento*, Florence, 1964, pp. 125 ff.

1409 Bazin, Germain, 'Naïveté et sentiment chez les classiques', in *Il Mito del Classicismo del Seicento*, Florence, 1964, pp. 165 ff.

1410 Blunt, Anthony, 'Poussin Studies XIV: Poussin's Crucifixion', *BM*, CVI, 1964, pp. 450 ff.

1411 Blunt, Anthony, 'Un tableau d'Eustache Le Sueur', *AF*, IV, 1964, pp. 293 f.

Bosse, Abraham, *Le Peintre converty . . .*, see No. 46a.

1412 Clark, Anthony M., 'Imperiali', *BM*, CVI, 1964, pp. 226 ff.

1413 Du Colombier, Pierre, 'Notes sur Nicolas Poussin—I. L'enlèvement des Sabines et Luca Cambiaso', and II. 'Un texte négligé sur les Sacrements de Cassiano dal Pozzo', *GBA*, 1964, I, pp. 81 ff. and 89 ff.

1414 Ebert, Hans, *Farbige Gemäldewiedergaben: Nicolas Poussin*, Leipzig, 1964.

1414.1 Glikman, A. S., *Nicolas Poussin*, Leningrad, 1964.

1415 Grassi, Luigi, 'La storiografia artistica del Seicento in Italia', in *Il Mito del Classicismo del Seicento*, Florence, 1964, pp. 61 ff.

1416 Ivanoff, Nicola, 'La parola "Idea" nelle "Osservationi di Nicolò Pussino sopra la pittura" ', in *Il Mito del Classicismo del Seicento*, Florence, 1964, pp. 91 ff.

1417 Kurz, Otto, 'La storiografia artistica del Seicento in Europa', in *Il Mito del Classicismo del Seicento*, Florence, 1964, pp. 47 ff.

1418 Medley, Robert, 'Poussin's "The Nurture of Jupiter" ', *The Listener*, 9.i.1964, pp. 56 ff.
Nicolas Poussin. Lettres et propos sur l'art, see No. 3e.

1419 Noehles, Karl, 'Francesco Duquesnoy: un busto ignoto e la cronologia delle sue opere', *Arte antica e moderna*, XXV, 1964, pp. 86 ff.

1420 Philipp, Franz, 'Poussin's "Crossing of the Red Sea" ', *In Honour of Daryl Lindsay. Essays and Studies*, Melbourne, etc., 1964, pp. 80 ff.

1420.1 Salerno, Luigi, and Paribeni, Enrico, *Palazzo Rondinini*, Rome, 1964.

1421 Schneider, Pierre, *Le voir et le savoir. Essai sur Nicolas Poussin*, Paris, 1964.

1422 Spear, Richard E., 'The source of an early falsification of Poussin', *BM*, CVI, 1964, p. 234.

1423 Thuillier, Jacques, 'Académie et classicisme en France: les débuts de l'Académie royale de peinture et de sculpture (1648–1663)', in *Il Mito del Classicismo del Seicento*, Florence, 1964, pp. 181 ff.

1964–1965

1424 *Albertina, Vienna: Claude Lorrain und die Meister der römischen Landschaft im XVII. Jahrhundert*, Vienna, November 1964–February 1965.
'Wahrheit und Wirklichkeit in der römischen Landschaftsdarstellung', Walter Koschatzky; *Introduction*: Eckhart Knab.

1965

1425 Alpatov, Michael, 'Poussins Landschaft mit Hercules und Cacus in Moskau (Zum Problem der heroischen Landschaft)', *Walter Friedlaender zum 90. Geburtstag*, Berlin, 1965, pp. 9 ff.

1426 Blunt, Anthony, 'Poussin and his Roman Patrons', *Walter Friedlaender zum 90. Geburtstag*, Berlin, 1965, pp. 58 ff.

1427 Blunt Anthony, *Poussin [The Masters]*, London, 1965.

1428 Boyer, Jean, 'Les Collections de peintures à Aix-en-Provence au XVIIe et XVIIIe siècles d'après des inventaires inédits', *GBA*, 1965, I, pp. 91 ff.

1428.1 Chiarini, Marco, 'Due mostre e un libro (Studi recenti sulla pittura di paesaggio a Roma fra Sei e Settecento)', *Paragone*, XVI, No. 187/7, 1965, pp. 62 ff.

1429 Costello, Jane, 'Poussin's *Annunciation* in London', *Essays in Honor of Walter Friedlaender*, New York, 1965, pp. 16 ff.

1430 Dempsey, Charles, 'Poussin's *Marine Venus* at Philadelphia: A re-identification accepted', *JWCI*, XXVIII, pp. 338 ff.

1431 *The Detroit Institute of Arts, Detroit: Art in Italy* 1600–
     1700 [Catalogue] Detroit, 1965. *Introduction* by R.
     Wittkower, *Commentaries* by Bonald Posner and others.

1431.1 Goldstein, Carl, 'Studies in seventeenth-century
     French art theory and ceiling painting', *AB*, XLVII,
     1965, pp. 231 ff.

1432 Holland, Ralph, 'Nicolas Poussin's "Rebecca al
     Pozzo" '. Letter in *Apollo*, LXXXI, 1965, p. 409.

1432.1 Huyghe, René, 'Le Tricentenaire de Poussin',
     Jardin des Arts, No. 132, 1965, pp. 32 ff.

1433 Kauffmann, Georg, 'Poussin's "Primavera" ', *Walter
     Friedlaender zum 90. Geburtstag*, Berlin, 1965, pp. 92 ff.

1434 Mahon, Denis, 'The dossier of a picture: Nicolas
     Poussin's "Rebecca al Pozzo" ', *Apollo* LXXXI, 1965,
     pp. 196 ff.

1435 Mahon, Denis, 'A Plea for Poussin as a Painter',
     Walter Friedlaender zum 90. Geburtstag, Berlin, 1965,
     pp. 113 ff.

1436 Mahon, Denis, 'Poussin's Rebekah', *Apollo* LXXXI,
     p. 147.

1436.1 Posner, Donald, 'A Poussin-Caravaggio connec-
     tion', *ZKG*, XXVIII, 1965, pp. 130 ff.

1437 Seznec, Jean, 'Falconet, Diderot et le Bas-Relief', *Walter
     Friedlaender zum 90. Geburtstag*, Berlin, 1965, pp. 151 ff.

1438 Spear, Richard E., 'The Literary Source of Poussin's
     "Realm of Flora" ', *BM*, CVII, 1965, pp. 503 ff.

1439 Teyssèdre, Bernard, *Roger de Piles et les débats sur le
     coloris au siècle de Louis XIV*, Paris, 1965.

1440 Thuillier, Jacques, 'Les "Observations sur la peinture"
     de Charles Alphonse Du Fresnoy', *Walter Friedlaender
     zum 90. Geburtstag*, Berlin, 1965, pp. 193 ff.

1441 Vitzthum, Walter, 'Zuschreibungen an François
     Perrier', *Walter Friedlaender zum 90. Geburtstag*, Berlin,
     1965, pp. 214, 216.

1442 Wild, Doris, 'Poussin: Lettres et propos sur l'art. Zu
     einer Publikation von Sir Anthony Blunt' (Review),
     Neue Zürcher Zeitung, 28.iii.1965.

1443 Zeitler, Rudolf, 'Il Problema dei "Modi" e la con-
     sapevolezza di Poussin', *Critica d'Arte*, XII, No. 69,
     1965, pp. 26 ff.

1966

1444 Friedlaender, Walter, *Nicolas Poussin, A new approach*,
     London, 1966.

SUPPLEMENT

When this catalogue was already in page proof, my attention was drawn to Mlle Mireille Rambaud's *Documents du Minutier Central concernant l'histoire de l'art* (1700–1750). This volume contains a number of important references to paintings by Poussin recorded in French collections during the first half of the eighteenth century. Where possible, I have incorporated Mlle Rambaud's documents in the relevant catalogue entries. In some cases this was not possible, but since the information which the documents contain is in many cases of great importance, I have summarized it in the following notes. I understand that a second volume is due for publication in the near future.

Nos. 12–14: A painting of *The Finding of Moses* after Poussin is listed in the inventory after death of Anne de Souvré, Marquise de Louvois, in 1715 (Rambaud, p. 545).

No. 14: Recorded in the inventory after death of Louis de Nyert, Marquis de Gambais, in 1736 and valued at 5000 livres (Rambaud, p. 584).

Nos. 14 and 19: Copies are recorded in the inventory after death of Anne de Souvré, Marquise de Louvois, in 1715 (Rambaud, p. 546).

Nos. 22–24: *Moïse frappant le Rocher dans le désert*, after Poussin, is recorded in the inventory after death of Anne de Souvré, Marquise de Louvois, in 1715 (Rambaud, p. 548).

No. 35: A copy is recorded in the inventory after death of Anne de Souvré, Marquise de Louvois, in 1715 (Rambaud, p. 545).

No. 38: An *Annunciation* attributed to Poussin is recorded among the pictures at Chantilly in the inventory after death of Henri-Jules de Bourbon, Prince de Condé, in 1709 (Rambaud, p. 527) and in that of his son, Louis Henri, in 1740 (*ibid.*, p. 595). In the first case it was valued at 400 livres and in the second at 100 livres.
It cannot be the picture now in the Musée Condé, which was in Naples till the late eighteenth century, but it may well be the version in the Hermitage, which in the middle of the eighteenth century belonged to members of the Crozat family in Paris.

No. 44: A copy is recorded in the inventory after death of the Sieur Gougenot in 1744 (Rambaud, p. 609).

No. 75: This may be the painting recorded in the inventory after death of Camille le Tellier, Abbé de Bourgueil et de Vauluisant, in 1718, valued at 1500 livres (Rambaud, p. 551).

Nos. 82–83: A painting of *Jésus-Christ que l'on va mettre au tombeau* after Poussin is recorded in the inventory after death of Francois, Duc de la Rochefoucauld, in 1728 (Rambaud, p. 562).

Nos. 88–89: A *Ravissement de Saint-Paul* after Poussin is recorded in the inventory after death of Anne de Souvré, Marquise de Louvois, in 1715 (Rambaud, p. 564).
Another is in the inventory after death of the Princesse de Conti in 1732 (*ibid.*, p. 570).

No. 100: The inventory taken after the death of the painter Nicolas de Plattemontagne in 1707 includes 'Saint François dans le désert, de Poussin (*toile de 25 s.*)', valued at 6 livres (Rambaud, p. 517). The low value suggests that this cannot be the original now in Jugoslavia, but it may well have been the copy at Montauban. This entry confirms the suggestion made in the catalogue that this composition actually represents St. Francis in his retreat at La Verna.

Nos. 105–111, 112–118: The inventory after death of Joachim de Seiglière, Sieur de Boisfranc, made in 1706 includes four large paintings of the Sacraments after Poussin, valued at 300 livres. No further details are given (Rambaud, p. 514).

Nos. 120–121: A copy of the *Pasteurs d'Arcadie*, probably No. 121, is listed in the inventory after death of Anne de Souvré, Marquise de Louvois, in 1715 (Rambaud, p. 545).
Another, 'dans un fond de paysage', after Poussin is mentioned in the inventory after death of Louis de Nyert, Marquis de Gambais, in 1736 (Rambaud, p. 585). This must be after the Louvre painting.

Nos. 130–131: '*Apollon et Daphne*, dans un fond de paysage', after Poussin, is listed in the inventory after death of Louis de Nyert, Marquis de Gambais, in 1736 (Rambaud, p. 584). This may be a copy of either the Munich or the Louvre painting.

No. 132: The inventory made of the possessions of Marie-Louise de la Rivière, widow of Paul de Vérani, Sieur de Varenne, after her death in 1713, includes an entry which reads as follows: 'Un grand Poussin: *La Naissance de Jupiter et la mort d'Adonis*', valued at 300 livres (Rambaud, p. 541). This title does not seem to make sense and it is possible that the picture in question may be the *Birth of Bacchus*, Adonis being a mistake for Narcissus. If so, it would mean that the Fogg painting belonged to Paul de Vérani and his widow after it had been sold by the Stella family and before it was bought by the Duke of Orleans. The problem is confused by another entry in the same inventory (*ibid.*), which mentions two paintings, one *La Naissance de Bacchus*, and the other *La Mort d'Adonis* 'à la manière de Poussin', valued at 800 livres.

The inventory made after the death of the Prince de Conti in 1709 includes among paintings in the Château of Issy '*La naissance de Bacchus*, copie d'après Poussin', valued at 100 livres.

No. 144:   Recorded in the inventory after death of Pierre d'Hariague in 1735 (Rambaud, p. 579).

No. 154:   A copy is listed in the inventory after death of Anne de Souvré, Marquise de Louvois, in 1715 (Rambaud, p. 548).

No. 155:   The inventory of Henri-Jules de Bourbon, Prince de Condé, drawn up after his death in 1709, includes among pictures at Chantilly '*Les Amours des dieux*, du même' (i.e. Poussin), valued at 1200 livres (Rambaud, p. 527). This may conceivably be the *Kingdom of Flora* which is first traceable at Dresden in 1722. This hypothesis is strengthened by the fact that the picture does not appear in the inventory made at the death of Louis-Henri, Prince de Condé, in 1740 (Rambaud, pp. 593 ff.).

No. 171:   Two paintings by Poussin, *À la Pie* and *L'Enlèvement du dieu Pan*, belonging to Amedée de Savoie, Prince de Carignan, are mentioned in documents of 1729 and 1732, which confirm that they were sold, with other paintings, to Pierre Dubreuil (Rambaud, pp. 567, 572). The *Pan and Syrinx* is probably the Dresden painting, but the other cannot be identified.

No. 182:   The inventory after death of Françoise Delens, wife of Jean Lemoyne, the painter, made in 1705, included: '*La Recherche des armes d'Achille*, original de Poussin', 3×4 feet, valued at 180 livres

(Rambaud, p. 513). The subject given is not one recorded and may well be a confusion with that of Theseus finding his father's arms. Since all the surviving versions are roughly the same size, there is no means of identifying any of them with the picture recorded in the inventory.

No. 183:   *Mars et Vénus avec plusieurs amours*, after Poussin, is listed in the inventory after death of Anne de Souvré, Marquise de Louvois, in 1715 (Rambaud, p. 546).

No. 209:   Recorded in the inventory after death of Louis de Nyert, Marquis de Gambais, in 1736 and valued at 800 livres (Rambaud, p. 586).

L87a: The inventory of Marie-Louise de la Rivière, widow of Paul Vérani, Sieur de Varenne, made at her death in 1713 includes 'Un grand tableau en longueur de Poussin: *Femme nue*', valued at 1000 livres (Rambaud, p. 542). This may possibly be connected with the *Danae* mentioned under L61.

R109:   Recorded in the inventory after death of Louis de Nyert, Marquis de Gambais, in 1736 (Rambaud, p. 584).

The inventory of Henri-Jules de Bourbon, Prince de Condé's, possessions, made after his death in 1709, includes among paintings at Chantilly '*Paysage*, de Poussin', valued at 1200 livres. No further details are given (Rambaud, p. 527).

The inventory after death of Mathieu Renard du Testa, made in 1738, also includes 'Un grand *Paysage*, de Poussin', valued at 300 livres (Rambaud, p. 590).

The inventory made after the death in 1709 of Henri-Jules de Bourbon, Prince de Condé, contains an entry '*Quatre petits enfants*, de Poussin', valued at 100 livres. It does not seem possible to connect this at all certainly with any recorded composition (Rambaud, p. 528).

INDEX OF EXTANT PAINTINGS

BY, AFTER OR ATTRIBUTED TO POUSSIN

PUBLIC COLLECTIONS AND CHURCHES

PRIVATE COLLECTIONS

INDEX OF SUBJECTS

ALLEGORY

CLASSICAL SUBJECTS

LANDSCAPES

SUBJECTS FROM TASSO

MISCELLANEOUS

INDEX OF PERSONS AND PLACES

All references are to catalogue numbers, except in the case of entries in the Supplement, where the page number is also given.

Abbreviations: d = drawing
e = engraving
c = copy
n = notes
L = Lost paintings
R = Paintings wrongly attributed to Poussin